A CENTURY OF CHARADE

THE INDIAN CITIZENSHIP ACT OF 1924

A CENTURY OF CHARADE
THE INDIAN CITIZENSHIP ACT OF 1924

ROBERTA CAROL HARVEY
A CITIZEN OF THE NAVAJO NATION

SUNSTONE PRESS
SANTA FE

Other books by Roberta Carol Harvey from Sunstone Press

The Earth Is Red: The Imperialism of the Doctrine of Discovery
The Eclipse of the Sun: The Need for American Indian Curriculum in High Schools
The Iron Triangle: Business, Government, and Colonial Settlers' Dispossession of Indian Timberlands and Timber
All That Glitters Is Ours: The Theft of Indian Mineral Resources
Social Contributions of Colorado's American Indian Leaders for the Seven Generations to Come
Warrior Societies A Manifesto
Brief Colorado Indian History of 1800's Through a Factual Lens
Stealing the Last Arrow The Department of Interior Indian Probate Proceedings
Colorado American Indian Civics

© 2025 by ROBERTA CAROL HARVEY
All Rights Reserved
No part of this book may be reproduced in any form or by any electronic or mechanical means including
information storage and retrieval systems without permission in writing from the publisher, except by a reviewer who may quote brief passages in a review.

Sunstone books may be purchased for educational, business, or sales promotional use. For information please write: Special Markets Department, Sunstone Press, P.O. Box 2321, Santa Fe, New Mexico 87504-2321.
Printed on acid-free paper
∞
eBook: 978-1-61139-787-1

Library of Congress Cataloging-in-Publication Data

Names: Harvey, Roberta Carol, 1950- author
Title: A century of charade : the Indian Citizenship Act of 1924 / Roberta Carol Harvey.
Description: Santa Fe, NM : Sunstone Press, [2025] | Includes bibliographical references. | Summary: "This book details the theft of Indian identity through Indian citizenship"-- Provided by publisher.
Identifiers: LCCN 2025051102 | ISBN 9781632937698 paperback | ISBN 9781632937704 hardback | ISBN 9781611397871 epub
Subjects: LCSH: Indians of North America | Indians of North America--Legal status, laws, etc.--History | Indians of North America--United States--Government relations--History | Citizenship--United States--History
Classification: LCC E93 .H3278 2025 | DDC 973.0497--dc23/eng/20251208
LC record available at https://lccn.loc.gov/2025051102

WWW.SUNSTONEPRESS.COM
SUNSTONE PRESS / POST OFFICE BOX 2321 / SANTA FE, NM 87504-2321 /USA
(505) 988-4418

DEDICATION

For Hidatsa Chief Old Dog (1851–1928)

A revered Hidatsa Chief, Old Dog, photographed in 1909 by Edward Curtis. Also served as a Judge at the Elbowoods Indian Court.

"I do not want the white man's offer of citizenship. I have lived a long life, and I have seen many of the Great White Fathers' promises vanish on the winds. I do not need the white man's government to tell me that I am free."

https://www.minotdailynews.com/news/local-news/2020/06/chief-old-dog-leader-among-hidatsa/ (accessed online December 15, 2024).

ACKNOWLEDGMENTS

This work would not have been possible without the outstanding research and scholarship done by so many on the topic of American Indian citizenship. For anyone who has written on this topic, thank you.

Family

Nobody has been more important to me in the pursuit of this project than the members of my family. Every day I wake up filled with joy, gratitude and love. I pray for every success and joy in their lives.

My oldest son asked me to write a book about the Indian Citizenship Act of 1924 in 2020 and here it is.

All of my family generously provided me with the protected academic time to pursue this project. They also made sure that whatever resources and assistance I needed for this project were available. Their encouragement and support were invaluable. Thank you to my most beloved husband, Dag, my sons, D.J. and Aaron, my daughter-in-laws, Malin and Marianne, and my grandchildren: Hadlie, Callan, Sander, Kennedy and Cooper, whose love provide such joy in my life.

The contribution of my husband in support of my writing is incredible. I cannot thank him enough for making breakfast, lunch and dinner for me and taking over family responsibilities when I am engaged in research and writing.

Thank you to Aaron for sharing his knowledge of Dandy's Band - Ho-Chunk Indians, and the reformers of the late 1800s and the early 1900s.

In the 1889 Proceedings of the Lake Mohonk Conference of the Friends of the Indian, they expressly signaled out their political influence as follows: "The first report of the Board of Indian Commissioners, twenty years ago, declared for nearly all the great reforms which this conference [Mohonk] has urged for many years. *I suppose that all other influences combined have not been equal to the power of the Mohonk conference in matters of legislation. Our committees have had influence with the committees in Congress, and with the President of the United States, and the Commissioner of Indian Affairs, aided by our uninterrupted and plentiful letter-writing to members of Congress....*" (Emphasis added). Report of the Annual Lake Mohonk Conference on the Indian and Other Dependent Peoples (1889), p. 7.

The Chapters below would not have been written without Aaron's support, and this book would have been wholly incomplete.

Dandy's Band, Ho-Chunk Indians Residing in Wisconsin; Reliance on Homestead Laws – Excerpts from "Their Civilization and Ultimate Citizenship": Land-ownership, Written and Unwritten Laws, and a Native American Path through Reconstruction, Stephen Kantrowitz, University of Wisconsin-Madison

Board of Indian Commissioners ("BIC")

Lake Mohonk Conferences ("LMC")

Society of American Indians ("SAI")

Dr. Carlos Montezuma

CONTENTS

49 // Preface
Primary Source Reliance
Different Names for Particular Tribe/Nation
Different Names for Land Areas in "America"
Personal Names; Spelling
Spelling Differed; Quotes Use Original Text
Real Property Terminology

51 // CHAPTER 1: "Charges Against American Civilization" (Article by Arthur Parker)

64 // CHAPTER 2: Focus of This Book - Indian Policy to Break Up Reservations, Destroy Tribal Relations, Settle Indians on Allotments, Deal with Them Not as Nations, but as Individual Citizens; American Indian Is to Become Indian American U.S. Citizen

67 // CHAPTER 3: Brief Review of U.S. Citizenship and Naturalization Policies

    English Roots: Theory of Natural Allegiance

    Colonial Experience: Theory of Volitional Allegiance Emerges

    Foreigners Perplexed by Use of Term 'Citizen'

    Need for Uniformity Obvious to Framers of United States Constitution

72 // CHAPTER 4: Citizenship under Treaties with Indian Nations

    U.S. Constitution's Treaty Power

    Methods of Indians Becoming U.S. Citizens by Treaty

    A. Become Citizen of State

    A.1. 1831: Choctaw Treaty of Dancing Rabbit Creek

    B. Dissolution of Tribal Organization

    C. Election to Dissolve Tribal Relations and Become U.S. Citizens

    C.1. 1855: Wyandot Treaty – Indians Sufficiently Advanced in Civilization, Become U.S. Citizens, Indian Tribe Terminated

    C.2. 1862: Treaty with the Ottawa

    D. Others Required Election and Proof of Competency

75 // CHAPTER 5: U.S. Constitution and Statutes on Naturalization
    U.S. Constitution on Naturalization

    1790: U.S.' First Naturalization Law Applied Only to "Free White Persons"

    1846: *United States v. Rogers*: Consensual Tribal Citizenship by White Person Intermarrying an Indian Not Sufficient to Make White Person an Indian for Purposes of Federal Law

    1870: Naturalization Eligibility Act for Former African Slaves

    1887: General Allotment Act

    1887: After Receiving Patent Every Allottee Subject to Civil and Criminal Laws of State or Territory of Residence; Imposed U.S. Citizenship; U.S. Citizenship Did Not Impair Rights in Tribal Property

    1887: Allotment Act: Ipso Facto Makes Citizens of Indians

    1890: Indian Territory Naturalization Act - Legislation Permitted Indians in Indian Territory to Apply for U.S. Citizenship

    1901: Congress Enacted Legislation Imposing U.S. Citizenship on Every Indian in Indian Territory

    1906: Burke Act

    Veterans of World War I

    1922: Citizenship re Indian Parents and Children

    1924: Indian Citizenship Act

    Indian Citizenship Act - Plenary Act of Congress

82 // CHAPTER 6: Citizenship under Fourteenth Amendment ("14th Amendment")

    A.1: 1866: Senate Debate on Including or Excluding Indians for Citizenship under 14th Amendment

    A.2: Opposition to Savages Becoming Citizens

    A.3: Indians Part of Quasi Foreign Nations

A.4: Senators Opposed to Indians Not Living under Tribal Jurisdiction for Citizenship - Not All Indians Associated with Tribe

A.5: Opposed to Mass Involuntary Imposition of Citizenship - Senator James Guthrie (D-KY)

A.6: Senators that Supported including Indians for Citizenship under 14th Amendment

A.7: 1866: Senator Maxey (D-TX) - "It Is Too Soon"

A.8: Conflict with State Liquor/Firearm Laws - Senator George H. Williams (R-OR)

A.9: "Exclude Indians Not Taxed"

A.10: Senator James Lane (R-KAN) - Confer Citizenship on "Indians Holding Lands in Severalty by Allotment"

A.11: 1866: Senator Lyman Trumbull (R-ILL) - Indians Not Object of Bill
14th Amendment to Constitution Submitted to States for Ratification

B. Decade of 1870s Produced Court Decisions regarding whether Indians Were Citizens under 14th Amendment (e.g., If They Had Abandoned Tribal Relations)

B.1. 1877: *United States v. Elm*, District Court, N.D.; Tribal Organization Defunct

B.2. 1878 *Ex parte Kenyon*, Circuit Court, W.D. ARK; Interpreting Cherokee Nation Constitutional Provision

B.3. 1884: *Elk v. Wilkins*, Individual Indian Voluntarily Leaving His Tribe Can Only Become Citizen by Treaty or Congressional Act

91 // **CHAPTER 7:** Presidential Views on Indian Civilization and Private Property

1789: Exclusive Indian Property Advocated by President Washington's Secretary of War Henry Knox

Executive Conflict of Interest

1798: President John Adams - Indian Trust Responsibilities Are Subordinate to Obligations to U.S. Citizenry

1801–1805: President Thomas Jefferson - Architect of Indian Removal

1809-1817: President James Madison - Civilize and Divide Up Indian Lands to Individuals

1816: Letters of Americanus to President Madison - For Citizenship, Indian Must Assimilate

Indians Will Be Stimulated to Industry by Separate Property

1817-1825: President James Monroe - Supported Land in Severalty; Tribes Not Sovereigns; Indians and Indian Property Subject to U.S. Control

1821: Second Inaugural Address of James Monroe, March 5, 1821 - Treatment of Indian Tribes as Sovereign Should Cease with Land Allocated to Individuals in Adequate Portions

1838: President Van Buren: Whites and Indians Cannot Safely Occupy Same Territory

1869: Presidential Inauguration of Ulysses S. Grant: Indian Conversion to Christianity and Education Seen as Solution; Federal Government Gave Money to Catholic and Protestant Churches to Christianize and Educate Indian Children

1880: President Grant's Peace Policy Failed to Bring about Indian Assimilation and Civilization

1885: President Cleveland - Guardianship over Indian Wards Test of Integrity and Honor

1901: President Theodore Roosevelt's Address to Congress - General Allotment Act Is Mighty Pulverizing Engine to Break Up Tribal Mass; Civilized Mankind Owes Debt to Settler

102 // CHAPTER 8: Removal Era

1824: Secretary of War Threatens Cherokees - They Will Be Left to Whims of Georgia

1827: Conflict between Creek Indians and State of Georgia Leads to Federal Threat of U.S. War against State

President John Quincy Adams: Indian Right of Possession Questionable

1828: Report of Thomas McKenney to Sec. of War - Indians Will Not Be Permitted to Hold Reservations on which They Live within States due to Covetous Illegal White Encroachment

1828: Secretary of War Porter Proposed to President J.Q. Adams Forming Contiguous Indian Colonies in West; Land Apportioned in Fee Simple Absolute to Individual Indians Willing to Pursue Civilization, with Temporary Restraints on Alienation of Land; Making Indians Subject to General Laws

1828: Andrew Jackson's Indian Removal Presidential Campaign

1829: Georgia Enacts Laws Abolishing Cherokee Indian Sovereignty, Self-Government and Right to Land

1829: Gold Discovered on Cherokee Lands

1829: War Generals - If Congress Rejects Cherokee Petition to Remain in Georgia and Georgia's Laws Are Enforced, Cherokee Will Move without Difficulty

Alternatives: Exterminate, Assimilate, Protect or Remove Indians

1829: President Jackson Recommends Setting Aside Western Lands for Indians

1830: Andrew Jackson's Justification for Indian Removal

1830: Tenor of Times - They May Begin to Dig Their Graves and Prepare to Die

1830: Indian Removal Bill Introduced in Congress

1830: Indian Removal Act Passed

Removal of Indian Nations Became Mandatory

1832: President Jackson - Acts Passed to Extinguish Indian Title in Illinois, Indiana, Missouri, and Territory of Michigan

113 // CHAPTER 9: 1831 - First Commissioner of Indian Affairs Elbert Herring - Absent Emigration, Indians Would Rapidly Become Extinct – Need Knowledge of Agriculture, Private Property, and Christianity

1831: Report of Chief Clerk Herring, Indian Bureau - Remove Indians, White Population Engulfing Them and Causing Their Total Extinction

~ 13

   1832: Supplant Savage for Social; Eradicate Absence of Meum ["What Is Mine"] and Tuum ["What Is Thine"]

   1834: Committee on Indian Affairs, H. Everett Report, Regulating the Indian Department; Establishing Western Indian Territory

115 // CHAPTER 10: Carey Allen Harris, Commissioner of Indian Affairs (July 4, 1836–October 19, 1838) – Statistical Data

   1838: Commissioner Harris Forced to Resign due to Land Speculation

116 // CHAPTER 11: Thomas Hartley Crawford, Commissioner of Indian Affairs (October 22, 1838–October 29, 1845) - Options for Indians – Integration, Emigrate to British Canada, Move West; Must Be Educated; Trade and Annuity Abuses Must Be Corrected

   1839: Commissioner Crawford - Contact of White Man Is Death to Indians

   1840: Commissioner Crawford - Indians Must Be Removed, Civilized and Christianized

   1844: Commissioner Crawford - Co-Education of Indians Mandatory; No Civilization without Individual Ownership of Property

118 // CHAPTER 12: William Medill, Commissioner of Indian Affairs (1845-1849) - U.S. Secured Oregon Country (1846), Annexed Texas (1845), and Acquired Southwest after Mexican War (1848) – Colonization, Civilization and Christianization of Indians Only Solution; U.S. beyond Reproach

   1845: Commissioner Medill - Education

   1846: Commissioner Medill - Annuities Prevent Improvement

   1846: Commissioner Medill - Chippewas of Mississippi and Lake Superior Still Own Valuable Mineral and Agricultural Land

   1846: Commissioner Medill's Position regarding Indian's Future

   1846: Senator Benton's (R-MO) Congressional Speech - White Race's Malevolent, Divine, Manifest Destiny

   1848: Commissioner Medill – Maintaining Order on Frontier - Establish Two Large "Colonies" (or Reservations) for Indians, One in North, One in South, Clear Central Unmolested Path for Emigrating Whites

   1848: Commissioner Medill - Strongest Propensities of Indian's Nature

Are Desire for War and Love of Chase; Labor Utterly Repugnant; Colonization of Indians Only Solution

1848: Treaty of Guadalupe Hidalgo Ended Mexican American War; U.S. Citizenship Offered to 100,000 Mexican Nationals; Mineral Resources of Southwest Territory Ceded to U.S. by Mexico Created U.S. Economic Boom

1848: Commissioner Medill - Indians Removed from Iowa; Removal Expected from Wisconsin

1848: Commissioner Medill - Bloodshed and Strife Inevitable between Different Races - Weaker Party Must Suffer; U.S. beyond Reproach

1849: Congress Creates Department of Interior; Thomas Ewing First Secretary of Interior

123 // CHAPTER 13: Orlando Brown, Commissioner of Indian Affairs (June 30, 1849–July 1, 1850) - Support for Indian Traders in Payment of Annuities Led to Forced Resignation; If Nothing Done for Indians – U.S. Legacy Will Be Constant Source of Regret, If Not Self-Reproach

1849: Commissioner Brown - Territory of Minnesota Being Overrun by White Settlers

1849: Commissioner Brown – Care of Indians by U.S. Required

125 // CHAPTER 14: Luke Lea, Commissioner of Indian Affairs (July 1, 1850–March 24, 1853) – Establishing Reservations Mandatory; Indians Must Resort to Agricultural Labor or Starve; Face Being Over-Run and Exterminated; Indians through Education, Capable of Civilization and U.S. Citizenship

127 // CHAPTER 15: George W. Manypenny, Commissioner of Indian Affairs (March 31, 1853–March 30, 1857) - Second Wave of Emigration Treaties - Allotment in Severalty; Relinquishment of Annuities; Forty-Three Ratified and Twenty-Three Unratified Treaties Opening More than 174 Million Acres of Land to White Settlement

1853: Indians' Future Grim

1853: Policy Must Be an Army or Annuity

1854: Michigan Agency, Henry C. Gilbert, Agent, Chippewas Destitute, Naked and Starving, One-Fourth of Band Dead

1854: Commissioner Manypenny - National Current of White Population Overwhelming Indians; Emigrated Tribes in Kansas Territory Permanently There to Be Civilized or Exterminated; No More Relocation Possible - on Ground They Occupy Crisis Must Be Met and Future Determined

1855: Commissioner Manypenny, Three Great Evils

1855: Indians Cheated of Annuities by "Shameful, Dishonorable, and Unlawful Means"

1855: Sioux Agency, No Agricultural Implements, Annuities Undelivered

1855: Fort Laramie Indian Agency, Agent Thomas S. Twiss – Indians Suffering, Thousands Die Annually

1856: Kansas Territory: Indians Endure Trespasses and Depredations of Every Conceivable Type; Despoiled of Their Lands and Annuities by Swarm of Audacious Speculators

1857: Oregon and Wash., Not Enough Agents, No Military Force, Indians Doomed to Extermination Unless Protected

1865: Indians Removed to Kansas Permanently, Subsequently Removed to Indian Territory

133 // CHAPTER 16: James W. Denver, Commissioner of Indian Affairs (April 17, 1857–December 2, 1857, and November 8, 1858–March 31, 1859) - Slavery Issue Resulting in "Bleeding Kansas"; Small Allotted Reservations; Indians - Hindrance to White Settlement; Commissioner Encouraged Tribes to Sell Land; Commissioner Denver's Family Speculated Heavily in Indian Allotments across West

Hurried Negotiation of Treaties Prior to Passage of Kansas-Nebraska Act

"Bleeding Kansas"

Commissioner Denver's Indian Policy

1857: Indian Title Extinguished to 13,658,000 Acres in Kansas, Lands Retained for Indians 1,342,000 Acres

Commissioner Denver's Perspective: Too Large Body of Land Assigned to Indians; Large Money Annuities Foster Dependence and Indolence

1857: Blue Earth, MN, Delay in Winnebagoes' Annuities, Rapid Settlement of Indian Land by Whites

1857: Oregon: Indians Cheated, No Fair Compensation

Commissioner Denver Pronounces that Indian Reservations Should Have Only Sufficient Allotted Land to Support Them, with Title to Land in Tribe

Commissioner Denver Views Indian Citizenship as Ultimate Goal

136 // CHAPTER 17: Charles E. Mix, Commissioner of Indian Affairs (June 14, 1858–November 8, 1858) - Recommended Small Reservations, Transition to Agrarian Culture; Ceasing Removal of Tribes; Assimilation Only Path Forward; Suggested Apprenticeship for Indian Orphans and Children Bound Out for Term of Years to Whites; Authored Office Laws, Regulations, Etc., for Indian Bureau

1858: Three Errors in Indian Policy: Continual Removal as White Population Advanced; Reservations Too Large; Payment of Cash Annuities

1858: Indian Policy Corrections Needed: Isolated Reservations with Good Lands, Allotted in Severalty; No Whites Permitted; Manual Labor and Mechanical Trade Schools

1858: Commissioner Mix Suggested that Indian Children Could Be Bound out to Whites for Apprenticeship with State Regulation

1858: Apache Character Demands Extermination

138 // CHAPTER 18: Alfred B. Greenwood, Commissioner of Indian Affairs (May 4, 1859–April 13, 1861) - Problems in Distinction between Treaty Tribes and Nontreaty Tribes; Treaty Tribes with Permanent Annuities and Those Without Annuities; Communal Landholding Tribes and Tribes with Allotted Reservations

1859: Traditional Subsistence by Indians Impossible in Colorado due to Gold Discoveries

1859: Massacres on Routes Through Utah Territory Planned, If Not Executed, by U.S. Citizens

1859: Westward Emigration, Upper Platte, Thomas S. Twiss, Agent

1859: Utah Territory, J. Forney, Superintendent Indian Affairs, Steal or Starve

1859: Carson Valley Agency, NEV, F. Dodge, Indian Agent, Steal or Starve

1859: Puget Sound Agency, Annuity - $1.41 Each

1859: WASH, Siletz Agency, R. B. Metcalfe, Indian Agent, To Civilize Indians, Separate Reservation for All Children over Three and Under Ten Years of Age, Never Allow Older Indians to Visit

1859: U.S. Policy - Restrict Indians to Small Reservations, Divide Lands Among Them in Severalty

1860: Utah, Superintendent Refuses Aid to Destitute Indians, Though He Had Funds in Hand, Indians Starved

1860: Oregon – Reservation System Last Resort

1860: Problems in Distinction between Treaty Tribes and Nontreaty Tribes; Treaty Tribes with Permanent Annuities and Those Without Annuities; Communal Landholding Tribes and Tribes with Allotted Reservations

1860: Indian Policy Must Be Based on Need for Private Property for White Settlers among Indians

1860: Policy of Severalty

1860: Squaksin Agency, V. B. Gosnell, Sub-Agent, Washington Territory, Increase to Annuities Suggested - $1 Per Capita

1860: Central Superintendency, Yancton Sioux, A. H. Redfield, Agent, Annuities $5 Each

1860: Ottoes and Missourias, Failures of Crops, Per Capita of Eighteen Dollars

1860: Annuities - Junk or Damaged, Overpriced, Huge Freight Charges

1860: Assimilation Policy, Individualizing Them as Agriculturists, Incorporation into U.S., Northern Superintendency, W.J. Cullen, Superintendent

1860: Remove Shawnees, Miamies, and Confederated Bands of Kaskaskias, Peorias, Weas, and Piankeshaws from Kansas; Rapidly Deteriorating

Transfer Supervision of Indian Bureau Back to War Department

States' Legislatures Petition President to Extinguish Indian Title

1860: SW States' Residents Petition President to Extinguish Indian Title

Reservations Swarm with Intimidating White Squatters

CHAPTER 19: William P. Dole, Commissioner of Indian Affairs (March 12, 1861–July 11, 1865)

1861: Annuities Short, Lafayette Head, Agent of Tubache Utahs

1861: NEV, Washoe Indians, James W. Nye, Gov. of Nevada Territory, ex officio Superintendent Indian Affairs, Relief Needed

1861: Oregon, Grand Ronde Agency, Need Aid

1862: NEV, Indians Eating Undigested Barley from Manure

1862: Upper Sioux Starving

1862: Yanktonais Sioux Starving

1862: New Mexico Superintendency: Exterminate, Starve or Provide for Indians

1862: Michigan Superintendency: Remove Indians or We Will Exterminate Them

1863: Northern Superintendency, Poncas Starving

Missouri Sioux Cheated, Robbed, Driven from Their Land

1863: Attack on Fort Ridgley by Sioux - They Must Be Whipped, Coerced into Obedience; Many Will Be Killed, More Must Perish from Famine and Exposure, and More Desperate Will Flee and Seek Refuge on Plains or in Mountains

1863: Tabequache Ute Cession to U.S. of Arable Land and Valuable Mining Districts

1863: Nez Perce Land Invaded by Whites due to Discovery of Gold

1863: Untutored, Uncivilized Barbarians, Savages, Yet Human Beings Must Be Treated As Wards of Government

1863: Annuities to Makahs (WASH) Nonsensical, If Not Dishonest

1863: Dakota Superintendency, Acting Gov. Dakota Territory, ex oficio Sup't Indian Affairs, John Hutchinson, Ponca Indians Destitute

1864: Nevada Territory Gold and Silver Discoveries

1864: Nevada, Discovery of Precious Minerals, Indians Must Be Provided for by U.S.

1864: Humboldt County, Nevada Territory, Lack of Subsistence for Indians

1864: AZ, Yumas, No Water, No Crops, Many Died from Hunger, Gave Them Damaged Hominy, which Horses Had Refused to Eat

1864: Apaches – Subjugate or Exterminate – Gold Field to Be Developed

1864: Blackfoot Agency, Montana, Chaos at Agency, No Agent, No Annuities

1864: Blackfeet Indians – Agent Insults

1864: Montana – Miners Trampling on Indian Rights

DOI Supports Whites Coveting Indian Agricultural and Mineral Lands

Commissioner Dole - Need to Concentrate Tribal Nations on Three to Five Large Reservations

159 // **CHAPTER 20: 1865 - Dennis N. Cooley, Commissioner of Indian Affairs (July 9, 1865–November 1, 1866)**

1865: Annual Report of Commissioner of Indian Affairs; Cost-Benefit Analysis of Total Destruction of Indians

1865: Treaties Abrogated with Tribes that Supported Confederacy during Civil War

1865: Washington, Spokane Indians – Gold Seekers Trampling on Indian Rights

1865: Yakama Reservation, WA, Former Agent Cheated Indians on Payment for Work Performed at Agency

1865: Kansas State Supreme Court Rules Miami Indian Lands Are Subject to State Taxation

1865: Fort Laramie Agency Indians Being Exterminated

1865: Washington Superintendency, W.H. Waterman, Superintendent, Paternal Government Needed to Avoid Demoralizing Influence of Corrupt White Men

1865: Utah, O.H. Irish, Superintendent, Settlers in Favor of Extermination

1865: Citizenship to Indians in Certain Treaties

163 // CHAPTER 21: Lewis V. Bogy, Commissioner of Indian Affairs (November 1, 1866–March 29, 1867) - House Investigated Commissioner Bogy's Award of Indian Contracts to Firms in which His Brother Had Connections

1866: Difficulties of Managing Indian Office, 300,000 Indians, More than 200 Tribes

1866: Nevada: Shoshonees, Destitute, Miners Demand Their Extermination

1866: Utah, Uintah Agency, Near Starvation

1866: Arizona, George W. Leihy, Indian Agent, Hualapais, Whites Threaten War of Extermination

1866: Dakota Superintendency, Execution of Treaties Negligent and Fraudulent

1866: Fetterman Massacre near Ft. Phil Kearney

1866: Pi-Utes - Walker River and Truckee River Reservations - All Arable Land Being Occupied by Whites

1866: Criminal Law Code Needed for Reservations

1866: H. G. Parker, Superintendent Indian Affairs, Nev., Purpose of Schools

March 1867: Commissioner Bogy under Investigation by House

167 // CHAPTER 22: Nathaniel G. Taylor, Commissioner of Indian Affairs (March 29, 1867–April 25, 1869)

1867: Report - Condition of Indian Tribes: Myriad Charges of Fraud

~ 21

and Corruption against Civilian and Military Forces; Blamed Indian Wars on "Aggressions of Lawless White Men"

1867: Mackinac Agency, Richard M. Smith, Indian Agent, Duty to Western Indians, Not Extermination as Some High in Authority Recommend

1867: Concentrate Indians on Reservations; Christianity and Civilization Spreading from Mississippi to Pacific; Indians Possess Land with Precious Metals and/or Agricultural Wealth

1867: Pottawatomies Applied for Citizenship, Want Patents and Share of Tribal Money

1867: Ottawas Not Yet Citizens, Can't Alienate Patents

1867: Wyandottes Restored to Tribal Citizenship

1867: Santee Sioux, NE, Utter and Complete Humiliation

1866: Idaho Gold and Silver - Governor D. W. Ballard, ex officio Superintendent Indian Affairs

1867: Nevada, Pyramid and Walker River Reserves, Segregate Mineral Lands, of No Value to Indians

1867: Arizona, Richest Mines of Gold, Silver, and Copper Located on Apaches' Land

1868: Idaho Governor Proposes Reservation for Bannocks Not Filled with Minerals

1868: Commissioner Report - Indian Population Decreasing due to (1) Intertribal Wars, (2) Loathsome Diseases Transmitted by Vicious Whites, and (3) Use of Liquor

1868: Dakota, Northern Cheyenne, Suffering beyond Endurance, Starving

1868: Shall Control of Indians Be Transferred to War Dept.

177 // CHAPTER 23: Ely S. Parker, Commissioner of Indian Affairs (April 26, 1869–July 24, 1871) - Helpless and Ignorant Wards, Not Independent Sovereigns, No More Treaties

1867: Colonel Ely Parker's Peace Policy

1869: Kickapoos - Unrestrained Power to Sell Their Lands Ought Not to Be Given to This Class of Indians; Remain under Guardianship

1869: Pottawatomies - Valuable Timber, Pure Water, Rich Prairie Soil, Containing Over Seventy-Five Thousand Acres, White Settlers Encroach – Reservation Could Never Have Been Intended as Home for Indians

Commissioner Parker Opposed to Treaty System

1869: Nevada, Pi-Utes, Destitute, Steal or Starve

1869: Montana, Bannacks, Half-Starved, Land Overrun by Miners

1869: Sisseton and Wahpeton Sioux, Upper Missouri Agency, Destitute, No Food, No Clothing

180 // CHAPTER 24: 1871: Acting Commissioner H. R. Clum

Issuing Patents will Result in Hastening Indians to Utter Extinction as Race; Pauperism and Crime in State

1871: NV, Indians on Pyramid Lake Reservation, Starvation and Intense Suffering

181 // CHAPTER 25: Francis A. Walker, Commissioner of Indian Affairs (November 27, 1871–January 1, 1873)

1871: Treaty-Making with Indian Nations Abolished

1871: Consolidation of All Tribes in Indian Territory; Release from Indian Occupancy 93,692,731 Acres for White Settlement

1871: NM, Grant County, Whites Threaten to Massacre Apaches on Reservations

April 30, 1871: Camp Grant Massacre, Arizona Territory

1871: Montana Territory, Assiniboines and Gros Ventres Indians, White Miners Over-Running Reservation

1871: Pottawatomies – Allotment Debacle; Retrograded into Intemperance and Poverty; Whites, like Leeches, Cling Until Divest Indians of Property

1872: Submission Is Only Hope of Indians

~ 23

1872: Freedom of Westward Expansion of Incalculable Value to U.S., to Indian - Incalculable Cost; Result for Indian - Wretchedness, Destitution, Beggary

1872: Army in Present Force Able to Deal with Few Marauding Bands

1872: Indians Justifiable Claim to Temporary Support as Left without Subsistence

1874: Former Commissioner Francis Walker - The Indian Question

Expenditures of Government 1861-1872

More Than Half, probably at Least Two-Thirds, of Tribes that Had Citizenship Imposed Are Homeless, and Must Be Re-Stored to Tribal Status

188 // CHAPTER 26: Edward P. Smith, Commissioner of Indian Affairs (March 17, 1873–December 11, 1875)

1873: Hindrances to Indian Civilization - Communal Land and Property, Cash Annuities, Absence of Law, Persistent Refusal to Remain upon Their Reservations, Intertribal Warfare

1873: Double Condition of Sovereignty and Wardship Absurd

1873: Difference between Barbarians and Civilized People Is Difference between Herd and Individual; Survey and Allot Indian Lands

1874: Individual Indians Can Only Become Citizens by Treaty or Congressional Act

191 // CHAPTER 27: 1874: Secretary of Interior Delano's Report – Enact Legislation for Indian Citizenship; Extend Homestead Laws to Indians

1874, Secretary's Report to President on Indian Question - Reservations; Instruction in Agriculture; Severity for Tribes Refusing to Accept Reservation; Temporary Subsistence Necessary

Recommends Extension of Homestead Laws to Indians; Break Up Tribal Organizations and Indian Communities; Indians Will Become Subject to U.S. Laws, Civil and Criminal

When Indian Tribe Is Dissolved and Its Tribal Relations Ended, with U.S. Consent, Either by Treaty or Legislative Enactment, Members Become Ipso Facto U.S. Citizens

Individual Indian by Voluntarily Withdrawing from His Tribe Cannot Become a Citizen without Government Approving His Citizenship

1874: Draft of Bill to Enable Indians to Become Citizens

1874: Most Indians Hesitate to Leave Tribal Condition

1874: Punishment for Being Off Reservation

194 // CHAPTER 28: Dandy's Band, Ho-Chunk Indians Residing in Wisconsin; Reliance on Homestead Laws – Excerpts from "Their Civilization and Ultimate Citizenship": Land-ownership, Written and Unwritten Laws, and a Native American Path through Reconstruction, Stephen Kantrowitz, University of Wisconsin-Madison

198 // CHAPTER 29: John Q. Smith, Commissioner of Indian Affairs (1875-1877)

1875: Relations of Indians to States - Indians Have to Be Civilized, Self-Supporting and Subject to Municipal Control

1875: Indians - Ignorant and Helpless People with Moral Claim upon U.S.; Must Be Driven to Toil by Cold and Hunger; Annuities for Labor Only

1876: Fate of Indians

1876: Concentration of All Indians on Few Reservations; Allot Land; Extend Jurisdiction of U.S. Courts over Indian Reservations

1876: Compulsory Education; Stop Raising Generations of Worthless and Costly Savages

201 // CHAPTER 30: 1877: (1) Secretary of Interior Carl Schurz - Code of Laws; Indian Police; Reservations Divided into Farms; Compulsory Education; Access of Christian Teachers and Missionaries to Reclaim Indians from Debasing Paganism; Contribution of Indian Labor in Return for Supplies; Concentration and Removal of Indians to Indian Territory (2) President Hayes Promises "Just and Humane Policy" regarding Indians

1876: Blanket Must Give Way

President Rutherford Hayes Promises "Just and Humane Policy" regarding Indians

CHAPTER 31: Ezra A. Hayt, Commissioner of Indian Affairs (September 20, 1877–January 29, 1880) - 1873 Modoc War, 1876 Sioux War, 1877 Nez Perce/Chief Joseph Flight, 1878 Bannack Outbreak, 1878 Flight of Northern Cheyenne from Indian Territory, and 1879 Ute Outbreak

1877: Commissioner Hayt - Dishonesty of Indian Agents, Traders, and Contractors

1877: Compulsory Education in Boarding Schools to Avoid Demoralization and Degradation of an Indian Home

1877: Commissioner Hayt - Remove Indians in Colorado and Arizona to Indian Territory to Facilitate Gold and Silver Mining and Farming by Whites

1877: Colorado Utes (Yampa, Grand River and Uinta Bands of Confederated Utes) Have Received No Annuities for Two Years

1877: Pottawatomies of Huron, MICH, Fast Dwindling Away, on Least Valuable Land, Wretchedly Poor

1877: Oneidas, Wisconsin - Not Ready for Citizenship, Being Robbed Systematically by Whites, Using Every Conceivable Method in Criminal Calendar

1877: San Carlos Reservation - Indian Agent Opened Three Indian Reservations to Ranchmen and Miners, Including Important Tracts of Agricultural and Mineral Lands

1878: Reduction of Indian Agencies, Consolidation of Indians on Small Reservations, Sale of Lands Vacated by Consolidation

1878: Even Most Advanced and Civilized Indians Not Capable of Defending Their Lands When Title in Fee Is Vested in Them, Assaulted by Class of Land-Sharks who Do Not Hesitate to Resort to Any Measure to Defraud Indians of Their Lands

1878: Nevada, Indians Are Complete Vagabonds

1878: State Imposes Unequal and Unjust Taxation which Indians Can't Pay and They Lose Their Lands

1878: To Make Them Citizens Too Quickly Is to Make Them Paupers or Result in Their Extermination

1878: "Outrageous Frauds" Committed at Isabella Reservation, Michigan, on Land Patented in Fee to Indians - Out of 1,735 Indians

Issued Patents in 1871 on Chippewa Reservation, Isabella County, Michigan, Fully Five-Sixths Have Sold or Have Been Cheated out of Their Lands; Agent Collusion; Agent Resigned without Any Legal Consequences

1879: Commissioner Hayt - Proposal for a General Allotment Law with Restrictions on Alienability

1879: Transfer of Indian Bureau to War Department under Consideration

1879: Commissioner Hayt under Investigation; Committee of Inquiry Led by General Fisk, Chairman of the Board of Indian Commissioners; Hayt Trying to Surreptitiously Purchase Mine on San Carlos Apache Tribal Land; Hayt Resigns

213 // CHAPTER 32: Rowland E. Trowbridge, Commissioner of Indian Affairs (March 15, 1880–March 19, 1881) - Advocated Strict Social Controls, including Institutionalizing Marriages between Indians, Prohibiting Polygamy; Employing Indian Police to Enforce Laws; Supported Government Boarding and Day Schools; Initiated Land Severalty on Crow and Fort Hall (Shoshone and Bannock) Reservations

1880: Well-Disciplined Indian Police Force Enables Agent to Be Informed of Noteworthy Occurrences within His Jurisdiction

1880: Issuance of Patents Disintegrates Tribal Relations, To Prepare Indians for Citizenship Land Must Be Safeguarded against Alienation

1880: Sioux Reservation Desolate and Barren

216 // CHAPTER 33: 1881: Secretary of Interior Schurz on American Indian Policy

1881: Secretary of Interior Schurz, Present Aspects of Indian Problem - Solution Is Assimilation

221 // CHAPTER 34: Hiram Price, Commissioner of Indian Affairs (May 6, 1881–March 26, 1885) - Indians Must Adopt Our Modes of Life; We Are Fifty Millions of People and They Are Only One-Fourth of One Million; Few Must Yield to Many; Establishment of Penal Reservations for Refractory Indians; Allotment and Issuance of Patents with Restrictions on Alienation; Eliminating Fees and Commissions on Homestead Entries by Indians; Survey of Indian Reservations and Arable Lands; Prohibition of Introduction of Liquor on Indian Reservations

1881: SD, Rosebud Sioux, Not Progressing, Barren Land, No Timber,

Severe Winter Killed Stock, Large Percentage of Deaths at Carlisle Boarding School

1881: MT, Blackfeet, Need Aid or Will Starve

Commissioner Price: Legislation Needed: Establishment of Penal Reservations for Refractory Indians; Allotment and Issuance of Patents with Restrictions on Alienation; Eliminating Fees and Commissions on Homestead Entries for Indians

1881: Allotment of Land in Severalty and Permanent Land Title

1882: Commissioner Price - All Agents Notified to Withhold Rations from Indians Unwilling to Work

1883: Starvation of Blackfeet, Blood, and Piegan Indians

1883: Commissioner Price - Survey Boundaries of Indian Reservations; Law to Punish Arms Sellers; Appropriations for Indian Police

1883: Commissioner Price - Whenever State Is Admitted into Union, Indians Should Become Citizens of State

1884: MT, Blackfeet, Issued Condemned Bacon to Prevent Starvation

1884: NV, Serious Starvation Destroying Indians

1884: Fort Belknap Reservation, MT, Starvation

1884: San Carlos Apache Reservation, Segregation of Coal Lands

226 // CHAPTER 35: John DeWitt Clinton Atkins, Commissioner of Indian Affairs (March 21, 1885–June 14, 1888) - Question of How to Relieve Indians from State of Dependence and Barbarism

1885: Indian Citizenship when Farm and School Familiar among Indians; Education to Regulate Conduct in Obedience to U.S. Laws

1885: Commissioner Atkins - English Language Only in Indian Schools to Americanize American Indians; Pupils Punished for Speaking Native Languages; Citizenship Was at Center of Federal Policies of Indian Assimilation

1885: Dakota Territory Governor Gilbert Pierce - Allotment, Sale of Surplus Land

1885: Puyallup Reservation, WA, Railroad Access and Excellent Land

1885: WASH, Yakama Reservation, A Story of One Suspended Despotic Indian Agent

1886: Cheyenne and Arapaho Agency, J.M. Lee, Captain Ninth Infantry, Acting Agent, Pioneers Not Fond of Indians

1886: MT, Assinnaboines at Wolf Point, 250-300 Died of Starvation in 1884, Much More Tractable

1886: Michigan - Isabella Reservation, Gross and Wanton Outrage, Mark W. Stevens, Indian Agent

1887: Commissioner Atkins' Three Tests of Progress Toward Civilization

1887: Omaha Allotment Results Disastrous, Advocated by La Flesches and White Ethnologist Alice Fletcher

231 // CHAPTER 36: John H. Oberly, Commissioner of Indian Affairs (October 10, 1888–June 30, 1889) [Eight Months]; Initiated Standardized Curriculum to Use in Boarding Schools to Socially Reengineer Indian Children; No More Degrading Communism; Citizenship with Complete Assimilation

1888: Indian Must Learn "I" Instead of "We," and "This Is Mine," Instead of "This Is Ours." If He Will Not Learn, Then Guardian Must Act for Ward; Compel Citizenship and Assimilation with Masses of Republic

1889: North Carolina Eastern Cherokees, Land Poor, Opposed to Allotment, Victims of Frauds and Outrages

233 // CHAPTER 37: Thomas Jefferson Morgan, Commissioner of Indian Affairs (July 1, 1889–March 3, 1893) Indian Policy - No Place for Independent, Alien Governments; Indians Must Surrender Their Autonomy and Become Merged in U.S. Nationality; Allotment, Compulsory Education, Destruction of Tribal Government, Citizenship Prerogative of U.S.

1890: Indian Agents Have Semi-Despotic Power Over Indians

1891: Citizenship Inevitable; Indian Reservations Dissolved; Tribal Autonomy Mere History

1891: Guardianship to Citizenship

1891: Reservations Cannot Remain Intact - Perpetual Abode of Savagery and Animalism

1892: Commissioner Morgan on Education - Common Schools on Reservations, Agency Boarding Schools, National Industrial Schools, Nonpartisan and Nonsectarian, English Only, Coeducation Essential

1892: Commissioner Morgan - Indian School Rules - Prepare Them for Duties and Privileges of American Citizenship

1892: Commissioner Morgan - Compulsory Education

1892: Montana, Flathead Agency, Chiefs Bitterly Oppose Allotment

1892: Criticism and Abuse Are Results of Honest Endeavor to Administer Business of Indian Office

1892: Thomas J. Morgan: A Plea for Papoose, An Address at Albany, N.Y., by Gen. T.J. Morgan

239 // CHAPTER 38: Capital Formation under GAA

1896: Wisconsin, Menominees, White Mill Operators Keep Price of Indian Logs Down

1900: Farming Potential

1900: NM, Jicarilla Apache Indians, No Money to Buy Stock

1901: Idaho, Lemhi Indians, No Advancement in Cattle Raising

1905: WASH, Tulalip Agency, Uncapitalized to Participate in Fishing and Lumbering

1906: WASH, Fishing and Lumbering, Need Capital and Technology

1912: Fort Belknap, MT, Reimbursable Funds ($25,000) for Promoting Agriculture

243 // CHAPTER 39: Daniel M. Browning, Commissioner of Indian Affairs (April 13, 1893–May 3, 1897) - Allotments to Unprepared Indians

1894: Commissioner Browning - Children of Indian Women Marrying Non-Indian Men Become U.S. Citizens
1895: Contests Initiated by Whites against Indian Homesteads

1895: ND, Devil's Lake, Death Rate Doubles, Unable to Satisfy Hunger

1896: Fort McDermitt Reservation, Nevada – Indians Not Qualified to Control Ownership of Land or Assume Responsibility of Citizenship

1896: Pawnee and Tonkawa Indians Not Prepared for Citizenship - Ignorant Indian Is Thrown upon Mercies of Cold World, in Their Location World Is Way below Zero

1896: Neither Colville nor Spokane Indians Prepared for Allotment or Citizenship; Prey for Whites who Will Not Hesitate to Drive Them from Allotments, and Force Them, if Possible, to Abandon Them

1896: Piegans, MT, Starving to Death

1896: Annual Report of Superintendent of Indian Schools – Indians Must Learn U.S. Social and Religious Customs

1896: NM, CO, Acting Indian Agent, V.E. Stottler, First Lt., Tenth Infantry, Placed Children in School through Firmness and Use of Guardhouse and Starvation of Parents

247 // CHAPTER 40: William A. Jones, Commissioner of Indian Affairs (May 3, 1897–January 1, 1905): Complete Extinguishment of Indian Race by Its Absorption into Body Politic Is Goal; Eastern Sentimentalist and Western Land Grabber Unitedly Sprung Trap that Has Been Undoing of Indians Who Had Lands of Value

1897: Commissioner Jones - Annual Lake Mohonk Conference; Indian Monies in Custody of Government Subject to Preying Men

1897: Sec. Bliss - Indian Leaders Not to Travel to Washington with Requests; Must Handle at Agency

1898: Otoes - Bitterly Opposed to Allotment

1898: Pawnees - As Qualified for Citizenship as 10-Year-Old Child

1898: Mexican Kickapoos Previously Self-Supporting, Became Entirely Dependent

1899: By Necessity, Indians Were Placed Upon Tracts of Land Reserved and Set Apart; Could Be under Absolute Control and Efficient Surveillance

1899: Poncas Accepted Allotments after Opposition

1899: Yakima Allotment Mistakes

1899: Commissioner Jones Disparages Educating Indians

1899: AZ, Colorado River Reservation, Drought, Irrigation Pumps Broken, Many Indians Compelled to Leave Reservation to Escape Starvation

1899: NM, Zuni, Point of Absolute Starvation

1900: No Middle Ground between Surveillance and Extermination

1900: Compulsory Education Will Hasten Accomplishment of Government's Plan of Complete Extinguishment of Indian Race by Absorption into Body Politic of U.S. and Extinguishment of Reservations

Entire Educational System of Indian Office Is Predicated upon Abolishment of Indian Reservation System

1900: Nebraska Indians, Rations Delivery Improved

1900: Law Requiring Indians to Work for Annuities

1900: Crow Creek Agency, SD, Unfair Allotting of Land

1900: Commissioner Jones – Rations Reduced as Much as Possible; except Where Needed to Prevent Indians from 'Dropping Out of Existence' (i.e., Starving)

1900: Indian "Movin' On" Until He Can Go No Further

1901: Commissioner Jones: Function of State: Assure Indian Has Opportunity for Self-Support; Protect Person and Property

1901: Klamath Indians, OR and CA, Allotted Sterile Lands

1901: Warm Spring Agency, OR – Allotment Mistakes

1901: Commissioner Jones Spiteful Report on Educating Indians

1901: Education - If He Is to Rise from His Low Estate, Germs of Nobler Existence Must Be Implanted in Him and Cultivated

1901: Industrial Training, Break Up Reservations, Indians Have to Rely on Their Own Resources

1902: Commissioner Jones - End Dancing, Feasts, Painting and Long Hair

1902: San Carlos Apache Reservation, AZ, Disastrous Drought, Need for Rations

1902: WIS, Winnebagoes, Annuity Amounting to $19.22 Per Year, Aged and Infirm Distressed

1903: *United States v. Rickert*, Allotted Lands Tax-Exempt

1903: North Dakota, Drought, No General Rations

1902: MINN, Leech Lake Agency, Indians Don't Know Where Allotments Are

1903: La Pointe Agency, WI, No Idea of Value of Money

1903: Commissioner Jones - Indian Choices - Toy for Tourist or Citizen

1903: Commissioner Jones - Cannot Exist as Cyst on Nation; Reduce Lands to What He Can Use; Open Remainder to White Settlement

1903: Commissioner Jones - Educate Indian - Prepare Him for Abolition of Tribal Relations; Take His Land in Severalty

1903: Commissioner Jones - Teach Its Indian Wards How to Farm

1903: Commissioner Jones – End Rations and Annuities - Are Disincentive to Work

1903: Commissioner Jones – Farm or Starve

1903: NM, Mescalero Apache Reservation, Starvation Basis for Years, Many Student Deaths

1904: North Dakota, Turtle Lake, Chippewa Refused to Move to Reservation, Starving - (i.e., 'Putting Indian into Civilization and Allowing Him to Starve There')

1904: SD, Sioux, Lower Brule Agency, Crops Failure

1904: Minnesota, Leech Lake Agency, Failure of Crops, Suffering among Young, Infirm and Elderly

Problem with Commissioner Jones Program: Indian Not Given White Man's Chance

1904: Commissioner Jones - Disposal of Indian Reservations Does Not Require Indian Consent; Guardian of Child Does Not Ask for Consent; Divide Reservations into Homesteads and Open Surplus to White Settlement

1904: Mescalero Apache Reservation, NM: Progressive Indians Rewarded for Good Behavior by Generous Issue of Government Largesse

1904: States Trying to Steal Indian Swamp Lands

1904: Wily Trader, Greedy Land Shark, and Heartless Money Lender; Insatiable Greed for "More Land," "More Free Homes," for Greater Riches, Unwilling to Respect Indian Rights

1904: Puyallup Agency - Valuable Agricultural Lands Lost to Unprincipled Schemer and Blackleg in Tacoma

1904: Jicarilla Apache Reservation, NM – 86% Allotments Undelivered

266 // CHAPTER 41: Francis E. Leupp, Commissioner of Indian Affairs (January 1, 1905–June 18, 1909) - Soon as Mixed or Full Blood Indian Competent, Sever Ties which Bind Him to Tribe – As to What Will Become of Indian's Land and Money - Man Never Lived who Did Not Learn More Valuable Lesson from One Hard Blow than from Twenty Warnings

1905: Uintah Reservation - Irrigation Project Paid with Six Hundred Thousand Dollars of Ute Tribe's Money; Blackfoot - Three Hundred Thousand Dollars - Same; Yakimas and Flatheads - Same

1905: Tulalip Reservation: Problem of Consolidation, Concentration, and Large Local Development; Encroachment by White Man into Fishing and Lumbering; Rushing Indians into Citizenship for Which They Are Unprepared

1905: Report of School Superintendent of Puyallup Agency, Citizenship Debacle

1905: In *Matter of Heff* - Indians Became American Citizens when They Accepted Their Land Allotment, under General Allotment Act, Not at Expiration of Trust Period

1906: Burke Act

BIC Opposes Burke Act

1906: Columbia Reserve - Wire-Pulling Efforts

1906: Puyallup Indian Agency, WA, Indians Target for Fraud

1906: Colville Agency, WASH, Cheating, Frightening Indians Out of Lands

No Official Definition of Competence or Incompetence

1906: Citizen Potawatomi, Absentee Shawnee, and Mexican Kickapoo: (1) Surrounding Country Had Not Been Settled and Indians Could Not Realize Importance of Their Allotment; (2) Did Not Understand What Title-in-Fee Land Meant; (3) Did Not Understand Value of Their Allotment; and (4) Did Not Understand that Disposing of Allotment Would Leave Them Homeless

1906: Flandreau Sioux Indians, SD, Moving in with Relatives on Other Reservations

1906: Umatilla Tribe, OR, Refuse to Approve Allotments

1907: Ethnically He Is Indian which Is a Source of Pride, But as a Citizen He Is Not an Indian but an American and Any Civil Distinctions Must Be Expunged

274 // CHAPTER 42: Indian Labor

1899: WASH, Puyallup Indians, Indians Labor as Hop Pickers

1899: NM, Jicarilla Apaches, Sell Indian Arts & Crafts (Bows & Arrows, Baskets & Bead Work)

1900: New York Indians, Common Laborers for Railroads, Timber Companies

1901: NY, Allegany Reservations, Common Laborers for Railroads, Timber Companies

1901: NV, Indian Labor, Ranch Hands

1901: Nevada, Western Shoshone, Common Labor as Ranch Hands

1901: Oregon, Grande Ronde Agency, Farm Laborers

1901: AZ, San Carlos Agency, Indian Labor – "Railroad Work to Washing Dishes"

1902: Utah, St. George, Indian Laborers – Ranch Hands, Farm Work, Lumber Jacks

1901-1902: AZ, Mohave Indians, Labor in Mines and Ranches

1902: AZ, Pima Indians - Railroad Work in NV

1902: AZ, Pima, Farm and Railroad Workers, No Better Laundresses than Pima Women; Sadly, Returned Students in Last Stages of Consumption

1902: AZ, Fort Apache Indian Agency, Legitimate Employment Difficult to Secure

1902: MT, Fort Peck Agency, Common Ranch and Railroad Workers, Women as Domestic Labor

1902: NV, Indian Women Domestic Labor

1903: MT, Crow Indians, Irrigation Canal Labor

1903: Utah, Men Work at Odd Jobs for Whites, Squaws Do Laundry for Whites

1903: WASH, Tulalip Agency, Work in Fish Canneries and Picking Hops

1903: WASH, Port Madison Reservation, Work in Logging Camps

1903: AZ, Papago Indians, Railroad Workers

1904: NM, Santa Fe Industrial School, Outing System - Railroad Workers, Migrant Farm Workers in CO

1904: AZ, San Carlos Agency, Dam Site Labor, Railroad Work

1904: Moapa Reservation, Moapa, Nev., Paiute Indians, Railroad Workers, Ranch Hands, Women are Domestic Help

1904: WASH, Neah Bay Agency, Migrant Farm Workers

1904: WY, Eastern Shoshoni Agency, Farm, Haul Military Freight

1905: Effect on Family Life of Breaking Up of Indian Homes by Organizing "Gangs of Indians" for Work at Distant Points – "Unfavorable"

1906: Commissioner Leupp Initiated Long-Term Leases of Tribal Lands to Sugar-Beet Companies in Exchange for Pledge to Employ Indian Laborers - Indian Takes to Beet Farming as Naturally as Italian Takes to Art or German to Science, Whole Family Can Work, Even Papooses

1906: Employment Bureau - Indian Laborers: Railroad Construction Laborers, Irrigation-Ditch Diggers, Beet Farm Help

1918-1919: Indian Employment – Common Labor, AZ, NM, CA, Cotton Picking

284 // CHAPTER 43: 1906: Conditions at White Earth Agency, Minn. - Land Speculators Plying Indians with Liquor to Secure Deeds or Mortgages to Valuable Timber Land for Small Amounts – Town Filled with Drunken Indians – 80% of Reservation Sold – "Ignorant Indians Were Fleeced"

288 // CHAPTER 44: Robert G. Valentine, Commissioner of Indian Affairs (June 29, 1909–September 10, 1912) - Severalty Primary Means of Transforming Indians into Self-Supporting, Independent Citizens - Indian Policy - Cross between Extermination and Citizenship; Pressure of Private Interest, Clutch of Private Greed, Political Interests of Public Men Are Too Omnipresent, Too Overwhelming, Unless Countered by U.S. Sentiment

    1910: No More Credit to Indians by Indian Traders Used to Get Indians into Debt

    Abolition of Tribal Relations Requires Allotment of Tribal Land

    1910: Commissioner Valentine Systematized Issuance of Fee Patents; Competency Commissions to Tour Indian Agencies and Issue Fee Patents to Qualified Allottees

    1910: Commissioner Valentine - Alienation of Allotted Land

    1910: Commissioner Valentine Gets Authority for Leasing of Minerals on Allotted Lands

    1910: Commissioner Valentine Gets Authority for Timber Leasing

    1911: Commissioner Valentine - Prepare Indians for Lifting of Government's Hand and Lift Hand

1911: Indian Affairs, Field for Grafter, Must Be Addressed Publicly

1912: Policy to Avoid Loss of Indian's Property Leading to Debasement and Pauperism

293 // CHAPTER 45: Cato Sells, Commissioner of Indian Affairs (June 2, 1913–March 29, 1921) - Indian Family Would Starve to Death if Required to Support Themselves on Many Allotments; Unprecedented Increase in Issuing Fee-Simple Patents, Sales of Trust Lands

1916: *U.S. v. Nice* - Legal Status of American Indians: Citizen/Ward Dichotomy Erased - Citizenship Not Incompatible with Tribal Existence or Continued Guardianship

Commissioner Sells – Unprecedented Increase in Issuing Fee-Simple Patents, Sales of Trust Lands

Commissioner Sells – Discontinue Guardianship of Competent Indians

Commissioner Sells – Aware of Corruption and Inefficiency within Government and Grafter Despoiling Indians of Land

1917: Commissioner Sells' Indian Policy - Release from Governmental Supervision (1) Indians with One Half or Less of Indian Blood; (2) Those Demonstrating Competency and All Students Who Get Diplomas, If Determined to Be Competent; (3) Liberal Sale of Indian Lands, including Inherited Lands; (4) Liberal Issuance of Certificates of Competency; and (5) Liberal Release of Pro-Rata Shares-Trust Funds

1917-1920: Commissioner Sells – Competency Commissions, Issue Patents in Fee

1919: Upon Application, Citizenship Open to World War I Honorably Discharged Indian Veterans

1919-1920: Compulsory Indian Education

1920: Commissioner Sells - Indian Education Must Enable Student to Acquire Citizenship

298 // CHAPTER 46: Charles Henry Burke, Commissioner of Indian Affairs (May 7, 1921–June 30, 1929)

1921: Commissioner Burke Aware of Whites Cheating Indians Out of Lands

1921: Commissioner Burke - Patents in Fee – Tax Foreclosures; Squandered Funds; Two-Thirds of Indians who Received Patents in Fee Lack Business Experience, Many Have Lost Every Acre They Had

1921: Commissioner Burke Revoked Cato Sells's Declaration of Policy – Resulted in Unnecessary Loss of Indian Lands

Commissioner Burke's Education Goal – "Every Indian School Filled to Its Limit"

Indian Religious Liberty Controversy

1924: Indian Citizenship Act

1924: Tribal Opposition to Indian Citizenship Act

Hidatsa Chief Old Dog (1851 – 1928): Opposed to Citizenship

1926: Commissioner Burke - Taxation of Restricted Indian Property

306 // CHAPTER 47: Board of Indian Commissioners ("BIC")

332 // CHAPTER 48: Lake Mohonk Conferences ("LMC")

    LMC Motive in Addressing Public on 'Indian Problem'

    LMC Goals

    Interrelationship of LMC Members, Board of Indian Commissioners and Indian Bureau

    LMC's Gargantuan Political Influence

    1885: Rev. Abbott - We Didn't Take Country from Indians

    1891: Indian Lands Could Be Legitimately Expropriated

336 // CHAPTER 49: Ethnic Cleansing of American Indians

    Assimilation of Indians

    #1 Using Military Action to Control Indians

    #2 Ignoring, Re-Negotiating, Abandoning and Abrogating Treaties Where Necessary - No More Treaties - No More Tribal Sovereignty

#3 Exterminating Indians, Such as Occurred in Texas, Dakotas, Pacific Northwest, and Wherever Indians Possessed Valuable Land

#4 Theft of Indian Land, Timber, Minerals, Agricultural Land, and Water, Leaving Indians Destitute

#5 Destruction of Indian Culture, Language, Religion and Customs

#6 Through Fear, Uncertainty, Starvation, Disease, Death, Causing Severe Psychological Harm, Where Indians Questioned Their Ability to Survive, Weakening Ability to Counter White Settlers' Encroachment and Settlement on Their Lands

#7 Withholding Federal Aid (e.g., Rations and Annuities), Even when Due Under Treaties

#8 Acquiescing in Death of Indians from Exposure and/or Starvation

#9 Running Railroad Routes across Indian Lands, Allowing Quick Military Transport to Control and Subdue Indians; Bisected Northern and Southern Plains Tribes from One Another Reducing Their Military Threat

#10 Abolishing Indian Reservations

#11 Disintegrating Indian Tribes

#12 Allotting Tribal Lands to Individual Indians

#13 Government Purchase, at Fair Rate, of Surplus Lands Left after Individual Allotment

#14 Opening Surplus Lands for White Purchase and Settlement

#15 Selling Indian Lands for Alleged Incompetent Indians or Fractionated Interests on Death of Allottee

#16 Leasing Indian Agricultural, Grazing and Mineral Lands

#17 Establishing Tribal Trust Fund Managed by Indian Bureau, with Cash Value of Surplus Lands Purchased and Sales and Leasing Revenues, to Be Used for Indians' Benefit, especially Education

#18 Taking No Action to Protect Indians from Graft and Corruption Resulting in Incalculable Loss of Land and Resources

#19 Inadequate Capital and Lack of Agricultural or Fishing Equipment and Education

#20 Extending Federal and State Law over Indians, especially those Relating to Crime, Marriage, and Inheritance

#21 Indian Access to Courts, Along with Making Them Subject to Litigation and Liability; 1881: President Chester A. Arthur on American Indian Policy - Access to Courts

#22 Terminating Government's Guardianship over Indians, Terminating Their Legal Status as Wards

#23 Abolishing Indian Bureau and Its Agencies

#24 Distributing Tribal Trust Funds ($50,000,000) to Individual Indians

#25 Eliminating Tax-Exempt Status of Individual Land and Property of Indians; Use Tribal Trust Funds to Pay Cost of Bureau Services

#26 Failure to Define Indian's Legal Status and Codify Laws Regarding Indians

#27 Permitting Indians to Bring Claims Against U.S. in Court of Claims, Subject to Offset of Any Federal Monies Previously Appropriated for Their Benefit and Counterclaims of Liabilities to Federal Government

#28 Acculturation to "American Ideals, American Schools, American Laws, Privileges and Pressure of American Rights and Duties" ... "All That Is Good in Our Life as a People"

#29 Indian Boarding Schools

#30 Imposing Involuntary U.S. Citizenship, with Concomitant Rights and Responsibilities – 'Manifest Destiny' for Any Man or Any Body of Men on Our Domain

440 // CHAPTER 50: Failures of Allotment Policy

448 // CHAPTER 51: Other Issues Raised by LMC

    Responsibility for Indian Affairs in Congress Is a Dereliction of Duty – Too Divided, No Help for Indian

    1901: Irrigation Should be Provided in Arid Districts

1905: No More Financing of Sectarian Schools

1907: LMC Opposed to Burke Act

1909: Catholic Indian Mission Statement: Obliteration or Demoralization of People Is Not Their Assimilation and Civilization

Industrial Landscape Transforms American Indian People and Lands

1911: Meeting of Society of American Indians

1916: Last LMC

452 // CHAPTER 52: 1885: National Indian Defence Association

National Indian Defence Association (NIDA) Opposed to Immediate Allotment

1885: President Cleveland Was Not in Favor of Immediate Severalty

1885: Russell Errett (R-PA) House of Representatives Minority Report Opposing GAA

1885: NIDA Splits Away from Other Reform Groups

1886: NIDA Protests against Lake Mohonk Conference's Allotment Resolution

1887: NIDA Opposed to General Allotment Act

1887: NIDA Plans to Test Constitutionality of GAA in Federal Court

1887: Bland's Injured in Deadly Train Collision

459 // CHAPTER 53: Society of American Indians ("SAI")

1911-1923: SAI's Annual Meetings

SAI's Quarterly Journals

SAI: Debate regarding Indian Bureau

OCTOBER 12, 1911: INAUGURAL ANNUAL SAI CONFERENCE, OHIO STATE UNIVERSITY

SAI's Plan to Develop Indian Leaders

    U.S. Strategy: Setting Indians against One Another

    Indians Have 72,535,862 Acres

    Wealth of "Government" Indians Is $1,066,106,427

    Leave Indian to (1) Sink or Swim or (2) Educate Indian to Economic System of Modern Civilization

    SAI Free to Speak Truth, Non-Partisan, Non-Secular

OCTOBER 1912: SECOND ANNUAL SAI CONFERENCE, OHIO STATE UNIVERSITY

    SAI 1912 Platform #1. *Codify Indian Laws*

    SAI 1912 Platform #2. *Commissioner of Indian Affairs Primary Object – Advancement of Indian*

    SAI 1912 Platform #3. *Investigations relative to Indian Affairs*

    SAI 1912 Platform #4. *Complaints of Wrongs Perpetrated upon Indians*

    SAI 1912 Platform #7. *Equal Indian Representation on BIC*

    SAI 1912 Platform #8. *Employment of Indians*

OCTOBER 1913: THIRD ANNUAL SAI CONFERENCE, DENVER, CO

SAI: Problem to Solve

    SAI 1913 Platform #1. *Legal Status of Indians in Nation*

    SAI 1913 Platform #2. *Open United States Court of Claims to All Tribes to Present Claims*

    SAI 1913 Platform #3. *Education*

    SAI 1913 Platform #4. *Prompt Division in Severalty of All Funds Held in Trust by United States for Any and All Indian Tribes*

    SAI 1913 Platform #6. *Need for Data*

    SAI 1913 Platform #8. President Taft to Secretary of Interior --

Indian Must Assume Responsibility if He Demands Rights

Key Information from SAI's Quarterly Journals

1913 Article: Teaching of Ethnology in Indian Schools by J.N.B. Hewitt (Tuscarora), Smithsonian Institution

1914: SAI Office in Washington, D.C.

OCTOBER 1914: FOURTH SAI CONFERENCE, UNIVERSITY OF WISCONSIN-MADISON

December 1914: SAI's Meeting with U.S. President Woodrow Wilson at White House

SAI April - June 2014 Edition - Editorial Comment: Equal Status of Indians Imperative; Legislative Needs of Indians Need to Be Understood
SAI July - September 1914 Edition: Rumor Started to Cause Dissension that SAI Has Hostile Attitude toward Indians in Federal Employ

OCTOBER 1915: FIFTH SAI CONFERENCE, LAWRENCE, KANSAS

SAI 1915 Platform: Define Legal Status of Indians; Open Court of Claims to Indians; Distribute Tribal Trust Funds to Individuals

SEPTEMBER 1918: SAI CONFERENCE, PIERRE, SOUTH DAKOTA – New Faction Elected

SAI 1918 Platform #1. Closing Indian Bureau

SAI 1918 Platform #3. Liquor Traffic an Evil

SAI 1918 Platform #5. *Former Principles Reaffirmed*

SAI Quarterly Journal (October-December 1917): "BREAK THE SHACKLES NOW, MAKE US FREE"

OCTOBER 1919 SAI EIGHTH CONFERENCE, MINNEAPOLIS, MINN.

Proceedings Weary and Disillusioned

SAI President Charles Eastman's Speech Excerpt

1923: LAST SAI CONFERENCE, CHICAGO

SAI's Legacy

1913-1915: SAI - Wanamaker Expedition of Citizenship – Offensive to Indians – Completely Discredited

484 // CHAPTER 54: Dr. Carlos Montezuma

September 1915: What Indians Must Do, Speech by Carlos Montezuma, M.D. (Apache)

Abolish Indian Bureau
Dr. Montezuma's WASSAJA Newsletter, 1916-22

WASSAJA, July 1916: Churches "Tolerate Monstrous, Conscienceless Devil-Fish Indian Bureau Which Squeezes and Sucks Life-Blood Out of Indians"

WASSAJA, October 1916: WASSAJA Attacks SAI Indians Employed by Indian Bureau; SAI "Arm in Arm" with Indian Bureau

Indian Bureau's Object – Save - Not Sever Ties of Bureauism; Helped by Indian Organizations Internal Squabbling

Indians Must Become Own Emancipators

WASSAJA, November 1916: Indian Reform Organizations in League with Indian Bureau

WASSAJA, December 1916: Dr. Montezuma Questioned Every Aspect of Indian Bureau

WASSAJA, January 1917: 6000 Indian Bureau Employees Used to Destroy other Indians

WASSAJA, February 1917: SAI Divided

WASSAJA Pigeon-Holed as "DESTRUCTIVE AND NOT CONSTRUCTIVE"

WASSAJA, May 1917: Half-White Indians Given Control of Their Property; Indians Judged "Competent" by Indian Office Will Also Be Given Such Control

WASSAJA, June 1917: Reservations Are Prisons

~ 45

WASSAJA, June 1917: Indian Bureauism is Kaiserism of America

WASSAJA, June 1917: How Reservation Indian Complaints Are Treated

WASSAJA, July 1917: When Are Indians Competent?

WASSAJA, September 1917 - What Indian Office or Reservation Life Does for the Indian; What Freedom, Rights and Citizenship Will Mean for the Indian; Constructive & Destructive Basis of Each

WASSAJA, January 1918: Plea to Indians for Unity

WASSAJA, March 1918: Indians Wake Up, Protect Your Rights

WASSAJA, March 1918: Indian Bureau Doesn't Want to Go out of Existence; Dr. Montezuma Opposed to Competency Determinations for Indians

1910: Competency Commission for Omaha's Divides Them into Three Groups

WASSAJA, April 1918: Reservation Indians Ruled by Czar of America

WASSAJA, July 1918: Dr. Montezuma Denounced Despotic Control Indian Bureau Exercised over Reservation Indians

WASSAJA, October 1918: SAI Condemns Indian Bureau

WASSAJA, November 1918: Demoralization of Reservation; Reservation Indians Lives Permeated with Fear

WASSAJA, December 1918: Reservation Indians Forced to Cower as Dogs at Dog Pound

WASSAJA, February 1919: Indian Bureau Cracks Whip

WASSAJA, March 1919: Indian Bureau Sells Indian Lands and Spends Indian Money without Approval of Indians

WASSAJA, June 1919: Is It Legal? Dr. Montezuma Questioned Indian Bureau's Tyrannical Authority over Indians

WASSAJA, July 1919: Bleeding Indians More; Indian Bureau Leasing Indian Mining Lands

WASSAJA, August 1919: Indian Bureau's Duty to Teach Indians to Manage Their Natural Resources

WASSAJA, January 1920: Indian Bureau's Leasing 30,000,000 Acres of Indian Mining Land

WASSAJA, December 1920: Who Would Like It? Reservation Indian Has No Rights

WASSAJA, February 1921: Indian Appropriations Are Mockery

WASSAJA, April 1921: Dr. Montezuma Despised Reservations

WASSAJA, April 1921: Indian Bureau Is Army of Blood-Sucking Grafters

WASSAJA, April 1921: Reservations Are Czars Siberia, Dungeon of Human Crimes

WASSAJA, September 1921: Indian Bureau Will Relinquish Its Throttle Hold on Indians Only when Every Indian Dollar Is Spent

WASSAJA, December 1921: Indian Bureau - Cold Blooded Greed

WASSAJA, March 1922: Indian Bureau - "Perpetual Machine"

1909: Board of Indian Commissioners - Is Indian Bureau No More than Well-Oiled Machine?

WASSAJA, October 1922: Dr. Montezuma Ill, End of WASSAJA Newsletter

504 // CHAPTER 55: 2024: Centennial Anniversary of Indian Citizenship Act

2024: Southern Ute Indian Tribe: "Indian Citizenship Act Offered Citizenship on Paper, But Also Sought to Dismantle Our Identity"

2024: Ute Mountain Ute Tribe: History Was Too Fraught To Warrant A "Celebration"

506 // APPENDICES

APPENDIX A: 1885: WASH, Yakama Reservation, A Story of One 'Suspended' Despotic Indian Agent

APPENDIX B: DECLARATION OF POLICY IN THE ADMINISTRATION OF INDIAN AFFAIRS By HON. CATO SELLS, Commissioner of Indian Affairs, Report of the Commissioner of Indian Affairs to the Secretary of the Interior, Office of Indian Affairs, 1917

APPENDIX C: Lake Mohonk Friends of the Indian Annual Conferences: Platforms

APPENDIX D: Lands in Severalty to Indians, Minority Report of Committee on Indian Affairs, Rep. Russell Errett, *et al.*, H.R. Rep. No. 1576, 46th Cong., 2nd Sess. (1880)

APPENDIX E-1: Society of American Indians Petitions to President of the United States
APPENDIX E-2: Society of American Indians Memorial to Congress
APPENDIX E-3: Highlights from Quarterly Journals of the Society of American Indians, 1912–1916

APPENDIX F: Excerpts from Charles Eastman's Books

PREFACE

~

Primary Source Reliance

The author's reliance on numerous direct citations from relevant historical documents is to provide factual evidence of the subject. This format derives from her view that the material under discussion here is best experienced by the contemporaneous voice unfiltered by time or personal interpretations and revisions.

Different Names for Particular Tribe/Nation

American Indian people describe their own cultures and the places they come from in many ways. Tribes often have more than one name. When Europeans arrived in the Americas, they used inaccurate pronunciations of the tribal names or used a name that another tribe used to refer to that tribe or renamed the tribes with European names. Following the preference of many Native peoples, when possible, we will refer to nations, tribes and bands by the English version of the name they use for themselves. [The use of the terms "tribe" and "nation" varies. Some groups prefer "nation" to emphasize their sovereignty. Others refer to themselves as a "tribe" in line with traditional usage.]

Different Names for Land Areas in "America"

The competition between Spain, France, Great Britain and the U.S. to establish "sovereignty" over lands inhabited by Indian peoples led to a variety of names for the same areas and 'alleged' jurisdiction over them. The U.S. would establish large Territories which would then be reduced in size to smaller territories and then become states, with modification of state lines as well.

Personal Names; Spelling

The names of historical American Indian people can cause much confusion for historians and readers. People often received several names over the course of their lives. A single person might have a birth name, a clan name, a name related to a good deed or act of bravery, and a French, Spanish, or English name used by Europeans or Americans. A tribal name could be spelled in numerous different ways.

Spelling Differed; Quotes Use Original Text

Spelling of words differed also. In this book, quotes used reflect original text, which may have different spellings, punctuation or mis-spellings or mis-punctuation. Please keep this in mind while reading this material.

Real Property Terminology

Fee simple: an estate in real property, meaning land, ownership of which is absolute, limited only by the four government powers of taxation, eminent domain, police power, and escheat, and by certain other encumbrances, or by a condition in the deed.

Trust patent: deed containing restrictions against alienation, especially one concerning land which is held in trust by the government for a period of years with an agreement to convey the land to the allottee at the end of the trust period - usually twenty-five years for Indian trust land.

Alienate: sell, exchange, or donate land, regardless of whether such sale, exchange, or donation is subject to a condition. In other words - Indians were not permitted to sell the land granted them until the trust period had passed - or until the government issued them "a patent in fee simple" before the expiration date - whichever came first.

Severalty: a sole, separate, and exclusive possession, dominion, or ownership.

CHAPTER 1: Charges Against American Civilization (Article by Arthur Parker)

~

This book must begin with Seneca Arthur Parker's blistering attack on the U.S. government's treatment of American Indians. Indigenous peoples will relate to this compendium of charges and denial of rights of indigenous peoples. Parker was a founding member of the Society of American Indians in 1911, its first Secretary-Treasurer and the Editor of the Quarterly Journal of the Society of American Indians.

The Society of American Indians was the first pan-Indian reform organization in the U.S. Most of the members were professional men and women. It was established to address the problems facing Indians which are set forth in Parker's "Charge Against American Civilization." *Though it is lengthy, every indigenous person should have a right to read it as part of their intellectual freedom to understand the conditions American Indians endured in the early twentieth century, and arguably still face. It is part of our history, part of our legacy of trauma.*

Certain of his most heinous charges include:

> Robbing a race of men-the American Indian-of their intellectual life;
> Robbing the American Indian of his social organization;
> Robbing the American Indian of his economic independence.

Among the denials, most blatant are:

> Denying the Indians a voice in their own affairs to such an extent that Indian councils may not now meet without the consent of the Commissioner of Indian Affairs;
> Denying the Indian a definition of his status in the country;
> Denying the Indian the right to submit his claims against the United States in the Court of Claims, without the special consent of Congress.

His call for restitution included:

Freedom;
Freedom of religion; and
Though he be stripped of land and possessions- the right to possess an honored name.

These charges and denials will be discussed herein. Each native person and Native nation must determine for themselves what restitution is due.

Certain Important Elements of the Indian Problem by Arthur C. Parker

There is little understanding of the blight that has fallen upon the red race within the United States. Notwithstanding the immense effort that is put forth by missionary bodies and by the federal government to remedy the unhappy situation of the Indians, neither of these forces acts as if it surely knew the elements with which it was dealing. But between the church and the state, if a comparison were drawn, the church understands better and responds more intelligently to the vital necessities of the race because its concern is with the man and not his property. Even so, there is no clearly defined philosophy that reveals causes and points out remedies.

The Indian Bureau of the Interior Department is charged by Congressional action with dealing with Indian affairs. Like some vast machine bulky with many ill-fitting, or inferior parts it grinds on, consuming huge sums of money for fuel and lubrication. Its constituted purpose is the protection of Indian property, the transformation of a race by civilization and its education, to the end that the Indians may become good citizens. Yet the Bureau is not achieving as great a measure of success as its Commissioner and earnest officials might wish.
(Emphasis added).

The church has a similar but broader object, expressed in its own words, "to save the souls of the Indians," in other words, to build manhood and character. But even the church in its various denominations has its trials and its missionaries pray for greater and more permanent influence over the morals of the red man whom they have set out to save.

Neither the church nor the state with all its powers for organization, however, proceeds as if it had discovered why its task was so greatly hampered or why it must apply so much unproductive effort. It appears that the Indians are perverse, are naturally inclined to degradation, are inferior and unmindful as a race, or that they were an accursed people as some of the early colonists thought. Yet both church and state labor on for they feel that Providence has entrusted a benighted people to their keeping. Each factor is an instrument of American civilization, the one a civic power, the other a moral force. Each sees the Indian problem through standards of its own race. Each translates its conception of the needs of the Indian in terms of its own liking. Each understands through its own system of thinking, and bases its acts upon the sure assumption of its correctness. No attempt is ever made to outline the plan of its action and to explain why it thinks thus and so, and to submit such a plan to a psychologist, a sociologist or an ethnologist for criticism and suggestion. Each has more or less definitely expressed the idea of "the white man's burden," or the obligation of American civilization and of Anglo-Saxon blood to lead mankind to higher goals. Each body resents any aspersion cast upon the integrity or the inherent moral qualities of the race it represents, for is not the Anglo-American the most charitable, the most conscientious of all races? Even so, there is a fundamental blindness, caused, shall we say, by a moral blind spot; there is a lack of feeling caused shall we say, by local anesthesia; there is a certain cerebral center in the cortices of the brain that seems insensible to certain impressions; there is a coating of the moral nature that is like, shall we say, a callous on the foot, covering an unsuspected nerve. A scratch gives no feeling, but when stepped upon there is a cry, "Keep off!" The development of the human race has not advanced to the point where men are uniformly fair minded. The people of the country who do have the welfare of an unhappy race at heart must come to understand the true nature of the injury the red man has sustained through his violent contact with civilization, and good men must learn to see the injury through the eyes and by the thoughts of the injured man.

For the sake of definiteness and to stimulate constructive argument *we wish to lay down seven charges, out of perhaps many more, that the Indian makes at the bar of American justice.* Whether the white man believes them just or not, true or not, he cannot discharge his obligation to the red man until he considers them and understands that the Indian makes them because he at least feels them just charges. There will be white Americans who will see the charges as rightfully made and there will no doubt be some Indians, who, trained in the philosophies of the narrow school of the conquerer [sic], will not admit them. (Emphasis added).

But notwithstanding objections we desire to submit the charges. The Indian's view must be known if his sight is to be directed to broader visions.

The Charge Against American Civilization

The people of the United States through their governmental agencies, and through the aggression of their citizens have:

1. Robbed a race of men-the American Indian-of their intellectual life;

2. Robbed the American Indian of his social organization;

3. Robbed the American Indian of his native freedom;

4. Robbed the American Indian of his economic independence;

5. Robbed the American Indian of his moral standards and of his racial ideals;

6. Robbed the American Indian of his good name among the peoples of the earth;

7. Robbed the American Indian of a definite civic status.

Each of the factors we have named is an essential to the life of a man or a nation. Picture a citizen of this republic without freedom, intellectual or social life, with no ability to provide his own food and clothing, having no sure belief in an Almighty being, no hero to admire and no ideals to foster, with no legal status and without a reputable name among men. Picture a nation or a people so unhappy. Yet civilization has conspired to produce in varying degrees all these conditions for the American Indians.

So much for the seven great robberies of the race. We have not even cared to mention the minor loss of territory and of resources - these are small things indeed, compared with the other thefts.

But though the robbery has been committed, the Government and great citizens will exclaim, "We have given much to atone for your loss, brother red man."

Let us examine the nature of these gifts. The Federal Government and the kind hearts of friends have

1. Given reserved tracts of land where the Indians may live unmolested;
2. Given agents and superintendents as guardians and constituted a division of the Interior Department as a special bureau for the protection of the red race;
3. Given schools with splendid mechanical equipment;
4. Given the ignorant and poor, clerks who will think and act for them, and handle their money;
5. Given food, and clothing and peace;
6. Given a new civilization;
7. Given a great religion.

So great and good gifts must have a price, for men cannot have these boons without suffering some disability. Measures are necessary to protect the Government itself from the results of its own charity and leniency to a people but lately regarded as enemies. The Government, therefore, as a price has-

1. Denied the Indians a voice in their own affairs to such an extent that Indian councils may not now meet without the consent of the Commissioner of Indian Affairs;

2. Denied the Indians the stimulus that springs from responsibility;

3. Denied the Indians the right to compete on the same terms as other men;

4. ***Denied the Indian a definition of his status in the country***;

5. ***Denied the Indian the right to submit his claims against the United States in the Court of Claims, without special consent of Congress***;

6. Denied the Indian a true and adequate education;

7. Denied the Indian the right to be a man, as other men of America are. (Emphasis added).

To be sure, the Indians were not at once denied these fundamental rights of human beings living in an organized civilized community. It was only as the seven great robberies became more or less complete and the reservation system grew, that the seven great denials took effect. The robberies and the denials are of a subtle psychological character and many there are who will ingeniously argue that the Indians still have all the things we have mentioned, or may have them if they will to do it, and that the seven gifts are but the gratuities of a charitable government.

But the men who so argue are devoid of finer spiritual perceptions, or perchance they are unable to see another man's viewpoint when they have one of their own. There are not wanting men and women who are unable to realize that another man can be hungry when their own stomachs are full. There are men having considerable mental endowments and a knowledge of the world who say, "If I were in his place, I would do thus and so. I would seize opportunity and soon all would be well." Men of this character are still mentally blind and spiritually dull, and are the first to deny that any great wrong has been done after all. ***They are insensible to the fact that the red man has felt his debasement and that his soul and his children's souls are bitter with a grief they cannot express.*** (Emphasis added).

The result of such denials of basic human rights to proud men and women is definite and deep. Whether he can express his thoughts in words or not, whether the turmoil in his heart finds voice or not, every American Indian who has suffered this oppression that is worse than death feels that civilization has:

1. ***Made him a man without a country;***
2. ***Usurped his responsibility and right of acting;***
3. ***Demeaned his manhood;***
4. ***Destroyed his ideals;***
5. ***Broken faith with him;***
6. ***Humiliated his spirit;***
7. ***Refused to listen to his petitions.*** (Emphasis added).

The old reservation Indian feels all these things, and they burn into his very soul leaving him unhappy and dispirited.

Only those who have had the comfort of education and the sustaining power of religion have been able to keep up hope, and even these often-times feel the sting the more and thus, a more painful recognition of their humiliation.

If these statements seem to tinge of irony or of invective to the civilized man with the moral blind spot, they are, nevertheless, very real things to the Indian who knows wherein he is wounded. To him this analysis will seem mild indeed for it speaks nothing of a thousand deeds that made the four centuries of contact years of cruel misunderstanding. Yet, to him these earlier years were better years than now, for he was then a free man who could boast a nation, who could speak his thought and who bowed to no being save God, his superior and guardian. Nor will we here mention the awful wars against Indian women and children, the treacherous onslaughts on sleeping villages, the murders of the old and helpless, broken promises, the stolen lands, the robbed orphans and widow, done by men professing civilization and religion-for this is aside from our argument. ***We mention what is more awful than the robbery of lands, more hideous than the scalping and burning of Indian women and babies, more harrowing than tortures at the stake; we mean the crushing of a noble people's spirit and the usurpation of its right to be responsible, self supporting and self governing.***

(Emphasis added).

Let it be affirmed as a deep conviction that until the American Indian is given back the right of assuming responsibility for his own acts, until his spirit is roused to action that re-awakened ideals will give him, all effort, all governmental protection, all gifts are of small value to him. **(Emphasis in original).**

The Indian must be given back the things of which he has been robbed with the natural accumulation of interest, that the world's progress has earned. American civilization and Christianity must return the seven stolen rights without which no race or community of men can live.

The Restitution of the Seven Stolen Rights

The people of the United States through the Congress, through the Indian Bureau and through the activities of its conscientious citizenship must return to the Indian:

1. *An Intellectual Life.* In his native state the Indians had things to think about. These things in their several subjects were a part of his organized mental and external activities. Using the thoughts that came, Indians could plan, organize, invent and promote their ideas. Their thoughts clustered about concepts with which they were familiar. All men must have thought nuclei. Rationally associated concepts become the basis of intellectual activity. Interest and desire are created and the man finds thoughts things that keep him alert. He knows his friends and associates are thinking along similar lines, because they are familiar with similar things. **Human beings have a primary right to an intellectual life, but civilization swept down upon groups of Indians and blighted or banished their intellectual life and left scattered groups of people mentally confused.** From thinking out of themselves they began to contemplate their own inward misery and act from the impulses that sprang from it. Yet nothing that could be easily or effectively understood was given to replace this mental life, "heathenish" though it was. The Indian must have his thought world given back. **(Emphasis in original).**

2. *Social Organization.* The Indians were always fond of mingling together. They had many councils and conferences. They had associations, societies, fraternities and pastimes. These things grew out of their social needs and each organization, game, dance, feast or custom filled some social need. They understood what they wanted and strove to meet the want. Civilization swept down upon them and with an iron hand broke up dances, forbade councils and ceremonies and refused to sanction customs, because they were barbarous. Yet nothing was given that ever effectually replaced these customs, speaking broadly and considering the social setting of the individual. *Civilization has not done its part until every Indian again finds a definite setting and an active part in the organized activities of communities of men.* Every man must have the right to be an exponent of a certain ideal or group of ideals. In these he finds himself and takes his keenest pleasure. (Emphasis in original).

3. *Economic Independence.* In his native state the Indian needed no government

warehouses wherein to contain his food and clothing, he needed no mills in New York to make his blankets, no plantations in Brazil to furnish his breakfast drink, no laboratory in Detroit to decant his medical extracts. Each Indian tribe, and to a large extent each individual was a master of his own resources. They could procure, cultivate or make their life necessities. They could make what they used, hunt or grow the food they ate. Civilization gave the Indians garments, and utensils they could not make. To get them they had to trade skins or lands. *When the hunting grounds were diminished and the Indians driven upon small barren tracts they became dependent for* food, dishes, tools and clothing, upon an external source. They were issued rations. Deep indeed was their humiliation. *From a self supporting people they had become abject paupers. Thousands died from eating decayed food, thousands froze because the clothing issued was stolen before it reached them, thousands without doubt, died from broken hearts. Then disease swept over them and reaped a full harvest, for the fields were ripe for the grim reaper.* (Emphasis added).

4. *The Right of Freedom*. The first and greatest love of the American Indian was his freedom. Freedom had been his heritage from time immemorial. The red man by nature cannot endure enforced servitude or imprisonment. By nature he is independent, proud and sensitive. Freedom to the red man is no less sweet, no less the condition of life itself than to other men. With Dryden the red man may exclaim:

"The love of liberty with life is given
And life itself the inferior gift of heaven!"

The fathers of the American Republic had suffered the hand of oppression. They could not endure the torment of being governed by a hand that wrote its laws across the sea. The will of the mother country was not the will of her children and there was a revolt. Patrick Henry arose and sounded the hearts of his compatriots when he shouted "Give me liberty or give me death." Benjamin Franklin, wrote; "Where liberty dwells, there is my country," and Thomas Jefferson in his Summary View of the Rights of British America laid down the principle, "The God who gave us life, gave us liberty at the same time." In how many instances do all these thoughts paraphrase the expression and the actions of the freedom-loving red men, who are governed not by their own kindred, or by their own volition, but by a hand that reaches out afar across the country.

The voice of great men rang out many times in the council halls of the nations of red men. The words of King Philip, Garangula, DeKanissora, Red Jacket, Tecumseh, Pontiac, Black Hawk, Osceola, Red Cloud and others, sound even yet, in eulogy of native freedom. The time was when red men were not afraid to speak for back of them was power. How masterful was the speech of Garangula in reply to the Governor of Canada, who came to intimidate the Five Nations and force them to trade with France alone, when he answered: "Hear, Yonondio, I do not sleep. I have my eyes open and the sun enlightens me. We are born free, we neither depend on Yonondio nor Corlear; we may go when we please and carry with us whom we please, buy and sell what we please. If your allies be your slaves, use them as such."

Imagine a reservation chief talking that way today to so small an official as a politically appointed agent set over his tribe! The chief would be sent to the lock up and the charge be labeled 'insubordination.' ...

A race of men and women to whom liberty was the condition of life itself must again have liberty restored, if it is again to live. (Emphasis in original).

5. *The God of Nations.* The American Indian must have restored to him moral standards that he can trust. A weak and hypocritical Christianity will make the red man of today what his ancestors never were-an atheist.

It has been difficult for some to realize what the disruption of an ancient faith can mean to the moral nature of a man. The old way is abandoned; its precepts and superstitions are cast to the scrap heap. Yet no wrath of the spirits comes as punishment. The new way is more or less not understood. Perhaps the convert may find that the magic and the taboos of the new religion have far less potency than he imagined, for no horrible calamity befalls him when he violates the laws of his new found religion. The convert may then become morally worse than before. All restraint has been eliminated and every sea seems safe to sail, for there are no monsters there, as superstition said. With his moral anchor torn from its moorings, he now is free and adrift. Thousands of Indians who have not understood Christianity, who have been unable to distinguish between the ethics of Christ and the immorality of some individual who was presumably a Christian, have become moral wrecks, just as thousands of others who have seen the light have gone their way rejoicing, singing:

"God's in his heaven, All's right with the world!"

The red man as he is today more than even he himself realizes, needs to know God. The basis of all his ancient faith was God. To him God was the beginning and the end of all human experience. Though he could not comprehend the deity, he could revere him as the Great Mystery, whose all-seeing eye looked upon his every act.

Civilization through its churches and mission agencies must restore the Indian to a knowledge of his Maker.

Civilization through its schools must give back the red man great ideals over which he may map his life and by which he may build his character. (Emphasis in original).

6. *The Right of an Assured Status.* Who is the Indian? What is he in the eyes of the law? The legal status of the Indian has never been defined. He is not an alien, he is not a foreigner, he is not a citizen. There is urgent need for a new code of law defining

the status of Indians and regulating Indian matters so that a definite program replaces chaos. A commission such as the Society of American Indians has petitioned for in its Memorial to the President should be empowered to draft a code of law and submit it to Congress. If a new day of friendship and cooperation has come, a new law should govern the red man in his relations with the federal government. The present laws in many instances are barriers to progress and conspire to produce conditions of life that make the assimilation of the Indians well nigh impossible.

As I have elsewhere stated *"Definite legal status in an organized community has an important psychological value. It is for want of this subtle psychological asset that the Indian suffers most grievously.* It is the root of most of his material evils. Witness the change that has come over the red man of the plains in the last fifty years. The old initiative has been crushed out, and in spirit 'the poor Indian' is low indeed …"

There can be nothing but bewilderment and anarchy when a man knows not what his status in his country is. This is especially true when the individual has property interests and matters at hazard in the courts-handled at the initiative of others. A group of people whose civic status is insecure becomes demoralized and the panic-spirit spreads to the individual. This fact is understood by thoughtful students of human progress. Hon. Franklin E. Lane, the Secretary of the Interior. summarizes this view in his annual report for 1914. He makes no attempt to excuse his country for its errors or lack of policy nor does he say that in spite of this "any Indian who desires can step through any day and stand clothed immediately with any legal right that is enjoyed by a citizen," as said an Indian school authority recently. The Secretary understands the psychic equation and candidly states:

> That the Indian is confused in mind as to his status and very much at sea as to our ultimate purpose toward him is not surprising. For a hundred years he has been spun round like a blindfolded child in a game of blindman's buff. Treated as an enemy at first, overcome, driven from his lands, negotiated with most formally as an independent nation, given by treaty a distinct boundary which was never to be changed 'while water runs and grass grows,' he later found himself pushed beyond that boundary line, negotiated with again, and then set down upon a reservation, half captive, half protege. What could an Indian, simply thinking and direct of mind, make of all this? To us it might give rise to a deprecatory smile. To him it must have seemed the systematized malevolence of a cynical civilization. And if this perplexed individual sought solace in a bottle of whiskey or followed after some daring and visionary Medicine Man who promised a way out of this hopeless maze, can we wonder?

Manifestly the Indian has been confused in his thought because we have been confused in ours. It has been difficult for Uncle Sam to regard the Indian as enemy, national menace, prisoner of war, and babe in arms all at the same time. The United States may be open to the charge of having treated the Indian with injustice, of having broken promises and sometimes neglected an unfortunate people, but we may plead by way of confession and avoidance that we did not mark for ourselves a clear course, and so, *'like bats that fly at noon,' we have spelled out our paths in syllables of pain.* (Emphasis added).

Professor F.A. McKenzie points out a number of pertinent facts entirely in harmony with this argument when he states:

> I maintain that the Indian has not been incorporated into our national life, and cannot be until we radically change a number of fundamental things. We must give him a defined status, early citizenship and control of his property, adequate education, efficient government and schools, broad and deep religious training and genuine social recognition. We must give him full rights in our society and demand from him complete responsibility.
>
> *The Indian today, the great mass of them, are still a broken and beaten people, scattered, isolated, cowed and disheartened, confined and restricted, pauperized and tending to degeneracy. They are a people without a country, strangers at home, and with no place to which to flee.* I know there are thousands of exceptions to these statements but yet they remain true for the great majority. The greatest injustice we do them - is to consider them inferior and incapable. The greatest barrier to their restoration to normality and efficiency lies in their passivity and discouragement. We have broken the spring of hope and ambition. (Emphasis added).

In [1846], the attorney-general of the United States said "there is nothing in the whole compass of our laws so hard to bring within any precise definition, or logical or scientific arrangement, as the relation in which the Indian stands toward the United States." Manypenny, George. Our Indian Wards. Vol. 215, Cincinnati, R. Clarke, 1880, p. xxiii.

7. *A Good Name among Nations.* No race of men has been more unjustly misrepresented by popular historians than the American Indian. Branded as an ignorant savage, treacherous, cruel and immoral in his inmost nature, the Indian has received little justice from the ordinary historian whose writings [American Journal of Sociology, 1913, reporting the Minneapolis meeting of the Sociological Society] influence the minds of school children. None of these popular writers tell of the white man's savagery, once he held the power over the red man's soul and body. The churchman would bid us be silent when we tell of the wars of Pilgrim Fathers on Indians. Some would not have us know that when the Pequot men, women and children had been murdered, the Pilgrim preacher rose in his pulpit to thank God the militia had "sent six hundred heathen souls to hell!" It is not considered good form to mention that Christian Indians were hunted and murdered like dogs in Pennsylvania and Ohio, and

even shot in church as they knelt to pray God's blessing on their persecutors. We are not allowed to know that Indians were hunted as wolves and that the states of Virginia, Ohio, Pennsylvania, North Carolina, New Jersey and even New York offered bounties for Indian scalps. The Pennsylvania schedule was as follows: "For every male above ten years captured, $150; for every male above ten years scalped, being killed, $134; for every female or male under ten captured, $130; for every female above ten years scalped, being killed, $50." Historians tell the white youth that Indians scalped their enemies and killed defenseless women, yet no mention is made that white men plundered, murdered, raped and tortured Indians. Nor are all these atrocities of an ancient day-Wounded Knee is not yet forgotten, and scores of local raids and unprovoked attacks, are remembered still. President Sherman Coolidge himself as a boy was saved as if by Providence from a machine gun attack on a peaceful Arapahoe village.

It may safely be said that most Indian raids or wars were provoked by a long series of contributing causes, which the patient Indians could no longer ignore. Proud people may not be forever goaded by abuse and broken promises.

A great nation like the United States needs not to vilify the history of its aborigines. They were men and brave men. Their cruelty and treachery was no more than that of the white men. They fought and each deed of violence they committed as "ignorant savages" can be matched by more revolting deeds committed by "educated, civilized men."

Why, then, may the truth not be known? Why besmear the pages of the red man's history with the blood that clots thick on the white man's own hidden record? Why not stand with Wendell Phillips and say to all the world,

> From Massachusetts Bay back to their own hunting grounds, every few miles is written down in imperishable record as a spot where the scanty, scattered tribes made a stand for justice and their right. Neither Greece nor Germany nor France, nor the Scotch can show a prouder record. And instead of searing it over with infamy and illustrated epithet, the future will recognize it as a glorious record of a race that never melted out and never died, but stood up manfully, man by man, foot by foot, and fought it out for the land God gave him.

The Indians have a right to know that their name as a people is not hidden forever from its place among the nations of the earth. They have a right to ask that the false statements and the prejudice that prevents historic justice be cast aside. They have a right to ask that their children know the history of their fathers and to know that the sins and savagery of their race were no worse than those of other races called great for bravery and conquest. Yet that the Indian youth in government schools are denied a true knowledge of their ancestors, may be judged from merely reading the essays of Indian students on the past history of their people.

The reservation Indian of today is not the noble red man of yesterday, though all elements of that nobility have not departed. The world is entitled to know why the change has come; the United States must know the facts we have pointed out and respond to the obligation that knowledge entails. The Indian must again be given a name that may be honored, else what sort of men and women will these future citizens be, who are to look to their ancestral blood as that of an accursed and inferior race?

Though he be stripped of land and possessions-give the red man the right to possess an honored name. How well may the red man exclaim with Iago:

Who steals my purse steals trash, 'tis something, 'tis nothing –
'Twas mine, 'tis his, and has been a slave to thousands;
But he that filches from me my good name
Robs me of that which not enriches him,
And makes me poor indeed! (Emphasis in original).

The End of the Old Life and the Hope of the New

Because of the emergencies that arose to make the mingling of the two races dangerous, undesirable or incompatible, special provisions were made for the treatment of the Indians. The Indian country as it became dissipated was replaced by reservations. It seemed eminently just that tribes of men having a common ancestry, language and interests should be placed together. Over these reservations, agents and later superintendents were placed to act for the government. The Indians having lost or bartered away their game lands secured by treaty or otherwise a supply of rations from the Government. They thus became abject dependents by very force of circumstances. To care for the young, schools were built by church organizations and by the Government. The ignorant, minor children and the incompetent, as in Oklahoma, were given guardians to act for them and to hold their estates. To a people so protected, civilization and religion were offered. But the depressing effect of the other conditions had evolved a people upon whom these agencies of human development took scant effect. Their very environment was adverse to refining influences. Thus the seeds of good had infertile soil in which to grow.

The great power for good among the Indians from the early contact period down to this day has been the school. Education in useful knowledge and the stimulation to industry has meant much to the Indian. So important have these things been that gentle hearted missionaries sent out by the Society of Friends and by the Moravians established schools and industrial stations long before they attempted to teach religion. Their principle followed that of Socrates who taught that an ignorant man cannot be truly virtuous.

The Indian has one door to true freedom-it is the door of education. Through it he may again find a greater life than that which his ancestors have lost. But the education which is provided and which he receives must be adequate. The value of education can hardly be overestimated, and the United States can do no better thing for the young Indians than to provide great opportunities for educational training. But the Indian schools provided by the government must see that their pupils are made to understand the need of a higher education than is now maintained. The eighth grade work of the ordinary boarding school for Indian children does not greatly expand the minds of its pupils. **Such schools may afford a basis upon which to rear an education, but *they do not provide an education.* (Emphasis in original).**

Ideals that spring from an awakened mind are not ordinarily developed through the study of primary text books because an intellectual background has not yet been created. The higher education that we advocate is that which will provide a mental growth from which great ideals may spring. In an Indian school it must be as clearly understood, as it is in any school, that the highest aim of education is the formation of character. Character comes from the inculcation of ideals, so that a man's character is but an expression of his ideals. So far as a school succeeds in establishing ideals and making character it has educated its student. The school that fails to do this has imposed upon those who trusted it to fulfill its assumed mission. It therefore remains for those who have assumed an interest in Indian education to see that schools do hold up ideals, develop individual responsibility and strengthen character by making knowledge so desirable that Indian students will press on to the higher goals of learning.

If the church and the state are sincere in their desire to bring moral and civic salvation to the American Indian each must manfully face the conditions that has made the red man a problem. The psychological character of the problem must be recognized, for most of the red man's woes are diseases of mental attitude. The miseries of his external life are the results of a bewildered, dispirited and darkened mind. The work of the agencies of good is to give order and hope, incentive and ambition, education and ideals. Every effort of the Federal Government should be directed to these ends, and men must be made to feel the thrill of manhood, the joy of having a part in the making of their country, and a sure faith in Him who holds all mankind in the hollow of His hand.

If our argument has seemed harsh it has only been so as all truth is hard that awakens men to a point where the truth is perceived, for it is our belief that if we would atone our injury to a suffering man we must see his trouble as he sees it, though it pricks our conscience and causes us renewed effort.

The Quarterly Journal of the Society of American Indians, V. III No. 1 (January-March 1915), Certain Important Elements of the Indian Problem, Arthur C. Parker, pp. 24-38. American Indian Digital History Project. https://aidhp.com/items/show/158 (accessed online April 29, 2024).

CHAPTER 2: Focus of This Book - Indian Policy to Break Up Reservations, Destroy Tribal Relations, Settle Indians on Allotments, Deal with Them Not as Nations, but as Individual Citizens; American Indian Is to Become Indian American U.S. Citizen

~

This book is to study the settled government policy of Indian U.S. citizenship, as declared numerous times by the federal government, Congress and reform groups, as generally stated below by Commissioner of Indian Affairs J.P. Morgan:

> It has become the settled policy of the Government to break up reservations, destroy tribal relations, settle Indians upon their own homesteads, incorporate them into the national life, and deal with them not as nations or tribes or bands, but as individual citizens. The American Indian is to become the Indian American. How far this process has advanced during the past year will be shown under the head of the reduction of reservations and allotment of lands.[1]

The plan to incorporate individual Indians as U.S. citizens involved a host of procedures as uniformly detailed by the Indian Bureau, the Board of Indian Commissioners, the Lake Mohonk Friends of the Indian, the Indian Rights Association and the other Indian policy reform groups of the late 1800's-early 1900's. These procedures were substantial. While not all of their recommendations were enacted, this was an enormous, extensive, epic, American Indian ethnic cleansing effort pursued by the U.S. government. The sanctioned guidance of these groups is presented herein under the following categories:

#1 Using Military Action to Control Indians

#2 Ignoring, Re-Negotiating, Abandoning and Abrogating Treaties Where Necessary - No More Treaties - No More Tribal Sovereignty

#3 Exterminating Indians, Such as Occurred in Texas, Dakotas, Pacific Northwest, and Wherever Indians Possessed Valuable Land

#4 Theft of Indian Land, Timber, Minerals, Agricultural Land, and Water, Leaving Indians Destitute

#5 Destruction of Indian Culture, Language, Religion and Customs

#6 Through Fear, Uncertainty, Starvation, Disease, Death, Causing Severe Psychological Harm, Where Indians Questioned Their Ability to Survive, Weakening Ability to Counter White Settlers' Encroachment and Settlement on Their Lands

#7 Withholding Federal Aid (e.g., Rations and Annuities), Even when Due Under

Treaties

#8 Acquiescing in Death of Indians from Exposure and/or Starvation

#9 Running Railroad Routes across Indian Lands, Allowing Quick Military Transport to Control and Subdue Indians; Bisected Northern and Southern Plains Tribes from One Another Reducing Their Military Threat

#10 Abolishing Indian Reservations

#11 Disintegrating Indian Tribes

#12 Allotting Tribal Lands to Individual Indians

#13 Government Purchase, at Fair Rate, of Surplus Lands Left after Individual Allotment

#14 Opening Surplus Lands for White Purchase and Settlement

#15 Selling Indian Lands for Alleged Incompetent Indians or Fractionated Interests on Death of Allottee

#16 Leasing Indian Agricultural, Grazing and Mineral Lands

#17 Establishing Tribal Trust Fund Managed by Indian Bureau, with Cash Value of Surplus Lands Purchased and Sales and Leasing Revenues, to Be Used for Indians' Benefit, especially Education

#18 Taking No Action to Protect Indians from Graft and Corruption Resulting in Incalculable Loss of Land and Resources

#19 Inadequate Capital and Lack of Agricultural or Fishing Equipment and Education

#20 Extending Federal and State Law over Indians, especially those Relating to Crime, Marriage, and Inheritance

#21 Indian Access to Courts, Along with Making Them Subject to Litigation and Liability; 1881: President Chester A. Arthur on American Indian Policy - Access to Courts

#22 Terminating Government's Guardianship over Indians, Terminating Their Legal Status as Wards

#23 Abolishing Indian Bureau and Its Agencies

#24 Distributing Tribal Trust Funds ($50,000,000) to Individual Indians

#25 Eliminating Tax-Exempt Status of Individual Land and Property of Indians; Use Tribal Trust Funds to Pay Cost of Bureau Services

#26 Failure to Define Indian's Legal Status and Codify Laws Regarding Indians

#27 Permitting Indians to Bring Claims Against U.S. in Court of Claims, Subject to Offset of Any Federal Monies Previously Appropriated for Their Benefit and Counterclaims of Liabilities to Federal Government

#28 Acculturation to "American Ideals, American Schools, American Laws, Privileges and Pressure of American Rights and Duties" … "All That Is Good in Our Life as a People"

#29 Indian Boarding Schools

#30 Imposing Involuntary U.S. Citizenship, with Concomitant Rights and Responsibilities – 'Manifest Destiny' for Any Man or Any Body of Men on Our Domain

There were many nuances to these and other activities required to erase Indian identity - a huge undertaking. Indians would be forcibly thrown into the "melting pot", melting together with the millions of immigrants, abandoning their individual cultures.

NOTES

1. J. Morgan, Thomas. "Statement on Indian Policy". Americanizing the American Indian: Writings by the "Friends of the Indian" 1880-1900, edited by Francis Paul Prucha, Cambridge, MA and London, England: Harvard University Press, 1973, pp. 74-76. https://doi.org/10.4159/harvard.9780674435056.c10 (accessed online April 29, 2024).

CHAPTER 3: Brief Review of U.S. Citizenship and Naturalization Policies

English Roots: Theory of Natural Allegiance

The concept of American citizenship and naturalization derived from English roots, as discussed by James H. Kettner, a renowned colonial and early American history scholar and professor.[1]

> The English notion of the process of naturalization flowed from the common law theory of natural subjectship, or birthright citizenship. Early English law held that persons born within the royal dominions were the king's subjects.[2]

In addition, the statute *De natis ultra mare* provided that foreign-born children of English subjects could inherit in England, thus giving such children the status of English subjects.[3]

Despite inconsistent interpretation of the statute *De natis*, English jurists consistently maintained that either birth or descent could identify the naturalborn subject.[4] The system combined the principles of *jus soli* and *jus sanguinis* in determining subjectship. Under jus soli, nationality is acquired through mere fact of birth within the territory of the state. Under jus sanguinis, nationality is acquired by descent following the status of at least one parent, regardless of place of birth.[5]

It was not until the early seventeenth century that a theory of allegiance and subjectship was fully articulated by Sir Edward Coke, in *Calvin's Case*.[6] The case was a test case brought primarily to determine the nature of the union that had been forged between Scotland and England by the accession of James I, who was already James VI of Scotland.[7]

Sir Coke began his analysis by noting that English law encompassed a number of different kinds of *"ligeance"* describing various kinds of relationships. Coke's primary concern was with the *"ligeantia naturalis"* that characterized the natural-born subject.[8] Coke conceived of the bond between the subject and the sovereign as involving reciprocal obligations, "for as the subject oweth to the king his true and faithful ligeance and obedience, so the sovereign is to govern and protect his subjects."[9]

Aliens born out of the protection of the English king and owing their natural allegiance to another sovereign could become adopted subjects and share the rights that others enjoyed as their natural inheritance. British parliamentary acts of naturalization incorporated foreigners on terms that generally conferred the full rights of subjectship.[10] The parliamentary act operated retrospectively to the birth of the party. It enabled him to inherit land; take lands by descent, purchase, or devise; and naturalized his alien-born children.[11]

In contrast to the parliamentary acts, *royal* patents of denization granted only limited rights to a non-native person, such as the right to live, work, own property, or engage in trade, making the denizen a sort of halfway member who ranked above the alien, yet below the native-born or naturalized subject.[12] The limited nature of the rights and benefits conferred upon aliens through denization resulted from the view that denization was a grant of *royal* prerogative or grace.[13] Denization did not operate retrospectively.[14]

Colonial Experience: Theory of Volitional Allegiance Emerges

To the colonists', naturalization was a contractual relationship based on consent and choice, with its origin based on the influential works of John Locke and William Blackstone. (Emphasis added).[15]

The competing principles of ascription and consent are explained below by legal scholars and in an early case:

> Generally, and in its purest form, the principle of ascription holds that one's political membership is entirely and irrevocably determined by some objective circumstance - in this context, birth within a particular sovereign's allegiance or territory. Sir Edward Coke's theory of natural allegiance embodied the ascriptive view of membership in which individual preference does not affect political membership; for example, place of one's birth.[16]

The principle of consent, on the other hand, holds that political membership can result only from free individual choice. The consent theory is embraced in John Locke's Second Treatise of Government.[17] Locke based the theory on the action of free individuals to enter into society and establish a government to preserve their natural rights.[18] According to Locke, individuals are not naturally subject to a sovereign. The state of nature is a "State of perfect Freedom, where each individual is free to act as he thinks fit, without depending on the will of others or any Subordination or Subjection."[19] For mutual protection of their lives and property, individuals voluntarily form a compact to establish a community.

Under the terms of the consensual compact, each individual foregoes its natural freedom of action "to be regulated by the Laws made by Society."[20] In turn, the individual assists the community as required, and receives "protection from [society's] whole strength."[21]

Thus, although Locke agreed with Coke that the subject owed allegiance to the sovereign who embodied and controlled the legal means of protection, Locke insisted that the community, not the king, was the ultimate sovereign. The resulting allegiance arose from the compact.[22]

According to legal scholar Jonathan Drimmer, William Blackstone's Commentaries on the Law of England synthesized these divergent views. He further asserts that Blackstone was generally recognized as the authoritative source of the common law by the American colonists.[23]

> Blackstone argued that it is "a maxim in the law, that protection and subjection are reciprocal" and arise from an individual's birth within the dominion of the crown. However, following Locke, he analyzed the "mutual bond" between subject and sovereign in terms of "the original contract of society." Blackstone, like Locke, stated that individuals formed a society for mutual protection, and argued that: The whole should protect all its parts, and that every part should pay obedience to the will of the whole; or, in other words, that the community should guard the rights of each individual member, and that (in return for this protection) each individual should submit to the laws of the community without which submission of all it was impossible that protection should be certainly extended to any.[24]

Thus, Blackstone proposed that the communal association itself constituted the sovereign, and the individual owed allegiance to "the community" in exchange for its protection.[25]

> For convenience it has been found necessary to give a name to this membership. The object is to designate by a title the person and the relationship he bears to the government. Citizen is employed as it has been considered better suited to the description of one living under a republican government...[26]

> The original citizens of the United States were those who were members or citizens of the States forming the same at the time the nation was established, and the natural-born citizens of the United States are the descendants of these. The colonists viewed the legal process of naturalization as a form of contract between an alien who chose a new allegiance and a community that consented to adopt him as a subject.[27]

Foreigners Perplexed by Use of Term 'Citizen'

In his article in The Atlantic Monthly in March 1888, Harvard Law School Professor James B. Thayer discussed the perplexing use of the term "citizen."

> It is interesting to notice that these words "citizen" and "citizenship," which we use so freely and familiarly today as indicating membership of a self-governing State, did not have that meaning in English speech until a little more than a hundred years ago; and it is we, on this side of the water, who have given them this sense, as it is we who have given prominence to the thing for which these words

now stand. ... The word "subject" was the English representative of our present term "citizen." ... In the Declaration of Independence we read it once: "He has constrained our fellow-citizens," etc.; and once in 1781, in the Articles of Confederation. In the treaty with France of 1778, the usual phrase is "subjects," "people." In the treaty with Great Britain of 1782, it is used in a marked way: "There shall be a ... peace between his British majesty and the said States, and between the subjects of the one and the *citizens* of the other." (Emphasis added).[28]

Need for Uniformity Obvious to Framers of United States Constitution

The need for uniformity was obvious to the framers of the United States Constitution. As a result, the Constitutional Convention adopted with little discussion article I, section 8, clause 4, which provides: "Congress shall have the power ... to establish an uniform rule of naturalization." Congress addressed the question of who should be offered citizenship in two ways: first, the law addressed what categories of immigrants should be offered U.S. citizenship; and second, the law addressed what characteristics and abilities individuals, within those categories, should have to be eligible for naturalization.

NOTES

1. James H. Kettner, The Development of American Citizenship 1608-1870 (1978), p. 3.
2. Ibid., 13.
3. Ibid., 14.
4. Ibid., 15.
5. Polly J. Price, Natural Law and Birthright Citizenship in Calvin's Case (1608), 9 YALE J.L. & Human. 73, 77 (1997).
6. 77 ER 377, Co. Rep. la (1608).
7. James H. Kettner, The Development of American Citizenship 1608-1870 (1978), p. 16.
8. Ibid., 17.
9. Ibid., 17.
10. Id.
11. Id.
12. Id.
13. Ibid., 30.
14. Ibid., 32.
15. Snowden, John Rockwell, Wayne Tyndall, and David Smith. "American Indian Sovereignty and Naturalization: It's a Race Thing." Neb. L. Rev. 80 (2001): p. 171.
16. Snowden, John Rockwell, Wayne Tyndall, and David Smith. "American Indian Sovereignty and Naturalization: It's a Race Thing." Neb. L. Rev. 80 (2001), pp. 186-187.
17. Id. (187) (citing John Locke, Two Treatises of Government, Peter Laslett ed.,

Cambridge Univ. Press. 1988).
18. Snowden, John Rockwell, Wayne Tyndall, and David Smith. "American Indian Sovereignty and Naturalization: It's a Race Thing." Neb. L. Rev. 80 (2001), p. 187.
19. Snowden, John Rockwell, Wayne Tyndall, and David Smith. "American Indian Sovereignty and Naturalization: It's a Race Thing." Neb. L. Rev. 80 (2001), p. 187.
20. Snowden, John Rockwell, Wayne Tyndall, and David Smith. "American Indian Sovereignty and Naturalization: It's a Race Thing." Neb. L. Rev. 80 (2001), p. 187.
21. Snowden, John Rockwell, Wayne Tyndall, and David Smith. "American Indian Sovereignty and Naturalization: It's a Race Thing." Neb. L. Rev. 80 (2001), p. 187.
22. Snowden, John Rockwell, Wayne Tyndall, and David Smith. "American Indian Sovereignty and Naturalization: It's a Race Thing." Neb. L. Rev. 80 (2001), pp. 187-188.
23. Snowden, John Rockwell, Wayne Tyndall, and David Smith. "American Indian Sovereignty and Naturalization: It's a Race Thing." Neb. L. Rev. 80 (2001), p. 188.
24. Snowden, John Rockwell, Wayne Tyndall, and David Smith. "American Indian Sovereignty and Naturalization: It's a Race Thing." Neb. L. Rev. 80 (2001), p. 188.
25. Id.
26. *Minor v. Happersett*, 88 U.S. (21 Wall.) 162 (1874).
27. Annual Report of the Department of the Interior, Volume 2, United States, Department of the Interior, U.S. Government Printing Office, 1891, pp. 22-23.
28. Thayer, James B., "The Dawes Bill and The Indians", Atlantic Monthly, March 1888.

CHAPTER 4: Citizenship under Treaties with Indian Nations

U.S. Constitution's Treaty Power

Under the Constitution's Treaty Power, some of the early treaties between the United States and Indian nations provided that Indians could obtain U.S. citizenship. The methodology varied.

> **U.S. CONST. art. VI, cl. 2 (Treaties)** This Constitution, and the Laws of the United States which shall be made in Pursuance thereof; and all Treaties made, or which shall be made, under the Authority of the United States, shall be the supreme Law of the Land; and the Judges in every State shall be bound thereby, any Thing in the Constitution or Laws of any State to the Contrary notwithstanding.

Methods of Indians Becoming U.S. Citizens by Treaty

A. Become Citizen of State

A.1. 1831: Choctaw Treaty of Dancing Rabbit Creek

The notion that Indians who did not move west of the Mississippi River could receive individual allotments, becoming citizens of the states where they lived, was embodied in Indian treaties as early as the Choctaw Treaty of Dancing Rabbit Creek in 1830. Under Article XIV of that Treaty, any Choctaw who elected not to move to Indian Territory could become a citizen of the State where they lived by *"signifying his intention to the Agent within six months from the ratification of this Treaty ... If they reside upon said lands intending to become citizens of the States for five years after the ratification of this Treaty, in that case a grant in fee simple shall issue..."* (Emphasis added).[1]

B. Dissolution of Tribal Organization

Some treaties merely dissolved the tribal organization. Article 5 of the Treaty of July 31, 1855, with the Ottawa and Chippewa provided: *The tribal organization of said Ottawa and Chippewa Indians ... is hereby dissolved.* (Emphasis added).[2]

After being made citizens under an 1843 statute, most Stockbridge Indians refused to accept it; they later persuaded Congress to revoke the legislation and enter into a treaty restoring their status as a tribe.[3]

C. Election to Dissolve Tribal Relations and Become U.S. Citizens
Some treaties required an election to dissolve the tribal organization itself.

C.1. 1855: Wyandot Treaty – Indians Sufficiently Advanced in Civilization, Become U.S. Citizens, Indian Tribe Terminated

The Wyandot Treaty in January 1855 is typical of such an agreement:

> Article 1. *The Wyandott Indians having become sufficiently advanced in civilization, and being desirous of becoming citizens, it is hereby agreed and stipulated, that their organization, and their relations with the United States as an Indian tribe shall be dissolved and terminated on the ratification of this agreement ... and from and after the date of such ratification, the said Wyandott Indians, and each and every one of them, except as hereinafter provided, shall be deemed, and are hereby declared, to be citizens of the United States.* (Emphasis added).[4]

C.2. 1862: Treaty with the Ottawa

The Ottawa Indians of the United Bands of Blanchard's Fork and of Certain Ottawa Roche de Boeuf, "*having become sufficiently advanced in civilization, and being desirous of becoming citizens of the United States, it is hereby agreed and stipulated that their organization, and their relations with the United States, as an Indian tribe, shall be dissolved and terminated...*" (Emphasis added).[5]

D. Others Required Election and Proof of Competency

Others required an election to become a U.S. citizen and proof of competency such as the 1866 Treaty with the Delaware Indians:

> Article IX. ... *any of said Delawares, being adults, may appear before the said judge in open court, and make the same proof and take the same oath of allegiance as is provided by law for the naturalization of aliens, and also make proof to the satisfaction of said court that he is sufficiently intelligent and prudent to control his own affairs and interests, that he has adopted the habits of civilized life, and has been able to support, for at least five years, himself and family*; when he shall receive a certificate of the same under the seal of the said court; and on the filing of the said certificate in the office of the commissioner of Indian affairs, the said Delaware Indian shall be constituted a citizen of the United States... (Emphasis added).[6]

NOTES

1. Treaty with the Choctaws, September 27, 1830, art. 14, 7 Stat. 333, 335.
2. Art. 5, 11 Stat. 621. Also, Treaty of July 31, **1855** with Ottawa and Chippewa, Art. 5, 11 Stat. 621; Act of March 3, **1839**, sec. 7, 5 Stat. 349, 351 (Brotherton); Act of March 3, **1843**, sec. 7, 5 Stat. 645, 647 (Stockbridge).
3. Treaty with the Stockbridge Tribe, Stockbridge-U.S., Nov. 24, 1848, 9 Stat. 955.
4. Article 1. Treaty with the Wyandot, 1855, 10 Stat. 1159.

5. Treaty with the Ottawa, June 24, 1862, art. 4, 12 Stat. 1237, 1238. Also, Treaty with the Cherokee, July 8, **1817**, art. 8, 7 Stat. 156; Treaty with the Delawares, art. 9, July 4, **1866**, 14 Stat. 793, 796; Treaty between the United States of America and the Senecas, Mixed Senecas and Shawnees, Quapaws, Confederated Peorias, Kaskaskias, Weas, and Piankeshaws, Ottawas of Blanchard's Fork and Roche de Boeuf, and certain Wyandottes, Feb. 23, **1867**, 15 Stat. 513.

6. Treaty with the Delaware Indians, art. 9, July 4, 1866, 14 Stat. 793. Also, Treaty with the Kickapoo, art. 3, June 28, **1862**, 13 Stat. 623; Treaty of November 15, **1861** with the Potawatomie, 12 Stat. 1191; Act of March 3, **1873** (Miami), 17 Stat. 631 (two competent witnesses and proof to the satisfaction of the circuit court of the United States for the State of Kansas). Treaty with the Potawatomie, February 27, **1867**, arts. 4 and 6, 15 Stat. 531-533 (certificate of the agent and business committee that he is fully competent to manage his own affairs).

CHAPTER 5: U.S. Constitution and Statutes on Naturalization

U.S. Constitution on Naturalization

Under the U.S. Constitution, Congress was clothed with the power to establish a uniform rule of Naturalization. U.S. CONST. art. I, § 8 (Naturalization): Clause 4. The Congress shall have Power * * * To establish an uniform Rule of Naturalization...

1790: U.S.' First Naturalization Law Applied Only to "Free White Persons"

The nation's first naturalization law, enacted in 1790, explicitly provided that only "free white persons" could naturalize.

1846: *United States v. Rogers*: Consensual Tribal Citizenship by White Person Intermarrying an Indian Not Sufficient to Make White Person an Indian for Purposes of Federal Law

In 1846, in *United States v. Rogers*, the court was presented with the question of whether an intermarried white citizen of the Cherokee Nation was an Indian. Rogers alleged that, as a mature adult, he had been adopted by the Cherokee Indian Nation. He had killed another intermarried white citizen.[1] At the time, the Trade and Intercourse Act of 1834 specifically excluded from its scope crimes committed by one Indian against another Indian.[2] Rogers argued that because both he and the victim were Cherokee citizens, they were both "Indians," and his crime was therefore exempt from the law.[3]

Justice Taney limited his review to two questions: first, was the country in which the crime is charged to have been committed a part of the territory of the U.S. and under its jurisdiction. He held though "occupied by the tribe of Cherokee Indians" it "has been assigned to them by the United States, as a place of domicile for the tribe, and they hold and occupy it with the assent of the United States, and under their authority." He disavowed decades of case and treaty law in asserting that: "The native tribes who were found on this continent at the time of its discovery have never been acknowledged or treated as independent nations." According to the Chief Justice's logic, the murder took place on lands within the jurisdiction of the U.S.

The second question was whether the alleged murderer and his victim were Indian and thus came under the exception to federal criminal jurisdiction which did not extend to crimes committed by one Indian against the person or property of another Indian. The Court rejected Rogers' assertion that he was an "Indian" for purposes of the statute. "...we think it very clear, that a white man who at mature age is adopted in an Indian tribe does not thereby become an Indian, and was not intended to be embraced in the exception above mentioned." ... The term "Indian" as used in the statute, Chief Justice Taney wrote for the Court, "does not speak of members of a tribe, but of the race generally - of the family of Indians..."[4]

1870: Naturalization Eligibility Act for Former African Slaves

After the Civil War, Congress amended naturalization requirements in 1870, extending naturalization eligibility to "aliens being free white persons, *and* to aliens of African nativity and to persons of African descent." (Emphasis added).[5]

1887: General Allotment Act

The General Allotment Act ("GAA") of 1887, divided Indian tribal land into individual allotments, forcing Indians into private property ownership. Up until this time the reservations had been held communally by all members of the tribe(s) living on the reservation. The alleged rationale for the GAA was that it would assimilate Indians into the mainstream of U.S. society by encouraging farming. Also, a transition to farming would lessen the amount of land needed by Indians such that it would justify reducing their land base. Alternatively, there was no need for a separate land base for Indians assimilated into the general society.[6]

To that end, individual Indians were given a certain number of acres, generally in 40-, 80- and 160-acre parcels, to be held in trust by the U.S. for the individual for 25 years and then patented in fee. Allotment was not new; certain treaties provided for it prior to the GAA, but the GAA enshrined it into U.S. statutory law.

After the twenty-five years that the allotment was held in trust by the U.S., it was expected that the Indian owner would be "civilized" and "competent enough" to manage his own affairs and the government would issue a fee patent for his allotment. (GAA § 5). The term "patent-in-fee" describes the title document issued by the U.S. to terminate the trust created by the trust patent issued to the allottee. The patent-in-fee operates to vest fee simple ownership in an allottee or his/her heirs.

Reservation lands not allotted or reserved for tribal or other use were considered surplus to Indian needs and opened to purchase and settlement by non-Indians.

Commissioner of Indian Affairs Atkins would expound from the bully pulpit:

> The advantages to the Indians of taking their lands in severalty are so important and far-reaching in their effects that I fear to dwell upon them in this report ...Every step taken, every move made, every suggestion offered, everything done with reference to the Indians should be with a view of impressing upon them that this is the policy which has been permanently decided upon by the Government in reference to their management. They must abandon tribal relations; they must give up their superstitions; they must forsake their savage habits and learn the arts of civilization; they must learn to labor, and must learn to rear their families as white people do, and to know more of their obligations to the Government and to society. In a

word, they must learn to work for a living, and they must understand that it is their interest and duty to send their children to school.[7]

Addressing "the inherent objection in the Indian mind against land in severalty," Senator Teller of Colorado explained that as long as the Indian "remains anything like an Indian in sentiment and feeling," you cannot make them take individual lands. It was part of their "religion not to divide his land." No matter what supporters said, this legislation was not "in the interest of the Indians" but "in the interest of [land] speculators." Issuing land in severalty would not civilize Indians, warned Senator Teller; instead, they first had to be civilized, educated, and Christianized to understand the value of a home.

It was said at the last session, speaking extravagantly, that the Indians were crying for lands in severalty. ... saying that they wanted a patent; asking that we should give them a fee-simple. There is not a wild Indian living who knows what a fee-simple is. There are a good many white men who do not know what it is, and there are certainly very few Indians, civilized or uncivilized, who understand it.

You propose to divide all this land and to give each Indian his quarter section, or whatever he may have, and for twenty-five years he is not to sell it, mortgage it, or dispose of it in any shape, and at the end of that time he may sell it. It is safe to predict that when that shall have been done, in thirty years thereafter there will not be an Indian on the continent, or there will be very few at least, that will have any land. That has been the experience wherever we have given land to Indians and guarded it as well as we might and as well as we could; they have eventually got rid of the land and the land has been of no particular benefit to them. I know it will be said, "Why, in twenty-five years they will be all civilized; these people will be church-going farmers, having schools and all the appliances of civilized life in twenty-five years."

It is in the interest of speculators; it is in the interest of the men who are clutching up this land, but not in the interest of the Indians at all;

If I stand alone in the Senate, I want to put upon the record my prophecy in this matter, that when thirty or forty years shall have passed and these Indians shall have parted with their title, they will curse the hand that was raised professedly in their defense to secure this kind of legislation, and if the people who are clamoring for it understood Indian character, and Indian laws, and Indian morals, and Indian religion, they would not be here clamoring for this at all.

> *This is a bill that, in my judgment, ought to be entitled "A bill to despoil the Indians of their lands and to make them vagabonds on the face of the earth."* (Emphasis added).[8]

1887: After Receiving Patent Every Allottee Subject to Civil and Criminal Laws of State or Territory of Residence; Imposed U.S. Citizenship; U.S. Citizenship Did Not Impair Rights in Tribal Property

An Indian became a U.S. citizen as soon as he received his allotment. The Act also declared that Indians could become citizens if they separated from their tribes and adopted the ways of civilized life, without this ending their rights to tribal or other property.

> After receiving his patent every allottee shall have the benefit of and be subject to the civil and criminal laws of the State or Territory in which he may reside; and no Territory shall deny any Indian equal protection of law; and every Indian born in the United States who has received an allotment under this or any other law or treaty, or who has taken up his residence separate from a tribe and adopted the habits of civilized life, is declared a citizen of the United States, but citizenship shall not impair any rights he may have in tribal property. General Allotment Act, 24 Stat. 388 (1887).[9]

1887: Allotment Act: Ipso Facto Makes Citizens of Indians

> I fail to comprehend the full import of the allotment act if it was not the purpose of the Congress which passed it and of the Executive whose signature made it a law ultimately to dissolve all tribal relations and to place each adult Indian upon the broad platform of American citizenship.

> Under this act it will be noticed that whenever a tribe of Indians or any member of a tribe accepts lands in severalty the allottee at once, ipso facto, becomes a citizen of the United States, endowed with all the rights and political privileges and subject to all the responsibilities and duties of any other citizen of the Republic.[10]

1890: Indian Territory Naturalization Act - Legislation Permitted Indians in Indian Territory to Apply for U.S. Citizenship

On May 2, 1890, Congress passed the Indian Territory Naturalization Act. *Members of tribes in the Indian Territory were allowed to apply for federal citizenship in federal court* without losing their tribal citizenship. The Act specified that in matters concerning members of a given Indian nation, the judicial tribunals of the Indian nation would continue to have jurisdiction. (Emphasis added).[11]

1901: Congress Enacted Legislation Imposing U.S. Citizenship on Every Indian in Indian Territory

The 1890 Indian Territory Naturalization Act was expanded in March 1901 by Congress declaring **every Indian in Indian Territory to be a citizen of the United States**. The 1901 Act accommodated a movement to raise the number of Oklahoma citizens in order for the Oklahoma Territory to apply for Statehood. (Emphasis added).[12]

1906: Burke Act

In 1906, the Burke Act postponed citizenship for the Indians until the end of the trust period, except for a provision allowing citizenship to be granted to an Indian who was deemed "competent and capable of managing his or her own affairs." Once an individual was certified competent, the Burke Act authorized the issuance of a fee patent to the allottee, immediately subjecting his/her lands to state property taxes and the option of sale to Indians or non-Indians.[13] While the GAA marked the destruction of a tribe's land base, the Burke Act of 1906 triggered the rapid loss of lands from individual Indian ownership.

Veterans of World War I

Congress enacted legislation on November 6, 1919, granting citizenship to Indian veterans of World War I, honorably discharged, upon application, who were not yet citizens. (H.R. 5007, An Act granting citizenship to certain Indians, September 27, 1919).

> BE IT ENACTED ... that every American Indian who served in the Military or Naval Establishments of the United States during the war against the Imperial German Government, and who has received or who shall hereafter receive an honorable discharge, if not now a citizen and if he so desires, shall, *on proof of such discharge and after proper identification before a court of competent jurisdiction*, and without other examination except as prescribed by said court, be granted full citizenship with all the privileges pertaining thereto, without in any manner impairing or otherwise affecting the property rights, individual or tribal, of any such Indian or his interest in tribal or other Indian property. (Emphasis added).[14]
>
> **INDIAN SOLDIERS.** It is estimated that considerably over 5,000 Indians have entered the military service of the Government.[15]

1922: Citizenship re Indian Parents and Children

In an opinion on Indian citizenship, the Solicitor of the Department of the Interior ("DOI") wrote as follows:

"(a) An Indian born in the United States of citizen Indian parents is born to citizenship. (b) Legitimate children born of an Indian woman and a white citizen father are born to citizenship."

"The solicitor of this department has held that where Indian parents became citizens upon allotment, their minor children became citizens with them, and that children born subsequent thereto were born to citizenship."[16]

1924: Indian Citizenship Act

ALL INDIANS ARE CITIZENS President Coolidge, on June 2, 1924, signed the Snyder Indian Citizenship Act and thereby conferred United States citizenship upon all noncitizen Indians, numbering some 125,000. The granting of citizenship to the 125,000 [Indians not yet citizens] ... did not change their relations as Federal wards; the United States still is their guardian and the trustee of their property and will continue in those relations until ... they are given unrestricted possession of the lands, funds, and other property which are now held in trust for them by the Federal Government.[17]

BE IT ENACTED by the Senate and house of Representatives of the United States of America in Congress assembled, That all non citizen Indians born within the territorial limits of the United States be, and they are hereby, declared to be citizens of the United States: Provided That the granting of such citizenship shall not in any manner impair or otherwise affect the right of any Indian to tribal or other property. (Approved June 2, 1924).[18]

Also known as the Snyder Act because it was proposed by Homer P. Snyder (R-NY), Representative of New York, the Indian Citizenship Act of 1924 was approved by Congress on June 2, 1924, and was signed into law by Calvin Coolidge as the 39th President of the United States, in a ceremony attended by representatives of a number of Indian nations.

The draft of the bill contained language granting "full citizenship" but the Senate removed the word "full", so that the "grant of full citizenship" was watered down to merely the grant of citizenship. The importance of this amendment is illustrated by the very brief legislative history that reveals the only floor discussion on the bill was one question from Congressman Garrett, from Tennessee, who asked Snyder if this bill meant that Indians could vote. Snyder assured him and the rest of the chamber that it did not and that this was still controlled by the states, when he answered: "[I]t is not the intention of this law to have any effect upon suffrage qualifications in any State."[19]

The Act did not include citizens born before the effective date of the 1924 Act, or outside of the United States as an indigenous person.

Indian Citizenship Act - Plenary Act of Congress

The Indian Citizenship Act was upheld when an Onondaga Indian challenged it in 1941. The Court of Appeals for the Second Circuit said the Act was binding, even if a treaty provided otherwise.[20]

NOTES

1. *United States v. Rogers*, 45 U.S. (4 How.) 567, 571-72 (1846).
2. 4 Stat. 729, 733.
3. *Rogers*, 45 U.S. (4 How.) at 571.
4. *Rogers*, 45 U.S. (4 How.) at 572-73.
5. 16 Stat. 254.
6. General Allotment Act, 24 Stat. 388, 389 (1887).
7. Report of the Commissioner of Indian Affairs to the Secretary of the Interior, United States. Office of Indian Affairs, 1885, p. 5.
8. Henry M. Teller, "Debate in the Senate on Land in Severalty," in *Americanizing the American Indians: Writings by the "Friends of the Indian," 1880–1900*, ed. Francis Paul Prucha (Cambridge, Mass).
9. Abstract in Report of the Commissioner of Indian Affairs to the Secretary of the Interior, United States. Office of Indian Affairs, 1887, p. VI.
10. Report of the Commissioner of Indian Affairs to the Secretary of the Interior, United States. Office of Indian Affairs, 1887, p. VIII.
11. 26 Stat. 81, 99-100 (1890).
12. Act of March 3, 1901, 31 Stat. 1447.
13. Act of May 8, 1906 (Burke Act), 34 Stat. 182, 183 (1906).
14. Act of November 6, 1919, 41 Stat. 350 (November 6, 1919).
15. Annual Report of the Board of Indian Commissioners, 1918-19 (Washington: Government Printing Office), p. 12. https://babel.hathitrust.org/cgi/pt?id=osu.32435064035710&seq=105 (accessed online October 5, 2024).
16. INDIAN CITIZENSHIP, OFFICE OF INDIAN AFFAIRS BULLETIN 20, (1922) reprinted in H.R. REP. NO. 68-222 (1924).
17. Annual Report of the Board of Indian Commissioners, 1923-24 (Washington: Government Printing Office), p. 2. https://babel.hathitrust.org/cgi/pt?id=umn.31951d02701465d&seq=3 (accessed online October 5, 2024).
18. Act of June 2, 1924, Public Law 68-175, 43 Stat. 253.
19. H.R. REP. NO. 222, 68th Cong., 1st Sess., Vol. 2, 1924, p. 1.
20. *Ex parte Green*, 123 F.2d 862 (2d Cir. 1941).

CHAPTER 6: Citizenship under Fourteenth Amendment ("14th Amendment")

The 14th Amendment to the U.S. Constitution debated by Congress in 1866 granted citizenship to all people born or naturalized in the United States, *including* formerly enslaved people. U.S. CONST. amend. XIV, § 1 (Fourteenth Amendment): All persons born or naturalized in the United States, and subject to the jurisdiction thereof, are citizens of the United States and of the state wherein they reside.

A.1. 1866: Senate Debate on Including or Excluding Indians for Citizenship under 14th Amendment

A lengthy Congressional debate ensued on whether Indians should be included under the 14th Amendment. Excerpts are included here because it addresses the multiplicity of views of Indian peoples at the time.

A.2. Opposition to Savages Becoming Citizens

1866: Senator Howard (R-MICH) – Opposed to Savages Becoming Citizens

> *I am not yet prepared to pass a sweeping act of naturalization by which all the Indian savages, wild or tame, belonging to a tribal relation, are to become my fellow-citizens and go to the polls and vote with me and hold lands and deal in every other way that a citizen of the United States has a right to do.* (Emphasis added).[1]

1866: Senator Hendricks (D-IND) – Opposed to Negroes, Coolies and Indians Becoming Citizens

> We have been justly proud of the rank and title of our citizenship, for we understood it to belong to the inhabitants of the United States who were descended from the great races of people who inhabit the countries of Europe, and such emigrants from those countries as have been admitted under our laws. The rank and title conferred honor at home and secured kindness, respect, and safety everywhere abroad: but if this amendment be adopted we will even carry the title and enjoy its advantages in common with the Negroes, the coolies, and the Indians.[2]

A.3. Indians Part of Quasi Foreign Nations

1866: Senator Jacob Howard (R-MICH) - Indians Part of Quasi Foreign Nations

> Indians born within the limits of the United States, are not, in the sense of this amendment, born subject to the jurisdiction of the United States. They are regarded, and always have been in our legislation and jurisprudence, as being quasi foreign nations.[3]

> ... Certainly, gentlemen cannot contend that an Indian belonging to a tribe, although born within the limits of a State is subject to [its] full and complete jurisdiction. That question has long since been adjudicated, so far as the usage of the Government is concerned. The Government of the United States have always regarded the Indian tribes within our limits as foreign Powers, so far as the treaty-making power is concerned, and so far especially as the commercial power is concerned.[4]

A.4. Senators Opposed to Indians Not Living under Tribal Jurisdiction for Citizenship - Not All Indians Associated with Tribe

Republican Senators John Conness of California and Alexander Ramsey of Minnesota raised a different objection. They noted that not all Indians were associated with a recognizable tribe; some lived on so-called "public" reservations, while others traveled in small nomadic groups.[5]

1866: Senator James Doolittle (R-WIS) - Not Prepared for Citizenship; If included, May Compel Some of Us to Vote against 14th Amendment

> If you make them citizens, of course they will not only have the privileges of citizens, but they will be subjected to the duties of citizens. They will not only have the right to sue, but they will be liable to be sued. They will not only have the right to make contracts, but they will be bound by their contracts; and that is a policy which the Government has resisted from the beginnings in its dealings with the Indians, except with those Indians who have become citizens and are liable to be taxed. Then they are regarded as citizens of the United States. Without going into the argument at length, I am decidedly of the opinion that if by declaring the Indians to be citizens you are going to bind them by their contracts and permit them to be sued as other citizens in the courts of the United States, the Indians are not prepared for citizenship.

> ... If you undertake to provide in this proposition that every Indian born in the United States who may not be for the time being incorporated in any tribe shall be a citizen of the United States you may compel some of us to vote against the amendment altogether. Although some of these Indians may be disconnected from their tribes, and may be wandering in bands and in families, as there are some in the State of Wisconsin and in other States, I do not think they are yet in a condition to be incorporated as part of the citizens of the United States and made liable to be bound by the contracts which they make and to be sued upon their contracts.

For example, Senator Doolittle argued: *It seems to me very clear that there is a large mass of the Indian population who are clearly subject to the jurisdiction of the United States who ought not to be included as citizens of the United States. ... by a constitutional amendment you propose to declare the Utes, the Tabahuaches, and all those wild Indians to be citizens of the United States, the great Republic of the world, whose citizenship should be a title as proud as that of king, and whose danger is that you may degrade that citizenship.* (Emphasis added).[6]

1866: Senator Alexander Ramsey (R-MINN) - Many Are Wild, Savage Indians

The Senator from Missouri seems to base his position upon the mistaken theory that all Indians who are no longer connected with their tribes or under a tribal government are civilized Indians, living as farmers, or in some other way earning a livelihood in the white settlements. This is an entire mistake. Where that happens to be the case, they are probably civilized Indians, holding property in that way. *But in all the border States there are large numbers of wild, savage Indians, as uncivilized and as untamed as any on the plains, who have no tribal government, who are outlaws from their tribes and their nations.* It certainly is not the intention of the Senator or the intention of the Senate to admit Indians of that class to citizenship. (Emphasis added).[7]

1866: Senator George Williams (R-OR) - Many Are from Fragments and Remnants of Destroyed Tribes Gathered Together - Not Competent or Qualified to Vote

... Thousands of Indians in the State that I have the honor to represent are collected upon reservations; they are not subject to tribal authority; their tribes are broken up and destroyed; they consist of the fragments and remnants of tribes gathered together upon these reservations; but they are no more competent or qualified to vote than they were when they existed in the original tribes. (Emphasis added).[8]

A.5. Opposed to Mass Involuntary Imposition of Citizenship - Senator James Guthrie (D-KY)

Senator Guthrie declared that "I cannot consent to impose citizenship and its liabilities and responsibilities upon a people without their assent [or the assent of their government]."[9]

A.6. Senators that Supported including Indians for Citizenship under 14th Amendment

1866: Senator John Henderson (R-MO)

> ... If citizenship be conferred upon the Indian, what right will be conferred that he objects to? The Indian, like the negro, was born upon our soil, and I say let him be declared a citizen also, unless some right will be thereby conferred upon him that will conflict with the general interests of the States.[10]
>
> My point is that the Indian, if he is connected with no tribe, whether he is taxed or not, ought to be a citizen of the United States. What harm can there be in declaring that fact? ... *The State need not admit him to the franchise. He may be a citizen of the United States, and yet not have all the privileges and all the immunities of a citizen of the State in which he may be. The State may deny him any of them that it chooses to deny.* But why not declare him a citizen of the United States? What harm can there be in that? It will enable him to sue in the courts of the United States to enforce his rights there. ... (Emphasis added).[11]
>
> Now that we are fixing the law on the subject, why not declare every man born in the United States to be a citizen of the United States, irrespective of race or previous condition? ...[12]
>
> To decide otherwise would be to conclude that "[the government is] made for the white man and the black man, but that the red man shall have no interest in it."[13]

1866: Senator Willard Saulsbury (D-DEL) - If Negroes Are to Be Citizens, I See No Reason for Excluding Indians

> I feel disposed to vote against [this] amendment because if these negroes are to be made citizens of the United States, I can see no reason in justice or in right why the Indians should not be made citizens.[14]

A.7. 1866: Senator Maxey (D-TX) - "It Is Too Soon"

Senator Samuel B. Maxey of Texas, though in favor of separate allotments, was against making Indians citizens "too soon."

> But here are people who but a few years ago were wild tribes roaming upon the prairies, engaged in raiding upon the settlements of the white people with the tomahawk and scalping-knife: we have gathered them up into reservations and now because we put them on separate tracts of land we are to say to them "You may become

citizens of the United States." It is too soon. I do not say and I do not wish to be understood as saying that the time may not come when I would favor the extension of citizenship to them: but I want first to educate them up to that standard.

A.8. Conflict with State Liquor/Firearm Laws - Senator George H. Williams (R-OR)

Republican Senator George H. Williams of Oregon warned that states typically banned sales of firearms and alcoholic beverages to Indians and, if Indians were granted citizenship, states would be powerless to enforce such bans.[15]

A.9. "Exclude Indians Not Taxed"

Senator Lyman Trumbull's (R-ILL) Proposal to Use Language from U.S. Constitution - "Exclude Indians Not Taxed"

Senator Lyman Trumbull proposed that only "Indians not taxed" be excluded from American citizenship. (Emphasis added).[16]

He argued that his proposal would only grant citizenship to those Indians "who are domesticated and pay taxes and live in civilized society," and thus had become "incorporated into the United States." Not everyone agreed.

1866: Senator George Williams (R-OR)

... The object is not to make taxation a criterion or a test of citizenship; but, although it is not absolutely certain and may operate with hardship in individual cases, it is the most certain way of defining the distinction between the wild, savage, and untamed Indians, and those who associate with white people, own property, and exercise the privileges that generally attend a citizen in the community.[17]

Senator Thomas A. Hendricks (D-IND) - Citizenship Should Not Depend on Payment of Taxes

Democratic Senator Thomas A. Hendricks of Indiana complained that the right to citizenship should not depend on whether a person pays taxes.[18]

A.10. Senator James Lane (R-KAN) - Confer Citizenship on "Indians Holding Lands in Severalty by Allotment"

To resolve any ambiguities, Senator Lane proposed an amendment that would have specifically conferred citizenship on "Indians holding lands in severalty by allotment." Trumbull objected to this proposal on the ground that some of these allotments remained wholly within the jurisdiction of the tribal government, and the amendment was rejected.[19]

A.11. 1866: Senator Lyman Trumbull (R-ILL) - Indians Not Object of Bill

...I wish this whole Indian question was out of the way. It is not the great object of the bill.[20]

14th Amendment to Constitution Submitted to States for Ratification

Whatever their reservations, mainstream Republicans were willing to acquiesce in the formulation "All persons born or naturalized in the United States, and *subject to the jurisdiction thereof.*" (Emphasis added).

Most senators agreed that, because the United States did not exercise complete jurisdiction over tribes, the phrase "All persons born in the United States, and subject to the jurisdiction thereof, are citizens of the United States" excluded members of Indian tribes.[21]

On June 16, 1866, the House Joint Resolution proposing the 14th Amendment to the Constitution was submitted to the states. On July 28, 1868, the 14th amendment, was declared ratified by the necessary 28 of the 37 States, and became part of the supreme law of the land.[22]

A December 1870 Senate resolution declared that tribal Indians were **not** citizens because they were not subject to U.S. jurisdiction as it was meant in the Amendment.

B. Decade of 1870s Produced Court Decisions regarding whether Indians Were Citizens under 14th Amendment (e.g., If They Had Abandoned Tribal Relations)

B.1. 1877: *United States v. Elm*, District Court, N.D.; Tribal Organization Defunct

The case of *United States v. Elm*, District Court, N.D. New York, Dec. 24, 1877, 25 F. Cas. 1006, involved an Indian seeking the right to vote. Elm was an Oneida Indian living in New York who voted in the congressional election of 1876. He was indicted and convicted of illegal voting on the grounds that as an Indian he could not be a citizen and only citizens could vote. The federal district court considered the question of whether Elm was, in fact, a citizen.

It must first be noted that this case involved members of a tribe whose "tribal organization had become defunct, and where the individual Indians had so far been recognized as citizens of the state that they had been authorized to acquire and hold real estate and subjected to taxation and to the civil jurisdiction of the courts."

> *The 20 families which constitute the remnant of the Oneidas reside in the vicinity of their original reservation. They do not constitute a community by themselves, but their dwellings are interspersed with the habitations of the whites. In religion, in customs, in language, in everything but the color of their skins, they are identified with the rest of the population.* In 1843, by an act of the legislature of this state, they were authorized to hold their lands in severalty, according to a partition which had theretofore been made. [In 1843 they were further] subjected to taxation and to the jurisdiction of the state courts in the same manner and to the same extent as other citizens. ...
>
> *They are natives, they owe no allegiance other than to the government of the United States, and they have been placed by the state upon an equality with its citizens respecting important rights denied to aliens.* As the state and the United States can impose upon them all the duties and obligations of subjects, they are entitled to the corresponding rights which spring from relation. (Emphasis added).[23]

The court found Elm was a citizen, was entitled to vote and had been improperly convicted.

B.2. 1878: *Ex parte Kenyon*, Circuit Court, W.D. ARK; Interpreting Cherokee Nation Constitutional Provision

The 1878 case of *Ex parte Kenyon,* Circuit Court, W.D. Arkansas, 1878, dealt with a white man married to a Cherokee Indian woman. His status as a white man was not key to the case. What was is whether the Cherokee Nation's court had jurisdiction over Kenyon to try, convict him of larceny and sentence him to five years imprisonment.[24]

It must first be noted that this case involved unique factual circumstances, including a Cherokee Nation constitutional provision.

If a court does not have jurisdiction over the person, the place, and the acts committed it does not have authority to try and convict a person. Article 1, § 2, of the Cherokee constitution provides *"that whenever any citizen shall remove with his effects out of the limits of this nation and become a citizen of any other government, all his rights and privileges as a citizen of this nation shall cease."* This principle applies to Indians of the full blood or by birth as well as to those by adoption. (Emphasis added).

The federal court held because he had voluntarily left the Cherokee Nation and became a citizen of the state of Kansas, he had been divested of all his rights and privileges as a citizen of the Cherokee Nation, under its own Constitution, including citizenship itself. As such, the Cherokee Nation did not have jurisdiction over the person, the subject matter or the place where the alleged larceny occurred. It could not try and sentence him to imprisonment.

B.3. 1884: *Elk v. Wilkins*, Individual Indian Voluntarily Leaving His Tribe Can Only Become Citizen by Treaty or Congressional Act

The 1884 *Elk v. Wilkins* case, decided by the U.S. Supreme Court, left the eastern wealthy, educated elite who had formed a highly influential group to support Indians, at odds with the exclusion of Native people from U.S. citizenship under the facts presented.

John Elk, a Winnebago Indian, was born on an Indian reservation and later resided with whites on the non-reservation U.S. territory in Omaha, Nebraska, where he renounced his former tribal allegiance and claimed citizenship under the 14th Amendment. He tried to register to vote on April 5, 1880, and was denied.

Speaking for the majority, Justice Horace Gray began with the premise that one could only become a citizen by virtue of either birth or naturalization. and plaintiff had not become a citizen through any statute or treaty. At the time of his birth, Elk was subject to the jurisdiction of an Indian tribe, which Gray described as "an alien, though dependent, power" and could therefore not claim birthright citizenship in the United States. Nor could Elk claim citizenship under any statute or treaty. Since Elk had never been naturalized, in Gray's view he failed both tests for citizenship.[25]

NOTES

1. Cong. Globe, 39th Cong., 1st Sess. (1866), 2895.
2. Cong. Globe, 39th Cong., 1st Sess. (1866), 2939.
3. Congressional Globe, 39th Cong., 1st Sess. (1866), 571–74, 2890–97.
4. Congressional Globe, 39th Cong., 1st Sess. (1866), 571–74, 2890–97.
5. Congressional Globe, 39th Cong., 1st Sess. (1866), 526-527.
6. Cong. Globe. May 30, 1866: 2893. Franz, Margaret E. *We Have Never Been Liberal: Legal Rhetoric and The Politics of Citizenship After Reconstruction.* Diss. The University of North Carolina at Chapel Hill, 2019, p. 55.
7. Congressional Globe, 39th Cong., 1st Sess. (1866), 571–74, 2890–97.
8. Congressional Globe, 39th Cong., 1st Sess. (1866), 571–74, 2890–97.
9. Id.
10. Congressional Globe, 39th Cong., 1st Sess. (1866), 571–74, 2890–97.
11. Congressional Globe, 39th Cong., 1st Sess. (1866), 571.
12. Congressional Globe, 39th Cong., 1st Sess. (1866), 571.
13. Congressional Globe, 39th Cong., 1st Sess. (1866), 574.
14. Congressional Globe, 39th Cong., 1st Sess. (1866), 571–74, 2890–97.

15. Congressional Globe, 39th Cong., 1st Sess. (1866), 574.
16. Gillman, Howard, Mark A. Graber, and Keith E. Whittington. "American Constitutionalism Volume II: Rights and Liberties." Supplementary Material, Chapter 6: The Civil War and Reconstruction—Equality/Native Americans, The Senate Debates Native American Citizenship (1866), (2013). https://global.oup.com/us/companion.websites/fdscontent/uscompanion/us/static/companion.websites/9780199751358/instructor/chapter_6/thedebatescitizenship.pdf (accessed online April 27, 2024). Congressional Globe, 39th Cong., 1st Sess. (1866), 571–74, 2890–97.
17. Congressional Globe, 39th Cong., 1st Sess. (1866), 571–74, 2890–97.
18. Cong. Globe, 39th Cong., 1st Sess., (1866), 2894.
19. Congressional Globe, 39th Cong., 1st Sess. (1866), 522, 526.
20. Congressional Globe, 39th Cong., 1st Sess. (1866), 571–74, 2890–97.
21. Congressional Globe, 39th Cong., 1st Sess. (1866), 571–74, 2890–97. https://global.oup.com/us/companion.websites/fdscontent/uscompanion/us/static/companion.websites/9780199751358/instructor/chapter_6/thedebatescitizenship.pdf (accessed online April 27, 2024).
22. 14th Amendment to the U.S. Constitution: Civil Rights (1868). https://www.archives.gov/milestone-documents/14th-amendment#:~:text=Passed%20by%20Congress%20June%2013,Rights%20to%20formerly%20enslaved%20people (accessed online November 1, 2024).
23. *United States v. Elm*, District Court, N.D. New York, Dec. 24, 1877, 25 F. Cas. 1006.
24. *Ex parte Kenyon*, Circuit Court, W.D. Arkansas, 1878, 14 F. Cas. 353 (1878).
25. *Elk v. Wilkins*, 112 U.S. 94, 103-109 (1884).

CHAPTER 7: Presidential Views on Indian Civilization and Private Property

1789: Exclusive Indian Property Advocated by President Washington's Secretary of War Henry Knox

The first Secretary of War, Henry Knox, advised President George Washington that to civilize the Indians: "Were it possible to introduce among the tribes a love for exclusive property, it would be a happy commencement of the business."[1]

Executive Conflict of Interest

The president's conflict of interest between the trust responsibilities to Indians and the obligations to the citizenry started early on.

1798: President John Adams - Indian Trust Responsibilities Are Subordinate to Obligations to U.S. Citizenry

President John Adams (1797-1801) captured the essence of the executive responsibility to its "white children" in this 1798 letter to the Cherokee Nation objecting to the invasion of squatters: His "stronger obligations" were to "hear the complaints, and relieve, as far as in my power, the distresses of my white children, citizens of the United States." These 'white children' had the right to vote, an important consideration for any elected official.[2]

1801–1805: President Thomas Jefferson - Architect of Indian Removal

Thomas Jefferson (1801–1805) would become the architect of (1) the U.S.' Indian removal policy, well before the Indian Removal Act of 1830; and (2) the "Manifest Destiny" of the U.S. to expropriate Indian lands.

His ideology of expansionism was voiced in 1780 when he coined the phrase "Empire of Liberty," while the American Revolution was still being fought. In his instructions to George Rogers Clark to take Fort Detroit he envisioned a future of commerce and expansion:

> We shall divert through our own Country a branch of commerce which the European States have thought worthy of the most important struggles and sacrifices and ... shall form to the American union a barrier against the dangerous extension of the British Province of Canada and add to the Empire of Liberty an extensive and fertile Country ...[3]

Later, in a letter from Thomas Jefferson to James Madison, April 27, 1809, Jefferson advocated for expansion, including Canada:

> ... we should have such an *empire for liberty* as she has never surveyed since the creation: & I am persuaded no constitution was ever before so well calculated as ours for extensive empire & self government...[4]

This false narrative of spreading liberty across the continent was used to justify removing Indians who were seen as obstacles to progress.

He also proclaimed his policy of drubbing the Indians and adopting the Spanish and English policy of bribery since it was cheaper than war.

> From Thomas Jefferson to James Monroe, 17 April 1791
>
> I hope we shall *drub the Indians well this summer and then change our plan from war to bribery*. We must do as the Spaniards and English do, keep them in peace by liberal and constant presents. They find it the cheapest plan, and so shall we. The expence of this summers expedition would have served for presents for half a century. ... Every rag of an Indian depredation will otherwise serve as a ground to raise troops... (Emphasis added).[5]

In a special message to Congress, January 18, 1803, he announced:

> Two measures are deemed expedient. First, to encourage them to abandon hunting, to apply to the raising stock, to agriculture and domestic manufacture. Second, to multiply trading houses among them, and place within their reach those things which will contribute to their domestic comfort. *In leading them thus to agriculture, to manufacture and civilization, in bringing together their and our sentiments, and in preparing them ultimately to participate in the benefits of our Government, I trust and believe we are acting for their greatest good.* (Emphasis added).[6]

In a private letter from Thomas Jefferson to William Henry Harrison on February 27, 1803, he proposes getting Indians into debt:

> ... we shall push our trading houses, and be glad to see the good & influential individuals among them run in debt, because we observe that *when these debts get beyond what the individuals can pay, they become willing to lop th[em off] by a cession of lands ...* (Emphasis added).[7]

1809–1817: President James Madison - Civilize and Divide Up Indian Lands to Individuals

The fourth President, James Madison, planned to complete the work of transitioning the Indians from the "habits of the savage to the arts and comforts of social life" by dividing up their communal land into individual property in a terrifying precursor to future allotment. By the political administration of Indians in reduced areas, land expropriation and exploitation would be easier.

> [T]he facility is increasing for extending that divided and individual ownership, which exists now in movable property only, to the soil itself, and of thus establishing in the culture and improvement of it the true foundation for a transit from the habits of the savage to the arts and comforts of social life.[8]

1816: Letters of Americanus to President Madison - For Citizenship, Indian Must Assimilate

The letters of "Americanus," addressed to President Madison and printed in the Philadelphia Democratic Press in April and May 1816, were a response to Secretary of War William Harris Crawford's 1816 report on Indian affairs. Much of Secretary Crawford's report was devoted to explaining the substantial increase in the cost of annuities during and immediately after the War of 1812, and describing the difficulties encountered in persuading Indian peoples to adopt notions of private property as an essential step in their progress from the "savage" state to that of "civilization." Future measures toward Indians, Secretary Crawford maintained, required either that the United States give up its long-standing efforts to manage Indian affairs and leave the business entirely to private enterprise or that it increase significantly its investment in the "civilizing" policies pursued after 1789. He added that intermarriage between U.S. citizens and Indians would ultimately incorporate "the natives of our forests in the great American family of freemen."

Americanus produced five essays written as letters, dated between 10 and 30 April 1816. *The first lambasted intermarriage between "blooming, healthy, hardy, active and enterprising" white frontier settlers and "dirty, draggle-tailed, blanketted, half human Squaws, or the filthy ferocious half naked Savages."* Secretary Crawford had compounded this latter offense by claiming that government support for intermarriage was a better way of populating the nation than encouraging immigration from Europe, whether or not the movement to the New World had been "the effect of their crimes or their virtues." (Emphasis added). [9]

The second and third Americanus essays, dated 13 and 16 April 1816, respectively, demeaned the customs of Indian peoples in order to prove that they were unfit for either citizenship or intermarriage.[10]

If President Madison had any reaction to these attacks, it has not been recorded. Unsurprisingly, Secretary Crawford was offended and noted on a copy of the Americanus essays he retained that they were written by an "Ignorant Man." "Criticism is Easy," he added, "but art is Difficult."[11]

Nonetheless, in his final message to Congress in December 1816, President Madison expressed his wish to treat Indian nations with "justice" rather than by taking advantage of "a feeble and untutored people," pointing out that the restoration of peace in 1815 favored "the resumption of the work of civilization which had made an encouraging progress among some tribes, and that the *facility is increasing for extending that divided and individual ownership*, which exists now in movable property only, to the soil itself..." (Emphasis added).[12]

Indians Will Be Stimulated to Industry by Separate Property

A House of Representatives Committee Report articulated it as follows:.

> As men and Christians, we should encourage and stimulate [the Indians] to the exertion of their own energies and faculties. It is believed that the history of all nations, Christian or heathen, will confirm the fact, that none of the sons and daughters of man ever did become extensively civilized, virtuous or happy, except they were stimulated to industry and enterprise ... by giving them an idea of separate property...[13]

1817-1825: President James Monroe - Supported Land in Severalty; Tribes Not Sovereigns; Indians and Indian Property Subject to U.S. Control

James Monroe, in his First Annual Message to Congress proclaimed his success in extinguishing Indian title in seven states: Ohio, Michigan, Indiana, Georgia, North Carolina, Tennessee and Alabama and pursuing his goal of individual Indian ownership of land:

> It is gratifying to know that the reservations of land made by the treaties with the tribes on Lake Erie were *made with a view to individual ownership among them* and to the cultivation of the soil by all ... (Emphasis added).[14]

In President Monroe's 1818 State of the Union address, he proclaimed:

> Experience has clearly demonstrated that independent savage communities cannot long exist within the limits of a civilized population. The progress of the latter has almost invariably terminated in the extinction of the former... To civilize them, and even to prevent their extinction, it seems to be indispensable that their independence as communities should cease, and that the control of the United States over them should be complete and undisputed.[15]

President Monroe appointed John C. Calhoun as his Secretary of War. In his 1818 Report to Congress, Secretary Calhoun recommended three policy changes: (1) Indian tribes should no longer be treated as independent nations; (2) Indian peoples should be made subject to U.S. law and civilized; and (3) their land should be allotted to save them from extinction. He stated:

> The time seems to have arrived when our policy towards them [the North American Indian peoples] should undergo an important change. ***They neither are, in fact, nor ought to be, considered as independent nations***. Our views of their interest, and not their own, ought to govern them. By a proper combination of force and persuasion, of punishments and rewards, ***they ought to be brought within the pales of law and civilization***. Left to themselves, they will never reach that desirable condition. Our laws and manners ought to supersede their present savage manners and customs. Beginning with those most advanced in civilization, and surrounded by our people, they ought to be made to contract their settlements within reasonable bounds, with a distinct understanding that the United States intend to make no further acquisition of land from them, and that the settlements reserved are intended for their permanent home. ***The land ought to be divided among families; and the idea of individual property in the soil carefully inculcated. ... It is only by causing our opinion of their interest to prevail, that they can be civilized and saved from extinction***. Under the present policy, they are continually decreasing and degenerating; notwithstanding the Government has, under all of its administrations, been actuated by the most sincere desire to promote their happiness and civilization. (Emphasis added).[16]

Secretary of War Calhoun created a separate office within the War Department to manage Indian affairs in 1824. The Office of Indian Affairs was given statutory authority in 1832 (4 Stat. 564) and remained within the War Department until its transfer to the Department of the Interior in 1849 (9 Stat. 395). Secretary of War Calhoun appointed Thomas L. McKenney to a vacant clerkship in the War Department and then directed that all matters relating to Indians be directed through his office. McKenney, in requesting funds from Congress to support Indian schools, proposed that if Indian youth are lifted to enter upon a course of civilized life sections of land be given them.

To the Hon. James Barbour, Secretary of War from Tho. L. McKenney:

> It is respectfully suggested whether, after the Indian children shall have passed through a course of instruction, and made capable thereby of taking care of themselves, some suitable provision of another kind ought not to be made for them. ... sections of land be given to them, and, a suitable present to commence with, of agricultural or other implements suited to the occupations in which they may be disposed... They will then have become, an "intermediate link between our own citizens, and our wandering neighbors, softening the shades of each, and enjoying the confidence of both." Tho. L. McKenney. (Emphasis added).[17]

1821: Second Inaugural Address of James Monroe, March 5, 1821 - Treatment of Indian Tribes as Sovereigns Should Cease with Land Allocated to Individuals in Adequate Portions

In his Second Inaugural Address, President Monroe reaffirmed his decision that Indian sovereignty over vast territories should cease, which should be superceded by individual Indian ownership of land in adequate portions.

> The care of the Indian tribes ... has not been executed in a manner to accomplish all the objects intended by it. We have treated them as independent nations, without their having any substantial pretensions to that rank. The distinction has flattered their pride, retarded their improvement, and in many instances paved the way to their destruction. The progress of our settlements westward, supported as they are by a dense population, has constantly driven them back, with almost the total sacrifice of the lands which they have been compelled to abandon. ***Their sovereignty over vast territories should cease, in lieu of which the right of soil should be secured to each individual and his posterity in competent portions.*** (Emphasis added).[18]

In 1825, he declared that the removal of the Indians was of paramount importance to the U.S. The state of Georgia was pressing for Indian removal which the U.S. had agreed to do whenever it could "be done peaceably and on reasonable conditions," in exchange for Georgia giving up its claims to western lands.

He ominously acknowledged that without protection, they were doomed to extermination.

> Being deeply impressed with the opinion that the removal of the Indian tribes from the lands which they now occupy within the limits of the several States and Territories ... is of very high importance to our Union ... the attention of the Government has been long drawn with great solicitude to the object. For the removal of the tribes within the limits of the State of Georgia the motive has been peculiarly strong, arising from the compact with that State whereby the United States are bound to extinguish the Indian title to the lands within it whenever it may be done peaceably and on reasonable conditions. ...
>
> "Experience has clearly demonstrated that in their present state it is impossible to incorporate them in such masses, in any form whatsoever, into our system," Monroe stated. "It has also demonstrated with equal certainty that without a timely anticipation of and provision against the dangers to which they are exposed,

under causes which it will be difficult, if not impossible, to control, ***their degradation and extermination will be inevitable***." (Emphasis added).[19]

The Monroe administration would eventually conclude a total of forty-one treaties with twenty-nine different Indian nations. All but eight involved a cession of Indian lands to the U.S. Of the eight remaining treaties, in accord with Secretary of War Calhoun's policies, six placed the signatory Indian nations under the protection, and de facto sovereignty, of the U.S.

1838: President Van Buren: Whites and Indians Cannot Safely Occupy Same Territory

In 1838, Van Buren defended the Cherokee removal in his second Message to Congress as follows:

> That a mixed occupancy of the same territory by the white and red man is incompatible with the safety or happiness of either is a position in respect to which there has long since ceased to be room for a difference of opinion. Reason and experience have alike demonstrated its impracticability.[20]

1869: Presidential Inauguration of Ulysses S. Grant: Indian Conversion to Christianity and Education Seen as Solution; Federal Government Gave Money to Catholic and Protestant Churches to Christianize and Educate Indian Children

President Grant announced in his First Inaugural Address that "I will favor any course towards them which tends to their civilization, Christianization and ultimate citizenship." He appointed his friend and former military secretary Ely Parker, a Seneca sachem, as the first American Indian Commissioner of Indian Affairs.[21]

1880: President Grant's Peace Policy Failed to Bring about Indian Assimilation and Civilization

> On Nov. 3, 1875, a mysterious meeting was convened at the White House with President Grant, Secretary of War Belknap and Generals Sheridan and Crook. Secretary of the Interior Chandler and General Cowen were sent for and the result was that President Grant ordered the military to not oppose miners invading the Black Hills promised to the Lakota in the Treaty of 1868. Grant, the Indian Peace Policy President, would breach the Treaty and instigate war.[22]

They came up with a three-phase plan. First, the DOI would concoct a report with complaints about the Lakotas justifying military action. Second, the Lakotas would be ordered to return to their reservation or be attacked by Jan. 31, 1876, a deadline they couldn't meet. Third, a winter U.S. military campaign would be promptly launched after the expiration of the deadline.[23]

By 1880, Congress came to the conclusion that Grant's Peace Policy had failed. It had failed to bring about Indian assimilation and civilization as quickly as had been hoped.[24]

1885: President Cleveland - Guardianship over Indian Wards Test of Integrity and Honor

In his inaugural address, President Cleveland stated: "The conscience of the people demands that the Indians within our boundaries shall be fairly and honestly treated, as wards of the Government, and their education and civilization promoted, with a view to their ultimate citizenship. The relation of a man to his wards tests his integrity and his sense of honor."[25]

1901: President Theodore Roosevelt's - General Allotment Act Is Mighty Pulverizing Engine to Break Up Tribal Mass; Civilized Mankind Owes Debt to Settler

President Roosevelt in his first annual message to Congress said:

> *"In my judgment the time has arrived when we should definitely make up our minds to recognize the Indian as an individual not as a member of a tribe. The general allotment act is a mighty pulverizing engine to break up the tribal mass. It acts directly upon the family and the individual. Under its provisions some 60,000 Indians have already become citizens of the United States. We should now break up the tribal funds, doing for them what allotment does for the tribal lands; that is, they should be divided into individual holdings. There will be a transition period during which the funds will in many cases have to be held in trust. This is the case also with the lands. A stop should be made to the indiscriminate permission to Indians to lease their allotments. The effort should be steadily to make the Indian work like any other man on his own ground. The marriage laws of the Indians should be made the same as those of the whites.* Teddy Roosevelt's Address to Congress, 1901. (Emphasis added).[26]

He is also quoted as saying:

> The most ultimately righteous of all wars is a war with savages, though it is apt to be also the most terrible and inhuman. The rude, fierce settler who drives the savage from the land lays all civilized mankind under a debt to him....[I]t is of incalculable importance that America, Australia, and Siberia should pass out of the hands of their red, black, and yellow aboriginal owners, and become the heritage of the dominant world races.[27]

And, further:

> "I don't go so far as to think that the only good Indians are the dead Indians, but I believe nine out of every ten are, and I shouldn't like to inquire too closely into the case of the tenth."[28]

NOTES

1. "To George Washington from Henry Knox, 7 July 1789," Founders Online, National Archives, https://founders.archives.gov/documents/Washington/05-03-02-0067. [Original source: The Papers of George Washington, Presidential Series, vol. 3, 15 June 1789–5 September 1789, ed. Dorothy Twohig. Charlottesville: University Press of Virginia, 1989, pp. 134–141.] (accessed online November 22, 2024).
2. "From John Adams to Cherokee Nation, 27 August 1798," Founders Online, National Archives. https://founders.archives.gov/documents/ Adams/99-02-02-2892 (accessed online Nov. 13, 2020).
3. "From Thomas Jefferson to George Rogers Clark, 25 December 1780," Founders Online, National Archives. https://founders.archives.gov/documents/Jefferson/01-04-02-0295. [Original source: The Papers of Thomas Jefferson, vol. 4, 1 October 1780 – 24 Feb. 1781, ed. Julian P. Boyd. Princeton: Princeton University Press, 1951, pp. 233–238.] (accessed online Nov. 13, 2020).
4. "Thomas Jefferson to James Madison, 27 April 1809," *Founders Online*, National Archives. https://founders.archives.gov/documents/Jefferson/03-01-02-0140. [Original source: *The Papers of Thomas Jefferson, Retirement Series,* vol. 1, *4 March 1809 to 15 November 1809*, ed. J. Jefferson Looney. Princeton: Princeton University Press, 2004, pp. 168–170.] (accessed online November 13, 2020).
5. "From Thomas Jefferson to James Monroe, 17 April 1791," *Founders Online*, National Archives. https://founders.archives.gov/documents/Jefferson/01-20-02-0051. [Original source: *The Papers of Thomas Jefferson*, vol. 20, *1 April–4 August 1791*, ed. Julian P. Boyd. Princeton: Princeton University Press, 1982, pp. 234–236.] (accessed online November 13, 2020).
6. "From Thomas Jefferson to the Senate and the House of Representatives, 18 January 1803," Founders Online, National Archives. https://founders.archives.gov/documents/Jefferson/01-39-02-0303. [Original source: The Papers of Thomas Jefferson, vol. 39, 13 November 1802–3 March 1803, ed. Barbara B. Oberg. Princeton: Princeton University Press, 2012, pp. 350–354.] (accessed online Nov. 13, 2020).
7. "From Thomas Jefferson to William Henry Harrison, 27 February 1803," *Founders Online*, National Archives, https://founders.archives.gov/documents/Jefferson/01-39-02-0500. [Original source: *The Papers of Thomas Jefferson*, vol. 39, *13 November 1802–3 March 1803*, ed. Barbara B. Oberg. Princeton: Princeton University Press, 2012, pp. 589–593.] (accessed online November 6, 2020).
8. "From James Madison to United States Congress, 3 December 1816," Founders Online, National Archives. https://founders.archives.gov/documents/Madison/99-01-02-5598 (accessed online Nov. 4, 2020).
9. "To James Madison from Americanus, 10 April 1816," Founders Online, National Archives. https://founders.archives.gov/documents/Madison/03-10-02-0380.

[Original source: The Papers of James Madison, Presidential Series, vol. 10, 13 October 1815–30 April 1816, ed. Angela Kreider, J. C. A. Stagg, Mary Parke Johnson, Katharine E. Harbury, and Anne Mandeville Colony. Charlottesville: University of Virginia Press, 2019, pp. 364–368.]

10. Founders Online, National Archives. https://founders.archives.gov/documents/Madison/03-10-02-0379 (accessed online September 22, 2024). [Original source: The Papers of James Madison, Presidential Series, vol. 10, 13 October 1815–30 April 1816, ed. Angela Kreider, J. C. A. Stagg, Mary Parke Johnson, Katharine E. Harbury, and Anne Mandeville Colony. Charlottesville: University of Virginia Press, 2019, pp. 358–364.]

11. "The William H. Crawford Archive," offered for sale by the Raab Collection, Ardmore, Pa., 2017.

12. Founders Online, National Archives. https://founders.archives.gov/documents/Madison/03-10-02-0379 (accessed online September 22, 2024). [Original source: The Papers of James Madison, Presidential Series, vol. 10, 13 October 1815–30 April 1816, ed. Angela Kreider, J. C. A. Stagg, Mary Parke Johnson, Katharine E. Harbury, and Anne Mandeville Colony. Charlottesville: University of Virginia Press, 2019, pp. 358–364.]

13. Hagan, William T. "Private Property, the Indian's Door to Civilization." Ethnohistory 3.2 (1956): 128, citing Register of Debates, 21 Congress, 1 session, p. 1087.

14. James Monroe, First Annual Message Online by Gerhard Peters and John T. Woolley, The American Presidency Project. https://www.presidency.ucsb.edu/node/205560 (accessed online November 4, 2020).

15. https://www.presidency.ucsb.edu/documents/second-annual-message-1 (accessed online November 25, 2024).

16. Report of the secretary of war, of a system, providing for the abolition of the existing Indian trade establishments of the United States, and providing for the opening of the trade with the Indians to individuals, under suitable regulations. December 8, 1818. p. 18. https://www.loc.gov/resource/gdcmassbookdig.reportofsecretar00unit_14/?sp=1&st=slideshow (accessed online November 22, 2024).

17. United States War Department, et al. Report of the Secretary of War. On Indian Affairs. [Washington, 1826], p. 71.

18. Second Inaugural Address of James Monroe, March 5, 1821. https://avalon.law.yale.edu/19th_century/monroe2.asp (accessed online November 14, 2020).

19. James Monroe, Special Message Online by Gerhard Peters and John T. Woolley, The American Presidency Project. https://www.presidency.ucsb.edu/node/206975 (accessed online November 22, 2024).

20. https://millercenter.org/the-presidency/presidential-speeches/december-3-1838-second-annual-message-congress (accessed online October 5, 2024).

21. https://avalon.law.yale.edu/19th_century/grant1.asp (accessed online October 5, 2024).

22. Gray, John Stephens. Centennial Campaign: The Sioux War of 1876, Vol. 8. University of Oklahoma Press, 1988, p. 26.

23. Military expedition against the Sioux Indians, July 18, 1876, H.R. Exec. Doc. No.

184, 44th Cong., 1st Sess.

24. 1880: Twelfth Annual Report Board of Indian Commissioners. https://babel.hathitrust.org/cgi/pt?id=hvd.32044021159991&seq=13 (accessed online November 8, 2024).

25. Annual Report of the Board of Indian Commissioners, 1885 (Washington: Government Printing Office), p. 7.

26. https://www.presidency.ucsb.edu/documents/first-annual-message-16 (accessed online December 11, 2024).

27. Roosevelt, Theodore. 1906. The Winning of the West, Volume 3.

28. Hagedorn, Hermann. 1921. Roosevelt in the Bad Lands, Volume 1. Houghton Mifflin.

CHAPTER 8: Removal Era

In 1817, in a letter to James Monroe, General Jackson refused to recognize Indian nations as sovereign. Jackson declared, "I have long viewed treaties with the Indians an absurdity not to be reconciled to the principles of our Government." The Indians, said Jackson, were subjects of the U.S., pure and simple, "inhabiting its territory and acknowledging its sovereignty." It was a fiction that the tribes were in fact separate and independent entities, and it was absurd to negotiate with them as such.[1]

1824: Secretary of War Threatens Cherokees - They Will Be Left to Whims of Georgia

In 1824, Secretary of War John Calhoun threatened to leave the Cherokees exposed to the discontent of Georgia and the pressure of her citizens if they continued to refuse to exchange their land in Georgia for land west of the Mississippi. They responded:

> ... the Cherokees are not foreigners, but original inhabitants of America; and that they now inhabit and stand on the soil of their own territory; and that the limits of their territory are defined by the treaties which they have made with the Government of the United States; and that the States by which they are now surrounded have been created out of lands which were once theirs; and that they cannot recognise the sovereignty of any State within the limits of their territory.[2]

Secretary Calhoun's seeming federal support led the Georgians to vigorously pursue inclusion of Indian land under state hegemony. In 1829, Calhoun's support for Georgia was confirmed by none other than President Andrew Jackson in his First Annual Message:

> I informed the Indians inhabiting parts of Georgia and Alabama that their attempt to establish an independent government would not be countenanced by the Executive of the United States, and advised them to emigrate beyond the Mississippi or submit to the laws of those States.[3]

1827: Conflict between Creek Indians and State of Georgia Leads to Federal Threat of U.S. War against State

In 1827, President John Quincy Adams, sent a message to Congress which he termed "most momentous." He informed Congress that the Creeks had invoked the protection of the federal government to defend their rights as guaranteed by a ratified treaty. "Their forbearance and reliance on the good faith of the United States will, it is hoped, avert scenes of violence and blood, which there is otherwise too much cause to apprehend." The message then delineated the stipulations of the Trade and Intercourse

Act of March 30, 1802, and the punishments prescribed for colonial settler intruders in Indian Country. There was no previous instance in which the disagreement between state and federal authority had been "urged into a conflict of actual force"—if not civil war, at least a potential prelude to it.

President Adams warned Georgia:

> ... it is my duty to say, that if the legislative and executive authorities of the State of Georgia shall persevere in acts of encroachment upon the territories secured by a solemn treaty to the Indians, and the laws of the Union remain unaltered, a superadded obligation, even higher than that of human authority, will compel the Executive of the United States to enforce the laws, and fulfill the duties of the nation by all the force committed for that purpose to his charge.[4]

In his fourth annual message, December 2, 1828, he criticizes, like Monroe, the system of dealing with Indian tribes as foreign and independent powers, and of negotiating with them by treaties.

> We have found them forming in the midst of ourselves communities claiming to be independent of ours, and rivals of sovereignty within the territories of the Union. This state of things requires a remedy which, while it shall do justice to these unfortunate children of nature, may secure to the members of our confederation their rights of sovereignty and of soil.[5]

The Adams administrations' saber rattling to protect the rights of the Creek Indians and Georgia's Governor to prevent precisely that meant that the potential for armed collision between different branches of the federal system fizzled, with the Adams' administration unwillingness to go to war. A select Senate committee chaired by the powerful Senator Thomas Hart Benton requested the President to take every action possible to convince the Creeks to accept payment for their lands. The Senate committee reported:

> The committee will not enlarge upon the frightful consequences of civil wars. They are known to be calamitous to single Governments, and fatal to confederacies. Reason tells us this, and history, with warning voice, confirms it. A contagious fury rages in Such contests. No matter how small the beginning, or how insignificant the cause, the dissension spreads, until the whole confederacy is involved.[6]

Negotiations commenced that summer with the Creeks, before Congress even approved funding for a cession of Indian lands, which allowed for a cooling off period. In the autumn, the Creeks ceded their lands.[7]

President John Quincy Adams: Indian Right of Possession Questionable

The sixth President, John Quincy Adams, proudly delivered his position regarding westward expansion:

> The United States would dominate the Americas, Adams said, and assert its hemispheric hegemony without challenge. He wrote, "We have it; we constitute the whole of it."[8]

On Indian land title, in his oration at the Jubilee of the Constitution, delivered at New York, April 30, 1839, before the New York Historical Society, he said the following:

> ***The Indian right of possession itself stands, with regard to the greatest part of the country, upon a questionable foundation.***
>
> Their cultivated fields, their constructed habitations, a space of ample sufficiency for their subsistence, and whatever they had annexed to themselves by personal labor, was undoubtedly by the laws of nature theirs.
>
> But what is the right of a huntsman to the forest of a thousand miles over which he has accidentally ranged in quest of prey? ...
>
> Shall the lordly savage not only disdain the virtues and enjoyments of civilization himself, but shall he control the civilization of a world? (Emphasis added).[9]

Henry Clay, Secretary of State under John Quincy Adams, claimed that "it was impossible to civilize Indians; that there never was a full-blooded Indian who took to civilization. It was not in their nature."

Adams recorded the moment:

> He [Clay] believed they were destined to extinction, and, although he would never use or countenance inhumanity towards them, *he did not think them, as a race, worth preserving*. He considered them as essentially inferior to the Anglo-Saxon race, which were now taking their place on this continent. They were not an improvable breed, and *their disappearance from the human family will be no great loss to the world*. In point of fact they were rapidly disappearing, and he did not believe that in fifty years from this time there would be any of them left. (Emphasis added).[10]

By portraying Indians as unimportant and destined to become extinct, Henry Clay is employing a perception of Indians which makes it easier to justify dispossession of their lands and extermination of them as a people.

1828: Report of Thomas McKenney to Sec. of War - Indians Will Not Be Permitted to Hold Reservations on which They Live within States due to Covetous Illegal White Encroachment

Thomas McKenney recognized in 1828, and warned Secretary of War Porter, that Indians wouldn't be able to hold onto their reservation lands due to the wave of emigration of white settlers occurring, who gave no cognizance to the rights of the Indians to their land. **It is a story repeated over and over across the U.S.** Game had been reduced beyond a subsistence level and the government would need to feed the Indians to avoid their starvation. Due to insufficient Congressional appropriations and/or delivery obstacles, many, many Indians starved to death.

> While some of our citizens, who are the advocates of primitive and imprescriptible rights in their broadest extent, contend that these tribes are independent nations, and have the sole and exclusive right to the property and government of the territories they occupy, others consider them as mere tenants at will, subject, like the buffalo of the prairies, to be hunted from their country whenever it may suit our interest or convenience to take possession of it. *Nothing can be more clear, to one who has marked the progress of population and improvement, and is conversant with the principles of human action, than that these Indians will not be permitted to hold the reservations on which they live within the States, by their present tenure, for any considerable period.* If, indeed, they were not disturbed in their possessions by us, it would be impossible for them long to subsist, as they have heretofore done, by the chase, as their game is already so much diminished, as to render it frequently necessary to furnish them with provisions, in order to save them from starvation. *In their present destitute and deplorable condition, and which is constantly growing more helpless, it would seem to be not only the right, but the duty of the Government, to take them under its paternal care; and to exercise, over their persons and property, the salutary rights and duties of guardianship.* (Emphasis added).[11]

In his 1828 Report to Sec. of War Porter, Thomas L. McKenney proposed the westward removal of Indians for their survival:

> Justice and Humanity. I forbear also to remark, except briefly upon measures of general policy in regard to our Indians. *What are humanity and justice, in reference to this unfortunate race?* Are these found to lie in a policy that would leave them to linger out a wretched and degraded existence, within districts of country already surrounded, and pressed upon by a population whose anxiety and efforts to get rid of them are not less restless and persevering than is that law of nature immutable, which has decreed that, under such circumstances, if continued in, *they must perish*? Or does it not

rather consist in withdrawing them from this certain destruction, and placing them, though even at this late hour, in a situation, where, by the adoption of a suitable system for their security, preservation, and improvement, and at no matter what cost, they may be saved and blest?[12]

1828: Secretary of War Porter Proposed to President J.Q. Adams Forming Contiguous Indian Colonies in West; Land Apportioned in Fee Simple Absolute to Individual Indians Willing to Pursue Civilization, with Temporary Restraints on Alienation of Land; Making Indians Subject to General Laws

Secretary Porter's 1828 proposal mirrored the General Allotment Act which would be enacted in 1877!!!

> If the project of colonization be a wise one, and of this, I believe ... Let such of the emigrating Indians as choose it continue, as heretofore, to devote themselves to the chase, in a country where their toils will be amply rewarded. Let those who are willing to cultivate the arts of civilization be formed into a colony, consisting of distinct tribes and communities, but placed contiguous to each other and connected by general laws, which shall reach the whole. ***Let the lands be apportioned among families and individuals in severalty, to be held by the same tenures by which we hold ours, with perhaps some temporary and wholesome restraints on the power [of] alienation.*** ... Letter to President John Quincy Adams from Peter B. Porter, Sec. of War, November 24, 1828. (Emphasis added).[13]

1828: Andrew Jackson's Indian Removal Presidential Campaign

Andrew Jackson's Presidential Campaign in 1828 made American Indian Removal his goal - relocating eastern Indians west of the Mississippi River.

> As cotton culture spread across Georgia, federal officials proved either unwilling or unable to extinguish quickly enough for land-hungry Georgians the claims of the Creeks and the Cherokees to lands within the state. Angered over the delay in fulfilling the terms of the Compact of 1802, Georgia's leaders, throughout the 1820s and 1830s, regularly prodded the President then in office to complete the process of Indian removal. ... Many Georgians were concerned that many Indian nations, particularly the Creek and the Cherokee, were not interested in selling land, much less leaving. What the Georgians refused to acknowledge was that 90 percent of Indian land claims within the state had been extinguished, at enormous cost, instead accusing the federal government of bad faith and threats of armed conflict.[14]

Just nineteen days into his presidency, Jackson stated his removal policy in a letter to the Creek Indians, on March 23, 1829.

> Where you now are, you and my white children are too near to each other to live in harmony and peace. Your game is destroyed and many of your people will not work and till the Earth. Beyond the great river Mississippi, where part of your nation has gone, your father has provided a country large enough for all of you, and he advises you to remove to it. There your white brothers will not trouble you; they will have no claim to the land, and you can live upon it, you and your children, as long as the grass grows or the water runs, in peace and plenty. It will be yours forever.[15]

The Creek Indians informed the federal government that, "We deem it impolitic and contrary to the true interests of this nation to dispose of any more of our country." The commissioners sent by Washington, D.C., offered a chilling reply: "If you wish to quit the chase, to free yourself of barbarism, and settle down in the calm pursuits of civilization, and good morals, and to raise up a generation of Christians, you had better go." If you choose otherwise, "You must be sensible that it will be impossible for you to remain for any length of time in your present situation as a distinct Society or Nations, within the limits of Georgia. Such a community is incompatible with our System and must yield to it."[16]

The continuing tension between Indian nations and states is but the continuing issue of an 'imperium in imperio.' No state wants another state within its boundaries.

1829: Georgia Enacts Laws Abolishing Cherokee Indian Sovereignty, Self-Government and Right to Land

The state of Georgia enacted laws abolishing the Cherokee's right to sovereignty, self-government and land. President Jackson and Congress refused the direct request of the Cherokee Nation for federal intervention to uphold their Hopewell Treaty (1785) rights against Georgia's legislative encroachments.

Georgia's first act was passed Dec. 12, 1829, and is entitled:

> An act to add the territory lying within the chartered limits of Georgia, and now in the occupancy of the Cherokee Indians, to the counties of Carroll, De Kalb, Gwinnett and Habersham, and to extend the laws of the State over the same, and to annul all laws made by the Cherokee Nation of Indians ... Resolved, Indians are tenants at her will, and that she may at any time she pleases, determine that tenancy, by taking possession of the premises.[17]

1829: Gold Discovered on Cherokee Lands

When gold was discovered on Cherokee land, the state of Georgia passed another act, entitled "An act to authorize the Governor to take possession of the gold, silver, and other mines lying and being in that section of the chartered limits of Georgia commonly called the Cherokee country, and those upon all other unappropriated lands of the State, and for punishing any person or persons who may hereafter be found trespassing upon the mines."[18]

In 1829, Hezekiah Niles, editor of the Niles Weekly Register newspaper, offered the starkest comment on removal: "The fate of the Indians within the present states and territories—is sealed." The eastern Indian nations would move or become extinct.[19]

1829: War Generals - If Congress Rejects Cherokee Petition to Remain in Georgia and Georgia's Laws Are Enforced, Cherokee Will Move without Difficulty

Arguments that the Indians would move if Congress did not respond favorably to their petitions to remain in the southeast were discussed by high-ranking military officials who recommended rejection of their petitions:

> In 1829, General Carroll described the difficulties he met with in inducing the Indians to emigrate to the secretary of war: "The truth is, they rely with great confidence on a favorable report on the petition they have before Congress. If that is rejected, and the laws of the States are enforced, you will have no difficulty of procuring an exchange of lands with them."

> General Coffee, upon the same subject says, "They express a confident hope that Congress will interpose its power, and prevent the States from extending their laws over them. Should they be disappointed in this, I hazard little in saying that the government will have little difficulty in removing them west of the Mississippi."[20]

Alternatives: Exterminate, Assimilate, Protect or Remove Indians

Four alternatives identified with regard to Indians included: exterminating them, assimilating them, protecting them or removing them. Exterminating them was not realistic. The U.S. Army was small, with only seven infantry regiments responsible for manning forty-nine military posts and arsenals from Maine to Florida and from Louisiana to Michigan. War would be too costly in money and American lives. Assimilation was considered impractical. Affording meaningful protection was impossible, militarily and, even more importantly, politically. The government lacked the finances and the U.S. Army lacked the will to fend off the squatting colonists. Removal, sanctioned from President Jefferson to Jackson, represented the only viable action. With the defeat of such renowned Indian leaders, as Pontiac, Tecumseh, Little Turtle, Blue Jacket, McGillivray, John Ross and Black Hawk, there remained no effective Indian resistance.

1829: President Jackson Recommends Setting Aside Western Lands for Indians

In 1829, President Jackson recommended to Congress setting aside western lands for the removed Indian tribes.

> [They were] to be guaranteed to the Indian tribes, as long as they shall occupy it; each tribe having a distinct control over the portion designated for its use. There, they may be secured in the enjoyment of governments of their own choice, subject to no other control from the United States, than such as may be necessary to preserve peace on the frontier and between the several tribes...[21]

1830: Andrew Jackson's Justification for Indian Removal

In 1830, President Jackson justified Indian removal based on his beliefs that the Indians were savages and had made no improvements to the U.S.:

> What good man would prefer a country covered with forests and ranged by a few thousand savages to our extensive Republic, studded with cities, towns, and prosperous farms, embellished with all the improvements which art can devise or industry execute, occupied by more than 12,000,000 happy people, and filled with all the blessings of liberty, civilization, and religion?[22]

1830: Tenor of Times - They May Begin to Dig Their Graves and Prepare to Die

In 1830, Alfred Balch, Jackson's Commissioner of Indian Treaties, echoed the tenor of the times: "...removal of Indians would be an act of seeming violence — But it will prove in the end an act of enlarged philanthropy. These untutored sons of the Forest, cannot exist in a state of Independence, in the vicinity of the white man. If they will persist in remaining where they are, they may begin to dig their graves and prepare to die."[23]

1830: Indian Removal Bill Introduced in Congress

Commissioner Balch's assurance to Jackson that he would ramrod Indian removal legislation through Congress was underway. On Feb. 24, 1830, Tennessee Rep. John Bell and the Indian Affairs committee introduced a removal bill—officially, H.R. 287. The Senate version of the bill, submitted at the same time by Bell's counterpart on the Senate's Indian Affairs committee, Hugh Lawson White, was known as S. 102.[24] The House version of the bill was preceded by a report of over 15,000 words that was part opposition to removal, part history of U.S. Indian policy, especially the peculiarities of the treaty system, and part assertion of the southern Indians' rapid decline and, should they remain, certain extinction.

The introduction of the Indian Removal Bill led to lengthy debates in the public and in Congress. President Jackson emphasized that the emigration of the Indians "should be voluntary, for it would be as cruel as unjust to compel the aborigines to abandon the graves of their fathers and seek home in a distant land."[25] In support of Georgia, those Indians who remained would be subject to the authority of local and state law and jurisdiction.

Reports from Indians that had moved west, however, were dismal and the southern Indians feared for their survival. In 1826, General Clark, Superintendent of Indian Affairs, credits the southern Indians fear of moving with the dire stories of the Indians who had moved west.

> The condition of many tribes west of the Mississippi is the most pitiable that can be imagined. During several seasons in every year, they are distressed by famine, in which many die for want of food, and during which the living child is often buried with the dead mother, because no one can spare it as much food as would sustain it through its helpless infancy.[26]

1830: Indian Removal Act Passed

In 1830, Congress passed the act titled: "An Act to provide for an exchange of lands with the Indians residing in any of the states or territories, and for their removal west of the river Mississippi," commonly referred to as the Indian Removal Act of 1830, 4 Stat. 411. It passed the Senate by a vote of 28-19. It passed the House by a vote of 102-97. It was signed by President Andrew Jackson on May 28, 1830. It included funds to pay for removal – $500,000 was appropriated to pay to move Indians west of the Mississippi River. The bill, conspicuously, contained no stipulation which allowed the Indian nations to refuse relocation or even any indication they might not wish to do so, and nothing further was said of assimilation. It made no mention of the use of force.

Three days later the House also passed the Preemption Act of 1830, giving squatters a right of first refusal to purchase land they had occupied prior to its being opened for sale.

Removal of Indian Nations Became Mandatory

Over 60 removal treaties were signed which resulted in the forced westward migration of approximately 80,000 American Indians. Although removal was supposed to be voluntary, relocation of Indian nations became mandatory whenever the government decided. Many of the eastern Indian nations were destroyed or decimated. Millions of acres of lands were opened to white settlers.

1832: President Jackson - Acts Passed to Extinguish Indian Title in Illinois, Indiana, Missouri, and Territory of Michigan

In 1832, President Jackson reported successfully extinguishing Indian title in Illinois, Indiana, Missouri, and the Territory of Michigan:

At the last session of Congress, acts were passed to extinguish the Indian title to land in Illinois, Indiana, Missouri, and the Territory of Michigan. Commissioners were accordingly appointed, and treaties have been concluded with the respective tribes claiming title, by which they have relinquished to the United States all their lands in Indiana, Missouri, and Illinois, with the exception of a few inconsiderable reservations; and by which the Potawatomies have also ceded to the United States all their land in the Territory of Michigan.[27]

NOTES

1. "Andrew Jackson to James Monroe, March 4, 1817," in The Papers of Andrew Jackson, vol. 4, 1816–1820, ed. Harold D. Moser, David R. Hoth, and George E. Hoemann (Knoxville: University of Tennessee Press, 1994), 95.
2. Excerpt from a letter from John Ross, et al., to John C. Calhoun, Sec. of War, during Pres. James Monroe's Administration. Feb. 11, 1824. https://teachingamericanhistory.org/document/letter-to-john-c-calhoun/ (accessed online November 22, 2024).
3. "Andrew Jackson, December 8, 1829, First Annual Message," The American Presidency Project. https://www.presidency.ucsb.edu/documents/first-annual-message-3 (accessed online September 7, 2024).
4. February 5, 1827: Message Regarding the Creek Indians. https://millercenter.org/the-presidency/presidential-speeches/february-5-1827-message-regarding-creek-indians (accessed online November 4, 2020).
5. https://www.presidency.ucsb.edu/documents/fourth-annual-message-2 (accessed online September 24, 2024).
6. Report of The [Senate] Committee to whom was referred the several messages of the President of the United States, of the 5th and 8th February, 1827, and a report and certain resolutions of the Legislature of Georgia, pp. 6-7. https://www.govinfo.gov/content/pkg/SERIALSET-00146_00_00-021-0069-0000/pdf/SERIALSET-00146_00_00-021-0069-0000.pdf (accessed online November 22, 2024).
7. Relinquishment of the Claims of the Creeks to the Lands in Georgia, American State Papers: Indian Affairs, 2: 871.
8. Adams, John Quincy. *Memoirs of John Quincy Adams: comprising portions of his diary from 1795 to 1848.* JB Lippincott & Company, 1874, 5:176.
9. Orations, John Quincy Adams, "The Jubilee of the Constitution, delivered at New York, April 30, 1839, before the New York Historical Society." https://www.gutenberg.org/files/896/896-h/896-h.htm (accessed online December 12, 2020).
10. Adams, John Quincy. *Memoirs of John Quincy Adams: comprising portions of his diary from 1795 to 1848.* JB Lippincott & Company, 1874, 7:89.
11. Report of the Commissioner of Indian Affairs to the Secretary of War, United States. Office of Indian Affairs, 1828, pp. 21-22. https://search.library.wisc.edu/digital/AEYQML7XLRVXUT8C (accessed online December 9, 2024).
12. Report of the Commissioner of Indian Affairs to the Secretary of War, United

~ 111

States. Office of Indian Affairs, 1828, p. 80. https://search.library.wisc.edu/digital/AEYQML7XLRVXUT8C/pages/ABFTILXMTFM4YR87 (accessed online November 22, 2024).

13. Report of the Commissioner of Indian Affairs to the Secretary of War, United States. Office of Indian Affairs, 1828, pp. 22-23.

14. Lamplugh, George R. "Rancorous Enmities and Blind Partialities: Factions and Parties in Georgia, 1807–1845." UPA, 2015, p. x.

15. https://www.presidency.ucsb.edu/documents/letter-the-creek-indians (accessed online November 22, 2024).

16. A Brief History of Land Transfers Between American Indians and the United States Government, Central Michigan University, Clarke Historical Library. https://www.cmich.edu/research/clarke-historical-library/explore-collection/explore-online/native-american-material/native-american-treaty-rights/land-transfers (accessed online November 22, 2024).

17. *Worcester v. Georgia*, 31 U.S. 515, 525 (1832).

18. A Digest of the Laws of the State of Georgia: Containing All Statutes and the Substance of All Resolutions of a General and Public Nature, and Now in Force, Which Have Been Passed in This State, Previous to the Session of the General Assembly of Dec. 1837 (Athens, GA: Oliver H. Prince, 1837), 560.

19. Niles' Weekly Register, December 19, 1829.

20. Letter from General John Coffee to Secretary of War Eaton, October 14, 1829. https://www.wcu.edu/library/DigitalCollections/CherokeePhoenix/Vol2/no42/we-insert-below-the-report-of-general-coffee-of-georgia-to-the-secretary-of-war-we-do-not-know-of-page-2-column-3c-5b.html (accessed online December 2, 2024).

21. See "Annual Message to Congress with Documents, President Jackson, December 8, 1829," *Senate Document 1*, Twenty-First Cong., First Sess., *Congressional Serial Set 192*.

22. President Jackson's Message to Congress "On Indian Removal", December 6, 1830. https://www.archives.gov/milestone-documents/jacksons-message-to-congress-on-indian-removal (accessed online November 22, 2024).

23. Alfred Balch to Andrew Jackson, January 8, 1830; Andrew Jackson Papers: Series 1, General Correspondence and Related Items, 1775-1885 (15,697).

24. Bills and Resolutions, Senate, 21st Cong., 1st Sess., February 22, 1830.

25. James D. Richardson, Messages and Papers of the Presidents, Vol. 2, 456-9.

26. Extracted from an official report of General Clark, Superintendent of Indian Affairs, dated March 1, 1826.

27. Message from the President to the Two Houses of Congress, at the Commencement of the Second Session of the Twenty-second Congress, December 4, 1832. Andrew Jackson, Duff Green, 1832, p. 162. Regulating the Indian Department, May 20, 1834. [To accompany bills H.R. Nos. 488, 489, & 490.] Everett, Horace. Gales & Seaton, 1834. United States, Congress, Bills and Resolutions of the House and Senate, H.R. 474 (20 May 1834), 23rd Cong., 1st. Sess., pp. 99-100.

CHAPTER 9: 1831 - First Commissioner of Indian Affairs Elbert Herring - Absent Emigration, Indians Would Rapidly Become Extinct – Need Knowledge of Agriculture, Private Property, and Christianity

1831: Report of Chief Clerk Herring, Indian Bureau - Remove Indians, White Population Engulfing Them and Causing Their Total Extinction

Elbert Herring, Chief Clerk (August 12, 1831–July 9, 1832), wrote to President Jackson in November 1831 claiming removal was the only option to save the tribes being engulfed by white settlers.

> Gradually diminishing in numbers and deteriorating in condition, incapable of coping with the superior intelligence of the white man, ready to fall into the vices, but unable to appropriate the benefits of the social state; the increasing tide of white population threatened soon to engulf them, and finally to cause their total extinction. ... [Only] salutary principle exists in the system of removal ... under the protection of the United States; connected with the benign influences of education and instruction in agriculture and the several mechanic arts, whereby social is distinguished from savage life.[1]

He continued this recommendation after his appointment as the first Commissioner of Indian Affairs on July 10, 1832, a position statutorily established by Congress.[2]

He warned, absent removal, the Indians would rapidly become extinct: "In the consummation of this grand and sacred object rests the sole chance of averting Indian annihilation."[3]

1832: Supplant Savage for Social; Eradicate Absence of Meum ["What Is Mine"] and Tuum ["What Is Thine"]

Commissioner Herring advocated for a code of laws based on separate and secure rights in property and person, coupled with youth education and Christianity to substitute "the social for the savage state."

> The unrestrained authority of their chiefs, and the irresponsible exercise of power, are of the simplest elements of despotic rule; while the absence of the meum ["what is mine"] and tuum ["what is thine"] in the general community of possessions, which is the grand conservative principle of the social state, is a perpetual operating cause of the vis inertiae of savage life.[4]

Commissioner Herring recognized that not all Indians should engage in agriculture; they needed to be exposed to all of the trades.[5]

~ 113

1834: Committee on Indian Affairs, H. Everett Report, Regulating the Indian Department; Establishing Western Indian Territory

The H. Everett Report #474, Committee on Indian Affairs, May 20, 1834, Regulating the Indian Department, recommended:

> A bill to provide for the organization of the Department of Indian Affairs.
> A bill to regulate trade and intercourse with the Indian tribes, and to preserve peace on the frontiers.
> A bill to provide for the establishment of the Western Territory, and for the security and protection of the emigrant and other Indian tribes therein.

The Everett Report continued:

> The rights of the Indians are to be secured in the possession of their lands, and in the exercise of self-government. The obligations of the United States are correlative: to secure them in the title and possession of their lands, in the exercise of self-government, and to defend them from domestic strife and foreign enemies; and powers ... Under the power to dispose of the territory of the United States, the Western territory is now to be dedicated to the use of the Indians...

A revised Non-Intercourse Act reflected new treaty boundaries and tribal obligations, including licensure of traders, while a reorganization of the Indian Office updated administrative lines of communication through the creation of a superintendent of Indian affairs based in St. Louis to oversee all western tribal affairs outside of any state or territory.[6]

NOTES

1. Annual Report of the Commissioner of Indian Affairs, United States. Office of Indian Affairs, 1831, p. 172.
2. The act of the 9th July, 1832, entitled "An act to provide for the appointment of a commissioner of Indian Affairs, and for other purposes," ... under... the Secretary of War.
3. Report of the Commissioner of Indian Affairs to the Secretary of War, United States. Office of Indian Affairs, 1832, p. 160.
4. Report of the Commissioner of Indian Affairs to the Secretary of War, United States. Office of Indian Affairs, 1832, p. 163.
5. Report of the Commissioner of Indian Affairs to the Secretary of War, United States. Office of Indian Affairs, 1835, p. 261.
6. "An Act to regulate trade and intercourse with the Indian tribes, and to preserve peace on the frontiers," 4 Stat. 929 (June 30, 1834); "An Act to provide for the organization of the department of Indian affairs," 4 Stat. 735 (June 30, 1834).

CHAPTER 10: Carey Allen Harris, Commissioner of Indian Affairs (July 4, 1836–October 19, 1838) – Statistical Data

The next Commissioner, Carey Harris, pointed out three principal goals: (1) the removal of all eastern tribes to lands west of the Mississippi River; (2) establishment of a territorial government for the tribes, including federal control and oversight of tribal governments; and (3) civilization of the Indians via education in the mechanical arts and agriculture. He reported on the amount of funds expended, the number of Indians removed, the operations of the Treaty Commissioners, and the number of schools established in the Indian Territory.

1838: Commissioner Harris Forced to Resign due to Land Speculation

By the fall of 1838, President Van Buren had evidence of Commissioner Harris's involvement in land speculation and requested his resignation.[1]

NOTES

1. See also "Message on the Creek Indians," July 3, 1838, *House Document 452*, Twenty-Fifth Cong., First Sess., *Congressional Serial Set 331*, 11:1–102.

CHAPTER 11: Thomas Hartley Crawford, Commissioner of Indian Affairs (October 22, 1838–October 29, 1845) - Options for Indians – Integration, Emigrate to British Canada, Move West; Must Be Educated; Trade and Annuity Abuses Must Be Corrected

President Martin Van Buren appointed Thomas Hartley Crawford as Commissioner of Indian Affairs, a position in which he remained for seven years. Commissioner Crawford served four presidents: Van Buren, William Henry Harrison, John Tyler, and James K. Polk. President Polk (Whig) asked for and received his resignation on October 29, 1845. During his tenure in office, Commissioner Crawford focused on expediting emigration of the tribes, correcting trade discrepancies and abuses, and accelerating civilization through coeducation. He concluded there were but three options for the Indians. (1) They could integrate with the white population, an option he thought individual Indians might accept but not whole tribes; (2) they could emigrate to British Canada; or (3) they could move west.[1]

1839: Commissioner Crawford - Contact of White Man Is Death to Indians

> The whole history of the race bears testimony to the fact that the contact of the white man is death to them. T. Hartley Crawford.[2]

1840: Commissioner Crawford - Indians Must Be Removed, Civilized and Christianized

Commissioner Crawford saw education as the strategy for their civilization and education.

> The sooner they are removed, the better. Permanency of location ... is the parent of all that is valuable in civilized life ... that the Indians must be civilized [and] Christianized. The great instrument of their moral elevation must be education...[3]

1844: Commissioner Crawford - Co-Education of Indians Mandatory; No Civilization without Individual Ownership of Property

> Unless the Indian female character is raised, and her relative position changed, such education as you can give the males will be a rope of sand, which, separating at every turn, will bind them to no amelioration.[4]

> Their great drawback is want of employment-want of incentive to exertion, of which they are deprived by the joint ownership of land and property. *It never has happened, and it never will happen ... that there can be much of civilization without separate and individual ownership of property...* (Emphasis added).[5]

NOTES

1. Report of the Commissioner of Indian Affairs to the Secretary of War, United States. Office of Indian Affairs, 1840, pp. 232-233.
2. Report of the Commissioner of Indian Affairs, Department of War, 1839, p. 346.
3. Report of the Commissioner of Indian Affairs to the Secretary of War, United States. Office of Indian Affairs, 1840, p. 242.
4. Report of the Commissioner of Indian Affairs to the Secretary of War, United States. Office of Indian Affairs, 1839, p. 344.
5. Report of the Commissioner of Indian Affairs to the Secretary of War, United States. Office of Indian Affairs, 1844, p. 11.

CHAPTER 12: William Medill, Commissioner of Indian Affairs (1845-1849) - U.S. Secured Oregon Country (1846), Annexed Texas (1845), and Acquired Southwest after Mexican War (1848) – Colonization, Civilization and Christianization of Indians Only Solution; U.S. beyond Reproach

1845: Commissioner Medill - Education

The succeeding Commissioner, William Medill, also asserted the need for a practical education which to him should include (1) manual labor; (2) mechanical arts; and (3) letters. This would enable the Indian to make a useful contribution to his community.

> He can make fences; plough and cultivate the fields; can raise all the necessaries of life; manufacture the requisite utensils; repair his gun; and in short supply all his own wants, and exert a useful influence among his people.[1]

1846: Commissioner Medill - Annuities Prevent Improvement

Continually the Office of Indian Affairs condemned cash annuities but as they were a treaty obligation, there was little that could be done.

> I have become satisfied that there is no evil so great to which a tribe can be subjected as the possession of resources, not the fruit of their own industry and frugality, in the form of large and extravagant annuities. They lead to indolence and to other habits, which not only prevent their moral and social improvement, but tend eventually to their corruption and diminution, if not extermination.[2]

Commissioner Medill opposed paying cash annuities to traders for Indian debt, arguing they intentionally kept Indians in indebtedness, leading to debauchery, disease, and shortened lives. He was unsuccessful due to Secretary of Interior Thomas Ewing's safeguarding of this practice.[3] Secretary Ewing strongly supported the traders, and in April 1849, he issued a policy allowing annuities to be paid directly to traders to cover Indian debt.

1846: Commissioner Medill - Chippewas of Mississippi and Lake Superior Still Own Valuable Mineral and Agricultural Land

The Indian Bureau's scheme in publishing the agricultural and mineral wealth of tribes would lead to their dispossession of these resources.

> *The Chippewas of the Mississippi and Lake Superior still own a considerable extent of country ... A portion is said to be so well adapted to agricultural purposes, and a part so rich in minerals and ores, that it will probably at an early day attract a considerable white population.* (Emphasis added).[4]

1846: Commissioner Medill's Position regarding Indian's Future

> [Indians represent] a barren field for the moral and intellectual teacher. ... Such a change can be brought about only by concentrating them within fixed and reasonable limits, where they are given to understand that they are to reside permanently, and where they will reap the benefit of any arrangements they may make for their subsistence and comfort. Game will soon become scarce, and they will be compelled gradually to resort to agriculture and other pursuits of civilized life, when a fruitful opening will be afforded for efforts for their moral, intellectual, and social improvement.[5]

1846: Senator Benton's (R-MO) Congressional Speech – White Race's Malevolent, Divine, Manifest Destiny

In 1846, Senator Thomas Hart Benton's speech to Congress epitomizes, in the most graphic, heinous and hideous exposition, the malevolence of the 'white race's' purported divine Manifest Destiny:

> *It would seem that the White race alone received the divine command, to subdue and replenish the earth, for it is the only race that has obeyed it-the only race that hunts out new and distant lands, and even a New World, to subdue and replenish. The Red race has disappeared from the Atlantic coast; the tribes that resisted civilization met extinction.* This is a cause of lamentation with many. For my part, I cannot murmur at what seems to be the effect of divine law. I cannot repine that this Capitol has replaced the wigwam—this Christian people, replaced the savages—white matrons, the red squaws— and that such men as Washington, Franklin, and Jefferson, have taken the place of Powhattan, Opechonecanough, and other red men, howsoever respectable they may have been as savages.
>
> Civilization, or extinction, has been the fate of all people who have found themselves in the trace of the advancing Whites, and *civilization, always the preference of the Whites, has been pressed as an object, while extinction has followed as a consequence of its resistance.* (Emphasis added).[6]

1848: Commissioner Medill - Maintaining Order on Frontier - Establish Two Large "Colonies" (or Reservations) for Indians, One in North, One in South, Clear Central Unmolested Path for Emigrating Whites

Colonizing the Indians. Commissioner Medill suggested a modification to Indian Country by proposing to establish two large "colonies" (or reservations) for the Indians, one in the north and one in the south. Border tribes in the middle would be relocated again to clear a path for the emigrants heading west. ...Commissioner Medill was sowing the seeds of the reservation policy.[7]

1848: Commissioner Medill - Strongest Propensities of Indian's Nature Are Desire for War and Love of Chase; Labor Utterly Repugnant; Colonization of Indians Only Solution

In support of his plan to 'colonize' the Indians, Commissioner Medill argued it would end their indolence. **The footing was reversed with the Indians being colonized in their own land by the European immigrants.** Their former traditional lands would be sold with a fund created for their aid.

> The strongest propensities of an Indian's nature are his desire for war and his love of the chase. ... But anything like labor is distasteful and utterly repugnant to his feelings and natural prejudices. He considers it a degradation... Nor can these be subdued in any other way than by the mode of colonization ...[8]

> The policy already begun and relied on ... *to colonize our Indian tribes beyond the reach, for some years, of our white population*; confining each within a small district of country, so that, as the game decreases and becomes scarce, the adults will gradually be compelled to resort to agriculture and other kinds of labor to obtain a subsistence, in which aid may be afforded and facilities furnished them out of the means obtained by the sale of their former possessions. (Emphasis added).[9]

1848: Treaty of Guadalupe Hidalgo Ended Mexican American War; U.S. Citizenship Offered to 100,000 Mexican Nationals; Mineral Resources of Southwest Territory Ceded to U.S. by Mexico Created U.S. Economic Boom

The Treaty of Peace, Friendship, Limits, and Settlement, better known as the Treaty of Guadalupe Hidalgo, was signed in 1848, and ended the Mexican American War. It increased the land mass of the U.S. by 50 percent and offered citizenship to the 100,000 Mexican nationals within the territory. The mineral resources from the territory conquered created an economic boom for the U.S.

General U. S. Grant, who had served as a young Lieutenant in the War, later commented on it as follows:

> I do not think there was ever a more wicked war than that waged by the United States on Mexico. ... I had a horror of the Mexican War, and I have always believed that it was on our part most unjust. The wickedness was not in the way our soldiers conducted it, but in the

conduct of our government in declaring war. ... We had no claim on Mexico. Texas had no claim beyond the Nueces River, and yet we pushed on to the Rio Grande and crossed it. I am always ashamed of my country when I think of that invasion.[10]

1848: Commissioner Medill - Indians Removed from Iowa; Removal Expected from Wisconsin

Commissioner Medill's colonization project resulted in cherry-picking the best lands for the U.S. and removing the Indians from their traditional lands. Indians from Iowa were to be removed from the "best and most desirable lands in the State" and those in Wisconsin were to be removed as well:

> The removal of [the Winnebagoes and the Pottawatomies], has entirely freed Iowa of her Indian population, which occupied *some of the best and most desirable lands in the State*, that will now be rapidly settled by our enterprising and industrious citizens. ... There is, probably no where within our limits a more desirable section of country than this - whether for soil or climate; and if opened to our hardy and enterprising pioneers, it would soon become densely settled with a prosperous and thriving white population. (Emphasis added).[11]

> Wisconsin, like Iowa, may also soon be relieved from the Indian population within her limits.[12]

1848: Commissioner Medill - Bloodshed and Strife Inevitable between Different Races - Weaker Party Must Suffer; U.S. beyond Reproach

With the further encroachment of the white population, the "prejudices led to bloodshed and strife – inevitable between different races under such circumstances – in which the weaker party must suffer."[13]

Akin to Senator's Benton pronouncement on white superiority in 1846, and the U.S.' manifest destiny, Commissioner Medill joined in this racial diatribe pardoning the U.S. for injuries to Indians as beyond reproach.

> Apathy, barbarism, and heathenism must give way to energy, civilization, and christianity; and so the Indian of this continent has been displaced by the European ... *If, in the rapid spread of our population and sway, with all their advantages and blessings to ourselves and to others, injury has been inflicted upon the barbarous and heathen people we have displaced, are we as a nation alone to be held up to reproach for such a result?* (Emphasis added).[14]

1849: Congress Creates Department of Interior; Thomas Ewing First Secretary of Interior

Congress created the Department of the Interior on March 3, 1849, and moved the Indian Office into the new executive department. In November 1848, Zachary Taylor was elected president and appointed Thomas Ewing as the first Secretary of the Interior.

NOTES

1. Commissioner of Indian Affairs to the Secretary of War, United States. Office of Indian Affairs, 1845, p. 453.
2. Report of the Commissioner of Indian Affairs to the Secretary of War, United States. Office of Indian Affairs, 1846, p. 6.
3. Report of the Commissioner of Indian Affairs to the Secretary of War, United States. Office of Indian Affairs, 1848, p. 15.
4. Report of the Commissioner of Indian Affairs to the Secretary of War, United States. Office of Indian Affairs, 1846, p. 8.
5. Report of the Commissioner of Indian Affairs to the Secretary of the Interior, Office of Indian Affairs, Printer: Ritchie & Heiss, 1846, p. 8.
6. Congressional Globe, May 28, 1846. http://www.historymuse.net/readings/benton.htm (accessed online September 30, 2024).
7. Dejong, David H. Paternalism to Partnership: The Administration of Indian Affairs, 1786–2021. University of Nebraska Press, 2022. Project MUSE. https://muse.jhu.edu/book/100035 (accessed online September 30, 2024).
8. Report of the Commissioner of Indian Affairs to the Secretary of War (1848), United States. Office of Indian Affairs, 1849, pp. 386-387. https://search.library.wisc.edu/digital/AFZWVMJ2YAVFXJ8T/pages/AQH6Y7NZBUHMMB8Y (accessed online September 30, 2024).
9. Report of the Commissioner of Indian Affairs to the Secretary of War (1848), United States. Office of Indian Affairs, 1849, p. 386.
10. Around the world with General Grant: a narrative of the visit of General U. S. Grant, ex-President of the United States, to various countries in Europe, Asia, and Africa, in 1877, 1878, 1879 to which are added certain conversations with General Grant on questions connected with American politics and history, John Russell Young, 1879: 448.
11. Report of the Commissioner of Indian Affairs to the Secretary of War (1848), United States. Office of Indian Affairs, 1849, p. 396.
12. Report of the Commissioner of Indian Affairs to the Secretary of War (1848), United States. Office of Indian Affairs, 1849, p. 397.
13. Report of the Commissioner of Indian Affairs to the Secretary of War (1848), United States. Office of Indian Affairs, 1849, pp. 385-386.
14. Report of the Commissioner of Indian Affairs to the Secretary of War (1848), United States. Office of Indian Affairs, 1849, p. 385.

CHAPTER 13: Orlando Brown, Commissioner of Indian Affairs (June 30, 1849–July 1, 1850) - Support for Indian Traders in Payment of Annuities Led to Forced Resignation; If Nothing Done for Indians – U.S. Legacy Will Be Constant Source of Regret, If Not Self-Reproach

Secretary Ewing continued to control the Indian Office, and because of his support for Indian traders in the payment of annuities, Congress investigated his actions and relationship with the traders. Commissioner Brown was guilty by association, and lost what little influence he had. On May 22, 1850, he offered his resignation, effective July 1.[1]

1849: Commissioner Brown - Territory of Minnesota Being Overrun by White Settlers

To dispossess the Minnesota Indians of their rich pine forests, the timber and lumber industries collaborated to secure timber contracts from individual Indians in advance of Indian title being extinguished and begin clearcutting.

> *Since the establishment of the new Territory of Minnesota, the attention of a large number of our enterprising citizens has been directed to that quarter, in consequence of the fine climate, and the richness and fertility of the lands on the Mississippi ... by the superabundant water-power afforded ... and by the superior advantages offered by the extensive forests of pine, convenient to water transportation, for a large and lucrative trade in timber. There has consequently been considerable emigration ... so that, in a very few years the population will be sufficient to justify a demand for admission into the Union as a State.* (Emphasis added).[2]

1849: Commissioner Brown – Care of Indians by U.S. Required

Before leaving office, Commissioner Brown did report on the need to care for the Indians who were declining in number, with the possibility of extinction.

> *[U]nless the fostering care of the Government be extended to them, [they] must continue to decline and soon disappear, leaving us as a legacy, a constant source of regret, if not self-reproach, in our having done too little to avert their melancholy fate.* (Emphasis added).[3]

NOTES

1. Dejong, David H. Paternalism to Partnership: The Administration of Indian Affairs, 1786–2021. University of Nebraska Press, 2022. Project MUSE. https://muse.jhu.edu/

book/100035 (accessed online September 30, 2024).
2. Report of the Commissioner of Indian Affairs to the Secretary of War, United States. Office of Indian Affairs, 1849, p. 9.
3. Report of the Commissioner of Indian Affairs to the Secretary of War, United States. Office of Indian Affairs, 1849, pp. 21, 22.

CHAPTER 14: Luke Lea, Commissioner of Indian Affairs (July 1, 1850–March 24, 1853) - Establishing Reservations Mandatory; Indians Must Resort to Agricultural Labor or Starve; Face Being Over-Run and Exterminated; Indians through Education, Capable of Civilization and U.S. Citizenship

Commissioner Lea believed Indians were just as capable as non-Indians and that they could take their place in the nation as productive citizens. He assumed office at a time of sectional strife over slavery that was temporarily appeased when Congress enacted into law a series of bills collectively referred to as the Compromise of 1850. More importantly, Indian wars in Texas and New Mexico, threats of extermination of the border tribes, and the near annihilation of the California Indians forced his hand in developing a policy to address the extermination and uprooting of the Indians. He advocated for reservations adapted to agriculture for all Indians.

> In the application of this policy to our wilder tribes, ***it is indispensably necessary that they be placed in positions where they can be controlled, and finally compelled, by stern necessity, to resort to agricultural labor or starve.*** ... There should be assigned to each tribe, for a permanent home, a country adapted to agriculture, of limited extent and well-defined boundaries, within which all, with occasional exceptions, should be compelled constantly to remain until such time as their general improvement and good conduct may supersede the necessity of such restrictions. ... In the meantime, ***the government should cause them to be supplied with stock, agricultural implements, and useful materials for clothing; encourage and assist them in the erection of comfortable dwellings, and secure to them the means and facilities of education***, intellectual, moral, and religious. The application of their own funds to such purposes would be far better for them than the present system of paying their annuities in money, which does substantial good to but few, while to the great majority it only furnishes the means and incentive to vicious and depraving indulgence, terminating in destitution and misery, and too frequently in premature death. (Emphasis added).[1]

> *If they remain as they are, many years will not elapse before they will be over-run and exterminated; or, uprooted and broken-spirited ... these Indians, if properly established, protected, and cherished, may at no distant time become intelligent, moral, and Christian communities ... and entitled to equal participation in the rights, privileges, and immunities of American citizens.* (Emphasis added).[2]

NOTES

1. Report of the Commissioner of Indian Affairs to the Secretary of the Interior, United States. Office of Indian Affairs, 1850, pp. 3-4.
2. Senate Executive document, no. 1, 31st Cong., 2d sess, serial 587, 35-37. Report of the Commissioner of Indian Affairs to the Secretary of the Interior, Office of Indian Affairs, 1850, p. 7.

CHAPTER 15: George W. Manypenny, Commissioner of Indian Affairs (March 31, 1853–March 30, 1857) - Second Wave of Emigration Treaties - Allotment in Severalty; Relinquishment of Annuities; Forty-Three Ratified and Twenty-Three Unratified Treaties Opening More than 174 Million Acres of Land to White Settlement

~

Commissioner Manypenny was known for his role in the second emigration of the border tribes. He was part of forty-three ratified and twenty-three unratified treaties that opened more than 174 million acres of land for settlement. Commissioner Manypenny also was active in the Pacific Northwest, executing seventeen treaties with the tribes in Washington and Oregon, where settlers were calling for the extermination of all Indians.[1]

1853: Indians' Future Grim

Tragically, as early as 1853, the Commissioner of Indian Affairs Annual Report proclaims what Indians had to look forward to with the extinction of game and the buffalo: starvation, death, gradual famine and disease (cholera and smallpox).

> The fact, startling as it may appear, was made manifest in my recent visit, that the Cheyennes and Arrapahoes, and many of the Sioux, are actually in a ***starving*** state. They are in abject want of food half the year, and their reliance for that scanty supply, in the ***rapid decrease of the buffalo***, is fast disappearing. ... ***Their women are pinched with want and their children constantly crying out with hunger***. Their arms, moreover, are unfitted to the pursuit of smaller game, and thus the lapse of a few years presents only the prospect of a ***gradual famine***. ... The same fate, too, ultimately awaits the tribes adjacent to New Mexico and Texas; and that will, in all probability, be hurried on with frightful rapidity. It will be seen that to leave them as they now are would be inhumanity; and that to isolate them in small strips of territory, where they cannot subsist under surrounding circumstances upon the large lands they now occupy, would be only to ***deliver them over to the ravages of disease***, in addition to the miseries of famine. If penned up in small secluded colonies they become hospital wards of ***cholera and smallpox***, and must lie supported at an immense annual cost to the government. If no alteration is effected in their present state, the future has only starvation in store for them. ... ***But one course remains which promises any permanent relief to them, or any lasting benefit to the country in which they dwell. That is, simply to make such modifications in the "intercourse laws" as will invite the residence of traders amongst them, and open the whole Indian territory to settlement.*** (Emphasis added).[2]

1853: Policy Must Be an Army or Annuity

Our relations with the wild tribes of the prairie and mountains resolve themselves, into a simple alternative. The policy must be either an army or an annuity. Either an inducement must be offered to them greater than the gains of plunder, or a force must be at hand able to restrain and check their depredations. Any compromise between the two systems will be only productive of mischief, and liable to all the miseries of failure. It will beget confidence, without providing safety; it will neither create fear, nor satisfy avarice; and, adding nothing to the protection of trade and emigration, will add everything to the responsibilities of the government. Thomas Fitzpatrick, Indian Agent, Upper Platte and Arkansas.[3]

1854: Michigan Agency, Henry C. Gilbert, Agent, Chippewas Destitute, Naked and Starving, One-Fourth of Band Dead

South of the Bad River settlement, and about Lakes Courteville and De Flambeau, are other bands, numbering in the aggregate from 1,200 to 1,500 persons, who are still in the lowest state of degradation. They have for several years been deprived of all participation in the benefit of existing treaties, and are in a state of poverty and destitution absolutely shocking. They came out en masse to the recent annuity payment, and were literally naked and starving. During the past year the smallpox has made fearful ravages among them, having carried off not less than one-fourth of their people.[4]

1854: Commissioner Manypenny - National Current of White Population Overwhelming Indians; Emigrated Tribes in Kansas Territory Permanently There to Be Civilized or Exterminated; No More Relocation Possible - on Ground They Occupy Crisis Must Be Met and Future Determined

The residence of the tribes who have recently ceded their lands, should, therefore be considered ... as permanently fixed. ... *It is therefore, in my judgment, clear, beyond doubt or question, that the emigrated tribes in Kansas Territory are permanently there—there to be thoroughly civilized, and to become a constituent portion of the population, or there to be destroyed and exterminated. ... They can go no further; on the ground they now occupy the crisis must be met, and their future determined* ... (Emphasis added).[5]

Commissioner Manypenny, Three Great Evils

In his 1855 Report, Commissioner Manypenny listed three problem areas:

Three great evils which have attended our Indian policy - large money annuities; excessive quantities of land held in common; and continued changes of location in advance of our frontier population.⁶

The conclusion to which I am tending, and which I would gladly impress upon the government, is, that one of three alternatives must be embraced. The first is, to wage a war of extermination against these unfortunate beings, and so be done with them at once and forever. However shocking to humanity such a course may appear, it is less so than the second, which is to let matters proceed as they are now going until, by the ***combined and gradual operation of famine, disease, domestic broil, and outside pressure, the same fate, that of utter extinction, shall have overtaken them***; the travel and commerce of the plains having, in the meantime, been subject to constant interruption and annoyance. ***The third, and it is in strict conformity to the humane and philanthropic spirit of the age, is to feed these people*** until such time as, by the introduction amongst them of knowledge and habits suitable to their condition, they shall be able to provide for their own subsistence. (Emphasis added).

Expensive as a compliance with these recommendations would undoubtedly be, it would yet prove less so than either a war of extermination or the maintenance of a sufficient force to hold these tribes constantly in check. Simply as a means of saving them from starvation, it is probably the most economical that could be devised, whilst on the score of humanity, it bears no comparison with a war, whether of extermination or of mere coercion. The fact must not be lost sight of, however, that, in order to do anything calculated to result in benefit to these deluded creatures, they must first be whipped into submission; at present they hold the American government and people in the utmost contempt, and until they shall be set right in this particular, it is folly, and worse than folly, to attempt to maintain friendly relations with them. J.A. Whitfield.⁷

1855: Indians Cheated of Annuities by "Shameful, Dishonorable, and Unlawful Means"

Commissioner Manypenny: When annuities are to be distributed, "a miserable class of men who deal in spirituous liquors, games, and other vices, and who, in despite of the vigilance of the officers, are enabled to carry off large amounts of the funds of the Indians, obtained by the most shameful, dishonorable, and unlawful means."⁸

1855: Sioux Agency, No Agricultural Implements, Annuities Undelivered

[A]s we had not sufficient farms opened to accommodate the mill, and the contractor having failed to perform his contract, (having broken only 63 acres instead of 500 above Yellow Medicine,) I shall be in the same position next year, unless you allow me to place in the hands of the farmer during this winter the ploughs, oxen, wagons, and other supplies necessary to commence in the spring in sufficient force ...

It is absolutely necessary that another blacksmith should be allowed the Sisetons and Wahpetons. ... This year's annuity goods and provision are still undelivered, and the time fixed by your contract is expired. It is impossible they can now be got up in time for the payment, late as it is. R. G. Murphy, Indian Agent.[9]

1855: Fort Laramie Indian Agency, Agent Thomas S. Twiss – Indians Suffering, Thousands Die Annually

It is evident to me, from my short experience, that the bands of Indians on the plains suffer greatly, at particular seasons, by cold and hunger. The buffalo is becoming scarce, and it is more difficult from year to year for the Indians to kill a sufficient number to supply them with food and clothing. The old and the very *young Indians are the greatest sufferers, for they are less able to bear the intense cold of winter and privation of food. Thousands die annually from these causes alone*; and the certain gradual disappearance of the buffalo is followed by the rapid, quick disappearance of the Indians. I would recommend to the department an increase, if possible, of the annuity to the tribes of this agency for the next year. There will be a greater degree of suffering than at any former period. (Emphasis added).[10]

1856: Kansas Territory: Indians Endure Trespasses and Depredations of Every Conceivable Type; Despoiled of Their Lands and Annuities by Swarm of Audacious Speculators

Trespasses and depredations of every conceivable kind have been committed on the Indians [inhabiting Kansas]. They have been personally maltreated, their property stolen, their timber destroyed, their possessions encroached upon, and divers other wrongs and injuries done them. (Emphasis added).[11]

1857: Oregon and Wash., Not Enough Agents, No Military Force, Indians Doomed to Extermination Unless Protected

The land laws which permit the occupation and settlement of both Washington and Oregon Territories, regardless of the rights of the Indians, render the intercourse laws, practically, a nullity. ... As the lands of the [Indian] are entirely occupied by the whites, their means of obtaining a living are greatly curtailed. ***The wants of those "untutored wards of the government" should be supplied, and their rights protected, unless the government has determined that they should be doomed to extermination at the hands of the whites.*** (Emphasis added).[12]

1865: Indians Removed to Kansas Permanently, Subsequently Removed to Indian Territory

The future of the Indians removed to Kansas was removal to Indian Territory. These included the Shawnee, Delaware, Ottawa, Miami, Chippewa, Kickapoo, Potawatomi, Sauk and Fox, Seneca, Wyandot, Confederated Tribes of the Kaskaskia, Peoria, Wea, and Piankashaw, Quapaw, Ioway, Otoe and Missouria and others.

Agent G.C. Snow documented in his 1865 Report the basis for the removal: (1) opening to white settlement four million acres of the best agricultural land in Kansas; and (2) removing the powerful Osage tribe.

> This movement, if accomplished, would open to white settlement four million acres of the best agricultural land in Kansas, and place these Indians in a country much better adapted to them in their present state. This plan I understand to be the policy of the government - to remove all the Indians from Kansas and form them into a confederacy in the Indian territory. By pursuing this course, one of the most powerful tribes (Osages) will be removed from the State.[13]

NOTES

1. Report of the Commissioner of Indian Affairs to the Secretary of the Interior (1855), United States. Office of Indian Affairs, 1856, p. 20.
2. Report of the Commissioner of Indian Affairs to the Secretary of the Interior, Upper Platte &c, Agency, United States. Office of Indian Affairs, U.S. Government Printing Office, 1853, p. 128.
3. Report of the Commissioner of Indian Affairs to the Secretary of the Interior, United States. Washington: Robert Armstrong, Printer, 1853, p. 122.
4. Report of the Commissioner of Indian Affairs to the Secretary of the Interior, 1854, Michigan Agency, Printer: A.O.P. Nicholson, 1855, p. 30.
5. Report of the Commissioner of Indian Affairs to the Secretary of the Interior, United States. Office of Indian Affairs, 1854, p. 10.
6. Report of the Commissioner of Indian Affairs to the Secretary of the Interior, 1855, United States. Office of Indian Affairs, U.S. Government Printing Office, 1856, p. 6.
7. Report of the Commissioner of Indian Affairs to the Secretary of the Interior, United States. Office of Indian Affairs. Printer: A.O.P. Nicholson, 1855, p. 117.
8. Report of the Commissioner of Indian Affairs to the Secretary of the Interior, 1855,

United States. Printer: A. O. P. Nicholson, 1856, p. 19.
9. Report of the Commissioner of Indian Affairs to the Secretary of the Interior, 1855, United States, Printer: A.O.P. Nicholson, 1856, pp. 59-60.
10. Report of the Commissioner of Indian Affairs to the Secretary of the Interior, United States, Printer: A.O.P. Nicholson, 1856, p. 83.
11. Report of the Commissioner of Indian Affairs to the Secretary of the Interior, Office of Indian Affairs, 1856, p. 21.
12. Report of the Commissioner of Indian Affairs to the Secretary of the Interior, 1857, United States. Office of Indian Affairs. Printer: William A. Harris, 1858, p. 218.
13. Annual Report of the Department of Interior, Report of the Commissioner of Indian Affairs to the Secretary of the Interior, United States. U.S. Government Printing Office, 1865, p. 293.

CHAPTER 16: James W. Denver, Commissioner of Indian Affairs (April 17, 1857–December 2, 1857, and November 8, 1858–March 31, 1859) - Slavery Issue Resulting in "Bleeding Kansas"; Small Allotted Reservations; Indians - Hindrance to White Settlement; Commissioner Encouraged Tribes to Sell Land; Commissioner Denver's Family Speculated Heavily in Indian Allotments across West

~

Hurried Negotiation of Treaties Prior to Passage of Kansas-Nebraska Act

In anticipation of the passage of the Kansas-Nebraska Act, treaties with various Indian tribes were hurried through, extinguishing their titles to the land. *Prior to the passage of the bill*, Commissioner Manypenny negotiated treaties with the Otoes, Delawares, Shawnees, Iowas, Sacs, Foxes, Kickapoos and the confederated tribes of Kaskaskias, Peorias, Piankeshaws and Weas. On June 5, 1854, a treaty was made with the Miami Tribe.

"Bleeding Kansas"

In May 1854, Congress passed the Kansas-Nebraska Act, which created the territories of Kansas and Nebraska, repealed the Missouri Compromise of 1850, and allowed the territory settlers to determine if they would allow slavery within their boundaries. Abolitionists poured in from the North to prevent Kansas from becoming a slave state and southerners poured across state lines to vote in the state election to determine the state's future.

For the next seven years, an internal civil war would be fought in Kansas over the issue, resulting in the Territory earning the nickname "Bleeding Kansas" as the death toll rose. Eventually, the anti-slavery settlers outnumbered pro-slavery settlers, and on January 29, 1861, just before the Civil War, Kansas was admitted to the Union as a free state

Commissioner Denver's Indian Policy

Commissioner Denver's tenure, though brief, saw radical changes in Kansas and Nebraska. His political philosophy with regards to Indian affairs was laid out in his only annual report in 1857. He believed each tribe was entitled to a unique but small reservation that was to be *allotted in severalty although still owned by the tribe*. He believed paying annuities to the Indians led to dependence and indolence. Consequently, he argued any annuities should be used for homes, farm buildings and equipment, and other basic supplies. While never charged with duplicity, Commissioner Denver and his family speculated heavily in Indian allotments, owning land across the West.

1857: Indian Title Extinguished to 13,658,000 Acres in Kansas, Lands Retained for Indians 1,342,000 Acres

Indian title *to about 13,658,000 acres* was extinguished for white settlement. *The Indians retained about 1,342,000 acres.* (Emphasis added).[1]

Commissioner Denver's Perspective: Too Large Body of Land Assigned to Indians; Large Money Annuities Foster Dependence and Indolence

I concur fully with those of my predecessors who have stated that there have been two great and radical mistakes in our system of Indian policy-the assignment of an entirely too large body of land in common to the different tribes which have been relocated, and the payment of large money annuities for the cessions made by them; the first tending directly to prevent the Indians from acquiring settled habits and an idea of personal property and rights, which lie at the very foundation of all civilization; the second causing and fostering a feeling of dependence and habits of idleness, so fatally adverse to anything like physical and moral improvement.[2]

1857: Blue Earth, MN, Delay in Winnebagoes' Annuities, Rapid Settlement of Indian Land by Whites

The Winnebagoes land in Minnesota was destined to be forfeited.

Their reservation comprises a body of land that possesses agricultural advantages of the highest character, though much larger than the requirements of the Indians demand. The rapid settlement of the country in the vicinity and the great demand for land for settlement create already *earnest appeals for the reduction of the reservation of these Indians* to that size which would be actually necessary to their mediate wants and requirements. (Emphasis added).[3]

1857: Oregon: Indians Cheated, No Fair Compensation

My own observation in relation to the treaties which have been made in Oregon leads me to the conclusion that in most instances the Indians have not received a fair compensation for the rights which they have relinquished to the government. It is too often the case in such negotiations that the agents of the government are over anxious to drive a close bargain; and when an aggregate amount is mentioned, it appears large, without taking into consideration that the Indians, in the sale and surrender of their country, are surrendering all their means of obtaining a living; and when the small annuities come to be divided throughout the tribe, it exhibits but a pitiful and meagre sum for the supply of their individual wants. The Indians, receiving so little for the great surrender which they have made, begin to conclude that they have been defrauded; they become dissatisfied, and finally resort to arms, in the vain hope of regaining their lost rights, and the government expends millions in the prosecution of a war which might have been entirely avoided by a little more liberality in their dealings with a people who have no very correct notions of the value of money or property. A notable instance of this kind is exhibited in the treaty of September 10, 1853, with the Rogue River Indians. That tribe has diminished more than one-half in numbers since the execution of the treaty referred to. They, however, number at present nine hundred and nine souls. The country which they ceded embraces nearly the whole of the valuable portion of the Rogue River valley, embracing a country unsurpassed in the fertility of its soil and value of its gold mines; and the compensation which those nine hundred and nine people now living receive for this valuable cession is forty thousand dollars, in sixteen equal annual instalments of two thousand five hundred dollars each, a fraction over two dollars and fifty cents per annum to the person, which is the entire means provided for their clothing and sustenance.[4]

Commissioner Denver Pronounces that Indian Reservations Should Have Only Sufficient Allotted Land to Support Them, with Title to Land in Tribe

Their reservations should be restricted so as to contain only sufficient land to afford them a comfortable support by actual cultivation, and should be properly divided and assigned to them, with the obligation to remain upon and cultivate the same. *The title should remain in the tribe...* (Emphasis added).[5]

Commissioner Denver Views Indian Citizenship as Ultimate Goal

[W]hen any of them become sufficiently intelligent, sober and industrious, [the U.S. will] grant them patents for the lands so assigned to them, but leaseable or alienable only to members of the tribe, until they [are] ... fitted for the enjoyment of all the rights and privileges of citizens of the United States.[6]

NOTES

1. Report of the Commissioner of Indian Affairs to the Secretary of the Interior (1857), Office of Indian Affairs, 1857, p. 3.
2. Report of the Commissioner of Indian Affairs to the Secretary of the Interior (1857), Office of Indian Affairs, 1857, p. 4.
3. Report of the Commissioner of Indian Affairs to the Secretary of the Interior, 1857, Mackinac Agency, Washington. Printer, William A. Harris, 1858, p. 47.
4. Report of the Commissioner of Indian Affairs to the Secretary of the Interior, United States, U.S. Government Printing Office, 1857, p. 609.
5. Report of the Commissioner of Indian Affairs to the Secretary of the Interior (1857), Office of Indian Affairs, 1857, p. 4.
6. Report of the Commissioner of Indian Affairs to the Secretary of the Interior (1857), Office of Indian Affairs, 1857, p. 4.

CHAPTER 17: Charles E. Mix, Commissioner of Indian Affairs (June 14, 1858– November 8, 1858) - Recommended Small Reservations, Transition to Agrarian Culture; Ceasing Removal of Tribes; Assimilation Only Path Forward; Suggested Apprenticeship for Indian Orphans and Children Bound Out for Term of Years to Whites; Authored Office Laws, Regulations, Etc., for Indian Bureau

Commissioner Mix supported the reservation policy, with each tribe entitled to a small reservation to aid it in transitioning to an agrarian culture. To him, removal interfered with the civilizing process and should cease. Only stability, good land, severalty, and isolation from unscrupulous white people would facilitate self-sufficiency and civilization, with *assimilation the only path forward*. He authored the 1850 Office Laws, Regulations, Etc., of the Indian Bureau, provided to all personnel.[1]

1858: Three Errors in Indian Policy - Continual Removal as White Population Advanced; Reservations Too Large; Payment of Cash Annuities

> Experience has demonstrated that at least three serious, and, to the Indians, fatal errors have, from the beginning, marked our policy towards them, viz: their *removal from place to place* as our population advanced; the assignment to them of *too great an extent of country, to be held in common*; and the allowance of large sums of money, as *annuities*, for the lands ceded by them.
>
> Holding the land in common prevented them from "acquiring a knowledge of separate and individual property." The large annuities "tended to foster habits of indolence and profligacy, but constantly made them the victims of the lawless and inhuman sharper and speculator." (Emphasis added).[2]

1858: Indian Policy Corrections Needed: Isolated Reservations with Good Lands, Allotted in Severalty; No Whites Permitted; Manual Labor and Mechanical Trade Schools

> No more reservations should be established than are absolutely necessary for such Indians as have been, or it may be necessary to displace, in consequence of the extension of our settlements, and whose resources have thereby been cut off or so diminished that they cannot sustain themselves in their accustomed manner. Great care should be taken in the selection of the reservations, so as to *isolate the Indians for a time from contact and interference from the whites*. They should embrace *good lands*, which will well repay the efforts to cultivate them. No white persons should be suffered to go upon the reservations, and after the first year the *lands should be divided and assigned to the Indians in severalty*, every one being

required to remain on his own tract and to cultivate it, no persons being employed for them except the requisite mechanics to keep their tools and implements in repair, and such as may be necessary, for a time, to teach them how to conduct their agricultural operations and to take care of their stock. They should also have the advantage of well conducted ***manual labor schools*** for the education of their youth in letters, habits of industry, and a knowledge of agriculture and the simpler mechanic arts. (Emphasis added).[3]

1858: Commissioner Mix Suggested that Indian Children Could Be Bound out to Whites for Apprenticeship with State Regulation

Much good could also probably be accomplished by the introduction of a judicious system of apprenticeship, by which the ***orphans and other children of both sexes, could be bound out for a term of years***, to upright and humane persons, to be taught suitable trades and occupations: provided the necessary State laws were enacted to authorize and regulate such a system. (Emphasis added).[4]

1858: Apache Character Demands Extermination

The testimony of all who have any knowledge of the Apache concurring in pronouncing him the most rascally Indian on the continent. Treacherous, bloodthirsty, brutal, with an irresistible propensity to steal, he has been for years the scourge of Mexico, as the depopulated villages and abandoned fields of Chihuahua and Sonora too faithfully attest, and grave doubts are expressed whether any process short of extermination will suffice to quiet him.[5]

NOTES

1. United States Bureau of Indian Affairs, *Office Copy of the Laws, Regulations, Etc., of the Indian Bureau, 1850.*
2. Report of the Commissioner of Indian Affairs to the Secretary of the Interior, Office of Indian Affairs, 1858, p. 6.
3. Report of the Commissioner of Indian Affairs to the Secretary of the Interior (1858), Office of Indian Affairs, 1858, p. 10.
4. Report of the Commissioner of Indian Affairs to the Secretary of the Interior (1858), Office of Indian Affairs, 1858, p. 11.
5. Report of Secretary of Interior. Printer: James B. Steedman, 1858, p. 558.

CHAPTER 18: Alfred B. Greenwood, Commissioner of Indian Affairs (May 4, 1859–April 13, 1861) - Problems in Distinction between Treaty Tribes and Nontreaty Tribes; Treaty Tribes with Permanent Annuities and Those Without Annuities; Communal Landholding Tribes and Tribes with Allotted Reservations

Commissioner Greenwood led the Indian Office during a time of sectional strife, with the Civil War looming on the horizon. To a Congress preoccupied with potential war, Indian affairs were of secondary importance. To Commissioner Greenwood land severalty was sound Indian policy, indispensable to the advancement of Indians. He also advanced the view of segregating Indians from non-Indians until such a time when the former were able to compete with the latter. His tenure was tumultuous, leading him to recommend in 1860 that the Indian Bureau be retransferred to the War Department. It was a dark time for Indians, leading to starvation, removal and military control.

(1) Gold discoveries in Colorado led to white encroachment on Indian lands leaving Indians without subsistence, starving and compelled to rob and plunder to survive.

(2) Massacres were executed by U.S. citizens on routes through the Utah Territory and Indians were blamed, to fan public sentiment to get rid of them.

(3) In Kansas, due to the increase of the white population, it was no longer possible to protect Indians in their rights. The Shawnees, Miamies, and Confederated Bands of Kaskaskias, Peorias, Weas, and Piankeshaws were removed from Kansas due to their rapid deterioration.

(4) Indians in Utah were desperate; there was no adequate subsistence and whites had taken control of the good lands. Indians were perishing from exposure and hunger.

(5) The Army had to be called up to protect the Indians the U.S. was removing from Texas due to the threat of their extermination.

(6) The Indian Bureau was without the ability to distinguish, much less fulfill, their obligations to treaty tribes and nontreaty tribes, treaty tribes with permanent annuities and those without annuities, communal landholding tribes and tribes with allotted reservations.

(7) All of this turmoil across the country led Commissioner Greenwood to recommend in 1860 that the Indian Bureau be re-transferred to the War Department.

1859: Traditional Subsistence by Indians Impossible in Colorado due to Gold Discoveries

In November 1859, Commissioner Greenwood informed the Secretary of the Interior, that the United States had essentially deprived the Indians living in or hunting and gathering or visiting spiritual sites in the Colorado area of any means of traditional subsistence.

> A crisis has now, however, arrived in our relations with them. Since the discovery of gold in the vicinity of "Pike's Peak," the emigration has immensely increased; the Indians have been driven from their local haunts and hunting grounds, and the game so far killed off or dispersed, that it is now impossible for the Indians to obtain the necessary subsistence from that source. In fact, we have substantially taken possession of the country and deprived them of their accustomed means of support. ... They have also been brought to realize that a stern necessity is impending over them; that they cannot pursue their former mode of life, but must entirely change their habits, and, in fixed localities, look to the cultivation of the soil and the raising of stock for their future support. *There is no alternative to providing for them in this manner but to exterminate them, which the dictates of justice and humanity alike forbid. They cannot remain as they are; for, if nothing is done for them, they must be subjected to starvation, or compelled to commence robbing and plundering for a subsistence.* (Emphasis added).[1]

1859: Massacres on Routes Through Utah Territory Planned, If Not Executed, by U.S. Citizens

> It cannot be doubted that the horrible massacres which have occurred during the past year on the routes leading through Utah Territory have been planned and directed, if not actually executed, by our own citizens.[2]

1859: Westward Emigration, Upper Platte, Thomas S. Twiss, Agent

> The Sioux chief stated pretty accurately the condition of things now in process of rapid development, which threaten the utter extinction of the wild tribes, by destroying the game on which they depend for subsistence. *This great wave of emigration to the prairie west is moving onward with greatly increased velocity. It is beyond human power to retard or control it, nor would it be wise to do so, even were it possible.* This process of development, this law of Anglo-Saxon progress, progress, is a necessity and a consequence of, and flowing directly from, our free institutions, which, in their strength, purity, and beauty, tend to stimulate and bring forth the vast resources of agriculture, mineral and commercial wealth, within the

boundaries of our great empire. (Empire added).³

1859: Utah Territory, J. Forney, Superintendent Indian Affairs, Steal or Starve

The balance of the Indians in Utah are extremely poor. The utmost ingenuity is put in requisition to sustain life; they eagerly seek after everything containing a life-sustaining element, such as hares, rabbits, antelope, deer, bear, elk, dogs, lizards, snakes, crickets, grasshoppers, ants, roots, grass-seeds, bark, &c. Many men, women, and children are entirely naked. With some of the Indians, stealing cattle, horses, mules, &c., is a matter of necessity-steal or starve.⁴

1859: Carson Valley Agency, NEV, F. Dodge, Indian Agent, Steal or Starve

The Humboldt Indians see by the experience of other tribes that roads are the harbingers of civilization, and the certain sign of their own subjugation and final extirpation. All they ask is something to eat. And here lies the true secret of most of the Indian depredations upon this great line of travel. The encroachments of the emigrant have driven away the game upon which they depend for a subsistence. They cannot hunt upon the territories of neighboring tribes, except at the risk of their lives. They must, therefore, steal or starve.⁵

1859: Puget Sound Agency, Annuity - $1.41 Each

Last winter, particularly, being unusually long and severe, and food scarce to begin with, they suffered much more than they ordinarily do. I had ordered the local and special agents to use a very strict economy in making distributions of food, clothing, &c.; and this caused this agency to be beset for six months by large numbers of sick and destitute, as well as lazy, Indians. Last year I paid the annuity to thirteen hundred and fifty-seven individuals belonging to this treaty, about one dollar and forty-one cents each.⁶

1859: WASH, Siletz Agency, R. B. Metcalfe, Indian Agent, To Civilize Indians, Separate Reservation for All Children over Three and Under Ten Years of Age, Never Allow Older Indians to Visit

My experience would lead us to conclude that the idea of civilizing the present race of Indians is utterly absurd, or, at least, all those who are over ten years of age. If the government would establish a separate reservation for all of the children over three and under ten years of age, and never allow the older Indians to visit them, we could then civilize the rising generation. The children could be taught to repeat the English language, and, forgetting their horrible superstitions, they would then be prepared to receive a Christian education. Let there be a manual labor school established, where all the mechanical arts, farming, &c., can be taught the boys, and the girls taught to spin and weave their own clothing. By a system of this kind, we could accomplish in a few years what a series of years have failed to do, in other parts of this country.[7]

1859: U.S. Policy - Restrict Indians to Small Reservations, Divide Lands Among Them in Severalty

At present, the policy of the government is to gather the Indians upon small tribal reservations, within the well-defined exterior boundaries of which small tracts of land are assigned, in severalty, to the individual members of the tribe, with all the rights incident to an estate in fee-simple, except the power of alienation.[8]

1860: Utah, Superintendent Refuses Aid to Destitute Indians, Though He Had Funds in Hand, Indians Starved

I would state that in consequence of the great damage to their crops by grasshoppers and crickets in 1859, the sufferings of these poor Indians during the past winter were horrible, many of them dying from starvation and exposure. It was a common circumstance to find them frozen to death.

I made frequent requisitions upon and earnest appeals to the superintendent. He steadily refused to relieve their sufferings, notwithstanding he had in his possession at the time some $5,000 or $6,000 worth of Indian goods. I was compelled to witness the sufferings and death of these poor creatures, without money, provisions, or clothing wherewith to relieve them. On several occasions I parted with my own blankets to bury them in.[9]

1860: Oregon – Reservation System Last Resort

As to Oregon, the Commissioner warned the reservation system was the "last resort to save the race from extermination; and, if it fails or is abandoned, their doom may then be pronounced."[10]

1860: Problems in Distinction between Treaty Tribes and Nontreaty Tribes; Treaty Tribes with Permanent Annuities and Those Without Annuities; Communal Landholding Tribes and Tribes with Allotted Reservations

In reviewing the results of the policy pursued by the government of the United States towards the Indian tribes within their limits, it should be borne in mind that, while the same general relation exists between the United States and all the tribes, that relation has been modified in respect to many of them by treaty stipulations and acts of Congress, and as these modifications vary in each case, and often in essential particulars, the subject becomes complicated, and the *difficulty of subjecting the Indians to a uniform policy greatly increased*. With the wild tribes in the heart of the continent, in Arizona, and in California, constituting, possibly, the majority, we have no treaties whatever. *With respect to policy, then, it is obvious that the Indians must be divided into two classes—those with whom we have treaties, and those with whom we have not.* (Emphasis added).[11]

Again, the treaty or annuity Indians may be arranged in two divisions. With one we have treaties of amity, and we pay them annuities, either in money, goods, or provisions, or perhaps all three, for a longer or shorter period, but without recognizing their title to any particular tract of country. ... This latter class, again, must be subdivided into those who hold their lands in common, whether in fee, or by the usual Indian title, and those whose lands are held in severalty by the individual members of the tribe. There is yet a further distinction to be made between those cases where the *several reservations are in a compact body, surrounded by a well-defined exterior boundary, constituting them a tribal reservation, over which the intercourse laws can be enforced, and those in which the individual reservations are scattered among the white settlements, and subjected to the operation of the laws of the State or Territory in which they are situated.* (Emphasis added).[12]

1860: Indian Policy Must Be Based on Need for Private Property for White Settlers among Indians

... the ideas of separate, or rather private property, and isolation, must form the basis alike of our diplomacy and our legislation.[13]

1860: Policy of Severalty

Private property in the soil and its products stimulates industry by guarantying the undisturbed enjoyment of its fruits, and isolation is an effectual protection against the competition, the cunning, and the corrupting influences of the white man. This is not mere theory, it has the sanction of successful application in practice. Divide these reservations into farms of moderate dimensions, to be held in severalty by the individual members of the tribe, with all the rights incident to an estate in fee simple, except that of alienation. Annuities should be paid, not in money but in goods, provisions, agricultural implements, and seeds, and authority should be given to the agents to discriminate in their distribution between the industrious and the idle, the orderly and the thriftless.[14]

1860: Squaksin Agency, V. B. Gosnell, Sub-Agent, Washington Territory, Increase to Annuities Suggested - $1 Per Capita

I will again take the liberty of suggesting to the department an increase to the annuities paid the Indians, parties to the treaty of Medicine creek. The present appropriation, when divided among all those who are really entitled to pay, does not realize to each individual over $1.[15]

1860: Central Superintendency, Yancton Sioux, A. H. Redfield, Agent, Annuities $5 Each

I have paid them in cash this year only $10,000, the same as last year; but as they then numbered less than 2,000, they received five dollars each, whereas this year they numbered over 2,000, and consequently the individual shares were less than five dollars. The chiefs earnestly desire to have paid them next year at least $15,000.[16]

1860: Ottoes and Missourias, Failures of Crops, Per Capita of Eighteen Dollars

Failure in his crops will make it barely sufficient to sustain him through the winter.

Their present money annuity, which is soon to be paid them, is thirteen thousand dollars. The amounts authorized to be withheld from this for specific purposes will not leave over nine thousand dollars to be paid per capita, or "otherwise, as the President may direct."

The tribe will enumerate about five hundred, which would give them per capita eighteen dollars. Now, by the failure of their crops, without anything within themselves to fall back upon excepting the uncertainty of the chase - flour at five dollars a sack, blankets six to eight dollars a piece, coffee twenty to twenty-five cents a pound, and sugar seven and eight pounds to the dollar, all of which are necessaries, and with only eighteen dollars to invest, is a practical demonstration that something should be done to prevent destitution and famine during a long and dreary winter.[17]

1860: Annuities - Junk or Damaged, Overpriced, Huge Freight Charges

The Department of the Interior entered into contracts with east coast vendors to supply food, clothing, farming implements and other goods for all of the tribes across the country. Huge freight charges were incurred. Many of the goods were junk or damaged. The graft and corruption in acquiring Indian goods is evident from the reforms made in the 1900's in Procurement.

The aggregate amount ... to be expended for ... the Indians east of the Cascade mountains ... is $231,000. Of this, the sum of $111,000 was expended in the purchase of dry goods, groceries, and hardware on the Atlantic side. These purchases, by which large sums have been diverted from their original intention ... occasion a loss to the several tribes ... Suitable goods of the best quality can be purchased in this market ... Thus the freight might have been saved ...[18]

1860: Assimilation Policy, Individualizing Them as Agriculturists, Incorporation into U.S., Northern Superintendency, W.J. Cullen, Superintendent

The means adopted to sustain this policy are,
First. Making their *agricultural system one of individual, instead of a tribal character*.
Second. By inducing a voluntary abandonment of their nationality in dress and costume.
Third. Furnishing them with houses and the comforts of civilized life.
Fourth. Protection by the government to those who assume the character of improvement Indians from all attacks upon their persons and property.
Fifth. Punishing by loss of annuities those who leave their reservations for the commission of depredations upon the white settlers, or to enter the war path against other tribes.
Sixth. By making intoxication an offense punishable by loss of annuity and degradation from prominent position in their community. (Emphasis added).[19]

1860: Remove Shawnees, Miamies, and Confederated Bands of Kaskaskias, Peorias, Weas, and Piankeshaws from Kansas; Rapidly Deteriorating

The Shawnees, Miamies, and the confederated bands of Kaskaskias, Peorias, Weas, and Piankeshaws, belong to that class of Indians whose lands have been divided among the individual members of the tribe, and are held in severalty. ... They are not only making no progress, but are rapidly deteriorating ...[20]

I would recommend that authority be given to this department to sell their lands, with their consent, and, with the proceeds, purchase them a home, either in the Cherokee neutral land, or in some part of, the Osage reservation. ... *Besides, it will open to settlement some of the richest and most productive lands in Kansas.* (Emphasis added).[21]

Transfer Supervision of Indian Bureau Back to War Department

I am of the opinion, therefore, that *the supervision of the Indian*

> *Bureau might be retransferred to the War Department with great propriety and advantage.* (Emphasis added).²²

States' Legislatures Petition President to Extinguish Indian Title²³

The following states' legislatures petitioned the then-sitting president to extinguish Indian title:

Georgia, Illinois, Indiana, Kentucky, Michigan Territory, Mississippi, Missouri, New York, North Carolina, Ohio, South Carolina and Tennessee. Others would follow.

1860: SW States' Residents Petition President to Extinguish Indian Title

In 1860, President Buchanan transmitted eight memorials to Congress from residents of New Mexico, Utah, Kansas, and Nebraska "for the early extinguishment of the Indian title, a consequent survey and sale of the public land, and the establishment of an assay office in the immediate and daily reach of the citizens of that region," along with granting territorial status.²⁴

Reservations Swarm with Intimidating White Squatters

> There is scarcely one of the ninety-two reservations at present established on which white men have not effected a lodgement: many swarm with squatters, who hold their place by intimidating the rightful owners; while in more than one case the Indians have been wholly dispossessed, and are wanderers upon the face of the earth. So far have these forms of usurpation been carried at times in Kansas, that *an Indian reservation there might be defined as that portion of the soil of the State on which the Indians have no rights whatsoever.* (Emphasis added).²⁵

NOTES

1. Report of the Commissioner of Indian Affairs to the Secretary of the Interior (1859), Office of Indian Affairs, 1859, p. 21.
2. Extract from Annual Report of the Secretary of the Interior to Congress, Dec. 1, 1859, p. 3.
3. Report of the Commissioner of Indian Affairs to the Secretary of the Interior (1859), Upper Platte Agency, United States. Office of Indian Affairs, 1860, p. 130.
4. Report of the Commissioner of Indian Affairs to the Secretary of the Interior, Utah Superintendency, United States. Office of Indian Affairs, 1860, p. 365.
5. Report of the Commissioner of Indian Affairs to the Secretary of the Interior, 1859, Carson Valley Agency, United States. Office of Indian Affairs, 1860, p. 376.
6. Report of the Commissioner of Indian Affairs to the Secretary of the Interior, Puget's Sound Agency, 1859. Washington: Printer, George W. Bowman, 1860, p. 393.
7. Annual Reports of the Department of the Interior, Report of the Secretary of the

Interior, 1859, United States. Office of Indian Affairs, U.S. Government Printing Office, 1860, p. 426.
8. Extract from Annual Report of the Secretary of the Interior to Congress, Dec. 1, 1859, p. 5.
9. The Abridgment: Containing Messages of the President of the United States to the Two Houses of Congress with Reports of Departments and Selections from Accompanying Papers, Report of the Secretary of Interior, 1860, p. 170.
10. Report of the Secretary of the Interior Ex. Doc., United States congressional serial set, United States. Department of the Interior, 1860, p. 389.
11. Extract from Annual Report of the Secretary of the Interior to Congress, 1860, p. 3.
12. Extract from Annual Report of the Secretary of the Interior to Congress, 1860, p. 4.
13. Id.
14. Report of the Commissioner of Indian Affairs to the Secretary of the Interior, Extract from the Annual Report of the Secretary of the Interior to Congress. Washington: Printer, George W. Bowman, 1860, p. 5.
15. Report of the Commissioner of Indian Affairs to the Secretary of the Interior, Squaksin Agency. Washington: Printer, George W. Bowman, 1860, p. 201.
16. Report of the Commissioner of Indian Affairs to the Secretary of the Interior, Yancton Sioux. Washington: Printer, George W. Bowman, 1860, p. 87.
17. Report of the Commissioner of Indian Affairs to the Secretary of the Interior, Ottoes and Missourias. Washington: Printer, George W. Bowman, 1860, p. 97.
18. Report of the Commissioner of Indian Affairs to the Secretary of the Interior, Puget's Sound Agency. Washington: Printer, George W. Bowman, 1860, p. 185.
19. Report of the Commissioner of Indian Affairs to the Secretary of the Interior, Northern Superintendency. Washington: Printer, George W. Bowman, 1860, p. 43.
20. Extract from Annual Report of the Secretary of the Interior to Congress, 1860, p. 6.
21. Extract from Annual Report of the Secretary of the Interior to Congress, 1860, p. 6.
22. Extract from Annual Report of the Secretary of the Interior to Congress, 1860, p. 7.
23. States' Legislatures Petition President to Extinguish Indian Title

GEORGIA
To James Madison from Georgia Legislature, 2 December 1816," *Founders Online*, National Archives. https://founders.archives.gov/documents/Madison/99-01-02-5597 (accessed online November 18, 2020).

ILLINOIS
"To James Madison from Thomas Worthington and Others, 18 March 1814," *Founders Online*, National Archives. https://founders.archives.gov/documents/Madison/03-07-02-0328. [Original source: *The Papers of James Madison*, Presidential Series, vol. 7, *25 October 1813–30 June 1814*, ed. Angela Kreider, J. C. A. Stagg, Mary Parke Johnson, Anne Mandeville Colony, and Katherine E. Harbury. Charlottesville: University of Virginia Press, 2012, pp. 375–378.] (accessed online November 18, 2020).

INDIANA
"To James Madison from Benjamin Lenover and Others, [ca. December 1815]," *Founders Online*, National Archives. https://founders.archives.gov/documents/

Madison/03-10-02-0055. [Original source: *The Papers of James Madison*, Presidential Series, vol. 10, *13 October 1815–30 April 1816*, ed. Angela Kreider, J. C. A. Stagg, Mary Parke Johnson, Katharine E. Harbury, and Anne Mandeville Colony. Charlottesville: University of Virginia Press, 2019, pp. 62–63.] (accessed online November 18, 2020).

KENTUCKY
"To James Madison from Matthew Lyon and Others, 20 February 1811 (Abstract)," *Founders Online*, National Archives, https://founders.archives.gov/documents/Madison/03-03-02-0232. [Original source: *The Papers of James Madison*, Presidential Series, vol. 3, *3 November 1810–4 November 1811*, ed. J. C. A. Stagg, Jeanne Kerr Cross, and Susan Holbrook Perdue. Charlottesville: University Press of Virginia, 1996, pp. 175–176.] (accessed online November 18, 2020).

MICHIGAN TERRITORY
"To Thomas Jefferson from Elijah Brush, 11 December 1805," *Founders Online*, National Archives, https://founders.archives.gov/documents/Jefferson/99-01-02-2799 (accessed online November 18, 2020).

MISSISSIPPI
"To James Madison from the Mississippi Territorial Legislature, 22 November 1809 (Abstract)," *Founders Online*, National Archives, https://founders.archives.gov/documents/Madison/03-02-02-0101. [Original source: *The Papers of James Madison*, Presidential Series, vol. 2, *1 October 1809–2 November 1810*, ed. J. C. A. Stagg, Jeanne Kerr Cross, and Susan Holbrook Perdue. Charlottesville: University Press of Virginia, 1992, p. 78.] (accessed online November 18, 2020).

MISSOURI
"To James Madison from Edward Hempstead, 31 March 1814," *Founders Online*, National Archives, https://founders.archives.gov/documents/Madison/03-07-02-0357. [Original source: *The Papers of James Madison*, Presidential Series, vol. 7, *25 October 1813–30 June 1814*, ed. Angela Kreider, J. C. A. Stagg, Mary Parke Johnson, Anne Mandeville Colony, and Katherine E. Harbury. Charlottesville: University of Virginia Press, 2012, pp. 402–403.] (accessed online November 18, 2020).

NEW YORK
"From James Madison to Alexander J. Dallas, 31 July 1815," *Founders Online*, National Archives, https://founders.archives.gov/documents/Madison/03-09-02-0483. [Original source: *The Papers of James Madison*, Presidential Series, vol. 9, *19 February 1815–12 October 1815*, ed. Angela Kreider, J. C. A. Stagg, Mary Parke Johnson, and Anne Mandeville Colony. Charlottesville: University of Virginia Press, 2018, p. 496.] (accessed online November 18, 2020).

NORTH CAROLINA
"To Thomas Jefferson from Joseph Anderson and William Cocke, 5 March 1801," *Founders Online*, National Archives, https://founders.archives.gov/documents/Jefferson/01-33-02-0136. [Original source: *The Papers of Thomas Jefferson*, vol. 33, *17 February–30 April 1801*, ed. Barbara B. Oberg. Princeton: Princeton University Press, 2006, pp. 174–175.] (accessed online November 18, 2020).

OHIO
"To James Madison from the Ohio Congressional Delegation, 3 February 1816," *Founders Online*, National Archives, https://founders.archives.gov/documents/Madison/03-10-02-0213. [Original source: *The Papers of James Madison*,

Presidential Series, vol. 10, *13 October 1815–30 April 1816*, ed. Angela Kreider, J. C. A. Stagg, Mary Parke Johnson, Katharine E. Harbury, and Anne Mandeville Colony. Charlottesville: University of Virginia Press, 2019, pp. 207–208.] (accessed online November 18, 2020).

SOUTH CAROLINA
"To James Madison from Henry Middleton, 31 December 1810," *Founders Online*, National Archives, https://founders.archives.gov/documents/Madison/03-03-02-0105. [Original source: *The Papers of James Madison*, Presidential Series, vol. 3, *3 November 1810–4 November 1811*, ed. J. C. A. Stagg, Jeanne Kerr Cross, and Susan Holbrook Perdue. Charlottesville: University Press of Virginia, 1996, pp. 88–89.] (accessed online November 18, 2020).

TENNESSEE
"To James Madison from the Tennessee Congressional Delegation, 17 April 1816," *Founders Online*, National Archives, https://founders.archives.gov/documents/Madison/03-10-02-0401. [Original source: *The Papers of James Madison*, Presidential Series, vol. 10, *13 October 1815–30 April 1816*, ed. Angela Kreider, J. C. A. Stagg, Mary Parke Johnson, Katharine E. Harbury, and Anne Mandeville Colony. Charlottesville: University of Virginia Press, 2019, pp. 397–398.] (accessed online November 18, 2020).

24. Message from the President of the United States, communicating four memorials of residents at and near the eastern slope of the Rocky Mountains, praying the extinguishment of the Indian title, a survey and sale of the public lands, the establishment of an assay office, and the erection of a new territory from contiguous portions of New Mexico, Utah, Kansas, and Nebraska, with his recommendation in relation thereto. S. Exec. Doc. No. 15, 36th Cong., 1st Sess. (1860). https://digitalcommons.law.ou.edu/cgi/viewcontent.cgi?article=8681&context=indianserialset (accessed online November 29, 2024).

25. Walker, Francis Amasa. The Indian Question. Boston: JR Osgood, 1874.

CHAPTER 19: William P. Dole, Commissioner of Indian Affairs (March 12, 1861–July 11, 1865)

Commissioner Dole's term was marked by the condemned practice of circumstances determining policy versus a uniform policy. "From a glance at the history of our relations with the Indians, it will appear that we have been governed by the course of events, rather than by the adoption of a well-settled policy."[1] It was further characterized by the frequent topic of extermination and/or starvation. With Indian subsistence on their land impossible, *Indians became subject to exposure, starvation, and extermination, with a need to rob and plunder*. It was clear that the government had to take action to provide for them.

1861: Annuities Short, Lafayette Head, Agent of Tubache Utahs

> You will see by the invoices that the amount of goods is only one-fourth in quantity of what is necessary for the annual issues to the Indians. *This country is the "gold region."* It is filling up with energetic gold-hunters, who make it their permanent home. The wild game is exterminated, and all sources of subsistence for the Indian extinct. *In the winter the Indian must be fed or die.* (Emphasis added).[2]

1861: NEV, Washoe Indians, James W. Nye, Gov. of Nevada Territory, ex officio Superintendent Indian Affairs, Relief Needed

> The streams in which the [Washoes] formerly fished are now all spoiled for that purpose by the operations of the miners and the washing of the ores and metals. They are indeed most all diverted from their original courses, or dammed so frequently that the fish have disappeared from them. Lake Bigler ... is now taken possession of by the whites. The hills and plains over which roamed plenty of game are now occupied by the whites, and the game has fled like the Indians from their presence. Their chief food in the short summer which we have is a large bug or cricket and a weed called tule, which disappears when snow or frost appears. To me, their condition is pitiful in the extreme, and such as to call upon the government for succor and relief.[3]

1861: Oregon, Grand Ronde Agency, Need Aid

Due to the lack of grain and cattle, "unless provided for by the government, there will be much suffering among them before spring."[4]

1862: NEV, Shoshone Indians Eating Undigested Barley from Manure

I found fifty or sixty half-starved Indians, and I observed from fifteen to twenty-five ... in a most deplorable condition, subsisting principally upon the undigested barley obtained by washing the manure from the overland stables in baskets, after the manner of separating gold from earth with a pan. Warren Wasson, Acting Indian Agent.[5]

1861: Upper Sioux Starving

The autumn of 1861 closed upon us rather unfavorably. The crops were light; especially was this the case with the Upper Sioux; they had little or nothing. As heretofore communicated to the Department, the cut-worm destroyed all the corn of the Sissitons, and greatly injured the crops of the Wahpetons, and Medewakaptons, and Wahpecutahs ... I made arrangements to feed the old and infirm men and the women and children of [Sissitons]. ... These people, it is believed, must have perished had it not been for this scanty assistance. Thomas J. Galbraith, Sioux Agent.[6]

1862: Yanktonais Sioux Starving

About the 25th of June, 1862, a number of the chiefs and headmen of the Sissitons and Wahpetons visited the agency and inquired about the payments, whether they were going to get any money ... and if so, how much, and when. I answered them that they would certainly be paid, exactly how much I could not say... I advised them to go home, and admonished them not to come back again until I sent for them. I issued provisions, powder and shot, and tobacco to them, and they departed.

I left them apparently satisfied ... on the 14th of July ... nearly all the upper Indians had arrived, and were encamped about the agency. I inquired of them why they had come, and they answered that they were afraid something was wrong they feared they would not get their money, because white men had been telling them so. ... How were over 4,000 annuity and over 1,000 Yanktonais Sioux, with nothing to eat, and entirely dependent on me for supplies, to be provided for? I supplied them as best I could, parsimoniously, indeed, from necessity it was, still I did all in my power. Our stock was nearly used up, and still on the 1st day of August no money had come. The Indians complained of starvation.[7]

They raided the warehouse and further hostilities resulted.

150 ~

1862: New Mexico Superintendency: Exterminate, Starve or Provide for Indians

Commissioner Dole: As the whites advance the only means by which the wild Indians can sustain life diminish. It is doubtful, even now, if game is not so scarce in New Mexico that, should the wild Indians wholly abstain from plunder a single season, the result would be starvation. That such would be the result a few years hence cannot be doubted. If, then, the Indians are not to be exterminated by violent means, or by the still more revolting method of starvation, nor yet by a combination of both, we must make some other provision for them.[8]

1862: Michigan Superintendency: Remove Indians or We Will Exterminate Them

We, the undersigned, citizens of Juneau county, would respectfully represent, that there are from one to two thousand Indians in this county and vicinity, who are murdering and constantly committing serious depredations upon our people ... Many families have already left their homes, and others are leaving them. We are kept in perpetual excitement, fear and dread, and a stop is being put to all regular business. We cannot endure this state of things much longer.

We therefore most earnestly petition the government, through you, to remove these barbarians from among us; pledging you all assistance in our power, and assuring you that unless government does remove them, we shall be compelled, in self-defence, to exterminate them. Signed by G. W. Bailie, Robert Henry, and one hundred and twenty-four others.[9]

1863: Northern Superintendency, Poncas Starving

Poncas p. 267 At one hour a famishing, begging, and half naked crowd would surround my office on a freezing cold morning and implore me to go to their lodges and see their old people and children, who from starvation or want of clothing were unable to come out. To these I doled out provisions in quantities barely sufficient to keep them alive. At another time, men wearing nothing but a stroud and robe or blanket, with a belt and knife in it, and carrying their tomahawks or other weapons, would come, and with loud, and, from starvation, hollow sounding voices, accompanied by exciting and threatening gestures demand the cattle or other food. These I met face to face and drove them back, never once yielding to any demand. To have yielded in the slightest degree would have been to give up all my authority and influence over them.

~ 151

> I have labored hard for three years to improve the condition of these Indians, having in view the great object of teaching them the use of tools and to labor, which when accomplished will reclaim them from their savage state, but, unfortunately for the success of my efforts, they have for more than three-fourths of the time been in a state of famishment, and this has not been from any fault of mine. J. B. Hoffman, United States Indian Agent.[10]

Missouri Sioux, Cheated, Robbed, Driven from Their Land

Those unfortunate savages [Missouri Sioux], *whom we have cheated, robbed, and driven from every desirable locality, disregarding their petitions and prayers-that we, by our superior strength, have forced back upon the border and sterile portions of the country, have claims upon our government, who alone can or will stand between them and complete annihilation.* Samuel N. Latta, U. S. Indian Agent, Fort Sully, Dakota Territory. (Emphasis added).[11]

1863: Attack on Fort Ridgley by Sioux - They Must Be Whipped, Coerced into Obedience; Many Will Be Killed, More Must Perish from Famine and Exposure, and More Desperate Will Flee and Seek Refuge on Plains or in Mountains

While the U.S. vacillated between control of the Indians by the Department of the Interior and the Department of the War, military chastisement continued. After the Sioux attack on Fort Ridgley, Indian Agent James Galbraith recommended the following:

> Article I, Section 8, Clause II, reserved the U.S.' power to make war.
>
> *The power of the government must be brought to bear upon them; they must be whipped, coerced into obedience. After this is accomplished, few will be left to put up on a reservation; many will be killed; more must perish from famine and exposure, and the more desperate will flee and seek refuge on the plains or in the mountains.* (Emphasis added).[12]

1863: Tabequache Ute Cession to U.S. of Arable Land and Valuable Mining Districts

At the same time as Indians were compelled to starve or steal necessities in order to live, the federal government continued negotiations for cessions of large tracts of Indian land. One such cession in Colorado included land of the Tabeguache, or "People of Sun Mountain," one of the largest of the ten nomadic bands of the Ute. They considered the Pike's Peak region their home. In October 1863, Commissioner Dole stressed the importance of the Treaty negotiated with the Tabequache band of Utahs extinguishing their title to white settlements in Colorado, and more importantly to valuable mining districts:

It will be seen that by the treaty negotiated with the Tabequache band of Utahs, as above stated, the *Indian title is extinguished to one among [sic] the largest and most valuable tracts of land ever ceded to the United States. It includes nearly all the important settlements thus far made in Colorado, and all the valuable mining districts discovered up to this time.* (Emphasis added).[13]

1863: Nez Perce Land Invaded by Whites due to Discovery of Gold

The rush of white persons, probably to the number of ten thousand, into the country of the Nez Perces, in search of gold, of which it is reported that valuable discoveries have been made, will require on the part of our agent great vigilance and care in order that collisions of the two races may be prevented, and *it will probably be necessary to negotiate an additional treaty with that tribe* ... (Emphasis added).[14]

1863: Untutored, Uncivilized Barbarians, Savages, Yet Human Beings Must Be Treated As Wards of Government

The government should, then, at once abandon the treaty system, and in lieu thereof take charge of the Indians [Yanktonais, annuity Sioux and other nomadic bands of Sioux] as wards or children, not as lunatics or madmen, and compel the Indians to submit to the authority of the government. Let the idea be abandoned in theory, as it has, indeed, been in fact, that Indians are an independent sovereign nation. Treat them just as we find them-*untutored, uncivilized barbarians, savages, yet as human beings not capable or fit to manage, their own affairs, but yet susceptible of being prepared by culture and discipline to become, in time, men, citizens, safe and good neighbors."*

Let a simple, clear, and well-digested code of laws be adopted for their government, in form and substance such as the laws regulating the relations of parent and child, guardian and ward, or teacher and pupil, and, of course, the means and the power to enforce these laws, and to punish their infractions, should be provided for, else the laws would be of no utility. More accurately, they would not be laws unless they were operative and of force. Thomas J. Galbraith, Sioux Agent. (Emphasis added).[15]

1863: Annuities to Makahs (WASH) Nonsensical, If Not Dishonest

[Annuity goods] *The high prices and inferior quality of the goods would seem to indicate that the main object of the persons engaged in furnishing them was simply to make as much money as possible, without regard to law or justice. ... To send these articles to fishermen, who live by catching whales and smaller fish for oil, is nonsense, if honest; if dishonest, the speculators should be attended to, as the matter is a serious evil and breeds disaffection among the tribes.* The invoice price of some of the articles is greater than the retail prices of the same things here. Such as they are, the packages are short. G.A. Paige. (Emphasis added).[16]

1863: Dakota Superintendency, Acting Gov. Dakota Territory, ex oficio Sup't Indian Affairs, John Hutchinson, Ponca Indians Destitute

I have just returned from a visit to the Ponca agency, and I find this tribe, numbering over eight hundred souls, in a most destitute condition. ... Something must be done for these Indians, or they will suffer; and *many, I fear, must starve during the ensuing winter*. The annuity money cannot support them through the winter. *Due to the drought "they have nothing, absolutely nothing."* (Emphasis added).[17]

1864: Nevada Territory Gold and Silver Discoveries

The Territory in gold and silver bearing quartz is fabulous in its extent and richness. Gold and silver are discovered in many portions of the Territory among large bands of Indians who have recently had undisturbed possession of the country. These discoveries being known, miners move in and settle up the country in a very short time. These miners drive away the game and cut down the pine-nut trees, upon which the Indians subsist. In this hurried manner of settling the country, of course many little difficulties arise. The mining interests have been of so much importance to the general government and the Territory, that every possible precaution has been taken to prevent an outbreak among the Indians, such as there was in 1860, which set the Territory back. Jacob T. Lockhart, Indian Agent.[18]

1864: Nevada, Discovery of Precious Minerals, Indians Must Be Provided for by U.S.

From the foregoing it will readily be seen, from the vast mineral resources of the country, the productiveness of the soil on the watercourses and in the valleys, and the natural influx of population consequent thereon, that the chances of subsistence of the Indians of this portion of the superintendency grow "small by degrees and beautifully (sic) less annually;" and where and how they are, in future, to subsist, in the absence of game, fish, pine-nuts, seeds, and roots, is altogether conjectural, unless their wants be supplied by the bounty of a protecting and beneficent government. John C. Burche, Local Agent, Humboldt County.[19]

1864: Humboldt County, Nevada Territory, Lack of Subsistence for Indians

> The approaching winter will be one of trying and peculiar hardship to all the Indians of this division, if not to those of the other portions of the territory caused by the great scarcity, or rather the utter failure, this year of all the principal productions of their subsistence, such as pine-nuts, seeds, roots, &c. Fish ... will also almost entirely fail them this season ... therefore rendering it imperatively necessary on the part of the government to administer promptly and liberally to their relief and support, to prevent starvation and disturbance. John C. Burche, Local Agent, Humboldt County.[20]

1864: AZ, Yumas, No Water, No Crops, Many Died from Hunger, Gave Them Damaged Hominy, which Horses Had Refused to Eat

> The Indians of the Colorado are as dependent upon the overflow of the river as the inhabitants of the Nile, but have no Joseph to provide for the years of famine. The river having entirely failed to overflow its banks the previous year, they had not planted, and consequently had not reaped: they were in a literal state of starvation, and *many of them absolutely died from the effects of hunger*. ... We had no food ... The bread and beef contractors to celebrate Christmas ... managed to give them an issue of damaged hominy, which the horses had refused to eat. ... The Yumas were formerly a powerful and manly tribe, numbering at the time of the American occupation some five thousand souls, but under the baneful effect of contact with the whites, are rapidly disappearing, and now only number some fifteen hundred.[21]

1864: Apaches – Subjugate or Exterminate – Gold Field to Be Developed

> The subjugation or extermination of this merciless tribe is a measure of stern justice, which ought not to be delayed. Their subjugation would open to our hardy miners an unexplored gold field north of the Gila ... A sickly sympathy for a few beastly savages should not stand in the way of the development of our rich gold fields, or the protection of our enterprising frontiersmen... The only one seen was hanging to a tree already scalped, and as harmless an Indian as Fennimore Cooper ever described.[22]

1864: Blackfoot Agency, Montana, Chaos at Agency, No Agent, No Annuities

> I found the affairs of the agency in a most deplorable condition, and the feelings of the Indians inclined to war and open hostilities-actual war existing among a portion of them; in fact, the whole field presented the appearance of unutterable confusion, wild chaos,

and a medley of unharmonious discords. No agent having been in the country for over eighteen months, the Indians began to feel as though they were forgotten by their "Great Father," and expressed themselves to that effect. This feeling was fostered and increased by the failure on the part of the contractors to deliver their annuities last year, and, to a certain extent, led the Indians to believe that the government was unable, or did not in good faith intend, to carry out the treaty obligations. The annuities paid to the tribes with whom treaties have been made are diminishing, and will soon cease. ... *Extensive gold fields have been discovered.* Gad E. Upson, Indian Agent, Montana Territory. (Emphasis added).[23]

1864: Blackfeet Indians – Agent Insults

The Blackfeet Indians present numbered one hundred lodges. These are the most impudent and insulting Indians I have yet met ... were it not that the treaty expires next year, would recommend that their next annuity be paid them in powder and ball from the mouth of a six-pounder, but as it is, I recommend that when the present treaty expires they be turned over to the tender mercies of the British crown, whose subjects they undoubtedly are. Gad E. Upson, Indian Agent, Montana Territory.[24]

1864: Montana – Miners Trampling on Indian Rights

Important changes have taken place in this country during the last two years. Extensive gold fields have been discovered, and millions of gold dust secured; emigration has wended its way here by thousands, and at this present time a population of not less than thirty thousand are within the limits of this Territory. The trade of the country is extensive and rapidly increasing; over one thousand tons of freight has passed through this place the present season, and this is but a very small portion of what has been received in the Territory. ... With these facts before us, the question naturally arises, what policy shall be pursued towards the Indians. This subject demands the most serious attention of the department, and I hope will receive that consideration the coming year which its importance demands. Gad. E. Upson, Indian Agent.[25]

DOI Supports Whites Coveting Indian Agricultural and Mineral Lands

DOI's policies swung between the arbitrary poles of coveting Indian agricultural and mineral lands with the obligation to secure Indian rights to their lands.

Commissioner Dole - Need to Concentrate Tribal Nations on Three to Five Large Reservations

Commissioner Dole also continued his recommendation that Indians be concentrated on three to five large reservations, isolated from non-Indian communities.[26]

NOTES

1. Report of t8he Commissioner of Indian Affairs to the Secretary of the Interior (1864), Office of Indian Affairs, 1864, p. 3.
2. Report of the Commissioner of Indian Affairs to the Secretary of the Interior, Colorado Superintendency, United States. Office of Indian Affairs, U.S. Government Printing Office, 1861, p. 102.
3. Report of the Commissioner of Indian Affairs to the Secretary of the Interior, Nevada Superintendency, United States. Office of Indian Affairs, U.S. Government Printing Office, 1861, p. 112.
4. Report of the Commissioner of Indian Affairs to the Secretary of the Interior, Oregon Superintendency, United States. Office of Indian Affairs, U.S. Government Printing Office, 1861, p. 170.
5. Report of the Commissioner of Indian Affairs to the Secretary of the Interior, 1862, Nevada Superintendency, United States. Office of Indian Affairs, U.S. Government Printing Office, 1863, p. 219.
6. HR, 37th Congress, 3d Session, Ex. Doc. No. 68, pp. 16-17.
7. HR, 37th Congress, 3d Session, Ex. Doc. No. 68, pp. 16-17.
8. Report of the Commissioner of Indian Affairs to the Secretary of the Interior, United States, 1862. Office of Indian Affairs, U.S. Government Printing Office, 1863, p. 36.
9. Report of the Secretary of the Interior, 1862, Vol. II, United States, 1863, p. 494.
10. Report of the Commissioner of Indian Affairs to the Secretary of the Interior, 1864, Dakota Superintendency, United States. Office of Indian Affairs, U.S. Government Printing Office, 1865, p. 273.
11. Report of the Commissioner of Indian Affairs to the Secretary of the Interior, 1864, Dakota Superintendency, United States. Office of Indian Affairs, U.S. Government Printing Office, 1865, pp. 273-274.
12. Report of the Commissioner of Indian Affairs to the Secretary of the Interior (1863), United States. Office of Indian Affairs, 1863, p. 296.
13. Report of the Commissioner of Indian Affairs to the Secretary of the Interior, Office of Indian Affairs, 1863, p. 17.
14. Report of the Commissioner of Indian Affairs to the Secretary of the Interior, Office of Indian Affairs, 1861, p. 26.
15. Report of the Commissioner of Indian Affairs to the Secretary of the Interior, United States. Office of Indian Affairs, 1863, p. 296.
16. Report of the Commissioner of Indian Affairs to the Secretary of the Interior, 1862, Washington Superintendency, U.S. Government Printing Office, 1863, p. 410.
17. Report of the Commissioner of Indian Affairs to the Secretary of the Interior, Dakota Superintendency, U.S. Government Printing Office, 1863, pp. 152-153.
18. Report of the Commissioner of Indian Affairs to the Secretary of the Interior, (1864) Nevada Superintendency, United States, Office of Indian Affairs, U.S. Government Printing Office, 1865, p. 142.

19. Report of the Commissioner of Indian Affairs to the Secretary of the Interior, (1864), Nevada Superintendency, United States, Office of Indian Affairs, U.S. Government Printing Office, 1865, p. 147.
20. Report of the Commissioner of Indian Affairs to the Secretary of the Interior, 1864, Nevada Superintendency, United States, Office of Indian Affairs, U.S. Government Printing Office, 1865, p. 148.
21. Report of the Commissioner of Indian Affairs to the Secretary of the Interior, 1864, Arizona Superintendency, United States. Office of Indian Affairs, U.S. Government Printing Office, 1865, p. 151.
22. Report of the Commissioner of Indian Affairs to the Secretary of the Interior, 1864, Arizona Superintendency, United States. Office of Indian Affairs, U.S. Government Printing Office, 1865, p. 155.
23. Report of the Commissioner of Indian Affairs to the Secretary of the Interior, 1864, Montana Superintendency, U.S. Government Printing Office, 1865, p. 293.
24. Report of the Commissioner of Indian Affairs to the Secretary of the Interior, 1864, Montana Superintendency, U.S. Government Printing Office, 1865, p. 300.
25. Report of the Commissioner of Indian Affairs to the Secretary of the Interior (1864), Office of Indian Affairs, 1865, p. 298.
26. Report of the Commissioner of Indian Affairs to the Secretary of the Interior (1864), Office of Indian Affairs, 1865, p. 5.

CHAPTER 20: 1865 - Dennis N. Cooley, Commissioner of Indian Affairs (July 9, 1865–November 1, 1866)

Commissioner Cooley entered office just months after the Sand Creek Massacre in eastern Colorado and a series of Indian wars in the West. Indian military campaigns in the west tended towards extermination. Thus, the military debacles with the failed internment of Navajos at Fort Sumner and the Sand Creek Massacre after the Arapaho Indians had begged for peace eleven times closed the debate over the Department of War getting jurisdiction over Indians. Gold discoveries continued the policy of removal of the Indians and concentration on reservations. Railroads lobbied for right-of-ways across Indian lands and the DOI supported closing this gap for the railroad companies. States fought out the right to tax Indian allotted lands in state court and won. Treaties with the option of citizenship were implemented, notwithstanding that the DOI became aware citizenship was being imposed on "Indians who are notoriously unfit for citizenship." Indians felt utterly hopeless.

1865: Annual Report of Commissioner of Indian Affairs; Cost-Benefit Analysis of Total Destruction of Indians

In an Extract from the 1865 Commissioner of Indian Affairs Report to the Secretary of the Interior, we find the following cost-benefit analysis of the total destruction of the Indians:

> The policy of the total destruction of the Indians has been advocated by gentlemen of high position, intelligence, and personal character; but no enlightened nation can adopt or sanction it without a forfeiture of its self-respect and the respect of the civilized nations of the earth.
>
> Financial considerations forbid the inauguration of such a policy. *The attempted destruction of three hundred thousand of these people, accustomed to a nomadic life, subsisting upon the spontaneous productions of the earth, and familiar with the fastnesses of the mountains and the swamps of the plains, would involve an appalling sacrifice of the lives of our soldiers and frontier settlers, and the expenditure of untold treasure.* It is estimated that the maintenance of each regiment of troops engaged against the Indians of the plains costs the government two million dollars per annum. All the military operations of last summer have not occasioned the immediate destruction of more than a few hundred Indian warriors. Such a policy is manifestly as impracticable as it is in violation of every dictate of humanity and Christian duty. (Emphasis added).[1]

1865: Treaties Abrogated with Tribes that Supported Confederacy during Civil War

"The following named nations and tribes have by their own acts, by making treaties with the enemies of the United States at the dates hereafter named, forfeited all right to annuities, lands, and protection by the United States."

The different nations and tribes having made treaties with the rebel government are as follows, viz: [Creeks, Choctaws and Chickasaws, Seminoles, Shawnees, Delawares, Wichitas and affiliated tribes, Comanches of the Prairie, Great Osages; Senecas and Shawnees (Neosho Agency), Quapaws, and Cherokees.]

By these nations having entered into treaties with the so-called Confederate States, and the rebellion being now ended, they are left without any treaty whatever or treaty obligations for protection by the United States.[2]

1865: Washington, Spokane Indians – Gold Seekers Trampling on Indian Rights

The [Spokane Indian country] is being traversed by the inevitable gold-seekers, and unpleasant collisions, arising from the reckless and unscrupulous manner in which the property and rights of Indians are trampled upon by the whites will doubtless compel a resort to the usual plan of reservation and concentration.[3]

1865: Yakama Reservation, WA, Former Agent Cheated Indians on Payment for Work Performed at Agency

When I took possession the Indians were very much dissatisfied with the doings of the former agent. They had been employed to work, and vouchers to the amount of thousands of dollars, had been issued to them, with, assurance that soon money would be received and payment would be made. *He had paid a large portion of said vouchers with annuity goods at extravagant prices. He had, directly and indirectly, influenced them to sell their vouchers at prices differing from twenty to fifty cents on the dollar.* He had taken their goods off the reservation (as the Indians believed) and sold them to the whites, and had used their goods in clothing himself and family. This breach of faith, with the influence brought to bear upon them from the enemies of our government, made it difficult to restore confidence. Soon after I took possession I received from the department [$1,321], which was still due the Indians on old claims. This was immediately paid out to them on dues that had been standing from one to five years. James H. Wilbur, Indian Agent. (Emphasis added).[4]

1865: Kansas State Supreme Court Rules Miami Indian Lands Are Subject to State Taxation

> A case in relation to the Miami Indians of Kansas has recently been decided by the supreme court of that State in favor of the right of the State to tax the lands, although the Indians still reside upon lands reserved to them by treaty.[5]

1865: Fort Laramie Agency Indians Being Exterminated

> From the latest advices from the region of hostilities, it would appear that so far as the Indians especially belonging to the Fort Laramie agency are concerned, the campaign against them is one tending towards extermination ...[6]

1865: Washington Superintendency, W.H. Waterman, Superintendent, Paternal Government Needed to Avoid Demoralizing Influence of Corrupt White Men

> Shall we accept the prevailing heresy, that the American Indian is a hopeless subject, doomed to extermination, bound to disappear before advancing civilization, and the sooner he becomes extinct the better; and that the true policy is to hasten his decay by giving facility to his demoralization, instead of striving to redeem him from it? This heresy, which is found in the mouths not only of unreflecting and unprincipled men, but of many men of high social position, can never be accepted by a Christian government; but the question must be continually asked, and an answer sought, how shall the Indian be reclaimed from his barbarism and his vices, and be made to enjoy the blessings of a Christian civilization? To this question there is but one answer to be made: Indians are like children; they require for their improvement similar care and guardianship as children, and the more nearly the relationship of parents can be represented by those officially appointed to be over them and among them, the more likely will they be to restrain them from evil habits, and induce them to adopt good ones.[7]

1865: Utah, O.H. Irish, Superintendent, Settlers in Favor of Extermination

> The cruelties practiced by hostile savages have prejudiced our people against the whole race. The emigrants who traverse these plains, the settlers in these mountains, and the officers and soldiers who are here for their protection, are almost entirely in favor of the extermination of all Indians, and the constant exhibition of this feeling in the presence of our peaceful Indians discourages them and leads them to distrust our professions of friendship. O.H. Irish, Superintendent of Indian Affairs.[8]

1865: Citizenship to Indians in Certain Treaties

Pottawatomies: The treaty with this tribe provides that, on application to the department by Indians who have taken out certificates of naturalization in the Kansas courts, they shall receive patents for their lands, and their pro rata share of the funds of the tribe, *and become citizens of the United States*. Under this provision about 150 applications for patents, &c., have been made to this office; but on careful inquiry *it was found that gross carelessness (or worse) had occurred in furnishing the certificates of good conduct, sobriety, and ability to conduct their own affairs*, which certificates were a necessary preliminary to naturalization. (Emphasis added). It has been decided to issue patents to such only as are certified by both the agent and a business committee, (appointed by the tribe to conduct its affairs, and composed of its best men,) to be thoroughly fitted for citizenship and the control of their own affairs, and patents are now in preparation for about fifty who come up to this standard; others will be furnished with patents as soon as they come up to the standard. (Emphasis added).[9]

NOTES

1. Extract from Report of the Commissioner of Indian Affairs to the Secretary of the Interior, Office of Indian Affairs, 1865, p. iv.
2. Report of the Commissioner of Indian Affairs to the Secretary of the Interior, Southern Superintendency, U.S. Government Printing Office, 1865, pp. 298-299.
3. Report of the Commissioner of Indian Affairs to the Secretary of the Interior, Office of Indian Affairs, 1865, p. 19.
4. Report of the Commissioner of Indian Affairs to the Secretary of the Interior, Washington Superintendency, U.S. Government Printing Office, 1865, p. 84.
5. Report of the Commissioner of Indian Affairs to the Secretary of the Interior, Office of Indian Affairs, 1865, p. 3.
6. Report of the Commissioner of Indian Affairs to the Secretary of the Interior, Office of Indian Affairs, 1865, p. 51.
7. Report of the Commissioner of Indian Affairs to the Secretary of the Interior, United States. Office of Indian Affairs, U.S. Government Printing Office, 1865, p. 67.
8. Report of the Commissioner of Indian Affairs to the Secretary of the Interior, Utah Superintendency, United States. Office of Indian Affairs, U.S. Government Printing Office, 1865, p. 147.
9. Report of the Commissioner of Indian Affairs to the Secretary of the Interior, Office of Indian Affairs, 1865, p. 44.

CHAPTER 21: Lewis V. Bogy, Commissioner of Indian Affairs (November 1, 1866–March 29, 1867) - House Investigated Commissioner Bogy's Award of Indian Contracts to Firms in Which His Brother Had Connections

~

President Johnson appointed Orville H. Browning of Ohio as Secretary of the Interior and Bogy as Commissioner. Commissioner Bogy's tenure was faced with the continuing diatribe for extermination of Indians and encroachment on their lands. He expressed the difficulties of managing the Indian Bureau and the need for a criminal code in Indian country.

> As the Kansas Daily Tribune stated in July 1866, "There can be no permanent, lasting peace on our frontiers till these devils are exterminated. Our eastern friends may be slightly shocked at such a sentiment, but a few year's residence in the West, and acquaintance with the continued history of their outrages upon the settlers and travelers of the west, disperses the romance with which these people are regarded in the East."[1]

1866: Difficulties of Managing Indian Office, 300,000 Indians, More than 200 Tribes

> It does not seem a great risk to attend to the business of directing the management of about three hundred thousand Indians; but when it is considered that these Indians are scattered over a continent, and divided into more than two hundred tribes, in [the] charge of fourteen superintendents and some seventy agents, whose frequent reports and quarterly accounts are to be examined and adjusted; that no general rules can be adopted for the guidance of those officers, for the reason that the people under their charge are so different in habits, customs, manners, and organization, varying from the civilized and educated Cherokee and Choctaw to the miserable lizard-eaters of Arizona; and that this office is called upon to protect the Indian, whether under treaty stipulations or roaming at will over his wild hunting-grounds, from abuse by unscrupulous whites, while at the same time it must be conceded every reasonable privilege to the spirit of enterprise and adventure which is pouring its hardy population into the western country; when these things are considered, the task assigned to this bureau will not seem so light as it is sometimes thought.[2]

1866: Nevada: Shoshonees, Destitute, Miners Demand Their Extermination

> These Indians are more destitute of the necessaries of life than any other under the care of this superintendency. ... The families and bands which dwell in this region are destitute of horses and

other domestic animals. They live in the depths of poverty, and are actuated from hunger when they steal horses, mules, and cattle, it is to appease the craving appetite to keep themselves and their families from starvation ... the miners almost universally demand their extermination. Acts of injustice, wrong, and cruelty are not unfrequent.³

1866: Utah, Uintah Agency, Near Starvation

Owing to the lack of funds, but little has been done during the present season toward preparing the Uintah valley to be the home for all the Utah tribes of Indians. Near starvation. ... Goshen Indians, were enraged at not having been fed during the winter, and the winter being an unusually severe one, many had nearly perished of starvation, and a great part of their animals had perished.⁴

1866: Arizona, George W. Leihy, Indian Agent, Hualapais, Whites Threaten War of Extermination

The Hualapais are supposed to number about 2,500. This tribe is located in the northeastern portion of the Territory. The feeling has already become deep seated among the whites, that if these tribes are not shortly cared for by the government a war of extermination against them will have to be inaugurated. It must be confessed that the *treatment of these Indians by the government has not been heretofore in exact accordance with justice or humanity. It has permitted its citizens to overrun and possess themselves of their best lands, without having so much as proposed to them any compensation therefor*, except that of a few acres upon the Colorado, which it kindly offers some day to help them improve and teach them to cultivate. George W. Leihy, Indian Agent. (Emphasis added).⁵

1866: Dakota Superintendency, Execution of Treaties Negligent and Fraudulent

In the preceding remarks we have said enough to show the very irregular and imperfect mode of our execution of treaties. Negligence and frauds have characterized this essential executive duty. Indians are like children, hopeful and anxious for the goods which the "Great Father" has promised as an annuity. Commissioners Newton Edmunds, S.R. Curtis, Orrin Guernsey, Henry W. Reed. (Emphasis added).⁶

1866: Fetterman Massacre near Ft. Phil Kearney

Commissioner Bogy agreed with the policy of concentrating the Indians on smaller reservations. The December 21, 1866, Fetterman Massacre near Ft. Phil Kearney added to the list of Commissioner Bogy's challenges. When he asked Congress for a $50,000 appropriation to negotiate treaties with the border tribes calling for their emigration to Indian Territory, the House refused.

1866: Pi-Utes - Walker River and Truckee River Reservations; All Arable Land Being Occupied by Whites

> Their country is rapidly passing from them. Every arable spot and tillable acre of land is now being sought out and occupied by white men. Their groves of pinon are disappearing before the strokes of his axe, their grass-seed is consumed by his herds, the antelope and mountain sheep are killed or driven away, and, although there is some compensation in the employment given in the harvest field and elsewhere, still the Indian must look for a reliable and permanent supply of his wants to the products of these lands sacredly set apart for him. But he has no skill in husbandry, and no implements of culture.[7]

1866: Criminal Law Code Needed for Reservations

> Among other subjects ... I refer to that of the necessity of providing some effectual code of laws for the arrest, conviction and punishment of crimes committed by whites against Indians, or by Indians against whites, or by Indians against each other, upon reservations, or in regions chiefly inhabited by Indians.[8]

1866: H. G. Parker, Superintendent Indian Affairs, Nev., Purpose of Schools

> Schools: It is only hoped that the race might be improved; that the child, when grown, would be less a savage and more of a true man than he would have been otherwise; that he might have a practical knowledge of agriculture; be able to read and write; *be a good law-abiding citizen*. H. G. Parker, Superintendent Indian Affairs, Nevada. (Emphasis added).[9]

March 1867: Commissioner Bogy under Investigation by House

By March 1867, the House was investigating Commissioner Bogy's award of Indian contracts to firms in which his brother had connections.

NOTES

1. Kearney (Nebraska) Herald in The Marysville (Kansas) Enterprise, July 14, 1866.
2. Report of the Commissioner of Indian Affairs to the Secretary of the Interior, Office of Indian Affairs, 1866, pp. 1-2.
3. Report of the Commissioner of Indian Affairs to the Secretary of the Interior,

Nevada Superintendency, United States. Office of Indian Affairs, U.S. Government Printing Office, 1866, p. 115.

4. Report of the Commissioner of Indian Affairs to the Secretary of the Interior, Utah Superintendency, United States. Office of Indian Affairs, U.S. Government Printing Office, 1866, pp. 125, 129.

5. Report of the Commissioner of Indian Affairs to the Secretary of the Interior, United States, 1866. Office of Indian Affairs, U.S. Government Printing Office, 1867, p. 154.

6. Report of the Commissioner of Indian Affairs to the Secretary of the Interior, Dakota Superintendency, U.S. Government Printing Office, 1866, p. 174.

7. Report of the Commissioner of Indian Affairs to the Secretary of the Interior, United States. Office of Indian Affairs, 1866, p. 116.

8. Report of the Commissioner of Indian Affairs to the Secretary of the Interior, Office of Indian Affairs, 1866, pp. 16-17.

9. Report of the Commissioner of Indian Affairs to the Secretary of the Interior, United States. Office of Indian Affairs, 1866, p. 117.

CHAPTER 22: Nathaniel G. Taylor, Commissioner of Indian Affairs (March 29, 1867–April 25, 1869)

Commissioner Taylor considered the government had duties to protect the Indians **and whites**. The 300,000 Indians possessed *"vast tracts of country, abounding in precious metals, or rich in sources of agricultural wealth"* which the whites commandeered for themselves. **His solution was the continued removal and concentration of Indians on small reservations.** Protecting the Indians meant civilizing them. At the same time, Indians were demanding patents to their land and their share in their tribal trust funds. The beginning cracks in the treaty severalty and citizenship process were already confronting the Indian Bureau. The Wyandotte's declared "incompetent" and those who had not applied for citizenship successfully petitioned for an 1867 treaty reversing their tribal dissolution and grant of citizenship. The Ottawas' citizenship was still at issue, complicated by their selling their 'inchoate' head rights to whites. As to the Pottawatomies, "Property has been taken by whites, which was notoriously the property of an Indian." The Indians were declining in number and the War Department wanted to take over jurisdiction of Indians which Commissioner Taylor opposed.

1867: Report - Condition of Indian Tribes: Myriad Charges of Fraud and Corruption Against Civilian and Military Forces; Blamed Indian Wars on "Aggressions of Lawless White Men"

In 1867, a committee appointed by Congress to investigate the treatment of Indian tribes leveled myriad charges of fraud and corruption against civilian and military forces and blamed Indian wars largely on "the aggressions of lawless white men."[1] In 1968, another Peace Commission further denounced the violation of tribal treaty and property rights, declaring that the United States had been "uniformly unjust."[2]

1867: Mackinac Agency, Richard M. Smith, Indian Agent, Duty to Western Indians, Not Extermination as Some High in Authority Recommend

> What then becomes the duty of the government towards this portion of its population [western Indians – whites demanding immense mineral wealth]. Most assuredly not, as many have demanded, and I regret to say some high in authority have recommended, to exterminate it or a part of it. To do so would be to make a very bad use of our civilization, as well as to render us justly liable to the charge of being civilized savages. Richard M. Smith, Indian Agent.[3]

1867: Concentrate Indians on Reservations; Christianity and Civilization Spreading from Mississippi to Pacific; Indians Possess Land with Precious Metals and/or Agricultural Wealth

> Our Indian relations have assumed a new and interesting aspect. The steady approach of emigration to the grounds heretofore devoted to

the chase, and the rapid progress of the railroads pointing towards the Pacific and traversing the country over which the Indians from time immemorial have roamed, imperiously demand that the policy of concentrating them upon reservations should, whenever practicable, be adopted. Until recently there was territory enough to supply the demands of the white race, without unduly encroaching upon the districts where the Indians subsisted by hunting. This condition of things no longer exists. Christianity and civilization, with the industrial arts, are spreading over the entire region from the Mississippi to the Pacific. *The Indians are in possession of vast tracts of country, abounding in precious metals, or rich in sources of agricultural wealth.* These invite the enterprise of the adventurous pioneer, who, in seeking a home and fortune, is constantly pressing upon the abode of the red man. (Emphasis added).

By an inevitable law, two races, one civilized and the other barbarous, are being brought face to face. The obligations which rest upon the government extend to both. Each is justly entitled to protection. Our duty requires us to devise a system by which civilization, with its attendant blessings, may be fostered and extended, and at the same time protection be secured to the tribes.

The estimated number of Indians is about three hundred thousand, spreading from Lake Superior to the Pacific ocean. (Emphasis added).[4]

1867: Pottawatomies Applied for Citizenship, Want Patents and Share of Tribal Money

Many of the Pottawatomie Indians have made application for citizenship, and want their patents and share of the national money as per their treaty of 15th November, 1861.

> Many of the Indians have complied with all the conditions required of them, and have been urging upon the government the payment of all moneys due them under the treaty. They have taken the oath of allegiance, made the necessary proof of competency before the United States court, and have been recommended by the business committee of the tribe, and by their agent, as fitted by sobriety, industry, intelligence, and general good conduct, to be entrusted with the management of their own affairs. L.R. Palmer, United States Indian Agent.[5]

> One hundred and ninety patents have been issued [to Pottawatomies], and the number will probably be increased to 250 within a year from this, and to 300 the year following.[6]

The white man (where an Indian only is concerned against him) with a high hand possesses himself of what he claims to be his, while the Indian must patiently suffer an infringement of his rights, or resort to force, in which he is sure to be beaten. Property has been taken by whites, which was notoriously the property of an Indian.[7]

1867: Ottawas Not Yet Citizens, Can't Alienate Patents

According to their treaty of 1862 the Ottawas were to become citizens of the United States on the 24th day of June last, and according to a treaty made by them with the United States last winter, which is now pending before the United States Senate, the time for becoming citizens has been extended; hence they are in doubt whether they are citizens or not. *They have been selling some of their head-rights to whites, promising to make warrantee deeds when they become citizens*. These whites are now pressing for the deeds, but if the treaty made by them last winter is ratified by the next Congress they are still Indians, and not citizens, and consequently cannot give warrantee deeds. (Emphasis added).[8]

1867: Wyandottes Restored to Tribal Citizenship

Two hundred Wyandots had been declared "unfit" for citizenship under their Treaty of 1855. Thus, there were Wyandottes who accepted citizenship and those deemed incompetent in the dissolved Wyandotte Tribe. By midsummer 1857, most of the "incompetents" had drifted to the Indian Territory of Oklahoma where they became guests of the Seneca. Also, there were Wyandottes deemed "competent" to become citizens in 1855 but who had not exercised that option, or who had been minors. Rival tribal councils of "citizen" and "non-citizen" Wyandottes further complicated who belonged to the restored Wyandotte Tribe. In 1867, the Kansas Wyandots were surveyed by special Indian agent Joel T. Olive to determine who wished to retain tribal status and who wished to renounce their opportunity to become United States citizens. The 'Olive Roll' was submitted to the Indian Bureau in 1871.

1867: Santee Sioux, NE, Utter and Complete Humiliation

All treaties with these Indians have been abrogated, their annuities forfeited, their splendid reservation of valuable land in Minnesota confiscated by the government, their numbers sadly reduced by starvation and disease; they have been humiliated to the dust, and in all of these terrible penalties the innocent have suffered with the guilty. The good that can result from this course of retribution has been realized ere this or it never will be. The loss of power, utter and complete humiliation and broken spirit of this tribe affords ample evidence that they have fully expiated their crime and will never again repeat it. Wisdom and humanity alike demand that the government should now adopt a different policy.[9]

1866: Idaho Gold and Silver - Governor D. W. Ballard, ex officio Superintendent Indian Affairs

The immense wealth of the Pacific coast has had the effect to people our shores with a vast population in advance of the extinguishment of what is called "the Indian title." Idaho is not an exception to other States and Territories west of the Rocky mountains, and all the unhappy consequences resulting from a promiscuous intermingling of whites with the Indians have been painfully experienced in our Territory. The mountains of Idaho, abounding as they do in *many rich deposits of precious metals, some of them, perhaps, the richest known to the world*, will still continue to invite an increasing population to our Territory. These deposits of mineral wealth not being confined to any particular locality, but abounding in both northern and southern Idaho, some of them almost fabulous in richness, will continue to present in the future, as now, the most profitable fields of labor for the active and industrious miner and tradesman, and as profitable investments for the capitalist as can be found in any other part of our Union.

The Indians of southern Idaho are fast fading away, and as we occupy their root grounds, converting them into fields and pastures, *we must either protect them or leave them to the destroying elements now surrounding them, the result of which cannot be doubtful*. (Emphasis added).[10]

1867: Nevada, Pyramid and Walker River Reserves, Segregate Mineral Lands, of No Value to Indians

I have no other recommendations to offer than those contained in my last annual report, except in relation to the *reduction of the Pyramid and Walker River reserves. At present they contain a large area of mineral land which is of no value to the Indians*. Miners will not be debarred from working thereon. Already mines have been discovered, but none of which will pay to work at present. Future discoveries, however, may prove better; if so, then there would be no boundary to warn them "thus far thou shalt come and no further."

I would propose that the reserves be resurveyed in such a manner as to exclude all mineral lands and the greater portion of both Pyramid and Walker lakes, and include within the reserves so much of the lakes as is necessary for fishing purposes, immediately adjacent to the mouths of the Truckee and Walker rivers, together with all of the arable land not contained within the limits of those reserves. Franklin Campbell, Indian Agent. (Emphasis added).[11]

1867: Arizona, Richest Mines of Gold, Silver, and Copper Located on Apaches' Land

Within the limits of the range of this tribe exist the richest mines of gold, silver, and copper that have yet been discovered in our Territory, some of which compared favorably in their prospecting with the richest of the Pacific coast. Many claims had been entered upon these veins or ledges, and the owners had gone to a very considerable expense in prospecting them and procuring machinery with which to work them, but the larger portion are now abandoned in consequence of these hostilities, and those who continue to work do so at a great disadvantage, from the necessity of being so constantly on their guard against the wily enemy. George W. Leihy, Superintendent, Arizona Territory.[12]

In 1874 the Commissioner of Indian Affairs persuaded President Ulysses S. Grant to restore the eastern portion of the Apache reservation in Arizona to the public domain by executive order. This portion of the reservation contained copper-bearing lands which non-Indians wished to mine. Both the Indian agent in Arizona and the Commissioner of Indian Affairs had financial holdings in the company which subsequently developed the copper mines. (Emphasis added).[13]

1868: Idaho Governor Proposes Reservation for Bannocks Not Filled with Minerals

Idaho Governor D. W. Ballard, ex officio superintendent Indian affairs"
I desire peace and good will between the white and red men. I desire to see all the Bannocks comfortable and happy, and so situated that they may become a prosperous people, skilled in the arts of civilization. To this end the President of the United States proposes to place you upon a reservation, and afford you the facilities for farming, thereby enabling you to make your livelihood by tilling the soil, raising and herding stock, &c., instead of depending upon roots and the uncertainties of the chase. The white people are numerous in the United States; *the mountains of your country are filled with minerals; the white people seek them; your valleys and plains are productive, they want to cultivate them; they are spreading all over this vast country, even as you see the grasshoppers and crickets around you; no power on earth can restrain them.* Common contact between the white and the red man has always resulted badly

to the latter; it always will; and while the white people increase in numbers, the Indians gradually disappear from the earth. (Emphasis added).[15]

1868: Commissioner Report - Indian Population Decreasing due to (1) Intertribal Wars, (2) Loathsome Diseases Transmitted by Vicious Whites, and (3) Use of Liquor

The Indian population within the bounds of the United States is about 300,000, exclusive of those in Alaska Territory. It is sad to think that they are decreasing from year to year, fading so rapidly away from the nations of the earth. The causes thereof, as well as of much of the misery and degradation prevailing, may be mainly attributed to inter-tribal wars, the entailment of loathsome diseases by vicious whites, and to the effects of indulgence in the use of spirituous liquors; and these evils, it is feared, will continue to exist....[16]

1868: Dakota, Northern Cheyenne, Suffering beyond Endurance, Starving

The Indians who have been thus subsisted and belong to this agency are the Brule Sioux, numbering about 350 lodges; the Ogallalla Sioux, numbering about 350 lodges; the Northern Arapahoes, numbering about 150 lodges; and the Northern Cheyennes, numbering about 150 lodges, all averaging about six persons to the lodge. Many of these Indians are in a suffering condition, and must perish if not aided in some way. They have learned to depend upon the government for support and have made no provision for the approaching winter, and their suffering will be beyond endurance unless they are supplied by the government. M. T. Patrick, Indian Agent.[17]

1868: Shall Control of Indians Be Transferred to War Dept.

On the question of whether the Indian Bureau should be transferred to the War Department or remain under the direction of the Secretary of the Interior, Commissioner Taylor penned a compelling review of the military's contemptible actions against Indians.

More than half the period in which this bureau was under the control of the War Office was spent in the prosecution of costly and unprofitable as well as unjust wars against the Seminoles and the Sacs and Foxes, and in vexatious and expensive troubles with the Creeks and Cherokees. It should not be forgotten, in this connection, that almost all the Indian wars which have depleted the treasury and desolated our frontiers ever since the bureau was given to the Interior

Department, had their origin in the precipitate and ill-considered action of the military stationed in the Indian country.[18]

On the Pacific coast the indiscretions of our military, I am informed, produced similar unfortunate results, and nearly all our troubles with the Indians there, marring our history with cruel massacres, and in some instances with the extermination of whole bands, had their origin in the presence and unwise action of our military. (Emphasis added).[19] In evidence of this statement, I refer to the letter of Mr. Anson Dart, Oregon and Washington Territory.

But besides the cost to the treasury, it is found by actual comparison, approximating closely the truth, that the slaying of every Indian costs us the lives of 25 whites, so that the extermination process must bring about the slaughter of 7,500,000 of our people. Extermination by arms is simply an absurdity, unless we could get the Indians under the protection of the flag in large masses, surround and butcher them as at Sand Creek. But admitting, for the argument, they deserve extermination without mercy, and that we might achieve the grand consummation, it seems to me that the glory of the result would bear no proportion to the fearful sum of the cost.[20]

If might makes right, we are the strong and they the weak; and we would do no wrong to proceed by the cheapest and nearest route to the desired end, and could, therefore, justify ourselves in ignoring the natural as well as the conventional rights of the Indians, if they stand in the way, and, as their lawful masters, assign them their status and their tasks, or put them out of their own way and ours by extermination with the sword, starvation, or by any other method.[21]

I know no exception to the rule that the presence of military posts in the Indian country is speedily subversive of even the sternest ideas of Indian domestic morals. Female chastity, the abandonment of which in some tribes is punished with death, yields to bribery or fear; marital rights are generally disregarded, and shameless concubinage, with its disgusting concomitants, spreads its pestiferous stench through camp and lodge. *The most loathsome, lingering, and fatal diseases, which reach many generations in their ruinous effects, are spread broadcast, and the seeds of moral and physical death are planted among the miserable creatures.*[22]

If you wish to exterminate the race, pursue them with the ball and blade; if you please, massacre them wholesale, as we sometimes have done; or, to make it cheap, call them to a peaceful feast, and feed them on beef salted with wolf bane; but, for humanity's sake save them from the lingering syphilitic poisons, so sure to be contracted about military posts. (Emphasis added).[23]

5. It is inhuman and unchristian, in my opinion, leaving the question of economy out of view, to destroy a whole race by such demoralization and disease as military government is sure to entail upon our tribes.[24]

If, however, they have rights as well as we, then clearly it is our duty as well as sound policy to so solve the question of their future relations to us and each other, as to secure their rights and promote their highest interest, in the simplest, easiest, and most economical way possible. But to assume they have no rights is to deny the fundamental principles of Christianity, as well as to contradict the whole theory upon which the government has uniformly acted towards them; we are therefore bound to respect their rights, and, if possible, make our interests harmonize with them. This brings us to the consideration of the question:[25]

Must we drive and exterminate them as if void of reason, and without souls? Surely, no. It is beyond question our most solemn duty to protect and care for, to elevate and civilize them. We have taken their heritage and it is a grand magnificent heritage. Now is it too much that we carve for them liberal reservations out of their own lands and guarantee them homes forever? Is it too much that we supply them with agricultural implements, mechanical tools, domestic animals, instructors in the useful arts, teachers, physicians, and Christian missionaries?

Our course has generally been to circumscribe, but not to localize them in the proper sense, and thus give them the certainty of fixed and permanent homes, but to hold them as pilgrims resting a year or two on this reservation, and then removing them to a new one on the outer verge of civilization, there to linger awhile in sad suspense till the remorseless rapacity of our race requires them to move farther back into darkness again.

If we find them fierce, hostile and revengeful; if they are cruel, and if they sometimes turn upon us and burn, pillage, and desolate our frontiers, and perpetrate atrocities that sicken the soul and paralyze us with horror, let us remember that two hundred and fifty years of injustice, oppression and wrong, heaped upon them by our race with cold, calculating and relentless perseverance, have filled them with the passion of revenge, and made them desperate. (Emphasis added).[26]

NOTES

1. Joint Special Comm. of the Two Houses of Cong., Condition of the Indian Tribes, S. Rep. No. 39-156, (1867), p. 5.
2. Indian Peace Comm'n, Report to the President (1868). Berger, Bethany, "Birthright Citizenship on Trial: *Elk v. Wilkins* and *United States v. Wong Kim Ark*" (2016), p. 1200. Faculty Articles and Papers 378. https://opencommons.uconn.edu/law_papers/378 (accessed online April 30, 2024).
3. Report of the Commissioner of Indian Affairs to the Secretary of the Interior, United States. Office of Indian Affairs, Mackinac Agency. U.S. Government Printing Office, 1867, p. 336.
4. H.R. Exec. Doc. No. 1, 40th Cong., 2nd Sess. (1867), p. 7. Extract from Report of Annual Report of the Secretary of the Interior, United States. Office of Indian Affairs, 1867, p. 7.
5. Report of the Commissioner of Indian Affairs to the Secretary of the Interior, United States. Office of Indian Affairs, 1867, p. 304.
6. Report of the Commissioner of Indian Affairs to the Secretary of the Interior, United States. Office of Indian Affairs, 1867, p. 305.
7. Report of the Commissioner of Indian Affairs to the Secretary of the Interior, United States. Office of Indian Affairs, 1867, p. 305.
8. Report of the Commissioner of Indian Affairs to the Secretary of the Interior, United States. Office of Indian Affairs, 1867, p. 291.
9. Report of the Commissioner of Indian Affairs to the Secretary of the Interior, United States. Office of Indian Affairs, U.S. Government Printing Office, 1867, p. 265.
10. Report of the Commissioner of Indian Affairs to the Secretary of the Interior, Office of Indian Affairs, 1866, p. 191.
11. Report of the Commissioner of Indian Affairs to the Secretary of the Interior, 1867, Office of Indian Affairs, 1868, p. 172.
12. Report of the Commissioner of Indian Affairs to the Secretary of the Interior, 1867, Office of Indian Affairs, 1868, pp. 152-153.
13. Ulysses S. Grant, Executive Order—Restoring Land in Arizona to Public Domain. Online by Gerhard Peters and John T. Woolley, The American Presidency Project. https://www.presidency.ucsb.edu/node/371202 (accessed online December 6, 2024).
14. Report of the Commissioner of Indian Affairs to the Secretary of the Interior, Office of Indian Affairs, 1877, p. 83.
15. Report of the Commissioner of Indian Affairs to the Secretary of the Interior, Office of Indian Affairs, 1868, p. 197.
16. Report of the Commissioner of Indian Affairs to the Secretary of the Interior, United States. Office of Indian Affairs, 1868, p. 1.
17. Report of the Commissioner of Indian Affairs to the Secretary of the Interior, Northern Superintendency, United States. Office of Indian Affairs, U.S. Government Printing Office, 1868, pp. 191, 250.
18. Report of the Commissioner of Indian Affairs to the Secretary of the Interior, United States. Office of Indian Affairs, 1868, p. 8.
19. Report of the Commissioner of Indian Affairs to the Secretary of the Interior, United States. Office of Indian Affairs, 1868, p. 9.

20. Report of the Commissioner of Indian Affairs to the Secretary of the Interior, United States. Office of Indian Affairs, 1868, p. 10.
21. Report of the Commissioner of Indian Affairs to the Secretary of the Interior, United States. Office of Indian Affairs, 1868, p. 16.
22. Report of the Commissioner of Indian Affairs to the Secretary of the Interior, United States. Office of Indian Affairs, 1868, pp. 10-11.
23. Report of the Commissioner of Indian Affairs to the Secretary of the Interior, United States. Office of Indian Affairs, 1868, p. 11.
24. Report of the Commissioner of Indian Affairs to the Secretary of the Interior, United States. Office of Indian Affairs, 1868, p. 10.
25. Report of the Commissioner of Indian Affairs to the Secretary of the Interior, United States. Office of Indian Affairs, 1868, p. 19.
26. Report of the Commissioner of Indian Affairs to the Secretary of the Interior, United States. Office of Indian Affairs, 1868, p. 19.

CHAPTER 23: Ely S. Parker, Commissioner of Indian Affairs (April 26, 1869–July 24, 1871) - Helpless and Ignorant Wards, Not Independent Sovereigns, No More Treaties

Colonel Ely Parker's Peace Policy

Colonel Ely Parker's 1867 plan, which he described as a program for the establishment of a permanent and perpetual peace *focused on oversight of policy administration by both Native and non-Native individuals. He also advocated bureaucratic reform through the transfer of the OIA back to the War Department.* He argued that this move would curb corruption, allow the military to enforce treaty stipulations (something civil agents failed to do), and insulate the OIA from the influence of land and business interests. (Emphasis added).[1]

1869: Kickapoos - Unrestrained Power to Sell Their Lands Ought Not to Be Given to This Class of Indians; Remain under Guardianship

By the treaty of 1861, the Kickapoos received their share of the tribal funds, and became citizens. ... Some half dozen have made proof of their competency, but have not yet been admitted to citizenship. ... A number of the most worthless members of the tribe are now ready to go before the court with ample proof. Should they become citizens they would squander their money and lands in a very few months. The unrestrained power to sell their lands ought not to be given this class of Indians. They should remain under guardianship, so that their lands at least should be preserved for their children. F. G. Adams, United States Indian Agent.[2]

1869: Pottawatomies - Valuable Timber, Pure Water, Rich Prairie Soil, Containing Over Seventy-Five Thousand Acres, White Settlers Encroach – Reservation Could Never Have Been Intended as Home for Indians

The idea seems to prevail among the white settlers that that particular reserve, with its valuable timber, pure water, and rich prairie soil, containing over seventy five thousand acres, within an hour's ride from the dome of our State capitol, could never have been intended as a home for the Indian, the land to remain, to a great extent, uncultivated, and forever free from taxation. They enter upon these lands stealthily and take away timber, or make a contract with some worthless Indian for such timber as they want, (the land being held in common they can buy of the same Indian in one part of the reserve as well as another,) and under this contract they go on defiantly cutting and destroying. L.R. Palmer, United States Indian Agent. (Emphasis added).³

Commissioner Parker Opposed to Treaty System

It has become a matter of imperious import whether the treaty system in use ought longer to be continued. ... *The Indian tribes of the United States are not sovereign nations*, capable of making treaties, as none of them have an organized government of such inherent strength as would secure a faithful obedience of its people in the observance of compacts of this character. *They are held to be the wards of the government, and the only title the law concedes to them to the lands they occupy or claim is a mere possessory one.*
... In regard to treaties now in force, justice and humanity require that they be promptly and faithfully executed so that the Indians may not have cause of complaint, or reason to violate their obligations by acts of violence and robbery. (Emphasis added).⁴

1869: Nevada, Pi-Utes, Destitute, Steal or Starve

The Pi-Utes are a very destitute tribe... They have no horses or any domestic animals; neither have they clothing to cover their nakedness... Their mode of living is principally on rabbits, lizards, snakes, sunflower seeds, flag-roots, and pine-tree nuts, gathered from dwarf pines on the mountains.

A few around the settlements engage in farming to a limited extent. They raise a small quantity of wheat, corn, and melons using sticks to plant and knives to harvest with; therefore, the crops raised amount to mere nothing.

The greater portion of them, say four-fifths, live by pilfering grain, melons, and occasionally horses and cattle from the whites. *There being no game for them to subsist on, starvation compels them to steal*. R.N. Fenton, Captain U.S.A., Special Indian Agent. (Emphasis added).⁵

1869: Montana, Bannacks, Half-Starved, Land Overrun by Miners

They were in a deplorable condition, half starved, many of them without lodges, and what few they had were miserable cotton affairs, which could hardly stand the wind.

But emigration has been gradually filling up the rich valleys of this country with towns and farms, and the miners have been pushing their way into the mountain regions. In consequence, game, the only means of support these Indians have, is becoming scarce in certain sections, and it is a mere question of time when all this country will be occupied with a scattered population, and the game all killed or driven off. *The country is undoubtedly rich in minerals*... (Emphasis added).[6]

1869: Sisseton and Wahpeton Sioux, Upper Missouri Agency, Destitute, No Food, No Clothing

Inclemency of the approaching winter. A very few of them had some corn, but the majority were without food or clothing and were living on roots. I had known them for thirteen years, in peace and plenty, in famine and war, and *never, at any time, was there so much suffering and utter destitution*. I immediately called the chiefs and headmen together and told them I wanted the number of their people. (Emphasis added).[7]

NOTES

1. "Letter from the Secretary of War, addressed to Mr. Schenck, chairman of the Committee on Military Affairs, transmitting a report by Colonel Parker on Indian affairs," House of Representatives, 39th Cong., 2nd sess., Misc. Doc. No. 37 (Washington, D.C.: Government Printing Office, 1867).
2. Report of the Commissioner of Indian Affairs to the Secretary of the Interior (1869), United States. Office of Indian Affairs, 1870, p. 369.
3. Report of the Commissioner of Indian Affairs to the Secretary of the Interior, United States. Office of Indian Affairs, 1869, pp. 373-374.
4. Report of the Commissioner of Indian Affairs to the Secretary of the Interior (1869), Office of Indian Affairs, 1870, p. 6.
5. Report of the Secretary of the Interior, 1869, Nevada Superintendency, United States, Office of Indian Affairs, U.S. Government Printing Office, 1870, p. 203.
6. Report of the Commissioner of Indian Affairs to the Secretary of the Interior, United States. Office of Indian Affairs, U.S. Government Printing Office, 1869, p. 289.
7. Report of the Commissioner of Indian Affairs to the Secretary of the Interior, 1869, Secretary of the Interior, United States. Office of Indian Affairs, U.S. Government Printing Office, 1870, p. 320.

CHAPTER 24: 1871: Acting Commissioner H. R. Clum

Issuing Patents will Result in Hastening Indians to Utter Extinction as Race; Pauperism and Crime in State

Grand River Ottawas and Chippewas, Mackinac Indian Agency. Indian Agent Richard M. Smith reported that even those these Indians may have seemed acceptable for receiving patents, that they were simply unable to protect their land.

And what is and will be true of this reserve will, in all probability, sooner or later be true of the other reserves of the agency, provided the like *patents shall be issued to the Indians located thereon. And most assuredly this will be the case if the greed of gain, whisky, the general taxation of the Indians, and other pernicious influences, can accomplish it. In my opinion, the general result of all this will be an unnecessary amount of poverty and wretchedness to the Indian and the hastening him to utter extinction as a race, and to the State of Michigan an increased amount of pauperism and crime within its borders.* (Emphasis added).[1]

1871: NV, Indians on Pyramid Lake Reservation, Starvation and Intense Suffering

Indians on Pyramid Lake Reservation - starvation and intense suffering among the Indians there.[2]

NOTES

1. Report of the Commissioner of Indian Affairs to the Secretary of the Interior, 1871, United States. Office of Indian Affairs, U.S. Government Printing Office, 1872, p. 510.
2. Report of the Commissioner of Indian Affairs to the Secretary of the Interior, 1871, United States. Office of Indian Affairs, U.S. Government Printing Office, 1872, p. 560.

CHAPTER 25: Francis A. Walker, Commissioner of Indian Affairs (November 27, 1871–January 1, 1873)

Commissioner Walker, an advocate of concentrating all Indians in the Indian Territory, underhandedly noted it would free over 93 million acres for white settlement. He vacillated between the U.S. obligation to provide for the Indians given the U.S. expropriation of their lands and the providential mercy in their rapid removal. He was adamant in the need to extend over them a legalized rigid reformatory discipline for a generation to get them on their feet. As more Indians became citizens or eligible for citizenship, 1,594 Winnebagoes and 250 Pottawatomies, 1,630 Chippewas of Saginaw, Swan Creek, and Black River, and 6,039, he was informed of the debacle, the failure of the allotment policy. Disreputable men cling to them like leeches until they get their property.

1871: Treaty-Making with Indian Nations Abolished

Formal treaty making ended when Congress, with a rider in the Appropriation Act of March 3, 1871 (16 Stat. 544), prohibited the federal government from making new treaties with American Indian tribes.

1871: Consolidation of All Tribes in Indian Territory; Release from Indian Occupancy 93,692,731 Acres for White Settlement

> Could the entire Indian population of the country, excluding Alaska and those scattered among the States ... be located in the Indian Territory, there would be 180 acres of land, per capita, for the entire number, showing that there is an ample area of land to afford them all comfortable homes. [S]uch a disposition of the now scattered tribes would release from Indian occupancy 93,692,731 acres of land, and throw it open to white settlement and cultivation.[1]

1871: NM, Grant County, Whites Threaten to Massacre Apaches on Reservations

> On the 30th of July, Hon. B. Hudson, probate judge of Grant County, New Mexico, inclosed to Colonel Pope the following series of resolutions passed by the citizens at a public meeting at Rio Mimbres, New Mexico, 19th July, 1871:
>
> "Resolved, That the people of Grant County, New Mexico, organize themselves into a posse and follow their stock to wherever it may be, and take it by force wherever found, even if it be at the sacrifice of every Indian man, women, and child, in the tribe.
> "Resolved, That if opposed by Indians or their accomplices, be they Indian agents, Indian traders, or Army officers, let them be looked upon as our worst enemies and the common enemies of New Mexico, and be dealt with accordingly."

And the Hon. B. Hudson wrote as follows:

"What we want to know is; whether our stock can be recovered or not from Indians on your reservation, when fully proved and identified, or if we are to be forever at the mercy of these thieving murderous Apaches, who have a 'house of refuge' at Alamosa; if so, the sooner we know it the better, because the citizens of this county are determined to put a stop to it, and if they carry out their programme *the Camp Grant massacre will be thrown entirely in the shade, and Alamosa will rank next to Sand Creek*! (Emphasis in original).²

April 30, 1871: Camp Grant Massacre, Arizona Territory

"On my arrival I found that I should have but little use for wagon or medicines. The work had been too thoroughly done.

The camp had been fired, and the dead bodies of some twenty-one women and children were lying scattered over the ground; those who had been wounded in the first instance had their brains beaten out with stones. Two of the best-looking of the squaws were lying in such a position, and from the appearance of the genital organs, and of their wounds, there can be no doubt that they were first ravished, and then shot dead. Nearly all of the dead were mutilated. One infant, of some ten months, was shot twice, and on leg hacked nearly off.³

1871: Montana Territory, Assiniboines and Gros Ventres Indians, White Miners Over-Running Reservation

The Milk River country is entirely unfit for farming purposes; there is no water for irrigation; in fact, none that is fit to drink in the summer season. ... Serious complaints are also made by the [Indians] in regard to the *whites*, who, in place of being compelled to leave the Crow reservation, as was agreed upon in the Crow treaty, are coming on to it by hundreds, killing and *chasing the game; feeding and destroying the best of their grazing country by bringing into the country herds of cattle and horses; roaming at will from one end to the other; searching for gold and silver mines, of which the mountainous portion of the reserve seems to be well supplied; and it is owing to this great thirst for gold that all white men have that prevents me from being able to protect the Indians in their rights.* (Emphasis added).⁴

1871: Pottawatomies – Allotment Debacle; Retrograded into Intemperance and Poverty; Whites, like Leeches, Cling Until Divest Indians of Property

Superintendent Enoch Hoag, Central Superintendency: This once powerful tribe has experienced great changes within the last three years. A large number have become citizens of the United States, and received their respective proportions of the tribal funds, as well as their allotments of land. A few of these have borne the change well, and are in a prosperous condition; but unfortunately a much larger proportion have retrograded into intemperance and poverty. *The policy of allowing Indians to become citizens in the midst of white people is ruinous to the former, and should no longer be pursued. They are not usually able to withstand the corrupting influences which are thrown around them by designing and dishonest men, who cling to them like leeches, until they have possessed themselves of all their property, and then abandon them to the charge of public or private charity.* (Emphasis added).[5]

1872: Submission Is Only Hope of Indians

If they stand up against the progress of civilization and industry, they must be relentlessly crushed. The westward course of population is neither to be denied nor delayed for the sake of all the Indians that ever called this country their home. They must yield or perish; and there is something that savors of providential mercy in the rapidity with which their fate advances upon them, leaving them scarcely the chance to resist before they shall be surrounded and disarmed. (Emphasis added).[6]

1872: Freedom of Westward Expansion of Incalculable Value to U.S., to Indian - Incalculable Cost; Result for Indian - Wretchedness, Destitution, Beggary

But another such five years will see the Indians of Dakota and Montana as poor as the Indians of Nevada and Southern California; that is, reduced to an habitual condition of suffering from want of food. The freedom of expansion which is working these results is to us of incalculable value. To the Indian it is of incalculable cost. Every year's advance of our frontier takes in a territory as large as some of the kingdoms of Europe. We are richer by hundreds of millions; the Indian is poorer by a large part of the little that he has. This growth is bringing imperial greatness to the nation; to the Indian it brings wretchedness, destitution, beggary. Surely there is obligation found in considerations like these, requiring us in some way, and in the best-way, to make good to these original owners of the soil the loss by which we so greatly gain. (Emphasis added).[7]

1872: Army in Present Force Able to Deal with Few Marauding Bands

... a general Indian war could not be carried on with the present military force of the United States. ... On the other hand, by the reservation system and the feeding system combined, the occasions for collision are so reduced by lessening the points of contact, and the number of Indians available for hostile expeditions involving exposure, hardship, and *danger is so diminished through the appeal made to their indolence and self-indulgence*, that the Army in its present force is able to deal effectively with the few marauding bands which refuse to accept the terms of the Government. (Emphasis added).[8]

1872: Indians Justifiable Claim to Temporary Support as Left without Subsistence

The people of the United States can never without dishonor refuse to respect these two considerations: 1st. That this continent was originally owned and occupied by the Indians ... 2d. That inasmuch as the progress of our industrial enterprise has cut these people off from modes of livelihood entirely sufficient for their wants and has left them utterly without resource, they have a claim on this account again to temporary support, to such assistance as may be necessary to place them in a position to obtain a livelihood by means which shall be compatible with civilization. (Emphasis added).[9]

1874: Former Commissioner Francis Walker - The Indian Question

In 1874, former Commissioner Francis Walker published The Indian Question, in which he criticized the corruption and graft of the Indian Office. He recommended:
- The reservation system should be the permanent policy of the government but **recast** by reduction and consolidation of Indians on two reservations.
- Legislation is needed to combat the organized expeditions invading Indian country. Many reservations swarm with squatters.
- A rigid reformatory control should be exercised by the government over the Indians, requiring them to learn and practise the arts of industry.
- The Indian service costs far less than fighting Indians.
- Subsistence must be provided to the Indians.
- *The experiment of citizenship is failing.*
- *Dispersing the Indian tribes would result in their complete vagabondage.* (Emphasis added).

- *First.* The reservation system should be made the general and permanent policy of the government. ...
- *Second.* ... consolidat[ing] the Indian tribes into one or two great

bodies would leave all the remaining territory of the United States open to settlement...

- *Third.* The intrusion of whites upon lands reserved to Indians should be provided against by legislation ... **There is scarcely one of the ninety-two reservations at present established on which white men have not effected a lodgement: many swarm with squatters, who hold their place by intimidating the rightful owners; while in more than one case the Indians have been wholly dispossessed, and are wanderers upon the face of the earth.** (Emphasis added).

- *Fourth.* Indians should not be permitted to abandon their tribal relations, and leave their reservations to mingle with the whites, except upon express authority of law. ...

- *Fifth.* A rigid reformatory control should be exercised by the government over the lives and manners of the Indians of the several tribes, particularly in the direction of requiring them to learn and practise the arts of industry...

- *Sixth.* The provision made by the government for the partial subsistence of Indian tribes ... for their instruction and equipment in industrial pursuits, and for starting them finally on a course of full self-support and economical independence, should be liberal and generous...

The experiment of citizenship, except with the more advanced tribes, is at the serious risk, amounting almost to a certainty, of the immediate loss to the Indians of the whole of their scanty patrimony, through the improvident and wasteful alienation of the lands patented to them, the Indians being left thus without resource for the future, except in the bounty of the general government or in local charity. (Emphasis added).

The dissolution of the tribal bands, and the dispersing of two hundred thousand Indians among the settlements, will devolve upon the present and future States beyond the Missouri an almost intolerable burden of vagabondage, pauperism, and crime. ... **Unless the system of reservations shall soon be recast, and the laws of non-intercourse thoroughly enforced, the next fifteen or twenty years will see the great majority of the Indians on the plains mixed up with white settlements, wandering in small camps from place to place, shifting sores upon the public body, the men resorting for a living to basket-making, beggary, and hog-stealing, the women to fortune-telling, beggary, and harlotry; while a remnant will seek to maintain a little longer, in the mountains, their savage** *independence, fleeing before the advance of settlement when they can, fighting in sullen despair when they must.* (Emphasis added).

We conclude, then, that Indian citizenship is to be regarded as an end, and not as a means; that it is the goal to which each tribe should in turn be conducted, through a course of industrial instruction and constraint, maintained by the government with kindness but also with firmness, under the shield of the reservation system.[10]

Expenditures of Government 1861-1872[11]

- Expensive as is the Indian service as at present, conducted in the interest of peace, it costs far less than fighting. The result of the year's [1865 military] campaign satisfied all reasonable men that war with Indians was useless and expensive. *Fifteen or twenty Indians had been killed at an expense of more than a million dollars apiece, while hundreds of our soldiers had lost their lives, many of our border settlers had been butchered, and their property destroyed.* (Emphasis added).

- The following table exhibits the expenditures of the government on account of the Indian service for the twelve years 1861 to 1872:

Year.	Expenditures on Indian Account.
1861	$2,865,481.17
1862	2,327,948.37
1863	3,152,032.70
1864	2,629,975.97
1865	5,059,360.71
1866	3,295,729.32
1867	4,642,531.77
1868	4,100,682.32
1869	7,042,923.06
1870	3,407,938.15
1871	7,426,997.44
1872	7,061,728.82

More Than Half, probably at Least Two-Thirds, of Tribes that Had Citizenship Imposed Are Homeless, and Must Be Re-Stored to Tribal Status

Former Commissioner Walker reported that of the tribes to whom citizenship had been extended, "more than half, probably at least two-thirds, are now homeless, and must be re-endowed by the government, or they will sink to a condition of hopeless poverty and misery." (Emphasis added).[12]

NOTES

1. Annual Report of the Secretary of the Interior, 1871, p. 6.
2. Report of the Secretary of the Interior, United States. Office of Indian Affairs, U.S. Government Printing Office, 1871, p. 46.
3. Report of the Commissioner of Indian Affairs to the Secretary of the Interior, 1871, United States. Office of Indian Affairs, U.S. Government Printing Office, 1872, p. 72.
4. Report of the Commissioner of Indian Affairs to the Secretary of the Interior, United States. Office of Indian Affairs, U.S. Government Printing Office, 1871, p. 418.
5. Report of the Commissioner of Indian Affairs to the Secretary of the Interior (1871), United States. Office of Indian Affairs, p. 462.
6. Report of the Commissioner of Indian Affairs to the Secretary of the Interior, Office of Indian Affairs, 1872, p. 9.
7. Report of the Commissioner of Indian Affairs to the Secretary of the Interior, Office of Indian Affairs, 1872, p. 10.
8. Report of the Commissioner of Indian Affairs to the Secretary of the Interior, Office of Indian Affairs, 1872, p. 6.
9. Report of the Commissioner of Indian Affairs to the Secretary of the Interior, Office of Indian Affairs, 1872, p. 10.
10. Walker, Francis Amasa. The Indian Question. Boston: JR Osgood, 1874, pp. 80, 81, 82, 139-143.
11. Francis A. Walker, The Indian Question (1874), p. 33.
12. Francis A. Walker, The Indian Question (1874), p. 141.

CHAPTER 26: Edward P. Smith, Commissioner of Indian Affairs (March 17, 1873–December 11, 1875)

1873: Hindrances to Indian Civilization - Communal Land and Property, Cash Annuities, Absence of Law, Persistent Refusal to Remain upon Their Reservations, Intertribal Warfare

Commissioner Smith professed what he considered hindrances to Indian civilization: (1) communal land and property, (2) cash annuities, (3) absence of law, (4) persistent refusal if Indians to remain upon their reservations, and (5) intertribal warfare. Also, the lack of access to citizenship was fatal to many Indians who would, otherwise, strike out for themselves.

He was adamant that the treatment of Indians as sovereigns had to end; they were wards, subjects of the government. He strongly endorsed allotting Indian lands, along with extending federal and state law over Indians. He was absolutely opposed to leniency to any Indians and believed it led to defiance by the Indians – in one case wilder and more unmanageable tribes "inaugurated hostilities by assassinating the clerk at the Cheyenne and Arapahoe agency, and by the murder of teamsters and the plunder of a train freighted with Indian supplies."[1]

His recommendations for legislation were heavily weighted to extending state and federal laws over Indians; state court jurisdiction; and prescribing for all tribes prepared an elective government. Also, he requested an executive order for annuities to be paid only for work performed.

1873: Double Condition of Sovereignty and Wardship Absurd

First. A radical hinderance is in the anomalous relation of many of the Indian tribes to the Government, which requires them to be treated as sovereign powers and wards at one and the same time. ... We have in theory over sixty-five independent nations within our borders, with whom we have entered into treaty relations as being sovereign peoples; and at the same time the white agent is sent to control and supervise these foreign powers, and care for them as wards of the Government. *This double condition of sovereignty and wardship involves increasing difficulties and absurdities* ... and as rapidly as possible, all recognition of Indians in any other relation than strictly as subjects of the Government should cease. To provide for this, radical legislation will be required. (Emphasis added).[2]

1873: Difference between Barbarians and Civilized People Is Difference between Herd and Individual; Survey and Allot Indian Lands

In 1873, Commissioner Smith stated:

> A fundamental difference between barbarians and a civilized people is the difference between a herd and an individual. All barbarous customs tend to destroy individuality. Where everything is held in common, thrift and enterprise have no stimulus of reward and thus individual progress is rendered very improbable, if not impossible. The starting point for an Indian is the personal possession of his portion of the reservation. ... *the survey and allotment in severalty of the lands belonging to the Indians must be provided for by congressional legislation*. (Emphasis added).[3]

1874: Individual Indians Can Only Become Citizens by Treaty or Congressional Act

> *Neither is there any provision of law by which an Indian can begin to live for himself as an American citizen*. ..... As a result of this restriction, many Indians are kept with the mass of their tribe who otherwise would strike out for themselves. (Emphasis added).

Commissioner Smith recommended qualified legislation for Indians and the following as well:
First, a suitable government of Indians:
(1.) By providing that the criminal laws of the United States shall be in force upon Indian reservations, and shall apply to all offenses, including offenses of Indians against Indians, and extending the jurisdiction of the United States courts to enforce the same.
(2.) By declaring Indians amenable to the police laws of the State or Territory for any act committed outside a reservation.
(3.) By conferring upon the President authority, at his discretion, to extend the jurisdiction of the State courts, or any portion of them, to any reservation, whenever, in his judgment, any tribe is prepared for such control.
(4.) By providing a sufficient force of deputy marshals to enforce law and order both among and in behalf of Indians.
(5.) By giving authority to the Secretary of the Interior to prescribe for all tribes prepared, in his judgment, to adopt the same, an elective government, through which shall be administered all necessary police regulations of a reservation.
(6.) By providing a distinct territorial government, or United States court, wherever Indians are in numbers sufficient to justify it.

Second. Legislation for the encouragement of individual improvement:

(1.) By providing a way into citizenship for such as desire it.

(2.) By providing for holding lands in severalty by allotment for occupation, and for patents with an ultimate fee, but inalienable for a term of years.

(3.) By providing that wherever per capita distribution provided by treaty has proved injurious or without benefit to its recipients, a distribution of the same may, in the discretion of the President, be made only in return for labor of some sort.[4]

NOTES

1. Report of the Commissioner of Indian Affairs to the Secretary of the Interior, Office of Indian Affairs, 1874, p. 10.
2. Report of the Commissioner of Indian Affairs to the Secretary of the Interior (1873), Office of Indian Affairs, 1874, p. 3.
3. Report of the Commissioner of Indian Affairs to the Secretary of the Interior, Office of Indian Affairs, 1873, p. 4.
4. Annual Report of the Secretary of the Interior, Office of Indian Affairs, 1874, p. 16.

CHAPTER 27: 1874: Secretary of Interior Delano's Report – Enact Legislation for Indian Citizenship; Extend Homestead Laws to Indians

In Secretary Delano's 1874 Report, the ***strong focus is on enacting legislation for Indian citizenship***. The reservation policy was in force, with instruction in agriculture. He recommended extending the Homestead laws to Indians which would serve to break up tribal organizations and Indian communities and bring them under federal law. Also, he issued a warning to Indians off the reservation – they would be subject to severe military treatment or the police of the State or Territory. Subsistence was necessary.

1874: Secretary's Report to President on Indian Question - Reservations; Instruction in Agriculture; Severity for Tribes Refusing to Accept Reservation; Temporary Subsistence Necessary

> The present method of dealing with the Indian race aims to induce, and when necessary to compel, the roaming tribes to accept reservations as rapidly as possible. On such reservations they are instructed in agriculture and in other pursuits incident to civilization, and with the aid of our Christian organizations their intellectual, moral and religious culture is advanced as rapidly as practicable. When a tribe refuses to accept a reservation, and continues to violate the laws of civilization, it is treated with all needful severity.
>
> The Indian race cannot be induced to abandon nomadic habits, where subsistence has been procured by hunting, and be placed upon reservations, unless supported and sustained by the Government while being taught the arts of civilization and habits of industry sufficiently to be self-supporting.[1]

Recommends Extension of Homestead Laws to Indians; Break Up Tribal Organizations and Indian Communities; Indians Will Become Subject to U.S. Laws, Civil and Criminal

> To aid in the prosecuting of work of Indian civilization I recommend the extension of the Homestead laws to Indians. ... ***It will rapidly break up tribal organizations and Indian communities; it will bring Indians into subjection to our laws, civil and criminal***; it will induce them to abandon roving habits, and teach them the benefits of industry and individual ownership, and thus prove highly advantageous in promoting their prosperity. (Emphasis added).[2]

When Indian Tribe Is Dissolved and Its Tribal Relations Ended, with U.S. Consent, Either by Treaty or Legislative Enactment, Members Become Ipso Facto U.S. Citizens

> The department has arrived at the conclusion that when an Indian tribe is dissolved and its tribal relations ended, with the consent of the United States, either by treaty or legislative enactment, the members of such tribe become ipso facto citizens of the United States, and entitled to all the privileges and immunities belonging to other citizens.[3]

Individual Indian by Voluntarily Withdrawing from His Tribe Cannot Become a Citizen without Government Approving His Citizenship

> The department has also decided that an Indian cannot voluntarily dissolve his relation with his tribe and thereby become a citizen of the United States; that before citizenship can be created the tribal relation must be dissolved by the tribe *as a tribe*, and that too, with the consent of the General Government, as shown by treaty or act of Congress.[4]

1874: Draft of Bill to Enable Indians to Become Citizens

Beginning in 1874, Congress repeatedly debated a bill that would allow individual Indians to become citizens if they proved they had "adopted the habits of civilized life."[5]

1874: Most Indians Hesitate to Leave Tribal Condition

> Pride of nationality, dread of competition with the enterprise of white men, and fear of loss of property by taxation or suit for debt cause this hesitation among the mass of the less educated.[6]

1874: Punishment for Being Off Reservation

> It is quite important that Indians throughout the country should thoroughly understand that when outside of their reservation-lines they are subject to severe treatment by the military, and to the police of the State or Territory, for depredations or mischief of any kind committed by them, either among white settlements or against other tribes which are at peace with the Government, and that agents have no responsibility or help for them except upon the reservations to which they belong.[7]

NOTES

1. Annual Report of the Secretary of the Interior to the President, Nov. 24, 1874. https://www.newspapers.com/article/chicago-tribune-indian-citizenship-1870s/38066224/ (accessed online October 2, 2024).

2. Report of Secretary Delano to the President: Department of the Interior, Washington, Oct. 31, 1874.
3. Annual Report of the Secretary of the Interior to the President, Nov. 24, 1874. https://www.newspapers.com/article/chicago-tribune-indian-citizenship-1870s/38066224/ (accessed online October 2, 2024).
4. Annual Report of the Secretary of the Interior to the President, Nov. 24, 1874. https://www.newspapers.com/article/chicago-tribune-indian-citizenship-1870s/38066224/ (accessed online October 2, 2024).
5. See Sec'y of the Interior, Letter Transmitting Draft of Bill to Enable Indians to Become Citizens of the United States, H.R. Exec. Doc. No. 43-228 (1874).
6. Report of the Commissioner of Indian Affairs to the Secretary of the Interior, Office of Indian Affairs, 1874, p. 6.
7. Annual Report of the Secretary of the Interior, Nov. 24, 1874. https://www.newspapers.com/article/chicago-tribune-indian-citizenship-1870s/38066224/ (accessed online October 2, 2024).

CHAPTER 28: Dandy's Band, Ho-Chunk Indians Residing in Wisconsin; Reliance on Homestead Laws – Excerpts from "Their Civilization and Ultimate Citizenship": Land-ownership, Written and Unwritten Laws, and a Native American Path through Reconstruction, Stephen Kantrowitz, University of Wisconsin-Madison

In the spring of 1873, "Dandy's Band," a group of several hundred Ho-Chunk Indians residing in Wisconsin, informed the federal Office of Indian Affairs that they wished to sever their tribal ties, "purchase real estate," and "adopt the habits and customs of civilized life." Their stated goal was to become citizens of the United States, securing "the constitutional and inalienable rights of men."[1]

They had resisted four decades of attempts to remove them from Wisconsin, and they still refused to join the tribe, now resident in Nebraska, to which officials thought they belonged. Some owned land, but their way of life more generally consisted of seasonal migrations around Wisconsin and a variety of activities that included farming, but also hunting, berrying, and various forms of market engagement. The Indian Office dubbed the Wisconsin Ho-Chunk a "stray band," and their constitutional status remained uncertain. As Wisconsin Republican Timothy Howe put it in a debate on the floor of the U.S. Senate, they were "not quite constitutionalized."[2]

They expediently adopted a key form of "civilization"—individual landholding. They ended up with land, citizenship, and the right to remain in the state.[3]

By the standards of many Wisconsin settlers, the Ho-Chunk were a nuisance. They allegedly begged and lived outside the regime of steady toil, violating the tenets of labor.[4] Substantial parts of Wisconsin's settler society were petitioning for the Ho-Chunks' removal to the Winnebago Reservation in Nebraska.

[A]s the threat of federal removal from Wisconsin seemed to grow greater during 1873, Ho-Chunks and their representatives tested the possibility that land-ownership could protect them. In May, "Dandy's Band" attorney, Henry Lee, told the Indian Office that "they do not wish to be removed, are willing to do anything to be allowed to stay, would gladly become citizens if there is any way for them to do so." "[S]ome of them now own real estate," he underlined. "Is there any law by which they can become citizens?"[5]

At a meeting near Sparta, Wisconsin in June 1873, Gov. Washburn told the four hundred Ho-Chunk people assembled that they could not legitimately own land in the state: "I am informed that some of you think you can avoid going by buying land here. In your present condition you are the wards of the government, and cannot hold lands without its consent."[6]

Charles A. Hunt, the special commissioner appointed to remove the Ho-Chunks from Wisconsin, even asked the federal Commission of Indian Affairs to have the state's land offices closed to them.[7]

On the other hand, some whites stood to gain economically from the Ho-Chunks' presence. They had come to play important roles as suppliers of berries and other goods, and as wage laborers at peak seasons. One trading partner and staunch political ally, Jacob Spaulding of Black River Falls, noted that the Ho-Chunks with whom he traded desired "swamp lands adapted to the raising of cranberries, huckleberries, and grass," and that some were even now picking hops and working in the pineries. The Ho-Chunks had sold as much as $30,000 worth of huckleberries during the 1873 season.[8]

In July 1873, shortly after "Dandy's Band" offered their petition, the Commissioner of Indian Affairs issued an order for the Ho-Chunks' removal "nolens volens." In late December 1873 Hunt and his men sprang into action, quickly capturing nearly two hundred people and sending them west by rail to the Winnebago Reservation. The prisoners, hurried out of their winter camps and corralled into freezing boxcars, suffered terribly. A number died en route or shortly after arriving in Nebraska. And soon, as after every previous removal, significant numbers of Ho-Chunk began to return.[9] "[N]early every Indian returning purchased small worthless tracts of land for the purpose of evading removal," Hunt fumed ... By the fall the Nebraska Winnebago agent glumly reported that as many as two-thirds of the removed Ho-Chunk population had returned to Wisconsin.[10]

A large group of Ho-Chunk retained Henry Lee to lobby Congress for a law to make Indians eligible for public lands, while Jacob Spaulding took part in a parallel movement to have the Ho-Chunk "declared citizens" of Wisconsin.[11]

On March 3, 1875, the last day of its session, Congress passed an appropriation act for Indian affairs that included a provision making Native Americans who abandoned tribal ties eligible to take up land under the Homestead Act of 1862. This "Indian Homestead Act" conveyed the land without the right of alienage. It also required Indians acquiring such land to abandon tribal relations, **while allowing them to retain their right to annuities and tribal funds**. (Emphasis added).[12]

In May 1875 a Ho-Chunk assembly (including Dandy's son and many members of the prominent Decora family) hired Henry Lee on a contingency basis to help them enter homesteads and obtain the money due them from the tribal funds—money without which many could not afford to take or hold such lands.[13]

It took six years to wrangle the money due the Ho-Chunk from the tribal funds, but finally in 1881, an "Act for the Relief of the Winnebago Indians in Wisconsin" mandated the creation of a tribal roll and the distribution of tribal funds to those who had entered homesteads under the 1875 act.[14]

The citizenship they claimed gave them the right to remain, immunity from removal, and insulation from the worst features of wardship.[15]

NOTES

1. Petition of "Indians of the Winnebago Tribe, and more particularly described as the descendants of what was known in the year 1837, and subsequent, as Dandy's Band." [May] 1873, Letters Received by the Office of Indian Affairs, 1824–1881, Microcopy No. 234, (Washington, 1956), Winnebago Agency, Roll 944. "Their Civilization and Ultimate Citizenship": Land-ownership, Written and Unwritten Laws, and a Native American Path through Reconstruction, Stephen Kantrowitz, University of Wisconsin-Madison, p. 1.
2. Congressional Globe, 42nd Cong., 3d sess., 1873, 374. "Their Civilization and Ultimate Citizenship": Land-ownership, Written and Unwritten Laws, and a Native American Path through Reconstruction, Stephen Kantrowitz, University of Wisconsin-Madison, p. 2.
3. "Their Civilization and Ultimate Citizenship": Land-ownership, Written and Unwritten Laws, and a Native American Path through Reconstruction, Stephen Kantrowitz, University of Wisconsin-Madison, p. 4.
4. "Their Civilization and Ultimate Citizenship": Land-ownership, Written and Unwritten Laws, and a Native American Path through Reconstruction, Stephen Kantrowitz, University of Wisconsin-Madison, p. 16.
5. Lee to Blum, May 1, 1873, Roll 944. "Their Civilization and Ultimate Citizenship": Land-ownership, Written and Unwritten Laws, and a Native American Path through Reconstruction, Stephen Kantrowitz, University of Wisconsin-Madison, p. 25.
6. "Indian Council," Madison Wisconsin State Register, June 21, 1873, p. 2. "Their Civilization and Ultimate Citizenship": Land-ownership, Written and Unwritten Laws, and a Native American Path through Reconstruction, Stephen Kantrowitz, University of Wisconsin-Madison, p. 25.
7. Telegram, C. A. Hunt to E.P. Smith, July 8, 1873, Roll 944. "Their Civilization and Ultimate Citizenship": Land-ownership, Written and Unwritten Laws, and a Native American Path through Reconstruction, Stephen Kantrowitz, University of Wisconsin-Madison, pp. 25-26.

8. Spaulding to Pres. U.S. Grant, Sept. 1, 1873, OIA-Winnebago, Roll 944. "Their Civilization and Ultimate Citizenship": Land-ownership, Written and Unwritten Laws, and a Native American Path through Reconstruction, Stephen Kantrowitz, University of Wisconsin-Madison, p. 27.

9. Telegram, C.A. Hunt to E.P. Smith, Dec. 26, 1873, Roll 944. "Their Civilization and Ultimate Citizenship": Land-ownership, Written and Unwritten Laws, and a Native American Path through Reconstruction, Stephen Kantrowitz, University of Wisconsin-Madison, p. 29.

10. Bradley to Smith, Nov. 5, 1874, Roll 945. "Their Civilization and Ultimate Citizenship": Land-ownership, Written and Unwritten Laws, and a Native American Path through Reconstruction, Stephen Kantrowitz, University of Wisconsin-Madison, p. 32.

11. "Stevens Point," *Milwaukee Daily News*, February 17, 1875. "Their Civilization and Ultimate Citizenship": Land-ownership, Written and Unwritten Laws, and a Native American Path through Reconstruction, Stephen Kantrowitz, University of Wisconsin-Madison, p. 33.

12. "An act making appropriations for the current and contingent expenses of the Indian Department, and for fulfilling treaty stipulations with various Indian tribes, for the year ending June thirtieth, eighteen hundred and seventy-six, and for other purposes," *U.S. Statutes at Large* 18, 1875, 420. "Their Civilization and Ultimate Citizenship": Land-ownership, Written and Unwritten Laws, and a Native American Path through Reconstruction, Stephen Kantrowitz, University of Wisconsin-Madison, pp. 33-34.

13. Henry W. Lee, 2–5. "Their Civilization and Ultimate Citizenship": Land-ownership, Written and Unwritten Laws, and a Native American Path through Reconstruction, Stephen Kantrowitz, University of Wisconsin-Madison, p. 35.

14. "An act for the relief of the Winnebago Indians in Wisconsin, and to aid them to obtain subsistence by agricultural pursuits, and to promote their civilization," *U.S. Statutes at Large* 21 Stat. 315.

15. "Their Civilization and Ultimate Citizenship": Land-ownership, Written and Unwritten Laws, and a Native American Path through Reconstruction, Stephen Kantrowitz, University of Wisconsin-Madison, p. 36.

CHAPTER 29: John Q. Smith, Commissioner of Indian Affairs (1875-1877)

~

Commissioner Smith echoed the recommendations of previous commissioners: concentration of all Indians on few reservations; allotting their land in severalty; and, to him the most important, extend the jurisdiction of U.S. laws and courts over Indian reservations. He also recommended *"committing the Indians at the earliest day possible to the care of the State."* This would eliminate the need for an Indian Bureau and change their status as wards of the federal government. He viewed the next 25 years as critical to the Indians – either they would learn to support themselves or become extinct. Congress enacted legislation that annuities be paid only for work. To Commissioner Smith, compulsory education for children four years and older should be mandated to *"stop raising generations of worthless and costly savages."* He proclaimed what was common knowledge - that *the "avarice and determination of the white man" prevailed whenever an Indian reservation had good land, timber or minerals*. (Emphasis added). Civilization was the gift the U.S. should give Indians, an "ignorant and helpless people."

1875: Relations of Indians to States - Indians Have to Be Civilized, Self-Supporting and Subject to Municipal Control

> The theory of Indian sovereignty has practically placed the Indians at a disadvantage in their relations to the several States where they are found. *Being held by the State authorities to be neither citizens nor paupers, nor criminals, nor wards in any sense, they come easily to be, regarded on all hands as outcasts and intruders, and a normal prey for anybody strong or cunning enough to defraud them.*

> The most potent and sure remedy for this evil will be found in *committing the Indians at the earliest day possible to the care of the State*. It is not probable that State authorities will be found ready to accept this care with its responsibilities, except in cases where the Indians have attained to such a degree of civilization as to become self-supporting, and in other respects ready to mingle with the citizens of the State, and be subject to the same municipal control. (Emphasis added).[1]

1875: Indians - Ignorant and Helpless People with Moral Claim upon U.S.; Must Be Driven to Toil by Cold and Hunger; Annuities for Labor Only

> They have been treated as if capable of acting for themselves in the capacity of a nation, whereas all history shows no record of a tribe, within our republic, able to assume and continue the character and relations of a sovereign people. ... Their own interests, more strongly even than those of the Government require that they should

be recognized and treated for what they are, ***an ignorant and helpless people, who have a large moral claim upon the United States-a debt which cannot be discharged by gifts of blankets and bacon, or any routine official care for their protection or relief.*** These are trifles compared with the ***one boon-civilization-***which every consideration of humanity requires that we should give them. We have taken from them the possibility of living in their way, and are bound in return to give them the possibility of living in our way - an obligation we do not begin to discharge when we merely attempt to supply their wants for food and clothing. They need to be taught to take care of themselves. ... (Emphasis added).

Congress, at its last session, recognizing the propriety that Indians, like other people, should toil for what they have, directed that ***all annuities should hereafter be paid only in return for some form of labor***, giving, however, to the Secretary of the Interior discretion which allows the exemption of certain tribes from the operation of this restriction. (Emphasis added).[2]

1876: Fate of Indians

The next twenty-five years are to determine the fate of a race. If they cannot be taught, and taught very soon to accept the necessities of their situation and begin in earnest to provide for their own wants by labor in civilized pursuits, they are destined to speedy extinction.[3]

1876: Concentration of All Indians on Few Reservations; Allot Land; Extend Jurisdiction of U.S. Courts over Indian Reservations

First. Concentration of all Indians on a few reservations.
Second. Allotment to them of lands in severalty.
Third. Extension over them of United States law and the jurisdiction of United States courts.[4]

1876: Compulsory Education; Stop Raising Generations of Worthless and Costly Savages

No healthy Indian child over four years old and under the jurisdiction of an agent, should be left out of school. ***The caprice of barbaric parents should not be permitted to interfere with the vastly important work of civilizing their children and of preparing them to become American citizens. Our Government has the right, power and ability, and it is time she should stop raising generations of worthless and costly savages.*** (Emphasis added).[5]

NOTES

1. Report of the Commissioner of Indian Affairs to the Secretary of the Interior, Office of Indian Affairs, 1875, pp. 16-17.
2. Report of the Commissioner of Indian Affairs to the Secretary of the Interior, Office of Indian Affairs, 1875, pp. 23-24.
3. Report of the Commissioner of Indian Affairs to the Secretary of the Interior, Office of Indian Affairs, 1876, p. vi.
4. Report of the Commissioner of Indian Affairs to the Secretary of the Interior, Office of Indian Affairs, 1876, p. vii.
5. Report of the Commissioner of Indian Affairs to the Secretary of the Interior, Office of Indian Affairs, 1877, p. 13.

CHAPTER 30: 1877: (1) Secretary of Interior Carl Schurz - Code of Laws; Indian Police; Reservations Divided into Farms; Compulsory Education; Access of Christian Teachers and Missionaries to Reclaim Indians from Debasing Paganism; Contribution of Indian Labor in Return for Supplies; Concentration and Removal of Indians to Indian Territory (2) President Hayes Promises "Just and Humane Policy" regarding Indians

~

The first thing in Secretary Schurz' opinion was keeping good faith with the Indians. At the same time, he, too, focused on removing the Indians in Colorado, Arizona, and New Mexico, to the Indian Territory. He provided a list to the President of the reforms being pledged.

> 1. A code of laws for Indian reservations, and appliances for dispensing justice, neither of which at present have any existence.
> 2. Provision for the preservation of order and the enforcement of laws by means of an Indian police, composed of Indians under white officers.
> 3. The endowment of the Indians with lands, divided into farms of convenient size, the title to which shall be vested in individuals and inalienable for twenty years; and the promotion in every feasible way of the knowledge of agriculture and a taste for agricultural pursuits among them.
> 4. The establishment of the common-school system (including industrial schools) among them, with provision for their compulsory education in such schools.
> 5. Opportunity for the free access to the Indians of Christian teachers and missionaries, in order to reclaim them from a debasing paganism, and to win them to a purer and more ennobling faith.
> 6. The institution of a wise economy in feeding and clothing them making sure that it is not wastefully done, and being careful especially not to make paupers of them by the encouragement of a system of gratuitous supplies, but to minister to their self-help by insisting on their contributing their labor in return for the supplies given them.
> 7. A steady concentration of the smaller bands of Indians upon the larger reservations, and a discontinuance of the removal of the northern Indians to the Indian Territory. Southern Indians, however, who are in Colorado, Arizona, and New Mexico, should be settled in the Indian Territory, the climate being favorable to them, and there being sufficient arable land for their maintenance.[1]

1877: Blanket Must Give Way

The blanket must give way. It is only tolerable in the rudest savage life. ... We should have a uniform material, made entirely of wool-like army-cloth-for Indian clothing; and the garments should consist of a coat and pantaloons, the coat to be in shape like the old fringed rifle-coat or blouse, with a belt at the waist. The object should be to secure the comfort of the wearer and uniformity in style of clothing ... (Emphasis added).[2]

1877: President Rutherford Hayes Promises "Just and Humane Policy" regarding Indians

December 03, 1877, First Annual Message

After a series of most deplorable conflicts--the successful termination of which, while reflecting honor upon the brave soldiers who accomplished it, cannot lessen our regret at their occurrence-- we are now at peace with all the Indian tribes within our borders. *To preserve that peace by a just and humane policy will be the object of my earnest endeavors.* Whatever may be said of their character and savage propensities, of the difficulties of introducing among them the habits of civilized life, and of the obstacles they have offered to the progress of settlement and enterprise in certain parts of the country, the *Indians are certainly entitled to our sympathy and to a conscientious respect on our part for their claims upon our sense of justice. They were the aboriginal occupants of the land we now possess. They have been driven from place to place. The purchase money paid to them in some cases for what they called their own has still left them poor.* In many instances, when they had settled down upon land assigned to them by compact and begun to support themselves by their own labor, they were rudely jostled off and thrust into the wilderness again. *Many, if not most, of our Indian wars have had their origin in broken promises and acts of injustice upon our part, and the advance of the Indians in civilization has been slow because the treatment they received did not permit it to be faster and more general.* We cannot expect them to improve and to follow our guidance unless we keep faith with them in respecting the rights they possess, and unless, instead of depriving them of their opportunities, we lend them a helping hand. (Emphasis added).

... I cannot too urgently recommend to Congress that prompt and liberal provision be made for the conscientious fulfillment of all engagements entered into by the Government with the Indian tribes.

... I see no reason why Indians who can give satisfactory proof of having by their own labor supported their families for a number of years, and who are willing to detach themselves from their tribal relations, should not be admitted to the benefit of the homestead act and the privileges of citizenship, and I recommend the passage of a law to that effect. (Emphasis added).[3]

He too called for "*preparing for the gradual merging of our Indian population in the great body of American citizenship.*" (Emphasis added).[4]

NOTES

1. Report of the Commissioner of Indian Affairs to the Secretary of the Interior, Office of Indian Affairs, 1877, pp. 1-2.
2. Report of the Commissioner of Indian Affairs to the Secretary of the Interior, Office of Indian Affairs, 1877, p. 5.
3. Rutherford B. Hayes, First Annual Message. Online by Gerhard Peters and John T. Woolley, The American Presidency Project. https://www.presidency.ucsb.edu/documents/first-annual-message-12 (accessed online September 6, 2024).
4. Rutherford B. Hayes, Fourth Annual Message, 1880. https://history.state.gov/historicaldocuments/frus1880/message-of-the-president (accessed online September 6, 2024).

CHAPTER 31: Ezra A. Hayt, Commissioner of Indian Affairs (September 20, 1877–January 29, 1880) – 1873 Modoc War, 1876 Sioux War, 1877 Nez Perce/Chief Joseph Flight, 1878 Bannack Outbreak, 1878 Flight of Northern Cheyenne from Indian Territory, and 1879 Ute Outbreak

~

Commissioner Hayt's tenure was tempestuous, as he dealt with the residual effects of the 1873 Modoc War, the Sioux War of 1876, the Nez Perce/Chief Joseph flight in 1877, the Bannack outbreak of 1878, the flight of the Northern Cheyenne from Indian Territory in 1878, and the Ute outbreak of 1879. While he urged a general allotment law, serious difficulties were ongoing. Whites were actively defrauding Indians of their allotted lands.

In regard to the administration of Indian lands, he advocated for the (1) **reduction** of Indian agencies; (2) **consolidation** of Indians on small reservations; (3) the **sale of lands vacated** by consolidation; (4) the **removal of Indians in Colorado and Arizona** to the Indian Territory due to the mining of gold and silver and the need for arable land to feed the white settlers; and (5) **compulsory education in Indian boarding schools.**

> The consolidation of Indian tribes upon fewer reservations, as recommended elsewhere, would enable the Army to concentrate and become more effective.[1]

He declared the government *impotent* to protect the Indians on their reservations and only by allotment with restrictions on alienability for twenty-five years, could the Indians be certain of securing land.

He sounded the alarm on citizenship - if conferred indiscriminately, it would be of incalculable damage to them. There were numerous instances of Indians being cheated out of their lands after they became citizens. Out of 1,735 Indians to whom patents were issued about the year 1871 on the Chippewa Reservation of Isabella County, Michigan, fully five-sixths sold, or in some manner were cheated out of their lands. An investigation alleged that this loss of lands could not have occurred without the collusion of the Indian Agent, who was forced to resign but faced no legal consequences. States were unjustly and unequally taxing allotments. Chaos ruled the Indian Service. **His warning went unheeded.**

1877: Commissioner Hayt - Dishonesty of Indian Agents, Traders, and Contractors

> Hayt: There is little hope of the civilization of the older wild Indian, and the only practical question is how to control and govern him, so that his savage instincts shall be kept from violent outbreaks. There is, however, much encouragement to work for the gradual elevation of the partially civilized adult Indians, and especially of the youths of both sexes; and considerable progress has been made,

notwithstanding the difficulties which a humane treatment of the Indians has had to encounter. *These difficulties may be stated as partially growing out of the dishonesty of Indian agents, traders, and contractors, by which Indians have been deprived of their just dues, and sometimes of the necessaries of life. Another and serious drawback is to be found in the encroachment of greedy white men, who surround them and continually plot to deprive them of their possessions. Unfortunately, Indians judge all white men by these specimens, with which they are only too familiar.* (Emphasis added).²

1877: Compulsory Education in Boarding Schools to Avoid Demoralization and Degradation of an Indian Home

Commissioner Hayt expressed his position on Indian education to the Secretary of the Interior in 1877, as follows:

> Undoubtedly our chief hope is in the education of the young... I would advise the establishment of a rule making it compulsory upon all Indian children between the ages of six and fourteen years to attend schools, and requiring English alone to be spoken and taught therein; and it is decidedly preferable that as many of them as possible should be placed in boarding-schools, which possess more advantages in every way than day-schools, for the reason that the *exposure of children who attend only day-schools to the demoralization and degradation of an Indian home neutralizes the efforts of the schoolteacher* ... (Emphasis added).³

1877: Commissioner Hayt - Remove Indians in Colorado and Arizona to Indian Territory to Facilitate Gold and Silver Mining and Farming by Whites

Commissioner Hayt reported to the Secretary of the Interior in 1877 that all Indians in Colorado and Arizona should be removed to the Indian Territory in what is now Oklahoma. Miners, in search of gold and silver, could claim lands without regard to Indian reservations established by the federal government by treaty, legislative or executive authority. He further stated that all of the arable land was required by white settlers and feeding them was of paramount importance.

> In this connection, I recommend the removal of all the Indians in Colorado and Arizona to the Indian Territory. In Colorado, gold and silver mines are scattered over a wide extent of territory, and are to be found in every conceivable direction, running into Indian reservations. Of course miners will follow the various leads and prospect new ones without regard to the barriers set up by an Indian reservation. Hence the sojourn of Indians in this State will be sure to lead to strife, contention, and war, besides entailing an enormous

expense to feed and provide for them. Again, there is no hope of civilizing these Indians while they reside in Colorado, *as all the arable land in the State is required for its white settlers*. A mining population needs in its immediate vicinity abundant facilities for agriculture to feed it. The question of feeding the white population of the State is one of paramount importance, and will certainly force itself on the attention of the government. (Emphasis added).[4]

1877: Colorado Utes (Yampa, Grand River and Uinta Bands of Confederated Utes) Have Received No Annuities for Two Years

None of their annuity goods (and but part of their supplies) have reached this agency during the year. Goods purchased in August of last year have been lying in the railroad depot, 175 miles away, since November last, a period of over nine months. Flour purchased the first of June is still at Rawlins. No clothing, blanket, tent, implement, or utensil of any kind has been issued at this agency for nearly two years; no flour, except once, 15 pounds to a family, since first May. E.H. Danforth, Indian Agent.[5]

1877: Pottawatomies of Huron, MICH, Fast Dwindling Away, on Least Valuable Land, Wretchedly Poor

Pottawatomies of Huron are the remnant of the once great and powerful tribe who wielded a century ago no mean influence in the councils of the nations. They are the possessors of 120 acres of perhaps the least valuable land to be found in Calhoun County, consisting of marshes and sand-knolls ... Upon this are living this little band, consisting at last pay-day of fifty-four persons, old and young, who eke out an existence by fishing and trapping along the river and its marshy banks, making baskets, and an occasional day's labor for the farmers in the neighborhood. They are wretchedly poor. The annuity of $400 from the Government which they receive helps to bridge over the chasm between the seasons, as it is usually paid about the time that winter reminds them most keenly of their needy condition, when it is most likely to afford them the greatest benefit. They have neither school nor church ... *They seem to be fast dwindling away; a few years, at the farthest, and history alone will tell of their part in the councils and wars of the Indians of Michigan.* (Emphasis added).[6]

1877: Oneidas, Wisconsin - Not Ready for Citizenship, Being Robbed Systematically by Whites, Using Every Conceivable Method in Criminal Calendar

The tribe is divided as to what course they would have the Government take with them, as the time cannot be far distant when some step must be taken for their relief. A large majority of them will petition at next Congress for a sale of the reserve, and the money received from such sale divided pro rata among the tribe, and they dissolve their tribal relation and become citizens of the United States. Others of their tribe will ask for a division of their lands, securing to each individual 120 or more acres, they to be governed by Wisconsin State laws. In the opinion of your agent, as a tribe they are not ready for citizenship. Again, the allotment of 120 acres to a family of four persons or less would be a mistake, as but few of them would till over 15 to 25 acres ... *Surrounded as their reservation is by unprincipled whites, the Indian and the government are being robbed systematically by short measures, unjust scaling, getting the Indian drunk and buying his merchandise at a fifth of its value, and by every conceivable method known in the criminal calendar.* (Emphasis added).[7]

1877: San Carlos Reservation - Indian Agent Opened Three Indian Reservations to Ranchmen and Miners, Including Important Tracts of Agricultural and Mineral Lands

The discovery of a valuable mineral belt in the northeastern portion of the reservation has caused the town of McMillan to be built, and a number of encroachments to obtain timber, herd stock. Until such survey is made the trespassers refuse to acknowledge any right to remove them

Since taking charge of the San Carlos agency in 1874 it has been my lot to consolidate five agencies into one, and to superintend the movement of about four thousand wild Indians to the San Carlos reservation; thus bringing together Indians, who, by their former locations, were separated by a distance of 600 miles; and also opening to ranchmen and miners three Indian reservations, including important tracts of agricultural and mineral lands. These movements have all been effected without the loss of a single life, and without destroying the property of citizens.[8]

1878: Reduction of Indian Agencies, Consolidation of Indians on Small Reservations, Sale of Lands Vacated by Consolidation

First. The reduction of the number of agencies, and consequently a large annual reduction of the expense attending the civilization of the Indians and the management of their affairs.

Second. The consolidation of the Indians upon reservations where they might be best protected in their personal and property rights.

[The various] tribes and bands of Indians embraced in the bill now occupy thirty-six reservations, containing 21,922,507 acres of land, under charge of twenty agents and the necessary attendant corps of teachers and other employees. Upon the reduction proposed in the bill they will occupy nine reservations containing 4,239,052 acres, under the charge of nine agents, all of whom are now provided for by law. *A reduction of twenty-five reservations and eleven agencies will thus be effected. There will be restored to the public domain 17,642,455 acres of land,* and an annual saving in agency expenses to the amount of $120,000 will be effected ... (Emphasis added).[9]

1878: Even Most Advanced and Civilized Indians Not Capable of Defending Their Lands When Title in Fee Is Vested in Them, Assaulted by Class of Land-Sharks Who Do Not Hesitate to Resort to Any Measure to Defraud Indians of Their Lands

But after the issue of patents, the difficulties surrounding them do not cease. A few, it is true, hold to their land and make rapid and encouraging progress in agricultural pursuits. The major portion of them, however, yielding to the pressure surrounding them, fall victims to the greed of unscrupulous white men, and, one by one, part with or are defrauded of their lands. Every means that human ingenuity can devise, legal or illegal, has been resorted to for the purpose of obtaining possession of Indian lands.

Experience has shown that even the most advanced and civilized of our Indians are not capable of defending their lands when title in fee is once vested in them. The reservations in such cases are at once infested by a class of land-sharks who do not hesitate to resort to any measure, however iniquitous, to defraud the Indians of their lands. Whiskey is given them, and while they are under its influence they are made to sign deeds of conveyance, without consideration. They are often induced to sign what they are informed is a contract of sale for a few trees growing on their land, with a receipt for the consideration paid; or some party goes to them claiming to be an agent of the State or county, distributing funds to the poor. This party will pay the Indian five or ten dollars, and procure his signature to a pretended receipt for the same, when in reality the paper signed is a warranty deed, which is recorded, and generally the land is sold to a third and innocent party before the Indian discovers the fraud which has been practiced upon him.

Again they are induced to mortgage their lands for small sums which they are told will enable them to make money and improve their farms as their white neighbors have done. These mortgages are made payable generally at a time when the Indians are likely to have no money; an attorney fee of seventy-five or one hundred dollars is inserted. At maturity if the mortgage is not satisfied, which generally happens, foreclosure is had, the land is sold, and the Indian is left homeless and hopeless, a pauper for the community to support.[10]

1878: Nevada, Indians Are Complete Vagabonds

Indians are scattered over a large tract of country; while many employed by the whites, yet others have become demoralized and are now roving vagabonds, living about mining camps and railroad towns, subsisting upon refuse food thrown away by restaurants and boarding houses; that they got drunk and committed crimes among themselves; that their squaws are prostitutes; that, loathsome diseases were spreading among them; that in consequence they were degenerating and would soon die off.[11]

1878: State Imposes Unequal and Unjust Taxation which Indians Can't Pay and They Lose Their Lands

In other cases the Indians complain, and, as it appears, not without cause, that they are subjected to unequal and unjust taxation which they are unable to meet, and are thus divested of the title to their lands.[12]

1878: To Make Them Citizens Too Quickly Is to Make Them Paupers or Result in Their Extermination

Commissioner Hayt, in 1878, urged caution:

Such citizenship, if conferred indiscriminately, would, in my judgment, while the Indians are in their present transition state, be of incalculable damage to them. We should move slowly in the process of making Indians citizens, until they are prepared to assume intelligently its duties and obligations. The experience of the past has shown us that to make them citizens hastily is to make them paupers. Indians of full age are infants in law; and in fact they need a long tutelage before launching them into the world to manage their own affairs. Entire civilization, with education, a knowledge of the English language, and experience in business forms and matters, especially such as relate to the conveyance of lands, should precede citizenship if it is the intention of the government to save the Indians from pauperism and extermination. (Emphasis added).[13]

1878: "Outrageous Frauds" Committed at Isabella Reservation, Michigan, on Land Patented in Fee to Indians - Out of 1,735 Indians Issued Patents in 1871 on Chippewa Reservation, Isabella County, Michigan, Fully Five-Sixths Have Sold or Have Been Cheated out of Their Lands; Agent Collusion; Agent Resigned without Any Legal Consequences

The effect of allotment was a period of fraud and calumny. An investigation by Special Agent Edwin Brooks in 1878 at the Isabella Reservation uncovered "outrageous frauds."

> Out of 1,735 Indians to whom patents were issued about the year 1871 on the Chippewa Reservation of Isabella County, Michigan, fully fivesixths have sold, or in some manner have been cheated out of their lands. ... others, in large numbers, sold their lands before the selections were approved or patents issued, receiving only a nominal price (about twenty-five cents per acre) for lands worth from $3 to $25 per acre. ... *All the circumstances connected with these sales point directly to collusion between the agent and the parties purchasing in the execution of these unmitigated frauds.* (Emphasis added).[14]

Eventually a government investigation forced the Isabella Reservation Indian Agent to resign, but not before five-sixths of the land he had allocated to Saginaw-Chippewa tribal members had been sold.

1879: Commissioner Hayt - Proposal for a General Allotment Law with Restrictions on Alienability

> Commissioner Hayt felt only by means of an individual patent to a given number of acres, with restrictions on alienability for twenty-five years, could the Indian be sure of his ownership and advance to a state of self-support that would relieve the government of continued appropriations for his care.

> The experience of the Indian Department for the past fifty years goes to show that the *government is impotent to protect the Indians on their reservations*, especially when held in common, from the encroachments of its own people, whenever a discovery has been made rendering the possession of their lands desirable by the whites.

> The system of *title in common has also been pernicious to them, in that it has prevented individual advancement* and repressed that spirit of rivalry and the desire to accumulate property for personal use or comfort which is the source of success and advancement in all white communities.

Where the fee has been granted by patent, as also in the cases of issuance of the restricted patents, the Indians have, with very few exceptions, owing to their ignorance of the English language and of business forms, particularly with reference to conveyances, fallen victims to the cupidity of the whites, and **have practically been defrauded of their lands.**

These facts demonstrate the necessity, if the problem of Indian civilization is ever to be solved, or if they are to become self-supporting, of *vesting in them and their heirs such a title that they cannot be ousted for a long term of years*, either by the government, its citizens, or by voluntary act of the Indians themselves. (Emphasis added).[15]

1879: Transfer of Indian Bureau to War Department under Consideration

Congress was considering the transfer of the Bureau of Indian Affairs to the War Department - during the year 1879 - and appointed a joint committee to survey the subject and make recommendations. In the final report of that committee, the recommendation was made that *"The Indian should have his land allotted and the permanent title thereto given, with the precaution provided that he is not despoiled of his rights; and in addition to this, a law should be enacted which will virtually prevent the Indians from selling or disposing of their lands and houses to sharp and designing persons for not less than 25 years."* (Emphasis added).[16]

1879: Commissioner Hayt under Investigation; Committee of Inquiry Led by General Fisk, Chairman of the Board of Indian Commissioners; Hayt Trying to Surreptitiously Purchase Mine on San Carlos Apache Tribal Land; Hayt Resigns

Committee of Inquiry. In January 1879 meeting, General Fisk, Chairman of the Board of Indian Commissioners, preferred charges against Commissioner Hayt. Hayt's former chief clerk, William Leeds, testified that Hayt spent much of his time on his private business interests. "Irregularities among the San Carlos Apache led to an investigation that uncovered evidence that Hayt's son, Edward Knapp Hayt, was surreptitiously seeking to sever a portion of the reservation so he could purchase a mine then located on tribal lands."[17] On January 29, 1880, Hayt resigned.

NOTES

1. Report of the Commissioner of Indian Affairs to the Secretary of the Interior, United States. Office of Indian Affairs, U.S. Government Printing Office, 1878, p. X1.
2. Report of the Commissioner of Indian Affairs to the Secretary of the Interior, United States. Office of Indian Affairs, U.S. Government Printing Office, 1877, p. 3.
3. Report of the Commissioner of Indian Affairs to the Secretary of the Interior, Office

of Indian Affairs, 1877, p. 3.

4. Report of the Commissioner of Indian Affairs to the Secretary of the Interior, Office of Indian Affairs, 1877, p. 6.

5. Report of the Commissioner of Indian Affairs to the Secretary of the Interior, Reports of Agents in Colorado, U.S. Government Printing Office, 1877, p. 46.

6. Report of the Commissioner of Indian Affairs to the Secretary of the Interior, Reports of Agents in Minnesota, U.S. Government Printing Office, 1877, p. 123.

7. Report of the Commissioner of Indian Affairs to the Secretary of the Interior, United States. Office of Indian Affairs, 1877, p. 202.

8. Report of the Commissioner of Indian Affairs to the Secretary of the Interior, United States. Office of Indian Affairs, 1877, p. 34.

9. Report of the Commissioner of Indian Affairs to the Secretary of the Interior, Office of Indian Affairs, 1878, pp. iv-v.

10. Report of the Commissioner of Indian Affairs to the Secretary of the Interior, Office of Indian Affairs, 1878, p. VIII.

11. Report of the Commissioner of Indian Affairs to the Secretary of the Interior, Reports of Agents in Nevada, United States. Office of Indian Affairs, U.S. Government Printing Office, 1878, p. 105.

12. Report of the Commissioner of Indian Affairs to the Secretary of the Interior, Office of Indian Affairs, 1878, p. VIII.

13. Report of the Commissioner of Indian Affairs to the Secretary of the Interior, Office of Indian Affairs, 1878, p. IX.

14. Report of the Commissioner of Indian Affairs to the Secretary of the Interior, Office of Indian Affairs, 1878, p. IX.

15. House Report No. 165, 45th Congress, 3 session, serial 1866, pp. 2-3.

16. U.S. 45th Cong., third sess. H. Rept. No. 93. Report of the Joint Committee Appointed to Consider the Expediency of Transferring the Indian Bureau to the War Department, 1879, p. 18.

17. Report of Committee to the Board of Indian Commissioners, January 31, 1880, in Records of the Board of Indian Commissioners, RG 75, NARA.

CHAPTER 32: Rowland E. Trowbridge, Commissioner of Indian Affairs (March 15, 1880–March 19, 1881) - Advocated Strict Social Controls, including Institutionalizing Marriages between Indians, Prohibiting Polygamy; Employing Indian Police to Enforce Laws; Supported Government Boarding and Day Schools; Initiated Land Severalty on Crow and Fort Hall (Shoshone and Bannock) Reservations

Commissioner Trowbridge never penned an annual report, with the 1880 report signed by E. M. Marble, Acting Commissioner, due to Commissioner Trowbridge's continued illness.

Commissioner Trowbridge advocated strict social controls, including institutionalizing marriages between Indians and prohibiting polygamy, employing Indian police to enforce such policies. He supported government boarding and day schools (boasting that some seven thousand children were enrolled in such schools by 1880), and he supported the Hampton Institute and Carlisle Indian School industrial models. For the latter, he favored not only agricultural education but also animal husbandry, with the Indian Office assigning 10,283 cattle to Indians to encourage ranching. He also initiated land severalty on the Crow and Fort Hall (Shoshone and Bannock) reservations.[1]

1880: Well-Disciplined Indian Police Force Enables Agent to Be Informed of Noteworthy Occurrences within His Jurisdiction

The duties performed by the [Indian] police are as varied as they are important. ... In Dakota, surveying parties have required no other escort than that furnished by detachments of police from the different agencies. In Arizona, the San Carlos police for six years past have rendered invaluable service as scouts; and, in general, at all agencies Indian policemen act as guards at annuity payments; render assistance and preserve order during ration issues; protect agency buildings and property; return truant pupils to school; search for and return lost or stolen property, whether belonging to Indians or white men; prevent depredations on timber, and the introduction of whiskey on the reservation; bring whiskey sellers to trial; make arrests for disorderly conduct, drunkenness, wife-beating, theft, and other offenses; serve as couriers and messengers; keep the agent informed as to births and deaths in the tribe, and notify him promptly as to the coming on the reserve of any strangers, white or Indian. *Vigilant and observant by nature, and familiar with every footpath on the reservation, no arrivals or departures, or clandestine councils can escape their notice, and with a well-disciplined police force an agent can keep himself informed as to every noteworthy occurrence taking place within the entire limit of his jurisdiction.* (Emphasis added).[2]

1880: Issuance of Patents Disintegrates Tribal Relations, To Prepare Indians for Citizenship Land Must Be Safeguarded against Alienation

> Following the issue of patents comes disintegration of tribal relations, and, if his land is secured for a wholesome period against alienation, and is protected against the rapacity of speculators, the Indian acquires a sense of ownership, and, learning to appreciate the results and advantages of labor, insensibly [sic] ***prepares himself for the duties of a citizen***. (Emphasis added).[3]

1880: Sioux Reservation Desolate and Barren

> This large reservation, excepting the Black Hills ... is a most inhabitable region, desolate and barren, and includes a large area of the well-known sterile and clayey tracts of "bad lands." Once abounding in buffaloes and smaller game, which afforded an abundant maintenance for the hunting Indians, it is now deserted... The buffaloes have been destroyed ... and this large population of 50,000 Indians is held in a tract of country whose natural resources are utterly inadequate to maintain even a tithe of the number. ... The agricultural possibilities of the Sioux Reservation may practically be considered as nothing.
>
> Many parts of the reservation afford excellent grazing during the summer, though water is deficient, but the rigors of a Dakota winter forbid any attempt at a systematic engagement in the grazing of stock, especially by the improvident Indians. It may be said with truth that the Black Hills include all the desirable land in the reservation and all the useful timber, and by those who view the treatment and future of the Indians in this region in a purely humanitarian spirit the presence of gold in the Black Hills has been regarded as unfortunate ...
>
> ...[t]hey are of necessity thrown upon the bounty of the government, which has taken all the desirable land they possessed in Minnesota and elsewhere, leaving them a desolate waste.
>
> The Black Hills are pre-eminently a gold-producing region: the metamorphic rocks constituting the gold-field cover an area of nine hundred square miles, extending north and south through the central portions of the Hills for a distance of seventy miles, with a breadth of from five to twenty-five miles. "There's gold from the grass roots down, but there's more gold from the grass roots up."[4]

NOTES

1. Agreement with the Bannack, Sheepeater, and Shoshone (Ft. Hall) Tribes, 25 Stat. 687 (May 14, 1880); Agreement with the Crow Tribe, 22 Stat. 42 (June 12, 1880).
2. Report of the Commissioner of Indian Affairs to the Secretary of the Interior, United States. Office of Indian Affairs, 1880, pp. ix–x.
3. Report of the Commissioner of Indian Affairs to the Secretary of the Interior, Office of Indian Affairs, 1880, p. xvii.
4. U.S. Department of the Interior, Geographical and Geological Survey of the Rocky Mountain Region; Report on the geology and resources of the Black Hills of Dakota: with atlas, Newton, Henry, 1845-1877, Jenney, Walter Proctor, 1849-1921. Washington: Govt. Print. Off., 1880, p. 225.

CHAPTER 33: 1881: Secretary of Interior Schurz on American Indian Policy

1881: Secretary of Interior Schurz, Present Aspects of Indian Problem - Solution Is Assimilation

Secretary Schurz indelibly stated his opinion supporting work, education, allotment, the opening and sale of surplus lands to white settlers, and the extension of U.S. law over Indians such that tribal cohesion would disappear and Indians would have made a big step in advancing to the "white man's way." "Their ultimate absorption in the great body of American citizenship" would be possible. Indians would have ceased to be an obstacle to development of the country. It was crystal clear - the Indian's choice was either civilization or extermination.

Secretary of the Interior Carl Schurz wrote in 1881 in Present Aspects of the Indian Problem the following:

> In the light of events, the policy of assigning to the Indian tribes large tracts of land as permanent reservations, within the limits of which they might continue to roam at pleasure, with the expectation that they would never be disturbed thereon, appears as a grand mistake, a natural, perhaps even an unavoidable mistake in times gone by, but a mistake for all that, for that policy failed to take into account the inevitable pressure of rapidly and irresistibly advancing settlement and enterprise. While duly admitting and confessing the injustice done, we must understand the real nature of the difficulty if we mean to solve it.[1]
>
> *The settler and miner are beginning, or at least threatening, to invade every Indian reservation that offers any attraction,* and it is a well-known fact that the frontiersman almost always looks upon Indian lands as the most valuable in the neighborhood, simply because the Indian occupies them and the white man is excluded from them. (Emphasis added).[2]
>
> As the settlements crowd upon the reservations, the population thickens, and the demand for larger fields of agricultural and mining enterprise becomes more pressing, the Government may still remain true to its purpose. But will those who are hungry for the Indian lands sit still? It will be easy for the rough and reckless frontiersmen to pick quarrels with the Indians. The speculators, who have their eyes upon every opportunity for gain, will urge them on. The watchfulness of the Government will, in the long run, be unavailing to prevent collisions. The Indians will retaliate. Settlers' cabins will be burned and blood will flow. *The conflict once brought on, the white man and the red man will stand against one another, and, in spite of all its good intentions and its sense of justice, the forces*

of the Government will find themselves engaged on the side of the white man. The Indians will be hunted down at whatever cost. It will simply be a repetition of the old story, and that old story will be eventually repeated whenever there is a large and valuable Indian reservation surrounded by white settlements. *Unjust, disgraceful, as this may be, it is not only probable, but almost inevitable. The extension of our railroad system will only accelerate the catastrophe.* (Emphasis added).³

It is needless to say that the rights of the Indians are a matter of very small consideration in the eyes of those who covet their possessions. The average frontiersman looks upon the Indian simply as a nuisance that is in his way. There are certainly men among them of humane principles, but also many whom it would be difficult to convince that it is a crime to kill an Indian, or that to rob an Indian of his lands is not a meritorious act. This pressure grows in volume and intensity *as the population increases, until finally, in some way or another, one Indian reservation after another falls into the hands of white settlers. Formerly, when this was accomplished, the Indians so dispossessed were removed to other vacant places farther westward. Now this expedient is no longer open.* The western country is rapidly filling up. A steady stream of immigration is following the railroad lines and then spreading to the right and left. The vacant places still existing are either worthless or will soon be exposed to the same invasion. The plains are being occupied by cattle-raisers, the fertile valleys and bottom-lands by agriculturists, the mountains by miners. *What is to become of the Indians?* (Emphasis added).⁴

I am profoundly convinced that a stubborn maintenance of the system of large Indian reservations must eventually result in the destruction of the red men, however faithfully the Government may endeavor to protect their rights. It is only a question of time. My reasons for this belief I have given above. What we can and should do is, in general terms, to fit the Indians, as much as possible, for the habits and occupations of civilized life, by work and education; to individualize them in the possession and appreciation of property, by allotting to them lands in severalty, giving them a fee simple title individually to the parcels of land they cultivate, inalienable for a certain period, and to obtain their consent to a disposition of that part of their lands which they cannot use, for a fair compensation, in such a manner that they no longer stand in the way of the development of the country as an obstacle, but form part of it and are benefited by it. The circumstances surrounding them place before the Indians this stern alternative: extermination or civilization. (Emphasis added).⁵

According to Schurz:

> To fit the Indians for their ultimate absorption in the great body of American citizenship three things were necessary: that Indians be taught to work; that their youth be educated; and that they be individualized in the possession of property by settlement in severalty with a fee simple title after which the lands they do not use may be disposed of for general settlement and enterprise without danger and with profit to the Indian.[6]

> Indians are [not] yearning for American citizenship, eager to take it if we will only give it to them. No mistake could be greater. ***An overwhelming majority of the Indians look at present upon American citizenship as a dangerous gift***, and but few of the more civilized are willing to accept it when it is attainable. And those who are uncivilized would certainly not know what to do with it if they had it. ... But full citizenship must be regarded as the terminal, not as the initial, point of their development. ***The first necessity, therefore, is not at once to give it to them, but to fit them for it.*** And to this end, nothing is more indispensable than the protecting and guiding care of the Government during the dangerous period of transition from savage to civilized life. (Emphasis added).[7]

> It has been my purpose merely to set forth those important points which, in the practical management of Indian affairs, should be steadily kept in view. I will recapitulate them:
> (1) The greatest danger hanging over the Indian race arises from the fact that, with their large and valuable territorial possessions which are lying waste, they stand in the way of what is commonly called "the development of the country."
> (2) A rational Indian policy will make it its principal object to avert that danger from the red men, by doing what will be most beneficial to them, as well as to the whole people: namely, by harmonizing the habits, occupations, and interests of the Indians with that "development of the country."
> (3) To accomplish this object, it is of pressing necessity to set the Indians to work, to educate their youth of both sexes, to make them small proprietors of land, with the right of individual ownership under the protection of the law, and to induce them to make that part of their lands which they do not need for cultivation, profitable to themselves in the only possible way, by selling it at a just rate of compensation, thus opening it to general settlement and enterprise.[8]

> The question is, whether the Indians are to be exposed to the danger of hostile collisions, and of being robbed of their lands in consequence, or whether they are to be induced by proper and fair means to sell

that which, as long as they keep it, is of no advantage to anybody, but which, as soon as they part with it for a just compensation, will be of great advantage to themselves and their white neighbors alike. No true friend of the Indian will hesitate to choose the latter line of policy as one in entire accord with substantial justice, humanity, the civilization and welfare of the red men, and the general interests of the country.[9]

As the third thing necessary for the absorption of the Indians in the great body of American citizenship, I mentioned their individualization in the possession of property by their settlement in severalty upon small farm tracts with a fee simple title. When the Indians are so settled, and have become individual property owners, holding their farms by the same title under the law by which white men hold theirs, they will feel more readily inclined to part with such of their lands as they cannot themselves cultivate, and from which they can derive profit only if they sell them, either in lots or in bulk, for a fair equivalent in money or in annuities. This done, the Indians will occupy no more ground than so many white people; the large reservations will gradually be opened to general settlement and enterprise, and the Indians, with their possessions, will cease to stand in the way of the "development of the country." The difficulty which has provoked so many encroachments and conflicts will then no longer exist. **When the Indians are individual owners of real property, and as individuals enjoy the protection of the laws, their tribal cohesion will necessarily relax, and gradually disappear. They will have advanced an immense step in the direction of the "white man's way."** (Emphasis added).[10]

NOTES

1. Carl Schurz, "Present Aspects of the Indian Problem," North American Review, 133 (July 1881), p. 3.
2. Carl Schurz, "Present Aspects of the Indian Problem," North American Review, 133 (July 1881), p. 3.
3. Carl Schurz, "Present Aspects of the Indian Problem," North American Review, 133 (July 1881), p. 5.
4. Carl Schurz, "Present Aspects of the Indian Problem," North American Review, 133 (July 1881), p. 4.
5. Carl Schurz, "Present Aspects of the Indian Problem," North American Review, 133 (July 1881), p. 6.
6. Carl Schurz, "Present Aspects of the Indian Problem," North American Review, 133, (July 1881), p. 9.
7. Carl Schurz, "Present Aspects of the Indian Problem," North American Review, 133 (July 1881), p. 8.
8. Carl Schurz, "Present Aspects of the Indian Problem," North American Review, 133

(July 1881), p. 23.
9. Carl Schurz, "Present Aspects of the Indian Problem," North American Review, 133 (July 1881), p. 24.
10. Carl Schurz, "Present Aspects of the Indian Problem," North American Review, 133 (July 1881), p. 17.

CHAPTER 34: Hiram Price, Commissioner of Indian Affairs (May 6, 1881– March 26, 1885) - Indians Must Adopt Our Modes of Life; We Are Fifty Millions of People and They Are Only One-Fourth of One Million; Few Must Yield to Many; Establishment of Penal Reservations for Refractory Indians; Allotment and Issuance of Patents with Restrictions on Alienation; Eliminating Fees and Commissions on Homestead Entries by Indians; Survey of Indian Reservations and Arable Lands; Prohibition of Introduction of Liquor on Indian Reservations

~

1881: SD, Rosebud Sioux, Not Progressing, Barren Land, No Timber, Severe Winter Killed Stock, Large Percentage of Deaths of Sioux Students at Carlisle Boarding School

Not progressing. Barren land. No timber. Severe winter killed stock.

> Owing to the large percentage of deaths among the scholars furnished by this people to the Carlisle school, it is extremely doubtful if any parents can hereafter be found who will permit their children to be sent to any distant point for the purpose of being educated; hence the establishment of a boarding school within the reservation, yet located far enough away from the agency as to be removed from family influences, seems to be the only true solution of the problem.[1]

1881: MT, Blackfeet, Need Aid or Will Starve

> Need appropriations or will starve. Increasing feeling of hostility on the part of cattle-owners and settlers concerned, to the presence of any Indians in the region mentioned, and recently several organizations of stock-owners have had meetings with apparent intent to prevent Indians from crossing the ranges; and some, no doubt, would not hesitate, if opportunity offered, to act with a purpose of bringing matters to a crisis in expectation of a final settlement resulting, by which the Indians would be confined to their reservations; and this applies as well to the settlers on the Yellowstone with respect to the Crows, Flatheads, &c.[2]

Commissioner Price: Legislation Needed: Establishment of Penal Reservations for Refractory Indians; Allotment and Issuance of Patents with Restrictions on Alienation; Eliminating Fees and Commissions on Homestead Entries for Indians

Commissioner Price's directives for legislation was brief:

> Establishment of penal reservations for refractory Indians.
> Allotment of lands in severalty and issue of patents therefor, with restrictions as to alienation.

~ 221

Remission of fees and commissions on homestead entries by Indians.
Survey of boundaries of Indian reservations and of arable lands therein.
Prohibition of introduction of liquor on Indian reservations.³

He was a proponent of using Indian police and courts to weaken tribal leadership. They were "a power entirely independent of the chiefs. It weakens and will finally destroy the power of tribes and bands."⁴

1882: Allotment of Land in Severalty and Permanent Land Title

Commissioner Price also boasted of how allotment would "break up tribal relations" and relieve the government of expenses:

> As stated in my report of last year, *The allotment system tends to break up tribal relations*. It has the effect of creating individuality, responsibility, and a desire to accumulate property. It teaches the Indians habits of industry and frugality, and stimulates them to look forward to a better and more useful life, and, in the end, it will relieve the government of large annual appropriations. (Emphasis added).⁵

Commissioner Price was limited to allotting reservations under treaty provisions. For instance, some treaties authorized severalty, but most did not; some authorized fee patents, while others provided simple allotment certificates.⁶

1882: Commissioner Price - All Agents Notified to Withhold Rations from Indians Unwilling to Work

Commissioner Price argued rations should be withheld unless Indians agreed to work for food. This was the only way to make them "self-supporting," Commissioner Price added, since the alternative resulted in vagabondage. On September 27, 1882, Commissioner Price issued a circular to all agents notifying them to withhold rations from those unwilling to work, and he encouraged Congress to reduce appropriations to only those guaranteed by treaty.

1883: Starvation of Blackfeet, Blood, and Piegan Indians

> Speaking of the Blackfeet, Blood, and Piegan Indians in a report dated July 26 last, an Indian inspector says:
> *There can be no doubt but many of the young children died from lack of food during last winter and spring*.
> In reference to the same Indians a special agent reports, under date of August 21 last: Last week 3,200 persons presented themselves as actually in need of subsistence ... *but one-fifth the established ration is being issued.* I am fearful that unless additional supplies are furnished *depredations must be expected to prevent starvation,*

and early action is necessary ... *It is not pleasant to be importuned, day after day, by hordes of half-fed women and children for something more to eat, and not have it in your power to alleviate their suffering.* (Emphasis added).⁷

1883: Commissioner Price - Survey Boundaries of Indian Reservations; Law to Punish Arms Sellers; Appropriations for Indian Police

Surveying the out boundaries of reservations had been advocated for decades, along with punishment of Indian arms-dealers and appropriations for tribal police. Commissioner Price continued the rhetoric:

> Among the things needed to secure success and efficiency in solving what is called the Indian problem are: First: *An appropriation to survey the out boundaries of Indian reservations*, so that both Indians and white men may know where they have rights and where they have none. This will save not only much trouble and expense, but also many lives of both white men and Indians. ... Second: *A law for the punishment of persons who furnish arms or ammunition to Indians.* No such law now exists. Third: *More liberal appropriations for Indian police.*⁸

1883: Commissioner Price - Whenever State Is Admitted into Union, Indians Should Become Citizens of State

Commissioner Price pushed for state control of Indians - frightening given the hostile attitude between Indians and states, with some states demanding extermination or removal.

> And I would particularly recommend that hereafter, whenever a State is admitted into the Union, the act of admission shall contain a provision giving to Indians within its limits all the rights, privileges, and immunities enjoyed by the citizens thereof, and subjecting them to like penalties, liabilities, restrictions, &c., except in cases specially otherwise provided for by treaty or act in Congress.⁹

1884: MT, Blackfeet, Issued Condemned Bacon to Prevent Starvation

> Their supplies had been limited and many of them were gradually dying of starvation. I visited a large number of their tents and cabins. All bore marks of suffering from lack of food, but the little children seemed to have suffered most; they were so emaciated that it did not seem possible for them to live long, and many of them have since passed away. To feed these Indians, I was reduced to such a strait that I was compelled to issue over 2,000 pounds of bacon which had been condemned. Indians stripped the bark from saplings to eat. The

buffalo, on which these people formerly subsisted, is now extinct.[10]

1884: NV, Serious Starvation Destroying Indians

Game, fish, wild fruits, are about exhausted, the former by the white man and the latter by the numerous herd of cattle and bands of horses who roam over the mountains and plains. An Indian is less capable of working on half allowance than a white man would be, yet the Government expects him to perform labor on, three pounds of flour a week, and two pounds of beef per week, and one pound of bacon, alternating beef and bacon; with coffee, one-fourth pound of sugar, and three-fourths pounds of beans per week. No man that lives can work on that small amount per week. *This serious starvation is fast destroying these people on the reservation.* (Emphasis added).[11]

1884: Fort Belknap Reservation, MT, Starvation

I had to feed a certain number of people for a period of fifty-two weeks and was allowed enough supplies to feed them but sixteen or seventeen weeks. (Without irrigation, no farming possible.)

Our wise Congress has appropriated lands, money, and legislation upon railroads, rivers, and harbors, public buildings, and monuments to the dead ... while within our own borders men, women, and children have been in a state of starvation, in actual want of sufficient to sustain life, and all this in the interest of economy. I believe the nation paid, and dearly, too, for the great crime of slavery and I believe that a just God will exact the tribute for our treatment of the Indian race."[12]

1884: San Carlos Apache Reservation, Segregation of Coal Lands

To the plan of segregation [of coal mineral land] urged by interested parties, I am unalterably opposed. By such an act the Indians would be deprived of whatever value may attach to property now admitted to be theirs; the limits of the reservation would be circumscribed so as to admit what may soon become a populous community of whites in close proximity to the agency, with all the allurements of vice so congenial to the Indians. P. P. Wilcox, Indian Agent.[13]

NOTES

1. Report of the Commissioner of Indian Affairs to the Secretary of the Interior, Reports of Agents in Dakota. Office of Indian Affairs, 1881, p. 53.
2. Report of the Commissioner of Indian Affairs to the Secretary of the Interior, United States. Office of Indian Affairs, U.S. Government Printing Office, 1881, p. XV.

3. Report of the Commissioner of Indian Affairs to the Secretary of the Interior, United States. Office of Indian Affairs, 1881, p. LXIX-LXX.
4. Report of the Commissioner of Indian Affairs to the Secretary of the Interior, United States. Office of Indian Affairs, 1881, pp. XVII-XVIII.
5. Report of the Commissioner of Indian Affairs to the Secretary of the Interior, United States. Office of Indian Affairs, 1882, p. XLIII.
6. Report of the Commissioner of Indian Affairs to the Secretary of the Interior, United States. Office of Indian Affairs, 1882, p. XLIII.
7. Report of the Commissioner of Indian Affairs to the Secretary of the Interior, United States, Office of Indian Affairs, U.S. Government Printing Office, 1883, p. LX.
8. Report of the Commissioner of Indian Affairs to the Secretary of the Interior, United States. Office of Indian Affairs, (1883), p. iv.
9. Report of the Commissioner of Indian Affairs to the Secretary of the Interior, United States. Office of Indian Affairs, 1883, p. xi.
10. Report of the Commissioner of Indian Affairs to the Secretary of the Interior, Vol. 2, United States, Office of Indian Affairs, U.S. Government Printing Office, 1884, p. 151.
11. Report of the Commissioner of Indian Affairs to the Secretary of the Interior, Report of Agents in Nevada, United States. Office of Indian Affairs, U.S. Government Printing Office, 1884, p. 129.
12. Report of the Commissioner of Indian Affairs to the Secretary of the Interior, United States, Office of Indian Affairs, U.S. Government Printing Office, 1884, p. 115.
13. Report of the Commissioner of Indian Affairs to the Secretary of the Interior, United States. Office of Indian Affairs, U.S. Government Printing Office, 1884, p. 8.

CHAPTER 35: John DeWitt Clinton Atkins, Commissioner of Indian Affairs (March 21, 1885–June 14, 1888) - Question of How to Relieve Indians from State of Dependence and Barbarism

Steeped in blind ignorance, abominable superstitions, and idleness, Commissioner Atkins policy for the management of the Indians was one word - agriculture.

> It requires no seer to foretell or foresee the civilization of the Indian race as a result naturally deducible from a knowledge and practice upon their part of the art of agriculture; for the history of agriculture among all people and in all countries intimately connects it with the highest intellectual and moral development of man. Historians, philosophers, and statesmen freely admit that civilization as naturally follows the improved arts of agriculture as vegetation follows the genial sunshine and the shower and that those races who are in ignorance of agriculture are also ignorant of almost everything else. The Indian constitutes no exception to this political maxim. Steeped as his progenitors were, and as more than half of the race now are, in blind ignorance, the devotees of abominable superstitions, and the victims of idleness and thriftlessness, the absorbing query which the hopelessness of his situation, if left to his own guidance, suggests to the philanthropist, and particularly to a great Christian people like ours, is to know how to relieve him from this state of dependence and barbarism, and to direct him in paths that will eventually lead him to the light and liberty of American citizenship. There are in the United States, exclusive of Alaska, about 260,000 Indians.[1]

1885: Indian Citizenship when Farm and School Familiar among Indians; Education to Regulate Conduct in Obedience to U.S. Laws

> When the farm and the school have become familiar institutions among the Indians, and reasonable time has intervened for the transition from barbarism or a semi-civilized state to one of civilization, then will the Indian be prepared to take upon himself the higher and more responsible duties and privileges which appertain to American citizenship.[2]

1885: Commissioner Atkins - English Language Only in Indian Schools to Americanize American Indians; Pupils Punished for Speaking Native Languages; Citizenship Was at Center of Federal Policies of Indian Assimilation

It was under Commissioner Atkins' watch that the Indian Office ordered all Indian schools to teach English only and forbade the use of tribal languages at schools, government or private. While he was not opposed to mission schools, he emphasized secular, federal control of Indian education.

Characterizing Indian students as "embryo citizens," Commissioner Atkins and other assimilationists believed that learning English was an essential component of the "citizenizing" process because it would allow American Indians to come into greater contact with non-Indian society and create a sense of unity needed for the perpetuation of a democratic society.[3]

The infamous practice of punishing pupils for speaking their native languages was a direct outgrowth of education for citizenship, with schools ordered to ensure children spoke "the language of the Republic of which they are to become citizens."[4]

1885: Dakota Territory Governor Gilbert Pierce - Allotment, Sale of Surplus Land

Governor Gilbert Pierce of Dakota Territory was among those demanding allotment and access to Indian reservations for white settlement, as he stated in his report of 1885:

> The Indian reservations located within the Territorial limits of Dakota are becoming sources of trouble and annoyance, both to the Government and to settlers on adjoining lands. It is quite impossible that two such distinct and entirely different modes of life should exist in close contact without difficulties; and that these difficulties will increase is quite inevitable. The Sioux Reservation embraces about 34,000 square miles, and contains much of the finest agricultural and grazing lands in the Territory. As the public lands decrease in quantity and become more valuable this section set apart for Indian occupation will become more and more an object of desire on the part of the white man, and the folly of leaving so vast a body of land unproductive will be loudly descanted upon. It is scarcely my province to discuss this question; but in view of the facts stated I venture to suggest that it would seem the part of wisdom strongly to encourage the dissolution of tribal relations and the granting of lands to the Indians in severalty. A reasonable quantity of land held by an Indian by direct grant would not become such an object of complaint or greed as enormous tracts occupied by tribes and claimed by no direct individual. Even if these entire reservations were thus cut up and divided among the Indians, it is believed the result would be better than to continue the present system.[5]

1885: Puyallup Reservation, WA, Railroad Access and Excellent Land

> It is situated on the Puyallup River, and is near to and adjoining the city of Tacoma. It has about 7 miles of railroad running through it. There is on it a large body of excellent land, which excites the envy and cupidity of the rich and the powerful. ... These Indians have certificates of allotment but as yet no patents to their land. Great

opposition has been, and still is being, made by outside parties to the issuing of their patents; but there is no reason for it, except that others want it.⁶

1885: WASH, Yakama Reservation, A Story of One Suspended Despotic Indian Agent

This story alone is sufficient to document the arbitrary and vicious authority of one agent, R.H. Milroy. It is critical to understanding not only the authority of one agent, but also the boarding school experience. See APPENDIX A. For more information on boarding schools see Federal Indian Boarding School Initiative Investigative Report, July 2024. https://www.bia.gov/sites/default/files/media_document/doi_federal_indian_boarding_school_initiative_investigative_report_vii_final_508_compliant.pdf (accessed online December 8, 2024).

1886: Cheyenne and Arapaho Agency, J.M. Lee, Captain Ninth Infantry, Acting Agent, Pioneers Not Fond of Indians

> All this high-sounding talk about the hardy pioneer coming and mingling among them "with the Bible in one hand" and a patent to their land in the other, the latter backed by force, means in effect the absolute dispersion and ultimate extermination of the Indian. Pioneers and frontier settlers are not missionaries, and they are not fond of close contact with the Indian race.⁷

1886: MT, Assinnaboines at Wolf Point, 250-300 Died of Starvation in 1884, Much More Tractable

> The Assinnaboines at Wolf Point are ... far more industrious, easier to manage. ***Possibly they were starved into thrift and tractability two years ago last winter, when it is said, they lost from 250 to 300 of their number by starvation.*** (Emphasis added).⁸

1886: Michigan - Isabella Reservation, Gross and Wanton Outrage, Mark W. Stevens, Indian Agent

> The prosperity of the Indians upon the Isabella Reservation has not been all that could be desired; indeed, it has not been what it might have been and what it would have been had their rights and their interests been protected and properly guarded by the Government. To illustrate: Take the Isabella Reservation, as above stated; the amount of land ceded to them under the treaty and subject to allotment was 98,760 acres. ***The amount patented to them in fee simple, which they had a right to dispose of, experience has shown was a gross and wanton outrage.*** These lands in Isabella County, a large portion of them at least, were valuable for their pine

timber. The timber upon the lands has been cut and taken away from the lands, and neither the Indians nor the Government have ever received the smallest pittance therefor. ...

A few years ago the Indians on the Isabella Reservation numbered in the neighborhood of 2,000; but because of the frauds, the intimidations, and the threats that have been brought to bear upon them by the whites in the vicinity, they have been compelled for their own safety and welfare to seek other places of abode. Thus, the Indians of this band are scattered all over Northern Michigan, mingled with other bands. Large numbers of them have gone West and many of them have gone to Canada. Had their interests been properly guarded, today they might be living upon the reservation with a large area of improved land, prosperous and happy. ...

In short, the Indians on the Isabella Reservation have been the victims of long and continuous frauds and outrages, without interruption and without measures of prevention being instituted, until they are entirely discouraged and disorganized and their identity nearly destroyed.[9]

1887: Commissioner Atkins' Three Tests of Progress Toward Civilization

In 1887, Commissioner J.D.C. Atkins in his Annual Report to the Secretary, proclaimed his "three tests of progress toward civilization, viz, the adoption of the dress of the white man, engaging in agriculture, and the education of their children."[10]

1887: Omaha Allotment Results Disastrous, Advocated by La Flesches and White Ethnologist Alice Fletcher

Dr. Susan La Flesche was a member of the western-educated elite. Her father Joseph La Flesche came from a Ponca/French fur trading family but had been adopted by and succeeded the Chief of the Omahas; her mother was the daughter of a white army doctor and an Omaha woman. Due to the advocacy of the La Flesches and white ethnologist Alice Fletcher, the Omahas were early experiments in allotment (1884) and citizenship (1887).[11]

The results were such a disaster that by December 1887, 158 Omahas had signed a petition to Congress asking for their citizenship to be revoked and their tribal status returned.[12]

One man pleaded, "*I want you to help us keep this thing citizenship, away from us.*" (Emphasis added).[13]

The petitioners claimed that Alice Fletcher had misled them. One wrote that Fletcher had told them that they would not be citizens or pay taxes for twenty-five years, but

~ 229

now, only three years later, they had become citizens.[14] "If there is a chance at all," he asked, "we want a little of our Indian ways for twenty-five years."[15]

She organized the Nez Perce tribe for allotment even with their strong resistance. **Of the Dawes Act, she wrote:**

> *The Indian may now become a free man; free from the thralldom of the tribe; freed from the domination of the reservation system; free to enter into the body of our citizens.* **This bill may therefore be considered as the Magna Carta of the Indians of our country.** (Emphasis added).[16]

NOTES

1. Report of the Commissioner of Indian Affairs to the Secretary of the Interior, United States. Office of Indian Affairs, 1885, p. iii.
2. Report of the Commissioner of Indian Affairs to the Secretary of the Interior, United States. Office of Indian Affairs, 1885, p. vi.
3. Report of the Commissioner of Indian Affairs to the Secretary of the Interior, United States. Office of Indian Affairs, 1885, p. vi.
4. J.D.C. Atkins, The English Language in Indian Schools, in Americanizing the American Indians, pp. 197, 203.
5. The Abridgment: Containing the Annual Message of the President of the United States to the Two Houses of Congress with Reports of Departments and Selections from Accompanying Papers, Secretary of the Interior, U.S. Department of the Interior, 1885, p. 900.
6. Report of the Commissioner of Indian Affairs to the Secretary of the Interior, Reports of Agents in Washington Territory, United States. Office of Indian Affairs, U.S. Government Printing Office, 1885, p. 193.
7. Report of the Commissioner of Indian Affairs to the Secretary of the Interior, United States. Office of Indian Affairs, U.S. Government Printing Office, 1886, p. 118.
8. Report of the Commissioner of Indian Affairs to the Secretary of the Interior, Report of Agents in Montana, United States, Office of Indian Affairs, U.S. Government Printing Office, 1886, p. 184.
9. Report of the Commissioner of Indian Affairs to the Secretary of the Interior, United States. Office of Indian Affairs, U.S. Government Printing Office, 1886, p. 167.
10. Report of the Commissioner of Indian Affairs to the Secretary of the Interior, Office of Indian Affairs, 1887, p. xxvi.
11. Judith A. Boughter, Betraying the Omaha Nation: 1790-1916, at 109-13 (1998).
12. Wa Hane Ga et al., Petition of Members of the Omaha Tribe of Indians in Regard to Citizenship and Taxation, S. Misc. Doc. 50-26 (1888).
13. Id. at 2 (statement of Pa-hang-ga-ma-ne).
14. Id. at 2 (statement of Wa-ha-na-zhe).
15. Id. at 3.
16. Alice Fletcher "The Crowning Act," Morning Star 7, 1887. https://sites.google.com/view/fulbrights-u-s-history/native-american-policy-case-study (accessed online August 14, 2024).

CHAPTER 36: John H. Oberly, Commissioner of Indian Affairs (October 10, 1888–June 30, 1889) [Eight Months]; Initiated Standardized Curriculum to Use in Boarding Schools to Socially Reengineer Indian Children; No More Degrading Communism; Citizenship with Complete Assimilation

~

In his brief tenure of eight months, Commissioner Oberly standardized regulations, conducted school inspections, implemented reforms, and initiated standardized curriculum intending to use boarding schools to socially reengineer Indian children. At the same time, he held demeaning, ugly stereotypical views of Indians:

1888: Indian Must Learn "I" Instead of "We," and "This Is Mine," Instead of "This Is Ours." If He Will Not Learn, Then Guardian Must Act for Ward; Compel Citizenship and Assimilation with Masses of Republic

> He should, therefore, be taught how to work, and all the schools that are opened for his children should be schools in which they will be instructed in the use of agricultural implements, the carpenter's saw and plane, the stonemason's trowel, the tailor's needle, and the shoemaker's awl. And the Indian should be taught not only how to work, but also that it is his duty to work; for *the degrading communism of the tribal reservation system gives to the individual no incentive to labor*, but puts a premium upon idleness and makes it fashionable. ... And he must be imbued with the exalting egotism of American civilization, so that he will say "I" instead of "We," and "This is mine," instead of "This is ours." But if he will not learn ...? Then the Guardian must act for the Ward, and do for him the good service he protests shall not be done—the good service that he denounces as a bad service. *The Government must then, in duty to the public, compel the Indian to come out of his isolation into the civilized way that he does not desire to enter—into citizenship—into assimilation with the masses of the Republic.* (Emphasis added).[1]

1889: North Carolina Eastern Cherokees, Land Poor, Opposed to Allotment, Victims of Frauds and Outrages

> 1899: These people are "land poor," i.e., the payment of taxes on and caring for, even meagerly, the large body of unoccupied land, is to a greater or less extent impoverishing them. Some of the land would scarcely bring, if on the market, the tax valuation. From some tracts valuable timber has already been removed. The small area of level land makes extensive agriculture impracticable.[2]

> The only cause that prevents the prosperity of these Indians is that a great many white citizens and land speculators claim title by entry to

much of their lands. It seems to me that they have been the victims of long and continuous frauds and outrages without the institution of any measures of relief, and it is a wonder they have not become discouraged and disorganized.[3]

1904: Their present peculiar condition, viz, that of being neither wards nor citizens, with no right of suffrage, yet paying taxes on their land to the State of North Carolina, under the laws thereof, is not one which is conducive to contentment or satisfaction with their environments, and makes impracticable an entirely successful administration of their affairs under Government supervision.[4]

NOTES

1. Report of the Commissioner of Indian Affairs to the Secretary of the Interior, Office of Indian Affairs, 1888, p. lxxxix.
2. Annual Reports of the Department of Interior, Report of the Commissioner of Indian Affairs to the Secretary of the Interior, Report Concerning Indians in North Carolina, Report of Superintendent in Charge of Eastern Cherokees, Office of Indian Affairs, United States. U.S. Government Printing Office, 1899, p. 267.
3. Report of the Commissioner of Indian Affairs to the Secretary of the Interior, United States. Office of Indian Affairs, U.S. Government Printing Office, 1889, p. 268.
4. Annual Reports of the Department of Interior, Report of the Commissioner of Indian Affairs to the Secretary of the Interior, 1904, Report Concerning Indians in North Carolina, Report of School Superintendent in Charge of Eastern Cherokee, Office of Indian Affairs, United States. U.S. Government Printing Office, 1905, p. 266.

CHAPTER 37: Thomas Jefferson Morgan, Commissioner of Indian Affairs (July 1, 1889–March 3, 1893) Indian Policy - No Place for Independent, Alien Governments; Indians Must Surrender Their Autonomy and Become Merged in U.S. Nationality; Allotment, Compulsory Education, Destruction of Tribal Government, Citizenship Prerogative of U.S.

~

Second.-The logic of events demands the absorption of the Indians into our national life, not as Indians, but as American citizens.

Third.-As soon as a wise conservatism will warrant it, the relations of the Indians to the Government must, rest solely upon the full recognition of their individuality. Each Indian must be treated as a man, be allowed a man's rights and privileges, and be held to the performance of a man's obligations. Each Indian is entitled to his proper share of the inherited wealth of the tribe, and to the protection of the courts in his "life, liberty, and pursuit of happiness." He is not entitled to be supported in idleness.[1]

1890: Indian Agents Have Semi-Despotic Power Over Indians

The entire system of dealing with them is vicious, involving, as it does, the installing of agents, with semi-despotic power over ignorant, superstitious, and helpless subjects; the keeping of thousands of them on reservations practically as prisoners, isolated from civilized life and dominated by fear and force; the issue of rations and annuities, which inevitably tends to breed pauperism; the disbursement of millions of dollars worth of supplies by contract, which invites fraud; the maintenance of a system of licensed trade, which stimulates cupidity and extortion, etc.[2]

1891: Citizenship Inevitable; Indian Reservations Dissolved; Tribal Autonomy Mere History

Nearly every year Congress has taken a step toward the full recognition of the individuality of the Indian, the final abolition of tribal organizations, and the total extinction of the tribal sovereignty ... *It may be remote, but the time is surely coming when these alien, quasi-independent nations within our territorial limits will have disappeared, and the individuals composing them will have been absorbed in our population, becoming fully and completely subject to the jurisprudence of the United States, both civil and criminal.* (Emphasis added).[3]

1891: Guardianship to Citizenship

The Government has now full care of the estates of the Indian tribes as represented by their land and by their trust funds upon which interest is annually paid to them and for their benefit, and, to a limited extent, it has control over and care of the persons of the Indians themselves. It is in these respects that our relations to the Indian tribes and to the Indians themselves have been said to resemble those of a guardian to his ward. ... ***When the Indians shall have become citizens of the United States this paternal control will ease.*** (Emphasis added).[4]

1891: Reservations Cannot Remain Intact - Perpetual Abode of Savagery and Animalism

The millions of acres of Indian lands now lying absolutely unused are needed as homes for our rapidly increasing population and must be so utilized. Whatever the right and title the Indians have in them is subject to and must yield to the demands of civilization. They should be protected in the permanent possession of all this land necessary for their own support, and whatever is taken from them should be paid for at its full market value. But it cannot be expected under any circumstances that these reservations can remain intact, hindering the progress of civilization, requiring an army to protect them from the encroachments of home-seekers, and maintaining a perpetual abode of savagery and animalism.[5]

1892: Commissioner Morgan on Education - Common Schools on Reservations, Agency Boarding Schools, National Industrial Schools, Nonpartisan and Nonsectarian, English Only, Coeducation Essential

The Indian school system Commissioner Morgan envisioned included three types of schools: common schools on reservations, agency boarding schools, and national industrial schools. A universal course of study patterned after public schools included standardized textbooks and teaching methods. It was to be nonpartisan and nonsectarian. Industrial education was the center of curriculum, but it also included cultural literacy; all schools receiving federal funds would be restricted to English only. Coeducation was essential to Commissioner Morgan's plan, as it was the means of lifting women out of servile roles.[6]

1892: Commissioner Morgan - Indian School Rules - Prepare Them for Duties and Privileges of American Citizenship

Commissioner Morgan published a detailed set of rules for Indian schools which stipulated a uniform course of study and the textbooks which were to be used in the schools. Instruction was to include "love of country, obedience to law, respect for civil rulers, fidelity to official trust, obligations of oaths, the ballot, and other duties involved in good citizenship."[7]

Commissioner T.J. Morgan's Order on the Course of Study in Indian Schools set forth the purpose of the schools as follows: "*The general purpose of the Government is the preparation of Indian youth for assimilation into the national life by such a course of training as will prepare them for the duties and privileges of American citizenship.*" The highest efficiency of the school is tested by its results in moral character, and hence its highest duty is effective moral training. (Emphasis added).

"The Indian pupils are taught that they are Americans, that the Government is their friend, that the flag is their flag, that the one great duty resting on them is loyalty to the Government, and thus the foundation is laid for perpetual peace between the Indian tribes in this country and the white people."[8] The 8th of February was celebrated as Franchise Day, the day the Dawes Act was signed into law - "it is worthy of being observed in all Indian schools as the possible turning point in Indian history, the point at which the Indians may strike out from tribal and reservation life and enter American citizenship and nationality."

In pursuing the assimilation process, Rule 93 specified as follows: "Pupils must be compelled to converse with each other in English, and should be properly rebuked or punished for persistent violation of this rule. Every effort should be made to encourage them to abandon their tribal languages." ... Corporal punishment or imprisonment in the guardhouse was permitted in certain situations as specified in Rule 116; expulsion was governed by Rule 117; and removal to state reform schools was permitted given certain circumstances under Rule 118.[9] *Any unnecessary reference to the fact that they are Indians was to be avoided.* (Emphasis added).[10]

Measures to assure all members of Indian family bear the same surname was stressed so that when the Indians became citizens, the inheritance of property would not cause needless confusion and probably considerable loss to the Indians if no attempt was made "to have the different members of a family known by the same family name on the records and by general reputation." Morgan's circular condemned some prevailing practices in naming the Indians [such as the English translation of Indian names]. Officials had permission to substitute English names for those too difficult to pronounce, to place English "Christian names" before the Indian surname, and to arbitrarily shorten any Indian name that was "unusually long and difficult." Also, -- stated: *it will tend strongly toward the breaking up of the Indian tribal system which is perpetuated by the Indian's own system of names.* (Emphasis added).[11]

1892: Commissioner Morgan - Compulsory Education

[I]n cases where parents, without good reason, refuse to educate their children, we believe that the Government is justified, as a last resort, in using power to compel attendance. We do not think it desirable to rear another generation of savages. ... I would withhold from them rations and supplies where those are furnished, if that were needed; and when every other means was exhausted, when I could not accomplish the work in any other way, I would send a troop of United States soldiers, not to seize them, but simply to be present as an expression of the power of the government. Then

I would say to these people, "Put your children in school"; and they would do it. There would be no warfare.[12]

1892: Commissioner Morgan, Change of Surnames

Morgan's circular condemned some prevailing practices in naming the Indians [such as the English translation of Indian names]. Officials had permission to substitute English names for those too difficult to pronounce, to place English "Christian names" before the Indian surname, and to arbitrarily shorten any Indian name that was "unusually long and difficult." Also, -- stated: *it will tend strongly toward the breaking up of the Indian tribal system which is perpetuated by the Indian's own system of names.* (Emphasis added).[11]

1892: Montana, Flathead Agency, Chiefs Bitterly Oppose Allotment

Allotments in severalty. The chiefs bitterly opposed the allotments of land in severalty, and are upheld in their prejudices by most of the full-blooded Indians of the reservation. No allotment has yet been made to any Indian within boundary. Great prejudice prevails against a survey of any kind, and the chiefs and Indians constantly state that a "measurement" of land means a robbery of the Indians. There are some of the young and more enlightened Indians who desire allotments and titles to their lands, but it is unpopular to discuss it, and they are silent on the subject. Peter Ronan, U.S. Indian Agent.[13]

1892: Criticism and Abuse Are Results of Honest Endeavor to Administer Business of Indian Office

> Any Commissioner who tries to administer this office honestly and fearlessly in the interest of the Indians; who attempts to maintain a fair state of discipline among 3,000 employees; to insist that agents shall discharge their duties faithfully; that evil-doers shall be punished and the weak and innocent shall be protected; that incompetent or unfaithful agents and employees shall be discharged; that spoilsmen shall not corrupt the service; that the land-grabber shall loose his clutches on Indian lands; that cattlemen shall not fatten their herds on Indian grass; that traders shall deal honestly; that contractors shall fulfill their contracts; that public moneys shall not be misappropriated; that attorneys shall not despoil the Indians; that gamblers shall not rob them nor whisky sellers debauch them; that they shall not be lured to vagabondage by "wild west" shows; who insists that the Government shall be just and keep its faith, and shall build schoolhouses to educate all Indian children; who tries to defeat the schemes of powerful lobbyists urging hurtful legislation; who demands that the adult Indians shall keep their agreements, give up their savagery, send their children to school, and go to work to earn an honest living, the Commissioner who insists on

progress and improvement, will be reminded very frequently of the utopian nature of his ideas. He will stir up opposition on every side. *Criticism and abuse are the inevitable results of an honest endeavor to rightly administer the business of the Indian Office. I believe it can be done, however, if a man is willing to pay the price.* (Emphasis added).[14]

1892: Thomas J. Morgan: A Plea for Papoose, An Address at Albany, N.Y., by Gen. T. J. Morgan

The term "savage" is often applied to them as carrying with it a condemnation of them as inhuman beings; bloodthirsty, gloating in war, rejoicing in revenge, happy in creating havoc, and irreconcilably hostile to all that is noble, true and good. But if the Indian babies could speak for themselves, they would say that whatever of savagery or brutishness there has been in the history of their people has been due rather to unfortunate circumstances, for which they were not always responsible, than to any inherent defect of nature. … Give the papoose a chance.[15]

NOTES

1. Report of the Commissioner of Indian Affairs to the Secretary of the Interior, United States. Office of Indian Affairs, 1889, pp. 3-4.
2. Report of the Commissioner of Indian Affairs to the Secretary of the Interior, United States. Office of Indian Affairs, U.S. Government Printing Office, 1890, p. V.
3. Report of the Commissioner of Indian Affairs to the Secretary of the Interior, United States. Office of Indian Affairs, 1891, p. 26.
4. Report of the Commissioner of Indian Affairs to the Secretary of the Interior, United States. Office of Indian Affairs, 1891, pp. 25-26.
5. Report of the Commissioner of Indian Affairs to the Secretary of the Interior, Office of Indian Affairs, 1891, p. 46.
6. Report of the Commissioner of Indian Affairs to the Secretary of the Interior, United States. Office of Indian Affairs, 1892, pp. 45-48.
7. Report of the Commissioner of Indian Affairs to the Secretary of the Interior. United States. Office of Indian Affairs. U.S. Government Printing Office, 1890, p. CLIX.
8. Congressional Record: 1891, p. 2821. From "Instructions to Indian Agents in Regard to Inculcation of Patriotism in Indian Schools," in House Executive Document No. 1, part 5, vol. II, 51st Congress, 2 session, serial 2841, p. clxvii.
9. Report of the Commissioner of Indian Affairs to the Secretary of the Interior, United States. Office of Indian Affairs, 1890, p. CLI.
10. Report of the Commissioner of Indian Affairs to the Secretary of the Interior, Office of Indian Affairs, 1890, p. CLXVII.
11. Report of the Commissioner of Indian Affairs to the Secretary of the Interior, Office of Indian Affairs, 1890, p. 1890, CLXI.
12. Proceedings of the Tenth Annual Meeting of the Lake Mohonk Conference of

Friends of the Indian (1892), pp. 51-54.
13. Report of the Commissioner of Indian Affairs, Reports of Agents in Montana, Report of Flathead Agency, Office of Indian Affairs, United States. U.S. Government Printing Office, 1892, p. 294.
14. Report of the Commissioner of Indian Affairs to the Secretary of the Interior, Office of Indian Affairs, 1892, p. 138.
15. Thomas J. Morgan: A Plea for Papoose, An Address at Albany, N.Y., 1892.

CHAPTER 38: Capital Formation under GAA

Of the land actually acquired 17,400,000 acres, or about one seventh of all the Indian lands in the United States, might seem like a somewhat rapid reduction of the landed estate of the Indians, but when it is considered that for the most part the land relinquished was not being used for any purpose whatever, that scarcely any of it was in cultivation, that the Indians did not need it and would not be likely to need it at any future time, and that they were, as is believed, reasonably well paid for it, the matter assumes quite a different aspect. The sooner the tribal relations are broken up and the reservation system done away with the better it will be for all concerned.[1]

Only ten percent of the lands in the West were ever developed by homesteading. The rest was monopolized by powerful corporations, making speculation the driving force in the market. (Emphasis added).[2]

The "surplus" land was to be sold, not homesteaded. The GAA was about making land available for purchase, about privatizing land in favour not of Indians or homeless white farmers but of people with money—people whom almost anyone would call land speculators. ... For capital to "accumulate" on the Great Plains, it had to come from somewhere else, and come it did. Since mortgage rates were high on the frontier, sometimes—through creative financing and in excess of usury laws—banks, mortgage companies, and other lenders in the East and in Europe were eager to make as many loans as they could. The land would always be there, they reasoned, and the world would always need food. Great Plains land would not, however, always produce food.[3]

1896: Wisconsin, Menominees, White Mill Operators Keep Price of Indian Logs Down

The mill men form a combination or trust and keep the price of the logs down by not bidding against each other. The only way to prevent these combinations is for the Government to erect a large sawmill on the reservation, in which can be sawed the entire cut of logs banked by the Indians on Wolf River and tributaries, if in the judgment of the Department the logs did not sell for what they were worth. A complete sawmill could be built for $20,000, and it is my opinion that it would break up the combination among the mill men and would more than pay for itself every year if a log was never sawed in it. If such a mill was erected it would give employment to the Indians and the lumber sell for many thousand dollars more than the logs do at present. Thos. H. Savage, Indian Agent. (Emphasis added).[4]

1900: Farming Potential

It is money that moves the world-money, as interpreted into such elemental terms of living as food, clothing, shelter. What makes the capitalist invest in the corporation is the desire to make his accumulated wealth earn him more of the comforts and luxuries of life; what the corporation works for is to keep itself alive by satisfying the investor; what the boss works for is to support himself and his dependents by satisfying the corporation that employs him, and what the laborer works for is to keep himself and his family fed and clad by satisfying the boss. That is where the Indian comes in when he is the laborer; and not all the governmental supervision, and all the schools, and all the philanthropic activities set afoot in his behalf by benevolent whites, if rolled into one and continued for a century, would begin to compare in educational value and efficiency with ten years of work under bosses whose own bread and butter depend upon their making him a success as a small farmer.[5]

1900: NM, Jicarilla Apache Indians, No Money to Buy Stock

Too poor to secure the necessary amount of stock to enable him to support himself by their care, and he will remain a burden upon the Government until they are provided.[6]

1901: Idaho, Lemhi Indians, No Advancement in Cattle Raising

Stock raising. In regard to cattle raising, I regret to say that hitherto nothing has been done, either by the Department or Indians, for their advancement along this line. This reservation is admirably adapted to this industry; besides this branch of agricultural life is more in keeping with Indian ideas, and for which he is most adapted.[7]

1905: WASH, Tulalip Agency, Uncapitalized to Participate in Fishing and Lumbering

Consolidation, concentration, and large local development are seriously depleting the natural larders of our Indians and cutting down their main reliance for support and subsistence. Living for them is becoming more precarious year by year. Encroachment of the white man into fishing and lumbering is driving the individual and uncapitalized Indian to the wall and making living for him indeed precarious.[8]

1906: WASH, Fishing and Lumbering, Need Capital and Technology

The two great industries of the State are fishing and lumbering, and their tremendous development, capitalization, and the application of all modern improvements, have left the Indian (dependent upon these industries for his livelihood) with his primitive methods well-nigh stranded and well-nigh destitute, and may give rise to an Indian problem where none has hitherto existed.[9]

1912: Fort Belknap, MT, Reimbursable Funds ($25,000) for Promoting Agriculture

In 1908 Congress appropriated the sum of $25,000 as a fund, reimbursable under conditions to be prescribed by the Secretary of the Interior, to aid the Indians at Fort Belknap, Mont. Wagons, implements, etc., as needed, are purchased and charged to the Indians to whom they are delivered. This property is carried in the Government accounts until paid for in full by the Indians, when title passes to them.[10]

NOTES

1. Report of the Commissioner of Indian Affairs to the Secretary of the Interior. United States. Office of Indian Affairs. U.S. Government Printing Office, 1890, pp. XXXVIII-XXXIX.
2. Love, Christopher J. "The Friends of the Indians and Their Foes: A Reassessment of the Dawes Act Debate." (1991), p. 59.
3. Kaye, Frances W. Goodlands: a meditation and history on the Great Plains. Athabasca University Press, 2011, p. 151. https://www.aupress.ca/app/uploads/120192_99Z_Kaye_2011-Goodlands.pdf (accessed online October 7, 2024).
4. Report of the Commissioner of Indian Affairs to the Secretary of the Interior, 1896, Vol. 2, Reports of Agents in Wisconsin, U.S. Government Printing Office, 1897, p. 323.
5. Annual Report of the Department of Interior, Report of the Commissioner of Indian Affairs to the Secretary of the Interior, Office of Indian Affairs, United States. U.S. Government Printing Office, 1900, p. 11.
6. Annual Report of the Department of Interior, Report of the Commissioner of Indian Affairs to the Secretary of the Interior, Miscellaneous Reports, Territory of New Mexico, Jicarilla Reservation, Office of Indian Affairs, United States. U.S. Government Printing Office, 1900, p. 252.
7. Annual Report of the Department of Interior, 1901, Part 1, Report of the Commissioner of Indian Affairs to the Secretary of the Interior, Reports Concerning Indians in Idaho, Report of Agent for Lemhi Agency, Office of Indian Affairs, United States. U.S. Government Printing Office, 1902, p. 212.
8. Annual Report of the Department of Interior, 1905, Part 1, Report of the Commissioner of Indian Affairs to the Secretary of the Interior, Reports Concerning Indians in Washington, Report of Superintendent in Charge of Tulalip Agency, Office of Indian Affairs, United States. U.S. Government Printing Office, 1906, p. 362.
9. Report of the Commissioner of Indian Affairs to the Secretary of the Interior, Reports

Concerning Indians in Washington, Report of Superintendent of Tulalip Reservation, Office of Indian Affairs, United States. U.S. Government Printing Office, 1906, p. 382.
10. Report of the Commissioner of Indian Affairs to the Secretary of the Interior, Office of Indian Affairs, United States. U.S. Government Printing Office, 1912, p. 14.

CHAPTER 39: Daniel M. Browning, Commissioner of Indian Affairs (April 13, 1893–May 3, 1897 - Allotments to Unprepared Indians

1894: Commissioner Browning - Children of Indian Women Marrying Non-Indian Men Become U.S. Citizens

The only significant policy resulting from Commissioner Browning's tenure was a departmental ruling that addressed the issue of Indian women marrying non-Indian men and the legal status of their children ... in marrying a citizen of the United States ... an Indian woman by such marriage separates herself from her tribe and becomes identified with the people of the United States, and her children are citizens of the United States in all respects, and in no respect can be deemed members of the tribe to which the mother belonged prior to her marriage. They would, therefore have no right to share in the property of the tribe except such as they might take by representation of the mother on her death.[1]

1895: Contests Initiated by Whites against Indian Homesteads

The whites in some sections of the country seem to have very little respect for the rights of Indians who have segregated themselves from their tribes and sought to avail themselves of the benefits of the Indian homestead and allotment laws enacted expressly for them by Congress, and I apprehend that the opposition to them will increase as the public domain grows less and less.[2]

The ever-greedy spirit of the white man is still abroad in the land, and his inordinate desire to seize upon, occupy, and appropriate to his own use and benefit the home of the Indian is manifested by the contests initiated by whites against the homestead entries of Indians. [It is our duty] to protect them in the use and occupancy of lands selected by them for homesteads or allotments. This Bureau has notice of numerous Indian homestead contests now pending...[3]

From the frequency of the contests it would seem that Indian lands have a peculiar attraction for a certain class of white men. They seek the home of an Indian because they apprehend that the land contains valuable minerals, water facilities, timber, or a soil better adapted to the purposes of agriculture or grazing than other portions of the surrounding country. This is the case not only with Indian homes upon the public domain, but also with Indian reservations upon which they too often trespass for prospecting and grazing.[4]

1895: ND, Devil's Lake, Death Rate Doubles, Unable to Satisfy Hunger

It has been my purpose as far as possible to prevent the killing of stock and to encourage the increase until such a time as they might have a sufficient number, so they could be permitted to kill each year enough for their use and still keep their number increasing. But with the failure of crops, the small number of animals here when I came, and their utter destitution, I have been unable to make any showing in this direction.

My first act was to forbid the dances and feasts and deny them the privilege of leaving the reservation or visiting other agencies except when urgently necessary.

Sanitary. The health of the people has not been what it should be, the *death rate being nearly double what it has been during the two preceding years, or nearly 70 to the 1,000; yet I can assign no cause except want and destitution. I have been compelled to use subsistence furnished me with a sparing hand, and I am satisfied that at times I have been unable to satisfy the demands of hunger.* With the failure of crops, the limited supply of Government assistance, and scarcity of game, they have become beggars for food, until the daily appeals, could they be seen and heard by Congress, would receive a better reward. (Emphasis added).[5]

1896: Fort McDermitt Reservation, Nevada – Indians Not Qualified to Control Ownership of Land or Assume Responsibility of Citizenship

It is my opinion that the allotment of these lands in severalty was premature. There are very few, if any, of the Indians in this State ready or qualified to control the ownership of land or assume the responsibility of citizenship.[6]

1896: Pawnee and Tonkawa Indians Not Prepared for Citizenship - Ignorant Indian Is Thrown upon Mercies of Cold World, in Their Location World Is Way below Zero

The Pawnees and Tonkawas have been allotted, their surplus lands sold to the Government and opened up to white settlement. With these two tribes can be seen the evil coming from premature citizenship. *The ignorant Indian is to a great extent thrown upon the tender mercies of a cold world, and let me assure you that right in this particular spot in this respect the world is way below zero.* (Emphasis added).[7]

1896: Neither Colville nor Spokane Indians Prepared for Allotment or Citizenship; Prey for Whites Who Will Not Hesitate to Drive Them from Allotments, and Force Them, If Possible, to Abandon Them

> I do not think the large majority of Indians on either the Colville or the Spokane reservation are prepared to take their lands in severalty and become citizens. The Indian is considered legitimate prey by a certain class of people who will not hesitate to employ any means to drive him from his allotment, and force him, if possible, to abandon it. These people religiously think an Indian has no rights a white man is bound to respect.[8]

1896: Piegans, MT, Starving to Death

> Upon the disappearance of the buffalo the Piegans passed through a period of distressing want-450 of them dying in one winter from starvation. At last the Government was brought to recognize their needs, and in May, 1888, bought of them a large tract of prairie land for $1,500,000. Shortly afterwards I was appointed as their agent.[9]

1896: Annual Report of Superintendent of Indian Schools – Indians Must Learn U.S. Social and Religious Customs

> *So long as Indians continue to maintain tribal relations and so long as they are confined to the limits of their reservations, the Indian question will continue to be a problem. They must become more intimate with our citizenship.* ... He should be induced to emulate the white man in all things that conduce to his happiness and comfort. (Emphasis added).[10]

1896: NM, CO, Acting Indian Agent, V.E. Stottler, First Lt., Tenth Infantry, Placed Children in School through Firmness and Use of Guardhouse and Starvation of Parents

> School.-There are 115 children at school, 96 at the reservation boarding school, 19 at Fort Lewis, Colo. This is 100 per cent of the children of school age and available. One girl was sent home during the year non compos mentis and one hopelessly crippled has not been required to attend school. *This showing has not been brought about except by firmness and a judicious use of the guardhouse and starvation of the parents*. (Emphasis added).[11]

NOTES

1. Report of the Commissioner of Indian Affairs to the Secretary of the Interior, United States. Office of Indian Affairs, 1894, p. 65.

2. Report of the Commissioner of Indian Affairs to the Secretary of the Interior, United States. Office of Indian Affairs, 1895, p. 22.
3. Report of the Commissioner of Indian Affairs to the Secretary of the Interior, United States. Office of Indian Affairs, 1895, p. 23.
4. Report of the Commissioner of Indian Affairs to the Secretary of the Interior, United States. Office of Indian Affairs, 1896, pp. 28-29.
5. Report of the Commissioner of Indian Affairs to the Secretary of the Interior, 1895, United States. Office of Indian Affairs, 1895, p. 130.
6. Report of the Commissioner of Indian Affairs to the Secretary of the Interior, United States. Office of Indian Affairs, 1896, p. 209.
7. Report of the Commissioner of Indian Affairs to the Secretary of the Interior, United States. Office of Indian Affairs, 1896, p. 265.
8. Report of the Commissioner of Indian Affairs to the Secretary of the Interior, United States. Office of Indian Affairs, 1896, p. 311.
9. Report of the Commissioner of Indian Affairs to the Secretary of the Interior, 1896, Reports of Agents in Montana, United States, Vol. 2, Office of Indian Affairs, U.S. Government Printing Office, 1897, p. 175.
10. Report of Superintendent of Indian Schools to the Secretary of the Interior, 1896, p. 18.
11. Annual Report of the Secretary of the Interior, 1896, Vol. II, Report of Agents in New Mexico, Office of Indian Affairs, U.S. Government Printing Office, 1897, p. 211.

CHAPTER 40: William A. Jones, Commissioner of Indian Affairs (May 3, 1897– January 1, 1905): Complete Extinguishment of Indian Race by Its Absorption into Body Politic Is Goal; Eastern Sentimentalist and Western Land Grabber Unitedly Sprung Trap that Has Been Undoing of Indians Who Had Lands of Value

Commissioner Jones worked with the leading reform groups of his day, including the Board of Indian Commissioners, Indian Rights Association, and the Lake Mohonk Conference. He was a speaker at the Lake Mohonk Conference in 1901 on the need for Indians to be self-supporting and self-reliant.

1897: Commissioner Jones: Annual Lake Mohonk Conference; Indian Monies in Custody of Government Subject to Preying Men

Commissioner Jones pointed out a fault that should have been addressed by the Treasury Department – the potential for theft of the 33 Million Dollars plus held in trust for Indian tribes.

> Commissioner Jones: there is now in the Treasury to the credit of Indian tribes $33,317,955.09, drawing interest at the rate of 4 and 5 per cent, the annual interest amounting to $1,646,485.96. Besides this several of the tribes have large incomes from leasing and other sources. *It is a safe prediction that so long as these funds exist they will be the prey of designing people.* (Emphasis added).[1]

1897: Sec. Bliss - Indian Leaders Not to Travel to Washington with Requests; Must Handle at Agency

The Secretary of Interior no longer wanted Indians visiting D.C. to complain about their problems. They were to be addressed at the agency. Agent was given complete authority over the Indians at his agency.[2]

1898: Otoes - Bitterly Opposed to Allotment

Indian Agent Asa Sharp, Otoe Tribe, reported the difficulties in resisting the pressure of local non-Indian cattlemen who put their interests for profit ahead of the Otoe Indians:

> *The Indians of this reservation have been bitterly opposed to the allotment of their lands in severalty, caused by the influence of the cattlemen, who are leasing their reservations for pasturage at the rate of 6 to 8 cents per acre, and in many instances subleasing it for 20 to 30 cents per acre, thereby making it profitable to them to*

> *induce the Indians to oppose allotments; and these same cattlemen apparently make it very warm for an agent who has nerve enough to administer the affairs of the agency in the interest of the Indians instead of the cattlemen.* (Emphasis added).³

1898: Pawnees - As Qualified for Citizenship as 10-Year-Old Child

The Indian Bureau continued to be advised of the inability of Indians to manage their business affairs. Yet the trustee for Indians took no action to protect them.

> Here the Indians have been allotted and their surplus lands sold to become homes of the white men. The Indians are considered citizens of the United States, are voters, and are amenable to the laws of the Territory in which they reside. *The majority of them are about as well qualified for citizenship as a 10-year-old child.* (Emphasis added).⁴

1898: Mexican Kickapoos Previously Self-Supporting, Became Entirely Dependent

> The Mexican Kickapoo Indians were allotted 80 acres per capita in 1894. A number of them have refused to accept their money or lands, and are known as the kicking Kickapoos. This portion of the tribe is under a special agent, who is supposed to be locating them on their several allotments. Before the allotments were made these Indians were virtually self-supporting, but under the present conditions they seem to be entirely dependent, receiving this year for their support $10,000.⁵

1899: By Necessity, Indians Were Placed Upon Tracts of Land Reserved and Set Apart; Could Be under Absolute Control and Efficient Surveillance

Commissioner Jones reported his assessment that the Indians needed to be under "absolute control" and surveillance at all times.

> The reservation system of the United States was the necessary outcome of conditions prevailing between the whites and Indians in the settlement and development of the country. The Government was forced to deal with large bands of Indians who were gradually driven back as the borders of civilization were extended, while the busy hum of industry began to be heard where all had been stillness under the ownership of this people. Angry and revengeful, their predatory attacks were inimical to the best interests of the settlers; therefore two alternatives presented themselves-extermination or *absolute control*. Humanitarian principles prevailed, and the latter was accepted. Hence as a matter of military and commercial

necessity the Indians were placed upon tracts of land reserved and set apart for their benefit, where ***they could be at all times under proper and efficient surveillance***. (Emphasis added).[6]

1899: Poncas Accepted Allotments after Opposition

Much of the land allotted to the Pottawatomie and Absentee Shawnee Indians is very poor. Many of them were absent when the allotments were made, so land was given to them as the allotting agent came to it, regardless of utility. The sale of this cheap land cuts down the average price very materially.[7]

1899: Yakima Allotment Mistakes

Trust patents. I received 1,818 trust patents from your office to deliver to the Indians. I have delivered 1,154. In many instances I find it a very difficult task to deliver these patents, as there are many that do not know the name they were allotted by, and in many instances their land was selected by some relative who is now dead. Disputes are also constantly arising as to the legal heirs of deceased Indians who have improved allotments, and there seems to be no way to have these estates probated through our State courts.[8]

1899: Commissioner Jones Disparages Educating Indians

In language, repeatedly and consistently demeaning Indians, Commissioner Jones' 1899 Annual Report describes educating Indians:

The educational system is therefore a broad and comprehensive one, and includes not only that which is taught the white boy and girl in our public schools, but also that which they learn at the fireside and in Christian homes. Their thoughts are turned from the tepee, the chase, and the barbaric ease of a savage life, when they would

Wallow naked in December snow
By thinking on fantastic summer's heat.[9]

His report continues:

The hope of the Indian race lies in taking the child at the ***tender age of four or five*** years, before the trend of his mind has become fixed in ancient molds or bent by the whims of his parents, and guiding it into the proper channel. (Emphasis added).[10]

1899: AZ, Colorado River Reservation, Drought, Irrigation Pumps Broken, Many Indians Compelled to Leave Reservation to Escape Starvation

The first half of the year was a peculiarly trying one. Not only did the Colorado River fail to make its annual overflow, but the old experimental irrigation pumps erected in 1892 broke down altogether in August, ruining all unmatured crops and leaving the Indians without any opportunity for self-support on the reservation. By September 1 there was not a spear of food-producing vegetation growing on the entire reservation. As the agent is only furnished rations to supply one-third of the population many of the Indians were compelled to leave the reservation to escape starvation. The unusual drought conditions prevailing for months over the surrounding country for the previous year had caused all the cattle to be driven out of adjacent territory. For this reason the Department could secure no bids for the delivery of beef cattle at the usual time of letting contracts nor for months afterwards. It was not until September that a bid was secured at nearly double former prices, and coupled with the conditions that the cattle should all be furnished at one delivery. The agent protested as soon as this condition was learned, but it was too late to prevent the contractor bringing results.[11]

1899: NM, Zuni, Point of Absolute Starvation

Every appearance points to the fact that through no fault of their own many of the Indians will be on the point of absolute starvation and it will be necessary to extend far more aid than last year to prevent numbers of them from dying from hunger.[12]

1900: No Middle Ground between Surveillance and Extermination

It was a matter of segregating and confining them, for political and commercial reasons, upon limited areas, where they could either be under definite surveillance or exterminated as a race. There appeared to be no middle ground between surveillance and extermination, and the former was adopted as a fixed policy, which has continued until the present time. The vicious ration and annuity system was its logical corollary. *However wise such a policy may have been during the past century, the condition of the Indian and his surrounding white neighbors at the beginning of a new century demand a change.* (Emphasis added).[13]

1900: Compulsory Education Will Hasten Accomplishment of Government's Plan of Complete Extinguishment of Indian Race by Absorption into Body Politic of U.S. and Extinguishment of Reservations

The old Indian must die out. The buffalo, the chase, the warpath, the ghost dance, must be forgotten as actual occurrences before many of the backward tribes will voluntarily take advantage of the schools. A compulsory school law will hasten the final accomplishment of the Government plan of absorption of tribes and extinguishment of reservations.[14]

[T]he Indian is not dying out, is not becoming extinct. He is in our population, but not of it, and there is only one course to pursue, and that is so to educate each generation that it will be a stepping-stone to the *final achievement of complete extinguishment of the Indian race* by its absorption into the body politic of the country. (Emphasis added).[15]

Entire Educational System of Indian Office Is Predicated upon Abolishment of Indian Reservation System

The entire educational system of the Indian Office is therefore predicated upon the final abolishment of the Indian reservation system.

1900: Nebraska Indians, Rations Delivery Improved

There has been a decided improvement in the method of issuing rations in late years. The old-fashioned way was for the Indians to assemble at a central supply station on ration day. At a given time the cattle, wild by nature, frightened and desperate by their surroundings, were turned loose to be chased by the Indians, yelling and whooping, and shot down upon the prairie in imitation of the savage method of buffalo hunting of the early days. When the animal was killed a motley assembly of Indians, ponies, and dogs of all sizes and ages gathered around where it lay. The bucks and squaws gorged themselves upon the raw entrails and smoking blood, the hide was taken to the traders, and the squaws divided up the carcass and took it away. To satisfy a morbid curiosity people used to travel sometimes a long distance to visit the agencies on ration day to witness these savage sights. ... All of that has been done away. ... Beef, with other supplies, is issued to them in a civilized way...

Notwithstanding all this, it is the consensus of opinion of those who from observation and experience are qualified to speak intelligently on the subject, that the gratuitous issue of rations, except to the old and helpless, is detrimental to the Indian. It encourages idleness and destroys labor; it promotes beggary and suppresses independence; it perpetuates pauperism and stifles industry; it is an effectual barrier to the progress of the Indian toward civilization.

> Yet, objectionable as it is, the system must continue as long as the present reservation system continues. Until the Indians are placed in a position where the way is open before them to support themselves they must be assisted. A civilized nation will not permit them to starve.[16]

1900: Law Requiring Indians to Work for Annuities

> In 1875, for the purpose of inducing Indians to labor and become self-supporting, Congress passed a law requiring all able-bodied Indians between the ages of 18 and 45, in return for supplies and annuities issued them, to perform services upon the reservation for the benefit of themselves or the tribe to an amount equal in value to the supplies to be delivered, and that such allowances should be distributed to them upon condition of the performance of such labor. The Secretary of the Interior, however, was authorized to exempt any particular tribe from its operations where he deemed it proper and expedient.[17]

1900: Crow Creek Agency, SD, Unfair Allotting of Land

> In the matter of allotments made to these Indians, in my opinion, a great injustice was done to more than three-fourths of the allottees-namely, in the allotting of timber, the timber being almost wholly along the Missouri River bottom and some families being allowed to take all of their allotments from the same.[18]

1900: Commissioner Jones, Rations Reduced as Much as Possible except Where Needed to Prevent Indians from 'Dropping Out of Existence' (i.e., Starving)

Commissioner Jones explained the need for the ration system where Indians could not farm due to the environment.

> To confine a people upon reservations where the natural conditions are such that agriculture is more or less a failure and all other means of making a livelihood limited and uncertain, it follows inevitably that they must be fed wholly or in part from outside sources or drop out of existence.

It cost at most $5 a year per person. The issues of net beef (or bacon), one-half pound of flour to each person, with three pounds beans, four pounds coffee, and seven pounds sugar to every one hundred rations does not make for a healthy subsistence. These were reduced as much as possible.[19]

1900: Indian "Movin' On" Until He Can Go No Further

> Originally and until a very comparatively recent period the red man was self-supporting. ... The advent of the white man was the

beginning of the end. From east to west, from one place to another ... the Indian has been "movin' on" until he can go no further. ***Surrounded by whites, located upon unproductive reservations often in a rigorous climate, he awaits the destiny which under existing conditions he is powerless to avert.*** (Emphasis added).[20]

1901: Commissioner Jones: Function of State: Assure Indian Has Opportunity for Self-Support; Protect Person and Property

Commissioner Jones speaking at LMC: What, then, is the function of the state? Briefly this: To see that the Indian has the opportunity for self-support, and that he is afforded the same protection of his person and property as is given to others. That being done, ***he should be thrown entirely upon his own resources to become a useful member of the community in which he lives, or not, according as he exerts himself or fails to make an effort.*** He should be located where the conditions are such that by the exercise of ordinary industry and prudence he can support himself and family; he must be made to realize that in the sweat of his face he shall earn his bread; he must be brought to recognize the dignity of labor and the importance of building and maintaining a home; he must understand that the more useful he is there, the more useful he will be to society; it is there he must find the incentive to work, and from it must come the uplifting of his race. (Emphasis added).[21]

1901: Klamath Indians, OR and CA, Allotted Sterile Lands

These people have, many of them, been given allotments in Harney Lake Valley, in Oregon, in Surprise Valley, in California, and elsewhere. Many of these allotments, I am informed, are on dry or sterile lands where irrigation is impossible and upon which the most industrious and progressive white man could not possibly make a living. O.C. Applegate, Indian Agent.[22]

1901: Warm Spring Agency, OR – Allotment Mistakes

About six years ago allotments were made to these Indians in severalty. The patents are still in this office, although the most of the Indians are living on the lands allotted to them and are making some improvements on it, but there has been so much trouble over boundary lines, so many unwise selections, allotments wholly unfit for any purpose, or two allotments of good land made to the same person under different names, that they refuse to accept the patents until corrections are made and these matters definitely settled. James E. Kirk, Superintendent and Special Disbursing Agent.[23]

1901: Commissioner Jones Spiteful Report on Educating Indians

In his 1901 Annual Report, Commissioner Jones reveals his distaste for the education program. His spite-filled analysis is quoted in full:

> There are in operation at the present time 113 boarding schools, with an average attendance of something over 16,000 pupils, ranging from 5 to 21 years old. These pupils are gathered from the cabin, the wickiup, and the tepee. *Partly by cajolery and partly by threats; partly by bribery and partly by fraud; partly by persuasion and partly by force, they are induced to leave their homes and their kindred to enter these schools* and take upon themselves the outward semblance of civilized life. They are chosen not on account of any particular merit of their own, not by reason of mental fitness, but solely because they have Indian blood in their veins. Without regard to their worldly condition; without any previous training; without any preparation whatever, they are transported to the schools-sometimes thousands of miles away-without the slightest expense or trouble to themselves or their people.
>
> The Indian youth finds himself at once, as if by magic, translated from a state of poverty to one of affluence. He is well fed and clothed and lodged. Books and all the accessories of learning are given him and teachers provided to instruct him. He is educated in the industrial arts on the one hand, and not only in the rudiments but in the liberal arts on the other. Beyond "the three r's" he is instructed in geography, grammar, and history; he is taught drawing, algebra and geometry, music, and astronomy, and receives lessons in physiology, botany, and entomology. Matrons wait on him while he is well and physicians and nurses attend him when he is sick. A steam laundry does his washing and the latest modern appliances do his cooking. A library affords him relaxation for his leisure hours, athletic sports and the gymnasium furnish him exercise and recreation, while music entertains him in the evening. He has hot and cold baths, and steam heat and electric light, and all the modern conveniences. All of the necessities of life are given him and many of the luxuries. All of this without money and without price, or the contribution of a single effort of his own or of his people. His wants are all supplied almost for the wish. The child of the wigwam becomes a modern Aladdin, who has only to rub the Government lamp to gratify his desires.
>
> Here he remains until his education is finished, when he is returned to his home-which by contrast must seem squalid indeed-to the parents whom his education must make it difficult to honor, and left to make his way against the ignorance and bigotry of his tribe. Is it any wonder he fails? Is it surprising if he lapses into barbarism?

Not having earned his education, it is not appreciated; having made no sacrifice to obtain it, it is not valued. It is looked upon as a right and not as a privilege; it is accepted as a favor to the Government and not to the recipient, and the almost inevitable tendency is to encourage dependence. (Emphasis added).[24]

1901: Education - If He Is to Rise from His Low Estate, Germs of Nobler Existence Must Be Implanted in Him and Cultivated

[T]he Indian youth ... Born a savage and raised in an atmosphere of superstition and ignorance, he lacks at the outset those advantages which are inherited by his white brother and enjoyed from the cradle. His moral character has yet to be formed. If he is to rise from his low estate the germs of a nobler existence must be implanted in him and cultivated. He must be taught the habits of civilized life.[25]

1901: Industrial Training, Break Up Reservations, Indians Have to Rely on Their Own Resources

The Indians cannot be made an integral part of the body politic or fitted for citizenship by herding them on limited areas, with a separate government, and feeding them in idleness; but they can be thus advanced by giving the children *industrial training, breaking up their reservations, and throwing them upon their own resources among the white people*. (Emphasis added).[26]

1902: Commissioner Jones - End Dancing, Feasts, Painting and Long Hair

Commissioner Jones observed that many Indians continued to wear their hair long, to "paint," and to participate in tribal dances. The commissioner objected to these traditions on a number of grounds, arguing that dancing and feasting were "simply subterfuges to cover degrading acts and to disguise immoral purposes," that painting caused people to go blind, and that long hair simply was not "in keeping with the advancement they are making ... in civilization."

Commissioner Jones sent a letter to superintendents of all federal reservations and agencies in January 1902, ordering Indians to cut their hair ("haircut order"). Commissioner Jones suggested that superintendents could induce compliance by holding back rations and required a report on the progress of these efforts by June 30, 1902. ... [I]f they become obstreperous about the matter a short confinement in the guardhouse at hard labor with shorn locks, should furnish a cure. The wearing of citizens' clothing, instead of the Indian costume and blanket, should be encouraged.[27]

1902: San Carlos Apache Reservation, AZ, Disastrous Drought, Need for Rations

Discontinuance of the ration issue. It was proposed at the end of June to stop the issue of rations at this agency. When this became generally known there was much opposition on the part of the people throughout Arizona. The military authorities were also apparently convinced that the Indians would go on the warpath if their rations were cut off. The commanding officer at Fort Grant was strongly opposed to the measure. ... *This year has been one of disastrous drought in this vicinity, and the Indians have suffered more than anyone else*, because their methods are not as good as the white peoples'. But methods will not make water when it does not rain, and the grain crop has been almost an entire failure. When the question of cutting off the rations was put before the Indians they said that they had nothing and did not know how they would be able to live. The drought also affected the demand for labor, and they could obtain very little remunerative employment. The Indians said they would have to go to the mountains and cook mescal and live in the old way on roots and nuts.[28]

1902: WIS, Winnebagoes, Annuity Amounting to $19.22 Per Year, Aged and Infirm Distressed

I feel it my duty again to call attention to the condition of the aged and infirm Indians of this tribe. *It is sad to see the look of distress on the faces of some of these sober and well-behaved people, who range in age from 50 to 100 years, as they take their annuity amounting to $19.22 per year and depart for their homes in November with the conviction that this sum must supply them with food and clothing during the cold winter.* Forsaken by the younger members of the tribe and with $19.22 a year, they are slowly wearing out their existence in actual starvation. (Emphasis added).[29]

1903: *United States v. Rickert*, Allotted Lands Tax-Exempt

In *United States v. Rickert*, 188 U.S. 432 (1903), the state of South Dakota attempted to tax farm improvements on land allotted to Indians. Farm improvements, the justices reasoned, were simply an extension of that instrumentality and therefore should also be tax-exempt. "It is evident," Justice John Harlan wrote for the majority, "that Congress expected that the lands ... allotted would be improved and cultivated by the allottee. ... that object would be defeated if the improvements could be assessed and sold for taxes." As for the county's claim that all citizens were obligated to support their government through taxes, Harlan responded, "It is for the legislative branch of the Government to say when these Indians shall cease to be dependent and assume the responsibilities attaching to citizenship." The *Rickert* decision settled disputes over the direct taxation of allottees, but the issue continued to plague the Indian Office because county governments often strapped for funds tried to enforce indirect levies.

1903: North Dakota, Drought, No General Rations

Drought and extreme heat of the summer resulted in the crop being nearly lost. Hail and the entire acreage more or less damaged by an August frost, thus materially lessening what had promised to be an abundant crop. No general rations have been issued during the summer, though I fear many will suffer during the winter unless we aid them.[30]

1902: MINN, Leech Lake Agency, Indians Don't Know Where Allotments Are

Many of the Indians do not know where their allotments are situated, and none seem to know anything about where the lines run. I believe all these lines must be established and corners plainly marked to prevent encroachment by settlers and loggers. G.L. Scott, Major, Tenth Cavalry, Acting Indian Agent. Leech Lake Agency, Minn. [Red Lake Chippewa, Leech Lake Pillager, Chippewa Cass and Winibigoshish Pillager Chippewa, White Oak Point Mississippi Chippewa].[31]

1903: La Pointe Agency, WI, No Idea of Value of Money

The Indian has no more conception of the value of money than a child. They are entirely in the hands of unprincipled whites, both business men and saloon men, who encourage and abet them secretly in obtaining their money, with the expectation of plundering them later. S.W. Campbell, Indian Agent.[32]

1903: Commissioner Jones - Indian Choices - Toy for Tourist or Citizen

By 1903, Commissioner Jones encapsulated his program for resolution of the "Indian question."

Education. There are only two phases of the Indian question: One, that the American Indian shall remain in the country as a survival of the aboriginal inhabitants, a study for the ethnologist, a toy for the tourist, a vagrant at the mercy of the State, and a continual pensioner upon the bounty of the people; the other, that he shall be educated to work, live, and act as a reputable, moral citizen, and thus become a self-supporting, useful member of society.

The latter is the policy of the present administration of Indian affairs, and if carried to its legitimate conclusion will settle for all time the "Indian question." Such a settlement will be an honor to the Government and a credit to the Indian. He will then pass out of our national life as a painted, feather-crowned hero of the novelist to add the current of his free, original American blood to the heart of this great nation.³³

1903: Commissioner Jones - Cannot Exist as Cyst on Nation; Reduce Lands to What He Can Use; Open Remainder to White Settlement

To educate the Indian in the ways of civilized life, therefore, is to preserve him from extinction, not as an Indian, but as a human being. *As a separate entity he cannot exist encysted, as it were, in the body of this great nation. The pressure for land must diminish his reservations to areas within which he can utilize the acres allotted to him, so that the balance may become homes for white farmers who require them.*³⁴

1903: Commissioner Jones - Educate Indian - Prepare Him for Abolition of Tribal Relations; Take His Land in Severalty

To educate the Indian is to prepare him for the abolishment of tribal relations, to take his land in severalty, and in the sweat of his brow and by the toil of his hands to carve out, as his white brother has done, a home for himself and family.³⁵

1903: Commissioner Jones - Teach Its Indian Wards How to Farm

Practical education is what he most requires-the knowledge of how to make a living, even under adverse circumstances. ... The Government must therefore advance a step further-toward paternalism, if you will-and *teach its Indian wards how intelligently to plant and cultivate crops and reap the harvest*. While doing this it must also instill a love for work, not for work's own sake, but for the reward which it will bring.³⁶

1903: Commissioner Jones – End Rations and Annuities - Are Disincentive to Work

By the issuing of rations and the payment of annuities, lease money, and grass funds, the incentive to work has been removed, the Government freely giving to the red man that for which the white, the black, and the yellow must toil early and late. These latter do no work unless compelled by necessity to do so; neither will the Indian. Rations were a necessity in the past, but that day has gone...³⁷

1903: Commissioner Jones – Farm or Starve

Give the Indian a white man's chance. Educate him in the rudiments of our language. Teach him to work. Send him to his home, and *tell him he must practice what he has been taught or starve.* It will in a generation or more regenerate the race. It will exterminate the Indian, but develop a man. Protect him only so far that he may gain confidence in himself, and let nature and civilized conditions do the rest.[38]

1903: NM, Mescalero Apache Reservation, Starvation Basis for Years, Many Student Deaths

The Mescalero School still enjoyed the unique distinction of showing an attendance exceeding 100 per cent of the scholastic population. Runaways and expulsions were unknown. This must not be attributed to a thirst for knowledge, but rather to a longing for something to eat and wear. The Indians have been on a starvation basis for years. They have subsisted largely on game, pinon nuts, mescal fruit, and by slaughtering stock of sheepmen and cattlemen whose herds were trespassing on the reservation. Many of them have suffered from hunger and cold... The mortality among the pupils, as well as among the Indians, was excessive, being attributable in almost every instance to tuberculosis.[39]

1904: North Dakota, Turtle Lake, Chippewa Refused to Move to Reservation, Starving – (i.e., 'Putting Indian into Civilization and Allowing Him to Starve There')

In this connection the small band of full bloods living off the reservation, near Dunseith, calls for special mention. After the reduction of the reservation to two townships nearly twenty years ago and the opening to settlement of all except those two townships, this little band has resolutely refused to leave their old home and move in on the reservation or consent to removal to any other reservation. It seems the policy was adopted not to extend any aid or protection to them except to dole out their small allowance of rations. *They starved for days before issue of rations*, and doubtless bartered, in some instances, their subsistence for poison and vice afterwards. At time of my first visit to them last spring, after taking charge of the agency department, I found them as absolutely destitute of food and clothing as it is possible to be and not experience actual starvation. It was about ten days until ration day and nowhere did I find more than three or four days subsistence in their homes. *This little band presents a most conspicuous example of "putting the Indian into civilization and allowing him to starve there."* (Emphasis added).[40]

1904: SD, Sioux, Lower Brule Agency, Crops Failure

The general condition of the Indians on this reservation is not

~259

good; they are very poor, having few cattle or horses. Their crops, owing principally to climatic conditions, were almost a failure. This summer the prospect is no better; so little dependence for future support can be looked for from agriculture.[41]

1904: Minnesota, Leech Lake Agency, Failure of Crops, Suffering among Young, Infirm and Elderly

General condition of the Indians. There was *some suffering among the Indians during the long hard winter, confined principally to the old and comparatively helpless and the young children.* The almost complete failure of the sugar, berry, and wild rice crops did much to bring this about. There was no case of actual starvation, but it was only prevented by the Department giving me a limited amount of money to buy pork and flour for them during the latter part of the winter. Conditions are more favorable this year. (Emphasis added).[42]

Problem with Commissioner Jones Program: Indian Not Given White Man's Chance

As reported by the BIA, in the years following the passage of the Allotment Act, tribal lands were allotted to individuals who were then expected to farm successfully. The problem was that they were without training, tools, or equipment.

In 1888 Congress appropriated $30,000 for seed, farming implements, and other things necessary for farming. *In that year there were 3,568 allotments, so that the fund provided an average of less than $10 to each allottee. In 1889 Congress again appropriated $30,000. In the following year nothing was appropriated; but in 1891, 1892, and 1894, annual appropriations of $15,000 were made. Thereafter until 1911, nothing was appropriated.* That year Congress established a loan fund. Approximately $250,000, or about $1.50 per capita of the Indian population, has been annually set aside for this purpose - a woefully inadequate amount to help the Indians to their feet. (Emphasis added).[43]

Practical assistance to the Indians was limited to the appointment of Government "farmers" and "stockmen." As is well known, these employees were often poorly qualified and even if they had been able to stimulate and assist the Indians in farm work, their number was inadequate. In 1900 there were only 320 farmers to 185,790 Indians, exclusive of the Five Civilized Tribes.[44]

1904: Commissioner Jones - Disposal of Indian Reservations Does Not Require Indian Consent; Guardian of Child Does Not Ask for Consent; Divide Reservations into Homesteads and Open Surplus to White Settlement

In the case of *Lone Wolf v. Hitchcock*, 187 U.S. 553 (1903), the Supreme Court announced that Congress had plenary authority over Indian nations. It can limit tribal powers, enhance them by delegating new powers to tribes, or even terminate tribal status. Congress' power comes from authority delegated to it by the Indian Commerce Clause of the U.S. Constitution. Pursuant to this plenary authority, Congress may unilaterally break treaties with the Indian nations in order to allot their reservations and sell the surplus land to non-Indians. Indian nations do not have recourse to the federal courts to remedy violations of treaties by the federal government.

After *Lone Wolf v. Hitchcock*, 187 U.S. 553 (1903), Congress immediately began to change the way that it dealt with Indian property. Commissioner of Indian Affairs William Jones in testimony before the House Indian Affairs Committee stated: "The decision in the *Lone Wolf* case will enable you to dispose of [Indian] land without the consent of the Indians. If you wait for their consent in these matters, it will be fifty years before you can do away with the reservations." ... "Supposing you were the guardian or ward of a child 8 or 10 years of age," he told, "would you ask the consent of a child as to the investment of its funds? No; you would not."[45] Congress followed Jones' suggestion and, without even initiating negotiations, proceeded to adopt allotment statutes for many Indian reservations.

1904: Mescalero Apache Reservation, NM: Progressive Indians Rewarded for Good Behavior by Generous Issue of Government Largesse

> The policy of rewarding the progressive by a generous issue of the articles furnished by the Government and imposing privation upon others who obstinately persist in refusing to adopt civilized habits has been productive of good results. It has brought forcibly to them an object lesson and the realization of the fact that, while the Government is disposed to be kind and generous to them if they will accept the instruction and advice imparted through its representatives, it will not support them in idleness. ... The past season has witnessed the most serious drought this section of country has experienced in fifteen years.[46]

1904: States Trying to Steal Indian Swamp Lands

> If the State is entitled to swamp lands, it should be restricted to that class of land. To take land not swamp now and never has been, and give it to the State, after same has by treaty been guaranteed to the Indian, is taking his property from him without compensation and giving it to the State, which is unjust, unfair, and unconstitutional. If the State owns the swamps, let them take them; but there is no justice in enriching the State at the expense of the Indian by bestowing upon it property which has been guaranteed by the Government to the Indian, and which the State claims only by virtue of field notes of survey fraudulently and inaccurately made and wholly unreliable.[47]

1904: Wily Trader, Greedy Land Shark, and Heartless Money Lender; Insatiable Greed for "More Land," "More Free Homes," for Greater Riches, Unwilling to Respect Indian Rights

Commissioner Jones reported the severe problems associated with allotment in 1904:

> The Indian has not yet been civilized. ... His white brother must bear his proportion of the burden of the Indians' failings. His insatiable greed for "more land," "more free homes," for greater riches, often blind his eyes to the right in dealing with these newborn citizens, who are encompassed by the wily trader, greedy land shark, and heartless money lender. Many white communities around Indian allotted reservations, or "sandwiched" among them, through purchases of inherited lands, fail to cooperate with the Government in holding up the hands of the educated Indians, who have become, in the eyes of the law, their equals. They appear to be unwilling to protect him so long as the Indian has lands to sell or annuities with which to buy.[48]

1904: Puyallup Agency - Valuable Agricultural Lands Lost to Unprincipled Schemer and Blackleg in Tacoma

> *The Puyallup tribe lives near Tacoma and are now, by act of Congress, citizens. The giving of unrestricted freedom to these Indians, ignorant and incapable as they are, and owning as they do the most valuable agricultural lands in the State of Washington, has made them the mark for every unprincipled schemer and blackleg in Tacoma and vicinity and will soon result in their destruction. They are continually being robbed, and several even now, who a very short time ago were owners of very valuable property, are entirely destitute.* (Emphasis added).[49]

1904: Jicarilla Apache Reservation, NM – 86% Allotments Undelivered

> **Allotments.** Some years ago allotments were made to the Indians then living, but owing to confusion of names it has been found impossible to deliver most of the patents, only about 14 per cent of them being delivered, the others remaining stored away in the agency office for lack of means to identify the Indians to whom the patents belong.[50]

NOTES

1. Report of the Annual Lake Mohonk Conference on the Indian and Other Dependent Peoples, Volumes 14-20, 1897, p. 691.
2. Report of the Commissioner of Indian Affairs to the Secretary of the Interior,

Office of Indian Affairs, 1897, p. 55.
3. Report of the Commissioner of Indian Affairs, Reports of Agencies in Oklahoma, 1898, pp. 245-246.
4. Report of the Commissioner of Indian Affairs, Reports of Agencies in Oklahoma, 1898, p. 245.
5. Report of the Commissioner of Indian Affairs, Office of Indian Affairs, United States. U.S. Government Printing Office, 1898, p. 251.
6. Report of the Superintendent of Indian Schools, Report of the Commissioner of Indian Affairs to the Secretary of the Interior, Office of Indian Affairs, 1899, Part 1, p. 6.
7. Report of the Commissioner of Indian Affairs, Office of Indian Affairs, United States. U.S. Government Printing Office, 1899, p. 306.
8. Report of the Commissioner of Indian Affairs, Office of Indian Affairs, United States. U.S. Government Printing Office, 1899, p. 363.
9. Report of the Commissioner of Indian Affairs to the Secretary of the Interior, Office of Indian Affairs, 1899, p. 4.
10. Report of the Commissioner of Indian Affairs to the Secretary of the Interior, Office of Indian Affairs, 1899, p. 5.
11. Annual Report of the Secretary of the Interior, Report of the Commissioner of Indian Affairs to the Secretary of the Interior, Reports Concerning Indians in Arizona, Report of Colorado River Agency, U.S. Department of the Interior, U.S. Government Printing Office, 1899, p. 145.
12. Annual Reports of the Secretary of the Interior, Part I, Report of the Commissioner of Indian Affairs, Reports of Agencies in New Mexico, Report of Agent for Pueblo Agency, Zuni Pueblo, U.S. Department of the Interior, United States. U.S. Government Printing Office, 1899, p. 253.
13. Report of the Commissioner of Indian Affairs to the Secretary of the Interior, 1901, United States. Office of Indian Affairs, U.S. Government Printing Office, 1902, p. 10.
14. Report of the Commissioner of Indian Affairs to the Secretary of the Interior, Office of Indian Affairs, 1900, p. 35.
15. Report of the Commissioner of Indian Affairs to the Secretary of the Interior, Office of Indian Affairs, 1900, p. 49.
16. Report of the Commissioner of Indian Affairs to the Secretary of the Interior, Part 1, Reports Concerning Indians in Nebraska, Report of Superintendent in Charge of Omaha Agency, U.S. Government Printing Office, 1900, pp. 8-9.
17. Report of the Commissioner of Indian Affairs to the Secretary of the Interior, United States. Office of Indian Affairs, U.S. Government Printing Office, 1900, p. 8.
18. Report of the Commissioner of Indian Affairs, Office of Indian Affairs, United States. U.S. Government Printing Office, 1900, p. 373.
19. Report of the Commissioner of Indian Affairs to the Secretary of the Interior, Office of Indian Affairs, 1900, p. 5.
20. Report of the Commissioner of Indian Affairs to the Secretary of the Interior, Office of Indian Affairs, 1900, p. 5.
21. Annual Report of the Board of Indian Commissioners, 1901 (Washington:

Government Printing Office), p. 56. https://babel.hathitrust.org/cgi/pt?id=mdp.39015039328276&seq=7 (accessed online October 5, 2024).
22. Report of the Commissioner of Indian Affairs (1901), Office of Indian Affairs, United States. U.S. Government Printing Office, 1902, p. 344.
23. Report of the Commissioner of Indian Affairs (1901), Office of Indian Affairs, United States. U.S. Government Printing Office, 1902, pp. 356-357.
24. Report of the Commissioner of Indian Affairs to the Secretary of the Interior, Office of Indian Affairs, 1901, pp. 1-2.
25. Report of the Commissioner of Indian Affairs to the Secretary of the Interior, Office of Indian Affairs, 1901, p. 4.
26. Report of the Commissioner of Indian Affairs to the Secretary of the Interior, Office of Indian Affairs, 1901, p. 12.
27. Annual Report of the Secretary of the Interior, Vol. II, Part 1, Report of the Commissioner of Indian Affairs, Office of Indian Affairs, 1902, p. 14.
28. Annual Report of the Secretary of the Interior, 1902, Part 2, Report of the Commissioner of Indian Affairs, Reports Concerning Indians in Arizona, United States. Office of Indian Affairs, U.S. Government Printing Office, 1903, p. 162.
29. Report of the Commissioner of Indian Affairs to the Secretary of the Interior, 1902, Part I, Office of Indian Affairs, U.S. Government Printing Office, 1903, p. 383.
30. Report of the Commissioner of Indian Affairs (1902), Office of Indian Affairs, United States. U.S. Government Printing Office, 1903, p. 222.
31. Annual Report of the Secretary of the Interior, 1903, Part 1, Report of the Commissioner of Indian Affairs, Reports Concerning Indians in North Dakota, United States. Office of Indian Affairs, U.S. Government Printing Office, 1904, p. 230.
32. Annual Report of the Department of Interior, Part 1, Report of the Commissioner of Indian Affairs to the Secretary of the Interior, 1903, Report of Agent for La Pointe Agency, Office of Indian Affairs, United States. U.S. Government Printing Office, 1904, p. 352.
33. Report of the Commissioner of Indian Affairs (1903), p. 435.
34. Report of the Commissioner of Indian Affairs to the Secretary of the Interior, Office of Indian Affairs, 1903, pp. 2-3.
35. Report of the Commissioner of Indian Affairs to the Secretary of the Interior, Office of Indian Affairs, 1903, pp. 2-3.
36. Report of the Commissioner of Indian Affairs to the Secretary of the Interior, Office of Indian Affairs, 1903, p. 3.
37. Report of the Commissioner of Indian Affairs to the Secretary of the Interior, Office of Indian Affairs, 1903, p. 3.
38. Report of the Commissioner of Indian Affairs to the Secretary of the Interior, Office of Indian Affairs, 1903, p. 3.
39. Report of the Commissioner of Indian Affairs to the Secretary of the Interior, Miscellaneous Reports, Part III, Report of Governor of New Mexico, James A. Carroll, Superintendent, Mescalero Indian Agency, Office of Indian Affairs, U.S. Government Printing Office, 1903, p. 498.

40. Annual Reports of the Secretary of the Interior, 1904, Part I, Report of the Commissioner of Indian Affairs, Reports Concerning Indians in North Dakota, Turtle Mountain Chippewa, U.S. Department of the Interior, United States. U.S. Government Printing Office, 1905, p. 269.
41. Annual Reports of the Secretary of the Interior, 1904, Part I, Report of the Commissioner of Indian Affairs, Reports Concerning Indians in South Dakota, Report of School Superintendent of Flandreau Sioux, U.S. Department of the Interior, United States. U.S. Government Printing Office, 1905, p. 327.
42. Annual Reports of the Secretary of the Interior, 1904, Part I, Report of the Commissioner of Indian Affairs, Reports Concerning Indians in Minnesota, Report of Agent for Leech Lake Agency, U.S. Department of the Interior, United States. U.S. Government Printing Office, 1905, p. 217.
43. INDIAN LAND TENURE, ECONOMIC STATUS, AND POPULATION TRENDS, PART X OF THE REPORT ON LAND PLANNING, Office of Indian Affairs, United States Printing Office, 1935, p. 8.
44. INDIAN LAND TENURE, ECONOMIC STATUS, AND POPULATION TRENDS, PART X OF THE REPORT ON LAND PLANNING, Office of Indian Affairs, United States Printing Office, 1935, p. 8.
45. House Report No. 443, 58-2, Serial 4578, p. 4.
46. Annual Report of the Secretary of the Interior, 1904, Report of the Commissioner of Indian Affairs, Part 1, Reports Concerning Indians in New Mexico, Office of Indian Affairs, United States. U.S. Government Printing Office, 1905, p. 251.
47. Annual Report of the Department of the Interior ... [with Accompanying Documents], 1904, United States. 1905, p. 218.
48. Report of the Commissioner of Indian Affairs to the Secretary of the Interior, Office of Indian Affairs, 1904, Part 1, p. 31.
49. Report of the Commissioner of Indian Affairs to the Secretary of the Interior (1904), Office of Indian Affairs, United States. U.S. Government Printing Office, 1905, p. 353.
50. Annual Report of the Department of the Interior, Report of the Commissioner of Indian Affairs, Part II, Miscellaneous Reports, Governor of New Mexico, Office of Indian Affairs, United States. U.S. Government Printing Office, 1904, p. 271.

CHAPTER 41: Francis E. Leupp, Commissioner of Indian Affairs (January 1, 1905–June 18, 1909) - Soon as Mixed or Full Blood Indian Competent, Sever Ties Which Bind Him to Tribe – As to What Will Become of Indian's Land and Money - Man Never Lived Who Did Not Learn More Valuable Lesson from One Hard Blow than from Twenty Warnings

~

Prior to his appointment as Commissioner, Leupp served on the Board of Indian Commissioners. During his tenure as Commissioner of Indian Affairs, Leupp would work to implement a new agenda; as he explained in his annual report, "The foundation of everything must be the development of character. Learning is a secondary consideration."[1]

The commonest mistake made by his white well-wishers in dealing with the Indian is the assumption that he is simply a white man with a red skin. The next commonest is the assumption that because he is a non-Caucasian he is to be classed indiscriminately with other non-Caucasians, like the negro, for instance. The truth is that the Indian has as distinct an individuality as any type of man who ever lived and he will never be judged aright till we learn to measure him by his own standards, as we whites would wish to be measured if some more powerful race were to usurp dominion over us.[2]

Moreover, as fast as an Indian of either mixed or full blood is capable of taking care of himself, it is our duty to set him upon his feet and sever forever the ties which bind him either to his tribe, in the communal sense, or to the Government. This principle must become operative in respect to both land and money. We must end the un-American absurdity of keeping one class of our people in the condition of so many undivided portions of a common lump. Each Indian must be recognized as an individual and so treated, just as each white man is.[3]

A second critic will doubtless air his fears as to what will become of the Indian's land and money under this "wide-open" policy. ... Swindlers will unquestionably lay snares for the weakest and most ignorant Indians, just as they do for the corresponding class of whites. ... In spite of all our care, however, after we have taken our hands off, he may fall a victim to sharp practices; but the man never lived—red, white or any other color—who did not learn a more valuable lesson from one hard blow than from twenty warnings.[4]

1905: Uintah Reservation - Irrigation Project Paid with Six Hundred Thousand Dollars of Ute Tribe's Money; Blackfoot - Three Hundred Thousand Dollars - Same; Yakimas and Flatheads - Same

While Commissioner Leupp was concerned with irrigation of Indians lands at the expense of the particular tribe, many of the projects were (1) poorly designed or constructed; or (2) did not benefit the Indians intended, but non-white citizens instead.

> In June 1905, the newly opened Uintah reservation in eastern Utah became the site for a two-hundred-thousand-acre irrigation project. Commissioner Leupp asked that Congress appropriate five hundred thousand dollars of the tribe's money for the project, arguing, "The future of these Indians depends upon a successful irrigation scheme, for without water their lands are valueless, and starvation or extermination will be their fate."[5]

Always generous with tribal funds, the lawmakers allocated six hundred thousand dollars. During the same session Congress authorized the Reclamation Service to include the Yakima agency in a large [irrigation] system being built on the Yakima River, and the following year three hundred thousand dollars from the Blackfoot treasury was earmarked for that tribe's reservation water system. In 1908 a similar project was launched for the Flatheads.[6]

1905: Tulalip Reservation: Problem of Consolidation, Concentration, and Large Local Development; Encroachment by White Man into Fishing and Lumbering; Rushing Indians into Citizenship for Which They Are Unprepared

> Problem of consolidation, concentration, and large local development are seriously depleting the natural larders of our Indians and cutting down their main reliance for support and subsistence. Living for them is becoming more precarious year by year. Encroachment of the white man into fishing and lumbering is driving the individual and uncapitalized Indian to the wall and making living for him indeed precarious.[7]

> Allotted. Patented. Citizens. Tulalip Agency, Washington, Report of Superintendent in Charge of Tulalip Agency, Charles M. Buchanan. **We are rushing the Indians too rapidly into a civilization and citizenship for which they have had little or no preparation.** (Emphasis added).[8]

The Superintendent listed the following obstacles: (1) Liquor, (2) undigested and unassimilated citizenship, (3) poor school and industrial training facilities, and (4) greedy white men.

1905: Report of School Superintendent of Puyallup Agency, Citizenship Debacle

> The Puyallup Indians have had citizenship for some time, and now have the reputation among our people here of being a worthless lot of drunken Indians, who have lost most of their property, self-respect,

health, homes, and all that they possessed, except their citizenship, which they still retain intact, but disfigured and shop worn from too much contact with exhilarating spirits.[9]

1905: In *Matter of Heff*, Indians Became American Citizens when They Accepted Their Land Allotment under General Allotment Act, Not at Expiration of Trust Period

In 1905 the U.S. Supreme Court in *Matter of Heff* held that Indians became American citizens as soon as they accepted their land allotment under the General Allotment Act, not at the end of the restriction on alienation period. As such

> ... when the United States grants the privileges of citizenship to an Indian, gives to him the benefit of and requires him to be subject to the laws, both civil and criminal, of the State, it places him outside the reach of police regulations on the part of Congress.[10]

The decision infuriated Congress and the Indian Bureau who had insisted that Indians who accepted allotments could not become citizens until the end of their trust period.

1906: Burke Act

The immediate uproar from the *Heff* decision caused Congress to pass the Burke Act in 1906, amending the citizenship section of the Dawes Act. The Burke Act postponed the acquisition of citizenship until the fee patent was issued which was 25 years after the allotment was made, unless the Indian could prove earlier that he was ready for citizenship. Citizenship was tied to the patent, not the allotment.

Commissioner Leupp was pleased that the power to terminate the trust period by issuing a patent in fee was placed under the control of the Secretary, whenever he was satisfied of the competency of an allottee to manage his own affairs. Also, the Indian Bureau was able to sell the allotment of a noncompetent allottee with the proceeds of the sale to go to the heirs, as determined by the Secretary.[11]

The Commissioner of Indian Affairs announced a policy of considering all applications with a view toward recommending issuance of a patent, in order to free Indians from the "shackles of wardship."[12]

BIC Opposes Burke Act

In no uncertain terms, the Board of Indian Commissioners strongly opposed the Burke Act which delayed citizenship until the twenty-five year restriction period ended, rather than on receipt of an allotment. It obstinately refused to support any action which would leave Indians untaxed wards of the government, with the machinery of the Indian Bureau perpetuated.

THE BURKE BILL OF MAY, 1906, SHUTTING OUT OF UNITED STATES CITIZENSHIP FOR TWENTY-FIVE YEARS ALL INDIANS ALLOTTED LAND AFTER MAY 8, 1906, EXCEPT AS THE DEPARTMENT MAY ALLOW INDIVIDUAL INDIANS TO BECOME CITIZENS, SEEMS A LONG STEP BACKWARD-AGAINST MAKING CITIZENS OF INDIANS AND IN FAVOR OF EXCLUSIVE DEPARTMENTAL CONTROL.

> *Most of all we deprecate the change because it involves the perpetuation for from twenty to fifty years longer of a distinct class of "Indians untaxed and not citizens," to be cared for as special wards of the nation by an Indian Bureau, with all the machinery essential to its maintenance.* (Emphasis added).[13]

1906: Columbia Reserve - Wire-Pulling Efforts

The act of March 8, 1906, authorizing the Secretary of the Interior to issue ten-year trust patents for the allotments made by Executive order dated May 1, 1886, to certain Indians of the Columbia or Moses Reserve was no doubt the result of *wire-pulling efforts on the part of certain white men who have for years coveted these lands, in some instances settling upon them and actually claiming ownership by right of mythical purchase from ignorant Indians, and by other devious means.* The proviso in the act that these allottees, or their heirs, may sell all except 80 acres of their holdings, under regulations to be established by the Secretary of the Interior, should receive careful attention from the Department, and every safeguard should be placed around such sales, which should be made in the same manner as those of inherited Indian allotments; otherwise the Indians will be swindled out of their lands, which are extremely valuable. Most of these allotments lie along the valleys of the Okanogan, Methow, and Columbia rivers, and on the shores of Lake Chelan. *Outrageous bargains have already been made*, and I would urge immediate action in the formulation of protective rules to govern their sale. (Emphasis added).[14]

1906: Puyallup Indian Agency, WA, Indians Target for Fraud

The Puyallup Reservation is no longer Indian country, and the members of the tribe are no longer wards of the Government. Their valuable lands, together with their ignorance of business methods, has made them an especial target for every rascal in Tacoma and vicinity, and their future is anything but bright. Harry F. Liston, Superintendent.[15]

1906: Colville Agency, WASH, Cheating, Frightening Indians Out of Lands

Some valuable water powers are going to waste within the limits of the two reservations, but the opening to the public for power and other purposes of the Spokane River, with its numerous rapids and occasional gorges has given an impetus to the promotion-legitimate and otherwise-of various industrial enterprises, some of which will be of decided benefit to this whole region, and it is only a question of time when the remaining forces of nature will be utilized for the general good and private gain. *The rich soil of the valleys of the Colville Reservation along the rivers has tempted the cupidity of numerous persons who have made thousands of entries of quartz and placer mining claims on splendid fruit, wheat, and timber lands. In this process many Indians have been cheated, frightened, cajoled, or bought out of their rightful possessions*, and it has been claimed by some eminently respectable people that such entries are justifiable on the ground that there is no other way in which the lands can be obtained within a reasonable time. (Emphasis added).[16]

No Official Definition of Competence or Incompetence

An official definition of competence or incompetence never surfaced.[17]

1906: Citizen Potawatomi, Absentee Shawnee, and Mexican Kickapoo: (1) Surrounding Country Had Not Been Settled and Indians Could Not Realize Importance of Their Allotment; (2) Did Not Understand What Title-in-Fee Land Meant; (3) Did Not Understand Value of Their Allotment; and (4) Did Not Understand that Disposing of Allotment Would Leave Them Homeless

Various acts of Congress have been past permitting these Indians to sell their allotments and, in my opinion, all have been detrimental to them, unless it be the act authorizing the sale of "heirship Indian land." It is true that a considerable number of them have the proceeds received from the sale of their land well invested; but these cases are the exception rather than the rule. ... At the time most of the Indians of this agency sold their own allotments the surrounding country had not as yet been settled up and the Indians could not realize the great importance of their holding the lands set aside to them by the Government. They did not know what the absolute title to a tract of land meant-that to dispose of such title and spend the proceeds of the sale, left them to live upon the section lines without a home or the means with which to buy one. Those who were unfortunate enough to sell all of their land are now, generally speaking, in this condition. They not only have no financial means with which to get a home, but they are also unable to compete with their white neighbors in the securing of such means, and therefore they seem to be left by the wayside in this seeming uncontrollable strife of the "survival of the fittest." Most of those of the Indians who have thus far held to their lands can now better understand what title to a tract of land-title to a home means, and there is a marked decrease in Indian lands placed upon the markets for sale. ...

Since the purchase of these lands the title thereto has past thru several hands, and mortgages have been recorded against nearly every tract. Why were these rapid transfers made? Plainly to get the title into the hands of so-called "innocent purchasers," with the hope of heading off any possible efforts in behalf of the Indians by the Department of Justice or by Congress. A "guilty conscience" seems to be clearly defined in a person taking such steps in regard to the title of land he may have purchased from an ignorant Indian. The only reason that the 50 Indians above mentioned have not disposed of their land is because the probate judges have been good enough to them to declare them "incompetents" and appoint a legal guardian over them. Frank A. Thackery, Superintendent and Special Disbursing Agent, Shawnee Training School, OK, Appointed July 1, 1893.[18]

1906: Flandreau Sioux Indians, SD, Moving in with Relatives on Other Reservations

These people [Flandreau Sioux Indians] vote, pay taxes, and are considered full citizens of the State of South Dakota. This Indian population is gradually decreasing, for many have sold, and others will sell their small real estate holdings, here and move to some of the larger reservations where they have relatives who have land in abundance, and will assist them in gaining a livelihood.[19]

1906: Umatilla Tribe, OR, Refuse to Approve Allotments

Charges of unfairness, and even dishonesty on part of the allotting agents, are still made, and adjustment being insisted upon. Quite a number of suits have been begun in the Federal courts to cancel allotments and secure them to the petitioners. The Indians, in council, have been presented these applications for allotments, and have in every instance refused to approve of them.[20]

1907: Ethnically He Is Indian which Is a Source of Pride, But as a Citizen He Is Not an Indian but an American and Any Civil Distinctions Must Be Expunged

Ethnically he will always remain an Indian ... and I see nothing to deplore in that indeed much that is gratifying, for he has abundant reason for all his pride of race. But as a citizen of our republic, and an equal sharer of his fellows of every blood in the privileges and responsibilities of this common citizenship, he is not an Indian but an American; and I should be glad to see every mark expunged which tends to keep alive in his mind any civil distinctions to confuse his sense of allegiance.[21]

NOTES

1. Report of the Commissioner of Indian Affairs, United States. Office of Indian Affairs, 1905, p. 3.
2. Report of the Commissioner of Indian Affairs to the Secretary of the Interior, United States. Office of Indian Affairs, 1905, p. 1.
3. Report of the Commissioner of Indian Affairs to the Secretary of the Interior, United States. Office of Indian Affairs, 1905, p. 3.
4. Report of the Commissioner of Indian Affairs to the Secretary of the Interior, United States. Office of Indian Affairs, 1905, p. 6.
5. See Report of the Commissioner of Indian Affairs to the Secretary of the Interior, United States. Office of Indian Affairs, 1905, p. 147.
6. See Report of the Commissioner of Indian Affairs to the Secretary of the Interior, United States. Office of Indian Affairs, 1906, p. 89.
7. Report of the Commissioner of Indian Affairs to the Secretary of the Interior, United States. Office of Indian Affairs, 1905, Part I, p. 362.
8. Report of the Commissioner of Indian Affairs to the Secretary of the Interior, United States. Office of Indian Affairs, 1905, p. 363.
9. Report of the Commissioner of Indian Affairs to the Secretary of the Interior, United States. Office of Indian Affairs, 1905, p. 364.
10. *Matter of Heff*, 197 U.S. 488, 509 (1905).
11. Report of the Commissioner of Indian Affairs to the Secretary of the Interior, United States. Office of Indian Affairs, 1906, p. 29.
12. Report of the Commissioner of Indian Affairs to the Secretary of the Interior, United States. Office of Indian Affairs, 1906, p. 30.
13. Annual Report of the Board of Indian Commissioners, 1906 (Washington: Government Printing Office), p. 8. https://babel.hathitrust.org/cgi/pt?id=hvd.32044097929715&seq=7 (accessed online October 5, 2024).
14. Annual Reports of the Department of the Interior … [with Accompanying Documents], United States. Office of Indian Affairs, U.S. Government Printing Office, 1906, p. 371.
15. Report of the Commissioner of Indian Affairs, Office of Indian Affairs, United States. U.S. Government Printing Office, 1906, p. 376.
16. Annual Reports of the Department of the Interior, Reports Concerning Indians in Washington, United States. Office of Indian Affairs, U.S. Government Printing Office, 1906, p. 371.
17. Franz, Margaret E. *We Have Never Been Liberal: Legal Rhetoric and The Politics of Citizenship After Reconstruction*. Diss. The University of North Carolina at Chapel Hill, 2019, p. 117.
18. Report of the Commissioner of Indian Affairs, Office of Indian Affairs, United States. U.S. Government Printing Office, 1906, pp. 325, 326.

19. Report of the Commissioner of Indian Affairs, Office of Indian Affairs, United States. U.S. Government Printing Office, 1906, p. 351.
20. Annual Report of the Department of the Interior, Report of the Commissioner of Indian Affairs, Office of Indian Affairs, United States. U.S. Government Printing Office, 1906, p. 355.
21. Report of the Commissioner of Indian Affairs to the Secretary of the Interior, United States. Office of Indian Affairs, 1907, p. 25.

CHAPTER 42: Indian Labor

1899: WASH, Puyallup Indians, Indians Labor as Hop Pickers

Hop picking begins in September and keeps a large number of children out of school until well into October. This not only occasions a serious loss of time from school but, what is of more importance, the free and easy manners attending these gatherings have very bad effect on children of all ages and especially on the older girls. After the first of December the boarding school is well filled, the average attendance after that time being about 230.[1]

1899: NM, Jicarilla Apaches, Sell Indian Arts & Crafts (Bows & Arrows, Baskets & Bead Work)

There is every prospect that conditions will be more severe this year, as their crops are almost a total failure, owing to the extraordinary drought of the past nine months, and they will be compelled to live upon the Government rations, which are not sufficient to keep them from want, supplemented with the small amount earned from the sale of bows and arrows, baskets and bead work.[2]

1900: New York Indians, Common Laborers for Railroads, Timber Companies

They are steadily improving as laborers. They are employed by the whites as track hands on the railroads, as workmen on the farms, as bark peelers and axmen in the lumber woods, and to some extent as skilled help in tanneries and other manufactories.[3]

1901: NY, Allegany Reservations, Common Laborers for Railroads, Timber Companies

About 11,000 acres is tillable land, but not one-half of this is cultivated or in pasturage. A large part of the male Indians on the Allegany reservations support themselves principally by working out among the whites. Many of them find employment in the *lumber woods, cutting timber and pealing bark. Others are track hands on the various railroads* which run through the reservation. They are good workers usually, and are growing in favor among the whites as common laborers.

Most of the valuable timber on the reservation has been cut off and sold. There are some good farmers on the reservation, and on the whole the Indian residents are making fair progress. (Emphasis added).[4]

1901: NV, Indian Labor, Ranch Hands

Industry. The Indians of this reserve have shown themselves to be sober and industrious. On the reservation proper whisky drinking is almost unknown. They are much sought after by the owners of cattle ranges in the surrounding country as ranch hands and to care for stock.[5]

1901: Nevada, Western Shoshone, Common Labor as Ranch Hands

They are in demand as sheepshearers, hay hands, ranch hands, vaqueros, and do all the freighting and irregular labor on the reservation. They earn several thousand dollars during the year, and work at such work with greater interest and regularity than at their farming, because the pay is more definite and in plainer view, it seems.[6]

1901: Oregon, Grande Ronde Agency, Farm Laborers

It is estimated that these Indians obtain from the sale of basket, a chitem bark, hay, wood, and other articles about $4,000 per annum. All of them are employed in the hop yards during September, making from $1 to $2 per day; most all of them have a garden; all own some stock, principally cattle, horses, and hogs.[7]

1905: Boys from 15 years up work through harvest, and all men, women, and children pick hops, prunes, and potatoes in season. But it must be admitted they do not make the most of their opportunities. They have not yet learned the value of steady labor nor to provide for the future.[8]

1901: AZ, San Carlos Agency, Indian Labor – "Railroad Work to Washing Dishes"

As a rule they are industrious, and eagerly seek work on the railroad, among the white farmers, at the mines, and, in fact, anywhere they can hear of a job. They have established a reputation as good workers, and their capacity runs from railroad work to washing dishes. There are several who are capable of running and caring for stationary engines, and quite a number are familiar with the use of drills and dynamite in mining. They learn very rapidly when thrown in contact with the whites.

Agriculture and Stock. The Indians have something over 1,200 head of cattle, but they are not good stockmen. The cravings of their stomachs overcome their desire for wealth.[9]

1902: Utah, St. George, Indian Laborers – Ranch Hands, Farm Work, Lumber Jacks

They have had, however, considerable work at fairly good wages in the surrounding neighborhood-riding after cattle and working on farms being the principal occupations of the younger men, while the older ones cut and haul to St. George large quantities of wood for fuel and some green cedar for posts. The women are somewhat better paid for their washing than formerly, and have made over $100 worth of baskets in the past year.[10]

1901-1902: AZ, Mohave Indians, Labor in Mines and Ranches

Opportunities for earning money adjacent to the reservation have increased through the development of mining claims and the opening up of ranches. These Indians have made acceptable workmen around the mining camps, especially in wheeling out ore and waste, in cutting wood, and in the transporting of supplies on the river. I have noted with increasing prosperity a greater disposition to shirk work on the part of certain Indians. Orders of the agent are not so quickly and explicitly obeyed as in the days when the agent and the Government flour house alone offered a means of assuaging hunger. The police have been less attentive to their duties, and it has required greater vigilance on the part of agent and employees to keep the Indians industrious and orderly. Some changes in the police force are being made with a view to securing better discipline and renewed activity.[11]

1902: The field of opportunity for these people [Mohave Indians] to earn anything is very limited indeed. The nearest railroad is 100 miles from his habitation, while the nearest town or settlement of any size, where he might find possible employment, is Needles, Cal., about the same distance from his home and little world. There are no markets within his reach, except what wild millet hay and a few hundred cords of wood he can sell to the Government, with an occasional bundle of hay or a few sacks of mesquite or screw beans that he can perchance dispose of to the passing prospector; and even though the Mohave should be so fortunate as to raise a surplus of any farm cereal, he is too far away from any market, unless provided with means of transportation up the Colorado River to Needles, Cal., and this surplus would not be of any benefit.[12]

1902: AZ, Pima Indians - Railroad Work in NV

Two hundred and fifty Indians from this reservation are at work on a railroad in Nevada. They were furnished transportation and receive $1.50 per diem, paid weekly.[13]

1902: AZ, Pima, Farm and Railroad Workers, No Better Laundresses than Pima Women; Sadly, Returned Students in Last Stages of Consumption

The men cut wood, hire out as laborers on the adjacent farms, and are in great demand on the railroad, where they are preferred as the most capable help to be found in that line. The women make good domestics, but unfortunately are tied down to families and cannot take permanent situations in town. But they work by the day and no better laundresses can be found than these Pima women, who are well aware of their own worth and charge for their services accordingly. The returned students do not go back to the old life on the reservation, but where their health will permit they work in town. *Those on the reservation are sent back from northern and eastern schools, usually in the last stages of consumption; too ill to work, not wanted in town, their only refuge is the reservation.* (Emphasis added).[14]

1902: AZ, Fort Apache Indian Agency, Legitimate Employment Difficult to Secure

If the Apache is patiently and properly directed, it seems that there is no doubt of his ability to earn his own living in the herding industry alone. It appears that this is his only salvation, and his future is dark without it.

From these facts it is and has been my determination to try to start these Indians in the business of raising stock, and from the Indian Office I have had some encouragement. But as the Indian here has not been able to sacrifice and take advantage of his natural resources by grazing the land himself, it appeared best to grant grazing permits to others who were glad to have that privilege.

However, I can truthfully say that the *year ensuing will be one of great hardship for them on account of the unusual drought*. They will not be able to sell the usual amount of forage except wild hay; and it may be impossible to create a legitimate opportunity for their employment that they may earn their bread. (Emphasis added).[15]

1902: MT, Fort Peck Agency, Common Ranch and Railroad Workers, Women as Domestic Labor

They were employed by the Government, the Great Northern Railroad, and by ranchmen living contiguous to the reservation.

They received from $1.25 to $1.50 per day, and from ranchmen $30 per month and board. A limited number of young women were secured positions in respectable families at good wages.[16]

1902: NV, Indian Women Domestic Labor

The people in Wadsworth employ Indian women to do almost all the housework, including washing and ironing. *The wages paid them consist, to a large degree, of scraps from the table and cast-off clothing.* This condition of things has a tendency to pauperize the Indians. The Indian men do nothing.[17]

1904: No material changes. Try to sell their basket and bead work, but this trade is controlled by a white woman, who has installed herself here with a table laden with Indian curios which she seldom if ever buys from the Paiute. This has been a great annoyance to our Indians. The white families of Wadsworth hire the Paiute women for housework, washing, and ironing.[18]

1903: MT, Crow Indians, Irrigation Canal Labor

Outside work. The chances for obtaining work outside for the Indians is very meager, as it is from 30 to 75 miles to white settlements. We have, however, obtained work on a large irrigation canal in the northern part of Rosebud County, and will send from 50 to 60 teams from the Black Lodge district, as they can be spared from this district on account of failure of crops. We have arranged with the contractor to pay the Indian and team 40 cents per hour, and he can work eight or ten hours a day.[19]

1903: Utah, Men Work at Odd Jobs for Whites, Squaws Do Laundry for Whites

The men work for the white people at odd jobs. The hay season is when they are most employed. Some few are herding sheep this year. The squaws have steady employment the year round washing for the white people.[20]

1903: WASH, Tulalip Agency, Work in Fish Canneries and Picking Hops

They also earn considerable money work in the fish canneries and in the hop fields.[21]

1903: WASH, Port Madison Reservation, Work in Logging Camps

Work in the adjacent logging camps.[22]

1903: AZ, Papago Indians, Railroad Workers

> There has been a continuous demand by railroad contractors and others for Papago laborers, and all who desire could find occupation at a compensation of from $1.50 to $2 per day.[23]

1904: NM, Santa Fe Industrial School, Outing System - Railroad Workers, Migrant Farm Workers in CO

> The outing system has been practiced for the past two years quite successfully, but the matter of finding employment for the boys as well as the girls has been quite a question. Last year, when the Santa Fe Central Railway was building a large number of our boys found work there, but this year they were sent to Colorado to work in the sugar-beet fields.[24]

1904: AZ, San Carlos Agency, Dam Site Labor, Railroad Work

> Funds at the disposal of the agent have been totally inadequate, but near the end of the last quarter the demand for labor at the Government dam site on Salt River and on railroads nearing the reservation has been such that every Indian desiring it has been supplied with work at good wages.[25]

1904: Moapa Reservation, Moapa, Nev., Paiute Indians, Railroad Workers, Ranch Hands, Women are Domestic Help

> Some are working on the railroad and some are working for ranchers. They work where they can find work to do, as a rule, though we have a few that will not work at all. The squaws are industrious and earn quite an amount making baskets, washing and working for ranchers.[26]

1904: WASH, Neah Bay Agency, Migrant Farm Workers

> Hop fields in central Washington, where they earn good wages. The women weave many beautiful baskets and mats.[27]

1904: WY, Eastern Shoshoni Agency, Farm, Haul Military Freight

> During the last few weeks notice has been received that the Indians of this reservation have secured the contract for hauling all of the military freight from the railroad to Fort Washakie, near this agency. This is the first time the hauling for this post has been let to other than a white contractor, and will furnish agreeable and profitable employment to these people. A substantial increase in the garrison

of the post mentioned was secured during the past winter, which will add greatly to the Indians' market for oats, hay, straw, wood, and coal. This increase in garrison was stated at the time to be only temporary, but, owing to the great need of a steady market for the products of these Indian farms, I hope the Department will see the advisability of asking that the garrison as now constituted be made permanent.[28]

1905: Effect on Family Life of Breaking Up of Indian Homes by Organizing "Gangs of Indians" for Work at Distant Points – "Unfavorable"

Unfavorable.[29]

1906: Commissioner Leupp Initiated Long-Term Leases of Tribal Lands to Sugar-Beet Companies in Exchange for Pledge to Employ Indian Laborers - Indian Takes to Beet Farming as Naturally as Italian Takes to Art or German to Science, Whole Family Can Work, Even Papooses

Commissioner Leupp's most successful scheme involved American sugar-beet companies who received long-term leases to tribal lands in exchange for a pledge to employ Indian laborers.

Our first duty to the Indian is to teach him to work. In this process the sensible course is to tempt him to the pursuit of a gainful occupation by choosing for him at the outset the sort of work which he finds pleasantest; and the Indian takes to beet farming as naturally as the Italian takes to art or the German to science. It has an attraction for him above all other forms of agriculture because it affords employment for his whole family at once; the wife-and children, who are so large factors in his life, can work in the beet fields side by side with him. Even the little papoose can be taught to weed the rows just as the pickanniny in the South can be used as a cotton picker. (Emphasis added).[30]

1906: Employment Bureau - Indian Laborers: Railroad Construction Laborers, Irrigation-Ditch Diggers, Beet Farm Help

This employment bureau has been in the care of Charles E. Dagenett, in whose veins is a strain of Indian blood, and whose efforts are therefore sympathetic as well as practical. The results of the first year's experiment have been most encouraging. During the last season some six hundred Indians, including both adults and schoolboys, have found employment in the open labor market as railroad construction laborers, irrigation-ditch diggers, beet farmers, and in other occupations.[31]

1918-1919: Indian Employment – Common Labor, AZ, NM, CA, Cotton Picking

Commissioner Ayer recommended that an agent in the Indian Service be detailed to look after the interests of Indian laborers and to cooperate with superintendents in Arizona, New Mexico, and eastern California in securing Indians for cotton picking and to see that the Indians not only receive adequate pay but are provided with decent living conditions.[32]

NOTES

1. Annual Reports of the Department of Interior, Part 1, Report of the Commissioner of Indian Affairs to the Secretary of the Interior, Reports of Agencies in Washington, Report of School Superintendent in Charge of Puyallup Consolidated Agency, Office of Indian Affairs, United States. U.S. Government Printing Office, 1899, p. 358.
2. Annual Reports of the Secretary of the Interior, Part I, Report of the Commissioner of Indian Affairs, Reports of Agencies in New Mexico, Jicarilla Reservation, U.S. Department of the Interior, United States. U.S. Government Printing Office, 1899, p. 255.
3. Annual Report of the Department of Interior, Part 1, Report of the Commissioner of Indian Affairs to the Secretary of the Interior, Reports Concerning Indians in New York, Report of Agent for New York Agency, Office of Indian Affairs, United States. U.S. Government Printing Office, 1900, p. 305.
4. Annual Report of the Department of Interior, 1901, Part 1, Report of the Commissioner of Indian Affairs to the Secretary of the Interior, Reports Concerning Indians in New York, Report of Agent for New York Agency, Office of Indian Affairs, United States. U.S. Government Printing Office, 1902, p. 285.
5. Annual Report of the Department of Interior, 1901, Part 1, Report of the Commissioner of Indian Affairs to the Secretary of the Interior, Reports Concerning Indians in Nevada, Report of School Superintendent in Charge of Nevada Agency, Office of Indian Affairs, United States, p. 276.
6. Annual Report of the Department of Interior, 1901, Part 1, Report of the Commissioner of Indian Affairs to the Secretary of the Interior, Reports Concerning Indians in Nevada, Report of School Superintendent in Charge of Western Shoshone Agency, Office of Indian Affairs, United States. U.S. Government Printing Office, 1902, p. 279.
7. Annual Report of the Department of Interior, 1901, Part 1, Report of the Commissioner of Indian Affairs to the Secretary of the Interior, Reports Concerning Indians in Oregon, Report of School Superintendent in Charge of Grand Ronde Agency, Office of Indian Affairs, United States. U.S. Government Printing Office, 1902, p. 341.
8. Annual Report of the Department of Interior, 1904, Part 1, Report of the Commissioner of Indian Affairs to the Secretary of the Interior, Reports Concerning Indians in Oregon, Report of School Superintendent in Charge of Grande Ronde Agency, Office of Indian Affairs, United States. U.S. Government Printing Office, 1905, p. 310.
9. Annual Report of the Department of the Interior, 1901, Part 1, Report of the Commissioner of Indian Affairs to the Secretary of the Interior, Reports Concerning

Indians in Arizona, Report of Agent for San Carlos Agency, Office of Indian Affairs, United States. U.S. Government Printing Office, 1902, p. 190.

10. Annual Report of the Department of Interior, 1902, Part 1, Report of the Commissioner of Indian Affairs to the Secretary of the Interior, Reports of Independent Schools, Report of School at St. George, Utah, Office of Indian Affairs, United States. U.S. Government Printing Office, 1903, p. 472.

11. Annual Report of the Department of Interior, 1901, Part 1, Report of the Commissioner of Indian Affairs to the Secretary of the Interior, Reports Concerning Indians in Arizona, Report of Agent for Colorado River Agency, Office of Indian Affairs, United States. U.S. Government Printing Office, 1902, p. 175.

12. Annual Report of the Department of Interior, 1902, Part 1, Report of the Commissioner of Indian Affairs to the Secretary of the Interior, Reports Concerning Indians in Arizona, Report of Agent for Colorado River Agency, Office of Indian Affairs, United States. U.S. Government Printing Office, 1903, p. 146.

13. Annual Report of the Department of Interior, 1902, Part 1, Report of the Commissioner of Indian Affairs to the Secretary of the Interior, Reports Concerning Indians in Arizona, Report of Agent for Pima Agency, Office of Indian Affairs, United States. U.S. Government Printing Office, 1903, p. 159.

14. Annual Report of the Department of Interior, Report of the Governor of Arizona to the Secretary of the Interior, United States. U.S. Government Printing Office, 1902, p. 177.

15. Annual Report of the Department of Interior, 1902, Part 1, Report of the Commissioner of Indian Affairs to the Secretary of the Interior, Reports Concerning Indians in Arizona, Report of Agent for Fort Apache Agency, Office of Indian Affairs, United States. U.S. Government Printing Office, 1903, p. 149.

16. Annual Report of the Department of Interior, 1902, Part 1, Report of the Commissioner of Indian Affairs to the Secretary of the Interior, Reports Concerning Indians in Montana, Report of Agent for Fort Peck Agency, Office of Indian Affairs, United States. U.S. Government Printing Office, 1903, p. 234.

17. Annual Report of the Department of Interior, 1902, Part 1, Report of the Commissioner of Indian Affairs to the Secretary of the Interior, Reports Concerning Indians in Nevada, Report of School Superintendent in Charge of Nevada Agency, Office of Indian Affairs, United States. U.S. Government Printing Office, 1903, p. 244.

18. Annual Report of the Department of Interior, 1904, Part 1, Report of the Commissioner of Indian Affairs to the Secretary of the Interior, Reports Concerning Indians in Nevada, Report of Field Matron at Wadsworth, Nevada, Office of Indian Affairs, United States. U.S. Government Printing Office, 1905, p. 247.

19. Annual Report of the Department of Interior, 1903, Part 1, Report of the Commissioner of Indian Affairs to the Secretary of the Interior, Reports Concerning Indians in Montana, Report of Agent for Crow Agency, Office of Indian Affairs, United States. U.S. Government Printing Office, 1904, p. 192.

20. Annual Report of the Department of Interior, 1903, Part 1, Report of the Commissioner of Indian Affairs to the Secretary of the Interior, Reports Concerning Indians in Utah, Report of Special Agent for Kaibab Indians, Office of Indian Affairs, United States. U.S. Government Printing Office, 1904, p. 329.

21. Annual Report of the Department of Interior, 1903, Part 1, Report of the

Commissioner of Indian Affairs to the Secretary of the Interior, Reports Concerning Indians in Washington, Report of Farmer, Swinomish Reservation, Office of Indian Affairs, United States. U.S. Government Printing Office, 1904, p. 340.

22. Annual Report of the Department of Interior, 1903, Part 1, Report of the Commissioner of Indian Affairs to the Secretary of the Interior, Reports Concerning Indians in Washington, Report of Teacher and Housekeeper, Port Madison, Reservation, Office of Indian Affairs, United States. U.S. Government Printing Office, 1904, p. 340.

23. Annual Report of the Department of Interior, 1903, Part 1, Report of the Commissioner of Indian Affairs to the Secretary of the Interior, Reports Concerning Indians in Arizona, Report of Farmer in Charge of Papago, Office of Indian Affairs, United States. U.S. Government Printing Office, 1904, p. 149.

24. Annual Report of the Department of Interior, 1904, Part 1, Report of the Commissioner of Indian Affairs to the Secretary of the Interior, Reports Concerning Indians in New Mexico, Report of School Superintendent in Charge of Pueblo, Office of Indian Affairs, United States. U.S. Government Printing Office, 1905, p. 259.

25. Annual Report of the Department of Interior, 1904, Part 1, Report of the Commissioner of Indian Affairs to the Secretary of the Interior, Reports Concerning Indians in Arizona, Report of Agent for San Carlos Agency, Office of Indian Affairs, United States. U.S. Government Printing Office, 1905, p. 152.

26. Annual Report of the Department of Interior, 1904, Part 1, Report of the Commissioner of Indian Affairs to the Secretary of the Interior, Reports Concerning Indians in Nevada, Report of Farmer in Charge of Paiute on Moapa Reservation, Office of Indian Affairs, United States. U.S. Government Printing Office, 1905, p. 244.

27. Annual Report of the Department of Interior, 1904, Part 1, Report of the Commissioner of Indian Affairs to the Secretary of the Interior, Reports Concerning Indians in Washington, Report of School Superintendent in Charge of Neah Bay Agency, Office of Indian Affairs, United States. U.S. Government Printing Office, 1905, p. 352.

28. Annual Report of the Department of Interior, 1904, Part 1, Report of the Commissioner of Indian Affairs to the Secretary of the Interior, Report Concerning Indians in Wyoming, Report of Agent for Shoshoni Agency, Office of Indian Affairs, United States. U.S. Government Printing Office, 1905, p. 383.

29. Report of the Board of Indian Commissioners to the Secretary of the Interior, 1905, United States. U.S. Government Printing Office, 1906, p. 10.

30. Report of the Commissioner of Indian Affairs to the Secretary of the Interior, United States. Office of Indian Affairs, 1906, p. 4.

31. Report of the Commissioner of Indian Affairs to the Secretary of the Interior, Indian Labor Outside Reservations, Office of Indian Affairs, United States. U.S. Government Printing Office, 1906, p. 6.

32. Annual Report of the Board of Indian Commissioners, 1918-19 (Washington: Government Printing Office), p. 5. https://babel.hathitrust.org/cgi/pt?id=osu.32435064035710&seq=105 (accessed online October 5, 2024).

CHAPTER 43: 1906: Conditions at White Earth Agency, Minn. - Land Speculators Plying Indians with Liquor to Secure Deeds or Mortgages to Valuable Timber Land for Small Amounts – Town Filled with Drunken Indians – 80% of Reservation Sold – "Ignorant Indians Were Fleeced"

> *Recent investigations at the White Earth Reservation in Minnesota have shown the existence there of conditions which require prompt and vigorous action by the Department of Justice. Beyond question great wrongs have been inflicted upon full-blood Indians and minors. Already, as a result of the removal of restrictions by the act of 1906, over 80 per cent of the Indian allotments have passed into the hands of whites.* (Emphasis added).[1]

The story of White Earth is a black page in American History. It is not pleasant reading. I have cast about earnestly to find some extenuating circumstances, but there are none. We are responsible for what has happened—all of us.[2]

Cat's Out of the Bag

On July 18, 1906, a Minneapolis newspaper reported that land speculators were plying the Indians with liquor in order to secure deeds or mortgages to their lands for small amounts; that the town had been filled with drunken Indians; and that 250 allotment mortgages had been filed at Detroit and many more in Norman County.

> The Office at once telegraphed its agent at White Earth to investigate the matter, and he answered by telegraph on July 19 that many of the mixed bloods had taken advantage of the provisions of the act to sell or mortgage their lands; that some of them were squandering the proceeds for intoxicants; but that this was true of only a limited number, and that no case had come under his observation where an Indian had first been plied with liquor to secure his consent to dispose of his land. Francis E. Leupp, Commissioner. Indians at White Earth Agency: (1) White Earth Mississippi Chippewa, (2) Gull Lake Mississippi Chipewa, (3) Removal White Oak Point Mississippi Chippewa, (4) Removal Mille Lac Mississippi Chippewa, (5) NonRemoval Mille Lac Mississippi Chippewa, (6) Removal Leech Lake Pillager Chippewa, (7) Cass and Winnebagoshish Chippewa, (8) Otter Tail Pillager Chippewa, (9) Removal Fond du Lac Chippewa, and (10) Pembina Chippewa.[3]

The subsequent Indian Commissioner, R.G. Valentine, ordered an investigation. Fully ninety per cent of the allotments to full-bloods had been sold or mortgaged and *eighty per cent of the whole acreage of the reservation had passed into private hands*. Full-bloods had received not more than ten per cent of the value of their land and timber. (Emphasis added).[4]

> *Commissioner of Indian Affairs at that time, under oath, states that he did not know his wards at White Earth were being robbed. The Indian Office cannot explain why the inspectors did not inspect. Yet here are steals of over 220,000 acres of pine and farm lands worth $8,000,000, cash value.* (Emphasis added).[5]

Stage Was Set to 'Get Rich Quick' Off of Indian Land

Anthropologist Warren Moorehead's first-person account discloses the confederation behind the scenes to 'get rich quick' off of White Earth Indian timber and arable land:

> The effect of the allotment on the Whites near White Earth was immediate. Mushroom banks sprang up in the surrounding small towns. The Indians in their affidavits (of which Linnen and myself took 505) testified that lawyers, banks, county officials, and business men of prominence in Detroit, Ogema, Mahnomen, and other towns, joined in the scramble to secure their pine lands and farm tracts... in the majority of cases, as the Indian could neither write nor read, he did not know whether he was signing receipts, mortgages, deeds or releases.[6]

In tandem with Moorehead, contemporary historian William Folwell reported:

> Purchases from adult mixed-bloods might be strictly legal, even though they were not equitable; but fullbloods and minors were not legally competent to sell. In utter violation of law, land sharks from near and far bought allotments of full-bloods and took their deeds and had them recorded. ... Some operators did not scruple to obtain conveyances from minors ... *Ignorant Indians were fleeced*. (Emphasis added).[7]

More than 2,000 suits were filed by the federal government involving over 2,500 allotments and 142,000 acres of land, asserting that White Earth allotments had been wrongfully obtained from both full-bloods and minors. The timber companies continued logging while the cases were being pursued.

In 1911, the Commissioner of Indian Affairs reported that:

> *Complete success means the recovery of 142,000 acres, valued at over $2,000,000, and for timber valued at $1,755,000, on behalf of more than 1,700 Indians, forming almost 34 per cent of the White Earth allottees.* (Emphasis added).[8]

The timber industry retained attorney Ransom Powell. *First*, he used the easiest and strongest defense of all: *delay*. Documents get lost; memories fade; witnesses can't be located; government attorneys turn over frequently versus having an attorney handling one issue for the long run; and parties give up. *Second*, he needed to establish mixed blood status since (a) they had the right to sell their allotments; and (b) they presented the majority of the cases. *Third*, knowing that most Indians didn't have the money to bring a case, he pursued a novel theory: the federal government didn't have the right to represent individual Indian defendants since they had a state court forum for their fraud cases and he won the case he filed.

Skull Studies

In 1914 with timber-company funds, Powell hired two anthropologists for the identification of Ojibwe full-bloods and mixed-bloods. Dr. Albert E. Jenks, a professor at the University of Minnesota, and Dr. Ales Hrdlicka examined 696 Ojibwe who claimed to be full bloods, comparing their physical attributes to the Pima Indians of the southwestern United States, whom the anthropologists considered the most racially "pure" American Indians. *They carefully measured and calibrated hair, eyes, nails, gums, head shapes, and teeth of White Earth Ojibwe and compared this data to measurements of the Pima.*[9]

Their studies narrowed the pool of full-bloods. *Of the 5,173 White Earth allottees, only 408 were considered to be full bloods - and 306 of them died before the roll was finalized in 1920.* Based on the government studies, in 1920, there were only *102 full-blood White Earth Ojibwes*. The results of this study still stand today given Judge Page Morris, Senior Judge of the United States District Court for the District of Minnesota, approving the roll and placing it on file with the Clerk of Court in Fergus Falls, Minnesota. In *Bisek v. Bellanger*, 5 F.2d 994, 995 (D. Minn. 1925), the "Blood Roll" was upheld.

Government's Cases Weakened by Powell's Advocacy

Due to Powell's *first defense* – delay – he won. The DOJ determined that it would be difficult to successfully prevail at trial given the *decade* that had passed since starting the litigation. They agreed on a settlement basis:

> Land would be restored to full bloods; the cases involving mixed bloods who were competent to sell would be dismissed; and others who were defrauded, such as minors, would receive the difference between their original payments and the fair value of the property at time of sale, plus six percent interest to the time of settlement [not their land]. Significantly, no remedy was established for mixed bloods who had been defrauded.[10]

Powell ensured that most of his clients' purchases were protected for a comparatively small cost. Nichols-Chisholm paid only $48,497 and its sister firm, Park Rapids Lumber, only $23,015.

NOTES

1. Annual Report of the Board of Indian Commissioners, 1909 (Washington: Government Printing Office), p. 7. https://babel.hathitrust.org/cgi/pt?id=hvd.32044097929384&seq=5 (accessed online October 5, 2024).
2. 30 Report of the Annual Lake Mohonk Conference on the Indian and Other Dependent Peoples (1912), p. 55.
3. Report of the Commissioner of Indian Affairs, Office of Indian Affairs, United States. U.S. Government Printing Office, 1906, p. 148.
4. Report of the Commissioner of Indian Affairs to the Secretary of the Interior, United States. Office of Indian Affairs, U.S. Government Printing Office, 1911, p. 42.
5. 30 Report of the Annual Lake Mohonk Conference on the Indian and Other Dependent Peoples (1912), p. 55.
6. Moorehead, Warren King. The American Indian in the United States, Period 1850-1914. Andover MA: Andover Press, 1914, pp. 73, 75.
7. William W. Folwell, History of Minnesota, rev. ed. (St. Paul: Minnesota Historical Society, 1969), 4: 278-279.
8. Report of the Commissioner of Indian Affairs to the Secretary of the Interior, United States. Office of Indian Affairs, U.S. Government Printing Office, 1912, p. 43.
9. Peterson, Ken. "Ransom Powell and the Tragedy of White Earth." Minnesota History 63.3 (2012): 96.
10. Id.

CHAPTER 44: Robert G. Valentine, Commissioner of Indian Affairs (June 29, 1909–September 10, 1912) - Severalty Primary Means of Transforming Indians into Self-Supporting, Independent Citizens – Indian Policy - Cross between Extermination and Citizenship; Pressure of Private Interest, Clutch of Private Greed, Political Interests of Public Men Are Too Omnipresent, Too Overwhelming, Unless Countered by U.S. Sentiment

WHAT THE PUBLIC SHOULD KNOW ABOUT THE INDIAN BUREAU. ADDRESS OF HON. ROBERT G. VALENTINE.

The people of the United States ought to know certain things about their Indian Bureau.

It is possible to do only two things with the Indians - to exterminate them, or to make them into citizens. Whichever we choose should be done in the most business-like manner. If we choose extermination, we should do it suddenly, painlessly and completely; but, instead of frankly engaging in that course, the country has set itself to make the Indians into citizens. It has no business to bungle this job as it is now doing, any more than, if the course of extermination were now to be decided on, it would have any business to bungle that. *Our present course is, as a matter of fact, a cross between extermination and citizenship.*

If we would escape a disgrace greater than any which has attended this Indian business yet, we must stop at the beginning of this twentieth century and think clearly about the Indians, and set ourselves resolutely to certain clean and high courses. The whole American people must do this thinking. No group, no section alone, can do it effectively. *The pressure of private interest, the clutch of private greed, the political interests of public men, unless smoothed for them by wide public demand, are too omnipresent, too overwhelming for anything less than the attention of the whole people turned to the Indian to avert.*

Finally, one great force, perhaps above all others must be met and overcome. It seems as if in many white men there existed a different moral code among themselves and between themselves and Indians. *Men who would not think of stealing from white men apparently consider it no crime to steal from Indians.* (Emphasis added).[1]

1910: No More Credit to Indians by Indian Traders Used to Get Indians into Debt

Another forward step of very great importance has been the absolute abolishment of the "credit system." Under the old arrangement of indiscriminate allowances to all Indians having income from their lands *it was the practice of licensed traders and other dealers to encourage the Indians to purchase on credit anything and everything invented or used by civilized man, thus obligating far ahead the funds they could hope to receive.* Due notice has been given that all claims contracted subsequent to the date of the departmental order referred to will not be allowed unless previously authorized. Many of the claims filed with the superintendent are now in the office, and final action is being expedited in every way. When these are disposed of the administration of Indian-land money will be considerably simplified and the financial resources of the Indians held in readiness for application to present necessities and future needs, instead of being obligated in advance to meet extravagant bills. (Emphasis added).[2]

Abolition of Tribal Relations Requires Allotment of Tribal Land

The essential feature of the Government's great educational program for the Indians is the abolition of the old tribal relations and the treatment of every Indian as an individual. The basis of this individualization is the breaking up of tribal lands into allotments to the individuals of the tribe. This step is fundamental to the present Indian policy of the Government. Until their lands are allotted, the Government is merely marking time in dealing with any group of Indians.[3]

1910: Commissioner Valentine Systematized Issuance of Fee Patents; Competency Commissions to Tour Indian Agencies and Issue Fee Patents to Qualified Allottees

As commissioner, Valentine supported land severalty.[4] Within his first year in office, Commissioner Valentine proposed legislation to systematize the issuance of fee patents. Commissioner Valentine's proposal provided for competency commissions to tour the agencies and issue fee patents to qualified allottees. Rather than wait for natives to apply for titles, the government would issue them on its own. Beginning in the summer of 1910, competency commissions began making the rounds of the reservations.

1910: Commissioner Valentine - Alienation of Allotted Land

Any Indian of 21 years or over who holds an allotment of land under a trust patent can-
1. Procure a patent in fee under the act of May 8, 1906 (34 Stat.,182), provided it is shown that he is competent to care for his own affairs.
2. Devise his land by will under the act of June 25, 1910 (36 Stat.,

855-856), provided the land is not located in Oklahoma.
3. Sell his land under the act of March 1, 1907 (34 Stat., 1015-1018).

If the Indian is shown to be fairly competent to care for his affairs, a considerable portion of the money will be turned over to him. If good use is made of the privilege, additional sums will be given. In all cases sufficient funds will be given the Indian allottee to meet his absolute needs. Commissioner Valentine.[5]

1910: Commissioner Valentine Gets Authority for Leasing of Minerals on Allotted Lands

Legislation for leasing the lands of allottees for mining was enacted.[6]

1910: Commissioner Valentine Gets Authority for Timber Leasing

The act of June 25, 1910 (36 Stat. 855), so amended the penal laws of the United States that it became a serious offense to unlawfully cut or wantonly injure timber on Indian reservations, as well as to set a fire on Indian reservation forests without exercising due care to extinguish the same. This act also authorizes the Secretary of the Interior under such regulations as he may prescribe to sell the mature living timber, as well as dead and down timber, on the unallotted lands of any Indian reservation, except those within the States of Minnesota and Wisconsin, and upon allotments of Indians held under trust or other patents containing restrictions upon alienation. Indians would receive the proceeds from the timber sales once deductions for maintenance and fire fighting had been made.[7]

Distribution of the pro rata share of tribal funds to an individual upon application was administered by the Indian Bureau, as well. Act of March 2, 1907 (34 Stat. 1221).

1911: Commissioner Valentine - Prepare Indians for Lifting of Government's Hand and Lift Hand

All activities employed in this steadily increasing encouragement of the Indians toward self-support are governed by the two main aims of the service-first, to prepare the Indians for the lifting of the Government's hand, and, second, to lift the hand.[8]

1911: Indian Affairs, Field for Grafter, Must Be Addressed Publicly

Commissioner Valentine admitted the defects of the agency with which he is obliged to work, stating that it was 'weak in the head, weak-eyed and hard of hearing.' Public oversight was needed.

Indian affairs are, even under the best possible administration, peculiarly a field for the grafter, and all other wrongdoers. The lands and the moneys of the Indians offer a bait which the most satiated fish will not refuse, and frequently a whole local community will get on the wrong track toward the Indians. I have heard genuinely respectable members of a community say that the best thing that could happen to the Indian was to lose all his lands and all his money, and have to go to work; they say this notwithstanding the fact that by such a time the Indian would have no physique left, for drink and disease are allies of those who seek to prey upon him. To offset all this, not only publicity as to Indian affairs, but the freest discussion of all divergent views with regard to them is essential. (Emphasis added).[9]

1912: Policy to Avoid Loss of Indian's Property Leading to Debasement and Pauperism

Thus it happens that present policies are comparatively recent developments—the policies which center upon individual Indians and individual Indian families, seeking to give each Indian the health and the knowledge of health which will enable him to associate and to compete with his fellow Americans, to place each Indian upon a piece of land of his own where he can by his own efforts support himself and his family, or to give him an equivalent opportunity in industry or trade, and to lead him to conserve and utilize his property as means to these ends rather than to have it as an unappreciated heritage, through the loss of which only moral and industrial debasement and eventually pauperism are to be derived.[10]

NOTES

1. Making Citizens of the Indians, Nov. 1909.
Indian Craftsman, Volume 2, Number Three, Indian School, Carlisle, PA. https://carlisleindian.dickinson.edu/sites/default/files/docs-publications/IndianCraftsman_v02n03c.pdf (accessed online November 26, 2024).
2. Report of the Commissioner of Indian Affairs to the Secretary of the Interior, United States. Office of Indian Affairs, U.S. Government Printing Office, 1910, p. 42.
3. Report of the Commissioner of Indian Affairs to the Secretary of the Interior, Office of Indian Affairs, U.S. Government Printing Office, 1910, p. 28.
4. Report of the Commissioner of Indian Affairs to the Secretary of the Interior, United States. Office of Indian Affairs, 1910, p. 28.
5. Report of the Commissioner of Indian Affairs (1910), Office of Indian Affairs, United States. U.S. Government Printing Office, 1911, p. 39.
6. Report of the Commissioner of Indian Affairs to the Secretary of the Interior, United States. Office of Indian Affairs, 1909, p. 72.

7. Report of the Commissioner of Indian Affairs to the Secretary of the Interior, United States. Office of Indian Affairs, 1910, pp. 25-26.
8. Report of the Commissioner of Indian Affairs to the Secretary of the Interior, United States. Office of Indian Affairs, 1911, p. 3.
9. Report of the Commissioner of Indian Affairs to the Secretary of the Interior, United States. Office of Indian Affairs, 1911, p. 149.
10. Report of the Commissioner of Indian Affairs to the Secretary of the Interior, United States. Office of Indian Affairs, 1912, pp. 5-6.

CHAPTER 45: Cato Sells, Commissioner of Indian Affairs (June 2, 1913–March 29, 1921) - Indian Family Would Starve to Death if Required to Support Themselves on Many Allotments; Unprecedented Increase in Issuing Fee-Simple Patents, Sales of Trust Lands

In 1915, Commissioner Cato Sells stated the truth about the majority of allotments:

> I know of many allotments depending entirely upon which an Indian family would starve to death and where no white family could be induced to attempt to make a living, and yet under these circumstances an unsuccessful Indian farm is apt to be declared a failure. There are thousands of acres of land on Indian reservations where 100 hundred acres would not feed a rabbit. I suggest that hereafter we photograph the "painted desert" more frequently and less often the small alfalfa patch on a great reservation. We should at least tell the whole truth. It is prejudicial to the Indian to emphasize the small part of their possessions that are productive and withhold from the public the very large unproductive portion. In this wise it becomes wrongfully understood that they have vast and valuable possessions unused by them which should be otherwise utilized.[1]

1916: *U.S. v. Nice* - Legal Status of American Indians: Citizen/Ward Dichotomy Erased - Citizenship Not Incompatible with Tribal Existence or Continued Guardianship

The Supreme Court transformed the conception of the citizen/ward dichotomy in 1916 when it decided *U.S. v. Nice*. Nice had sold liquor to a Sioux Indian on his trust allotment on the Rosebud Sioux Reservation in violation of an 1897 federal statute regulating liquor transactions with Indians. The questions presented to the Court were (1) whether the Indian had been granted citizenship under section 6 of the Allotment Act when his trust allotment was issued in 1889 and (2) whether the federal government retained power to regulate liquor transactions with Indians in this situation.[2]

As to the first question, the Court overruled its decision in *Heff* and concluded that citizenship is not incompatible with tribal existence or continued guardianship, and so may be conferred without completely emancipating the Indians, or placing them beyond the reach of congressional regulations adopted for their protection.[3] It then concluded that Congress had not totally dissolved tribal status under the General Allotment Act. The "allottees remain tribal Indians, and under national guardianship."[4] The prohibition of alcohol sales to allottee Indians, would be effectively upheld.

Commissioner Sells – Unprecedented Increase in Issuing Fee-Simple Patents, Sales of Trust Lands

In the first four years of his administration, more than 155,000 acres of trust lands had been sold; during the second four years (1917–20) that figure more than doubled. The same increase occurred in sales of inherited allotments. *By the time he left office, Commissioner Sells had presided over the sale of more than 1 million acres of trust land.* (Emphasis added).⁵

Commissioner Sells – Discontinue Guardianship of Competent Indians
The time has come for discontinuing guardianship of all competent Indians and giving even closer attention to the incompetent that they more speedily achieve competency.⁶

Commissioner Sells – Aware of Corruption and Inefficiency within Government and Grafter Despoiling Indians of Land

While corruption and inefficiency may find its way into the rank and file of Government employees, the greatest danger to the Indian lies in the greed of the white man for his land and money. Where a tribe has these the grafter is sure to be in evidence. He comes from every breed known to mankind, and in the past has despoiled the Indian with a ruthlessness unparalleled.⁷

1917: Commissioner Sells' Indian Policy - Release from Governmental Supervision (1) Indians with One Half or Less of Indian Blood; (2) Those Demonstrating Competency and All Students Who Get Diplomas, If Determined to Be Competent; (3) Liberal Sale of Indian Lands, including Inherited Lands; (4) Liberal Issuance of Certificates of Competency; and (5) Liberal Release of Pro-Rata Shares-Trust Funds

Broadly speaking, a policy of greater liberalism will henceforth prevail in Indian administration to the end that every Indian, as soon as he has been determined to be as competent to transact his own business as the average white man, shall be given full control of his property and have all the lands and moneys turned over to him, after which he will no longer be a ward of the Government.

1. Patents in fee. To all able-bodied adult Indians of less than one-half Indian blood, there will be given as far as may be under the law full and complete control of all their property. Patents in fee shall be issued to all adult Indians of one-half or more Indian blood who may, after careful investigation, be found competent, provided, that where deemed advisable patents in fee shall be withheld for not to exceed 40 acres as a home. Indian students, when they are 21 years of age, or over, who complete the full course of instruction in the Government schools, receive diplomas and have demonstrated competency will be so declared.
2. Sale of lands. A liberal ruling will be adopted in the matter of

passing upon applications for the sale of inherited Indian lands where the applicants retain other lands and the proceeds are to be used to improve the homesteads or for other equally good purposes. A more liberal ruling than has hitherto prevailed will hereafter he followed with regard to the applications of noncompetent Indians for the sale of their lands where they are old and feeble and need the proceeds for their support.

3. Certificates of competency. The rules which are made to apply in the granting of patents in fee and the sale of lands will be made equally applicable in the matter of issuing certificates of competency.

4. Individual Indian moneys. Indians will be given unrestricted control of all their individual Indian moneys upon issuance of patents in fee or certificates of competency. Strict limitations will not be placed upon the use of funds of the old, the indigent, and the invalid.

5. Pro-rata shares-trust funds. As speedily as possible their pro rata shares in tribal trust or other funds shall be paid to all Indians who have been declared competent, unless the legal status of such funds prevents. Where practicable the pro rata shares of incompetent Indians will be withdrawn from the Treasury and placed in banks to their individual credit.

6. Elimination of ineligible pupils from the Government Indian schools. In many of our boarding schools Indian children are being educated at Government expense whose parents are amply able to pay for their education and have public school facilities at or near their homes. Such children shall not hereafter be enrolled in Government Indian schools supported by gratuity appropriations, except on payment of actual per capita cost and transportation.

It means the ultimate absorption of the Indian race into the body politic of the Nation. It means, in short, the beginning of the end of the Indian problem.[8]

By the end of 1917, his "aggressive steps" had produced a two-hundred-thousand-acre increase in the amount of land under lease. By 1920, 4.5 million acres of trust land were under lease. (Emphasis added).[9]

1917-1920: Commissioner Sells – Competency Commissions, Issue Patents in Fee

During the fiscal year competency commissions have investigated the qualifications of Indian allottees to manage their own affairs on the following Indian reservations: Cheyenne and Arapaho, Crow, Crow Creek, Devil's Lake, Kickapoo, Lower Brule, Oneida, Sac and Fox, Seneca, Shawnee, and Sisseton. These commissions are composed of men who are well qualified for the work and who have had long experience in the Indian Service. Numerous fee patents, involving an area of about 50,000 acres of land, have been issued on the recommendation of these commissions.[10]

1919: Upon Application, Citizenship Open to World War I Honorably Discharged Indian Veterans

> During World War I, about 9,000 American Indians served in the armed services. They fought and died in defense of a nation that still denied most of them the right to participate in the political process. Congress, as a result, enacted legislation on November 6, 1919, granting citizenship to Indian veterans of World War I who were not yet citizens.[11]

The 1919 American Indian Citizenship Act did not grant automatic citizenship to American Indian veterans who received an honorable discharge. The Act merely authorized those American Indian veterans who wanted to become American citizens to apply for and be granted citizenship. Few Indians actually followed through on the process, but it was another step towards citizenship.

1919-1920: Compulsory Indian Education

Compulsory Indian education was imposed pursuant to the act of February 14, 1920, which authorized the Secretary of the Interior to make and enforce such rules and regulations as might be necessary to secure the enrollment and regular attendance of eligible Indian children who are wards of the Government in schools maintained for their benefit by the United States or in public schools.[12]

1920: Commissioner Sells - Indian Education Must Enable Student to Acquire Citizenship

> The primary object of education is to prepare the individuals to be worthy citizens and to live happy and useful lives. Indian education requires more. It must enable the Indian to acquire citizenship and then prepare him to be a worthy citizen and qualify him to compete in the activities of life. [Indian Schools of New Mexico Lack Capacity to Accommodate All Needing Education, Superintendent of Albuquerque Indian School, Rueben Perry].[13]

NOTES

1. Report of the Commissioner of Indian Affairs, (1915), Office of Indian Affairs, United States. U.S. Government Printing Office, 1916, p. 62.
2. 241 U.S. 591-597 (1916).
3. Ibid, 598.
4. Ibid, 601.
5. Hoxie, Frederick E. A final promise: The campaign to assimilate the Indians, 1880-1920. U of Nebraska Press, 2001, p. 182.
6. Indian Commissioner Sells, A Declaration of Policy. Report of the Commissioner of Indian Affairs, 1917, pp. 3-4.

7. Annual Report of the Secretary of the Interior, Vol. II, Report of the Commissioner of Indian Affairs, Office of Indian Affairs, United States. U.S. Government Printing Office, 1917, p. 71.

8. Indian Commissioner Sells, A Declaration of Policy. Report of the Commissioner of Indian Affairs, 1917, p. 4.

9. Frederick E. A final promise: The campaign to assimilate the Indians, 1880-1920. U of Nebraska Press, 2001, p. 184.

10. Report of the Commissioner of Indian Affairs to the Secretary of the Interior, United States. Office of Indian Affairs, 1917, p. 49.

11. H.R. 5007, An Act granting citizenship to certain Indians, September 27, 1919.

12. Annual Report of the Board of Indian Commissioners, 1919-20 (Washington: Government Printing Office), p. 6. https://babel.hathitrust.org/cgi/pt?id=uc1.a0002912087&seq=5 (accessed online October 5, 2024).

13. Albuquerque, NM Journal, 12/6/1920, p. 5.

CHAPTER 46: Charles Henry Burke, Commissioner of Indian Affairs (May 7, 1921 – June 30, 1929)

~

While serving in the House, on the Committee on Indian Affairs, Commissioner Burke authored the Burke Act, which amended the General Allotment Act, delayed U.S. citizenship until the end of the trust period, unless the Indian Service determined an allottee competent to handle his own affairs.

Burke served as Commissioner of Indian Affairs under Secretary of the Interior Albert B. Fall whose two years as head of the Interior Department were marred by scandals and a conviction and prison term for Fall. **Commissioner Burke was not involved in these scandals.** Secretary Fall became involved in the Teapot Dome scandal after exclusively leasing naval oil reserves in California to the Pan-American Petroleum Company, owned by Edward Doheny, and reserves at Teapot Dome, Wyo., to Mammoth Oil Company, owned by Harry Sinclair. These reserves were to be used only in a national emergency. The investigation revealed that Fall received a $100,000 interest-free "loan" from oilman Doheny to purchase land for a New Mexico ranch. Doheny admitted to the Senate that he had his son, Ned Doheny, deliver the cash— arranged in five $20,000 stacks in a black parcel bag — directly to Fall, accompanied by Ned's friend, Hugh Plunkett. Sinclair also delivered a large herd of livestock to Fall's ranch, and his company transferred some $300,000 in Liberty bonds and cash to Fall's son-in-law. Before the rulings came down, in a murder-suicide, Hugh Plunkett killed Doheny's son, Ned, and Plunkett then killed himself. It's believed Plunkett grew fearful that authorities would charge him and Ned Doheny for their role in delivering the cash to Fall. Secretary Fall resigned his appointment in disgrace in 1923.[1]

1921: Commissioner Burke Aware of Whites Cheating Indians Out of Lands

Commissioner Burke was fully aware of white settlers attempts to cheat Indians out of their fee patents and the *more than two-thirds of the Indians who had received patents in fee and lost every acre they had to these 'white schemers.'* A method for determining competency had still not been devised leaving it to the Indian agents across the country.

> *The Government should not be expected to shirk its trust. It should not be made easy for young men to squander their substance and drift into vagrancy, nor for successful landholders to remain under restrictions not justified by their qualifications for citizenship.* (Emphasis added).[2]

The situation, therefore, suggests the need of some revision of practice as a *check upon the machinations of white schemers who covertly aid the issuance of fee patents in order to cheat the holders out of their realty*, and as a restraint upon those who are not so lacking in competency as in the disposition to make the right use of it, and also as a stimulant to the thrifty holder of a trust title to accept the entire management of his estate with the full privileges and obligations that follow. (Emphasis added).³

1921: Commissioner Burke - Patents in Fee –Tax Foreclosures; Squandered Funds; Two-Thirds of Indians Who Received Patents in Fee Lack Business Experience, Many Have Lost Every Acre They Had

It is doubtful if a satisfactory method has been found for determining the competency upon which to base a termination of the trust title. Applications for patents in fee have too often been adroitly supported by influences which sought to hasten the taxable status of the property or to accomplish a purchase at much less than its fair value, or from some other motive foreign to the Indian's ability to protect his property rights.

Notwithstanding the sincere efforts of officials and competency commissions to reach a safe conclusion as to the ability of an Indian to manage prudently his business and landed interests, *experience, shows that more than two-thirds of the Indians who have received patents in fee have been unable or unwilling to cope with the business acumen coupled with the selfishness and greed of the more competent whites, and in many instances have lost every acre they had.* It is also true that many of the applications received for patents in fee are from those least competent to manage their affairs, while the really competent Indians are in large numbers still holding their lands in trust. It is evident to the careful observer that degree of blood should not be a determining factor. Chas. H. Burke. (Emphasis added).⁴

1921: Commissioner Burke Revoked Cato Sells's Declaration of Policy – Resulted in Unnecessary Loss of Indian Lands

Commissioner Burke revoked Cato Sells's Declaration of Policy in 1921, acknowledging it had resulted in an unnecessary loss of land for Indian landowners. In its place, Burke instituted procedures that better protected land, going so far as to ask Congress to cancel all patents issued since 1917, a matter that Congress agreed to but that did nothing to recover the alienated lands.⁵

1923: Commissioner Burke's Education Goal – "Every Indian School Filled to Its Limit"

In 1923, Commissioner Burke outlined his goals: "Every eligible Indian child in school every day" and "Every Indian School filled to its limit."⁶

In 1920, the year before Commissioner Burke started his "every pupil in some school" campaign, the number of Indian children eligible for school attendance was reported to be 82,856; this number increased to 85,689 in 1922. The total of attendance in all schools in 1920 was 61,800; this leaped to 64,943 in 1922. *Comparing the situation to-day with what it was 15 or 20 years ago, when it was necessary to resort almost to kidnapping to get Indian children into school, when parents obstinately refused to send their boys and girls to a white teacher, the contrast is startling.* (Emphasis added).[7]

Indian Religious Liberty Controversy

In response to lobbying by the Indian Rights Association and missionaries who were opposed to the growing influence of peyote and threatened to remove the right of Pueblo Indians to perform their traditional dances and ceremonies in New Mexico, Commissioner Burke issued a letter to all BIA superintendents discouraging any dances the agent deemed immoral, indecent or dangerous. Charles H. Burke to All Indians, 24 February 1923. (Circular 1665 aka 'Dance Order').[8]

In 1923, Burke issued a supplement to the Dance Order that endorsed six recommendations made by a 1922 conference of missionaries. Hoping to use moral influence, Burke's supplement called for a year's trial to determine if the Indians would voluntarily give up the "worst features" of their dances and threatened to "*take some other course*" of action if the Indians did not.

>Charles H. Burke to All Indians, 24 February 1923
>Department of the Interior Office of Indian Affairs
>Segments from the Circular No. 1665 and Supplement to Circular No. 1665 April 26, 1921 and February 14, 1923 Washington
>
>Indian Dancing
>
>To Superintendents: It is not the policy of the Indian Office to denounce all forms of Indian dancing. It is rather its purpose to be somewhat tolerant of pleasure and relaxation sought in this way or of ritualism and traditional sentiment thus expressed. The dance per se is not condemned. It is recognized as a manifestation of something inherent in human nature, widely evidenced by both sacred and profane history, and as a medium through which elevated minds may happily unite art, refinement, and healthful exercise. It is not inconsistent with civilization. *The dance, however, under most primitive and pagan conditions is apt to be harmful, and when found to be so among the Indians we should control it by educational processes as far as possible, but if necessary, by punitive measures when its degrading tendencies persist*. (Emphasis added).

The sun-dance and other similar dances and so-called religious ceremonies are considered "Indian Offences" under existing regulations, and corrective penalties are provided. I regard such restriction as applicable to any dance which involves acts of self-torture, immoral relations between the sexes, the sacrificially destruction of clothing or other useful articles, the reckless giving away of property, the use of injurious drugs or intoxicants and frequent and or prolong periods of celebration which bring the Indians together from remote points to the neglect of their crops, livestock, and home interests; in fact any disorderly or plainly excessive performances that promotes superstitious cruelty, licentiousness, idleness, danger to health, and shiftless indifference to family welfare.

At a conference in October, 1922, of the missionaries of the several religious denominations represented in the Sioux country, the following recommendations were adopted and have been courteously submitted to this office:

1. That the Indian form of gambling and lottery known as the "ituranpi" (translated "give away") be prohibited.
2. That the Indian dances be limited to one in each month in the daylight hours of one day in the midweek, and at one center in each district; the months of March and April, June, July and August be excepted.
3. That none take part in the dances or be present who are under 50 years of age.
4. That a careful propaganda be undertaken to educate public opinion against the dance and to provide a healthy substitute.
5. That a determined effort be made by the Government employees in cooperation with the missionaries to persuade the management of fairs and "round-ups" in the town adjoining the reservations not to commercialize the Indian soliciting his attendance in large numbers for show purposes.
6. That there be close cooperation between the Government employees and the missionaries in those which affect the moral welfare of the Indians.

February 14, 1923,

Then on February 24, 1923, the Commissioner broadcasted a 'Message to All Indians.' It read: 'I could issue an order against these useless and harmful performances, but I would rather have you give them up of your own free will, and, therefore, I ask you in this letter to do so. If at the end of one year the reports which I receive show that you are doing as requested, I shall be glad, for I shall know that you are making progress—but if the reports show that you reject this plea, then *some other course will have to be taken.*' (Emphasis added).

Although Burke pulled back from further public statements on the dance subject during the remainder of 1923, he released the secret dance file to S.M. Brosius of the Indian Rights Association of Philadelphia, who began to circulate copies among sympathetic parties. One of these apparently found its way to Gustavus E.E. Lindquist, who referred to it in his The Red Man in the United States. Lindquist claimed the file documented "obscenities and barbarisms in Indian religious rites," and Burke, who wrote the introduction to the book, praised the missionary influence that sought to lead the Indians away from their "benighted and sometimes degrading" traditions.

Earlier in the year at the suggestion of his supervisor of education, Burke had ordered a ban on the performance of native dances at the commencement exercises of the Santa Fe Indian school. Shortly afterward, he received a request from the Taos authorities to withdraw two boys from the government school for eighteen months of religious instruction. Failing to find a record of similar requests in the past, Burke called upon Northern Pueblo Superintendent C.J. Crandall for explanation and advice. Crandall's reply was that a government school had just been constructed at Taos and for the first time an effort was being made to enroll all the children. To grant the Indians' request would "almost mean a surrender of our attempt to educate these Pueblos in our Christian civilization," Crandall replied, but to deny it completely would only arouse the Indians. A compromise permitting the absence of the students for two weeks each year was suggested and Burke concurred. The Taos Indians, however, refused to accept it, and on April 18 Burke and Secretary Work appeared in New Mexico to confer with the Taos authorities. What transpired at the April 18 meeting became thereafter a matter of dispute.

During the summer, Commissioner Burke decided not to force compulsory attendance of the boys at Taos and he ruled in favor of the Pueblos' right to demand community work from their members. Superintendent Crandall ... advised Birke that "If the demands of the Taos council were to be publicly accepted," he warned, "we virtually surrender to the Indian government and they become dictators ..."9

On July 13, the New York Times reported on the restrictions on religious liberty. A similar article, "Persecuting the Pueblos," appeared in the July issue of Sunset Magazine.

The Dance Order was ultimately withdrawn.

1924: Indian Citizenship Act

In 1924, during Commissioner Burke's term, Congress approved the Indian Citizenship Act, which granted U.S. citizenship to all American Indians, whether competent or incompetent, allotted or unallotted.

1924: Tribal Opposition to Indian Citizenship Act

One group who opposed the Bill was the Onondaga Nation. They believed acceptance of this act was "treason" because the United States Senate was forcing citizenship on all Indians without their consent. According to the Iroquois, the Bill disregarded previous treaties between the Indian Tribes and the United States. On May 19, 1924, Snyder said on the House floor, "*The New York Indians are very much opposed to this, but I am perfectly willing to take the responsibility if the committee sees fit to agree to this.*" The historical records do not contain any explanation for why Mr. Snyder felt that this unsolicited grant of citizenship did not include the guarantee of the right to vote, but his statement does make it clear, along with the removal of the word "full", that this Indian citizenship was something less than that enjoyed by non-Indians. (Emphasis added).

On December 30, 1924, the Chiefs of the Onondaga sent a letter to President Calvin Coolidge:

> Therefore, be it resolved, that we, the Indians of the Onondaga Tribe of the Six Nations, duly depose and sternly protest the principal and object of the aforesaid Snyder Bill, ... Wherefore, we ... recommend the abandonment and repeal of the Snyder Bill.[10]

Hidatsa Chief Old Dog (1851 – 1928): Opposed to Citizenship

A revered Hidatsa Indian Chief, Old Dog, photographed in 1909 by Edward Curtis, was born in 'the old world' and died, in 1926, in an era of modernization that his own parents could not have imagined. He never spoke a word of English, and when citizenship was offered him in 1922, he declined, saying that he had never needed the white man's blessing to make him a free man.

> I do not want the white man's offer of citizenship. I have lived a long life, and I have seen many of the Great White Fathers' promises vanish on the winds. I do not need the white man's government to tell me that I am free.[11]

1926: Commissioner Burke - Taxation of Restricted Indian Property

As reported in 1921 by Commissioner Burke, the loss of Indian allotments continued.

> Numerous tracts of land bought for homes for Indians with their restricted nontaxable funds, and conveyed with restrictions against alienation or incumbrance without the consent of the Secretary of the Interior, have been taxed by local authorities, and some of the lands were sold for nonpayment of assessments. Chas. Burke, Commissioner of Indian Affairs.[12]

> *The records show that the lands of a vast majority of Indians who have been given absolute control of their allotments have passed from Indian ownership in various ways-by sale for small values, through unredeemed mortgages, and in some instances by tax deeds.* Therefore a very decided halt was necessary to protect allottees appearing to be competent, and in no cases are fee patents now granted or restrictions on lands otherwise removed unless the evidence from the field clearly justifies the belief that the applicant is competent. (Emphasis added).[12]

NOTES

1. *U.S. v. Albert B. Fall*: The Teapot Dome Scandal, Jake Kobrick, Associate Historian, Federal Judicial History Office, Federal Judicial Center, 2020. https://www.fjc.gov/history/cases/famous-federal-trials/us-v-albert-b-fall-teapot-dome-scandal (accessed online November 27, 2024). Teapot Dome Scandal, History.Com. https://www.history.com/topics/1920s/teapot-dome-scandal (accessed online November 27, 2024).
2. Report of the Commissioner of Indian Affairs to the Secretary of the Interior, United States. Office of Indian Affairs, 1921, p. 26.
3. Report of the Commissioner of Indian Affairs to the Secretary of the Interior, United States. Office of Indian Affairs, 1921, pp. 25-26.
4. Report of the Commissioner of Indian Affairs to the Secretary of the Interior, United States. Office of Indian Affairs, 1921, pp. 25–26.
5. "An Act to authorize the cancellation, under certain conditions, of patents in fee simple to Indians for allotments held in trust by the United States," 44 Stat. 1247 (February 26, 1927).
6. Report of the Commissioner of Indian Affairs to the Secretary of the Interior, United States. Office of Indian Affairs, 1923, p. 1.
7. Annual Report of the Board of Indian Commissioners, 1922-1923 (Washington: Government Printing Office), p. 3. https://babel.hathitrust.org/cgi/pt?id=umn.31951d027014679&seq=3 (accessed online October 5, 2024).
8. Report of the Commissioner of Indian Affairs to the Secretary of the Interior, United States. Office of Indian Affairs, 1923, pp. 20-21.
9. The Religious Freedom Issue, (1924-25), Chapter 9. https://ia601509.us.archive.org/32/items/in.ernet.dli.2015.117914/2015.117914.The-Assault-On-Assimilation_text.pdf. Chapter 9 pp. (accessed online November 28, 2024).

10. https://www.onondaganation.org/news/2018/the-citizenship-act-of-1924/ (accessed online April 30, 2024). Robert B. Porter, The Demise of the Ongwehoweh and the Rise of the Native Americans: Redressing the Genocidal Act of Forcing American Citizenship upon Indigenous Peoples, 15 Harvard BlackLetter Law Journal 107 (Spring, 1999).

11. https://www.minotdailynews.com/news/local-news/2020/06/chief-old-dog-leader-among-hidatsa/ (accessed online April 30, 2024).

12. Report of the Commissioner of Indian Affairs to the Secretary of the Interior, United States. Office of Indian Affairs, 1926, p. 10.

13. Report of the Commissioner of Indian Affairs to the Secretary of the Interior, United States. Office of Indian Affairs, 1926, pp. 10-11.

CHAPTER 47: Board of Indian Commissioners ("BIC")

PART 1: 1869: Congress Enacts Legislation Establishing BIC to Advise Indian Bureau

In 1869, Congress enacted legislation for establishing the Board of Indian Commissioners to advise the Indian Bureau, in response to the growing feeling that nongovernmental oversight of the Indian Bureau was essential. Without it, graft and inefficiency would complicate the Indian problem and plunge the nation into a series of brutal and devastating Indian wars. Thus the Board of Indian Commissioners would provide sorely needed supervision.[1]

The 1869 Indian Appropriation Bill stated, in part:

And for the purpose of enabling the President to execute the power conferred by this act, he is authorized, at his discretion, to organize a board of Commissioners, to consist of not more than ten persons, to be selected by him eminent for their intelligence and philanthropy, to serve without pecuniary compensation, who may, under his direction, exercise joint control with the Secretary of the Interior over the disbursement of the appropriations made by this act, or any part thereof, that the President may designate.

BIC Appointed, Presidential Instructions

President Grant appointed the Board to cooperate with the Interior Department in securing a sound and progressive administration of Indian affairs. In his initial instructions to the Board, President Grant listed the regulations to govern the Board's joint supervision of the Indian Bureau.[2]

The BIC was to:

1. Establish its own organization and to employ its own clerical assistants.
2. Have the ability to inspect the records of the Indian Office and to obtain full information from it.
3. Have full power to inspect the various Indian superintendencies and agencies; to be present at the payment of annuities, councils, and negotiations; and to advise the agents and superintendents.
4. Be present at the purchase of goods for Indian purposes.
5. Make recommendations for changes and advisement of the agents through the Interior Department and Commissioner of Indian Affairs.
6. Determine the plans of civilizing or dealing with the Indians.

7. Make all requests for expenditures through the Treasury Department and their approval was subject to the law.
8. Have the complete cooperation of the offices associated with the Indian Service.
9. Maintain records or minutes of their meetings.[3]

NOTES: PART 1

1. Annual Report of the Board of Indian Commissioners, 1870 (Washington: Government Printing Office), p. 1. https://babel.hathitrust.org/cgi/pt?id=nyp.33433081889085&seq=12 (accessed online October 5, 2024).
2. Ulysses S. Grant, Executive Order, June 3, 1869.
3. Ulysses S. Grant, Executive Order Paraphrased; Report of the Commissioner of Indian Affairs to the Secretary of the Interior, 1869, Accompanying Papers, Report of the Board of Indian Commissioners to the Secretary of the Interior (1869), United States. Office of Indian Affairs, p. 44.

PART 2: BIC Castigates U.S. Treatment of Indians

1869: BIC Report – Treatment Received by Indians Unjust and Iniquitous Beyond Words

While it cannot be denied that the government of the United States, in the general terms and temper of its legislation, has evinced a desire to deal generously with the Indians, *it must be admitted that the actual treatment they have received has been unjust and iniquitous beyond the power of words to express.* ... (Emphasis added).[1]

... The history of the Government connections with the Indians is a shameful record of broken treaties and unfulfilled promises. The history of the border, white man's connection with the Indians is a sickening record of murder, outrage, robbery, and wrongs committed by the former, as the rule, and occasional savage outbreaks and unspeakably barbarous deeds of retaliation by the latter, as the exception.[2]

In addition to the class of robbers and outlaws who find impunity in their nefarious pursuits upon the frontiers, there is a large class of professedly reputable men who use every means in their power to bring on Indian wars, for the sake of the profit to be realized from the presence of troops and the expenditure of government funds in their midst. They proclaim death to the Indians at all times, in words and publications, making no distinction between the innocent and the guilty. They incite the lowest class of men to the perpetration of the darkest deeds against their victims, and, as judges and jurymen, shield them from the justice due to their crimes. Every crime committed by a white man against an Indian is concealed or palliated ... (Emphasis added).³

1869: BIC Blistering, Scathing Report Denouncing Federal Government and Those Cheating Indians under Its Aegis

In the BIC 1869 Report they pronounced the first of many blistering and scathing attacks against the federal government and those cheating the Indians under its aegis:

> Paradoxical as it may seem, the white man has been the chief obstacle in the way of Indian civilization. The benevolent measures attempted by the government for their advancement have been almost uniformly thwarted by the agencies employed to carry them out. *The soldiers, sent for their protection, too often carried demoralization and disease into their midst. The agent*, appointed to be their friend and counsellor, business manager, and the almoner of the government bounties, *frequently went among them only to enrich himself in the shortest possible time, at the cost of the Indians*, and spend the least available sum of the government money with the least ostensible beneficial result. *The general interest of the trader was opposed to their enlightenment as tending to lessen his profits*. Any increase of intelligence would render them less liable to his impositions; and, if occupied in agricultural pursuits, their product of furs would be proportionally decreased. *The contractor's and transporter's interests were opposed to it, for the reason that the production of agricultural products on the spot would measurably cut off their profits in furnishing army supplies. The interpreter knew that if they were taught, his occupation would be gone. The more submissive and patient the tribe the greater the number of outlaws infesting their vicinity; and all these were the missionaries teaching them the most degrading vices of which humanity is capable. If in spite of these obstacles a tribe made some progress in agriculture, or their lands became valuable from any cause, the process of civilization was summarily ended by driving them away from their homes with fire and sword, to undergo similar experiences in some new locality.* Whatever may have been the original character of the aborigines, many of them are now precisely what the course of treatment received from the whites must necessarily have made them-suspicious, revengeful, and cruel in their retaliation. (Emphasis added).⁴

1871: BIC's Scorching Attack on U.S. as Cause of Most Indian Wars

Probably all will agree that the rapid development of our western Territories, by which the Indians have been gradually driven from one reservation to another, together with dishonest management, and execution of treaties by bad agents, have caused most of our Indian wars. John V. Farwell, Felix R. Brunot.[5]

BIC's Report Lists Grievances with U.S.' Treatment of Indians

1. The dissatisfaction of the Indians in consequence of having sometimes been betrayed into the cession of their lands by pretended treaties.
2. The constant failure of the government to fulfill in good faith its treaty obligations with the tribes.
3. The frequent and unprovoked outrages and murders of Indians by soldiers and white citizens.
4. The impossibility of obtaining justice in local courts, or of punishing white criminals, for the reason that the testimony of Indians is not allowed in those courts.
5. The unlawful occupation, by the whites, of lands not ceded nor treated for.
6. The shameful fact, that of all the appropriations made by Congress for their benefit but a small part ever reaches them.

It is also affirmed, by the same authorities, that the Indian race is becoming not only morally degraded, but also physically undermined, by the most loathsome disease [syphilis] which infests our civilization; that one of the finest physical types of man has already become seriously enfeebled; and that tribes, originally comparatively pure, are fast sinking into a grossness of vice which threatens their utter extinction.

This latter evil, in all its destructive extent, seems to be an inevitable attendant of the presence of our troops in the Indian country. All these, and many other disgraceful facts, are attested by respectable officers of the government, by a large number of Indian chiefs, and by many trustworthy private citizens.

The unprovoked butchery of several hundred peaceable Indians, chiefly women and children, by Colonel Chivington, [perpetrated under the authority and in the name of the United States] ... is enough to brand with lasting infamy any nation that could suffer it to pass unpunished. ...

No nation can safely disregard the just claims of even the humblest class of its citizens. The promise made by General Sherman to the Indians, that their rights should be respected, and that they should be justly compensated for the necessary infringement of those rights, found an echo in the hearts of all honorable men. No nation is more sensitive to the claims and obligations of justice than our own; and we are sure that when the true history of the Indians' wrongs is laid before our countrymen, their united voice will demand that the honor and the interests of the nation shall no longer be sacrificed to the insatiable lust and avarice of unscrupulous men.

The good intentions of Congress toward the Indians have, in great measure been frustrated by the want of honest and faithful agents, with sufficient power to control the rapacity of frontier practice.[6]

NOTES: PART 2

1. Report of the Commissioner of Indian Affairs to the Secretary of the Interior, 1869, Accompanying Papers, Report of the Board of Indian Commissioners to the Secretary of the Interior (1869), United States. Office of Indian Affairs, p. 47.
2. Id.
3. Report of the Commissioner of Indian Affairs to the Secretary of the Interior, 1869, Accompanying Papers, Report of the Board of Indian Commissioners to the Secretary of the Interior (1869), United States. Office of Indian Affairs, p. 47.
4. Report of the Commissioner of Indian Affairs to the Secretary of the Interior, 1869, Accompanying Papers, Report of the Board of Indian Commissioners to the Secretary of the Interior (1869), United States. Office of Indian Affairs, p. 48.
5. Report of the Commissioner of Indian Affairs to the Secretary of the Interior, 1869, Accompanying Papers, Report of the Board of Indian Commissioners to the Secretary of the Interior (1869), United States. Office of Indian Affairs, pp. 43-44.
6. Report of the Commissioner of Indian Affairs to the Secretary of the Interior, 1869, Accompanying Papers, Report of the Board of Indian Commissioners to the Secretary of the Interior (1869), United States. Office of Indian Affairs, pp. 49-50.

PART 3: Overlap of Duties between Indian Bureau and BIC to Cause Troubled Rivalry

1869: Commissioner Parker Submits Questions to BIC – Mirrors His Own Duties – Evidences Overlapping Conflict to Occur between Indian Bureau and Oversight BIC

Commissioner Parker submitted questions to BIC in his bailiwick by letter of May 26, 1869. It demonstrated the COMPLETE overlap of duties between the Indian Bureau and BIC! Seeking to demonstrate the authority of the Secretary of the Interior, **BIC's responses were to be submitted to the Secretary who would choose, when necessary, to forward them to the President and Congress.**

A determination or settlement of what should be the legal status of the Indians; a definition of their rights and obligations under the laws of the United States, of the States and Territories and treaty stipulations; whether any more treaties shall be stipulated with the Indians, and if not, what legislation is necessary for those with whom there are existing treaty stipulations, and what for those with whom no such stipulations exist; should the Indians be placed upon reservations, and what is the best method to accomplish this object; should not legislation discriminate between the civilized and localized Indians, and the united roving tribes of the plains and mountains; what changes are necessary in existing laws relating to purchasing goods and provisions for the Indians, in order to prevent fraud, &c; should any change be made in the method of paying money annuities; and if so, what. Great mischief, evils, and frequently serious results follow from friendly Indians leaving the reservations, producing conflicts between the citizens, soldiers, and Indians. At what time and point shall the civil rule cease and military rule begin.

Is any change required in the intercourse laws by reason of the present and changed condition of the country? I respectfully suggest that inspection should be made by your commission of as many Indian tribes, especially the wild and roving ones, as the time of the honorable commissioners will permit, and their conditions and wants be reported on, with, any suggestions that each case may seem to require. Also, the accounts of superintendents and agents should be examined, and the efficiency or inefficiency of those officers should be reported upon. All suggestions, recommendations, and reports from the commission should be made to the honorable Secretary of the Interior, to be by him submitted, when necessary, to the President and Congress.[1]

1869: BIC's Indian Policy Recommendations to Commissioner Parker Critical – Set Entire Agenda for Indian Bureau

The BIC, unafraid to respond to the enormous task set by Commissioner Parker, unhesitatingly responded to his questions, **ESSENTIALLY,** *setting the Indian policy agenda for the Indian Bureau into the twentieth century*. The BIC had enormous authority and wielded it boldly, visiting tribes across the country, repeatedly. The President and the Secretary of the Interior engaged BIC members to constitute Peace Commissions to negotiate for reductions of tribal lands or the outright removal of tribes, primarily to the Indian Territory. It is no wonder that Commissioner Parker was abrasive to the BIC, as he saw his authority diminished. With BIC's authority to award government contracts pertaining to Indians, it exercised influence in the commercial sector, as well.

The BIC dictated (1) the consolidation of tribes on smaller reservations, preferably in the Indian Territory; (2) allotment of land in severalty; (3) breaking-up tribal relations; (4) abandoning and abrogating treaties; (5) taxing civilized tribes in Indian Territory; (6) duty to educate Indians in industry, civilization and the principles of Christianity; (7) establishing judicial tribunals for punishment of crime; (8) eliminating payment of money annuities; (9) clothing and sustaining them temporarily; and (10) the aim of citizenship. With the President's concurrence, it was postulated that "**the religion of our blessed Saviour is believed to be the most effective agent for the civilization of any people.**" Let there be no doubt, the BIC's Indian policy resulted in the destruction of tribal sovereignty, possession of communal tribal land, language, culture and religion of the tribes – they were at an end. Each year the BIC literally crusaded for Indian allotment in severalty, and U.S. citizenship to eradicate tribal bonds. To it, this pinnacle of achievement, in the total assimilation of the Indians into the U.S. body politic and nation would solve the Indian problem. No further entanglement in tribal or individual Indian affairs would be required. A huge expense of administration and support would evaporate. Each Indian would be siphoned off from its tribe, until there were no Indians or tribes. They would christen this as the Vanishing Indian Policy.

> *The treaty system should be abandoned, and as soon as any just method can be devised to accomplish it, existing treaties should be abrogated.*
>
> The payment of money annuities to the Indians should be abandoned, for the reason that such payments encourage idleness and vice, to the injury of those whom it is intended to benefit. Schools should be established, and teachers employed by the government to introduce the English language in every tribe. It is believed that many of the difficulties with Indians occur from misunderstandings as to the meaning and intention of either party. The teachers employed should be nominated by some religious body having a mission nearest to the location of the school. The establishment of Christian missions should be encouraged, and their schools fostered. The pupils should at least receive the rations and clothing they would get if remaining with their families. **The religion of our blessed Saviour is believed to be the most effective agent for the civilization of any people**.
>
> The honest and prompt performance of all the treaty obligations to the reservation Indians is absolutely necessary to success in the benevolent designs of the administration. ...
>
> There should be some judicial tribunal constituted within the Indian territory competent to the prompt punishment of crime, whether committed by white man, Indian or negro. ... (Emphasis added).[2]

The BIC's indictment of federal Indian policy must be studied repeatedly to understand the gravity of the implications.

The United States first creates the fiction that a few thousand savages stand in a position of equality as to capacity, power and right of negotiation with a civilized nation. They next proceed to impress upon the savages, with all the forms of treaty and the solemnity of parchment, signatures and seals, the preposterous idea that they are owners in fee of fabulous tracts of country over which their nomadic habits have led them or their ancestors to roam. The title thus being settled, they purchase and promise payment for a portion of territory, and further bind themselves in most solemn manner to protect and defend the Indians in the possession of some immense remainder defined by boundaries in the treaty, thus becoming, as it were, *particeps criminis* with the savages in resisting the "encroachments" of civilization and the progressive movement of the age. Having entered into this last-named impracticable obligation, the fact of its non-performance becomes the occasion of a disgraceful and expensive war to subdue their victims to the point of submission to another treaty. ***And so the tragedy of war and the farce of treaty have been enacted "again and again, each time with increasing shame to the nation.***" (Emphasis added).[3]

Particeps criminis is a Latin term that refers to someone who is involved in a crime, either as an accomplice or a co-conspirator - a person who is aware of criminal activity and may have played a role in planning or carrying out the crime.

1870: Congress Continues BIC, Expansion of Duties in 1871

A Congressional Act in 1870 extended the life of the BIC until such a time when Congress no longer appropriated funds for its expenses. "It shall be the duty of said commissioners," this Act declared, "to supervise all expenditures of money appropriated for the benefit of the Indians in" the U.S., and to inspect all the goods purchased for said Indians, in connection with the Commissioner of Indian Affairs, whose duty it shall be to consult said committee in making purchases of such goods.[4]

The powers of the BIC were further expanded under the provisions of the Congressional Act of March 1, 1871, which provided: That hereafter no payments shall be made by any officer of the United States to contractors for goods or supplies of any sort to be furnished to the Indians, or for the transportation thereof, or for any building or machinery erected or placed on their reservations ... until the accounts and vouchers have been submitted to the executive committee of the Board of Indian Commissioners ... and it shall be the duty of said board of commissioners, without unnecessary delay, to forward said accounts and vouchers ... to the Secretary of the Interior, with the reasons for their approval or disapproval of the same, in whole or in part, attached thereto; and said Secretary shall have the power to sustain, set aside or modify the action of said board and cause payment to be made or withheld, as he may designate.

1871: Interior Secretary Delano Inordinately Praises BIC

In reporting to the President, Secretary of the Interior Columbus Delano inordinately praised the BIC: they had "shrunk from no self-sacrifice, toil or danger in endeavoring to make the policy you [Congress] have adopted toward the Indian an entire success."[5] This didn't help the clash between the OIA and the BIC in overlapping responsibilities, where the OIA had been accused of graft and inefficiency.

1871: BIC Undertakes Campaign to Remove Commissioner Parker

The BIC resented Commissioner Parker's authority and undertook a campaign to remove him from office. They undertook a personal investigation! Feeling that his authority had been undermined, Parker resigned from office in 1871.[6]

1872: BIC Demands Board of Inspectors, Under Its Control, to Enable It to Fulfill Congressional Duties; Advises Extension of Law over Indians for Punishment of Crimes

> BIC's request in 1869 for a Board of Inspectors of "capable and reliable men, independent of political or party bias, who shall not be remunerated from the public treasury, and who shall have no pecuniary interest to swerve them from the objects of their appointment" was approved in 1872.[7]
>
> The experience of three years has convinced us of the inexpediency of attempting any general legislation to supersede the present laws regulating the Indian service. The great diversity of circumstances and conditions, and degrees of barbarism or civilization of the tribes, suggest difficulties which can only be fully estimated from personal observation of their differences. Laws suitable for the Sioux are totally inapplicable to the Indians of Puget Sound, and a code adapted to the latter would be absurd if applied to the Apaches. To attempt to extend civil law over the Apaches or the Sioux would simply be to inaugurate a state of continuous warfare.
>
> The measures which seem to us the most important to the welfare of the Indians, and the success of the efforts for their advancement, are—
> 1st. Extending the civil law of the United States over Indians.
> 3d. A more stringent law for the punishment of trespassers upon Indian reservations, and some effective mode by which it may be enforced. Also, to make Indian testimony lawful in all courts of the United States.
> 4th. As of great importance to maintain and perfect the system of reform in the Indian service, we recommend a board of inspectors, not less than five in number, to be selected by the President from

> such persons as shall be recommended by the annual meetings of the various religious denominations of the United States, who shall see proper to make such recommendation, to hold office during good behavior, or until removed by the President. They shall be charged with the duty of visiting each tribe at least once a year, to examine into the accounts, mode of doing business, and the conduct and management of the officers by and employes of the Government; see that treaty stipulations are kept by the United States, adopt such measures as will preserve the peace, examine into the educational progress of the Indians, hear their complaints, and right their wrongs, and witness the proper delivery of their annuities. They should have power to suspend agents or employes, subject to the President's approval, making immediate report of such suspension; to administer oaths, examine and report on claims for depredations, eject trespassers or improper persons from reservations, and call upon the military for aid when necessary. The board should be constituted of men of high character and ability, and should be paid a proper compensation, and give their exclusive attention to their duties. In connection with this, it is also recommended that the superintendencies, most of which we deem to be of doubtful utility in any case, be discontinued.[8]

The position held by the BIC that law must be extended over tribes, as they were prepared for it, did not undergo significant change in subsequent years. Many of the complex legal problems remained unsolved into the 1880's. In its demand, the BIC lists the laws that should be enacted, including "making the fraudulent practices of Indian agents, superintendents, employees and contractors felonies, and *imposing severe penalties of imprisonment.*" **The chasm between the BIC and the Indian Bureau became ever wider.** (Emphasis added).[9]

1872: Conflict between Indian Bureau and BIC Escalates; BIC Advocates for Independent Indian Department outside of DOI

With the rift widening between the Indian Bureau and the BIC, the BIC went so far as to seek the eradication of the Bureau.

> The conflict between the two groups led to a determined effort by the Board to establish an independent Indian Department with cabinet status. Opposition by members of Congress, politicians, and the existent Indian and Interior Departments thwarted the further development of the concept. With the defeat of the proposal, the Board members recognized that the system had changed only minimally.[10]

1874: BIC Gripes over Conflict with Indian Bureau

It was obvious, towards the close of 1873, that the original members of the Board of Indian Commissioners could not serve much longer. BIC Chairman Brunot wrote to President Grant of the difficulty in working within the constraints imposed by its duties:

> Experience has shown that a Board of Indian Commissioners clothed with proper authority, and acting in cooperation with the Department of the Interior, but not under its direction or control, can hardly maintain harmonious relations with that Department. On the other hand, a Board not so constituted, and under the influence or control of the Interior Department would be a comparatively useless appendage to the service.[11]

As a result, at the end of 1874, the original BIC members resigned in protest. Felix R. Brunot, Robert Campbell, William E. Dodge, John V. Farwell, Nathan Bishop, Edward S. Tobey, and George H. Stuart left the Board. The other two original members, Henry S. Lane and Vincent Colyer, had already left in 1870 and 1873 respectively.

1876: BIC Pressures for Independent Indian Department outside of DOI

BIC continued its dead-in-the-water proposal for a separate Indian Department, with Cabinet status.

> Our Indian affairs should be managed by an independent department. ... The head of the Department of the Interior is already burdened with five distinct bureaus, viz, Pension, Patent, Land, Education, and Indian. He cannot give to Indian affairs that patient attention which is necessary to success. The War Department, as its name indicates, is unsuited for the work of civilization.[12]

NOTES: PART 3

1. Report of the Commissioner of Indian Affairs to the Secretary of the Interior, 1869, Accompanying Papers, Report of the Board of Indian Commissioners to the Secretary of the Interior (1869), United States. Office of Indian Affairs, pp. 43-44.
2. Report of the Commissioner of Indian Affairs to the Secretary of the Interior, 1869, Accompanying Papers, Report of the Board of Indian Commissioners to the Secretary of the Interior (1869), United States. Office of Indian Affairs, pp. 49-50.
3. Report of the Commissioner of Indian Affairs to the Secretary of the Interior, 1869, Accompanying Papers, Report of the Board of Indian Commissioners to the Secretary of the Interior (1869), United States. Office of Indian Affairs, pp. 58-59.
4. United States Statutes at Large, XVI, p. 360.
5. Annual Report of the Secretary of the Interior, 1871, House Executive

Document No. 1, part 5, 42 Congress, 2 session, serial 1505, p. 3.
6. https://www.nps.gov/articles/000/president-ulysses-s-grant-and-federal-indian-policy.htm (accessed online October 2, 2024).
7. Report of the Commissioner of Indian Affairs to the Secretary of the Interior, 1869, Accompanying Papers, Report of the Board of Indian Commissioners to the Secretary of the Interior (1869), United States. Office of Indian Affairs, p. 96.
8. Annual Report of the Board of Indian Commissioners to the Secretary of the Interior, 1872 (Washington: Government Printing Office), pp. 19-20. https://babel.hathitrust.org/cgi/pt?id=ucl.31175 031092938&view=1up&seq=12 (accessed online October 2, 2024).
9. Annual Report of the Board of Indian Commissioners to the Secretary of the Interior, 1873 (Washington: Government Printing Office), p. 6. https://babel.hathitrust.org/cgi/pt?id=coo.31924071981298&seq=14 (accessed online October 2, 2024).
10. Annual Report of the Board of Indian Commissioners to the Secretary of the Interior, 1873 (Washington: Government Printing Office), p. 81. https://babel.hathitrust.org/cgi/pt?id=coo.31924071981298&seq=89&q1=winked (accessed online October 2, 2024).
11. Brunot el at. to President Grant, May 27, 1874.
12. Eighth Annual Report of the Board of Indian Commissioners, 1876 (Washington: Government Printing Office), pp. 18-19. https://babel.hathitrust.org/cgi/pt?id=mdp.39015027938565&seq=7 (accessed online October 2, 2024).

PART 4: Notwithstanding Danger and Death Staring Indians in Face, BIC Focuses on Individualizing Indians, Tearing Them Away from Only Source of Protection

1874: BIC's Policy of Visiting Indian Agencies Enables Witnessing Deadly Conditions Facing Indians

The broad Indian country encompassed by the BIC's annual Indian Agency visits and reports is unfathomable. Yet, the BIC would be fully aware of the poverty; exposure, starvation and diseased conditions facing Indians; and the private wars being fought to exterminate them. It must be classified as *particeps criminis*, along with the Indian Bureau.

1874: BIC Inspections and Surveys

Indian agencies in New York, Minnesota, Nebraska, Dakota, the Indian Territory, California, Oregon, and Washington Territory were visited and inspected.[1]

1878: BIC Inspections and Surveys

Indian agencies in Wisconsin; Colorado, Indian Territory; and Pacific Coast were visited and inspected.

1918-1919: BIC Inspections and Surveys

Indian agencies in Montana, ND, SD, CA, WIS, NY., Idaho, Nebr., Okla. and NM were visited and inspected.

1921- 1922: BIC Inspections and Surveys

Indian agencies in NM, AZ, CO, ND, SD, SO CA, WA, WIS, MISS, and OK were visited and inspected.

1922-1923: BIC Inspections and Surveys

Indian agencies in NM, SD, OK, ID, OR, IO, NEBR, WA, NY, and MT were visited and inspected.

1923-1924: BIC Inspections and Surveys

Eighteen reservations, agencies, and other branches of the Indian Service in AZ, NM, CO, UT, CA, KAN, MISS, NC, and NY were visited and inspected.[2]

NOTES: PART 4

1. Annual Report of the Board of Indian Commissioners to the Secretary of the Interior, 1874 (Washington: Government Printing Office), p. 5. https://babel.hathitrust.org/cgi/pt?id=mdp.39015039328144&seq=22 (accessed online October 2, 2024).
2. Annual Report of the Board of Indian Commissioners, 1923-1924 (Washington: Government Printing Office).

PART 5: BIC's Resolute Indian Policies

1874: Indians Should Be Encouraged to Renounce Tribal Relations for Individual Property and U.S. Citizenship until All Merged in Nation

> Isolation from the demoralizing influence of the class of white persons always found upon border settlements has been considered a condition requisite to the early improvement of the savage tribes until a certain period of advancement shall have been reached; the history of the world, however, demonstrates the fact that no community can ever reach an advanced stage of civilization without recognition of the right of individual property, and it is believed that whenever any tribe of Indians has reached such a stage of advancement in intelligence and good conduct as will enable the various members to transact their own business and participate in the affairs of the community with which they are surrounded, the policy of the Government should be to encourage such persons to

renounce their tribal relations and to establish individual homes for themselves and become invested with all the privileges of citizenship; that this process should continue from year to year, stimulated by every inducement the Government can properly offer, until the entire Indian race shall become merged in the community at large, and further intervention by the Government for their special care shall become unnecessary....[1]

1875: BIC - Abandon Tribal Relations, Individualizing Indians, No Bands or Tribes

The BIC's classification of Indians as 'wards' to be cared for is simply a mockery – 'disingenuous' in the extreme.

> The Indian, regarded as a "ward" of the government, needed guardianship in such a way to imply care and culture. The aim of the government, stated the Board, was "to reclaim the Indian from his rude, wild and savage state by the kindly influence of just dealing; by an undeviating observance of good faith; by a firm but kind and paternal rule over him; by protecting him from wrongs and aggressions; and by educating him ..."[2]

Reviewing the treatment of the Indians in Kansas is only one of the horrible stories of how Indians were 'cared for.' The Kansas state government and populace clamored for their removal. *The government's plan to remove the Indians in Kansas to the Indian Territory would open four million acres of prime agricultural land for white settlement and remove the powerful Osage tribe.*[3]

1876: Comprehensive, Expansive, Resolute BIC Indian Policy from 1869 Reaffirmed – (1) Indians Are Wards, Tribes Not Sovereignties; (2) Consolidate on Few Reservations; (3) Abolish Tribal Relations; (4) Allot Tribal Land in Severalty; (5) Impose U.S. Citizenship; (6) Yield Obedience to Law; (7) Establish Industrial and Agricultural Boarding Schools with Compulsory Attendance; and (8) Cease Disbursement of Annuities which Encourage Idleness and Vice

> The policy of collecting the Indian tribes upon small reservations contiguous to each other, and within the limits of a large reservation, eventually to become a State of the Union, seems to be the best that can be desired. Many tribes may thus be collected in the present Indian Territory. The larger the number that can thus be concentrated the better for the success of the plan, care being taken to separate hereditary enemies from each other. When upon the reservation, they should be taught as soon as possible the advantage of individual ownership of property, and should be given land in severalty, and the tribal relations should be discouraged...[4]

Since its inception, the BIC continually and persistently advocated for:

- treating Indians as wards of the U.S., not independent sovereignties;
- consolidating them upon few reservations;
- abolishing tribal relations;
- allotting lands in severalty;
- Indians becoming U.S. citizens speedily, that they may enjoy the protection of law, and *be required to yield obedience thereto*;
- educating Indian students in industry and the arts of civilization; and
- distributing appropriations in a manner discouraging idleness and vice.

> The commission has uniformly during the eight years of its existence, steadily and emphatically labored to uplift the Indian by all the institutions of civilization and religion. They believe the *Indians are the wards* of the Government, and in no sense should they be regarded or treated as independent sovereignties, that they should, so far as practicable, be *consolidated upon few reservations*, and provided with permanent individual homes; that the *tribal relation should be abolished*; that *lands should be allotted in severalty*, and not held or occupied in common; that the *Indians should become citizens of the United States speedily*, that they may enjoy the protection of law, and be required to yield obedience thereto; and that it is the duty of the Government to afford them all reasonable aid in their preparation for citizenship, by educating them in industry and the arts of civilization, and to so disburse appropriations for their benefit as to discourage idleness and vice.[5]

1876: BIC – Obstacle to Indian Progress, Absence of Laws Protecting Indians

The BIC's obstacle to Indian Progress – the lack of laws protecting Indians – was a subterfuge for its policy of making Indians comply with U.S. laws. It was well-known that whites refused Indians access to the courts to seek redress from the many injuries they suffered at the hands of whites. A paper law protecting them was illusory – a sleight of hand.

> The great obstacle to its complete success is that no change has been made in the laws for the care of Indians. The Indian is left without the protection of law in person, property, or life. He has no personal rights. He has no redress for wrongs inflicted by lawless violence. He may see his crops destroyed, his wife or child killed. His only redress is personal revenge. There is not a member of either house of Congress who does not know that, even with all the influences of Christian civilization, schools, churches, and social restraint, there is not a community of whites which could protect itself from lawless violence under the same conditions; and yet we take it for granted that the superior virtue of a savage race will enable it to achieve

civilization under circumstances which would wreck our own. In the Indian's wild state he has a rude government of chiefs and headmen, which is advisory in its character. When located upon reservations under the charge of a United States agent, this government is destroyed, and we give him nothing in its place.[6]

1899: Principles Advocated by BIC - A Vanishing Policy - Let Laws of States and Territories Govern Indians

It is the conviction of this board that all legislation for Indians, and the entire administration of affairs should look steadily to doing away with the away Indian problem - with the special administration of Indian affairs as a distinct bureau – at as early as a date as is consistent with justice. We have entire faith that before very many years shall have passed the Indians of the United States will be better off under the general laws of our States and Territories, and by incorporation with the great body of our American citizens, than they can possibly be under any system of 'paternal' government and peculiar and separate administration which could be devised to keep them permanently separate from the rest of our people.[7]

NOTES: PART 5

1. Annual Report of the Board of Indian Commissioners to the Secretary of the Interior, 1874 (Washington: Government Printing Office), p. 6. https://babel.hathitrust.org/cgi/pt?id=mdp.39015039328144&seq=22 (accessed online October 2, 2024).
2. Annual Report of the Board of Indian Commissioners, 1875 (Washington: Government Printing Office), p. 6. https://babel.hathitrust.org/cgi/pt?id=mdp.39015039328151&seq=12 (accessed online October 2, 2024).
3. Annual Report of the Department of Interior, Report of the Commissioner of Indian Affairs to the Secretary of the Interior, United States. U.S. Government Printing Office, 1865, p. 293.
4. Eighth Annual Report of the Board of Indian Commissioners, 1876 (Washington: Government Printing Office), p. 4. https://babel.hathitrust.org/cgi/pt?id=mdp.39015027938565&seq=7 (accessed online October 2, 2024).
5. Eighth Annual Report of the Board of Indian Commissioners, 1876 (Washington: Government Printing Office), p. 4. https://babel.hathitrust.org/cgi/pt?id=mdp.39015027938565&seq=7 (accessed online October 2, 2024).
6. Eighth Annual Report of the Board of Indian Commissioners, 1876 (Washington: Government Printing Office), p. 18. https://babel.hathitrust.org/cgi/pt?id=mdp.39015027938565&seq=7 (accessed online October 2, 2024).
7. Annual Report of the Board of Indian Commissioners, 1899 (Washington: Government Printing Office), pp. 18-19. https://babel.hathitrust.org/cgi/pt?id=mdp.39015081128962&seq=54&q1=citizenship&start=1 (accessed online October 5, 2024).

PART 6: BIC's Moral Indian Philosophy

1879: BIC - "Irrepressible Conflict" between Civilization and Barbarism; Barbarism Must Yield

In a moral tone eerily reminiscent of the past eras, the BIC pronounced as dogma that barbarism must yield to civilization.

> *It is as evident to every reflecting mind that civilization and barbarism cannot long live side by side as it was to President Lincoln that the country could not long remain "half slave and half free." There is the same "irrepressible conflict" between civilization and barbarism as between freedom and slavery. Barbarism must yield to and accept civilization, flee before it, or sooner or later be overborne by it.* As friends of the Indians, our efforts are directed to induce them to accept civilization, while as loyal citizens we use what influence we have to induce the government to be just, patient, kind, and even generous to this weak and ignorant race. ... (Emphasis added).

> *We may moralize over the natural rights of the Indian as much as we please, but after all they have their limit. His right to the soil is only possessory. He has not title in fee. If he will cultivate it and use it as civilized men use their possessions, it will and shall be well with him; but it is evident that no 12,000,000 acres of the public domain whose hills are full of ores, and whose valleys are waiting for diligent hands to "dress and keep them," in obedience to the divine command, can long be kept as a park, in which wild beasts are hunted by wilder men.* This Anglo-Saxon race will not allow the car of civilization to stop long at any line of latitude or longitude on our broad domain. If the Indian in his wileness plants himself on the track, he must inevitably be crushed by it. But when he sets his face and heart towards civilization, as many have done and are doing, then it becomes alike the interest and duty both of the government and the people to afford all needed aid. (Emphasis added).[1]

1880: Indians Not Going Away

Since Indians aren't dying out, the BIC advises the public that they should accept it.

> The most reliable statistics prove conclusively that the Indian population taken as a whole, instead of dying out under the light and contact of civilization, as has been generally supposed, is steadily increasing. The Indian is evidently destined to live as long as the

white race, or until he becomes absorbed and assimilated with his pale brethren. We should accept the situation, and go resolutely at work to make him a safe and useful factor in our body politic.

We hear no longer advocated among *really civilized men* the theory of extermination, a theory that would disgrace the wildest savage.

As we must have him among us, self-interest, humanity, and Christianity require that we should accept the situation, and go resolutely at work to make him a safe and useful factor in our body politic.

As a savage we cannot tolerate him any more than as a half-civilized parasite, wanderer, or vagabond. The only alternative left is to fit him by education for civilized life.

The public sentiment of our country appreciates as it never has before our duty and responsibility in this respect. *It is unwilling to perpetuate in our midst a race of paupers and pagans, groping in a superstition and barbarism unknown in the darkest ages.* The nation learned by costly experience that "it was cheaper to feed than to fight the Indian," and the same common sense teaches "it is cheaper to teach than to feed them." ... (Emphasis added).[2]

The important measure to encourage productive industry is a sure title. ... Our opinion is still unchanged, and our conviction becomes more decided with each year's; experience, that no people will reach a high state of civilization under the communistic system, and without the incentive to labor and enterprise that the right to individual ownership... of property inspires. *To many Indian tribes we are bound by treaty stipulations to grant these individual rights, and yet these solemn treaties remain a dead letter...* (Emphasis added).[3]

NOTES: PART 6

1. Annual Report of the Board of Indian Commissioners, 1879 (Washington: Government Printing Office), pp. 11-12. https://babel.hathitrust.org/cgi/pt?id=mdp.39015039328169&seq=18 (accessed online October 5, 2024).
2. Twelfth Annual Report of the Board of Indian Commissioners (1880), p. 8. https://babel.hathitrust.org/cgi/pt?id=hvd.32044021159991&seq=14 (accessed online October 5, 2024).
3. Twelfth Annual Report of the Board of Indian Commissioners (1880), pp. 7-8. https://babel.hathitrust.org/cgi/pt?id=hvd.32044021159991&seq=14 (accessed online October 5, 2024).

PART 7: 1880: BIC Faltering – New York Times Denounces BIC as Failure

On January 8, 1880 the New York Times denounced the Board a failure. It noted that the duties assigned to the Board were much too broad to be dealt with effectively. The Board had become merely a sanctioning body for all that the Commissioner of Indian Affairs had done. ... The Times article proved just the beginning of the battle for the Board's survival. (Emphasis added).[1]

1880: House of Representatives Refuses to Fund BIC; Senate Secretly provides Funds

The House refused to fund the BIC. But the Senate came to the rescue. The Senate ingeniously hid the appropriation for the Board within another bill to be sent to the House. Since the bill did not pass through the House Committee on Indian Affairs, no one noticed the appropriation rider until after approval had been granted. However, the scheme backfired, for the House provided no funds whatsoever for the Board in 1881, and carefully watched for any Senatorial attempt to circumvent its wishes.[2]

1882: Congress Restricts BIC's Power to Visiting Agencies and Inspecting Goods

A Congressional Act of May 17, 1882 provided that, "Hereafter the Commission shall only have power to visit and inspect agencies and other branches of the Indian Service, and to inspect goods purchased for such service and the Commissioner of Indian Affairs shall consult with the Commission in the purchase of supplies. By this action Congress removed the supervision of the expenditures of the Indian Service from the duties of the Board."

Without the authority to award government contracts, the Board lost much of its prestige and power.[3]

1882: BIC Coordinates Efforts with Lake Mohonk Friends of Indian

After Congress declined to fund the BIC, they joined hands with the Lake Mohonk Friends of the Indian. Year after year, they attended, congratulated themselves and even printed the Proceedings of the Lake Mohonk Conferences in their entirety in their Annual Reports to the Secretary.

NOTES: PART 7

1. New York Times, January 8, 1880, p. 4. Cartwright, Charles Edward. "The Board of Indian Commissioners: hope, failure and abandonment 1869-1887." (1980), p. 160.

2. Congressional Record, X, April 28, 1880, 46 Congress, 2 session, pp. 2823-2829. Cartwright, Charles Edward. "The Board of Indian Commissioners: hope, failure and abandonment 1869-1887." (1980), p. 161.
3. Cartwright, Charles Edward. "The Board of Indian Commissioners: hope, failure and abandonment 1869-1887." (1980), p. 163.

PART 8: 1885: Delegation from BIC and Lake Mohonk Conference Meets with President Cleveland: Recommend Land in Severalty; Renegotiating Treaties; Imposition of Law; Citizenship

This meeting held on Nov. 10, 1885, with President Grover Cleveland, demonstrates the interlocking relationship of the BIC and the LMC members. The highest dignitaries coupled positions within the BIC and LMC. Officials with the Indian Bureau also attended. The BIC and LMC policies were brought front and center to President Cleveland to be consummated as soon as possible, hastening the transition of Indians to citizenship... This is clear and convincing evidence of the political clout of the BIC and LMC and the danger they represented to Indians in hastening the completion of their objectives. These included:

citizenship of the emancipated Indians;
land in severalty;
abrogation of the reservation;
cessation of annuities;
protection of law (i.e., obedience to); and
renegotiating treaties.

The committee from the Mohonk conference, General Clinton B. Fisk [Chairman of BIC, President of LMC], Hon. Erastus Brooks [State Board of Health, NY and LMC], Hon. Albert K. Smiley [BIC and LMC], Rev. Lyman Abbott, D. D. [LMC], Mrs. A. S. Quinton, [Woman's National Indian Association and LMC]; Miss Alice C. Fletcher [Peabody Museum Archeology and Ethnography and LMC], Mrs. J. C. Kinney [CONN Indian Rights Association and LMC], together with Hon. William H. Lyon [BIC and LMC], Hon. Merrill E. Gates [BIC and LMC], Hon. John Charlton [BIC and LMC], Hon. E. Whittlesey [BIC and LMC]; Maj. John H. Oberly, Superintendent of Indian Education and LMC; Mr. A. B. Upshaw and Miss M. S. Cook, of the Indian Bureau, were received by the President, and introduced by General Fisk.

> Mr. President: The questions which, in the briefest reference, seem to us to demand the most immediate attention are those which relate to land and education, homes and families, and which in these relations seem to us to be what is now known as the new Indian policy. ... The time has now come to ... make the Indian a ***self-supporting citizen***, and with all the rights, privileges, and duties which belong to citizenship. ... What is now needed in regard to ***lands is severalty*** and individuality, with the ***protection of law*** ...

Rev. Abbott: *Wherever treaties stand in the way of reform; the present administration can negotiate for changes in those treaties.*[1]

1885: BIC and LMC Delegates Meeting with Secretary Lamar; Secretary Equates Immediate Citizenship with a War of Indian Extermination

Thereafter, the same group met with Secretary of Interior Lamar. It is only the Secretary that realized the gravity of the harm that would occur to Indians, if the BIC/LMC policies were hastily enacted, equating it with a war of extermination of the Indians:

> The SECRETARY. My idea is that the Indian cannot stand it to be thrown out; unprotected into the civilization of this country. *It would be almost as bad as a war of extermination, and until he is fitted to protect himself he should be kept under reservation influences, and the tribal system should not be entirely broken up.*
>
> General FISK. You also believe that it is best to *hasten that transition as fast as possible*?
>
> The SECRETARY: *Those that are ready; I will push on, and those that are not I will protect.*
>
> Mr. ABBOT. I would like to emphasize this, that there are quite a number of Indians now who desire to get lands in severalty.
>
> The SECRETARY: We could solve the problem as far as we are concerned by making him a citizen and giving him the right of suffrage. ... We could do that; but in my opinion *it would be most sad service to the Indian, and there would not be much of him left if that were done suddenly.*[2]

BIC/LMC Letter to President

> LMC Letter to President: the *abrogation of the reservation system* and the *citizenship of the Indian* are the two great ends to be steadily kept in view and immediately, vigorously, and continuously pursued...
>
> We therefore unite in recommending that Congress be asked to provide for the creation of an executive commission, to be appointed by the President, to open negotiations with the various tribes, as rapidly as in the judgment of the President is compatible with the safety and well-being both of the Indians and their white neighbors, in order to *secure their consent to the abrogation of the reservation, to land in severalty, to the cessation of annuities, and to the citizenship of the emancipated Indians.* Gen. Fisk

We believe that the time is fully ripe for the inauguration of such a policy. This is no sudden conclusion; we have come to it gradually, as the result of study and deliberation. And it is our profound conviction; that this administration can render no greater service to the nation than by inaugurating, and if possible carrying through to its consummation, a policy which shall solve the Indian problem by emancipating the Indian from his present condition of pupilage and pauperism, and his white neighbor from their alternate experiences of terror and of wrath. (Emphasis added).[3]

NOTES: PART 8

1. Annual Report of the Board of Indian Commissioners, 1885 (Washington: Government Printing Office), pp. 111-117. https://babel.hathitrust.org/cgi/pt?id=mdp.39015081128962&seq=5 (accessed online October 5, 2024).
2. Id.
3. Id.

PART 9: BIC's Legislative Position with Congress

1887: BIC Praises GAA

In 1880, 1881, 1883, 1883 and every year to 1887 the Board had urged the passage of legislation providing for individual allotments of land to those Indians capable of receiving them.

> In a speech before the Conference of the Board of Indian Commissioners, in Washington, last winter, the author of this bill, Senator Dawes, said: "If my land-in-severalty bill should become a law, it will depend entirely on the character of the Government agents who execute its provisions, whether it is a success or a failure. If it be intrusted to men of unflinching honesty and broad views, the Indians will be secure in the possession of homes on the best lands of the reservations; but *if it is intrusted to dishonest men, the Indians will be cheated out of their lands.*" (Emphasis added).[1]

BIC was pleased with the GAA in its 1887 report.

> The bill is a great step in advance in our Indian policy, and the day when it was approved by the President may be called the Indian emancipation day. The measure gives the Indian the possibility to become a man instead of remaining a ward of the Government. ... "The law is only the seed, whose germination and growth will be a slow process, and we must wait patiently for its mature fruit."[2]

Some whole tribes are unprepared for the execution of the law or to profit by it if it were by force applied to them. Hence we are pleased to notice that the Executive has begun the work of allotments under the provisions of the new act upon some of the smaller reservations where the Indians are somewhat advanced in education and habits of industry. Twenty-seven reservations have been selected.³

Our recommendations therefore include: (1) The establishment of courts at points accessible to all Indians. (2) Provision for the expenses of courts and public improvements, so long as Indian lands are exempt from taxation. (3) The application of civil-service principles to all appointments in the Indian service.⁴

1894: Abolishing Indian Bureau Is Idle Talk

The talk of abolishing all agencies and the Indian Bureau is, in existing conditions, idle talk. We recommend extreme caution in this direction. (Emphasis added).⁵

1895: Legislation Needed - Indian Service Should Be in Nonpartisan Commission, Not DOI; Prohibiting Sales of Allotted Lands

(1) To provide, as recommended by the Secretary of the Interior, for placing the Indian service in the hands of nonpartisan commissioners ...
(5) To provide for better regulating of leases and prohibiting sales of allotted lands
(6) To provide for the payment of depredation claims without encroaching upon Indian trust funds which are needed for their support and education.⁶

1900: Greatest Need - Comprehensive and Unified Indian Policy

> *... this board wishes to record its conviction that there is great need of a comprehensive and continuous policy of administration in Indian affairs which shall look to the speedy extinction of a separate bureau for Indians and a separate Indian administration.* (Emphasis added).

THE NEW METHOD RECOGNIZES THE INDIVIDUAL. When Congress, in 1871, voted to make no more treaties with Indian tribes as tribes, it erected a notable milestone at a turning point in the history of our Indian policy. For nearly a century the Government had proceeded upon the theory that each Indian tribe in the territory of the United States was to be regarded as a political entity, an imperium-in-imperio which might demand of its equal before international law the Government of the United States, something of the formal consideration accorded to a civilized and established State. To do away with this hollow pretense was a great gain. The laws and institutions of the United States should not be suspended by the interference of any other governmental power in any part of the territory of the United States.⁷

1908: Pressure by White Citizens to Get Hold of Restricted Indian Lands Is Constant and Intense

We respectfully commend to the Department and to Congress great caution in legislation and in administrative acts which look to the further removal of restrictions upon the alienation of the homesteads and severalty holdings of Indians, and particularly of Indian women and minor children. *The pressure on the part of white citizens to get hold of such lands is constant and intense. Petitions to Congress, resolutions of boards of trade passed in the interest of white settlers rather than from considerations of what is best for the Indians and for the public domain, are evidence of the intense economic pressure for land and lumber as the States and Territories of the West become more densely settled.* (Emphasis added).⁸

1912-1913: Open Court of Claims to Indian Claims

In line with the Society of American Indians, BIC recommended legislation to permit the proper presentation of Indian claims before the Court of Claims under contracts with attorneys that properly safeguard the rights of the Indians.⁹

1918: Turning Indians Loose Should Receive Scant Attention

TURNING THE INDIANS LOOSE. *For a number of years there has been more or less agitation for Congress to abolish the Bureau of Indian Affairs by releasing all Indians, without regard to degree of blood competency, from Government supervision.* ... The removal of restrictions from Indians is an individual, not a group, question, excepting as respects those people who have a larger proportion of white than of Indian blood and who are under Federal supervision to a greater or lesser degree. Such people should be given full control of any money and property which the Government holds in trust for them as soon as possible, and thus be entirely released from Federal supervision. But *where a person is of one-half or more Indian blood the greatest care should be exercised in the removal of restrictions, else in turning him loose the Government may be handing an unprotected incompetent over to an unscrupulous exploiter who had made his plans to rob the Indian even before the latter had received his certificate of independence. We are informed there have been many such instances* ... Almost all of the full-blood and three-quarter-blood and many of the half blood Indians will need intelligent supervision of their personal and property affairs by their guardian, the United States, for a number of years. In considering this most important question it is well to bear in mind that 73 per cent of the Indians, exclusive of those in the Five Civilized Tribes, are full-blood, three-quarter-blood, and half-blood, and that this percentage is about 50 in the Five Civilized Tribes. Also that only 55 per cent of all Indians under Federal supervision, exclusive of the Five Tribes, are reported as being able to speak the English language, and that only 37 per cent can read and write English. *With this showing of the Indians' ignorance of the language of the United States and of the large percentage of half and better Indian bloods, the cry from interested quarters to turn all Indians loose immediately should receive scant attention.* (Emphasis added).[10]

1922: BIC for Hastening End of Government's Supervision of Indians

Whereas in 1918, BIC counseled against immediate termination of the Indians guardianship, by 1922, BIC was for "hastening the time when the Government's supervision over Indians will come to an end."

> The Indian problem to-day, therefore, has in it something of the character of salvage, of reconditioning, of the building up of this dependent population group into American citizens who will be the equal of the white citizenry of the Nation. It follows, then, that to prepare, *to train our Indian people for the best type of American citizenship, and their absorption into the citizenship of the Nation, is the prime duty of the Government toward its Indian wards.* (Emphasis added).[11]

NOTES: PART 9

1. "Head of the National Indian Defense Association Opposes the Dawes Act." Issues & Controversies in American History. Infobase Learning, Web. 10 Dec. 2015.
2. Annual Report of the Board of Indian Commissioners to the Secretary of the Interior. Yr. 1887, p. 6. https://babel.hathitrust.org/cgi/pt?id=uc1.a0002911840&seq=13 (accessed online October 7, 2024).
3. Annual Report of the Board of Indian Commissioners to the Secretary of the Interior. Yr. 1887, p. 7. https://babel.hathitrust.org/cgi/pt?id=uc1.a0002911840&seq=13 (accessed online October 7, 2024).
4. Annual Report of the Board of Indian Commissioners to the Secretary of the Interior. Yr. 1887, p. 14. https://babel.hathitrust.org/cgi/pt?id=uc1.a0002911840&seq=13 (accessed online October 7, 2024).
5. Annual Report of the Board of Indian Commissioners, 1894 (Washington: Government Printing Office), p. 11. https://babel.hathitrust.org/cgi/pt?id=hvd.32044097929665&seq=7 (accessed online October 7, 2024).
6. Annual Report of the Board of Indian Commissioners, 1895 (Washington:

Government Printing Office), pp. 10-11. https://babel.hathitrust.org/cgi/pt?id=mdp.39015081128962&seq=54&q1=citizenship&start=1 (accessed online October 5, 2024).

7. Annual Report of the Board of Indian Commissioners, 1900 (Washington: Government Printing Office), p. 7. https://babel.hathitrust.org/cgi/pt?id=hvd.32044097929566&seq=7 (accessed online October 5, 2024).

8. Annual Report of the Board of Indian Commissioners, 1908 (Washington: Government Printing Office), p. 11. https://babel.hathitrust.org/cgi/pt?id=hvd.32044097929491&seq=5 (accessed online October 5, 2024).

9. Annual Report of the Board of Indian Commissioners, 1912 (Washington: Government Printing Office), p. 14. https://babel.hathitrust.org/cgi/pt?id=osu.32435064035769&seq=61 (accessed online October 5, 2024).

10. Annual Report of the Board of Indian Commissioners, 1918-19 (Washington: Government Printing Office), p. 8. https://babel.hathitrust.org/cgi/pt?id=osu.32435064035710&seq=105 (accessed online October 5, 2024).

11. Annual Report of the Board of Indian Commissioners, 1922-23 (Washington: Government Printing Office), p. 2. https://babel.hathitrust.org/cgi/pt?id=umn.31951d027014679&seq=3 (accessed online October 5, 2024).

CHAPTER 48: Lake Mohonk Conferences ("LMC")

In the autumn of 1883, Mr. Albert K. Smiley, the wealthy, philanthropic owner of a hostelry overlooking Lake Mohonk, situated on 1,325 acres of mountainous, wooded land beside a lake, invited a number of prominent men and women to meet as his guests for discussion of Indian policy. In 1879, President Hayes had appointed him as a member of the Board of Indian Commissioners. Mr. Smiley, concerned about the great diversity of opinion and practice prevailing, and the one day spent annually to discuss Indian policy, decided more time and debate was needed to advise the government administration on this pressing issue.

Mohonk was the ideal spot for lengthy debates. He invited the Board of Indian Commissioners, the Senate and House Committees on Indian Affairs, leading members of the Indian Bureau, War Department officers dealing with the Indian, the Indian Rights Association, Women's National Indian Association, heads of Indian schools, editors of leading papers, religious societies, and prominent philanthropic men all over the country.[1] A Platform was unanimously adopted each year, which was presented to the U.S. President.

LMC Motive in Addressing Public on 'Indian Problem'

> The motive, therefore, which has urged the members of the Mohonk Conference to issue their address to the public is twofold:
> 1st. To inform the people of the United States as to the most direct practicable way in which the Indian question may be solved. It was felt by all those who took part in the work of the Conference that a calm, definite, and earnest appeal made to the conscience and intelligence of the country in behalf of a poor and helpless people, and for the righting of a national wrong, would not be uttered in vain.
> 2. To stimulate the thoughtful and right-minded citizens of the country to take immediate steps toward the solution of the problem.[2]

LMC Goals

The Mohonk Conference Friends of the Indian ("Mohonk" or "LMC Members") goals for Indians remained constant from 1883 forward. Their planned, calculated program of assimilating an entire race of people was based on the following interrelated measures:

> The Platform. ... the object of all legislative and executive action hereafter should be not the isolation of the Indians, but the **abrogation of the Indian reservations as rapidly as possible,** the permitted diffusion of the Indians among the people in order that they may become acquainted with civilized habits and modes of life; the **ultimate discontinuance of annuities**, so promotive of idleness

and pauperism; the *subjection of the Indians to the laws of the United States, and of the States and Territories* where they may reside, and their protection by the same laws as those by which citizens are protected; the *opening of all the territory of the United States to their possible acquisition and to civilization,* and the early admission *of Indians to American citizenship.*[3]

The Mohonk plan of action ("POA") was deliberated at their annual three-to-five-day conferences and pronounced in their annual Platforms reached by consensus and vote. The "Proceedings of the Mohonk Lake Conference" published the debates on pertinent issues and the Annual Mohonk Platforms were published in their "Report of the Annual Lake Mohonk Conference on the Indian and Other Dependent Peoples," delivered to the U.S. president. The POA included the following:

> We must as rapidly as possible break up the tribal organization and give them law, with the family and land in severalty as its central idea. We must not only give them law, we must force law upon them. We must not only offer them education, we must force education upon them.[4]

> The uncivilized tribe enforces no law. The tribal relation dwarfs family life and weakens family ties. The reservation shuts off the Indians from civilization, and rations distributed unearned tend to pauperize them. Therefore we are convinced that the sooner family ties and family homesteads replace tribal relations and unsettled herding upon the reservation, the better. Give to every Indian family a home, where needful, with a protected title.[5]

See APPENDIX C: Lake Mohonk Friends of the Indian Annual Conferences: Platforms.

Interrelationship of LMC Members, Board of Indian Commissioners and Indian Bureau

Indian Bureau officials routinely attended, spoke at and were welcomed by the LMC that went on for thirty years. After Congress declined to fund the Board of Indian Commissioners, they joined hands with the LMC. Year after year, they attended, congratulated themselves and even printed the Proceedings of the Lake Mohonk Conferences in their Annual Reports to the Secretary, including their Platforms.

Dr. Carlos Montezuma, an Apache Indian reformer, castigated for his rhetoric, described this relationship aimed at ending the Indian existence:

The Indian Office, the Indian Rights Association and other organizations to "help" the Indians, have worked together so long that they seem to have been cemented or glued together, so that it is impossible to separate them. They see together, they move together and they speak together.⁶

LMC's Gargantuan Political Influence

In the 1889 Proceedings of the Lake Mohonk Conference, their political influence was proclaimed as follows:

> *...The first report of the Board of Indian Commissioners, twenty years ago, declared for nearly all the great reforms which this conference [Mohonk] has urged for many years. I suppose that all other influences combined have not been equal to the power of the Mohonk conference in matters of legislation. Our committees have had influence with the committees in Congress, and with the President of the United States, and the Commissioner of Indian Affairs, aided by our uninterrupted and plentiful letter-writing to members of Congress....* (Emphasis added).⁷

1885: Rev. Abbott - We Didn't Take Country from Indians

In 1885, Lyman Abbot, a well-known Congregational clergyman and LMC member, called for the end to the reservation system. He said: "It is sometimes said that the Indians occupied this country and that we took it away from them; that the country belonged to them. This is not true. The Indians did not occupy this land. A people do not occupy a country simply because they roam over it."⁸

1891: Indian Lands Could Be Legitimately Expropriated

LMC's President, Merrill Gates, pronounced that the Indian lands could legitimately be expropriated given the Indians using them merely to roam about:

> **But it is not possible that one hundred and eighty-one thousand miles of territory, more than all the New England and the Middle States, a territory almost as large as France or Spain, shall be forever kept out of civilization. It is too much to ask that the teeming life of America shall be shut out of this great territory, in order that the Indian may remain a savage and roam over it.** (Emphasis added).⁹

NOTES

1. Smiley, Alfred and Albert, Redlands Area Historical Society, Illustrated Redlands, 1897, pp. 50-51. https://rahs.org/photo/smiley-alfred-h-albert-k/ (accessed online November 12, 2024).
2. 2 Report of the Annual Lake Mohonk Conference on the Indian and Other Dependent Peoples (1884), pp. 3-4.
3. 3 Report of the Annual Lake Mohonk Conference on the Indian and Other Dependent Peoples (1885), p. 48.
4. E. Gates, Merrill. "6. Land and Law as Agents in Educating Indians". Americanizing the American Indian: Writings by the "Friends of the Indian" 1880-1900, edited by Francis Paul Prucha, Cambridge, MA and London, England: Harvard University Press, 1973.
5. 4 Report of the Annual Lake Mohonk Conference on the Indian and Other Dependent Peoples (1886), Business Committee Resolutions.
6. WASSAJA, Vol. 1, No. 8, November 1916. https://d1rbsgppyrdqq4.cloudfront.net/prism/s3fs-public/c195/WHS_Wassaja_V1_No8OCR.pdf?VersionId=WNDTI_ao1mQnxShGoO6tpw4TEvgOlq9L (accessed online October 10, 2024).
7. 7 Report of the Annual Lake Mohonk Conference on the Indian and Other Dependent Peoples (1889), p. 7.
8. 3 Report of the Annual Lake Mohonk Conference on the Indian and Other Dependent Peoples (1885), p. 51.
9. 9 Report of the Annual Lake Mohonk Conference on the Indian and Other Dependent Peoples (1891), p. 12.

CHAPTER 49: Ethnic Cleansing of American Indians

Assimilation of Indians

Speaking at the Lake Mohonk Conference in 1886, Phillip C. Garret, a member of the (1) Executive Committee of the Indian Rights Association, (2) elected President of the Mohonk Conference and a (3) member of the Board of Indian Commissioners, counseled for the destruction of the distinctions between Indians and non-Indians.

> *1886: If an act of emancipation will buy them life, manhood, civilization, and Christianity, at the sacrifice of a few chieftain's feathers, a few worthless bits of parchment, the cohesion of the tribal relation, and the traditions of their races; then, in the name of all that is really worth having, let us shed the few tears necessary to embalm these relics of the past, and have done with them; and, with fraternal cordiality, let us welcome to the bosom of the nation this brother whom we have wronged long enough.* (Emphasis added).[1]

A. 1887: Report of LMC Business Committee, Chair Rev. Dr. Lyman Abbott, Editor Christian Union, New York, Indian Must Become an American

Mohonk's philosophy of assimilation is summed up briefly by Chair of the Mohonk Business Committee, Rev. Lyman Abbott:

> The child must become a man, the Indian must become an American; the pagan must be new created a Christian.[2]

B. 1891: LMC Address of Dr. Merrill Gates: Solution of Indian Problem, Christianization of Whole Race

In his Address to the 1891 LMC Conference, Dr. Gates stated:

Our pleasure is the immediate and full preparation of all Indians for the duties and privileges of Christian citizenship in the United States.[3]

> *We can hereafter deal with them as they should be dealt with, not with each tribe as a little imperium in imperio, but with Indians as men and women dwelling upon our soil, subject to and supervised by the central government, where they are not yet intrusted to the States, and to be governed by law. ... It has become a profound conviction that the only way to deal with the Indian question, the only way to solve it, is by the education, the Christianization, of the whole race.* (Emphasis added).[4]

C. 1902: LMC Remained Persistent in Its Drive to Christian Manhood for Indian

The one effort of the Mohonk Indian Conference, and of all intelligent philanthropic effort for the Indian, has been and must be to develop in him a true Christian manhood, and to secure him a position as an American citizen. Here is the center of all wise legislation, all reasonable education, and all missionary labor.[5]

NOTES

1. 4 Report of the Annual Lake Mohonk Conference on the Indian and Other Dependent Peoples (1886), p. 11. HeinOnline.

2. 5 Report of the Annual Lake Mohonk Conference on the Indian and Other Dependent Peoples (1887), p. 104. https://babel.hathitrust.org/cgi/pt?id=uc1.a0012443123&seq=7 (accessed online September 26, 2024).

3. 9 Report of the Annual Lake Mohonk Conference on the Indian and Other Dependent Peoples (1891), p. 7.

4. 9 Report of the Annual Lake Mohonk Conference on the Indian and Other Dependent Peoples (1891), p. 8.

5. 20 Report of the Annual Lake Mohonk Conference on the Indian and Other Dependent Peoples (1902).

#1 Using Military Action to Control Indians

~

The U.S. Army used the methods outlined by Prussian General and military theorist Carl von Clausewitz: The *first* of these is invasion, that is the seizure of enemy territory; not with the object of retaining it but in order to exact financial contributions, or even to lay it waste. The immediate object here is neither to conquer the enemy country nor to destroy its army, but simply to cause general damage. The *second* method is to give priority to operations that will increase the enemy's suffering. The *third*, and far the most important method, judging from the frequency of its use, is to wear down the enemy. ... Wearing down the enemy in a conflict means using the duration of the war to bring about a gradual exhaustion of his physical and moral resistance.[1]

Lieutenant General John M. Schofield, commander of the Department of Missouri from 1869 to 1870, stated his career goal as follows: "With my cavalry and combined artillery encamped in front, I wanted no other occupation in life than to ward off the savage and kill off his food until there should no longer be an Indian Frontier in our beautiful country."[2]

The military tactic to "awe the Indians" by exposing them to the U.S.' military capabilities was used to intimidate Indians into realizing there was no way they could defeat the U.S. They would, thus, realize it was in their best interest to succumb to the will of the federal government.

Negotiators with Indian tribes realized that their remoteness might obscure the potent power of the U.S., such that it would be helpful to make them aware of this by hosting tribal leaders in Washington, D.C. Treaty commissions appointed by Congress through the DOI routinely included military generals.

A. General George Washington

The military tactic to "awe the Indians" was first stated by General George Washington: "First. A regular and standing force, for Garrisoning West Point & such other Posts upon our Northern, Western, and Southern Frontiers, as shall be deemed *necessary to awe the Indians*..."(Emphasis added).[3]

General George Washington: Sullivan Campaign of 1779 – Chastise and Intimidate

In 1779, General Washington planned an expedition of destruction and devastation of the Six Nations. Generals John Sullivan, James Clinton and Horatio Gates were to "chastise and intimidate" the Haudenosaunee. The fact that four brigades of Continental troops totaling around 4,469 men were earmarked for this expedition underlines just how important General Washington considered this enterprise. Hundreds of U.S. troops marched north to "extirpate those hell-hounds off the face of the Earth."[4] General Washington's instruction to General Sullivan were as follows:

> The Expedition is undertaken to Destroy those Indian Nations & **to Convince others that we have it in our power to Carry the war into their Country whenever they Commence hostilities.** (Emphasis added).[5]

Further instructions followed a month later:

> From George Washington to Major General John Sullivan, 31 May 1779
>
> The expedition you are appointed to command is to be directed against the hostile tribes of the six nations of Indians, with their associates and adherents. *The immediate objects are the total destruction and devastation of their settlements and the capture of as many prisoners of every age and sex as possible. It will be essential to ruin their crops now in the ground and prevent their planting more.*
>
> ... parties should be detached to lay waste all the settlements ... *that the country may not be merely overrun but destroyed.* But you will not by any means listen to (any) overture of peace before the total ruin of their settlements is effected ... Emphasis added).[6]

This government sanctioned destruction of the Six Nations was not only to affect them, but to prevent other Indians from challenging the U.S. authority.

General George Washington: Americans' Sole Lords and Proprietors, Revolutionary War Victory Foundation of Empire

Prior to becoming President, General Washington referred to Americans as "the sole Lords and Proprietors of a vast Tract of Continent" and believed winning the Revolutionary War was nothing less than the "foundation of our Empire[.]" (Emphasis added).[7]

His rhetoric is clear in announcing the status of the U.S. as owners of the Continent.

B. Meriwether Lewis to Inform Indians of U.S. Sovereignty over Louisiana Territory

President Thomas Jefferson continued this tactic in the Lewis and Clark Military Expedition. Meriwether Lewis' new duties included informing the Indians that the U.S. was now sovereign over the Louisiana Territory, their "Great Father," and the Indians, his "children," were mere occupants of their land.

> *Being now become sovereigns of the country, without however any*

~ 339

> *diminution of the Indian rights of occupancy* ...that henceforward we become their fathers and friends, and that we shall endeavor that they shall have no cause to lament the change. (Emphasis added).[8]

To "awe the Indians" Lewis demonstrated the Girandoni air rifle's capabilities to them. There are no fewer than 39 separate entries in the Military Expedition's journals mentioning the Girandoni.

> With a muzzle velocity of 1,000 feet per second, the windbuchse, literally "wind rifle," could put a lead ball clean through a one-inch pine board at 100 yards. Its full magazine (22 lead balls) could be discharged completely in less than 30 seconds. ...The Indians, he said, considered the rifle "something from the gods."[9]

C. State Militias Would Also Use Threat of Military Action against Indians

1831: Governor of Illinois John Reynolds to Sec. of War – State Militia Will Exterminate All Indians who Will Not Let Us Alone

State militias would also use their threat of military power against Indians. Illinois Governor Reynolds wrote to Secretary of War Porter that "if I am again compelled to call on the militia of this State, I will place in the field such a force as will exterminate all Indians who will not let us alone."[10]

Thereafter, he wrote to President Jackson that all Indians in Illinois should be removed west of the Mississippi. He insinuated that if President Jackson would inform the Indians that the State had the power to remove them of its own accord, they would voluntarily leave. The State had no such authority.

> For the good of all concerned, I would respectfully suggest to you the propriety of removing all the Indians in the State of Illinois to the west of the Mississippi. This ought to be effected in a peaceable manner, and could be, if the proper measures were taken with them. *I am informed that the impression made on the Indians is, that the United States will protect them in living and hunting in the State. If they were informed that the State had the power from the General Government, or otherwise, to remove them, they would, in my opinion, go off, of their own accord, in peace*. John Reynolds. (Emphasis added).[11]

First Colorado Cavalry – Sand Creek - Mayhem

On Nov. 29, 1864, John M. Chivington, First Colorado Cavalry, reported as follows:

> In the last ten days my command has marched 300 miles, 100 of which the snow was two feet deep. After a march of forty miles

> last night I, *at daylight this morning, attacked Cheyenne village of 130 lodges, from 900 to 1,000 warriors strong; killed Chiefs Black Kettle, White Antelope, Knock Knee, and Little Robe [Little Raven], and between 400 and 500 other Indians,* and captured as many ponies and mules. Our loss, 9 killed, 38 wounded. All died nobly. Think I will catch some more of them eighty miles, on Smoky Hill. Found white man's scalp, not more than three days' old, in one of lodges. (Emphasis added).[12]

In Congressional testimony, the mayhem at Sand Creek is vividly described:

> In going over the battle-ground next day I did not see a body of man, woman, or child but was scalped, and in many instances their bodies were mutilated in the most horrible manner—*men, women, and children's privates cut out,* &c. I heard one man say that he had cut a woman's private parts out, and had them for exhibition on a stick. I heard another man say that he had cut the fingers off of an Indian to get the rings on the hand. According to the best of my knowledge and belief, these atrocities that were committed were with the knowledge of J.M. Chivington, and I do not know of him taking any measures to prevent them. I heard of one instance of a child a few months' old being thrown in the feed-box of a wagon, and after being carried some distance left on the ground to perish. I also heard of numberless instances in which *men had cut out the private parts of females and stretched them over the saddle bows, and wore them over their hats while riding in the ranks*. (Emphasis added).[13]

Oregon, Militia, Walla Walla Indians, Dismemberment of Chief Pu-pu-mux-mux

The volunteer goons fighting against the Walla-Walla Indians in Oregon engaged in the following atrocity:

> *Chief Pu-pu-mux-mux met them under a flag of truce, and declared "He was for peace ... He, however, was taken prisoner, and afterwards barbarously murdered, scalped, his ears and hands cut off, and these preserved and sent to the friends of the volunteers in Oregon, all which was reported by volunteers."* (Emphasis added).[14]

D. Indian Bureau Advocated for Threat of Military Power against Indians to Control Them

1852: Commissioner Lea – Indians Need to Know Power of U.S.

Commissioner Lea was willing to use the U.S. military against the Indian barbarians, whether employed justly or not, even if a 'vast amount of human suffering' might be the result.

> When civilization and barbarism are brought in such relation that they cannot coexist together, it is right that the superiority of the former should be asserted and the latter compelled to give way. ... That the means employed to effect this grand result have not always been just, or that the conquest has been attended by a vast amount of human suffering, cannot be denied.[15]

> *One of the surest guarantees for the good conduct of our Indians is an adequate knowledge of the power of the government. Where such knowledge prevails, it is comparatively easy to control them.* (Emphasis added).[16]

E. 1872: Commissioner Mix: Military Force Essential to Prevent Intrusion of Improper Persons; Also, Needed to Prevent Indians from Leaving Reservation

Commissioner Mix, instead of going along with the party line that military protection was impossible, averred that a military presence would (1) prevent the intrusion of improper persons; (2) protect Indian agents; and (3) aid in controlling the Indians. Relying on the military to control the Indians was not war, but "discipline."

This was in line with the reservation policy previously announced:

> In the first announcement made of the reservation system, it was expressly declared that the Indians should be made as comfortable on, and as uncomfortable off, their reservations as it was in the power of the Government to make them; that such of them as went right should be protected and fed, and such as went wrong should be harassed and scourged without intermission. ... Such a use of the strong arm of the military is not war, but discipline.[17]

> Commissioner Mix: By the adoption of this course, it is believed that the colonies can very soon be made to sustain themselves, or so nearly so that the government will be subjected to but a comparatively trifling annual expense on account of them. But it is essential to the success of the system that there should be a *sufficient military force* in the vicinity of the reservations *to prevent the intrusion of improper persons* upon them, to afford protection to the agents, and *to aid in controlling the Indians and keeping them within the limits assigned to them*. (Emphasis added).[18]

E. Private Citizen Vigilante Groups Would Also Use Threat of Military Power against Indians

Knights of the Forest

The members of the secret Knights of the Forest took a solemn oath to do everything in their power to remove "all tribes of Indians from the State of Minnesota." A group of them would lie in ambush on the outskirts of the Winnebago Reservation, and shoot any Indian who might be observed outside the lines.[19]

The state of terror imposed on Winnebagoes to relinquish their lands is confirmed by the DOI: "The hostile feelings of the white people are so intense that I am necessitated to use extra efforts to keep the Indians upon their own lands, for the reason that *I have been notified by the whites that the Indians will be massacred if they go out of their own country;* and it is but a few days since *a Winnebago was killed* while crossing the Mississippi river for no other reason than that he was an Indian, and such is the state of public opinion that the murderer goes unpunished." (Emphasis added).[20]

NOTES

1. Von Clausewitz, Carl. On war. Vol. 1. Jazzybee Verlag, 1950.
2. John M. Schofield, Forty-six years in the Army, 1869, p. 428. https://www.perseus.tufts.edu/hopper/text?doc=Perseus%3Atext%3A2001.05.0131%3Achapter%3D23%3Apage%3D428 (accessed online March 25, 2023).
3. Washington, George. "Washington's sentiments on a peace establishment." Founders Online (1783) (accessed online April 20, 2022).
4. Mann, Barbara Alice. "Extirpate Those Hell-Hounds from off the Face of the Earth: The Sullivan-Clinton Campaign, 9 August – 30 September 1779" in *George Washington's War on Native America*. Lincoln: University of Nebraska Press, 2009, pp. 51-110.
5. "To George Washington from Major General John Sullivan, 16 April 1779," *Founders Online*, National Archives, https://founders.archives.gov/documents/Washington/03-20-02-0089. [Original source: *The Papers of George Washington*, Revolutionary War Series, vol. 20, *8 April–31 May 1779*, ed. Edward G. Lengel. Charlottesville: University of Virginia Press, 2010, pp. 716–719.] (accessed online November 13, 2020).
6. "From George Washington to Major General John Sullivan, 31 May 1779," *Founders Online*, National Archives, https://founders.archives.gov/documents/Washington/03-20-02-0661. [Original source: *The Papers of George Washington*, Revolutionary War Series, vol. 20, *8 April–31 May 1779*, ed. Edward G. Lengel. Charlottesville: University of Virginia Press, 2010, pp. 716–719.] (accessed online November 13, 2020).
7. "From George Washington to The States, 8 June 1783," *Founders Online,* National Archives, https://founders.archives.gov/documents/Washington/99-01-02-11404 (accessed online November 13, 2020).
8. "From Thomas Jefferson to Meriwether Lewis, 22 January 1804," *Founders Online*, National Archives, https://founders.archives.gov/documents/Jefferson/01-42-02-0285.

[Original source: *The Papers of Thomas Jefferson*, vol. 42, *16 November 1803–10 March 1804*, ed. James P. McClure. Princeton: Princeton University Press, 2016, pp. 325–326.] (accessed online November 16, 2020).

9. The Air Rifle of Captain Meriwether Lewis: "Something From the Gods." https://warfarehistorynetwork.com/article/lewis-and-clarks-girandoni-air-rifle/ (accessed online November 16, 2024).

10. Annual Report of the Commissioner of Indian Affairs, United States. Office of Indian Affairs, 1831, pp. 190-191. https://search.library.wisc.edu/digital/AEYQML7XLRVXUT8C/text/AKVAKACN74EFCG8E (accessed online September 30, 2024).

11. The War of the Rebellion: A Compilation of the Official Records of the Union and Confederate Armies, United States War Department, U.S. Government Printing Office, 1891. Series I, Vol. XLI, Part I, LOUISIANA AND THE TRANS-MISSISSIPPI, Chapter LIII0, p. 948.

12. Condition of the Indian Tribes: Report of the Joint Special Committee, Appointed Under Joint Resolution of March 3, 1865, United States. Congress. Joint Special Committee to Inquire into the Condition of the Indian Tribes, Kraus Reprint Company, 1973, p. 57.

13. Indian hostilities in Oregon and Washington. Message from the President of the United States, communicating information relative to Indian hostilities in the Territories of Oregon and Washington, H.R. Rep. No. 93, 34th Cong., 1st Sess. (1856), p. 33.

14. Report of the Commissioner of Indian Affairs to the Secretary of the Interior, United States. Office of Indian Affairs, 1852, p. 3.

15. Ibid., p. 4.

16. Report of the Commissioner of Indian Affairs to the Secretary of the Interior, Office of Indian Affairs, United States. 1872, pp. 5-6.

17. Report of the Commissioner of Indian Affairs to the Secretary of the Interior, Office of Indian Affairs, 1858, p. 10.

18. Mankato Review, April 27, 1886; Mankato Daily Review, April 18, 1916. Coats, Catherine M., "Extermination or Removal: The Knights of the Forest and Ethnic Cleansing in Early Minnesota" (2017). Culminating Projects in History, p. 62.

19. Ibid., p. 4.

20. Report of the Commissioner of Indian Affairs to the Secretary of the Interior, United States. Office of Indian Affairs. U.S. Government Printing Office, 1863, p. 92.

#2 Ignoring, Re-Negotiating, Abandoning and Abrogating Treaties Where Necessary - No More Treaties - No More Tribal Sovereignty

1852: Commissioner Lea – Treaty Compliance Impossible due to Conflicting Terms; Should Be Abrogated, Replaced with "Reservation" Treaties

> *The want of uniformity in our Indian treaties is a source of much confusion and embarrassment. They have been made from time to time to meet the emergency of particular occasions, and without reference to system or general principles. They, however, constitute an important part of the supreme law of the land, and there are peculiar reasons why they should be carried faithfully into effect. But this it is extremely difficult to do, in consequence of their discordant and multifarious provisions.* (Emphasis added).[1]

> If a large number of existing treaties were swept away, and others substituted in their stead, containing only a few plain, necessary, and assimilated provisions, serving as models for future treaties, and all looking mainly to the concentration of the several tribes; to their permanent domiciliation within fixed and narrow limits; to the establishment of efficient laws for the protection of their persons and property; and to a more judicious administration of the means provided for their support and improvement, the day would not be distant when the whole subject of our Indian affairs would assume a far more consistent and systematic form, presenting to the eye of the philanthropist and Christian a spectacle no longer cheerless. L. Lea.[2]

B. 1886: LMC, Philip C. Garrett - Treaties Were Not Real Treaties

> To those who held to an absolute fulfillment of all the treaties signed with the Indian nations, *he subtly proposed that perhaps some of the treaties were not in fact real treaties and therefore not binding*, and that they should not be allowed to prevent drawing the Indians into the bosom of the nation. Ultimate protection for the Indians, he argued, rested in individual citizenship.

> Treaties - these arrangements were in no sense regarded by us as treaties made with a party possessed of equal rights, but were simple arrangements between superior intelligence on the one hand and superior brute force on the other, which were to stand until we were in position either to persuade or enforce better.[3]

> *We have made, more than one thousand treaties with the various Indian tribes, and have not kept one of them; and we never intended to keep them. They were not made to be kept, but to*

~ 345

serve a present purpose, to settle a present difficulty in the easiest manner possible, to acquire a desired good with the least possible compensation, and then to be disregarded as soon as this purpose was gained and we were strong enough to enforce a new and more profitable arrangement. That this has been the history of our treaty making no one can deny. Some will charitably claim that we were sincere in our professions... (Emphasis added).[4]

Our treaties were made primarily to extinguish Indian titles to land; then to establish trade, and then to adjust difficulties or lessen dangers excited by our too great greed and unscrupulous methods of gaining land and pelf. These, and these alone, have been the objects for which treaties were made, and for which they were broken as soon as they ceased to subserve these purposes; and nowhere can we find intentions wise or generous with reference to the welfare of the Indian, except in some philanthropic plausibilities with which we concealed our real purpose, as made clear by subsequent events. And these treaties in many of their provisions constitute one of the greatest obstacles in the way of Indian civilization.[5]

1877: BIC Attributes Indian Wars to Unfulfilled Treaties; Encroachment of White Settlers

We have had the Apache war, the Modoc war, the Sioux war, and the Nez Perces war. But it is equally true that every one of these wars can be traced to wanton aggressions or broken treaties on the part of the whites. Even the last, with a small band of the Nez Perces, was not an unprovoked outbreak. Wrongs unredressed, crimes committed by white men upon Indians unpunished, treaty stipulations left many years unfulfilled by our government, and encroachments of settlers upon lands claimed never to have been ceded, were causes for uneasiness, and excited constant irritation, which at last broke out in revengeful war....[6]

1878: BIC - Treaties Violated when Greedy Whites Demand Land

After ten years of experience under its belt, BIC's utterances carried weight, and could not merely be attributed to sentiment.

It becomes more and more evident every year that reservations, though set apart by the government and guaranteed by solemn treaties as the possession of the Indians forever, do not and cannot secure to them a permanent home. Treaties do not execute themselves. Too often they are regarded by the dominant race as mere expedients for quieting disturbances, to be set aside and forgotten whenever the wants or the greed of the white man may demand it. Lands assigned to Indians and promised in perpetuity have been occupied by white settlers, and overrun by miners in search of gold....[7]

A. To Escape Evils of Treaties Persuade Indians to Modify Them

1884, Second Annual Address to Public, Lake Mohonk Conference: Resolved, That we are bound by many treaties with various Indian tribes. *These treaties are the bases of our relations with them, and yet are in some instances prejudicial to the best interests of both the Government and the Indians.* Nevertheless, the treaties are binding upon the Government and the tribes until they can be modified by mutual agreement. *The only way, therefore, to escape their evils is to persuade the Indians to agree to some modification of their provisions.* We rejoice that since March 3d, 1871, it has been the policy of the Government to make no fresh treaties with the Indians. (Emphasis added).[8]

... wherever necessary, negotiations should be entered into for the modification of the present treaties, and these negotiations should be pressed in every honorable way *until* the consent of the Indians be obtained. (Emphasis added).[9]

1903: Lone Wolf: Treaty Abrogation Unilateral Power of Congress

The Kiowa, Comanche, and Apache (KCA) tribes in Oklahoma opposed the allotment of their treaty-guaranteed reservation and subsequent opening of tribal lands to non-Indian settlement on the grounds that the Treaty of Medicine Lodge required a three-fourths vote of all adult males in the affected tribes before further land cessions could take place. But the Interior Department - acting on the instructions of Congress - began to prepare for the opening of the reservation. Unable to persuade the government to reconsider, the Kiowa's principal chief brought suit in federal court.[10]

The U.S. Supreme Court held treaty abrogation to be a unilateral power of Congress, and found that "the status of the contracting Indians and the relation of dependency they bore and continue to bear towards the government of the United States" meant that Congress's unilateral decision to allot the reservation was essentially a political question beyond the capacity of the federal courts to adjudicate. "Plenary authority over the tribal relations of the Indians has been exercised by Congress from the beginning," the justices explained, "and the power has always been deemed a political one, not subject to be controlled by the judicial department of the government."[11]

Society of American Indians Opinion of *Lone Wolf* Case

The decision of the Supreme Court of the United States rendered on January 5, 1903, in the appeal taken by Lone Wolf, representing the Kiowas, from the decision of the Court of Appeals of the District of Columbia, came with startling significance to the friends of the Indians. It had always been supposed by those interested in the welfare of the Indians that when the United States Government entered into treaty relations with them and by its treaty ostensibly secured them in certain rights therein enumerated, they were absolutely protected under the Constitution and laws of the United States from any abrogation of those rights, except in the manner prescribed by the treaty or in some such constitutional method as that which would be requisite when the rights of any other person in the community were sought to be infringed.

It is now distinctly understood that Congress has a right to do as it pleases; that it is under no obligation to respect any treaty, for the Indians have no rights which command respect. What is to be hoped for by an appeal to Congress can readily be anticipated from the history of the legislation by which Lone Wolf and his tribe have been deprived of that which had by express treaty stipulation apparently been secured to them. It is frequently said that the Indian question has been solved, but until public opinion has been so far educated as to require Congressmen to respect moral, if not legal rights, there would seem still to be room for a campaign of education in this regard. (Emphasis added).[12]

1914-1915: Indians Will Be Glad to Change Treaties

BIC is convinced that many of the Indian treaties are ill adapted to the present needs and conditions on Indian reservations and that the Indians themselves when fully and freely consulted will be glad to agree to changes suggested in their interest. (Emphasis added).[13]

NOTES

1. Report of the Commissioner of Indian Affairs to the Secretary of the Interior, United States. Office of Indian Affairs, 1852, p. 11.
2. Report of the Commissioner of Indian Affairs to the Secretary of the Interior, United States. Office of Indian Affairs, 1852, pp. 11-12.
3. 4 Report of the Annual Lake Mohonk Conference on the Indian and Other Dependent (1886), p. 19.
4. 4 Report of the Annual Lake Mohonk Conference on the Indian and Other Dependent (1886), p. 19.
5. "Our Indian Policy as Related to the Civilization of the Indian," 4 Report of the Annual Lake Mohonk Conference on the Indian and Other Dependent Peoples (1886), p. 19.
6. Annual Report of the Board of Indian Commissioners, 1877 (Washington: Government Printing Office), p. 6.

https://babel.hathitrust.org/cgi/pt?id=coo.31924105308997&seq=11 (accessed online October 2, 2024).

7. Annual Report of the Board of Indian Commissioners, 1878 (Washington: Government Printing Office), p. 7. https://babel.hathitrust.org/cgi/pt?id=mdp.39015034324361&seq=12 (accessed online October 2, 2024).

8. 1884, Second Annual Address to Public, Lake Mohonk Conference, p. 15.

9. 3 Report of the Annual Lake Mohonk Conference on the Indian and Other Dependent Peoples (1885), pp. 48-50.

10. *Lone Wolf*, 187 U.S. 553 (1903).

11. *Lone Wolf*, 187 U.S. 565 (1903).

12. Society of American Indians, "The American Indian Magazine, v. 6 no. 4 (Winter 1918)," 175-178. American Indian Digital History Project, https://www.aidhp.com/items/show/173 (accessed online September 10, 2024).

13. Annual Report of the Board of Indian Commissioners, 1914-15 (Washington: Government Printing Office), p. 6. https://babel.hathitrust.org/cgi/pt?id=osu.32435064035769&seq=115 (accessed online October 5, 2024).

#3 Exterminating Indians, Such as Occurred in Texas, Dakotas, Pacific Northwest, and Wherever Indians Possessed Valuable Land

1870: Montana's Governor James M. Ashely Castigated Indian Race as "Unmitigated Curse to Civilization"

The Indian race on this continent has never been anything but an unmitigated curse to civilization, while the intercourse between the Indian and the white man has been only evil, and that continually, to both races, and must so remain until the last savage is translated to that celestial hunting ground for which they all believe themselves so well fitted, and to which every settler on our frontier wishes them individually and collectively a safe and speedy transit. ... In Montana we want no more Chinamen or Indians or barbarians of any race; we already have enough and to spare. (Emphasis added).[1]

1870—1871: Congressional Debate on Indian Appropriation Bill – Exterminate Indians

The heated Congressional debate on the Indian Appropriation Bill for 1870-1871, included uncompromising arguments for exterminating Indians due to continuing Indian attacks. In defending extermination, Republican Representative Edward Degener of San Antonio, Texas, described civilization as the manifest destiny of mankind and stated: "*He who resists gets crushed. That is the history of the wild Indian.*" (Emphasis added).[2]

A. Texas

> *The removal of the Indians [from Texas by the U.S. Army] was demanded under a threat of extermination...* (Emphasis added).[3]

B: Dakota Territory

Governor Gilbert Pierce of Dakota Territory was among those demanding allotment and access to Indian reservations for white settlement, as he stated in his report of 1885:

> The rapidity with which the entire area of the western part of the country is being opened up and settled brings settlers to the very doors of the Indian reservations, often times introducing a class of men none too scrupulous regarding the rights of others; *men who regard the property of the Indian as lawful prey, and the life of the Indian as no obstacle to the possession of it...* (Emphasis added).[4]

C. 1855: Commissioner Manypenny - White Population of Pacific Territories Anxious for Extermination of Indians

> *It cannot be disguised that a portion of the white population of the Pacific Territories, entertain feelings deeply hostile to the Indian tribes of that region, and are anxious for the extermination of the race.* The existing laws for the protection of the persons and property of the Indian wards of the government are sadly defective. ... Trespasses and depredations of every conceivable kind have been committed on the Indians. They have been personally maltreated, their property stolen, **their timber destroyed**, their possessions encroached upon, and divers other wrongs and injuries done them. (Emphasis added).[5]

"Private War"

By early 1856, it was obvious to the U.S. military that the warfare occurring in Oregon was due to the desire of settlers to rid Oregon of Indians, and not the actual threat imposed by the Indians. As a result, lives were needlessly lost, Indians were deliberately exposed to cruel and barbarous suffering—exposure, starvation and death—while federal dollars were being expended on a private war.

In a deplorable Report from General Wool to Lieutenant Colonel L. Thomas, Assistant Adjutant General, U.S. Army, Benicia Headquarters, Department of the Pacific, dated January 19, 1856, he cited the frightening motives of the white settlers:

> In Oregon, as well as in the northern part of California, *many whites are for exterminating the Indians*. This feeling is engendered by two newspapers that go for extermination, and is more or less possessed by the volunteers as well as others not enrolled under the banners of Governor Curry. *As long as individual war is permitted and paid for by the United States, and which is expected by all the citizens of Oregon, we shall have no peace*, and the war may be prolonged indefinitely, especially as *it is generally asserted that the present war is a God-send.*[6]

In a subsequent letter to the Governor of Oregon, General Wool reiterated the "private" war being fought by the citizens.

> It is, however, greatly to be regretted that there are too many white inhabitants, both in Oregon and northern California, who go for exterminating the Indians, and, consequently, do not discriminate between friends and foes; the result of which has been the cause of the death of many innocent and worthy citizens, both in southern Oregon and in northern California. *Could the citizens be restrained from private war, I have no doubt peace and quiet would soon be restored to the people of that region of country*. (Emphasis added).[7]

A letter from Agt. Ambrose to Sup't Palmer, dated February 29, 1856, repeated the wish of certain citizens to prolong the war, which would mean more loss of lives and property.

> *It is the desire of many persons here to protract the war*, men who

have no interest in the country and might properly be considered vagrants in any country in the world but this. That our country is infested with such a set of men none will question who are acquainted with the country. (Emphasis added).[8]

A letter from Joel Palmer, Sup't, to Commissioner Manypenny, dated April 11, 1856, elucidated the strategy to keep the settlers up in arms, at the cost of Indian lives. Importantly, it highlights the dissension between the governing entities in the War. It is a well-known fact that the easiest way to prevent success in war is the inability to express and act upon a unified plan. No decisive victory was possible due to the splintered approach for war. The political infighting led to the Indians out maneuvering, outflanking, and soundly beating the disunited forces fighting them.

> These outrages and those in Southern Oregon have created a state of feeling among our citizens almost uncontrollable. ... Not a little of this unnecessary excitement, I am forced to believe, grew out of efforts of disappointed politicians who strove ... by circulating the most outrageous, exaggerated and groundless reports in regard to the acts of Indians and the agents in this Department to excite the fears and prejudices of the people. Meetings were held by the citizens simultaneously in different parts of the Territory ... petitions and memorials, resolutions and remonstrances were drawn up by the few present and passed condemnatory of almost every movement made by the Indian Department, tending to inflame the minds of the people (who were ignorant of the facts) and drive them to acts of desperation.
>
> The ***dissensions between the different functionaries of the government***, civil and military, tends greatly to destroy the efficiency of the service: crimination & recrimination but adds to the flame, and whilst a considerable portion of the energies of the respective parties are exhausted in striving to gain the ascendancy and convince others of the correctness of their policy, the enemy goes unwhipped, their forces continually augmenting, our citizens slaughtered, and our settlers cut off and destroyed. (Emphasis added).[9]

> ... The existing laws for the protection of the persons and property of the Indian wards of the government are sadly defective. ... Trespasses and depredations of every conceivable kind have been committed on the Indians. They have been personally maltreated, their property stolen, ***their timber destroyed***, their possessions encroached upon, and divers other wrongs and injuries done them. (Emphasis added).[10]

NOTES

1. The National Standard, Oct. 1, 1870.
2. 41st Cong., 3d sess., 1870-1871, Part 1, 656.
3. Extract from Annual Report of the Secretary of the Interior to Congress, Dec. 1, 1859, p. 5.
4. The Abridgment: Containing the Annual Message of the President of the United States to the Two Houses of Congress with Reports of Departments

and Selections from Accompanying Papers, Secretary of the Interior, U.S. Department of the Interior, 1885, p. 900.
5. Report of the Commissioner of Indian Affairs to the Secretary of the Interior, Office of Indian Affairs, 1857, p. 21.
   6. Senate Documents, Otherwise Publ. as Public Documents and Executive Documents: 14th Congress, 1st Session-48th Congress, 2nd Session and Special Session, Volume 10, 1856, p. 50. But see Communication from C. S. Drew, late Adjutant of the Second Regiment of Oregon Mounted Volunteers, giving an account of the origin and early prosecution of the Indian War in Oregon. S. Misc. Doc. No. 59, 36th Cong., 1st Sess. (1860). Letter to California Governor J. N. Johnson, from Major Gen. John E. Wool, Jan. 21, 1856.
   7. Indian hostilities in Oregon and Washington. Message from the President of the United States, communicating information relative to Indian hostilities in the Territories of Oregon and Washington. H.R. Rep. No. 93, 34th Cong., 1st Sess. (1856), pp. 35-36; Ex. Doc. 76, 34th Congress, 3rd session, 1857, pp. 103-104.
8. *Indian Affairs 1848–1873, Reel 14; Letters Received, 1856, No. 95.*
9. *NARA Series M234, Letters Received by the Office of Indian Affairs, Reel 609 Oregon Superintendency 1856, frames 647-662.* To James Clugage Esq. Grand Ronde *NARA Series M2, Microcopy of Records of the Oregon Superintendency of Indian Affairs 1848–1873, Reel 6; Letter Books E:10, pages 184-185.*
10. Report of the Commissioner of Indian Affairs to the Secretary of the Interior, Office of Indian Affairs, United States. A.O.P. Nicholson, Printer, 1857, p. 18.

#4 Theft of Indian Land, Timber, Minerals, Agricultural Land, and Water, Leaving Indians Destitute

1876: Constant Struggle to Dispossess Indian; Avarice and Determination of White Man Prevails

> *Wherever an Indian reservation has on it good land, or timber, or minerals, the cupidity of the white man is excited, and a constant struggle is inaugurated to dispossess the Indian, in which the avarice and determination of the white man usually prevails.*
> Commissioner Smith. (Emphasis added).[1]

A. Author's Book on Theft of Indian Land – Doctrine of Discovery

The Earth Is Red, The Imperialism of the Doctrine of Discovery, Publisher Sunstone Press. In 1823, United States Supreme Court Chief Justice John Marshall, based on his analysis of custom, not precedential law, proclaimed the "doctrine of discovery" as the supreme law of the land in the case, *Johnson v. M'Intosh*. This "doctrine" held that whichever European nation first "discovered" land, then not ruled by a Christian prince or people, could claim ownership. Indigenous people in this New World, as it was called, were a mere obstacle to be eliminated or moved out of the way of colonial settlers in their westward expansion.

B. Author's Book on Theft of Indian Timber Resources

The Iron Triangle: Business, Government, and Colonial Settlers' Dispossession of Indian Timberlands and Timber

The treatment of Indians timber lands in various states in the Great Lakes region and the Pacific Northwest is discussed in depth in *The Iron Triangle: Business, Government, and Colonial Settlers' Dispossession of Indian Timberlands and Timber*. The Iron Triangle centers on the massive cession of lands, removal, concentration and consolidation of tribes on small tracts, establishment of reservations, and allotment of tribal land in the theft of Indian timberlands and timber resources such that Indian Nations once self- sufficient became destitute paupers.

B.1. Michigan

In the summer of 1831, Alexis de Tocqueville, exploring America's wilderness traveled from Detroit to Saginaw, with two Indian guides. "A mile out of town," he wrote, "the road goes into forest and never comes out of it." Yet he knew the westward movement was already started. Saginaw was settled with thirty people.

> "In a few years these impenetrable forests will have fallen; the sons of civilization and industry will break the silence of the Saginaw; its

echoes will cease.... So strong is the impetus that urges the white man to the entire conquest of the New World."[2]

Michigan was deforested by 1910.

B.2. Minnesota

> As I stood upon the brow of Embarrass Hill...one of the grandest sights I ever looked upon was in view, a veritable ocean of pine. One could see for miles and miles in nearly every direction over the tops of the tall waving forests of virgin pine and a variety of other trees. I will never forget that sight or the impression it left upon my mind, as I stood there gazing upon this wonderful forest...inexhaustible, enough to last for ages as I thought at that time, yet within the course of a very few years not to exceed fifteen, this great forest was laid bare, leaving only a few scattering stands of pine in patches here and there. — Richard Louis Griffin, reminiscing in 1930 about seeing northern Minnesota's pine forests for the first time in the winter of 1890–1891.[3]

Minnesota was deforested by 1905.

B.3. Wisconsin

B.4. Timber of No Value to Chippewas of Wisconsin

In 1879, Commissioner E.A. Hayt repeated a common refrain within the DOI and elsewhere, that natural resources had no value to Indians, in this case the timber to the Chippewa Indians in Wisconsin.

> The Chippewas in Wisconsin "occupy three reservations, embracing a territory largely in excess of their actual wants, covered with a heavy growth of very valuable pine timber, which is deteriorating in value every year of being destroyed by forest fires. Large quantities of timber have also been removed in years past by trespassers. ***There are probably 600,000,000 feet of merchantable pine timber on these reservations, which, under present circumstances, is of no value to the Indians.*** ... Commissioner Hayt went on to advise consolidating the Indians by removing them to two reservations containing the "best agricultural lands. (Emphasis added).[4]

While the massive amount of timber was considered without value to the Chippewas, much of this land would be ceded and opened to white settlement. From 1899–1905, Wisconsin led nation in lumber production. Logging peaked in Wisconsin 1892 with over 4 billion board feet. Millions of dollars would be made by lumber companies.

According to the 1890 U.S. census, more than 23,000 men worked in Wisconsin's logging industry and another 32,000 worked at the sawmills that turned timber into boards. Each winter, the lumberjacks occupied nearly 450 logging camps. In the spring, they drove their timber downstream to more than 1,000 mills. Logging and lumbering employed a quarter of all Wisconsinites working in the 1890s.[5]

Wisconsin's forests were depleted by 1920.

C. Author's Book on Theft of Indian Mineral Resources

All That Glitters Is Ours, The Theft of Indian Mineral Resources centers on the theft of Indian mineral resources in the Great Lakes region, the Pacific Northwest, the Great Plains region and the Southwest.

Cheyenne and Arapaho Removed from Colorado

A commission was sent to negotiate a treaty with the surviving Arapaho and Cheyenne after the Sand Creek Massacre. Their instructions were as follows: "Agreements to pay money will not be approved. If a treaty is made, it will be one of occupancy only - no title to lands will be acknowledged in the Indians of the country they abandon, nor will any be conferred upon them in the country they are to inhabit…"

On Oct. 13, 1865, the surviving Arapaho and Cheyenne chiefs met with the U.S. treaty commissioners. The Arapaho didn't want to agree on land at the time - few were present, the rest were up north. They were still reeling from the Sand Creek Massacre:

> ***Little Raven stated:***
>
> *There is something very strong for us-that fool band of soldiers that cleared out our lodges, and killed our women and children. This is strong (hard) on us. There, at Sand creek, is one chief, Left Hand; White Antelope and many other chiefs lie there; our women and children lie there. Our lodges were destroyed there, and our horses were taken from us there, and I do not feel disposed to go right off in a new country and leave them.* (Emphasis added).[6]

Nonetheless, the Commissioners pressed the Arapaho and Cheyenne to relinquish their Colorado home:

> We all fully realize that it is hard for any people to leave their homes and graves of their ancestors; but, **unfortunately for you, gold has been discovered in your country**, and a crowd of white people have gone there to live, and a great many of these people are the worst enemies of the Indians - men who do not care for their interests, and

who would not stop at any crime to enrich themselves. These men are now in your country - in all parts of it - and there is no portion where you can live and maintain yourselves but what you will come in contact with them. The consequences of this state of things are that you are in constant danger of being imposed upon, and you have to resort to arms in self defence. ... *We want to give you a country that is full of game and good for agricultural purposes, and where the hills and mountains are not full of gold and silver.* In such a country as this the government can fully provide for your wants ... We are sorry that we have bad people among us, as you are sorry that you have bad people among you; but this is *unfortunately* the case with all people, and however severe we make laws *it is impossible to prevent crime.* You may accede to our wishes, and be happy and prosperous, or you may refuse to make a treaty, and be ruined in health and happiness. (Emphasis added).[7]

Indian Nations: Beware the Commissioner

In letter from General Crook to Mr. Tibbles, journalist, Indians' rights activist, and politician, Crook stated emphatically that Indians regarded commissioners with something akin to disgust:

> But I am very sorry to say they have, to a very great degree, lost confidence in our people and their promises. Indians are very much like white men in being unable to live upon air. ... *We send them too many commissioners; there is no class of men for whom the Indian has less respect.* (Emphasis added).[8]

"The Lobo"

In January 1859, the New York Times reported on the incendiary convergence of popular opinions, mining schemes, and government policies:

> The Apache is as near the lobo, or wolf of the country, as any human being can be to a beast. ... They neither cultivate nor hunt to any extent, but exist mainly ... by plunder. ... This is the greatest obstacle to the operations of the mining companies. ... [W]hipping these wild tribes ... into submission, and driving them into reservations ... with the penalty of death sternly enforced if they pass their limits, is the only prompt, economical, and humane process. ... My greatest hopes for Arizona, however, rest on the army. ... Officers of various grades are becoming interested in mines throughout that region. They ... have connections of influence and capital.[9]

This type of inflammatory rhetoric ignited vigilante and military campaigns between 1859 and 1874 that killed over 380 Pinal Apaches—including many women and children. Mining across Pinal Apache land followed promptly.[10]

Low Ball

Gold was discovered near the boundary line of the Shoshone Reservation. According to the DOI, "The best gold mines in the district had been found to be located within the reservation." Felix R. Brunot was appointed as a commissioner to negotiate with the Shoshone Indians for the cession of the part of the reservation located in the gold-mining district.

The DOI subsequently reported on the negotiations:

> As a result, ***Brunot obtained an agreement from the Shoshones ceding 700,642 acres of the reservation for a total consideration of $27,500 [25 cents/acre]. At that time the Indians had no conception of the value of money or the value of the property they were surrendering to the Government and they accepted, without question, Brunot's first offer of the amount stated.*** "Acting upon my experience of the general habit of Indians, the Shoshones were offered a sum as the basis of further negotiation, and which *I supposed would have to be increased to meet the demand of the Indians. When the terms first offered were promptly accepted, I did not feel at liberty to make an addition.*" (Emphasis added).[11]

D. Author's Book on Theft of Indian Agricultural Resources (Coming Soon)

> America's strength as a nation was substantially derived from its strength as an agricultural power. The huge expanse of American land and the vast number of climates across the country allowed the U.S. to grow a more diverse set of crops and raise more kinds of animals than its competitors. "The United States is the most self-sustaining nation in the world," Armour and Co. bragged.[12]

The U.S.' strength as an international power was based on the wealth generated from agricultural lands expropriated from Indian tribes and peoples.

E. Water for Indian Reservations Appropriated by 'White Water Users'

The Walker River Reservation's water supply was inadequate due to whites appropriating water upstream before it could reach the Reservation. The Agent thought the only way Indians could get relief was through the DOJ suing the white users.

> Due to a shortage of supply, the ***white water users*** along the stream above the Indian reservation are utilizing practically all of the available water, so that very little other than seeped and return flow reaches Indian lands. The situation became so serious last spring

that aid from the Department of Justice was sought. It is apparent from existing conditions that court action will be necessary in this case before the Indians will be granted their full rights, owing to the location of their lands with relation to lands of the *whites* subject to irrigation. (Emphasis added).[13]

In *Winters v. United States*, 207 U.S. 564 (1908), non-Indians had built large and substantial dams and reservoirs and, by means of canals and ditches and waterways, diverted waters of the Milk River from its channel, above the points of diversion by the U.S. and the Indians on the Fort Belknap Reservation in Montana, which deprived the U.S. and the Indians of the use of water. The U.S. Supreme Court explained that lands provided under the Fort Belknap agreement for the purpose of developing an agrarian society "were arid and, without irrigation, were practically valueless." Water was thus necessary for agriculture. The Supreme Court held that the federal government reserved water rights for the Fort Belknap Reservation and for a use which would be necessarily continued through the years. The amount must satisfy the present and future needs of the reservation. The water rights vest on the date that Congress reserves the land and are not lost if a tribe does not maintain continuous use.

As for the holding in the *Winters* decision, Utah's Senator George Sutherland spoke for many others when he dismissed it as "one of those unfortunate statements that sometimes courts, and the highest court, lapse into." Sutherland was a renowned legal scholar and politician, having served in the Utah State Senate, U.S. Congress, and U.S. Senate.[14]

"Whiskey Is for Drinking, Water Is for Fighting"

The real battle in mining was over the water, scarce in the desert and made even more valuable by the high stakes of gold mining. When water was scarce, mercury had to be used to separate the gold, but this method was considerably more expensive. It cost more than most miners could afford, thus, placing a premium on water. As *in western agriculture and ranching, whoever controlled the water supply controlled production, in this case, of gold*. Mark Twain's adage, "Whiskey's for drinking, water's for fighting," would be played out in the arid west.

In 1876, the DOI reported on the lack of water for farming for Indians in eastern Nevada: *the water used for irrigating purposes has been taken from them, and their crops have dried up and become worthless*. (Emphasis added). This story was repeated over and over across Indian country.[15]

NOTES

1. Report of the Commissioner of Indian Affairs to the Secretary of the Interior, Office of Indian Affairs, 1876, p. VIII.
2. Extract from the Memoir, Letter, and Remarks of Alexis De Tocqueville. Specifically, "A Fortnight in the Wilderness." Written on board the Steamboat Superior, August of

1831.

3. www.mnhs.org/foresthistory/learn/logging (accessed online July 17, 2022).

4. Report of the Commissioner of Indian Affairs to the Secretary of the Interior, Vol. 1, United States. Office of Indian Affairs, U.S. Government Printing Office, 1879, p. 102.

5. Edmonds, Michael. Out of the Northwoods: The Many Lives of Paul Bunyan, With More Than 100 Logging Camp Tales. Wisconsin Historical Society, 2010, p. 25.

6. Report of the Commissioner of Indian Affairs to the Secretary of the Interior, United States. Office of Indian Affairs. U.S. Government Printing Office, 1865, p. 525.

7. Ibid., p. 523.

8. George Crook, The Council Fire 2, No. 12 (December 1879): 178-79.

9. Welch, J. R. (2017). Earth, Wind, and Fire: Pinal Apaches, Miners, and Genocide in Central Arizona, 1859-1874. SAGE Open, 7(4).

10. Annihilationist Government Policy and Miner Bombast Targeting Pinal Apaches Welch, J. R. (2017). Earth, Wind, and Fire: Pinal Apaches, Miners, and Genocide in Central Arizona, 1859-1874. SAGE Open, 7(4).

11. Report of the Commissioner of Indian Affairs to the Secretary of the Interior, United States. Office of Indian Affairs. U.S. Government Printing Office, 1872, p. 126. H.R. Exec. Doc. No. 1, 42nd Cong., 3rd Sess. (1872).

12. 40 maps that explain food in America, Ezra Klein and Susannah Locke, June 9, 2014. https://www.vox.com/a/explain-food-america (accessed online May 6, 2023). Gilpin, William. Mission of the North American People, Geographical, Social, and Political (1874). De Bow, James Dunwoody Brownson, et al., eds. *De Bow's Review and Industrial Resources, Statistics, Etc: Devoted to Commerce, Agriculture, Manufactures*. Vol. 14., 1853.

13. Report of the Commissioner of Indian Affairs to the Secretary of the Interior, United States. Office of Indian Affairs. U.S. Government Printing Office, 1920, p. 18.

14. Hoxie, Frederick E. A final promise: The campaign to assimilate the Indians, 1880-1920. U of Nebraska Press, 2001, p. 184.

15. Report of the Commissioner of Indian Affairs to the Secretary of the Interior, United States. Office of Indian Affairs. U.S. Government Printing Office, 1876, p. 117.

#5 Destruction of Indian Culture, Language, Religion and Customs

1863: Assimilation Will Require Laws Forcing Them to Abandon Accursed Paraphernalia of Indian War, Murder, Superstition; Abstain Totally from Medicine, War, Scalp, and Other Barbarous, Superstitious, and Bloody Dances; Eschew Paint and Feathers; Force Them to Adopt Christian Civilization

> *[Our] code of laws should require the Indian novice to disarm and keep disarmed till otherwise ordered; to abstain totally from the medicine, war, scalp, and other barbarous, superstitious, and bloody dances; to eschew paint and feathers; in short, to abandon and throw away the accursed paraphernalia of Indian war, murder, superstition, jugglery, and bigotry; and, on the other hand, to adopt and practice the habits and customs of enlightened Christian civilization; and this should be not only required and taught, but rigidly enforced.* Indian Agent James Galbraith. (Emphasis added).[1]

1864: Unless Indian Nationality Is Abolished, Entire Race Must Become Extinct

> The need for assimilation would guide policy as it became clear to the U.S. that "unless Indian nationality is abolished, the Indian race must, ere long, be known only in history." Report of U.S. Indian Agent Thomas J. Galbraith to Clark W. Thompson, Superintendent of Indian Affairs, St. Paul, Minnesota.[2]

1885: No Indian Progress until Given Gospel of our Lord Jesus Christ

Rev. C.C. Painter:

> We believe that nothing adequate can be done-whatever may be done in giving citizenship, land in severalty, the ballot, industrial and mental training-until the gospel of our Lord Jesus Christ has been given to all these people.[3]

1881: Only Choice for Indians Is Civilization or Extermination

Continuing the domineering bombast of the Indian Bureau, he, too pronounced civilization or extermination to the Indian.

> There is no one who has been a close observer of Indian history and the effect of contact of Indians with civilization, who is not well satisfied that *one of two things must eventually take place, to wit, either civilization or extermination of the Indian*. Savage and civilized life cannot live and prosper on the same ground. One of the

two must die. If the Indians are to be civilized and become a happy and prosperous people, which is certainly the object and intention of our government, they must learn our language and adopt our modes of life. *We are fifty millions of people, and they are only one-fourth of one million. The few must yield to the many.* (Emphasis added).[4]

1883: Commissioner Price - To Further Promote Law and Order, Commissioner Price Argued for Code of Indian Offenses Prohibiting "Heathenish Dances," Plural Marriages, Medicine Men, Payment for Any Indian Girl or Woman

Given his stance on law and order, Commissioner Price authored rules prohibiting traditional dances and practices, which were approved by the Secretary of Interior.

> On December 2, 1882, the Secretary called the attention of the Commissioner to what he regarded as a great hinderance to the civilization of the Indians, viz: (1) "The continuance of the old heathenish dances, such as the sun dance, etc.; (2) marriages during pleasure, and plural marriages; (3) the influence of the medicine men, who are always found with the anti-progressive party; (4) the custom of destroying or distributing property on the death of an Indian." In concluding his communication the Secretary said: "I suggest whether it is not practicable to formulate certain rules for the government of the Indians on the reservations that shall restrict, and ultimately abolish, the practices I have mentioned."
>
> Acting upon this suggestion the Commissioner prepared certain rules for the guidance and direction of Indian agents, and they were approved by the Secretary on April 10, 1883.[5]

A. LMC, Charles C. Painter, Forget Once and Forever, Word 'Indian' and All that it Has Signified

> *... it is clear to one who studies the situation that the most urgent necessity of the Indian to-day is that he shall cease to be an Indian* ... that by allotment he shall get, at the earliest possible moment, a sufficiency of his best land for the support of his family, then strip himself of the residue which would otherwise surround him as an excluding wall, shutting out his civilized neighbors; convert this value, which would otherwise be a dead weight, into facilities for opening up and cultivating his farm, and put himself at once, free of all burdensome and entangling wrappings, in fullest and freest contact with the civilization he must embrace and absorb, or perish. (Emphasis added).[6]
>
> He pleaded for full emancipation of the Indians. **"Let us forget once and forever,"** he said, **"the word 'Indian' and all that it has**

signified in the past, and remember only that we are dealing with so many of the children of a common Father." (Emphasis added).⁷

B. LMC, Judge Strong, Indians Should Not Maintain Their Own Language and Habits, Be Americanized

> Judge Strong I am desirous to promote the Christianization and civilization of all the Indians in this country, and I am one of those who think it desirable that the Indians should be dispersed or diffused throughout our population; that they should not be preserved on reservations, if it is possible to avoid it; that they should not be encouraged to live in bodies; that they should not maintain their own language and habits, but be brought into contact with the better portion of our communities scattered throughout the land, where they might be brought under good influence, and ultimately be Americanized. I would not desire to see a great body of Irishmen herded together, but scattered throughout the country; and it is the same with the Indian.⁸

C. LMC, Philip Garrett, Let Indian Lay Aside His Picturesque Blanket for American Citizenship

LMC, Philip Garrett, Let Indian Lay Aside His Picturesque Blanket for American Citizenship

> Let him lay aside his picturesque blanket and moccasin, and, clad in the panoply of American citizenship, seek his chances of fortune or loss in the stern battle of life with the Aryan races. It will be no hardship, no unkindness to ask this of him. If civilization is a blessing, then in the name of Christianity let us offer it as a boon, even to the untutored savage.⁹

1905: Bring Best Indian Characteristics into American Civilization

VALUABLE RACE CHARACTERISTICS ARE PRESERVED AND STRENGTHENED BY CIVILIZATION - BRING THE BEST INDIAN CHARACTERISTICS INTO AMERICAN CIVILIZATION - DO NOT SHUT THE AMERICAN INDIAN OUT OF CIVILIZATION FOR THE SAKE OF PRESERVING HIS PECULIAR RACE TRAITS.

> In the objectionable "Indian dances" which are breaking out afresh at many points we see not a desirable maintenance of racial traits, but a distinct reversion toward barbarism and superstition. We believe that while the effort should never be made to "make a white man out of an Indian," ... it is still most desirable that all the Indians on our territory should come as speedily as possible to the white

man's habits of home-making, industry, cleanliness, social purity, and family integrity.¹⁰

Morality Policing by BIC

> *We believe that much can be accomplished in the way of moral rehabilitation of those Indian reservations where moral laxity is on the increase if Congress would pass a law conferring jurisdiction on State courts to try cases arising from offenses against the moral laws on reservations. It would enable the Bureau of Indian Affairs to put an end to sexual immoralities, such as illicit cohabitation, adultery, and other open offenses of like character, and of the "secret" and pseudo-religious dances and ceremonies which cloak bestial practices and gross immoralities and which would be particularly severe in its punishment of white men who prey on Indian women.* (Emphasis added).¹¹

NOTES

1. Report of the Commissioner of Indian Affairs to the Secretary of the Interior, United States. Office of Indian Affairs, 1863, p. 296.
2. HR, 37th Congress, 3d Session, Ex. Doc. No. 68, p. 39.
3. Annual Report of the Board of Indian Commissioners, 1885 (Washington: Government Printing Office), p. 50. https://babel.hathitrust.org/cgi/pt?id=mdp.39015081128962&seq=5 (accessed online October 5, 2024).
4. Report of the Commissioner of Indian Affairs to the Secretary of the Interior, United States. Office of Indian Affairs, 1881, p. IV.
5. Report of the Commissioner of Indian Affairs to the Secretary of the Interior, United States. Office of Indian Affairs, 1888, p. XXIX.
6. Report of the Annual Lake Mohonk Conference on the Indian and Other Dependent Peoples (1889), p. 87.
7. 7 Report of the Annual Lake Mohonk Conference on the Indian and Other Dependent Peoples (1889), p. 88.
8. 3 Report of the Annual Lake Mohonk Conference on the Indian and Other Dependent Peoples (1885), p. 32.
9. "Indian Citizenship," 4 Report of the Annual Lake Mohonk Conference on the Indian and Other Dependent Peoples (1886), p. 11.
10. Annual Report of the Board of Indian Commissioners, 1905 (Washington: Government Printing Office), p. 17. https://babel.hathitrust.org/cgi/pt?id=hvd.32044097929459&seq=7 (accessed online October 5, 2024).
11. Annual Report of the Board of Indian Commissioners, 1918-19 (Washington: Government Printing Office), p. 10. https://babel.hathitrust.org/cgi/pt?id=osu.32435064035710&seq=105 (accessed online October 5, 2024).

#6 Through Fear, Uncertainty, Starvation, Disease, Death, Causing Severe Psychological Harm, Where Indians Questioned Their Ability to Survive, Weakening Ability to Counter White Settlers' Encroachment and Settlement on Their Lands

A. 1824: U.S. Government Policy to Weaken Indians Successful

Governor William Clark and ex officio Superintendent of Indian Affairs for the Missouri Territory was responsible for negotiating treaties with the Indian tribes in his jurisdiction. He served as Governor three times. He negotiated thirty-seven treaties ratified by Congress. In fact, if the treaties completed by agents under his supervision, such as his nephew Benjamin O'Fallon are included, Clark was involved in more than twenty percent of all Indian treaties ratified by the U.S. Indian under which tribes surrendered over 100,000 acres of ancestral homelands. Some 75,000 Indians set out on countless trails of tears to reservations in the West.

> *"Their power has been broken, their warlike spirit subdued, and themselves sunk into objects of pity and commiseration," he wrote to his superiors in Washington. "While strong and hostile, it has been our obvious policy to weaken them; now that they are weak and harmless, and most of their lands fallen into our hands, justice and humanity require us to cherish and befriend them".* (Emphasis added).[1]

B: 1854: Alfred J. Vaughan, Indian Agent, Fort Pierre, SD, Famine

> In the winter of 1846, the buffalo disappeared from this district. After eating up their reserves of dried berries and roots, *they subsisted on the flesh of their dogs and horses; these failing, actual famine came upon them. ... Many died of disease and hunger; old persons were left behind to perish, and in several instances they ate their own children*. (Emphasis added).[2]

C: 1855: Council Grove, Kansas Territory, Indian Agent, John Montgomery, Kansa Indians Extinction

> I am constrained to say that the Kansas are a poor, degraded, superstitious, thievish, indigent, tribe of Indians; their tendency is downward, and, in my opinion, they must soon become extinct, and the sooner they arrive at this period, the better it will be for the rest of mankind. (Emphasis added). John Montgomery, Indian Agent. (Censured by Commissioner Manypenny).[3]
>
> *Many of the Indians are impressed with the idea that they belong to a race that shall become extinct, and this opinion produces such*

gloom, despondency and even despair, as to wither their energies and destroy their aspirations. (Emphasis added).[4]

1860: Texas Frontier Whites – No More a Crime to Kill an Indian than to Shoot a Deer

[T]hey have been kept in [constant alarm] by the threats and excitement of the people on the frontier of Texas, some of whom, it would seem, regard it as no more a crime to kill an Indian than to shoot a deer, and take a scalp of man or woman with the same sense of exhilaration and triumph with which a free hunter takes the brush of the animal run down by his dogs. If they are justly dealt with, not permitted to be hunted down as game and exterminated, but encouraged and rewarded, they will soon become self-supporting, and triumphantly vindicate the wisdom of the policy of colonization.[5]

D: 1866: Dakota Superintendency, Eating Offal from Slop Buckets, Grains of Corn on Ground

Even now, when they have nothing but dry buffalo meat, and not much of that, and when they had reason to expect a feast on our coming, and when the *commissary of the army has a very special order not to feed the Indians coming in to make a treaty*, they will run like chickens to *gather the offal from the slop buckets that are carried from the garrison kitchens*, while they pass a pile of corn and hundreds of loose cattle without touching a thing except when told they may gather up the grains of corn from the ground, where the rats in their depredations have let it fall from the sacks, (for corn is plenty for horses, mules, and cattle, where grass is abundant,) but not a pound can be issued to the craving Indians, whose hunting grounds we occupy. (Emphasis added).[6]

E. 1872: U.S.' Manifest Destiny Is Paramount

Debasing Indians to the category of an animal permitted horrific treatment by others, even to the point of wantonly killing them. This wasn't a localized problem. Acting Commissioner Mix stated the following in 1867 regarding the "vicious, unscrupulous whites" on page one of his Report to Secretary Browning:

No doubt the greatest obstacle to the consummation [progress of Indians] is to be found mainly in his almost constant contact with the vicious, unscrupulous whites, who not only teach him their base ways, but *defraud and rob him, and, often without cause, with as little compunction as they would experience in killing a dog, take even his life*. Another cause or hindrance is the fact that the Indian has no certainty as to the permanent possession of the land he occupies and which he is urged to improve, for he knows not how long he may be permitted to enjoy it. Should it be in a region of remarkable fertility, or in a country abounding in rich mineral ores, it may be wanted for the white man's occupancy or use. The plea of *"manifest destiny" is paramount and the Indian must give way, though it be at the sacrifice of what may be as dear as life.* (Emphasis added).[7]

Commissioner Walker, the guardian (trustee) for the Indians, bluntly stated in 1872 his support for fulfilling the U.S.' Manifest Destiny:

> *The westward course of population is neither to be denied nor delayed for the sake of all the Indians that ever called this country their home. They must yield or perish...* (Emphasis added).[8]

NOTES

1. Civilization of the Indians, March 23, 1824, ASP: Indian Affairs, 2: 458.
2. Report of the Commissioner of Indian Affairs to the Secretary of the Interior, 1854, Central Superintendency, United States. Printer: A.O.P. Nicholson, 1855, p. 83.
3. Report of the Commissioner of Indian Affairs to the Secretary of the Interior, 1855, United States. Office of Indian Affairs. Printer: A.O.P. Nicholson, 1856, p. 114. (Censured by Commissioner Manypenny).
4. Report of the Commissioner of Indian Affairs to the Secretary of the Interior (1855), Office of Indian Affairs, 1856, pp. 17-18.
5. Report of the Commissioner of Indian Affairs to the Secretary of the Interior, Southern Superintendency, United States. Office of Indian Affairs, 1860, p. 118.
6. Report of the Commissioner of Indian Affairs to the Secretary of the Interior, United States, Dakota Superintendency, Office of Indian Affairs. U.S. Government Printing Office, 1866, p. 167.
7. United States. Office of Indian Affairs. Report of the Commissioner of Indian Affairs to the Secretary of the Interior. U.S. Government Printing Office, 1872, p. 9.
8. https://merehistory.weebly.com/uploads/1/5/1/5/15155754/ccr-- heartland_ transcript. pdf (accessed April 17, 2022).

#7 Withholding Federal Aid (e.g., Rations and Annuities), Even when Due Under Treaties

~

... Government aid extended to Indians in the form of rations, implements, clothing, etc., is in many instances not a gratuity, but is given simply in fulfillment of treaty stipulations and in payment for land ceded by the Indians to the United States.[1]

A. 1856: Sioux Agency, Withholding Annuities, P. Prescott, Superintendent for Farming for Sioux

> The treaties say these funds shall be annually expended, whereas, large amounts have been kept back, and are now in arrears and that after repeated applications to have them expended. These arrears are not mere petty sums, surplusses or remnants of funds remaining unexpended, but *large amounts, thousand and tens of thousands*, and in some cases the whole fund appropriated for a special purpose. (Emphasis added).[2] [Commissioner Manypenny was upset over Agent Prescott's Report and accepted his resignation.]

Annuities in monies and goods that were a federal obligation were used as economic sanctions to get Indians to cede lands and to move out of the State of Wisconsin. Governor Ramsey and John Watrous, an Indian Agent at La Pointe, conspired to lure the Ojibwe's to Minnesota and then extend the time for payment, making it impossible for them to return home in the dead of winter. They were forced to travel three to five hundred canoe and portage miles to Sandy Lake in Minnesota to receive their annuities. While waiting to receive their annuities at Sandy Lake, Agent Watrous wrote to Governor Ramsey that as many as 150 Ojibwe had died. With the waterways frozen over, the Ojibwe abandoned their canoes and returned home to Wisconsin on foot in what is referred to as the Wisconsin Death March. Chief Buffalo told Commissioner Luke Lea that another 230 died during the long, cold march home.

The disease and starvation the Ojibwe experienced strengthened their resolve to remain in Wisconsin. Governor Ramsey was allowed to engage in a battle of wills, requiring the Ojibwe to travel to Sandy Lake for their annuities, but he lost. In 1854, the Lake Superior Ojibwe signed a new treaty at La Pointe that promised permanent reservations and on-site annual payments in their homeland.

1876: Idaho, Fort Hall, Starving

> The Indians present in November remained upon the reservation all winter, and of course had to be subsisted by the Government. Although the strictest economy was used in the distribution of food, only half rations of flour, beef, and potatoes being issued, by the 1st of March all the flour and nearly all the beef had been consumed.
>
> Had it not been for the wheat crop raised on the agency-farm,

from which 60,000 pounds of flour was made, the Indians must have starved. As it was, I had to stop the general issue on the 20th of April, and from that date furnish food only to the families of farmers, agency-laborers, the old and infirm, making in all about three hundred persons to be fed during the summer.

The rations of more than a thousand Indians were thus cut off, and they were thrown upon their own resources for a living. This in a season of the year when the mountains and foot-hills were covered with snow, and in a country where, under the most favorable circumstances, game is hard to obtain. *Large numbers came to the office begging most piteously for food, stating that their children were crying for bread, which I well knew was the truth* ... (Emphasis added).[3]

1877: Nez Perce War

Upon the discovery of gold, in the fall of 1860, the reservation was soon overrun by settlers rushing to the mines…

To this another grievance was added in the distribution of annuities, articles being supplied in inadequate quantities. In 1862, only 247 blankets were furnished the tribe, or *one blanket to six Indians*, and 4,393 yards of calico, which was less than two yards to each Indian. Giving a blanket to one Indian works no satisfaction to the other five, who receive none, and *two yards of calico to each Indian* affords but little help and no advancement; yet this was all that could be distributed owing to the *meagre appropriations allowed*. (Emphasis added).[4]

B. 1898: Sac and Fox Tribes – Land Allotted; Abolish Annuities, Force Them to Work

The only way, in my opinion, to compel them to farm or work their lands and send their children to school is to abolish the payment to them of annuities and thus force them to go to work.[5]

1885: LMC: Adult Indians should be brought under preparation for self-support. To this end the *free ration system should be discontinued as rapidly as possible*, and a sufficient number of farmers and other industrial teachers should be provided meantime to teach them to earn their own living.[6]

C. 1902: Cutting Off Rations

In the discussion of the Indian's progress and the difficulties to be

~ 369

overcome on his way to civilization. It was pointed out that among the obstacles to his self-support the first and perhaps the principal one was the then prevailing ration system, which was justly condemned as encouraging idleness with its attendant vices and as foreign in its results to the very purpose for which it was designed. At the same time, while an evil, it was admitted to be a necessary evil, to be endured only while the Indian was learning the art of self-support, or at least put in a way where, by the exercise of ordinary industry, he could support himself. The continuance, however, of the practice of the indiscriminate issue of rations to all alike, without regard to their worldly condition was earnestly opposed, and it was laid down as a correct rule of action that only the old and helpless should be supported, while the able-bodies, if not already self-supporting, should be given the opportunity to work and should then be required to take care of themselves

Faith without works is dead. Realizing this the office set to work to show by its acts the sincerity of its belief.

And here it is proper to say that this change in the manner of dealing with the Indians was not a hasty conception on the part of the office. Indeed, it was not new at all. It has been the hope and desire of enlightened men for many years. But inasmuch *as it has been the subject of some harsh criticism and severe condemnation*, and as the Indian Office has been freely charged with ignorance and blunders, it is simply fair that the motive which governed it and the principles which actuated it should be known and understood in order that the public may form an intelligent judgment on the matters involved. ... *The ration system and the reservation system are doomed.* (Emphasis added).[7]

NOTES

1. 2 Report of the Annual Lake Mohonk Conference on the Indian and Other Dependent Peoples (1884).
2. Report of the Commissioner of Indian Affairs to the Secretary of the Interior, 1856, United States, U.S. Government Printing Office, 1857, p. 588.
3. Report of the Commissioner of Indian Affairs to the Secretary of the Interior, Reports of Agents in Idaho, United States. Office of Indian Affairs, U.S. Government Printing Office, 1876, p. 43.
4. Report of the Commissioner of Indian Affairs to the Secretary of the Interior, Nez Perce War, U.S. Government Printing Office, 1877, p. 10.
5. Report of the Commissioner of Indian Affairs, Office of Indian Affairs, United States. U.S. Government Printing Office, 1898, p. 250.
6. 3 Report of the Annual Lake Mohonk Conference on the Indian and Other Dependent Peoples (1885).
7. Report of the Commissioner of Indian Affairs to the Secretary of the Interior, United States. Office of Indian Affairs, U.S. Government Printing Office, 1902, pp. 1-2, 12.

#8 Acquiescing in Death of Indians from Exposure and/or Starvation

1858: Indians Will Be Left to Starve or Steal if Not Provided for by U.S.

Commissioner Mix presumed Indians would be left to starve or steal. The government had no choice other than to providing for or exterminate them.

> We have no longer distant and extensive sections of country which we can assign them, abounding in game, from which they could derive a ready and comfortable support; a resource which has, in a great measure, failed them where they are, and in consequence of which they must, at times, be subjected to the pangs of hunger, if not actual starvation, or obtain a subsistence by depredations upon our frontier settlements. If it were practicable to prevent such depredations, the alternative to providing for the Indians in the manner indicated, would be to leave them to starve; but as it is impossible, in consequence of the very great extent of our frontier, and our limited military force, to adequately guard against such occurrences, the only alternative, in fact, to making such provision for them, is to exterminate them.[1]

1859: Condition of Indians in Utah Desperate; No Adequate Subsistence; Whites in Possession of Good Country

> *The reports of the condition of the Indians in Utah present a melancholy picture. The whites are in possession of most of the little comparatively good country there is*, and the game has become so scarce as no longer to afford the Indians an adequate subsistence. They are often reduced to the greatest straits, particularly in the winter, which is severe in that region; and when *it is no uncommon thing for them to perish of cold and hunger.* Even at other seasons, numbers of them are compelled to sustain life by using for food reptiles, insects, grass seed, and roots. (Emphasis added).[2]

1865: Crow Creek Sioux – Kept in Semi-Starvation for Two Years

> The undersigned deem it proper also to represent the miserable state of the Sioux Indians, principally women and children, who were taken prisoners in 1862, after the outbreak in Minnesota, and transported the following spring to the Crow Creek reservation, on the Missouri river. Concurrent evidence, of the most reliable character, shows these helpless creatures to have been kept in *a condition of semi-starvation for the two years following their arrival* at their new home, during which period *several hundred have died from actual want, or from disease superinduced by it.*

There are about a thousand remaining on the reservation, of whom only one-tenth are men, mostly aged and infirm. Even now, although every effort seems to have been made by the superintendent and agent to secure a proper supply, these people are receiving an amount of subsistence barely sufficient to sustain life, the liberal appropriation made by Congress for their benefit not having been expended for that purpose sufficiently early in the season to secure the delivery of the provisions at so high a point on the river. Treaty Commission. (Emphasis added).[3]

The **Blackfeet Indians** endured starvation in the Winters of 1881-1882 and 1883-1884. Men, women and children died. A Special Agent reported the extensive numbers in need of food: Last week 3,200 persons presented themselves as actually in need of subsistence.

Again, as to the Blackfeet:

Their supplies had been limited and many of them were gradually dying of starvation. I visited a large number of their tents and cabins. All bore marks of suffering from lack of food, but *the little children seemed to have suffered most; they were so emaciated that it did not seem possible for them to live long, and many of them have since passed away*. To feed these Indians, I was reduced to such a strait that *I was compelled to issue over 2,000 pounds of bacon which had been condemned*. Indians stripped the bark from saplings to eat. The buffalo, on which these people formerly subsisted, is now extinct. (Emphasis added).[4]

1887: OR, Warm Springs Reservation - Ultimatum - Nothing but Gradual Starvation

Uncertain boundary. White trespassers. Whites disagree with boundary line set by agent. Indians were fraudulently cheated out of their fishery by the Huntington treaty. It is their principal source of subsistence, and they never intended to part with it, but were cheated and swindled out of it by a cunning and unprincipled United States official. ... Barren and sterile condition of the reservation. There is not a sufficient amount of arable land for Indians or anybody else to maintain a living upon. *What is their ultimatum - nothing but gradual starvation.* (Emphasis added).[5]

1890: AZ, Mohaves, No Irrigation, Condemned to Slow Starvation

Expecting them to remain here without furnishing water for any them to irrigate their land with is of the same principle of confining a man in prison and *condemning him to slow starvation*. When I arrived here last April these Indians were in a starving condition, having scarcely anything to live on. A little cactus was all they had to eat last winter besides what few rations were issued to them. The cactus only serves to fill up one with scarcely any nutrient. .... To all appearances the only means of civilization the Government has furnished the Mohaves for several years was starvation. (Emphasis added).[6]

Also, please see the other numerous previous references.

NOTES

1. Annual Report of the Department of the Interior ... [with Accompanying Documents], Part 1, Printer: Wm. A. Harris, 1858, p. 9.
2. Report of the Commissioner of Indian Affairs to the Secretary of the Interior (1859), Office of Indian Affairs, p. 21.
3. Report of the Commissioner of Indian Affairs to the Secretary of the Interior, Appendix, United States. Office of Indian Affairs, U.S. Government Printing Office, 1865, p. 541.
4. Report of the Commissioner of Indian Affairs to the Secretary of the Interior, United States. Office of Indian Affairs, U.S. Government Printing Office, 1884, pp. 106-107.
5. Report of the Commissioner of Indian Affairs to the Secretary of the Interior, United States, Office of Indian Affairs, U.S. Government Printing Office, 1887, p. 277.
6. Report of the Commissioner of Indian Affairs to the Secretary of the Interior, Vol. 2, United States, Office of Indian Affairs, U.S. Government Printing Office, 1890, p. 3.

#9 Running Railroad Routes across Indian Lands, Allowing Quick Military Transport to Control and Subdue Indians; Bisected Northern and Southern Plains Tribes from One Another Reducing Their Military Threat

A. 1862: Pacific Railway Act

The Pacific Railway Act of 1862 (12 Stat. 489) provided federal subsidies in land and loans for the construction of a transcontinental railroad across the U.S. The legislation authorized two railroad companies, the Union Pacific and the Central Pacific, to construct the lines. Under the Act, the U.S. would extinguish any Indian title along the route.

1865: Secure Railroad Right-of-Ways from Indians

> Whatever can properly be done by the government of the United States in paving the way for railroads should, in my judgment, be done now, and thus avoid difficulties which may arise in the future.[1]

B. 1867: General Sherman

General Sherman believed military protection of the railroad construction parties was a task for the Army.

> These roads, although in the hands of private corporations have more than the usual claim on us for military protection, because the general government is largely interested pecuniarily (sic). They aid us materially in our military operations by transporting troops and stores rapidly across a belt of land hitherto only passed in the summer by slow trains drawn by oxen, dependent on the grass for food.[2]

In 1867, he wrote to General Ulysses S. Grant, *"we are not going to let thieving, ragged Indians check and stop the progress of the railroads."* (Emphasis added).[3]

Land Speculation and Atchison, Topeka and Santa Fe Railway

Cyrus Holliday secured a charter from the Kansas legislature in 1859 to build the Atchison, Topeka & Santa Fe Railway, but it needed land close to Topeka. Led by Senator Pomeroy, the Railway Company entered into negotiations with the Potawatomi resulting in an 1868 Treaty (15 Stat. 531), approved by Congress, whereby it purchased 338,766 unallotted acres from the Potawatomi at $1 an acre, with easy six-year, 6 percent terms. The Railway Company turned around and put this land on the market to settlers for 20 percent down and the balance in five equal installments. Some tracts were sold for as much as $16 per acre, but others went to insiders like Pomeroy and his brother-in-law at only $1 per acre.[4]

Railroads Spur Western Settlement with Pioneer Vigilantes

In his 1871 Report to the Secretary of the Treasury, the U.S. Commissioner of Mining Statistics, captured the *carte blanche approval for settlers* to deal with the Indians "*in their own way.*"

> But what the Government has not been able to do in the past the South Pacific or Texas Pacific Railroad will certainly do. As in the case of the Union and Central Pacific roads, it will attract population, and *the citizens, less hampered in regard to Indians than the military powers, will soon dispose of the question in their own way*. (Emphasis added). ... *Emigration pouring in would soon solve the Indian problem by the extermination or complete subjugation of the hostile tribes*. (Emphasis added).[5]

C: 1872: Commissioner Walker

As the railways expanded, they allowed the rapid transport of troops and supplies to areas where Indian battles were being waged. Commissioner Francis A. Walker reported:

> Indeed, the progress of two years more, if not of another summer, on the Northern Pacific Railroad will of itself completely solve the great Sioux problem, and leave the ninety thousand Indians ranging between the two transcontinental lines as incapable of resisting the Government as are the Indians of New York or Massachusetts. *Columns moving north from the Union Pacific, and south from the Northern Pacific, would crush the Sioux* and their confederates as between the upper and the nether millstone; while the rapid movement of troops along the northern line would prevent the escape of the savages, when hard pressed, into the British Possessions, which have heretofore afforded a convenient refuge on the approach of a military expedition. (Emphasis added).[6]

D: 1874: General G. M. Dodge, Chief Engineer, Union Pacific

In an 1874 Report of General G. M. Dodge, Chief Engineer, Union Pacific, he wrote: "*Experience proves the Railroad line through Indian Territory a Fortress as well as a highway.*" (Emphasis added).[7]

E. 1882: Senator Dawes – Congress' Determination to Run Railroads through Indian Territory

> In the United States, railroads were suspiciously in need of Indian land to expand across the country. The government wanted not only the excess land from reservations after giving each Indian a small

amount of land, but it also wanted to put Indians fully under the power of the United States Congress.

In his letter to Senator Teller, Dawes himself detailed this exact motivation in admitting "the determination by Congress to put Railroads through the Indian Territory under the power of 'Eminent Domain' regardless of treaty stipulations puts the whole territory hereafter at the mercy of a majority in Congress..."[8]

NOTES

1. Report of the Commissioner of Indian Affairs to the Secretary of the Interior (1865), Arizona Superintendency Office of Indian Affairs, 1865, p. 42.
2. THE REPORT OF GENERAL-IN-CHIEF, REPORT OF LIEUTENANT GENERAL SHERMAN. HEADQUARTERS MILITARY DIVISION OF THE MISSOURI, St. Louis, Mo., October 1, 1867. *Annual Report of the Secretary of War to Congress-1867 Report of General Sherman-Division of the Missouri Combined Arms Research Library, Ft. Leavenworth, KS D00998 roll no. 3 1867 page 33.* https://freepages.rootsweb.com/~familyinformation/history/fpk/sow67.html (accessed online September 27, 2023).
3. The Papers of Ulysses S. Grant: January 1-September 30, 1867, Volume 17 of Papers of Ulysses S. Grant, Ulysses Simpson Grant, Editor John Y. Simon, SIU Press, 1991, p. 162. https://digitalcommons.law.ou.edu/ cgi/viewcontent.cgi?article=2714&context=indianserialset (accessed online September 2, 2022).
4. Railroads of Kansas. Kathy Alexander, Feb. 2023. https://legendsofkansas.com/kansas-railroads/ (accessed online March 14, 2023).
5. Statistics Of Mines And Mining In The States And Territories West Of The Rocky Mountains: Being The 6th Annual Report Of U.S. Commissioner Of Mining Statistics to Secretary of Treasury, 1871, pp. 278, 280.
6. Report of the Commissioner of Indian Affairs to the Secretary of the Interior, United States. Office of Indian Affairs. U.S. Government Printing Office, 1872, p. 9.
7. William T. Sherman to Grenville M. Dodge, January 16, 1867, in Grenville Mellen Dodge, Personal Recollections of President Abraham Lincoln, General Ulysses S. Grant and General William T. Sherman (Glendale, CA: Arthur H. Clark, 1914), 195; Grenville Dodge to T. Scott, January 12, 1874, Letterbooks, Texas Pacific Railroad, Box 160, Grenville M. Dodge Papers, MS 98, State Historical Society of Iowa, 72–73, 77.
8. Letter from Henry L. Dawes to Henry M. Teller (Commissioner of Indian Affairs), September 19, 1882. Dawes Papers, Library of Congress, Washington, D.C. Reproduced in: Washburn, Wilcomb E. The Assault on Indian Tribalism: The General Allotment Law (Dawes Act) of 1887. Philadelphia: J.B. Lippincott Co., 1975. Meyer, Morgan. *A SETTLER COLONIAL FRAMEWORK DEVELOPED THROUGH THE DAWES ACT AND THE NATIVES LAND ACT.* Diss. 2017, p. 31.

#10 Abolishing Indian Reservations

A. LMC, Merrill Gates - Break Up Reservation

In his address on Land and Law as Agents in Educating Indians, in 1885, Mr. Gates took a straightforward approach to accomplishing this objective:

> *Break up the reservation. Its usefulness is past. Treat it as we treat the fever-infected hospital when life has so often yielded to disease ... it has proved to be a curse; away with it! burn it!* (Emphasis added).[1]

B: LMC, Rev. Abbott, Reservation System Should Be Uprooted

> Rev. Abbott stated: The Indian reservation prevents all these desirable results [labor and family virtues], insulates Indians from civilization, cultivates vice, is a domain for lawlessness licensed by the United States. *The reservation must go* but the rights of the Indian must be protected.
>
> I declare my conviction then that the reservation system is hopelessly wrong; that it cannot be amended or modified; that *it can only be uprooted, root, trunk, branch and leaf*, and a new system put in its place. (Emphasis added).[2]

C. LMC, Charles C. Painter – Break Down Reservation Walls; Remove Irresponsible Despot – Indian Agent

One of the most powerful men in the movement for Indian reform was Charles C. Painter, who from 1884 until his death early in 1895 was the full-time agent of the Indian Rights Association in Washington.

> As we grew stronger and the Indian weaker, and as the business of the agent became more and more that of a large disburser of provisions and annuities, with which we have made them helpless and pauperized dependents, his power has grown to the overthrow of all self-government, and *he is now an irresponsible despot, who has no laws to execute as related to the growth and development of the Indians.* (Emphasis added).[3]
>
> So we have, as parts of our civilizing machine, a reservation which excludes civilization and law and social order, and the institutions of organized society; which shuts in savagery and lawlessness. *Also, as the guardian of its gates, the agent who has power to shut out every one excepting the officer duly authorized to inspect him, has power even of life and death over those under his care, with*

no restraint upon him except what restraint fear may exert, with no body of laws to execute, with no institutions of government or social order to uphold, with immense facilities for demoralizing those under his power, and the duty of doing so largely as his business, under orders of the Department; and the temptation to do so in individual cases, to gain his own private ends, always upon him, with little fear of detection; also, until within a few years, unbounded opportunity to enrich himself at the expense of those who had no protector but himself; with no temptation in the way of reward for good conduct, and a wise use of power to advance his people, because continuance in office does not depend upon this, but upon the permanence in power of the political party to which he belongs, and with the assurance that if his wards outgrow the necessity of a guardian that his occupation is gone. (Emphasis added).[4]

What would you put in place of this? ***I would at once break down the reservation walls and let civilization go in***; I would secure the Indians for the present inalienable possession of sufficient land, by personal title, for the use of each one; I would sell the remainder for their benefit, and, in place of the agent's irresponsible will, make them subject to the laws and give them their protection; I would give them without delay citizenship with all its privileges and duties, and for the present place their property under the administration of a wise commission of such men as have been charged with the Peabody and like funds; with all the safeguards that can be thrown around it—a commission which should be removable only by death or impeachment or proved incapacity, and require that within a reasonable time this fund should be exhausted and there should nothing remain to separate the Indian from other citizens except the bronze of his skin and the memory of his great wrongs softened and made tender by the grace and sufficiency of our tardy atonement. (Emphasis added).[5]

Explaining the viewpoint of those who viewed the usurpation of Indian lands as only proper, Congregational clergyman Lyman Abbott wrote in 1885:

They did not occupy the coal mines, nor the gold mines, into which they never struck a pick; nor the rivers which flow to the sea, and on which the music of a mill was never heard. The Indians can scarcely be said to have occupied this country more than the bisons and the buffalo they hunted. Three hundred thousand people have no right to hold a continent and keep at bay a race able to people it and provide the happy homes of civilization. We do owe the Indians sacred rights and obligations, but one of those duties is not the right to let them hold forever the land they did not occupy, and which they were not making fruitful for themselves or others.[6]

Prof. Painter: I think there is no question but that the reservation system, the system of isolation and absorption, has held the Indian aloof from our civilization and denied him the opportunities of a citizen and a man. This process continued indefinitely will continue the problem. The difficulties of this reservation system are immense; it is an incubus upon every effort for the advancement of the Indian.[7]

D. 1886: LMC Business Committee Resolutions - Reservation and Agency System Impedes Civilization of Indian Race

We are convinced that the advancement of the Indian race in civilization is impeded rather than helped by a continuance of the reservation and agency system; and that their progress will be aided by its abandonment, as soon as practicable, with due consideration of all rights in the land acquired by the Indians. For this outgrown system would be substituted the rights and responsibilities of citizenship with individual ownership of homestead farms, or grazing ranges, and the protection of the equal laws made for all citizens as administered by the courts of the country. This change of the relations between the Government and the Indians is especially urgent in the case of tribes already surrounded or closely approached by a population of white citizens. Under these conditions the segregation of the Indians on reservations and their confinement thereon, under the arbitrary control of an agent and his subordinates, and subject to the existing laws regarding intercourse and trade with the whites, operate to keep them ignorant, barbarous, poor, dependent, and deprived of those inducements to industry and prudence which are potent forces in developing the saving aspirations and energies of every race of mankind. (Emphasis added).[8]

E. 1891: Captain Pratt Would Blow Reservations to Pieces

I would blow the reservations to pieces. I would not give the Indian an acre of land. When he strikes bottom, he will get up. I never owned an acre of land, and I never expect to own one. (Emphasis added).[9]

F. 1893: LMC Platform Item No. 4 - Break Up Reservations

LMC Platform *4. The breaking up of the reservations as rapidly as the interests of the Indians will allow, and the incorporation of the Indians in the mass of American citizens.* (Emphasis added).[10]

G. 1905: Indian Reservation System Should Be Abolished

The reservation system is an insuperable obstacle to civilization, and should be abolished, the tribal organization destroyed, the lands allotted in severalty, the Indians intermingled with the whites, and the Indians treated as other men. (Emphasis added).[11]

NOTES

1. E. Gates, Merrill. "6. Land and Law as Agents in Educating Indians". Americanizing the American Indian: Writings by the "Friends of the Indian" 1880-1900, edited by Francis Paul Prucha, Cambridge, MA and London, England: Harvard University Press, 1973.
2. 3 Report of the Annual Lake Mohonk Conference on the Indian and Other Dependent Peoples (1885), p. 53.
3. 4 Report of the Annual Lake Mohonk Conference on the Indian and Other Dependent Peoples (1886), p. 26.
4. 4 Report of the Annual Lake Mohonk Conference on the Indian and Other Dependent Peoples (1886), p. 20.
5. "Our Indian Policy as Related to the Civilization of the Indian," 4 Report of the Annual Lake Mohonk Conference on the Indian and Other Dependent Peoples (1886).
6. 3 Report of the Annual Lake Mohonk Conference on the Indian and Other Dependent Peoples (1885), p. 51. Shannon, B. Clay. Still Casting Shadows: A Shared Mosaic of US History: Volume 1: 1620-1913. iUniverse, 2006. https://archive.org/stream/StillCastingShadowsASharedMosaicOfU.s.HistoryVol.I1620-1914/StillCastingShadows1_djvu.txt (accessed online December 8, 2024).
7. 3 Report of the Annual Lake Mohonk Conference on the Indian and Other Dependent Peoples (1885), p. 29.
8. 4 Report of the Annual Lake Mohonk Conference on the Indian and Other Dependent Peoples (1886), p. 41.
9. 9 Report of the Annual Lake Mohonk Conference on the Indian and Other Dependent Peoples (1891), p. 67.
10. 11 Report of the Annual Lake Mohonk Conference on the Indian and Other Dependent Peoples (1893), pp. 5-6.
11. 13 Report of the Annual Lake Mohonk Conference on the Indian and Other Dependent Peoples (1895), p. 105.

#11 Disintegrating Indian Tribes

1885: Destroy Tribal Relations; Agents Allowed to Punish for Minor Offenses by Imprisonment or Withholding Rations

> Commissioner J.D.C. Atkins: The policy of the Government for many years past has been to destroy the tribal relations as fast as possible, and to use every endeavor to bring the Indians under the influence of law. To do this the agents have been accustomed to punish for minor offenses, by imprisonment in the guard-house and by with holding rations. ...[1]

A. LMC: Every Effort Should Be Made to Secure Disintegration of All Tribal Organizations

> II. WHAT IS NECESSARY TO SECURE INDIAN CITIZENSHIP? 1st. Resolved, That the organization of the Indians in tribes is, and has been, one of the most serious hindrances to the advancement of the Indian toward civilization, and that every effort should be made to secure the disintegration of all tribal organizations; that to accomplish this result the Government should, except where it is clearly necessary either for the fulfillment of treaty stipulations or for some other binding reason, cease to recognize the Indians as political bodies or organized tribes. (Emphasis added).[2]

B. 1885 Speech by Merrill Gates at LMC: Tribal Organization Must Be Broken Up

Land and Law as Agents in Educating Indians

> *Two peculiarities which mark the Indian life, if retained, will render his progress slow, uncertain and difficult. These are: (1) The tribal organization. (2) The Indian reservation.*
>
> *THE TRIBAL ORGANIZATION MUST BE BROKEN UP.* I am satisfied that no man can carefully study the Indian question without the deepening conviction that these institutions must go if we would save the Indian from himself. And first, the tribe. Politically it is an anomaly an imperium in imperio. Early in our history, when whites were few and Indians were relatively numerous and were grouped in tribes with something approaching to a rude form of government, it was natural, it was inevitable, that we should treat them as tribes. It would have been hopeless for us to attempt to modify their tribal relations. But now the case is entirely different. There is hardly one tribe outside the five civilized tribes of the Indian Territory which

can merit the name of an organized society or which discharges the simplest functions of government. Disintegration has long been the rule.

There is an utter barbarism in which property has almost no existence. *The tribal organization tends to retain men in such barbarism*. It is a great step gained when you awaken in an Indian the desire for the acquisition of property of his own, by his own honest labor

THE TRIBAL SYSTEM PARALYZES LABOR. But the tribal system paralyzes at once the desire for property and the family life that ennobles that desire. Where the annuities and rations that support a tribe are distributed to the industrious and the lazy alike, while almost all property is held in common, there cannot be any true stimulus to industry.

IT PREVENTS ALL ACCUMULATION OF PROPERTY FOR THE BENEFIT OF CHILDREN.
The gravest charge against the tribal organization, then, is that it tends to dwarf and blight the family. Tribal relations interfere with family grouping, and there is no sound progress in civilization until land begins to be held and property to be accumulated by groups at least as small as the family. (Emphasis added).[3]

NOTES

1. Report of the Commissioner of Indian Affairs, Vol. 2, Department of the Interior, United States. Office of Indian Affairs, U.S. Government Printing Office, 1885, p. XXI.
2. 1884 Second Annual Address to the Public of the Lake Mohonk Conference (Philadelphia: 1884), p. 6.
3. E. Gates, Merrill. "6. Land and Law as Agents in Educating Indians". Americanizing the American Indian: Writings by the "Friends of the Indian" 1880-1900, edited by Francis Paul Prucha, Cambridge, MA and London, England: Harvard University Press, 1973.

#12 Allotting Tribal Lands to Individual Indians
~

1838: Office of Indian Affairs (aka Indian Bureau) Advocacy for Allotment

As early as 1838, allotment of Indian lands was seen as the mechanism for eliminating "savagism." No effort was made whatsoever to understand the internal governance of the tribes or their heritage and culture.

> Unless some system is marked out by which there shall be a separate allotment of land to each individual whom the scheme shall entitle to it, you will look in vain for any general casting off of savagism. Common property and civilization cannot co-exist.[1]

1886: Reformers stressed the need for Indians to be self-reliant and self-supporting, and they sought a policy that would deal with Indians as individuals, rather than as part of a tribe. Owning land in severalty was one aspect of this policy. In 1886, Senator Dawes, addressing the Lake Mohonk Conference averred to another reason: white settlers would steal all Indian land, and Indians should at least be guaranteed 160 acres per family *"before every acre disappears from under him forever."*

2. Immediate measures should be taken to break up the system of holding all lands in common, and each Indian family should receive a patent for a portion of land to be held in severalty, its amount dependent upon the number of members of the family and the character of the land, whether adapted for cultivation or for grazing.
3 Report of the Annual Lake Mohonk Conference on the Indian and Other Dependent Peoples (1885), pp. 48-50.

A. 1885 Speech by Merrill Gates at LMC: Land in Severalty Patented to Indian as an Individual

> 1885 Gates Speech Land In Severalty.
> *First of all, he must have land in severalty*. ... It shall be patented to him as an individual. He shall hold it by what the Indians who have been hunted from reservation to reservation pathetically call, in their requests for justice, "a paper-talk from Washington, which tells the Indian what land is his so that a white man cannot get it away from him." (Emphasis added).

> 2. Immediate measures should be taken to break up the system of holding all lands in common, and each Indian family should receive a patent for a portion of land to be held in severalty, its amount dependent upon the number of members of the family and the character of the land, whether adapted for cultivation or for grazing.[2]

1887: BIC Praises GAA

In 1880, 1881, 1883, 1883 and every year to 1887 the Board had urged the passage of legislation providing for individual allotments of land to those Indians capable of receiving them.

BIC was pleased with the GAA in its 1887 report.

> The bill is a great step in advance in our Indian policy, and the day when it was approved by the President may be called the Indian emancipation day. The measure gives the Indian the possibility to become a man instead of remaining a ward of the Government. ... "The law is only the seed, whose germination and growth will be a slow process, and we must wait patiently for its mature fruit."[57]

> Some whole tribes are unprepared for the execution of the law or to profit by it if it were by force applied to them. Hence we are pleased to notice that the Executive has begun the work of allotments under the provisions of the new act upon some of the smaller reservations where the Indians are somewhat advanced in education and habits of industry. Twenty-seven reservations have been selected.[3]

1881: President Chester A. Arthur on American Indian Policy: Allotment with Alienability Restriction

The following is extracted from President Chester A. Arthur's First Annual Message to Congress, delivered December 6, 1881.

> Prominent among the matters which challenge the attention of Congress at its present session is the management of our Indian affairs. ...
> Second. ... The enactment of a general law permitting the allotment in severalty, to such Indians, at least, as desire it, of a reasonable quantity of land secured to them by patent, and for their own protection made inalienable for twenty or twenty-five years...

B. 1882: Senator Dawes - Lake Mohonk Conference: We Are Blind, Deaf, Insane if We Don't Protect Indian by Allotting Land to Him; Civilization Has Got After Indian Lands with a "Greed Never Before Equaled"

In a letter to Senator Teller, Senator Dawes himself detailed this exact motivation:

> An uncontrollable spirit is abroad in the land to appropriate what is called the "demands of civilization" every foot of desirable land now occupied by the Indians. You cannot resist it; Congress instead of resisting it will help it on.

What can you do with them? We may cry out against the violation of treaties, denounce flagrant disregard of inalienable rights and the inhumanity of our treatment of the defenseless ... [but the fact remains there is] "no practical answer to this question."

Indians could not even comprehend what civilization expects of them: Two hundred thousand savages who cannot read a word of any language or speak a word of English, who were never taught to work and don't know how to earn their living nor care to learn, who can't read or be made to comprehend the laws they are expected to obey as citizens or know what is meant by a Court of Justice instituted to enforce them or even the law of *meum et tuum*, the foundation of society, cannot be set up in severalty and left to stand alone ... Without doubt these Indians are going to be absorbed into and become a part of the 50,000,000 of our people.

I do not write this because I have any plan of my own but because I have none and at the same time see a combination of irresistible forces driving the Indians in upon us a great deal faster than we shall be prepared to deal with them.

Senator Dawes (R-MASS), the namesake of the final bill, speaking of the land and resources of Native Americans stated that *"civilization has got after these possessions with a greed never before equaled but it is idle to expect to stay it...."* (Emphasis added).[4]

Our work must be done now and without delay, for the greed for the Indian's land is growing every day, and it is impossible to resist it under the forms of our Government as to stop the flow of the river. We may guide and direct it, but we cannot stop it. We are blind, we are deaf, we are insane if we do not take cognizance of the fact that there are forces in this land driving on these people with a determination to possess every acre of their land, and they will lose it unless we work on and declare that the original owner of this land shall, before every acre disappears from under him forever, have 160 acres of it when he shall be fitted to become a citizen of the United States and prepared to bear the burdens as well as share the rights of our Government. (Emphasis added).[5]

Senator Dawes: *The idea, is to take the Indians out one by one from under the tribe, place him in a position to become an independent American citizen, and then before the tribe is aware of it its existence tribe is gone.* (Emphasis added). As Dawes put it, *The idea [behind the Act] is to take the Indians out one by one from under the tribe, place him in a position to become an independent American citizen, then before the tribe is aware of it its existence as a tribe is gone.*[6]

C. 1886: Rep. Skinner Favored Allotment in Congressional Debate on Indian Citizenship

The debate on the Allotment legislation echoed the sentiment of the social reformers. One sponsor argued that the Indian must either perish, depend upon the Government for support, or abandon his thriftless habits, learn to eat bread in the sweat of his face, and finally rise to the level of the civilization that surrounds him and take upon himself the duties and responsibilities of American citizenship. Starvation, pauperism, or independent self-supporting citizenship - between these the Indian must take his choice, or, rather, we as his guardians, must choose for him ...

What shall be his future status? Shall he remain a pauper savage, blocking the pathway of civilization, an increasing burden upon the people? Or shall he be converted into a civilized tax-payer, contributing toward the support of the Government and adding to the material prosperity of the country?

The tribal relations must be broken up ... the practice of massing large numbers of Indians on reservations must be stopped ... lands must be allotted in severalty ... [and] where there is more land in any reservation than the Indians on that reservation can profitably use, such surplus lands must be so disposed of that the white man may get possession of them and come into contact with the Indians. (Emphasis added).[7]

While the General Allotment Act established a mandate for allotting Indian lands, separate legislation was required to actually allot the lands of a particular Indian nation. Usually, government officials would negotiate with a tribe's leaders to secure their cooperation in the allotment process. In addition to the grant of individual lands and monetary compensation to the tribe, other incentives were given to induce Indians to relinquish their tribal lands. Often, however, these incentives failed to have their desired effect. But the government proceeded to allot the reservations anyway, even when doing so violated prior treaties with the affected Indian nation.[8]

D. LMC: Dawes Severalty Bill Should Be Speedily Passed by House

Resolved, ... the Dawes land and severalty bill ... which [has] passed the Senate and have been favorably reported by the Committee on Indian Affairs, should in the interest of the Indian race be speedily passed by the House.[9]

E. 1887: Passage of Dawes Act

Senator Dawes: For a good many years the Mohonk conference and the friends of the Indian have believed that the Indian problem could never be solved until there was a law giving to the Indian land in severalty and citizenship...[10]

To-day the law confers upon every Indian in this land a homestead of his own; and if he will take it, it makes him a citizen of the United States, with all the privileges and immunities and rights of such a citizen, and opens to him the doors of all the courts in the land, upon the same terms that it opens them to every other citizen, imposing upon him the obligations and extending to him the protection of all the laws, civil and criminal, of the State or Territory in which he resides.[11]

Two hundred thousand Indians have been led out, as it were, to a new life, to a new pathway, which is to them all a mystery; they do not know whither it leads or how to travel it. In the darkness they are groping about, and they are wandering away. They do not embrace this new life as by magic, and come out citizens of the United States.[12]

With the passage of the Dawes Act], we have brought them to this condition-and it is not too much to say that there would never have been such a law had it not been for the Mohonk conference-and the Mohonk conference is responsible to-day for what shall take place in consequence of it. If the Mohonk people, and those who have sent them here, shall feel that they have done their duty and have accomplished their work by simply enacting such a law as this, they have brought upon the Indian a calamity instead of a blessing. (Emphasis added).[13]

If he starts wrong; if when he comes upon the homestead which is offered to him he does not know what homestead means; if he comes upon that homestead and is left there with no house to put himself in; nobody to tell him what to do with it; nobody to guide him; nobody to help by a word of encouragement; nobody to speak to him so that he can understand it, what is to become of him? He had better never have been put there. (Emphasis added).[14]

President Cleveland said that he did not intend, when he signed this bill, to apply it to more than one reservation at first, and so on, which I thought was very wise. But you see he has been led to apply it to half a dozen. The bill provides for capitalizing the remainder of the land for the benefit of the Indian, but the greed of

> *the landgrabber is such as to press the application of this bill to the utmost, as was said by Dr. Ellinwood last night. There is no danger but this will come most rapidly, - too rapidly, I think, the greed and hunger and thirst of the white man for the Indian's land is almost equal to his 'hunger and thirst for righteousness.' That is going to be the difficulty in the application of this bill. He is going to press it forward too fast.* (Emphasis added). There should not be any Indian located until he has had some provision made for a fair start.[15]

> *It should be called the Mohonk bill, that is the name of the bill; it is the inspiration of the people; you are responsible for it, and I want you to understand the scope of it.* (Emphasis added).[16]

> *There is danger that we may go too fast in hurrying Indian children into public schools; that we may travel too fast in issuing patents in fee to competent Indians; as we doubtless have gone too slow in permitting Indians to handle their individual Indian moneys and make their own leases.* (Emphasis added).[17]

F. 1890: General Nelson A. Miles Opposed Dawes Act - Will Lead to Greater Poverty and Problems on Reservations; Federal Government Had Failed to Live Up to Its Promises

A few years after the Dawes Act was passed, General Nelson A. Miles (1825–1923) expressed his opposition to the Dawes Act in a telegram addressed to Senator Dawes. Miles was an Army officer who had fought in the Civil War, had forced the Lakotas onto a reservation, had led the Army against Chief Joseph of the Nez Perce, and captured the Chiricahua Apache leader, Geronimo. Like many officers, Miles believed that the Army, not Congress, should be in charge of Indian policy. However, he also believed that the Dawes Act would only lead to greater poverty and problems on reservations. Part of the problem was that the federal government had failed to live up to its promises. Miles wrote:

> *First. The forcing process of attempting to make large bodies of Indians self-sustaining when the government was cutting down their rations and their crops almost a failure, is one cause of the difficulty.*

> *Second. While the Indians were urged and almost forced to sign a treaty presented to them by the commission authorized by Congress, in which they gave up a valuable portion of their reservation which is now occupied by white people, the government has failed to fulfill its part of the compact, and instead of an increase or even a reasonable supply for their support, they have been compelled*

to live on half and two-thirds rations, and received nothing for the surrender of their lands, neither has the government given any positive assurance that they intend to do any differently with them in the future.

Congress has been in session several weeks and could, if it were disposed, in a few hours confirm the treaties that its commissioners have made with these Indians and appropriate the necessary funds for its fulfillment, and thereby give an earnest of their good faith or intention to fulfill their part of the compact. Such action, in my judgment, is essential to restore confidence with the Indians and give peace and protection to the settlements. If this be done, and the President authorized to place the turbulent and dangerous tribes of Indians under the control of the military, Congress need not enter into details, but can safely trust the military authorities to subjugate and govern, and in the near future make self-sustaining, any or all of the Indian tribes of this country. (Emphasis added).[18]

1904: Report of School Superintendent, Tulalip Agency – Allotments Done - Break Up Last Semblances of Tribal Life

Allotments. This phase of the work is a very important one, serving, as it does and as few other things do, to **break up the last semblances of a tribal life** and the seeking of family homes in severalty. It inculcates the primary principles of ownership, and **here lies the foundation of citizenship and of responsibility**. The entire Muckleshoot Reservation of the agency has been surveyed, subdivided, and allotted directly under the supervision of this office, and the President of the United States has directed patents to issue therefor. With a very slight exception all of the unallotted lands of the Tulalip Reservation have been allotted. (Emphasis added).[19]

NOTES

1. Report of the Commissioner of Indian Affairs to the Secretary of the Interior, United States. Office of Indian Affairs. Blair & Rives, Printers. 1838, p. 17.
2. E. Gates, Merrill. "6. Land and Law as Agents in Educating Indians". Americanizing the American Indian: Writings by the "Friends of the Indian" 1880-1900, edited by Francis Paul Prucha, Cambridge, MA and London, England: Harvard University Press, 1973. 3 Report of the Annual Lake Mohonk Conference on the Indian and Other Dependent Peoples (1885), pp. 48-50.
3. Annual Report of the Board of Indian Commissioners to the Secretary of the Interior. Yr. 1887, p. 7. https://babel.hathitrust.org/cgi/pt?id=uc1.a0002911840&seq=13 (accessed online October 7, 2024).

4. Letter from Henry L. Dawes to Henry M. Teller (Commissioner of Indian Affairs), September 19, 1882. Dawes Papers, Library of Congress, Washington, D.C. Reproduced in: Washburn, Wilcomb E. The Assault on Indian Tribalism: The General Allotment Law (Dawes Act) of 1887. Philadelphia: J.B. Lippincott Co., 1975.
5. 4 Report of the Annual Lake Mohonk Conference on the Indian and Other Dependent Peoples (1886), p. 34.
6. (1) L.B. Priest, Uncle Sam's Step-children: The Reformation of U.S. Indian Policy, 1865-87 (New York: Octagon, 1973), 246-47. (2) Sovereignty Reconstituted: Governmentality and the Indian Reorganization Act John French DePaul University Department of Political Science Presented at the Annual Meeting of the Western Political Science Association San Diego, California March 24-26, 2015, p. 8. https://www.wpsanet.org/papers/docs/JFrench%20WPSA%202016.pdf (accessed online December 1, 2024). (3) Dawes Act. https://www.vaia.com/en-us/explanations/history/us-history/dawes-act/ (accessed online December 1, 2024). (4) ON 'MODEST PROPOSALS' TO FURTHER REDUCE THE ABORIGINAL LAND BASE BY PRIVATIZING RESERVE LAND© Susan Campbell Montreal, Quebec Canada, p. 223. https://cjns.brandonu.ca/wp-content/uploads/27-2-01Campbell.pdf (accessed online December 1, 2024).
7. 18 CONG. REC. 190 (1886) (Statement of Representative Skinner).
8. See *Lone Wolf v. Hitchcock*, 187 U.S. 553 (1903) (upholding federal plenary power over Indian affairs so as to allow land allotment even though such action was a unilateral abrogation of the Treaty with the Kiowa).
9. 4 Report of the Annual Lake Mohonk Conference on the Indian and Other Dependent Peoples (1886). [Resolutions and Statement] Business Committee Resolutions.
10. 5 Report of the Annual Lake Mohonk Conference on the Indian and Other Dependent Peoples (1887). Business Committee Resolutions, p. 63.
11. 5 Report of the Annual Lake Mohonk Conference on the Indian and Other Dependent Peoples (1887). Business Committee Resolutions, p. 63.
12. 5 Report of the Annual Lake Mohonk Conference on the Indian and Other Dependent Peoples (1887). [Resolutions and Statement] Business Committee Resolutions, p. 63.
13. 5 Report of the Annual Lake Mohonk Conference on the Indian and Other Dependent Peoples (1887). [Resolutions and Statement] Business Committee Resolutions, pp. 63-64.
14. Report of the Annual Lake Mohonk Conference on the Indian and Other Dependent Peoples (1887). [Resolutions and Statement] Business Committee Resolutions, p. 65.
15. 5 Report of the Annual Lake Mohonk Conference on the Indian and Other Dependent Peoples (1887). [Resolutions and Statement] Business Committee Resolutions, p. 67.
16. 5 Report of the Annual Lake Mohonk Conference on the Indian and Other Dependent Peoples (1887). [Resolutions and Statement] Business Committee Resolutions, p. 63.
17. 30 Report of the Annual Lake Mohonk Conference on the Indian and Other Dependent Peoples (1912), p. 43.
18. Telegram, December 19, 1890, from General Miles to Senator Dawes, Report of the Secretary of War for 1891, Vol. I, pp. 133, 134, and 149. https://faculty.etsu.edu/history/documents/miles.htm (accessed online October 7, 2024).
19. Report of the Commissioner of Indian Affairs(1904), Office of Indian Affairs, United States. U.S. Government Printing Office, 1905, p. 358.

#13 Government Purchase, at Fair Rate, of Surplus Lands Left after Individual Allotment

1885: LMC Platform. All portions of the Indian reservations which are not so allotted should, after the Indians have selected and secured their lands, be purchased by the Government at a fair rate, and be thrown open to settlement.[1]

NOTES

1. 3 Report of the Annual Lake Mohonk Conference on the Indian and Other Dependent Peoples (1885).

#14 Opening Surplus Lands for White Purchase and Settlement

~

1885 Speech by Merrill Gates at LMC: Open Surplus Lands for Sale Using Money Obtained to Promote Indians' Education and Civilization

Where the reservations include more land than the Indians need for ample homesteads, the Government, making allotments of the best to the Indians in severalty, should *open the rest to settlers* for the benefit of the Indians, using the money thus obtained to promote their education and civilization. (Emphasis added).[1]

The ideal plan (which I believe to be also a practicable plan) is to *reserve alternate sections, ranges, or townships among the Indian allotments for white settlers*, of character approved by a philanthropic and experienced commission. Offer special inducements to reputable white settlers to occupy these farms. Thus "object teaching" in thrifty farming will go forward on a large scale. (Emphasis added).[2]

Funds from Sale of Allotments in Hands of Indian Superintendents

The rapidly increasing funds from the sale of Indian allotments and from leases of Indian lands, held by superintendents for the individual Indians to whom they belong, and to whom they must ultimately be paid, have now reached such amounts as to throw a very heavy responsibility upon the superintendents at many of the more important agencies and schools. ... The demand which these property interests make on superintendents of Indian schools is so great that it should be clearly recognized by the department in the allowance of needed clerical assistance, and in insisting upon full, regular, and methodical accounting for all these funds. The question of how to disburse to individual Indians the funds held in trust by superintendents is not settling itself yet in a very satisfactory way. (Emphasis added).[3]

NOTES

1. 1885, Merrill E. Gates, Land and Law as Agents in Educating Indians, p. 55.
2. 1885, Merrill E. Gates, Land and Law as Agents in Educating Indians. p. 56.
3. Annual Report of the Board of Indian Commissioners, 1909 (Washington: Government Printing Office), p. 21. https://babel.hathitrust.org/cgi/pt?id=hvd.32044097929384&seq=5 (accessed online October 5, 2024).

#15 Selling Indian Lands for Alleged Incompetent Indians or Fractionated Interests on Death of Allottee

1902: Sale of Indian Lands The Indians whom the law allows to sell their lands are disposing of them rapidly. The seductions of ready cash, and the importunities of land grabbers are irresistible.[1]

1902: Sale of Inherited Allotments Legislation at the last session of Congress permitting the sale of inherited allotments, will still further illustrate the adapted proverb that an Indian and his land are soon parted unless the land is inalienable.[2]

1903: Puyallup Indians Defrauded and Swindled Out of Lands

The case of the Puyallup Indians illustrates the fact that it is bad policy to remove the restrictive clause from the sale of Indian lands and permit allottees and owners to sell them without any Government supervision. These Indians are disposing of their lands for an inadequate consideration and are being defrauded and swindled. I am of the opinion that Indians in all cases should be aided and protected by the Government in making land sales. Commissioner Jones.[3]

1917: Commissioner Sells Pledged He Would "Not Be Outdone By Anyone" Issued 17,376 Fee Patents, 504, 661 Non-Competent Land and 498,398 Acres of Inherited Land Sold

Commissioner Sells issued 17,376 fee patents between 1917 and 1920, nearly double the number of the previous ten years. He pledged he would "not be outdone by anyone who would hasten Indian progress by the extension of freedom and obligation."[4]

By the time he left office, 504,661 acres of "non-competent" land and 498,398 acres of inherited land had been alienated, excluding the Five Tribes.

NOTES

1. 20 Report of the Annual Lake Mohonk Conference on the Indian and Other Dependent Peoples (1902), p. 17.
2. 20 Report of the Annual Lake Mohonk Conference on the Indian and Other Dependent Peoples (1902), p. 17.
3. Report of the Commissioner of Indian Affairs (1903), Office of Indian Affairs, United States. U.S. Government Printing Office, 1904, p. 110.
4. Dejong, David H. Paternalism to Partnership: The Administration of Indian Affairs, 1786–2021. University of Nebraska Press, 2022, pp. 246-253. Project MUSE. https://muse.jhu.edu/book/100035 (accessed online November 28, 2024), citing Report of the Commissioner of Indian Affairs to the Secretary of the Interior, United States. Office of Indian Affairs, 1920, p. 8.

#16 Leasing Indian Agricultural, Grazing and Mineral Lands

1894: LMC - Leasing of Indian Allotments - Dispossessing Ignorant Indians of Their Property Rights, without an Adequate Return

Mohonk Platform Recent laws permitting Indians to lease their lands are widely resulting in dispossessing ignorant Indians of their property rights, without an adequate return, to their great disadvantage and the enriching of designing white men. We recommend, therefore, that the law be so modified as to render it possible for Indians to sell or lease their lands only by permission of a judge of the United States District Court, upon the same principles which protect the lands of minor heirs among the whites from alienation.[1]

1901: Leasing of Allotments Bad

To the thoughtful mind it is apparent that the effect of the general leasing of allotments is bad. Like the gratuitous issue of rations and the periodical distribution of money it fosters indolence with its train of attendant vices. By taking away the incentive to labor it defeats the very object for which the allotment system was devised, which was, by giving the Indian something tangible that he could call his own, to incite him to personal effort in his own behalf.[2]

Merrill Gates Certain groups of Indians who ten years ago were working upon their own land, are now leasing their lands, securing enough yearly rental to supply them with the mere necessities of life, and not doing a stroke of work for the last few years. We are thus sending them back to barbarism, by allowing them to lease their lands. We had lifted them a little way by land and labor; we are letting them fall back again. From the issue of rations, from a share in 'annuity payments,' and from leasing their lands, they get enough to enable them to live in idleness.[3]

1912: Fraud in Leasing Indian Allotted Land

The white man takes advantage of the Indian's poverty and necessities and inveigles him into a lease contract by the terms of which the allottee receives from ten to fifty cents an acre per annum for land worth a rental of from $2.00 to $7.50 per acre. Many valuable tracts are thus held under so-called deeds or leases, void in law, upon which a consideration of $5.00 or $10.00 was paid to the indigent full-blood owner, and persons so holding will continue in possession appropriating the rents and profits until evicted after much delay and a prolonged lawsuit. Indeed, there is displayed by a few men dealing with these helpless and dependent people a species of rapacity, a disregard of truth, a lack of conscience and a defiance of legal precedent that is shocking in the extreme and lawyers are well represented in the class. They have resorted to all forms of chicanery, fraud, and misrepresentation in transactions affecting the land of both minors and adults.[4]

1899: Pottawatomie and Great Nemaha, Kansas, Leasing Negative Result

Their lands are leased to a very large extent with discouraging and dangerous results. As at first proposed, the ill results might have been checked, but with the numerous modifications that have been adopted an agency is becoming a machine through which large sums of money are disbursed to immoral, dissipated, and utterly thoughtless persons, who have neither occasion nor disposition to resort to labor, and many of whom are without moral perception.[5]

Omaha and Winnebago Agency, Nebr., Leasing Negative Result

The lands are leased to the full limit of possibilities under the law and regulations, and of 140,000 acres allotted 112,000 acres are leased, with the result that the Indians have or should have an income from their allotted lands-Winnebagoes, $55,000; Omahas, $40,000 and their tribal lands bring them -Omahas, $15,800; Winnebagoes, $4,000 - divided yearly among members of the tribe, all of which is, in my opinion, *a premium on laziness and a discouragement to industrious effort and self-support among the Indians*. (Emphasis added).[6]

NOTES

1. 2 Report of the Annual Lake Mohonk Conference on the Indian and Other Dependent Peoples (1894), p. 149.
2. Report of the Board of Indian Commissioners, 1901, p. 13.
3. Report of the Annual Lake Mohonk Conference on the Indian and Other Dependent Peoples (1901), p. 8.
4. 30 Report of the Annual Lake Mohonk Conference on the Indian and Other Dependent Peoples (1912), p. 245.
5. 30th Annual Report of the Board of Indian Commissioners, Office of Indian Affairs, United States. U.S. Government Printing Office, 1899, p. 24.
6. 30th Annual Report of the Board of Indian Commissioners, Office of Indian Affairs, United States. U.S. Government Printing Office, 1899, p. 24.

#17 Establishing Tribal Trust Fund Managed by Indian Bureau, with Cash Value of Surplus Lands Purchased and Sales and Leasing Revenues, to Be Used for Indians' Benefit, especially Education

> 1878: Third. The sale of the lands vacated by the consolidation, and the use of a portion of the funds arising therefrom in the removal and settlement of the Indians, now residing on the reservations to be vacated, on the reservations where the consolidation is to be effected, the balance of the money to be funded for their use, the interest thereon to be expended in lieu of direct appropriations for the benefit of all the Indians on the reservation as created by the bill.[1]

A. 1885: LMC Platform included Establishing Tribal Trust Fund Managed by Indian Bureau

> Platform The cash value of the lands thus purchased should be set aside by the Government as a fund to be expended as rapidly as can be wisely done for their benefit, especially their industrial and educational advancement.[2]

> *The protection of Indian trust funds against unjust claims, and their expenditure as far as possible for the education and civilization of the Indians.* (Emphasis added).[3]

A "tribal trust fund" refers to money held by the U.S. government in trust for Indian tribes, essentially acting as a fiduciary to manage funds generated from tribal lands.

B. 1884: Tribal Trust Funds to Be Used for Indians' Benefit, especially Education

> The Indian is to be prepared for citizenship by giving him his land in severalty in the manner provided for by the Coke Bill, *by larger appropriations for Indian education* and the careful use of such appropriations in the establishment and support of schools, industrial and otherwise, and by the *education* of the race in the broadest and largest sense of the word. (Emphasis added).[4]

The measures we recommend for their accomplishment are the following:
1. The present system of Indian education should be enlarged, and a comprehensive plan should be adopted, which shall place all Indian children in schools under compulsion if necessary, and shall provide industrial education for a large proportion of them.[5]

C. 1853: Commissioner Manypenny; Paying for Depredations Committed by Individual Indians Out of Tribal Annuities Unjust

A "depredation claim" is a legal claim filed against a tribe by non-Native individuals alleging that the tribe damaged or took their property. Depredation claims could result in significant financial burdens on tribes, even if the claims were ultimately unsuccessful.

> Paying for depredations committed by Indians out of their annuities, instead of operating as a check upon them, serves, with the viciously inclined, rather as an incentive to the practice. The criminal alone is not made to pay the penalty, as, in all cases of any consequence, his proportion of the annuity is wholly inadequate for that purpose. The loss falls upon the whole tribe.
>
> *The conversion of the debts due by individual Indians to their traders into what is known or denominated as "National Debts," and the appropriation of the annuities for their payment, is unjust to all the Indians who pay their obligations, and who are endeavoring by their own application and labor to sustain themselves, and is the fruitful source of corruption and fraud, and should meet with no favor from the officers of the government.* (Emphasis added).[6]

D. Early Part of Twentieth Century Dominated by Debate on Payment of Time-Worn Depredation Claims Asserted by Non-Indians

The early part of the twentieth century is dominated by depredation claims by non-Indians, over property disputes involving individual Indians and Indian tribes

> The act of March 3, 1891, entitled "An act to provide for the adjudication and payment of claims arising from Indian depredations," makes a radical change in the laws upon the subject of Indian depredations, especially in regard to the remedies, and is a departure from all preceding Congressional action. This act confers upon a branch of the Judiciary Department, the Court of Claims, jurisdiction and authority to inquire into, and finally adjudicate, all claims for Indian depredations …
>
> *Most of the injuries for which actions are brought were committed by the ancestors of the present generations of Indians, and it seems peculiarly unjust to them that their funds should be taken to pay for the misdoings of their forefathers.* (Emphasis added).
>
> These funds have been placed in the Treasury of the United States, under the sacred stipulations of solemn treaties, to be used for the support, education, and civilization of a people who are

acknowledged to have many characteristics worthy of preservation and adoption by the present dominant race. National good faith will not permit their diversion to other purposes, and the adjudications upon legal principles administered in the courts for centuries are in accord with the requirements of good faith.[7]

Gen. Colby then added:

> The aggregate amount claimed in the 9,706 suits brought up to August 1 was $37,533,374.15. This is continually increasing, and must now reach nearly **$40,000,000**, while the trust funds of all the tribes of Indians aggregate less than $24,000,000 and are constantly diminishing.[8]
>
> LEGISLATION NEEDED. First. The act of March 3, 1891, which provides for the adjustment and payment of claims arising from Indian depredations, should be so amended as to protect the tribal funds now held in trust by the Government, which are threatened with entire destruction.[9]
>
> Claims have been filed in the Court of Claims amounting to more than $34,000,000, and many others in addition have been filed in the Indian Office, making the whole amount probably not less than $40,000,000.
>
> Second. The laws of 1871 and 1872 relating to contracts of agents and attorneys with Indians should, we believe, be repealed. Great abuses have grown up under this system of contracts, and large amounts of money appropriated for the benefit of Indians have gone into the hands of claim agents.[60]
>
> For the Indians in general the Government holds a billion of dollars in property and funds, all open to constant attack from the cupidity and greed of the whites and recreant red men. There is no hope of ultimate justice save through an improvement in our laws and in more rigid enforcement of them.[10]
>
> Another danger that we have seen is the danger that the funds of the Indians shall disappear under the operation of this law which refers depredations to the Court of Claims.

NOTES

1. Report of the Commissioner of Indian Affairs to the Secretary of the Interior, Office of Indian Affairs, 1878, p. iv.

2. Report of the Annual Lake Mohonk Conference on the Indian and Other Dependent Peoples (1885).
3. 11 Report of the Annual Lake Mohonk Conference on the Indian and Other Dependent Peoples (1893), pp. 141-143.
4. 2 Report of the Annual Lake Mohonk Conference on the Indian and Other Dependent Peoples (1884), p. 21.
5. 2 Report of the Annual Lake Mohonk Conference on the Indian and Other Dependent Peoples (1884).
6. Report of the Commissioner of Indian Affairs to the Secretary of the Interior, Office of Indian Affairs, 1853, p. 21.
7. Annual Report of the Board of Indian Commissioners to the Secretary of the Interior, 1893, pp. 81-85.
8. Annual Report of the Board of Indian Commissioners to the Secretary of the Interior, 1893, pp. 134-135.
9. Annual Report of the Board of Indian Commissioners, 1891 (Washington: Government Printing Office), p. 10. https://babel.hathitrust.org/cgi/pt?id=mdp.39015011917955&seq=7 (accessed online September 20, 2024).
10. 33 Report of the Annual Lake Mohonk Conference on the Indian and Other Dependent Peoples (1915), pp. 7-8.

#18 Taking No Action to Protect Indians from Graft and Corruption Resulting in Incalculable Loss of Land and Resources

1857: Commissioner Denver Confessed that Protecting Indians from Lawless Whites, Greedy Traders and Land Speculators Was Impossible

> With large reservations of fertile and desirable land, entirely disproportioned to their wants for occupancy and support, it will be impossible, when surrounded by a dense white population, to protect them from constant disturbance, intrusion and spoliation by those on whom the obligations of law and justice rest but lightly; while their large annuities will subject them to the wiles and machinations of the inhuman trafficker in ardent spirits, the unprincipled gambler, and the greedy and avaricious trader and speculator.[1]

1859: Kansas - Due to Increase of White Population, No Longer Possible to Protect Indians in Their Rights

> In Kansas, where good land and timber have become so valuable and desirable, so long as they continue to hold, as some of them still do, far more than they can occupy and use, it will be impossible to protect them from constant intrusion and spoliation, by which they will be continually fretted and harassed, and their improvement seriously interfered with and delayed. ... from the increase of population, it was no longer possible, in their scattered condition, to protect them in their rights.[2]

1877: Secretary of Interior Carl Schurz

Secretary Schurz acknowledged the broken treaties and injustices to Indians. He called for a special service to investigate the fraud in the performance of contracts and the delivery and distribution of supplies and annuity goods.

There is no doubt that fraud in the performance of contracts, and dishonest practices in the delivery and distribution of supplies and annuity goods, have frequently been the cause of just discontent among the Indians, sometimes resulting in trouble and disaster. I do not deem the present machinery of the Indian service sufficient for the prevention or discovery of abuse and fraudulent practices. The Inspectors and Superintendents who are charged, among other things, with such duty, have in but rare instances been successful in ferreting out the wily expedients resorted to by dishonest contractors or agents. The records of the Indian Office bear out this assertion.[3]

1878: BIC Reforms Prevent Fraud in Purchasing Indian Supplies

> Formerly there was nothing to prevent contractors putting in straw bids, or withdrawing after a contract had been awarded to them, in

order that a bidder at a higher price (oftentimes the same party under another name) might receive the award.

Formerly contracts were so drawn that those to whom beef and flour contracts were awarded could and did habitually take advantage of the necessities of the Indians to accept grades inferior to those called for by the contracts.

Formerly agents hired as many employes as they saw fit and paid them such salaries as they chose. Now all employes must be approved by the Secretary of the Interior, and legal limits are fixed to the amounts which may be expended for agency employes.

Formerly agents' accounts ran on for years without settlement. Now, their accounts are settled quarterly.

Formerly funds were remitted quarterly to agents, even though their accounts might not have been sent in for two or three years. Now remittances to agents are not made and the salaries of their employee cannot be paid until their accounts for the preceding quarter have been received in the Indian Office.

Formerly the unexpended balances of funds which remained in the hands of agents at the end of a fiscal year were carried over by them to succeeding years until their retirement from the service. Now balances are covered into the Treasury at the end of each fiscal year.

Formerly agents expended government property in such manner as they thought best. Now sufficient reasons must be given for the disposal of any government property, and authority must be obtained from the Secretary of the Interior before any expenditure can be made.

Formerly supplies issued to Indians by Indian agents were receipted for by the chiefs. Now each head of a family and each individual Indian who is of age must receipt for himself.

Formerly when annuity moneys were paid to Indian tribes in fulfillment of treaty stipulations a large percentage of the whole sum was divided (or supposed to be) among a few prominent chiefs. Now each individual Indian, including chiefs, receives his per capita share.

Formerly flour was accepted at an Indian agency without any inspection. Now it is inspected before shipment and again upon its arrival at the agency.

Formerly when beef cattle were delivered at agencies two or three head were selected for their weights and an estimate was made for the weight of the whole herd. Now the agent must render a certified weigher's return for all animals received.

Formerly Indian traders were permitted to charge whatever prices they might elect to put upon their goods. Now their prices are controlled by the Indian Office.

Formerly a trader might charge an Indian two or three times the price charged a white man for the same kinds of goods. Now traders are forbidden to make any distinction in prices, under pain of the forfeiture of their licenses.

Formerly contracts wore made with Indians collecting claims against the government, by which attorneys took from one-half to two-thirds of the sums which were collected. Now all contracts made with Indians must be approved by the Commissioner of Indian Affairs.[4]

1902: Without BIC Reforms – Cheating by Indian Agents

BUSINESS REFORMS. It is difficult to realize now how great was the need of reform in the Indian Service thirty-four years ago. The Commission found under the old system such things as partnerships between the agent and trader, or the agent and contractors; receipting for supplies never delivered; overestimating; the weight of cattle for the contractor; taking vouchers in blank to be filled with fraudulent sums; carrying false names upon the rolls; paying employees for whom there was no employment; reporting employees at higher or lower salaries than provided by law, and using the difference for other purposes; farming out the appointments controlled by the agent; using annuity goods for the agents or employees; trading with the Indians; selling them their own goods; selling annuity goods to whites; conniving with others to swindle the Indians out of annuities after distribution; and many other *abuses had become so general that honesty and morality in the Indian Service were the exception*. (Emphasis added).[5]

NOTES

1. Report of the Commissioner of Indian Affairs to the Secretary of the Interior (1857), Office of Indian Affairs, 1857, p. 4.
2. Report of the Commissioner of Indian Affairs to the Secretary of the Interior (1859), Office of Indian Affairs, p. 16.

3. Report of the Secretary of the Interior on the Operations of the Department (1877), U.S., p. XIII. https://en.wikisource.org/wiki/Page:U.S._Department_of_the_Interior_Annual_Report_1877.djvu/15 (accessed online December 13, 2024).

4. Annual Report of the Commissioner of Indian Affairs, The Work of the Purchasing Committee of the Board of Indian Commissioners, Methods of Conducting Business in Indian Office, Office of Indian Affairs, United States. U.S. Government Printing Office, 1878, p. LXV.

5. Annual Report of the Board of Indian Commissioners, 1902 (Washington: Government Printing Office), p. 4. https://babel.hathitrust.org/cgi/pt?id=hvd.32044097929541&seq=7 (accessed online October 5, 2024).

#19 Inadequate Capital and Lack of Agricultural or Fishing Equipment and Education

A. 1891:

> Multitudes of them have no true conception of the value of good land, and moreover a large proportion of that which it is proposed to divide up among them is practically worthless. In some instances it consists of vast tracts of sandy plain, absolutely sterile and unfit for cultivation without extensive and costly irrigation; in others, of mountainous tracts fit only for grazing purposes and suitable for this only when fenced and guarded from the encroachments of the cattle of the white man; in other cases it is heavily timbered and valuable only for its lumber, which too frequently the Indians are unable to utilize. *In a large number of instances, therefore, giving an Indian 80 acres of land and asking him to make it his home and gain from it a subsistence, when he has no farming implements, no horses or cattle, no house but a tepee, no knowledge of farming, no ability to bring the wild land under cultivation, seems but a mockery.* (Emphasis added).[1]

B. 1900: South Dakota, Sisseton, Lack of Capital, Impeded by Debt

> The distance from the place of living is not the only reason why the Indian does not cultivate his allotment. The lack of means to buy large horses, machinery, and grain to sow, are three good reasons. It takes considerable capital to open up a prairie farm, even after it is broken up, which is being done now by white men, who are leasing the allotted lands. Large horses and machinery are what is needed by the Indian. But he is so heavily involved in debt that to possess a good horse and be seen in town with it would make him a shining mark for every collector in the neighborhood.[2]

1900: Sioux – No Water, No Fuel, No Capital, No Training, Sell or Lease Allotments

> The true idea of allotment is to have the Indian select, or to select for him, what may be called his homestead, land upon which by ordinary industry he can make a living either by tilling the soil or in pastoral pursuits. The essentials for success are water and fuel, but above all the former, for fuel can if necessary be procured and brought from a distance. To put him upon an allotment without water and tell him to make his living is mere mockery. His allotment having been selected he should be required to occupy it and work it himself. In this he must have aid and instruction. If he has no capital to begin on, it must be given him; a house must be built, a supply of water

must be assured and the necessaries of life furnished, at least until he can get a start and his labor become productive. The better to assist them the allottees should be divided into small communities, each to be put in charge of persons who by precept and example would teach them how to work and how to live.

This is the theory. The practice is very different. The Indian is allotted and then allowed to turn over his land to the whites and go on his aimless way.³

C. 1900: Nevada, Fishing Industry

An important industry of these Indians is that of fishing. Pyramid Lake is filled with a very fine species of edible trout which find ready sale. At present parties living outside the reservation furnish the Indians with boats, charging them an annual rental, and fix the price paid the Indians for their fish at whatever figure they see fit to pay, thus practically compelling the Indians to take whatever they feel like paying. At a comparatively small expense the Government could provide them with a small wharf or float and a shed or building, under which boats and gear could be sheltered from the weather, and fishing boats of the "dory" type. These boats are inexpensive, but strong and well adapted for fishing in the waters of this lake. The superintendent could then dispose of their catch for them at the prevailing market prices and materially increase their receipts. I would respectfully suggest that something be done in the near future to assist them in this industry.⁴

NOTES

1. Report of the Commissioner of Indian Affairs, Department of the Interior, Vol. 1, United States. Office of Indian Affairs, U.S. Government Printing Office, 1891, p. 39.
2. Annual Report of the Department of Interior, Part 1, Report of the Commissioner of Indian Affairs to the Secretary of the Interior, Reports Concerning Indians in South Dakota, Report of Agent for Sisseton Agency, Office of Indian Affairs, United States. U.S. Government Printing Office, 1900, p. 385.
3. Report of the Commissioner of Indian Affairs, Office of Indian Affairs, United States. U.S. Government Printing Office, 1900, pp. 12-13.
4. Report of the Commissioner of Indian Affairs to the Secretary of the Interior, Reports Concerning Indians in Nevada, Report of School Superintendent in Charge of Nevada Agency, Office of Indian Affairs, United States. U.S. Government Printing Office, 1900, p. 282.

#20 Extending Federal and State Law over Indians, especially those Relating to Crime, Marriage, and Inheritance

A. 1873: Hindrances to Indian Civilization - Absence of Law

> Commissioner Smith was adamant that the treatment of Indians as sovereigns had to end; they were wards, subjects of the government. He strongly endorsed allotting Indian lands, along with extending federal and state law over Indians.[1]

1881: President Chester A. Arthur on American Indian Policy: Extension of State Law to Reservations

The following is extracted from President Chester A. Arthur's First Annual Message to Congress, delivered December 6, 1881.

> Prominent among the matters which challenge the attention of Congress at its present session is the management of our Indian affairs. ...
>
> For the success of the efforts now making to introduce among the Indians the customs and pursuits of civilized life and gradually to absorb them into the mass of our citizens, sharing their rights and holden to their responsibilities, there is imperative need for legislative action. ...
>
> First. I recommend the passage of an act making the laws of the various States and Territories applicable to the Indian reservations within their borders and extending the laws of the State of Arkansas to the portion of the Indian Territory not occupied by the Five Civilized Tribes.[2]

1882: BIC - Reduce Indian Agencies; Turn Indians over to States

BIC surmised that land in severalty to individual Indians and requiring them to care for themselves, would reduce the number of Indian agencies required and effect "a large saving of expense." Based on their expertise, the agencies in New York, Michigan, Iowa, Nebraska, and Kansas, and some in Wisconsin, Minnesota, and the Northwest could be closed.

> No one supposes that the reservation system is to be kept up; forever and a race of people kept forever distinct and perpetually dependent upon the government for support while occupying vast tracts of fertile land that lies waste and uncultivated. Let the Indians first have all they can use; then, rigidly guarding all their treaty rights, let them be turned over to the States, to become a part of the people of the States, with all the rights and duties of freemen; and citizens.

... So the best way, probably the only way, to prepare the Indian for citizenship will be to make him a citizen.[3]

B. 1883: LMC

The [Lake Mohonk] Conference recommends: 1st, that the laws of any State or Territory relating to crime, marriage, and inheritance, be extended over the Indians on reservations within the limits of such State or Territory, except in the case of ...[4]

C. 1898: LMC

1898: LMC Platform We further recommend that special attention be paid to the subject of marriage and divorce among the Indians, so as to bring their family relations under the laws of the States or Territories within whose bounds they reside.[5]

NOTES

1. Report of the Commissioner of Indian Affairs to the Secretary of the Interior, Office of Indian Affairs, 1874, p. 10.
2. The America Presidency Project. https://www.presidency.ucsb.edu/documents/first-annual-message-13 (accessed online September 30, 2024).
3. 50 Annual Report of the Board of Indian Commissioners, 1882 (Washington: Government Printing Office), p. 8. https://babel.hathitrust.org/cgi/pt?id=hvd.32044021159983&seq=16 (accessed online October 5, 2024).
4. 1883 Address to the Public, Lake Mohonk Conference, pp. 8-9.
5. 16 Report of the Annual Lake Mohonk Conference on the Indian and Other Dependent Peoples (1898), p. 113.

#21 Indian Access to Courts, Along with Making Them Subject to Litigation and Liability; 1881: President Chester A. Arthur on American Indian Policy - Access to Courts

1879: General O.O. Howard remarked in an article written in 1879 that the slow process of civil law, and the prejudice against Indians in all frontier courts, almost invariably prevented the punishment of crimes against the Indians.[1]

1881: The following is extracted from President Chester A. Arthur's First Annual Message to Congress, delivered December 6, 1881.

> The Indian should receive the protection of the law. He should be allowed to maintain in court his rights of person and property. He has repeatedly begged for this privilege. Its exercise would be very valuable to him in his progress toward civilization.

1888: LMC: Make Indian Subject to Law and Extend Right to Sue in Our Courts

> *Resolved,* That immediate efforts should be made to place the Indian in the same position before the law as that held by the rest of the population ... **to give him at once the right to sue in our courts...**
>
> It remains for the Nation to protect him in them by some adequate system of courts organized by and vested with the authority of the Federal Government, and easily accessible to the poorest, the least influential and the most remote. ***During the present transition period, the Indian cannot with either safety or justice be given over to the protection of State and local courts, which are often inaccessible and not always impartial, nor left to petty police tribunals organized by and dependent on the will of the Indian agent; tribunals essentially inconsistent with the fundamental provisions of the Constitution.*** (Emphasis added).[2]

The real purpose for this recommendation was to make Indians amenable to suits in courts.

NOTES

1. O. O. Howard, "The True Story of the Wallowa Campaign," *The North American Review,* 129 (1879), p. 56.]
2. 6 Report of the Annual Lake Mohonk Conference on the Indian and Other Dependent Peoples (1888), pp. 104-106.

#22 Terminating Government's Guardianship over Indians, Terminating Their Legal Status as Wards

1894: LMC - The unfortunate relation which he has held as a ward of the nation is a relation which is incompatible with his manhood, and should be brought to an end as soon as possible.[1]

1912: Commissioner Valentine - Indians Should Be Made Subject to Laws of Their States

> With all the expedition compatible with the Indians' welfare they should be made subject to the laws of their States and be taught to look to their local government instead of the National Government.[2]

NOTES

1. 12 Report of the Annual Lake Mohonk Conference on the Indian and Other Dependent Peoples (1894).
2. Report of the Commissioner of Indian Affairs, United States Office of Indian Affairs, 1912, p. 16.

#23 Abolishing Indian Bureau and Its Agencies

~

1892: Commissioner Morgan - Wind Up Affairs of Indian Bureau

The present policy of dealing with the Indians, which is all summed up in the one word citizenship, should be accepted as final, and should be carried into execution as rapidly as practicable. *The one great thought which should dominate Indian administration is that the end is in sight, and that everything reasonable should be done to hasten the winding up of the affairs of the Indian Bureau*. It ought not, under wise management, to take many years to complete this work. (Emphasis added).[1]

LMC - Look Forward to Abolition of Indian Bureau

1894: LMC - That the work of transition be expedited by discontinuing some of the Indian agencies and introducing the district-school system among the Indians; while we look forward to the eventual *abolition of the Indian Bureau* and the relegation of Indian schools to the care of the individual States (Emphasis added).[2]

1894: Indian matters are now in a period of transition. The operation of the Severalty Law is steadily breaking up the reservation system and scattering Indians on individual holdings. The Indians are rapidly becoming citizens, with local rights and duties. In view of these facts, some of the Indian agencies should now be discontinued, the district-school system should be introduced as rapidly as possible; and the *time is coming when the Indian Bureau, as a distinct department of government, may well be abolished*, and the education of the Indian be placed - where it naturally belongs in the Bureau of Education, until it shall ultimately be relegated to the individual States. (Emphasis added).[3]

1901: BIC

... the object of the Indian Bureau [is to] help forward ... the civilization of the Indians and as soon as possible shall make all Indians self-supporting, self-respecting, and useful citizens of the United States. This means that... the Indian Bureau should always aim at its speedy discontinuance. Its success is to be shown not in self-perpetuation, but in self-destruction. (Emphasis in original).[4]

1908: Abolish Indian Bureau

Abolish Indian Bureau. For years in our annual reports we have advocated measures which should as soon as possible do away with the need of an Indian Bureau. The present Commissioner of Indian Affairs in his last annual report says: "All my work is guided by my general aim of preparing the whole Indian office for going out of existence."[5]

NOTES

1. Report of the Secretary, 1892, p. 140.
2. 12 Report of the Annual Lake Mohonk Conference on the Indian and Other Dependent Peoples (1894).
3. 12 Report of the Annual Lake Mohonk Conference on the Indian and Other Dependent Peoples (1894), pp. 150-151.
4. Annual Report of the Board of Indian Commissioners, 1901 (Washington: Government Printing Office), p. 4. https://babel.hathitrust.org/cgi/pt?id=mdp.39015039328276&seq=7 (accessed online October 5, 2024).
5. Annual Report of the Board of Indian Commissioners, 1908 (Washington: Government Printing Office), p. 10. https://babel.hathitrust.org/cgi/pt?id=hvd.32044097929491&seq=5 (accessed online October 5, 2024).

#24 Distributing Tribal Trust Funds ($50,000,000) to Individual Indians

1901: LMC - Break Up Tribal Funds

The tribal funds held in trust for Indians by the Government of the United States should be placed to the credit of individual Indians, who are entitled to share in them as rapidly as lists of such individuals in each tribe can be prepared and recorded.[1]

1902: LMC - Break Up Tribal Funds to Protect Indian from Machinations of Designing White Men

The next great step necessary for the good of the Indian, and for his protection from the machinations of designing white men, is to *break up the great tribal funds held by the Government into individual holdings*. A share should be apportioned to each individual member of the tribe, and placed to his credit on the books of the Treasury of the United States, interest being paid thereon, while as soon as practicable the principal itself of each individual share should be paid to the Indian to whom it belongs. (Emphasis added).[2]

1904: Maintenance of Trust Funds Opportunity for Unscrupulous Persons

Prolonged observation of the effect upon Indians - tribes and individuals of the retention of undivided tribal funds in the hands of the Government long ago convinced this Board that *the maintenance of such funds for an indefinite time has been and will be productive of great evils. Such tribal funds in the eyes of many unscrupulous persons have always been unexploited mines of money.* (Emphasis added).[3]

1905: BIC - Break Up Tribal Funds

(6) We suggest the wisdom of a plan which shall look to the breaking up of tribal funds into individual holdings to be credited now to the individual Indians of the tribes which have such funds, the share of the principal fund thus assigned to each such Indian to be made payable to him at any time after he has received his allotment of land, at the discretion of the Secretary.[4]

Indian tribal funds have too long been regarded as mines of money into which claim agents and contract lawyers might bore their way to take out masses of money. Too large a part of such tribal money has already gone to lawyers and claim agents by way of "contract fees." ... The funds should be broken up into individual holdings. (Emphasis added).[5]

Division of Tribal Funds into Individual Holdings

> The United States Government holds, in trust funds, about $62,000,000 belonging to tribes of Indians in their tribal capacity, and about $13,000,000 which belongs to individual Indians. Everyone who is familiar with legislation and administration for Indians knows that *attempts are frequently made to chisel out from these tribal funds large sums of money*. Such attempts often seem to be made in the selfish interest of lawyers and claim agents, who concern themselves with the matter because they hope to get a large percentage of the money in commissions and fees if they succeed in securing the legislation desired. (Emphasis added).[6]

At the same time the BIC complained about the continuation of the Indian Bureau, it recognized local Indian superintendents controlled huge sums of monies, again posing a risk of theft. It argued for increasing clerical staff to assure accurate accounting.

1900: BIC Recommendations – Records Needed to Determine Heirship; Tribal Funds Should Be Distributed to Tribal Members

After the passage of the GAA and allotting tribal land to individual Indians, the BIC foresaw the need for records to determine heirship. Further, they advanced distributing tribal funds to tribal members. Also,

> 2. We argued at length the imperative need of a system of permanent records of all marriages, births, and deaths of Indians, to be kept at each agency ...
> 4. We suggested a plan for determining and recording the heirs of deceased Indians.
> 6. We advised the breaking up of tribal funds into separate holdings. In addition to these nine points of our last report we wish to ask attention to -
> *(a) The need of a comprehensive, unified policy* in Indian affairs.
> *(b) The new method in dealing with Indians, the recognition of the individual, not the tribe, and the strengthening of personality and of the family.*
> *(c) To the wisdom of doing away with needless agents* and letting Indians learn to manage their own property and their own affairs.
> *(g)* For the 20,000 Navaho, with but 200 children in school, a system of industrial day schools should be begun at once.
> *(h)* The New York Indians should be brought under the allotment act.
> *(i)* [Appointing] *Indian agents without regard to their experience or their fitness for the place is responsible for a very large part of what is worst in the Indian service.*[7]

1905: LMC - Break Up Tribal Funds

We heartily commend the effort made in the last Congress to provide for the distribution of tribal funds, in accordance with recommendations made by President Roosevelt in his first annual message to Congress...[8]

NOTES

1. 19 Report of the Annual Lake Mohonk Conference on the Indian and Other Dependent Peoples (1901).
2. 20 Report of the Annual Lake Mohonk Conference on the Indian and Other Dependent Peoples (1902), p. 9.
3. Annual Report of the Board of Indian Commissioners, 1904 (Washington: Government Printing Office), p. 7. https://babel.hathitrust.org/cgi/pt?id=hvd.32044097929442&seq=7 (accessed online October 5, 2024).
4. 36th Annual Report of the Board of Indian Commissioners, Office of Indian Affairs, United States. U.S. Government Printing Office, 1905, p. 5.
5. Annual Report of the Board of Indian Commissioners, 1908 (Washington: Government Printing Office), p. 21. https://babel.hathitrust.org/cgi/pt?id=hvd.32044097929491&seq=5 (accessed online October 5, 2024).
6. Annual Report of the Board of Indian Commissioners, 1909 (Washington: Government Printing Office), p. 19. https://babel.hathitrust.org/cgi/pt?id=hvd.32044097929384&seq=5 (accessed online October 5, 2024).
7. Annual Report of the Board of Indian Commissioners, 1900 (Washington: Government Printing Office), pp. 17-18. https://babel.hathitrust.org/cgi/pt?id=hvd.32044097929566&seq=7 (accessed online October 5, 2024).
8. 23 Report of the Annual Lake Mohonk Conference on the Indian and Other Dependent Peoples (1905).

#25 Eliminating Tax-Exempt Status of Individual Land and Property of Indians; Use Tribal Trust Funds to Pay Cost of Bureau Services

LMC - Unrepublican and Un-American to Permit Any Landed Class Exemption from Taxation

> III. *It is unrepublican and un-American to permit the existence of any landed class in the community exempt from taxation. Such exemption is equally unjust to the taxed and to the untaxed. The taxes otherwise due on the allotment of the Indian citizen, so long as by a protected title his land is exempt, should be provided for out of Indian funds in the hands of the national government, or, if there are no such funds, out of the general treasury.* (Emphasis added).[1]

1903: Taxation Exclusion Problems

The BIC regularly, continually, repeatedly, undermined the tax-exempt status of Indian allotted and tribal lands. They felt sorry for the whites bearing the burden of infrastructure costs though their tax dollars, without Indians contributing. They proposed having the Indian Bureau use the tribal fund to fund the tax emption of Indians.

> But where the larger part of the land of a county is thus exempt from taxation, the white settlers who are taxed for the support of the local courts, the schools, and the highways, as well as for the care of paupers and the insane, must of necessity feel their burden an exceptionally heavy one. And it is perfectly natural that the objection on the part of the white taxpayers to increasing the burden of taxation which they already bear should make them very slow to admit Indians to the full protection of the courts and the law. Such white taxpayers say, not without reason, that it is not fair to have the machinery of their courts used, and bills of expense to the county incurred, to protect the person or the property rights of Indians who do not themselves pay any part of the cost of such courts.[2]

Can United States Retain from Tribes Mining Revenue Monies to Pay Local Government Taxes from which They Are Exempt?

Again, the BIC continued its mischief to have taxes on tax-exempt properties paid from the Indians' mineral and oil income held in trust by the Indian Bureau.

> While Congress is considering measures of legislation looking to the retaining by the General Government of the mining interests in Indian lands, should not consideration be given to plans which

propose the setting apart of a portion of the income from the leasing of such mining land to support schools, roads, and courts in counties and townships where there is much nontaxable Indian land?³

Pay Local Taxes

Again in 1908, the BIC continued its subversive activities to tax Indian lands.

> AN EQUIVALENT FOR TAXATION SHOULD BE PROVIDED BY CONGRESS TO MEET EXPENDITURES FOR ROADS, SCHOOLS, AND THE LOCAL ADMINISTRATION OF JUSTICE, WHERE INDIAN LANDS ARE NOT TAXED.
>
> Each year makes more evident the inequality of conditions and the consequent injustice imposed upon white citizens whose taxable farms and homesteads are surrounded by the nontaxable allotments of Indians. Schools, roads, and the administration of local courts are to be maintained by taxes, and the white citizens in such a township or county of necessity pay altogether too large a proportion of these expenses. Indeed the Indians whose lands are inalienable and nontaxable do not furnish any share of the revenue for the support of the local government and the local schools.⁴

The BIC, with the influence of the Mohonk Indian Friends, subversively again, attempted to draw money from the tribal trust fund to pay the costs of the Indian Bureau, irrigation and forest management.

> Recognizing the high costs of administering Indian property, BIC proposed *"shifting of the burden of cost of administering Indian property from the Government to the shoulders of the owners. Indian property should begin to protect and preserve itself by bearing its own administrative burdens.* ... Indian land under irrigation should bear the cost of reclamation and the operation of the projects, and that Indian forests should be charged with the cost of their protection and preservation. ... Indian moneys deposited in banks should earn enough interest to pay the employees who handle the funds, and that the cost of leasing Indian land should be paid from the income from the leases. *In short, we recommend a system of law and of administration which will make Indian property, by means of taxation and otherwise, automatically self-supporting..."* (Emphasis added).⁵

NOTES

1. 13 Report of the Annual Lake Mohonk Conference on the Indian and Other Dependent Peoples (1895), p. 106.

2. Annual Report of the Board of Indian Commissioners, 1903 (Washington: Government Printing Office), p. 10. https://babel.hathitrust.org/cgi/pt?id=hvd.32044097929434&seq=7 (accessed online October 5, 2024).
3. Annual Report of the Board of Indian Commissioners, 1907 (Washington: Government Printing Office), p. 19. https://babel.hathitrust.org/cgi/pt?id=hvd.32044097929608&seq=5 (accessed online October 5, 2024).
4. Annual Report of the Board of Indian Commissioners, 1908 (Washington: Government Printing Office), p. 23. https://babel.hathitrust.org/cgi/pt?id=hvd.32044097929491&seq=5 (accessed online October 5, 2024).
5. Annual Report of the Board of Indian Commissioners, 1913-14 (Washington: Government Printing Office), p. 8. https://babel.hathitrust.org/cgi/pt?id=osu.32435064035769&seq=79 (accessed online October 5, 2024).

#26 Failure to Define Indian's Legal Status and Codify Laws Regarding Indians

1. 1874: Indian Relations to General Government Undefined

The condition of the Indian population is anomalous, and their relations to the General Government undefined.

> The time has arrived when some general law regulating Indian citizenship is, in my judgment indispensable.[1]

A. 1888: LMC – Professor Thayer, Harvard Law School - Indian's Legal Status - Neither Fish, Flesh, Fowl, Nor Good Red Herring; Not Citizen and Not Foreigner

> Professor Thayer, Harvard Law School Professor: The relation of the tribal Indian on his reservation to our Constitution and laws is, as you know, very singular. *He is, legally speaking, as the phrase goes, neither fish, flesh, fowl, nor good red herring; not citizen and not foreigner*. It was formerly true that we recognized them as a separate people, who had the right to live under their own laws and usages, with whom we dealt by treaties and by war. This is still true partly and in a sense, but it has also come to be true that these people do not really live under their own laws; that their institutions have mainly gone to pieces, and that they have become a set of neglected dependents of our country; that we now legislate for them whenever we please,-that is to say, by fits and starts. We ceased making treaties with them seventeen years ago. But not yet do we fairly take the next step. We do not yet say, as we should and as we must, "If they are not a separate people, to be dealt with by treaty, then they are a subject people, to be fully legislated for and to be absorbed. They must come in out of the rain under the cover of our Constitution with the rest of us." (Emphasis added).[2]

B. Without Defining Indian's Legal Status, Indian Is as Far from Help as Limbo Is from Bliss

> Without this protection, Thayer described the situation of Indians as follows: He has lost his old surroundings, and has not yet acquired any new ones; he has passed into a sort of limbo. "As far from help as limbo is from bliss."[3]

2. Codification of Laws Pertaining to Indians

A. 1915 LMC - Codification of Laws Pertaining to Indians

We urge the defining of his legal status and the codification of the laws regarding him, that the confusion and uncertainty now existing may be done away.[4]

B. 1922-23 BIC - Still No Codification of Laws Pertaining to Indians

> **1922-1923: CODIFICATION OF LAWS.** The codification of all laws and treaty obligations relating to the Indians, with a view to the removal of the present complexity and confusion, has become a necessity. *There are now on the statute books about 370 Indian treaties and 2,000 special laws relating to Indians and their affairs. It is plainly evident there is need for clarification, condensation, and elimination in this mass of legislation.* (Emphasis added).[5]

NOTES

1. Annual Report of the Secretary of the Interior to the President, Nov. 24, 1874. https://www.newspapers.com/article/chicago-tribune-indian-citizenship-1870s/38066224/ (accessed online October 2, 2024).
2. 6 Report of the Annual Lake Mohonk Conference on the Indian and Other Dependent Peoples (1888), p. 42.
3. 6 Thayer, James B., "The Dawes Bill and The Indians;" in Atlantic Monthly, March 1888, p. 321.
4. 33 Report of the Annual Lake Mohonk Conference on the Indian and Other Dependent Peoples (1915), pp. 7-8.
5. Annual Report of the Board of Indian Commissioners, 1922-23 (Washington: Government Printing Office), p. 8. https://babel.hathitrust.org/cgi/pt?id=umn.31951d027014679&seq=3 (accessed online October 5, 2024).

#27 Permitting Indians to Bring Claims Against U.S. in Court of Claims, Subject to Offset of Any Federal Monies Previously Appropriated for Their Benefit and Counterclaims of Liabilities to Federal Government

> Under existing law Indian tribes are without general authority to submit their claims to the Court of Claims for final adjudication. *The Court of Claims appears to be open to all other persons in the United States except the Indians who have claims against the Government.* (Emphasis added).[1]

NOTES

1. Report of the Annual Lake Mohonk Conference on the Indian and Other Dependent Peoples (1912), p. 66. https://babel.hathitrust.org/cgi/pt?id=wu.89066407354&seq=70&q1=All+Indian+claims+ (accessed online September 30, 2024).

#28 Acculturation to "American Ideals, American Schools, American Laws, Privileges and Pressure of American Rights and Duties" ... "All That Is Good in Our Life as a People"

1888: Stereotypical View of Indian Expressed by Commissioner Oberly

Commissioner Oberly, in his 1888 Report, wrote the following:

> The Indian has indeed begun to change with the changing times. He is commencing to appreciate the fact that he must become civilized-must, as he expresses it, "learn the white man's way" - or perish from the face of the earth. He cannot sweep back with a broom the flowing tide. The forests into which he ran whooping from the door of "William and Mary" have been felled. The game on which he lived has disappeared. The war-path has been obliterated. He is hemmed in on all sides by white population. The railroad refuses to be excluded from his reservation-that hot-bed of barbarism, in which many noxious social and political weeds grow rankly. The Christian missionary is persistently entreating him to abandon paganism. Gradually the paternal hand of the Government is being withdrawn from his support. His environments no longer compel him, or afford to him opportunities, to display the nobler traits of his character. On the warpath and in the chase he was heroic: all activity; patient of hunger; patient of fatigue; cool-headed-a creature of exalted fortitude. "But," says a writer, sketching his character, "when the chase was over, when the war was done, and the peace-pipes smoked out, he abandoned himself to debauchery and idleness. To sleep all

day in a wigwam of painted skins, filthy and blackened with smoke, adorned with scalps, and hung with tomahawks and arrows, to dance in the shine of the new moon to music made from the skin of snakes, to tell stories of witches and evil spirits, to gamble, to sing, to jest, to boast of his achievements in war, and to sit with a solemn gravity at the councils of his chiefs constituted his most serious employment. His squaw was his slave. With no more affection than a coyote feels for its mate, he brought her to his wigwam that she might gratify the basest of his passions and minister to his wants. It was Starlight or Cooing Dove that brought the wood for his fire and the water for his drink, that plowed the field and sowed the maize."[1]

A. 1900, LMC, President Merrill Gates: Acculturate Indians

1900, LMC, President Merrill Gates: At last, as a nation, we are coming to recognize the great truth that if we would do justice to the Indians, *we must get at them, one by one, with American ideals, American schools, American laws, the privileges and the pressure of American rights and duties*. With as much of kindness and patience as can find scope in general laws, we must break up the tribal mass, destroy the binding force of savage tribal custom, and bring families and individuals into the freer, fuller life where they shall be directly governed by our laws, and shall be in touch with all that is good in our life as a people. (Emphasis added).[2]

B. LMC, Merrill Gates, They Should Be Got Out of Blanket and into Trousers with Pocket that Aches to Be Filled with Dollars

In his address at the Lake Mohonk Conference in 1896, Merrill Gates propounded:

To bring him out of savagery into citizenship we must make the Indian more intelligently selfish before we can make him unselfishly intelligent. We need to awaken in him wants. …They should be "got out of the blanket and into trousers," he said, "and trousers with a pocket in them, and with *a pocket that aches to be filled with dollars!*" (Emphasis in original).[3]

C. LMC Meeting with President Cleveland, President Said Solution of Indian Question Rests in Gospel of Christ

When the committee appointed by this board two years ago visited President Cleveland, he said to them, among other things: 'No matter what I may do; no matter what you may do; no matter what Congress may do; no matter what may be done for the education of the Indian, after all, the *solution of the Indian question rests in the Gospel of Christ*.' Rev. Chas. W. Shelton. (Emphasis added).[4]

D. 1899: LMC- For a Vanishing Policy in Indian Affairs

> We are for a *vanishing policy* in Indian affairs-a policy that shall press Indian peculiarities to the vanishing point, and shall speedily give to all Indians the laws, the privileges, the schools and the opportunities which are good enough for all other American citizens, and are good enough, and none too good, for Indians![5]

> Our highest hope for the Indians is to see them on their own lands, admitted into American citizenship, and living as Christian citizens among white neighbors under the system of American schools and American law.[6]

E. Indian Rights Association: Assimilation and Citizenship - Transform Savage to Industrious American Citizen

The IRA's agenda was unmistakably clear:

> The Association seeks to secure the civilization of the ... Indians of the United States ... and to prepare the way for their absorption into the common life of our people. *The Indian as a savage member of a tribal organization cannot survive, ought not to survive, the aggressions of civilization, but his individual redemption from heathenism and ignorance, his transformation from the condition of a savage nomad to that of an industrious American citizen, is abundantly possible.* (Emphasis added). This change can be fully accomplished only by means of legislation.[7]

> *Our North America will rapidly accumulate a population equalling that of the rest of the world combined: a people one and indivisible, identical in manners, language, customs, and impulses: preserving the same civilization, the same religion; imbued with the same opinions, and having the same political liberties.* Of this we have two illustrations now under our eye, the one passing away, the other advancing. The aboriginal Indian race ... and, second, in the instinctive fusion into one language and into one new race of immigrant Germans, English, Norwegians, Celts, and Italians, whose individualities are obliterated in a single generation. *thus held in unity by the American people, is a supreme, a crowning mercy.* (Emphasis added).[8]

NOTES

1. Report of the Commissioner of Indian Affairs to the Secretary of the Interior, Office of Indian Affairs, 1888, p. lxxxix.
2. 18 Report of the Annual Lake Mohonk Conference on the Indian and Other

Dependent Peoples (1900), p. 14.
3. 14 Report of the Annual Lake Mohonk Conference on the Indian and Other Dependent Peoples (1896), p. 11. (accessed online September 30, 2024).
4. 6 Report of the Annual Lake Mohonk Conference on the Indian and Other Dependent Peoples (1888), p. 32.
5. 17 Report of the Annual Lake Mohonk Conference on the Indian and Other Dependent Peoples (1899), p. 11.
6. 17 Report of the Annual Lake Mohonk Conference on the Indian and Other Dependent Peoples (1899), p. 18.
7. Indian Rights Association, The Second Annual Report of the Executive Committee of the Indian Rights Association. (Philadelphia: Office of Indian Rights Association, 1885).
8. Gilpin, William. Mission of the North American People, Geographical, Social, and Political (1874).

#29 Indian Boarding Schools

~

This topic is extensively covered in the press. I have addressed a few salient points. A great debt of gratitude is owed to Secretary of the Interior Deb Haaland, Laguna Pueblo.

> From 1819 to 1969, the U.S. government separated Native American children from their families to eradicate their cultures, assimilate them into White society and seize tribal land.[1]
>
> These were not schools," said Judi Gaiashkibos, executive director of the Nebraska Commission on Indian Affairs, whose relatives were sent to Indian boarding schools. "They were prison camps. They were work camps.[2]
>
> *"More than 3,100 students died at schools built to crush Native American cultures."*[3]
>
> Across all of Indian country, survivors and their descendants continue to suffer the consequences of a policy that was created to annihilate their way of being.[4]
>
> "Indigenous populations have lived through these horrific life tragedies, which then replay endlessly through the generations in cycles of substance abuse, addictions, generational disparities, chronic illnesses, violence, self-hatred, survivor's guilt, cultural dissociation and unremitting grief." – J.C. Seneca, Seneca Nation of Indians.[5]

For more information on boarding schools see (1) Federal Indian Boarding School Initiative Investigative Report, July 2024. https://www.bia.gov/sites/default/files/media_document/doi_federal_indian_boarding_school_initiative_investigative_report_vii_final_508_compliant.pdf (accessed online December 8, 2024); (2) Washington Post, https://www.washingtonpost.com/investigations/interactive/2024/native-american-deaths-burial-sites-boarding-schools/ (accessed online December 28, 2024); and (3) media coverage by Indian Country Today, Native News Online and other news sites.

Boarding School Policy: Repeatedly Reported in Report of the Commissioner of Indian Affairs to the Secretary of the Interior

Time to go out of the business of raising ignorant, lazy, worthless but costly savages.
Forced education for students as young as four years of age.
Deaths and illness of students.
Students cannot take colder climates, returned home on death bed.

The instances of using force, including military troops, to get students in school.
Withholding rations, annuities and using guard house to get parents to send children to school.
Keeping students for years, without returning home.
Schools should be located far from reservations.
Students must be separated from their languages, traditions and customs.
Take upon themselves the outward semblance of civilized life.
Change of names.
Military discipline in regimentation and strictness.
Outing system for Indian student labor in menial labor jobs.
Not elaborate or laborious brain-workers by inheritance or otherwise, and must be muscle-workers and "hewers of wood and drawers of water" for generations to come, and for this they need preparation and training.
One school reported that runaways were jailed for one-two weeks and fed limited rations.
School burial grounds were constructed at 53 schools, more may be identified.[6]
Unsanitary conditions.
Students of 'tender age' forget own language, able to speak English fluently, without an accent.
Inculcation of patriotism to ensure peace with Indians.
Reported rampant cases of physical, sexual and emotional abuse.[7]
Degrading view of Indians at highest level of government.
Ostracization of students from their tribes.

1885: Why Education of Indians Should Be Compulsory

> (1) Because it is high time for our Government to go out of the business of raising ignorant, lazy, worthless but costly savages to furnish material for occasional Indian wars, or rather hunts for the amusement of our Army, which wars it is estimated have on an average cost our Government $1,000,000 and the lives of 20 whites for every Indian killed.

> (2) Because our half million of Indians, though natives of the country, with their ancestors, from time immemorial, yet none of them can be enfranchised with the rights and privileges of citizenship, for the reason that the mass of them are ignorant and barbaric below the degree of civilization required by the duties of citizenship; and as they cannot cure themselves of ignorance and barbarism, which can only be reached and effaced in the rising generation through teachers in industrial boarding schools, and as it is both the duty and interest of the Government to civilize and citizenize all Indians as speedily as possible, and melt them into the body politic of our nation, and thus terminate the expensive and troublesome Indian Bureau; and as the Government has the right, power, and ability to put all Indian children as fast as they become of school age into

such schools, and thus rescue them from the low barbarism of their parents, and bring them up to citizenship, self-government, self-support, and independence, the Government should not permit the ignorance and superstition of parents to interfere with this high duty, and Indian children thereby held down in the barbarism of their parents. Education being compulsory upon white children, who could without education absorb sufficient civilization from their surroundings to qualify them for citizenship in a low degree, should surely be compulsory upon Indian children, who can only absorb barbarism from their parents and surroundings.[8]

1885: Where Should Indian Schools Be Located, and What Kind

I am convinced from thirteen years' continuous observation and experience among Indians that all Indian schools, to be successful, should be located off and away from reservations and the homes of the pupils, and the further away the better, and that all schools should be industrial boarding schools, where, besides the common English branches, the necessary industrial branches of civilized life are taught, for the following reasons: The greatest obstacle to education and civilization of Indians is their barbaric languages. No Indian children educated on a reservation, surrounded by and in daily contact with their people will ever get away from their mother tongues sufficiently to enable them to speak, write, and understand the English language correctly. ...

Their intellectual ability as a race is less than that of the white race. Indian children will acquire the elementary branches of education as readily as white children; will learn to handle pen and pencil fully if not more easily and skillfully than white children; in short, they will readily acquire those branches of education that require the use of the eye, the hand, and close observation only. But when they come to those branches that require a strong exercise of the reasoning powers, such as the higher branches of mathematics, natural and moral philosophy, logic, &c., they fall far behind the whites. They readily acquire a practical knowledge of the common mechanical arts, such as carpentering, blacksmithing, harness and shoe making, wagon and plow mending—not making-but they are deficient in the higher branches of carpentering requiring intricate planning, calculations, &c. In short, they are not elaborate or laborious brain-workers by inheritance or otherwise, and must be muscle-workers and "hewers of wood and drawers of water," and earn their bread by the sweat of their faces for generations to come, and for this they need preparation and training.[9]

1886: New Mexico, Police Required to Seize Indian Children, Take Them to School

Schools I found the attendance at the boarding school about half what it should be ... it became necessary to visit the camps unexpectedly with a detachment of police, and seize such children as were proper and take them away to school, willing or unwilling. Some hurried their children off to the mountains or hid them away in camp, and the police had to chase and capture them like so many wild rabbits. This unusual proceeding created quite an outcry. The men were sullen and muttering, the women loud in their lamentations, and the children almost out of their wits with fright. It was some time before the older ones became reconciled ... When first brought in they are a hard-looking set. Their long tangled hair is shorn close, and then they are stripped of their Indian garb, thoroughly washed, and clad in civilized clothing. The metamorphosis is wonderful, and the little savage made proud of his appearance.[10]

1886: Albuquerque Boarding School, One-Half of Students Died

About one-half that attended, while, as a matter of fact, the cause of this great loss of lives is attributed to diseased condition of the children, hereditary in its nature.[11]

1889: Outing System

Last year the number sent out was 225 boys and 101 girls, so that this year shows the usual growth. These young Indians have been placed in all the counties of southeastern Pennsylvania, and in others of the interior-Cumberland, Columbia, Luzerne, Junata. Some have gone to New Jersey and Maryland, a few to Ohio and Massachusetts. A larger part of the boys, however, have been placed with the farmers of Bucks County, and many of the girls in Montgomery, Chester, and Delaware. (The two sexes are not sent to the same neighborhood, nor is it usual to place two of the same tribe in one family.) It is a common thing, therefore, to see, at this time, Indian lads and Indian young men at work in the fields of Bucks County, and to find Indian girls cooking and waiting on table in farm houses of the counties adjoining. Here are the aboriginal people returned![12]

1891: Inculcation of Patriotism

Special attention is paid in the Government schools to the inculcation of patriotism. The Indian pupils are taught that they are Americans, that the Government is their friend, that the flag is their flag, that the one great duty resting on them is loyalty to the Government, and thus the foundation is laid for perpetual peace between the Indian tribes in this country and the white people.[13]

1892: Commissioner Morgan, Use Troops to Fill Schools

My opinion-pardon me, Mr. Secretary for expressing it, of the Indian educational question is that the only certain method of filling the schools with children is to use troops, and they should be used effectively. Winter is the best time for the troops to be out, for then the parents and their children could not scatter over the country and live on berries and roots. If the backbone or the rebellion is once broken and the Indians convinced that the Government is in earnest, I believe that the Indians would be reduced to submission and that very little trouble would be encountered in the future. The plan is at least worthy of trial on one reservation, and this agency or the Uintah and Ouray Agency would be a good place to test the matter.[14]

1892: Students Kept for Series of Years, without Returning Home

It seems desirable that Indian children taken from their homes to these distant institutions should remain there for a series of years without returning to their parents.[15]

1895: Montana, Blackfeet Agency Boarding School

Respect for the dead leads me to say that two years ago, thinking that at some time the school might need a burial ground, I selected a site to be reserved for that purpose.[16]

1896: Fort Mohave School, AZ, Deaths

The Hualapais positively refuse to send their children to distant schools, having sent some 12 or 15 to the Fort Mohave school during its first session, and these children were taken to a distant school (at Albuquerque) and a colder climate, without the knowledge or consent of their parents, where all but 3 died in a short time. This occurrence has had the effect of unalterably prejudicing these Indians against school.[17]

1896: Montana, Flathead Indians, Kindergarten Students Forget Own Language

The kindergarten is, in my opinion, doing the most important work of the school. When a child is taken from its Indian surroundings at a tender age it soon forgets its language, learns to speak English without accent and with fluency; thus the most difficult part of an Indian's education is accomplished in the kindergarten. This department has been in operation for six years and has proved a success beyond expectation. The Indians are anxious to send their children to the kindergarten, and offer them at 2 and 3 years of age. ... An annual vacation is given the pupils, but *as few as possible are allowed to go home, it being deemed detrimental to their progress and sometimes difficult to obtain their return*... (Emphasis added).[18]

1896: Mescalero Apaches, NM – Police Used to Round Up Males who Had Attended School, Cut Hair, Citizen Dress

I then sent the police, who were ripe for it, to bring in every male Indian who had ever been to school and I compelled them to cut off their hair and abandon breech clout and blanket and put on hat, coat, vest, shirt, pants, and shoes. In ten days I had one-third of the males in this condition.[19]

1896: Mescalero School, Industrial Work, Students Allowed to Go Home for One Week

All children were retained at school during the summer, and put at industrial work. This action was taken after approval by the Indian Office. The children went home by installments for a week at a time and returned. Outings were given them so as to vary the monotony. Thus retaining them under the eye of their natural protectors, they did not lapse into the filthy and Indian ways of the camp, and there was eliminated any desire on the part of the old people to marry off the large girls or hold out any of the children. The experiment was a success and will be continued as part of the settled policy of the school.[20]

1897: Education of Indian Children into Citizenship, Best Schools Far Removed from Reservation

It is scarcely necessary to add now that in my judgment, other things being equal, the best Indian schools are those which are farthest removed from the reservation, away from the influence of tribe and family over the Indian youth.[21]

1898: Ute Tribe, Colorado, 50% at Albuquerque School Died; 25% at Fort Lewis Rendered Sightless Due to Eye Disease

They are, as a whole, indolent, difficult to reason with, and excessively stubborn when resisting conditions tending to a betterment of their condition, and particularly schools and agriculture. ... Of the Ute children sent to the Albuquerque School 50 per cent died while 25 per cent of those contributed to Fort Lewis school were rendered sightless by transfer of a loathsome disease to the eyes.[22]

1898: Annual Report of Superintendent of Indian Schools, Indian Must Be Separated from All Traditions and Customs

How can we best discharge the obligation we owe this people? In the first place, the Indian must be separated from all traditions and customs, and he must be stimulated by a purer and more invigorating social and moral atmosphere. We must bring him into closer touch with the civilization of the age, into more intimate fellowship with our social and religious customs.[23]

1898, Fort Hall School, Idaho, Troops Used to Get Children in School

Lieut. F. G. Irwin, Jr., put nearly every child on the reservation in some school. There was great opposition on the part of the parents, and it became necessary to ask for troops to settle matters. The presence of a troop of cavalry proved effectual. Forty children were put in school in one day.[24]

1898: Pottawatomie School, KAN, Runaways Jailed for One-Two Weeks, Limited Rations

It took severe punishment to break up running away. One of the rooms in the main building was made into a quasi jail. After confining the worst cases in there for a week or two on limited rations, they generally preferred staying with us.[25]

1898: Isleta School, NM, Unsanitary Conditions

Isleta.-The school here is in a rented building and there are no seats, excepting some old benches of antediluvian pattern, which are ready to fall down. The building is adjoining the graveyard where smallpox victims and others have been buried on top of each other for hundreds of years, bones and decayed animal matter being thrown up with each new grave. This place is in the center of the smallpox region and there are few months when the disease is not prevalent. I beg that I may be allowed to relieve this unsanitary condition.[26]

1889: Five, Eight or Ten Years of Government Training School Needed

One thing is conclusively settled, that the brief period of three years at a government training school is not enough to establish a young Indian in a new type of character, and prepare him to return and withstand the downward gravitation of the old reservation life. The supposition is absurd. The period must be extended to five, eight, or ten years, and it should be coupled with a more extensive "outing" system.[27]

1898: Fort Lewis, CO; High Student Death Rate Due to Climate Change

Fort Lewis. Health. The health of all pupils. except those coming from the low altitude and hot climate of Arizona and New Mexico has been remarkably good. There has been no epidemic of any kind, although contagious diseases have been raging all about us in places of lower altitude and warmer climate. The rather high death rate among pupils from the locality mentioned should not be charged up to the climate, as the probable cause is the inherited tendency to scrofula and consumption.[28]

1899: Important to Get Students at Four of Five Years of Age

The hope of the Indian race lies in taking the child at the tender age of four or five years, before the trend of his mind has become fixed in ancient molds or bent by the whims of his parents, and guiding it into the proper channel.[29]

1899: Fort Hall School, ID, Unhealthy Location Responsible for High Death Rate

With an attendance of 175 pupils, however, the school is greatly overcrowded, and this fact, together with the unhealthy location of the institution, is, in my opinion, responsible for the high death rate among the children. The erection of a new school plant needed.[30]

1899: Warm Springs, SD, Several Children Died; Others Sent Home Still Sick

Several children have died during the year. Some sent home are still sick, and in most instances will not return this fall. The school was very poorly equipped for caring for its sick.[31]

1900: Report of Superintendent of Indian Schools - Compulsory Education – Students Should Be Kept until Contact with Our Life Has Taught Him to Abandon His Savage Ways and Walk in Path of Christian Civilization

General compulsory law for the Indian schools should be enacted at once and stringently enforced. The number of Indian children of school age in the United States is between 35,000 and 40,000, the average attendance being 21,558.
With education will come morality, cleanliness, self-respect, industry, and, above all, a Christianized humanity, the foundation stone of the world's progress and wellbeing.

> If we would be successful in our work, the Indian child must be placed in school before the habits of barbarous life have become fixed, and there he must be kept until contact with our life has taught him to abandon his savage ways and walk in the path of Christian civilization.[32]

1901: Umatilla School, Deaths in School from La Grippe

> There were more deaths among the children at school and in the camps during last spring than during the entire eight years of my incumbency, all of whom died from the effects of la grippe.[33]

1901: Commissioner Jones

> There are in operation at the present time 113 boarding schools, with an average attendance of something over 16,000 pupils, ranging from 5 to 21 years old. These pupils are gathered from the cabin, the wickiup, and the tepee. *Partly by cajolery and partly by threats; partly by bribery and partly by fraud; partly by persuasion and partly by force, they are induced to leave their homes and their kindred to enter these schools and take upon themselves the outward semblance of civilized life.* (Emphasis added).[34]

1903: Pima Indians, AZ, Students Cannot Take Colder Climates, Returned Home on Death Bed

> The Pima cannot live in the colder climates, and it is simply murder to send the children to northern and eastern schools. *More than once in the short time I have been here I have been requested to send a mattress to the station to convey a dying pupil to her home.* (Emphasis added).[35]

1903: Mescalero School, NM, Student Mortality from Tuberculosis Excessive

> The mortality among the pupils, as well as among the Indians, was excessive, being attributable in almost every instance to tuberculosis.[36]

NOTES

1. https://www.washingtonpost.com/investigations/interactive/2024/native-american-deaths-burial-sites-boarding-schools/ (accessed online December 28, 2024).
2. Id.
3. Id.
4. https://www.npr.org/2022/05/12/1098455535/burial-sites-linked-to-native-

american-boarding-schools-idd-in-government-report (accessed online Dec. 28, 2024).

5. U.S. Department of the Interior, Bureau of Indian Affairs, Indian Boarding School Initiative Tribal Consultation, Written Comment, December 23, 2021. https://www.bia.gov/sites/default/files/dup/inline-files/appendix_d_bsi_tribal_consultation_report_508_3.pdf (accessed online Dec. 28, 2024).

6. https://www.npr.org/2022/05/12/1098455535/burial-sites-linked-to-native-american-boarding-schools-idd-in-government-report (accessed online Dec. 28, 2024).

7. Federal Indian Boarding School Initiative Investigative Report, July 2024. https://www.bia.gov/sites/default/files/media_document/doi_federal_indian_boarding_school_initiative_investigative_report_vii_final_508_compliant.pdf (accessed online December 8, 2024).

8. Report of the Commissioner of Indian Affairs to the Secretary of the Interior, Reports of Agents in Washington Territory, Office of Indian Affairs. U.S. Government Printing Office, 1885, pp. 201-202.

9. Report of the Commissioner of Indian Affairs to the Secretary of the Interior, Reports of Agents in Washington Territory, Office of Indian Affairs. U.S. Government Printing Office, 1885, p. 202.

10. Report of the Commissioner of Indian Affairs to the Secretary of the Interior, Reports of Agents in New Mexico, Office of Indian Affairs. U.S. Government Printing Office, 1886, p. 199.

11. Report of the Commissioner of Indian Affairs to the Secretary of the Interior. Office of Indian Affairs. U.S. Government Printing Office, 1886, p. 49.

12. Report of the Commissioner of Indian Affairs to the Secretary of the Interior, Office of Indian Affairs. U.S. Government Printing Office, 1889, p. 7.

13. Report of the Commissioner of Indian Affairs to the Secretary of the Interior, Part 1, United States. Office of Indian Affairs, U.S. Government Printing Office, 1891, p. 69.

14. Report of the Commissioner of Indian Affairs to the Secretary of the Interior, Appendix, U.S. Office of Indian Affairs. U.S. Government Printing Office, 1892, p. 175.

15. Report of the Commissioner of Indian Affairs to the Secretary of the Interior, Office of Indian Affairs. U.S. Government Printing Office, 1892, p. 615.

16. Report of the Commissioner of Indian Affairs to the Secretary of the Interior, Reports of Agents in Montana (1895), Blackfeet Agency Boarding School, Office of Indian Affairs. U.S. Government Printing Office, 1896, p. 183.

17. Report of the Commissioner of Indian Affairs to the Secretary of the Interior, Office of Indian Affairs. U.S. Government Printing Office, 1896, p. 109.

18. Report of the Commissioner of Indian Affairs to the Secretary of the Interior, Reports of Agents in Montana, Flathead Agency, Office of Indian Affairs. U.S. Government Printing Office, 1896, p.187.

19. Report of the Commissioner of Indian Affairs to the Secretary of the Interior, Reports of Agents in New Mexico, Report of Superintendent of Mescalero School, Office of Indian Affairs. U.S. Government Printing Office, 1896, p. 213.

20. Report of the Commissioner of Indian Affairs to the Secretary of the Interior,

Reports of Agents in New Mexico, Report of Superintendent of Mescalero School, Office of Indian Affairs. U.S. Government Printing Office, 1896, p. 212.

21. Report of the Board of Indian Commissioners to the Secretary of the Interior, The Education of Indian Children into Citizenship, The Most Effective School, Rev, J.A. Lippincott, Vol. 29, Part 1897, U.S. Government Printing Office, 1898, pp. 46, 58-59.

22. Report of the Commissioner of Indian Affairs to the Secretary of the Interior, Office of Indian Affairs. U.S. Government Printing Office, 1898, p. 127.

23. Report of the Commissioner of Indian Affairs to the Secretary of the Interior, Office of Indian Affairs. U.S. Government Printing Office, 1898, p. 346.

24. Report of the Commissioner of Indian Affairs to the Secretary of the Interior, Office of Indian Affairs. U.S. Government Printing Office, 1898, p. 144.

25. Report of the Commissioner of Indian Affairs to the Secretary of the Interior, Report of the Agency in Kansas, Report of the Superintendent at the Pottawatomie School, Office of Indian Affairs. U.S. Government Printing Office, 1898, p. 179.

26. Report of the Commissioner of Indian Affairs to the Secretary of the Interior, Office of Indian Affairs. U.S. Government Printing Office, 1898, p. 218.

27. Report of the Commissioner of Indian Affairs to the Secretary of the Interior, Office of Indian Affairs. U.S. Government Printing Office, 1889, p. 378.

28. Report of the Commissioner of Indian Affairs to the Secretary of the Interior, Office of Indian Affairs. U.S. Government Printing Office, 1898, p. 373.

29. Report of the Commissioner of Indian Affairs to the Secretary of the Interior, Office of Indian Affairs. U.S. Government Printing Office, 1899, p. 5.

30. Report of the Commissioner of Indian Affairs to the Secretary of the Interior, Reports of Agencies in Idaho, Office of Indian Affairs. U.S. Government Printing Office, 1899, p. 181.

31. Report of the Commissioner of Indian Affairs to the Secretary of the Interior, Reports of Agencies in South Dakota, Report of Superintendent of Warm Springs School, Office of Indian Affairs. U.S. Government Printing Office, 1899, p. 327.

32. Report of the Commissioner of Indian Affairs to the Secretary of the Interior, Report of the Superintendent of Indian Schools, Office of Indian Affairs. U.S. Government Printing Office, 1900, p. 426.

33. Report of the Commissioner of Indian Affairs to the Secretary of the Interior, Part 1, Reports Concerning Indians in Oregon, Report of the Superintendent of Umatilla School (1901), Office of Indian Affairs. U.S. Government Printing Office, 1902, p. 354.

34. Report of the Commissioner of Indian Affairs to the Secretary of the Interior, United States. Office of Indian Affairs, U.S. Government Printing Office, 1902.

35. Report of the Commissioner of Indian Affairs to the Secretary of the Interior, 1903, Office of Indian Affairs. U.S. Government Printing Office, 1904, p. 131.

36. Report of the Commissioner of Indian Affairs to the Secretary of the Interior, 1903, Office of Indian Affairs. U.S. Government Printing Office, 1904, p. 216.

#30 Imposing Involuntary U.S. Citizenship, with Concomitant Rights and Responsibilities – 'Manifest Destiny' for Any Man or Any Body of Men on Our Domain

~

A. LMC – Merrill Gates – There Is No Other 'Manifest Destiny' for Any Man or Any Body of Men on Our Domain

1885: LMC President Merrill Gates - *What should the Indian become? To this there is one answer - and but one. He should become an intelligent citizen of the United States. There is no other 'manifest destiny' for any man or any body of men on our domain ... We are, as a matter of course, to seek to fit the Indians among us as we do all other men the responsibilities of citizenship.* (Emphasis added).[1]

Gates acknowledged a downside of granting citizenship - "the dangers that would beset Indian voters solicited by the demagogue" - but was more concerned about the dangers to Indians "unprotected by law, the prey of sharpers, and too often the pauperized, ration-fed pensioner of our Government, which when it has paid out all the sums it has promised to pay to Indians, has paid them in such a way as to undermine what manhood and self-respect the Indian had."[2]

[The Indians] are the wards of the Government. Is not a guardian's first duty so as to educate and care for his wards as to make them able to care for themselves? It looks like intended fraud if a guardian persists in such management of his wards and such use of their funds entrusted to him as in the light of experience clearly unfits them and will always keep them unfit for the management of their own affairs and their own property.[3]

B. John H. Oberly, Superintendent of Indian Schools, Educate before Citizenship

Mr. John H. Oberly, Superintendent of Indian Schools, Department of the Interior: With Dr. Abbott, and with your declaration of principles, I agree, that the Indian should be admitted to American citizenship, that the reservation system should be destroyed; that lands should be allotted to the Indians in severalty; and that the Indian should be compelled to work; but I would reverse the order of, and in some slight manner change this declaration. I would first teach the Indian how to work; then I would teach him our ideas of the rights of property, and give him lands in severalty; then I would abolish the reservation system; and then make the Indian a citizen and enfranchise him. I would prepare him for the unharmful exercise of the rights of a property-holder, a citizen, and a voter. How can this be done? You have said by enlarging the present system of Indian education.⁴

One great political truth has been made absolutely clear by the march of events, and that is that the people of the United States constitute one nation. There is no place within our borders for independent, alien governments, and the Indians must of necessity surrender their autonomy and become merged in our nationality. (Emphasis added). The allotment of land, the restriction of the power of alienation, the compulsory education of their children, the destruction of the tribal organization, the bestowment of citizenship, the repression of heathenish and hurtful practices, the suppression of outbreaks, and punishment for lawlessness are among the things which belong unmistakably to the prerogatives of the National Government.⁵

C. 1893: LMC – Hasten Absorption of Indians into U.S. Body Politic

1893: LMC - *We believe that the United States government should apply to the Indian problem a well-defined purpose to hasten, as rapidly as possible, the complete absorption of the Indians into the body politic.* (Emphasis added).⁶

1895: Umatilla Agent George W. Harper - Allotted Indian Is Full-Fledged Citizen; Turned Over in Primitive State of Ignorance into Hands of Parties Who Think That There Are No Good Indians except Dead Ones and Indians Have No Rights which White Man Is Bound to Respect

Within the past year it has been discovered that the allotted Indian is a full-fledged citizen of the United States, with all the rights and privileges of a citizen. He is no longer amenable to the agent or any tribunal on the reservation; no one on the reservation has authority to control him. For all this the Indian is not to blame. ... *Indian societies in the East and those who really wanted to benefit him honestly thought the best thing to do for him was to make him a citizen, a position he is utterly incapable of filling. It turns him over in his almost primitive state of ignorance into the hands of parties who religiously think that there are no good Indians except dead ones and that an Indian has no rights which a white man is bound to respect. The Indian has two enemies, and of the two it is a question which is the worst. One is the "set" of people who live around him; the other, the Eastern Indian societies, who are honestly endeavoring to do him good. ... I believe the date of the approval of the act is called "the Dawes emancipation day." So far as a great majority of my Indians are concerned, it should more appropriately be called "the Dawes bondage day..."* (Emphasis added).⁷

1901: Charles C. Parker Tonawanda - Majority of Indians Opposed to Citizenship and Division of Lands in Severalty

> *Citizenship. A majority of the Indians are opposed to citizenship and the division of lands in severalty.* The uneducated Indians feel that they are unprepared for citizenship and the responsibilities which would go with it. They fear that they would be crowded to the wall if they had to engage in the competition which would result from the breaking up of the tribal relation. The Indians who by industry and thrift have acquired considerable property fear that they would suffer loss if there should be a division of the lands among the members of the tribe. Those who are prominent in the tribe fear that they would lose their prominence and influence if the reservation should be broken up and the Indians absorbed into the body politic of the State. These several classes comprise a large majority of the people, hence it is easy to see that if division of lands and citizenship ever comes it will be from pressure from outside rather than from a movement in that direction by the Indians themselves. (Emphasis added).[8]

1904: Commissioner Jones - Allotment, Citizenship, and Opening of Reservations Came Too Soon - Eastern Sentimentalist and Western Land Grabber Unitedly Sprung Trap

> Reservations are being broken up. Inherited lands are being sold, and sturdy American citizens are buying them and settling among the Indians, and following the wake of all comes the public school, wherein time the white and Indian will mingle. ... Effort is constantly being made to "give the Indian a white man's chance." *The logical results will be the extermination of the Indian as an Indian.* (Emphasis added).[9]

> *The remedy has passed out of Government control; allotment, citizenship, and opening came too soon.* It can be seen now. *The eastern sentimentalist and the western land grabber unitedly sprung the trap that has been the undoing of the Indians who had lands of value.* Greed on the one hand and childishness that looks only to the wants of today on the other hand is completing the work. Retribution-that is not the adequate word-will come at the end of the twenty-five-year probation; when the community will have to bear the burdens of the paupers it has made. Unfortunately, I fear that most of those who have been successful plunderers will escape the responsibility by removing elsewhere. W.A. Jones. (Emphasis added).[10]

D. With No Vote, Indian Is of No Political Significance

1884: Humiliating as the acknowledgment may be, most of the placid indifference on the part of public men to dishonesty and injustice toward the Indian is due to the simple fact that he is not a voter: he is of no political significance.

With citizenship comes not only all the privileges, but also all the duties and responsibilities of citizenship. If we extend over the Indian the law of the State or Territory in which his reservation may be situated, we instantly and without his consent subject him to a complex system of law, in many respects utterly unsuited to his condition, and of which he is in absolute ignorance; we force on him public and private duties and responsibilities of which he has not the remotest comprehension. ... In justice to the Indian and to ourselves, I certainly think we should insist on one thing. There must be at least an approximate fitness in the individual Indian for the duties of citizenship before he is made a citizen. There must be some education, some elevation of the Indian toward our standard of right and morality, before we can with any justice punish him under laws which he had no part in making, and of which he is now blindly ignorant. This education should be general and immediate: every effort should be made to fit the individual Indian to take his place as soon as possible as an American citizen. But it is idle to dream that the mistake of a hundred years can be canceled by a dozen lines upon our statute book.[11]

NOTES

1. 3 Report of the Annual Lake Mohonk Conference on the Indian and Other Dependent Peoples (1885), p. 17.
2. 3 Report of the Annual Lake Mohonk Conference on the Indian and Other Dependent Peoples (1885), p. 17.
3. 3 Report of the Annual Lake Mohonk Conference on the Indian and Other Dependent Peoples (1885), p. 18.
4. 3 Report of the Annual Lake Mohonk Conference on the Indian and Other Dependent Peoples (1885), p. 58.
5. Report of the Commissioner of Indian Affairs to the Secretary of the Interior, Office of Indian Affairs, 1891, p. 7.
6. 11 Report of the Annual Lake Mohonk Conference on the Indian and Other Dependent Peoples (1893), p. 141.
7. Report of the Commissioner of Indian Affairs to the Secretary of the Interior, United States. Office of Indian Affairs, 1895, p. 274.
8. Report of the Commissioner of Indian Affairs to the Secretary of the Interior, Office of Indian Affairs, 1901, Part I, p. 293.

9. Report of the Commissioner of Indian Affairs to the Secretary of the Interior, Office of Indian Affairs, 1904, Part I, p. 29.

10. Report of the Commissioner of Indian Affairs to the Secretary of the Interior, Office of Indian Affairs, 1904, Part I, p. 43.

11. Henry S. Pancoast, From The Indian Before the Law (Philadelphia, Indian Rights Association, 1884). https://babel.hathitrust.org/cgi/pt?id=hvd.32044009975152&seq=19 (accessed online October 3, 2024).

CHAPTER 50: Failures of Allotment Policy

~

1889: Over 55,000 Indians Take Allotments

While Dawes may have initially assumed Indian lands would be allotted slowly, the lamentable fact was that, by 1899, 55,067 natives had already taken allotments.[1]

Land Loss Due to GAA

At the time of the bill's passage in 1887, Native Americans held 138 million acres, but by 1934 when the allotment process was halted forever, 91 million acres had been lost. (Emphasis added).[2] *Of all native lands held in trust by the government for the twenty-five-year period, two-thirds were lost by sale.* (Emphasis added).[3]

Former Commissioner Manypenny - Allotment Sponsored by "Railroad Monopolists, Land-Grabbers, [and] Cattle Kings"

Former Commissioner Manypenny charged that allotment was sponsored by a motley collection of "railroad monopolists, land-grabbers, [and] cattle kings or cowboys, who all have their covetous eyes set upon" Indian lands. Referring to the allotment treaties he had negotiated with the Delawares, Shawnees, Miamis, Kickapoos, and others in the 1850s, Manypenny pointed out that the agreements had served to dispossess the tribes of "their noble lands in Kansas." He had been convinced at the time that allotment would produce favorable results but freely admitted that he had been wrong. Manypenny's treaties, made in good faith and ignorance, had only tragic consequences for the Indians:

"SHALL WE PERSIST IN A POLICY THAT HAS FAILED?" In 1885, Manypenny wrote of his disillusionment with the allotment program.

When I made those treaties I was confident that good results would follow. Had I not so believed I would not have been a party to the transactions. Events following the execution of these treaties proved that I had committed a grave error. *I had provided for the abrogation of the reservations, the dissolution of the tribal relation, and for lands in severalty and citizenship; thus making the road clear for the rapacity of the white man. I had broken down every barrier. I had committed a grievous [sic] mistake, and entailed on the Indians a legacy of cruel wrong and injury. Had I known then, as I now know, what would result from those treaties, I would be compelled to admit that I had committed a high crime.* (Emphasis added).[4]

1885: Imprudent Allotment Sales of Kickapoo Indians, Shawnees and Pottawatomies, and Tribes in Michigan and Wisconsin – Given Lands in Severalty without Restriction on Alienation; Disposed of Them, Now Pensioners upon Government; Few Indians Ready for Allotment without Restriction on Alienation

The treaty of the United States with the Kickapoo Indians provided a mode by which aspiring Indians could become citizens of the United States, which was to accept or receive their part of the reservation lands in severalty in fee-simple, with power of alienation, they being first required to appear in open court and take the oath of allegiance (as in the case of the naturalization of foreigners), and also by proof to satisfy the court that they were able to manage their own affairs, had adopted the habits of civilized life, and had been able for five years to support themselves and families.[5]

The history of the Kickapoos and some of the Shawnees and Pottawatomies, and some tribes in Michigan and Wisconsin, who have taken lands in severalty without a restrictive power of alienation, and who have disposed of them, and are now for the most part pensioners upon the bounty of the Government, or are without visible means of support, is sufficient to demonstrate the fact that the Indians in general are not sufficiently advanced in education and civilization to make it safe, and to their best interest, to give them citizenship and title to their lands with unrestricted power of alienation. What I would impress is the fact that there are but few Indians outside of the civilized tribes, who are prepared to own lands in severalty without the Government retaining a lien upon the same as trustee for twenty-five or thirty years, allowing no power of alienation by them either to white men or to their own race.[6]

1886: Senator Dawes, National Indian Defence Association, Senator Teller Fear Land in Severalty Policy Embraced by LMC

Senator Dawes: *[A]lmost at the last moment, when I see this bill so near the end, I begin to fall back and ask myself seriously, whether, after all, too much risk is not being taken with him, because if the bill becomes a law, and it is administered in bad faith, and by bad men, it first wipes out all of the heritage of the Indian, and then it scatters him among our people without preparation for citizenship, and without the capability of maintaining himself, really in a worse condition than he can be in now.* (Emphasis added).[7]

In a speech before the Conference of the Board of Indian Commissioners, in Washington, last winter, the author of this bill, Senator Dawes, said: "If my land-in-severalty bill should become a law, it will depend entirely on the character of the Government agents who execute its provisions, whether it is a success or a failure. If it be intrusted to men of unflinching honesty and broad views, the Indians will be secure in the possession of homes on the best lands of the reservations; but *if it is intrusted to dishonest men, the Indians will be cheated out of their lands*." (Emphasis added).[8]

1891: LMC - Concern with Rapidity of Allotments Being Made

Platform: We look with satisfaction upon the allotments of lands in severalty, but with concern upon the rapidity with which they are being made.[9]

Finally, the Indian has lost much, but much remains. *Our policy, weak but well-meaning, has plunged thousands of our wards into poverty.* Let us give the Indian what we ourselves enjoy - full rights and privileges of citizenship, and the pursuit of happiness — not merely empty words. (Emphasis added). Otherwise, history will record our short-sighted and disastrous policy in its true light, and we shall be condemned by future generations. (Applause.)[10]

1892: LMC, C.C. Painter - Some Dangers which Now Threaten Interests of Indians

Prof. C. C. Painter was invited to speak as a representative of the Indian Rights Association. I have recently returned from a visit to the Cheyenne and Arapahoe and Kiowa and Comanche and Wichita reservations in Oklahoma ... There are certain dangers threatening the Indian service just now to which attention should be called and in regard to which the friends of the Indians should be fully awake. *The severalty law wisely provided that allotments of land should be made only to Indians who were living on agricultural lands and so far advanced in civilization that it was wise to make such allotments. ... allotments should be made only as the law contemplated - to those who are so far advanced that when the intercourse laws are removed by which they have been guarded they will still be safe. ... but these wise restrictions and limitations have been steadily disregarded in many cases.* Take these Cheyennes and Arapahoes among whom I have been. The idea of allotting land to over thirty-three hundred blanket Indians, 160 acres to each individual, within ninety days, as would have been done but that the funds were exhausted and they had to wait for more money. Mistakes are continually coming up, to the irritation of the Indian, and promising in the future, difficulties, collisions, conflicts between the whites and the Indians. Then the character of the allotting agents has sometimes been bad, as was the case with some at this agency. ... I think it is time that this body should insist that a long step be taken in advance of any that has yet been taken in regard to the emancipation of Indian civilization from low political control. If those in power please to put the material interests of the country in the hands of politicians for political ends, let them do it, though that is bad enough; but when the civilization of a people is to be trodden under foot simply to subserve the interest of politicians it is time that we should, with emphasis and directness and with specification, call attention to it. (Emphasis added).[11]

It was clearly in the minds of those urging the enactment of this law, as it was also made one of its provisions, that it should be applied only to those who, in the enlightened judgment of the President, had reached that point in their progress toward civilization where individual titles to land and citizenship were necessary to their further development. It was also provided that reasonable time should be given to the backward and reluctant, even on reservations where the majority were progressive, to accept the new regime. *These wise provisions of the law have been in a number of cases disregarded.* Reservations have been subjected to the operation of this law which are not "agricultural." *Allotments have been made, not because the tribes were "so far advanced in civilization" that their progress required it, but because the neighboring whites, for reasons of their own, have demanded it, and, when begun, have been pushed to a rapid conclusion, regardless of the reluctance of the Indians to accept them.* In some cases, agents totally unfit for the delicate and difficult duties with which they are charged have added unnecessary complications to a problem already sufficiently complex and perplexing; and thus have been engendered irritation, distrust, and bitter opposition, where there should have been only the reluctance of the ignorant to accept the untried. (Emphasis added).[12]

1892: LMC - Allotments Have Been Made to Blanket Indians, Wholly Unfit for Citizenship

Allotments have been made to blanket Indians, wholly unfit for citizenship, forced to a rapid conclusion within a few months, and by an agent who gave the valuable lands on which a few had built homes, and were cultivating crops, to be opened up for settlement; and who, allotted poorer lands, several miles from where they had built homes, to the Indians. (Emphasis added).[13]

1895: Indian Allottees Need Protection from Land Robber, Gambler, and Liquor-Dealer

LMC Platform II. Until the Indian comes into complete ownership of his allotment, he should have the special protection of the

~ 443

federal government, special federal officers should be endowed with magisterial authority for the administration of local justice, the bureau should have power and means to employ and assign counsel for the legal protection of his rights, he should be guarded by adequate legislation from the land robber, the gambler, and the liquor-dealer, he should not be allowed to sell or lease his lands except upon permission first obtained from a federal judge, and provision should be made for the secular and industrial education of all Indian children of school age in schools supported by and under the exclusive control of the government, State or federal.[14]

LMC Platform The habit of leasing allotments converts the lessee from an industrious worker into an idle and improvident landlord. It should, therefore, be permitted only to allotees who suffer from an infirmity or disability which incapacitates them from obtaining in any other way the benefit of their allotment; and the power of the agent to authorize such leases should be strictly limited by law to such carefully defined exceptions.[15]

In his History of Indian Policy, Lyman Tyler of the Bureau of Indian Affairs provided this summary:

The refusal of the United States to adequately protect Indians in their rights against non-Indians played an important part in the failure of the concentration policy, the reservation policy, and the allotment policy. During each of the three periods mentioned, the Congress, time after time, responded to local non-Indian voters to the detriment of the Indians. Policies that failed to achieve the goals of civilization and assimilation set for the Indians often succeeded in securing the land or other resources as planned for the non-Indians. (Emphasis added).[16]

1895: LMC – Allotment Law Fallen among Thieves

Now, what is the matter with this severalty law? It has fallen among thieves... If you can get the Indian set out in severalty, the white men will get the rest of it; and they will not have anything to do but see to it that the rest of it is the best part of the reservation. *Instead of trying the experiment upon one single reservation, as the President supposed it would be, when we came to Washington in December, seven reservations were in process of being allotted; and the poor Indians were crowded out into the poorest part of the land, and the white men were gathering around them, as the eagles round a carcass, waiting for the opportunity to get the best lands. When the attention of the President was called to that fact, he ordered a halt...* (Emphasis added).[17]

Why, twelve of the twenty-five years of probation for the Omahas are already passed; and today they are in a worse condition than they were when they were allotted. You may say what you please about it. I have been there. *The poor fellows have lost their land to these land-grabbers, who have paid them only just enough to supply them with whiskey; and that is all they get for it. They know no more about the duties and obligations and work of a civilized citizen today than they did when they began.* (Emphasis added).[18]

1899: Senator Dawes remarked that if the Conference would turn its guns on those who were trying to skin the allottees he should feel encouraged.[19]

Resolved, That the attention of the Board of Indian Commissioners be called to the condition and needs of the allottees under the Severalty Act, with the request that they consider and adopt such measures as will more surely protect them from outside encroachment, and more effectively stimulate in them the development of self-sustaining citizenship.[20]

1913-1914: Deficiencies in Allotment and Distribution of Tribal Funds to Tribal Members

The BIC began to see the deficiencies in allotment and distribution of tribal funds to tribal members. Restrictions for alienation were removed too soon and Indians were not educated regarding the handling and disposition of their individual property.

The property of the 300,000 Indians of the United States is estimated at about $1,000,000.000. *It is our conviction that the haste of Congress and of the Indian Bureau to individualize the land holdings of Indians, who have had centuries of life under the communistic system of land ownership ... are responsible for much of the fraud and graft from which Indians have suffered in a large majority of the cases where the restrictions upon alienation have been removed.* ... The Government's policy has been to coddle the restricted Indian, transact his business for him, do his thinking for him, giving him no opportunity to grow strong by assuming responsibility, and then suddenly, after he has become thoroughly emasculated from nonuse of his powers, when he has obtained a certain knowledge of the English language in the schools, restrictions have been removed from his property, and in most cases it has been quickly dissipated. (Emphasis added).[21]

1914-1915: Competency Commission Appointed

The Secretary appointed a commission of three experienced men to determine the competency of individual Indians on various reservations.⁹⁰

> *It is a fact that a majority of Indians who in the past have been declared competent were not really competent, and too frequently their applications have been made upon the urging of creditors or persons having an unworthy design upon Indian property.* (Emphasis added).²²

NOTES

1. Hoxie, "End of the Savage," 168; Henry Laurens Dawes, "Have We Failed the Indian?" Atlantic Monthly, 84 (August 1899): 283.
2. Wilcomb E. Washburn, The Indian in America (New York: Harper and Row, 1975), 243; Elizabeth S. Grobsmith, "The Plains Culture Area," in Native North Americans: An Ethnohistorical Approach, ed. Daniel L. Boxberger (Dubuque, Iowa: Kendall/Hunt Publishing Company, 1990), 189.
3. Washburn, Indian In America, 243.
4. See George W. Manypenny, "Shall We Persist in a Policy That Has Failed?" in Wilcomb E. Washburn, The Assault on Indian Tribalism: The General Allotment Law (Dawes Act) of 1887, edited by Harold M. Hyman (Philadelphia: J. B. Lippincott Company, 1975), 61–67.
5. 13 Stat., p. 624, Art. III.
6. The Abridgment: Containing the Annual Message of the President of the United States to the Two Houses of Congress with Reports of Departments and Selections from Accompanying Papers, Secretary of the Interior, U.S. Department of the Interior, 1885, p. 888. Report of the Commissioner of Indian Affairs to the Secretary of the Interior, United States. Office of Indian Affairs, 1885, p. viii.
7. Annual Report of the Board of Indian Commissioners, 1886 (Washington: Government Printing Office), p. 131. https://babel.hathitrust.org/cgi/pt?id=mdp.39015081128962&seq=54&q1=citizenship&start=1 (accessed online October 5, 2024).
8. 9 Report of the Annual Lake Mohonk Conference on the Indian and Other Dependent Peoples (1891), p. 113.
9. "Head of the National Indian Defense Association Opposes the Dawes Act." Issues & Controversies in American History. Infobase Learning, Web. 10 Dec. 2015.
10. 30 Report of the Annual Lake Mohonk Conference on the Indian and Other Dependent Peoples (1912), p. 61.
11. 10 Report of the Annual Lake Mohonk Conference on the Indian and Other Dependent Peoples (1892), p. 72.
12. 10 Report of the Annual Lake Mohonk Conference on the Indian and Other Dependent Peoples (1892), p. 71.

13. 10 Report of the Annual Lake Mohonk Conference on the Indian and Other Dependent Peoples (1892), p. 71.
14. 13 Report of the Annual Lake Mohonk Conference on the Indian and Other Dependent Peoples (1895), p. 106.
15. 19 Report of the Annual Lake Mohonk Conference on the Indian and Other Dependent Peoples (1901), pp. 7-8.
16. Tyler, S. Lyman A History of Indian Policy. Bureau of Indian Affairs (Dept. of Interior), Washington, D.C., Superintendent of Documents, U.S. Government Printing Office, Washington, D.C. 20402.
17. 13 Report of the Annual Lake Mohonk Conference on the Indian and Other Dependent Peoples (1895), p. 49.
18. 13 Report of the Annual Lake Mohonk Conference on the Indian and Other Dependent Peoples (1895), p. 51.
19. 17 Report of the Annual Lake Mohonk Conference on the Indian and Other Dependent Peoples (1899), p. 55.
20. 17 Report of the Annual Lake Mohonk Conference on the Indian and Other Dependent Peoples (1899), p. 75.
21. Annual Report of the Board of Indian Commissioners, 1913-14 (Washington: Government Printing Office), p. 7. https://babel.hathitrust.org/cgi/pt?id=osu.32435064035769&seq=79 (accessed online October 5, 2024).
22. Annual Report of the Board of Indian Commissioners, 1914-15 (Washington: Government Printing Office), p. 8. https://babel.hathitrust.org/cgi/pt?id=osu.32435064035769&seq=115 (accessed online October 5, 2024).

CHAPTER 51: Other Issues Raised by LMC

~

Responsibility for Indian Affairs in Congress Is a Dereliction of Duty – Too Divided, No Help for Indian

> **Prof. Painter:** *When responsibility for Indian matters is so divided that it rests nowhere. It is over in the Treasury Department, and it is not in the Treasury Department. It is in the Indian Bureau, and it is not in the Indian Bureau. It is in the Department of Justice, and it isn't there-it is somewhere else.* I will not undertake to say how the Commissioner of Indian Affairs makes his estimates as to money needed for the Indians, and how it goes to the Appropriation Committee. If you take the estimates of the Indian Commissioner, and then take the bill prepared by the House Committee on Appropriations, you will see that the latter take the liberty to think they know more about the Indian than the Indian Commissioner himself, and they cut down his estimates fearfully. (Emphasis added).[1]
>
> The Committee make the report, and it goes into the House. Somebody there concludes he knows more about it than the Committee, and insists upon cutting it down still further.
>
> *They know nothing about the merits of the bill, but they must make a record for economy, no matter if it cuts down into the life of the people, as it did two years ago in Montana, where 482 Indians, out of a population of a little less than 2000, died in nine months.* (Emphasis added).[2]
>
> The Commissioner makes his report to them, unless that appropriation is made before the holiday recess, or at least, by the middle of January, the probabilities are that the Indians will not get the benefit of it till they have had to go through their sufferings again. The Commissioner makes his estimates again and recommends an appropriation of $50,000 for the Montana Indians. I went to Washington to see if that measure would be taken up by Congress. I went to the Commissioner, and he said he had made his estimate. I went to the chairman of the Committee of the House, and he had never heard of it. I went back to find where it was and was told that Congress had made a law the year before regarding all such estimates; they were to be sent to the Treasury Department, and by them to be referred so and so, and to be printed so and so, and to be sent so and so. Well, it hadn't been sent there. The question was, where was it? In a few weeks Congress would adjourn, and the time was coming when these goods could not go in, so I start through

the departments to find out about it. I go through the Indian Bureau; I chase it round and round, and after a while, find it in charge of a certain clerk who has the estimates for deficiencies till just about the close of Congress, when this will be sent there in a batch. *I go to him to see if some action cannot be taken lest these people starve; but he cannot help me, and I go back, and back, and back. Instructions are issued that this be sent over.* Mr. Dawes goes around and makes an impression on the Department that it is essential that this be done. He also goes to the Treasury Department for action. It comes from there. *Understand that unless the Indian has a friend, it lies there.* The clerk has done his duty when he has made a record of it, and when, in the course of time, he has sent it along. I go there and find they have been sent over all in a lump. I follow it up through three or four different rooms and at last find it. Estimates have been made for about $4,000,000 for the Interior Department. There is nothing to indicate that it is a matter of pressing urgency any more than the deepening of the channel for the Podunk River. You undertake to get this detached and sent out and are informed that it can't be done except by a letter from the Secretary of the Interior. I go to him, and I go to his representative. He says there need be no trouble; just send the whole back here. I go back on a fool's errand; he says this can't go back except in such and such a way. After more than a day's work I write a letter myself asking that this be sent back, because they wish to take special action, and it is sent back. It goes over; it goes through the Treasury Department. What is it there for? We get it over to the Chairman of the House. He has said that when it reaches him he will introduce it at once. We get it to the Speaker's desk, and to the Committee, and finally to the chairman of the Committee of Appropriations a day or so before Congress adjourns. It has taken nearly two weeks and then he declines to do anything about it, and Congress adjourns. (Emphasis added).[3]

1901: Irrigation Should be Provided in Arid Districts

LMC Platform Where allotments are made in arid districts an ample supply of water for purposes of irrigation and domestic requirements should be provided under such arrangements as, within their natural possibilities, will secure its permanence and will make its subsequent diversion impossible.[4]

1905: No More Financing of Sectarian Schools

In 1905, the Lake Mohonk Conference came out against tribal funds being used for financing sectarian schools. The move was basically anti-Catholic and was intended to prevent the financing of Catholic schools.[5]

1907: LMC Opposed to Burke Act

LMC opposed to Burke Act.[6]

1909: Catholic Indian Mission Statement: Obliteration or Demoralization of People Is Not Their Assimilation and Civilization

> I take it that it is the first principle of all Indian work that the Indian should be fitted as soon as possible for citizenship. The Catholic missionary will welcome this assimilation of the Indian with the white citizen but *we should not be too precipitate in the process. The obliteration or demoralization of a people is not their assimilation and civilization.* (Emphasis added). **Catholic Missions Among the Indians Extract from the Lake Mohonk Conference** Address by Rev. William Hughes.[7]

Industrial Landscape Transforms American Indian People and Lands

The arrival of the railroad, the conversion of forests into lumber, increased agricultural production, and pervasive mining activity transformed the landscape and marginalized the people who had inhabited it for thousands of years. The federal government was trying to make farmers out of Indians when the profitability of the agricultural sector had already switched to the mechanized mass production of the Industrial Age.

1911: Meeting of Society of American Indians

> *Mr. Smiley: Just about a week ago a Conference was held at Columbus, Ohio. It is exclusively an Indian Conference; no white man is allowed to take part in it. They invited some white men to come and listen, but it was exclusively an Indian Conference. The leaders of that meeting were men who have been here year after year, and I know a dozen or more of them.* (Emphasis added).[8]

1916: Last LMC

> The last annual meeting of the Lake Mohonk Conference was held in 1916.[9]

NOTES

1. 3 Report of the Annual Lake Mohonk Conference on the Indian and Other Dependent Peoples, 1885, p. 12.
2. 3 Report of the Annual Lake Mohonk Conference on the Indian and Other Dependent Peoples, 1885, p. 13.
3. 3 Report of the Annual Lake Mohonk Conference on the Indian and Other Dependent Peoples (1885), p. 13.

4. 19 Report of the Annual Lake Mohonk Conference on the Indian and Other Dependent Peoples (1901), p. 7.
5. 23 Report of the Annual Lake Mohonk Conference on the Indian and Other Dependent Peoples (1905).
6. 25 Report of the Annual Lake Mohonk Conference on the Indian and Other Dependent Peoples (1907), pp. 7-8.
7. 27 Report of the Annual Lake Mohonk Conference on the Indian and Other Dependent Peoples, (1909), pp. 877-78.
8. 29 Report of the Annual Lake Mohonk Conference on the Indian and Other Dependent Peoples (1911), p. 88.
9. 34 Report of the Annual Lake Mohonk Conference on the Indian and Other Dependent Peoples (1916), pp. 7-8.

CHAPTER 52: 1885: National Indian Defense Association

On November 28, 1885, the National Indian Defense Association ("NIDA") was organized joining the battle over allotment of Indian tribal lands.

> From its inception, the group's membership was comprised more of scholars than of politicians. Contained within their numbers were prominent late-nineteenth-century intellectual figures as well as general lay-sympathizers. ... The NIDA grew rapidly, and on the eve of the severalty bill's passage in March, 1887, NIDA membership was nearly equal to that of the IRA. *The group fundamentally opposed immediate severalty because dissolution of tribal rights was inherent in the policy's intent. To the scholarly NIDA, severalty became an impediment to the Indians' civilization process because tribal government was the only form of community control with which natives were familiar. Without it, they lacked the ability to preserve order among themselves.* (Emphasis added).[1]

> [To NIDA] simply granting the Indians title to their land would not give them either the motive or the means to contend with the disadvantages of reservation status. On the other hand, the pressures to part with their land would be numerous and irresistible. Hence, immediate severalty would only bring about the loss of the individual native's land before he acquired the capacity to manage it. *While they learned the virtues of land ownership, Native Americans should have the right to maintain self-government under the protection of United States laws, and they should communally control their lands with patents issued to the tribes.* (Emphasis added).[2]

National Indian Defense Association (NIDA) Opposed to Immediate Allotment

NIDA's platform, opposing immediate allotment of Indian tribal lands, was published in *Council Fire*, its pro-Indian rights journal, edited by Dr. Thomas Bland.

> *The Indians should be allowed to hold their lands in common or divide them in severalty as they see fit.* Justice says, let *land in severalty and citizenship* be given to Indians when they ask for them, but to force them upon them before they are capable of appreciating them and protecting themselves in them, would be palpably unjust. It *has been tried repeatedly and in every case resulted disastrously to the Indians*. Land in severalty, and citizenship must come and will come to the Indians. It is the ultimate solution to the Indian problem, but if justice is to guide the nation in this matter, it will demand that the change shall be made only so fast as the Indians shall

become educated into the world wisdom and practical habits of the white men. (Emphasis added).³

At the LMC debating the draft GAA, Mr. Porter, Member of the National Indian Defence Association stated: the NIDA differs from [Mohonk]. I am opposed to the allotment of lands in severalty to any individuals, or the extension of the laws of any State of any state or country over any Indians at present. ... The idea of lands in severalty has been for the last fifty years a pet scheme for the solution of the question as to the civilization and the Christianization of Indians.

> I tell you what you will see is a fact, by reference to the reports of the Commissioner of Indian Affairs, that in numbers of instances where the Indians have taken the lands in severalty, where the benefits of law have been extended, that in every instance it has failed, and will fail to the end of time. ... If Mr. Dawes, who has no doubt thought more about this subject than any of us here, has such grave doubts about the wisdom of the measure as to almost withdraw his support from the bill, why may not we? ... His land [Indians] must go: tell him the truth; tell him: "You have got too much land; the advances of civilization do not allow of your occupying so much." ... Tell him the truth; don't tell him that you are going to lift him up to citizenship, give him land in severalty, and make him a Christian gentleman. You cannot do it. He has got to do it himself.⁴

1885: President Cleveland Was Not in Favor of Immediate Severalty

Allotment lacked the backing of the new Democratic administration. President Grover Cleveland declined to take a stance favoring immediate severalty. He believed legislation could not force whites to mingle with the Indians. (Emphasis added).⁵

President Cleveland added that natives should not be forced from their reservations either, but rather should be educated toward civilization in their present locales. (Emphasis added).⁶

> *Like President Chester Arthur before him, Cleveland had only vague ideas about Indian policy and left the specifics to his secretary of the interior, Lucius Q.C. Lamar. Cleveland, who generally refused to see any reporters, nonetheless, sought Bland's advice on allotment and, like Bland, Cleveland concluded it would be many years before Native Americans were ready to hold individual land titles.* (Emphasis added).⁷

> *Lamar also ... believed that Native Americans must gradually accept civilization. For the time being, he said they should remain on their reservations and take collective titles to their lands.* (Emphasis added).⁸

> *Even after the reservations were allotted, Lamar believed large areas should remain tribally controlled, because Indians were not ready for the rigors of land ownership, and severing their tribal relations would be fatal.* (Emphasis added).[9]

1885: Russell Errett (R-PA): House of Representatives Minority Report Opposing GAA

In the October 1885 issue of the Council Fire, Bland published the transcript of a minority report filed in the House of Representatives by Russell Errett of Pennsylvania, Charles Hooker of Mississippi, and T M. Gunter of Arkansas, all opposing the GAA.

> From the time of the discovery of America, and for centuries probably before that, the North American Indian has been a communist. Not in the offensive sense of modern communism, but in the sense of holding property in common. The tribal system has kept bands and tribes together as families, each member of which was dependent on the other. The very idea of property in the soil was unknown to the Indian mind.
>
> *The main purpose of this bill* is not to help the Indian, or solve the Indian problem, or provide a method of getting out of our Indian troubles so much as it *is to provide a method for getting at the valuable Indian lands and opening them up to white settlement*. ... The provisions for the apparent benefit of the Indian are but the pretext to get at his lands and occupy them. With that accomplished, we have securely paved the way for the extermination of the Indian races upon this part of the continent. If this were done in the name of Greed, it would be bad enough; but to do it in the name of Humanity, and under the cloak of an ardent desire to promote the Indian's welfare by making him like ourselves, whether he will or not, is infinitely worse.

Errett went on to say that Indian progress toward "civilization" had hitherto been made under the "tribal system": "Gradually, under that system they are working out their own deliverance, which will come in their own good time if we but leave them alone and perform our part of the many contracts we have made with them."[10] See APPENDIX D for the full document.

1885: NIDA Splits Away from Other Reform Groups

NIDA had been on friendly terms with other reform groups until the 1885 Lake Mohonk Conference, Friends of the Indian, when the Indian Rights Association, the Women's National Association and the Indian Committee of Boston, accepted the Mohonk platform by which allotment would be forced upon the Indians.

A.J. Willard, the former chief justice of the South Carolina Supreme Court, articulated NIDA's stance that American Indians needed to own their land base permanently and use their own judgments in decisions affecting their future.[11]

> They should be permitted to reach civilization through the development of their own institutions under the motives afforded by advanced surrounding civilization. An Act of Congress cannot lay the basis of civilization. While there should be a general conformity to the conditions and habits of the nation at large, there is abundant room for Indian individuality to display itself in the growth of those institutions. *It is also essential that time should be allowed for the consumption of these transformations.* Sudden changes in methods and manners are contrary to the course of nature. (Emphasis added).[12]

> *In that reality lies the importance of the NIDA ... [which] championed gradual assimilation and retention of tribal government, while vigorously opposing immediate severalty.* (Emphasis added).[13]

1886: NIDA Protests against Lake Mohonk Conference's Allotment Resolution

NIDA protested against the 1886 Lake Mohonk Conference's Allotment Resolution, criticizing the reform group:

> It is to be deplored that a body of professed philanthropists should have adopted and published a series of resolutions so entirely in harmony with the sentiments of those who openly denounce the Indians as incorrigible savages, who have no rights save such as the white man may choose to grant, and who denominate as sentimental cranks those who demand that the Government shall stand by the treaty rights of the Indians. (Emphasis added).[14]

When Bland spoke at the January 1886 meeting of the Board of Indian Commissioners, he proposed an alternative course in Indian policy - "that patents to their lands be issued by the Government to the Indian tribes, to be held in common until by education ... they should be prepared to safely have the land divided and patented to them in severalty."[15]

Those pushing for the General Allotment Act castigated tribes for monopolizing vast tracts of land in the West, making it impossible for 'poor' white citizens to acquire land. However, corporations, which held considerably more land than the Indian tribes, were accomodated. NIDA published opposing arguments of various tribal spokesman, such as Col. G.W. Harkins, of the Chickasaws:

> *Is it a crime for an Indian tribe to hold more land than its people can use at once, but all of which will be needed for its increasing population? Then why not declare it a crime for corporations to own and hold for speculation large bodies of land, and why allow foreigners to buy up and hold vast estates in this country? Indeed, why not say that it is an outrage on those who have no homes for a rich farmer to own more land than he can cultivate or to hold land for his children and grandchildren. There is no scarcity of public land open to people at nominal price; then why this clamor for the Indians' lands?* (Emphasis added).[16]

Late in the summer of 1886, as pressure to open Indian lands reached a fever pitch among Westerners and their congressmen, Bland warned, *"If land is given to the Indian in severalty, the mass of Indians will soon be deprived of its possession, even though their power of alienating their title is taken away for many years to come, and they will inevitably become pauperized."* (Emphasis added).[17]

1887: NIDA Opposed to General Allotment Act

After Congress enacted the General Allotment Act, NIDA charged it with violating the U.S. Constitution:

> Said act is not only opposed to the principles of common law, but a flagrant violation of the Constitution of the United States ... The government proposes by this law to take the property of the several tribes without their consent and without compensation ... This is as clearly a usurpation of power, a disregard of constitutional limitations as it would be to take the property of any land syndicate and divide that among the members and families of said body. With this additional aggravation, that in the case of the Indians, it is exercising its power over a people beyond its jurisdiction, except within the limits named by express treaty stipulations. (Emphasis added).[18]

1887: NIDA Plans to Test Constitutionality of GAA in Federal Court

Judge A.J. Willard, in an 1887 Council Fire article, stated that the land rights of Native people "are vested in the tribe as a corporate body." And furthermore, that the tribes held political authority over these lands in the same ways that private corporations and municipalities held their property. This was significant, Willard wrote, because, if Congress could arbitrarily "distribute the tribal property among the members of the tribe," through the allotment program, then it could just as easily divide the lands held by municipal corporate charters or private companies "among the individuals constituting such corporate bodies." With this precedent, Congress could dispossess city governments and private landholders alike. Willard asked rhetorically if the people of the United States were willing to extend such extraordinary powers to Congress. He concluded most directly that the issue was no longer simply a question "of robbing the Indian, but ... a question whether Congress shall enter upon a career of legislation that embodies the worst principles ... upon the stability of social institutions."[19]

The GAA, Willard asserted, "destroys the tribal condition and assumes to place the Indian on the same footing within the States as their white citizens." Willard also asserted that the history of Indian-white contact demonstrated that when Native communities fell under the jurisdiction of a state or territory, there was often little interest by local politicians or settlers to protect them and their lands. He concluded that the allotment program broke the "solemn trust" between Congress and Indian people, and more importantly for his larger argument, undermined the power of Congress and the federal government more generally to pass the GAA.[20]

1887: Bland's Injured in Deadly Train Collision

On June 22, 1887, the Bland's were severely injured in a deadly train collision in Maryland. Bland was badly scalded on his head and right arm and escaped through the window of a mangled train car.[21] The couple spent the remainder of the summer regaining their strength on the southern coast of Massachusetts. Because Bland himself was the nucleus of communication among practical philanthropists (just as was Herbert Welsh to the IRA), the forward momentum of NIDA's plan to test the constitutionality of the GAA in the courts ground to a halt, and Council Fire ceased publication during a most critical period.[22]

NOTES

1. Behrens, Jo Lea Wetherilt. "The National Indian Defense Association and Council Fire." Chronicles of Oklahoma 75.2 (1997): p. 137.
2. Behrens, Jo Lea Wetherilt. "The National Indian Defense Association and Council Fire." Chronicles of Oklahoma 75.2 (1997): pp. 137-138.
3. Council Fire Journal (Jan. 1882) (Dec. 1885). https://books.google.com/books?id=K69GAAAAMAAJ&printsec=frontcover#v=onepage&q&f=false (accessed online April 29, 2024). Council Fire (Washington, DC: T. A. and M. C. Bland, 1883), p. 122.
4. Annual Report of the Board of Indian Commissioners, 1886 (Washington: Government Printing Office), pp. 134-135. https://babel.hathitrust.org/cgi/pt?id=mdp.39015081128962&seq=54&q1=citizenship&start=1 (accessed online October 5, 2024).

5. "The New York Independent," Council Fire, 8 (December 1885): 186.
6. "The Constitution of the National Indian Defence [sic] Association," Council Fire, 9 (June 1886): 98.
7. Behrens, Jo Lea Wetherilt. "The National Indian Defense Association and Council Fire." Chronicles of Oklahoma 75.2 (1997): p. 136.
8. Annual Meeting of the N.I.D.A., Council Fire, 10: 17-18.
9. Ibid., 18; Hagan, Indian Rights Association, 45, 47.
10. Russell Errett (US Congress, House Committee on Indian Affairs, Lands in Severalty to Indians: Report to Accompany H.R. 5038, 46th Cong., 2d Sess., May 28, 1880, H. Rept. 1576, pp. 7–10), quoted in Washburn, Assault on Indian Tribalism, 39, 40.
11. Our Reception to Chief Red Cloud, Council Fire, 8 (April 1885): 55.
12. Our Reception to Chief Red Cloud, Council Fire, 8 (April 1885): 55.
13. Behrens, Jo Lea Wetherilt. "The National Indian Defense Association and Council Fire." Chronicles of Oklahoma 75.2 (1997): p. 129.
14. Council Fire. https://search.worldcat.org/title/The-Council-fire-and-arbitrator/oclc/702601696 (accessed online April 29, 2024).
15. Cowger, Thomas W. "Dr. Thomas A. Bland, critic of forced assimilation." American Indian Culture and Research Journal 16.4 (1992).
16. COL. G. W. HARKINS, OF THE CHICKASAWS, ON THE DAWES BILL.
17. "Congress Laid The Bad Bills Aside," Council Fire, 9 (August-September 1886): 120.
18. "An Address to the Friends of Justice," Council Fire, March 1887, p. 38.
19. A.J. Willard, "Annual Report of Judge Willard," Council Fire, 10 (December 1887): 99-100.
20. A.J. Willard, "Indian Jurisdiction After Division in Severalty," Council Fire, 12 (Mar. 1889): 46–47.
21. "Homeward Bound-A Railroad Collision," Council Fire, 10 (November 1887): 77.
22. Love, Christopher J. "The Friends of the Indians and Their Foes: A Reassessment of the Dawes Act Debate." (1991), p. 65.

CHAPTER 53: Society of American Indians ("SAI")

The Society of American Indians ("SAI") was formed in Columbus, Ohio, in 1911 by 50 American Indians, most of them educated professional men and women. *It sought U.S. citizenship, thinking this would give Indians freedom and equality, without realizing the powerful forces of racism and prejudice entrenched against them.* The BIC and LMC had been collaborating for twenty-nine years with the legislation for achieving their objectives already enacted.

> *We note the organization during the past year of a society composed of Indians themselves whose object it is to direct public attention to present needs and to the righting of existing wrongs.* (Emphasis added).
> **29 Report of the Annual Lake Mohonk Conference on the Indian and Other Dependent Peoples (1911), pp. 7-9.**

At the same time other forces pushed for Indian citizenship for other motives: destroying reservations; eradicating tribal relations, and opening surplus lands for settlement for a wave of increasing white emigration. With the Commissioner of Indian Affairs, the Board of Indian Commissioners, the Indian Rights Association, the Lake Mohonk Friends of the Indians, the SAI and individuals such as Dr. Carlos Montezuma, all pushing for Indian U.S. citizenship for their own purposes, it was a foregone conclusion.

The SAI founders created a problem for themselves with one of their first actions. They passed a unanimous resolution inviting General Pratt to become their first white associate member. Many of the founders had attended Carlisle or other eastern boarding schools. Pratt favored immediate citizenship for Indians.

> In a country like America, composed of people from all races, it has seemed to me both the highest privilege and a sacred duty devolving upon our government and people to see that the original inhabitants, from whom we were wresting so much, should be admitted to the very best opportunities to prove their worth. *What brighter glory could shine from our national escutcheon than to give the native people we found here foremost privileges to become a very part of our citizenry under our benign Declaration of Independence and Constitution!* (Emphasis added).[1]

Commissioner Valentine favored pan-Indian groups such as the SAI only if *"the proper element of the Indians" attended, and if it brought "together really progressive Indians" and the "wise members of the race."* (Emphasis added).

The SAI's constitution stipulated that only Indians could be active, voting, office-holding members. Whites interested in the welfare and advancement of Indians could become associate members and attend meetings as observers. *It outlined seven goals: 1) to advance Indian understanding; 2) to provide a forum for discussion of differing opinions; 3) to present to whites an accurate picture of Indians and their history; 4) to obtain citizenship for Indians; 5) to provide legal advice and assistance for Indians; 6) to oppose anything felt to be detrimental to Indians; and, 7) to remain a free and independent organization, unencumbered by personal or political entanglements.* (Emphasis added). Article VII of the constitution stated that a conference of the general membership was to be held annually for the consideration of topics pertaining to Indians and for the presentation and discussion of papers on Indian subjects.

1911-1923: SAI's Annual Meetings

SAI members convened in annual meetings between 1911 and 1923, and for much of that period the Society's executive offices in Washington, D.C., were a hub for political advocacy, lobbying Congress and the Office of Indian Affairs. publishing a journal, offering legal assistance to Indian individuals and tribes, and maintaining a voluminous correspondence across the country with American Indians.

SAI's Quarterly Journals

SAI's Quarterly Journal was the first twentieth-century forum for professional American Indian writers. It covered a wide array of topics on national and local reservation problems. The first issue of the *Quarterly Journals'* masthead carried on one side the Society's emblem, the American Eagle, and on the other a lighted torch. Underneath was the legend, taken from the Society's statement of purposes: "The honor of the race and the good of the country shall be paramount." It stated its plan: "Never before has an attempt been made on the part of a national Indian organization to publish a periodical devoted to the interest of the entire race. The open plan is to develop race leaders."[7]

Thereafter, the Society published the *Quarterly Journal of the American Indian* (1913–1915), renamed the *American Indian Magazine* (1916–1920), for seven years.

SAI: Debate regarding Indian Bureau

The Indian Bureau was a topic of constant and divisive debate within the SAI. Many Indians regarded the Bureau with contempt and viewed it as representing white oppression and control, and that Indians affiliated with the Bureau worked against the race. At the first Columbus conference, Charles Edwin Dagenett, who as Supervisor of Employment was the highest ranking Indian in the Bureau, was elected Secretary-Treasurer. This contributed to suspicion among Indians of white control of the SAI. SAI leaders debated whether the Bureau and the federal reservation system should be abolished and whether employees of the Bureau holding offices could be loyal to the "race" and the SAI. They feared the SAI would be a puppet of the Bureau.

OCTOBER 12, 1911: INAUGURAL ANNUAL SAI CONFERENCE, OHIO STATE UNIVERSITY

The Society of American Indians held its Inaugural Conference at Ohio State University during the first week of October 1911. The quotes below are from the SAI QUARTERLY JOURNAL, v. 1, no. 1 (January-April 1913).

> *"An Indian must say with a man of any race who has risen, I am proud of my race. It is not an inferior race. It can advance; it can achieve; and by God's help I shall do my utmost to prove it."* (Emphasis added).[8]

SAI's Plan to Develop Indian Leaders

> The open plan is to develop race leaders, to give hope, to inspire, to lead outward and upward, the Indian American as a genuine factor in his own country and lead him to see that upon his individual effort depends his share in the salvation of his race and his value to his country. ... The plan is so transparent, so simple, that those inclined to be sordid cannot believe that there is not some deep and hidden evil. Here lies a grave danger. Good men and good women fear.[9]

U.S. Strategy: Setting Indians against One Another

> Long ago, this principle of setting Indians against one another was understood and in the heat of the early contest for the Indians' country, it was no less than George Washington who said: "Unless we have Indians to oppose Indians we may expect but small success." For four hundred years this opposing of one's own people has been cleverly fostered. (Emphasis added).[10]

Indians Have 72,535,862 Acres

> **Indians under government supervision, have in individual right, 31,383,354 acres of land and in tribal right 40,263,445 acres, making a total of 71,646,799. With the public domain added, the total swells to 72,535,862 acres.** (Emphasis added).[11]

Wealth of "Government" Indians Is $1,066,106,427

> **According to government appraisers the value of this property, together with the houses, barns, tools, lumber, furniture, stock and other properties, in the possession of government-controlled Indians is $387,542,166. Undivided tribal property amounts to $687,564,253. The grand total of the wealth of "government" Indians is $1,066,106,427.** (Emphasis added).[12]

The BIC recognized the *tens and hundreds of millions of dollars tied up in Indian lands and pushed to resolve the question of ownership, sabotaging the Indians lawful possession.*

> *The entire Indian population of the United States is not greater than that of the District of Columbia.* The total area of lands still reserved to the Indians is greater than the combined area of half a dozen of the States of the Union. The dangers and difficulties which surround attempts at legislation for the true welfare of the Indians are to no small degree connected still with the question of the land in Indian reservations, and the lands already allotted in severalty to Indians. *The involved problems of ownership and administration of lands held in common, of great tracts of pasturage, of forest and timber lands, and of mines of minerals, oil and asphalt, still embarrass the administration of Indian affairs. The values involved in the resulting questions of the ultimate ownership and administration of Indian lands and mines can be estimated only in tens and hundreds of millions of dollars.* (Emphasis added).[13]

Leave Indian to (1) Sink or Swim or (2) Educate Indian to Economic System of Modern Civilization

> Unskilled, as yet in sharp business methods, and unfamiliar with values and indeed with the whole economic system of civilization, the Indian holds his property by only a slender grasp. This immense property protected only by the filmy tissue of law affords a tempting bait to the shrewd speculator, for, as Washington said of the white race, "our people are not to be restrained by any law now in being, or likely to be enacted." Until the Indian can be educated and adjusted to the economic system of modern civilization, he will suffer from constant exploitation. How shall he learn? "Throw every Indian upon his own responsibility now say some. Educate him more, allow him to develop, grow and gradually accustom him to independence by withdrawing supports one by one," say others.[14]

SAI Free to Speak Truth, Non-Partisan, Non-Secular

> *Our great advantage is that we are free from any connection with political bodies, from churches and from the government or its dictation. Nobody may say what we shall do or say, save the Indian people themselves. We exist to afford them a right and an opportunity to speak out. We ask every Indian to speak, to voice his wrongs, to tell of injustice where he knows it to be, to mention his fears of any factor affecting the Indian. ... Your officials are but your servants, your society your means for work. ... We stand*

> as the founders of the Society have said *"for broad interests, not selfish interests."* (Emphasis added).

What is best for the American Indian as a race? How shall his condition be bettered? How may he have justice and secure his natural rights? Who are his enemies? What forces are holding him down? Who are his friends? Who will help in his uplift? Should not the Indian people themselves be the chief factors in placing their own race on a solid foundation and in demanding for it a definite status in the country?

The Society of American Indians is not a political or a partisan organization.[15]

OCTOBER 1912: SECOND ANNUAL SAI CONFERENCE, OHIO STATE UNIVERSITY

SAI 1912 Platform #1. *Codify Indian Laws*

> That we reiterate the petition of our First Annual SAI Conference *asking Congress to pass a law, authorizing the President to name an Indian Code Commission to codify the laws relative to Indians taxed and not taxed, and to define more exactly the privileges and abilities of the several classes of Indians in the United States* ... This request is substantially that contained in House Bill 18334 introduced on January 19, 1912, by Hon. Chas. D. Carter, at the instance of the society. (Emphasis added).[16]

Justification:

Repeatedly within the Bureau, reference is made to the lack of a code of laws.[17]

In 1915, the LMC jumped on the codification of laws bandwagon. In the 1922-23 BIC Report, this is still highlighted as a problem!![18]

SAI 1912 Platform #2. *Commissioner of Indian Affairs Primary Object – Advancement of Indian*

> That we respectfully urge that the Commissioner of Indian Affairs have as his primary object the advancement of the Indian...

Justification:

> The second difficulty in the way of formulating and pursuing a wise and uniform policy ... has been the persistent pressure by partisan politicians to use positions in the Indian service as places to which

men might be appointed for political service, without any regard whatever to their fitness for the duties of these positions.[19]

SAI 1912 Platform #3. *Investigations relative to Indian Affairs*

> *That all investigation relative to Indian affairs be carried on through public hearings where affidavits can be submitted by Indians, and that copies of such proceedings be put on file for the use of all Indians.* (Emphasis added).[20]

Justification:

An investigation by Special Agent Edwin Brooks in 1878 at the Isabella Reservation uncovered "outrageous frauds." His handwritten Report is 38 pages long. He urged that the DOI consider criminal prosecution, finding in particular that in issuing 1,735 patents at Isabella, Indian Agent George Betts had deemed a mere 24 allottees as "not so competent" to receive their patents in fee. It was not printed or released.

> *The facts discovered by the brief investigation made, in my opinion, conclusively show that the [competency] schedule ... is in the main fraudulent, that it was prepared by an Agent in collusion with, and in the interest of a pack of unscrupulous land sharks seeking and conspiring to defraud the Government and the Indians of a large tract of valuable land* ...(Emphasis added).

Eventually a government investigation forced Agent Betts to *resign*, but not before five-sixths of the land he had allocated to Saginaw-Chippewa Tribal members had been sold.[21]

SAI 1912 Platform #4. *Complaints of Wrongs Perpetrated upon Indians*

> *That when complaints are made to the Society of American Indians, of wrongs perpetrated upon Indians who need aid or representation in adjusting their claims or righting their wrongs, the President of the Society of American Indians requests of the President of the United States, authority to investigate, and he be furnished with necessary information and facilities to make such investigation*, and that such authority be asked only in such specific cases as shall to the President of the Society seem proper. (Emphasis added).[22]

Justification: Past Experiences of Tribes

The Secretary of War's investigation of the Fort Berthold Tribes' complaints would have horrific consequences for them. In six months, the Indians would lose 4,686,612 acres.[23]

1893: AZ, Navajo Agency, Fort Defiance, Bordering on Starvation, Warned Not to Complain which Could Cause Reduction in Land

> The condition of the Navajo Indians is worse than it has been for a number of years. This is due, partly, to a succession of very dry seasons, which have caused a great scarcity of forage, very poor crops, loss of many sheep and ponies from starvation during the winters, and a very poor yield of wool. Many of the Navajos are in a condition bordering on starvation.[24]

Many times, on the verge of starvation, they received $5,000 in appropriations for 16,000-17,000 Navajoes, amounting to twenty-five cents per capita. Other tribes, in the same region, received $60 per capita or more. Their federal agent counseled them not to complain and to "behave better than ever," due to the covetous eyes of those who would take any opportunity to divest them of their lands.

> But in the face of these shameful facts, these Indians still listen to their agent, when I tell them *they must behave better than ever before, for evidently the plotters and the large majority of the whites and Mexicans residing in the Territories of New Mexico and Arizona desire their 6,000,000 acres of reserved lands.* (Emphasis added).[25]

SAI 1912 Platform #7. *Equal Indian Representation on BIC*

> That we respectfully urge that if the Board of Indian Commissioners is to be retained as a body, the Indian be given equal representation on that Board, and that we further urge this be accomplished at an early date.[26]

Justification: Board of Indian Commissioners ("BIC") Joined Hands with Lake Mohonk Conferences after Congress Declined to Fund BIC in 1882

As previously stated: Indian Bureau officials routinely attended, spoke at and were welcomed by the Indian Rights Association's Lake Mohonk Conferences that went on for thirty years. After Congress declined to fund the BIC, they joined hands with the Lake Mohonk Conferences, as well. Year after year, they attended, congratulated themselves and even printed the Proceedings of the Lake Mohonk Conferences in their Annual Reports to the Secretary, including their Platforms.

In the 1889 Proceedings of the Lake Mohonk Conference, the BIC expressly signaled out their political influence as follows:

> *...The first report of the Board of Indian Commissioners, twenty years ago, declared for nearly all the great reforms which this conference [Mohonk] has urged for many years. I suppose that*

all other influences combined have not been equal to the power of the Mohonk conference in matters of legislation. Our committees have had influence with the committees in Congress, and with the President of the United States, and the Commissioner of Indian Affairs, aided by our uninterrupted and plentiful letter-writing to members of Congress.... (Emphasis added).[27]

SAI 1912 Platform #8. *Employment of Indians*

That we endorse that portion of the Circular, CED. No. 673, August 23, 1912 ... referring to the employment of Indians who are trying to make a living, and who show themselves capable and qualified for certain positions in the Indian Service; that this organization feels that such appointment of efficient Indians, wherever possible, is entirely in accord with the general policy of the Indian department to put the Indian on his feet.[28]

Justification: Indians Employed as Common Laborers

To complement the government's work in vocational training, Commissioner Leupp established an Indian employment bureau early in his term. He placed Charles Dagenett, a thirty-three-year-old Carlisle graduate, in charge of the program, instructing him, "Gather up all the able-bodied Indians who ... have been moved to think that they would like to earn some money and *plant them on ranches, on railroads, in mines* wherever in the outer world, in short, there is an opening for a dollar to be gotten for a day's work." (Emphasis added).[29] In general, Indians were employed as common laborers, not in professional capacities.

OCTOBER 1913: THIRD ANNUAL SAI CONFERENCE, DENVER, CO

By 1913, active members grew to the high point of nearly 230 individuals representing almost 30 tribes. Arthur C. Parker, its Secretary, envisioned an organization composed of American Indian men and women from all tribes in the U.S. He proposed that the SAI adopt an organizational format like that of "friends of Indians" organizations, meet at academic institutions rather than on reservations, maintain a Washington headquarters, publish a quarterly journal, conduct annual conferences and be a vehicle for the expression of a pan-Indian identity.

The Platform promulgated at SAI's Third Annual Conference in Denver in October 1913, was considered the premier statement of the organization. With a membership of one thousand in equal representation of native and white Americans, the Society recognized the responsibility resting upon it. *In later years, SAI's Secretary Arthur Parker often referred to the "Denver Platform" as the ideal statement of the organization's goals*. (Emphasis added).[30]

SAI: Problem to Solve

The problem which the Society is attempting to solve is one that vitally concerns the red race; and that vitally affects the white race. Our labors involve:

More than a billion dollars of Indian property;
More than seventy-one million acres of land remaining to the Indian;
Six hundred eighty-seven million dollars in trust funds;
Ten million dollars in taxes paid by citizens to support the Indian Bureau;
The millions of dollars used by the Interior Department and by the various missionary bodies for the welfare of Indians;
The health and usefulness of 300,000 Indians;
The fulfillment of all treaties and contracts with the Indians;
The bringing of hope and ambition to the hearts of thousands;
The salvation of the American Indian, industrially, socially and morally;
The provision of just laws, like the Carter Code Bill and the Amended Stephens Bill, through which the Indian may be freed from unjust conditions and reach out by his own strength as a man and an American.[31]

The Platform is as follows with a statement justifying the need for the SAI Platform position:

SAI 1913 Platform #1. *Legal Status of Indians in Nation*

Of all the needs of the Indian one stands out as primary and fundamental. So long as the Indian has no definite or assured status in the nation; so long as the Indian does not know who he is and what his privileges and duties are, there can be no hope of substantial progress for our race. With one voice we declare that our first and chief request is that Congress shall provide the means for a careful and wise definition of Indian status through the prompt passage of the Carter Code Bill. (Emphasis added).[32]

SAI 1913 Platform #2. *Open United States Court of Claims to All Tribes to Present Claims*

Our second request is based on the second great legislative need of our race. Many of our tribes have waited for many years for money owed them, as they believed, by the United States. Without a standing in court, our tribes have waited for years and decades for a determination and settlement of their claims through Con-

gressional action, and the hope of justice has almost died within their hearts. They ought to know soon and once for all, what their claims are worth. We urge upon Congress the removal of a great source of injustice, a perpetual cause of bitterness, through the passage of the amended Stephens Bill, which will open the United States Court of Claims to all the tribes and bands of Indians in the nation. (Emphasis added).[33]

Justification: Legislation to Permit Indians to Submit Claims to U.S. Court of Claims

On February 3, 1912, Mr. Stephens of Texas introduced H.R. 19414, authorizing any nation, tribe or band of Indians to submit claims against the United States to the Court of Claims. (According to existing law, Indians cannot enter the United States courts without special enabling acts. This bill, on becoming law, would be the enabling act for all tribes suing the government for any moneys due or misappropriated under any treaties or laws.) It is provided that either party may appeal to the United States Supreme Court and a statute of limitation clause demands that all claims, based on facts, happening prior to the passage of this act, shall be barred unless suit is brought within five years after the passage of this act. ... The rights in the claims are to be settled by the Court of Claims regardless of the lapse of time or statutes of limitation prior to the passage.[34]

Letter from Charles H. Burke (Rep. SD) to Chairman Committee on Indian Affairs, House of Representatives. March 1, 1912. Department would prefer H.R. 19414 enacted into law.

> In this connection, however, your attention is respectfully invited to H. R. 19414, introduced on February 3, 1912, the purpose of which is to authorize any nation, tribe, or band of Indians to submit their claims against the United States to the Court of Claims for adjudication. While the department would have no objection to interpose to the approval of H. R. 4578, if amended as suggested above, *it would prefer to see the general jurisdictional bill (H. R. 19414) enacted into law.* (Emphasis added).[35]

Commissioner Cato Sells Recommends Legislation to Allow Indian Tribes to Submit Claims to Court of Claims

> I find that there is need for additional legislation by Congress to meet the problems arising, such as legislation authorizing ... the submission of claims of Indian tribes to the Court of Claims, and other additional legislation which will be prepared and ready for submission to the Congress at its regular session in December.[36]

SAI 1913 Platform #3. *Education*

> Realizing that the failure of the Indian to keep pace with modern thought is due to the inadequacy and ineffectiveness of the Indian schools, we demand the complete reorganization of the Indian school system.[37]

Justification: Education - Senator John J. Ingalls (R-KAN) - Promoting Indian Literacy and Training Absurd and Futile

> Senator John J. Ingalls of Kansas believed that the millions of dollars wasted on trying to promote Indian literacy and training "is just as absurd and would be as futile in its results as it would be to go among a heard of Texas broad horn steers and endeavour to turn them into Durhams and thoroughbreds by reading Alexander's herd book in their cattle pens at Dodge City or Wichita."[38]

> Senator Ingalls of Kansas:

> Some races are plastic and can be molded; some races are elastic and can be bent; but the Indian is neither; he is formed out of rock, and when you change his form you annihilate his substance… Civilization destroys the Indian … and the sooner the country understands that all these efforts are valueless unless they are based upon force supplemented by force and continued by force, the less money we shall waste and the less difficulty we shall have.[39]

Indian Schools: Expenditure of Five or Six Million Dollars for Education over Fifteen-Year Period Would Make Indian, "If Not a Valuable Citizen, at Least One from Whom Danger Need Not Be Apprehended;" Contracts and Jobs Might Be Distributed for Greatest Political Benefit

> Sec. Teller defended the new schools in coldly practical terms. *In his first annual report he estimated that the expenditure of five or six million dollars for education over a fifteen-year period would make the Indian, "if not a valuable citizen, at least one from whom danger need not be apprehended." The Indian would thus "cease to be a tax on the government."* Better to "civilize" the tribes than dispute with them over boundaries and property. Better also to establish new schools under a Republican administration so that contracts and jobs might be distributed for the greatest political benefit. (Emphasis added).[40]

SAI 1913 Platform #4. *Prompt Division in Severalty of All Funds Held in Trust by United States for Any and All Indian Tribes*

> *For reasons long evident and incontrovertible and in harmony with the policy of land allotments, we urge the prompt division in severalty upon the books of the nation of all funds held in trust by the United States for any and all Indian tribes. We further urge that these individual accounts be paid at as early a date as wisdom will allow.* (Emphasis added).[41]

Justification: Board of Indian Commissioners, Maintenance of Trust Funds Opportunity for Unscrupulous Persons

> Prolonged observation of the effect upon Indians - tribes and individuals of the retention of undivided tribal funds in the hands of the Government long ago convinced this Board that *the maintenance of such funds for an indefinite time has been and will be productive of great evils. Such tribal funds in the eyes of many unscrupulous persons have always been unexploited mines of money.* (Emphasis added).[42]

SAI 1913 Platform #6. *Need for Data*

> *We reiterate our belief that the data concerning Indians gathered by the United States Census Bureau are so essential to Indian progress that failure to complete the tabulation and publication would be a calamity to our race, as well as a great extravagance to the nation.* (Emphasis added).[43]

Justification: Board of Indian Commissioners

> **In our last annual report we presented letters and reports from all the Indian agencies, showing the great need of regulations to govern the licensing and solemnizing of marriages among Indians, and to provide for such records of births, deaths, and family relationship as are absolutely essential to the delivering of a clear title to the lands of allotted Indians when the period of protected title expires.** (Emphasis added).[44]

SAI 1913 Platform #8. President Taft to Secretary of Interior -- Indian Must Assume Responsibility if He Demands Rights

> **We realize that hand in hand with the demand of our rights must go an unwavering desire to take on new** responsibility. (Emphasis added).[45]

Justification: President Taft to Secretary of Interior -- Indian Must Assume Responsibility if He Demands Rights

Hon. William Howard Taft, Letter of President Taft to Secretary of Interior, 1912.

> Citizenship involves more than benefits to the individual. There are obligations and burdens toward the community which he must recognize and assume. Any plan for the development of the Indian as an individual must, to be successful, include efforts to impress upon him the fact that he must accept the responsibilities if he demands the benefits of citizenship.

Key Information from SAI's Quarterly Journals

1913 Article: The Teaching of Ethnology in Indian Schools by J.N.B. Hewitt (Tuscarora), of the Smithsonian Institution

The well-attested fact that not one American Indian in 5,000 knows what his own tribe, not to say the American Indian race, has done in the past as expressed in terms of human culture, makes this question one that should receive the attention of this Society of American Indians, at this Conference.

> Among the objects mentioned in the Statement of Purpose of this Society of American Indians are, to promote the advancement of the American Indian in enlightenment, to conserve the history of the American Indian race, without distortion from ignorance, misconception, or misinterpretation, and to promote all honorable means the social, ethical, political, and economic welfare and betterment of not only its members but also that of their other brothers of the American Indian race, by conserving and developing what is congruous to their attainment, and eliminating what is not. It is true that before this great work can be done intelligently and effectively the past history and the culture of the people must be known.[46]

1914: SAI Office in Washington, D.C.

In 1914, the SAI established its headquarters in Washington, D.C., across the street from the Indian Office, and lobbied for the passage of "two great objects of immense importance to the Indians and to the nation", the "Carter Bill" and the "Stephens Bill". It held its Fourth Annual Conference at the University of Wisconsin in Madison, Wisconsin, in October 1914.

The Carter Bill, introduced by Oklahoma Congressman Charles D. Carter, (Chickasaw and Cherokee), Chairman of the House Indian Committee, codified the laws relating to Indian citizenship, and provided "that every Indian born within the territorial limits of the United States is hereby declared to be a citizen of the United States, entitled to all the rights, privileges, and immunities of such citizens." The Stephens Bill called for opening to Indian tribes the United States Court of Claims to facilitate settlement of long neglected Indian land claims.[47]

OCTOBER 1914: FOURTH SAI CONFERENCE, UNIVERSITY OF WISCONSIN-MADISON

The 1914 meeting produced a document, called a "memorial," which was to be presented to President Woodrow Wilson. Unexpectedly, the SAI was invited to meet with U.S. President Woodrow Wilson at the White House in December 1914.

December 1914: SAI's Meeting with U.S. President Woodrow Wilson at White House

Dennison Wheelock presented the written Society's petition in support of the Carter Bill and Stephens Bill to President Wilson. This was followed by an address by William Kershaw. Congressman Charles D. Carter, former chief of the Chickasaw Council and now vice-president on legislation of the Society, made the closing address.

Neither bill would garner political traction in Washington. The entirety of SAI's written Petition to U.S. President Wilson is set forth in APPENDIX E-1, SAI's Address to U.S. President Wilson, made by William Kershaw, APPENDIX E-2 and SAI's Platforms in APPENDIX E-3.

President Wilson expressed his pleasure in receiving the delegation, stating that he had not given special thought to the Indian, though he had appointed the best man he could find as Secretary of the Interior and as Commissioner of Indian Affairs. He promised to give the memorial his most earnest consideration and to study the measures advocated by the Society.

SAI April - June 2014 Edition - Editorial Comment: Equal Status of Indians Imperative; Legislative Needs of Indians Need to Be Understood

> The Indian cannot compete in civilization unless placed on the same footing as other men. An equal status is imperative. If the Indian does not become an equal before the law he will be robbed, plundered, trampled upon, and finally die out. This will not be alone his fault. To obtain legal equality the law must pave the way. There is a primary need, therefore, for legislative action. The legislative needs of the race need a thorough understanding. We have many times pointed out these needs. ... We are not to demand a dozen new laws. In our endorsement of laws let us stick to those already demanded. ... The Society of American Indians' three great ideals for the American Indian are equal rights, equal responsibility and equal education.[48]

SAI July - September 1914 Edition: Rumor Started to Cause Dissension that SAI Has Hostile Attitude toward Indians in Federal Employ

A rumor has gone forth that "the Society" has a hostile attitude toward Indians in Federal employ. Some one seems to have spread the idea that, through our members so employed, "the Bureau" was endeavoring to control the Society. Of course this is untrue and unjust. ... our Indian membership employed by the Bureau is absolutely loyal to the race.[49]

OCTOBER 1915: FIFTH SAI CONFERENCE, LAWRENCE, KANSAS

SAI 1915 Platform: Define Legal Status of Indians; Open Court of Claims to Indians; Distribute Tribal Trust Funds to Individuals

> (1) *Congress, thus far has taken no action on the Carter Code Bill, introduced in 1912 at the instance of this Society. So long as the Indian has no definite or assured status in the nation, so long as the Indian does not know who he is and what his privileges and duties are, there can be no hope of substantial progress of our race*. (Emphasis added).
>
> (2) Our second request is based on the second great legislative need of our race. Our tribes have waited for many years for money owed them, as they believed, by the United States. We therefore *urge upon Congress the passage of the amended Stephens Bill,* or some similar measure, which will *directly open the United States Court of Claims to all the tribes and bands of Indians in the country*. (Emphasis added).
>
> (5) For reasons long evident and incontrovertible and in harmony with the policy of land allotments, we urge the prompt *division in severalty upon the books of the nation of all funds held in trust by the United States for any and all Indian Tribes*. (Emphasis added).[50]

SEPTEMBER 1918: SAI CONFERENCE, PIERRE, SOUTH DAKOTA – New Faction Elected

At the September 1918 SAI Conference in Pierre, South Dakota, Dr. Montezuma's "faction" secured leadership of the SAI. In the January 1919 issue the new SAI president Charles Eastman published a letter charging that "the mass of Indian people" suspected that the Indian Bureau had had a "controlling interest" in the activities of the Society. But, with his election as president, he would lead the Society toward what he takes as his and the Society's "ultimate project": "THE FREEDOM OF THE INDIAN FROM BONDAGE."

> **SAI 1918 Platform #1. Closing Indian Bureau.** We believe the time has come when we ought to call upon the country and upon Congress to look to the closing of the Indian Bureau, so soon as trust funds, treaty rights and other just obligations can be individualized, fulfilled or paid.[51]

SAI 1918 Platform #3. *Liquor Traffic an Evil.* We commend the efforts of the officials of the Bureau for the suppression of the liquor traffic among Indians and we urge upon our own people the adoption of habits of total abstinence which we are convinced are conducive to happiness and prosperity. We urge unequivocally upon Congress the passage of the Gandy bill to prohibit the commerce in and use of peyote among our people, because of its known baneful effects upon the users in mind and morals.⁵²

SAI 1918 Platform #5. *Former Principles Reaffirmed.* We reaffirm the principles so ardently and justly urged by former Conferences of this Society. We reiterate our pleas made in our Denver, Madison and Lawrence platforms calling for *(a) a definition of the legal status of the Indians; (b) for the individualization of trust funds; (c) and the early adjudication of all tribal claims.* We renew our appeal as made in our memorial to the President of the United States, December 11, 1914. (Emphasis added).⁵³

SAI Quarterly Journal (October-December 1917): Dr. Carlos Montezuma - "BREAK THE SHACKLES NOW, MAKE US FREE"

MORE than once the platforms of the Society of American Indians have pointed out the glaring defects of the Indian Bureau system, and, more than this, at least two Conferences of the Society have expressed a belief that the Indian Bureau must be eliminated.

This doctrine is founded upon an intimate knowledge of the evils of the reservation system, the failures of a paternal policy and the incompetence of the Bureau itself. We doubt than any sort of "reform" within the Bureau would root out its defects.

The fundamental errors of the Bureau are those of its attitude toward the Indians, whom it is supposed to protect and serve. These errors are paternalism, segregation, autocratic action, amounting to tyranny, politics. Out of these major evils have grown minor evils, some menacing, others actually criminal.

A paternal attitude held by the Bureau or by its Agent will not develop virile citizenship or respect for the order of society that permits this paternalism. A policy of segregation of Indians prevents these Indians from mingling normally with the rest of the country. Society generally looks upon the segregated as pests and treats them accordingly. ... Indians affected by such conditions have an enormous handicap to overcome. The wonder is that any ever become accepted as citizens, the wonder is that any can be found "competent."

The mistake is that the Indian Bureau has the power over the souls and minds of its "wards." This is the grip that is fatal to their mental growth and their moral welfare.

The Bureau is supposed to *protect* the Indians, and yet because it was indifferent or incapable, millions of dollars and millions of acres of land have been filched from the Indians under the very nose of the Bureau and before its very eyes. One will hear the excuse, "Oh, well, that was in the former administration." But right now the work goes on, and the next Commissioner of Indian Affairs, if there be one, will say the same thing.

The Bureau may have protected certain interests and even certain Indian interests, but it has never given adequate protection. The misery that has been unable to mitigate, the thieving that it has not prevented, the thousand and one evils it has not stopped stand as its indictment. May it not be true that if there had been no Bureau whatsoever that the evils that the Indians would have suffered would not have been more, and that perhaps their fitness for citizenship would today have been far greater because of the virility of an uncrushed spirit and the experience of coping with the world? Might it not be true that the unfit and sub-normal would not have been bred and that the incompetents would not have been produced in the numbers by which they are now counted?

But, it will be argued, "The Government has certain obligations to fulfill to the Indians, certain monies to pay out and certain treaties to execute." This is true, but these things could be done without the vast, self-perpetuating machine, that beside paying out money, dictates to the Indians what they shall do, where they shall go, what they shall think, and denies them the right of discussion.

The Indian Bureau is an un-American institution; it must go. No longer must it be an institution of tyranny. If any vestige of it remains it must simply be a disbursing office which shall have the order of Congress to pay the Indians their due and say nothing more, because the Indians have become citizens and are free to think and discuss and participate in their mutual affairs and in the affairs of the Nation.

Make the Indian a citizen, eliminate the Bureau, demonstrate that America is a safe place for every American citizen, whether he has studied at Harvard or has learned of Nature out on the plains, and whether he happens to be the First American or of a later importation.

We believe that an equitable plan could be worked out by which the Indians could have the monies due them paid or apportioned, their interests conserved and real protection given them, without the necessity of a bulky bureau and all its red tape. In advocating the closing up of the Bureau we are not advocating the abandonment of the legal and moral obligations of Government to the Indians, but a recognition of these obligations in such a manner that the first Americans shall become, indeed, real Americans in every sense, and that they may become the good citizens they ought and would like to be.[54]

WHO FOOTS THE INDIAN BILL Somehow most people get it into their heads that the people of the United States, through Congress, each year take twelve millions of dollars out of the treasury each year and give it to the Indians, or to "agents" who "look after and civilize the Indians."

It is never quite generally known that millions of Indian money is used to pay for the administration of tribal affairs, and that the Government makes the Indians pay for the System that rules them, whenever it can. It is sometimes lost sight of that much of the money appropriated by Congress is simply in payment of treaty funds and contracts made by the United States; and which the Government is, therefore, bound to pay.

An example of how the Indians are made to pay for the administration is the case of the Ute Six Million Dollar fund, of the 1910 settlement. When the money was appropriated a bill was prepared itemizing every dollar and every cent ever paid out by the Government for the administration, support, sustenance, etc. of these Indians and charging for the salaries of every and all employees that had ever served them. The Utes had this money taken out from their fund. They paid it. Generally speaking the Red Man pays in one way or an another,-but does he really ever get what he wants?

Considering the quality of "sustenance," the foetid civilization and the grade of the "employees" that the Indian is given, doesn't it seem like a hideous crime to make him pay for these what should only be paid for sanitary and nourishing food, real industrial and educational training and decently civilized employees?

And still the robbery goes on, still the Red Men foots the bill.[55]

OCTOBER 1919 SAI EIGHTH CONFERENCE, MINNEAPOLIS, MINN

Proceedings Weary and Disillusioned

The tone of the October 1919 SAI Conference in Minneapolis proceedings was weary and disillusioned. (Emphasis added). When calling for Bureau abolition, the 1919 SAI conference issued the following statement which, in comparison to previous statements, was angry in tone:

> *SAI Editorial Comment: Indians who attended the Eighth Annual Conference of the Society of American Indians at Minneapolis are*

> *firm in the belief that there is no hope of fair treatment, honest reforms, just administration of the laws to their personal and property rights, the enactment of laws for the benefit of the Indians or receiving the rights and benefits of citizenship according to the laws of the land without abolishing the Indian Bureau.* (Emphasis added).

> Agents in charge of reservations are thought to be dishonest. That they have no respect for the rights of the Indians and their property. They ignore the laws and exercise arbitrary and illegal power over the person and property of the Indians. Their property, out of which they have made the living for themselves and families, have been ruthlessly taken from them. They have been left destitute, their work destroyed, their initiative broken. Independent men have been made dependent, repressed and oppressed. Comfort and reasonable affluence has been changed to need and want. Such is the hopelessness of reservation supervision under the Indian Bureau.[56]

SAI President Charles Eastman's Speech Excerpt

> Indians have power in their hands to get citizenship. We must stand on our treaty rights. We must stand on our constitutional rights and force the Bureau to cease its shameless bluffing, put it right out. So long as we let it rule, we are playing an ignorant Indian.[57]

See APPENDIX F: Excerpts from Charles Eastman's Books.

1923: LAST SAI CONFERENCE, CHICAGO

In 1923, the organization met in Chicago. By this time, the Society was almost completely inactive and differences regarding the Indian Bureau and the Native American Church had alienated most of the leadership. The meeting in Chicago was overshadowed by the Indian encampment held in connection with the [SAI] conference in the forest preserve near the city. Thousands of Chicagoans journeyed to the camp to see the Indians "informal gala" and watch Indian dances and ceremonials. William Madison, a Minnesota Chippewa who was treasurer of the Society, "expressed his regrets that it is only when he exhibits Indian war dances in ancient ceremonies that the public evinces any interest in the Indian."[58] The Society disbanded with little fanfare after the Chicago meeting.[59]

SAI's Legacy

The SAI was the first national American Indian rights organization run by and for American Indians and pioneered twentieth century Pan-Indianism. Former Society leaders continued to influence Indian affairs serving with the American Indian Defense Association, the Committee of One Hundred and authoring the Meriam Report of 1928.

In 1924 Congress passed the Indian Citizenship Act. In 1946, Congress established an Indian Claims Commission, not a court, and successful claims could only result in monetary compensation, not regained lands.

1913-1915: SAI - Wanamaker Expedition of Citizenship – Offensive to Indians – Completely Discredited

The SAI completely discredited the 1913 Rodman Wanamaker Expedition of Citizenship which circled the entire country in a clockwise direction, covering more than 20,000 miles. It had no notice of this Expedition. The SAI stated: "Where, oh, where, has every one been, that through the merits of a six months' trip this information has for the first time been made available! Of what use is an Indian Bureau, an Ethnological Bureau, an Indian organization, where they have been so blind?"[60]

The Expedition's letter to the President of the United States, the Secretary of the Interior, the Commissioner of Indian Affairs and the people of the U.S. stated:

> For the first time the nation may have the full, unvarnished truth, at first hand, from a neutral authority-the truth about lands,-the truth about starvation,-the truth about education,-the truth about health,-the truth about intemperance,-the truth about unjust allotments,-the truth about irrigation and water rights,-the truth about agriculture,-land that may be tilled and land that is desert,-the truth about the industrial problem, supervising farmers who do not supervise,-the truth about the extent of the Indian police control,-the truth about a waste of funds, the open market versus bids,-the truth about warehouse folly,-the truth about the vexed question of half-breeds,-the truth about blanket orders for school supplies, a failure to recognize climatic conditions,-the truth about the abolition of Indian ceremonies and regalia,-the truth about the supreme struggle for existence,-and the truth about the actual living conditions of the Indian.

> It included the 1913 Wanamaker DECLARATION OF ALLEGIANCE TO THE GOVERNMENT OF THE UNITED STATES BY THE NORTH AMERICAN INDIAN, signed by 31 'Chiefs,' Attested by President Taft. Wanamaker stated: "I took the flag in my hands, I ordered the Indians to bow their heads, I dedicated the Indians to the flag; I dedicated the flag to the Indians."

> We, the undersigned representatives of the various Indian tribes of

the United States, through our presence and the part we have taken in the inauguration of this memorial to our people, renew our allegiance to the glorious flag of the United States, and offer our hearts to our country's service. We greatly appreciate the honor and privilege extended to us by our white brothers who have recognized us by inviting us to participate in the ceremonies on this historical occasion.

The Indian is fast losing his identity in the face of the great waves of Caucasian civilization which are extending to the four winds of this country, and we want fuller knowledge, in order that we may take our places in the civilization which surrounds us.

Though a conquered race, with our right hands extended in brotherly love, and our left hands holding the Pipe of Peace, we hereby bury all past ill feeling and proclaim abroad to all the nations of the world our firm allegiance to this nation and to the stars and stripes, and declare that henceforth and forever in all walks of life and in every field of endeavor we shall be as brothers, striving hand in hand, and will return to our people and tell them the story of this memorial, and urge upon them their continued allegiance to our *common* country. *[Thirty-one signatures of the "Chiefs" including some with thumbprints.]*[61]

Wanamaker also sponsored three other western expeditions. The first was devoted to the filming of a dramatization of "Hiawatha" on the Blackfoot reservation. The second was for a "last council of the chiefs," a gathering of old warriors that was also filmed. The final trip was a visit to 169 Indian communities by a special railroad car that carried recorded greetings and patriotic messages from President Woodrow Wilson and Secretary of the Interior Franklin K. Lane. The last two of these projects are described in Joseph K. Dixon, The Vanishing Race. Multitudes of photographs of Indians in native dress were taken during the expeditions.

Wanamaker proposed building a giant statue of an Indian at Fort Tomkins. The groundbreaking ceremony and Taft's speech were described in the New York Times on February 23, 1913. Wanamaker's Indian statue was never completed. Work was postponed by the world war—apparently because of a shortage of bronze—and later abandoned for lack of interest. The War Department did not want one of its harbor forts marked so conspicuously. The Staten Island Society of Natural Science was invited to take it as a relic.[62]

NOTES

1. Pratt, Richard Henry. Battlefield and classroom: Four decades with the American Indian, 1867–1904. University of Oklahoma Press, 2023, p. 195.
2. Annual Report of the Board of Indian Commissioners to the Secretary of the Interior

(1877), p. 7.

3. Lake Mohonk Conference - Third Annual Meeting, The Report of the Annual Lake Mohonk Conference on the Indian and Other Dependent Peoples, 3, 1885, p. 53.

4. Annual Report of the Commissioner of Indian Affairs, United States. Office of Indian Affairs. Printer: A.O.P. Nicholson, 1889, p. 3.

5. Society of American Indians, "The Quarterly Journal of the Society of American Indians v. 2 no. 3 (July-September 1914)," pp. 187-189, 232. American Indian Digital History Project. https://aidhp.com/items/show/156 (accessed online October 8, 2024).

6. WASSAJA, Vol. 1, No. 9, December 1916. https://d1rbsgppyrdqq4.cloudfront.net/prism/s3fs-public/c195/CHM_Wassaja_V1_No9OCR.pdf?VersionId=GKeIQidk6YlNTpaQyXY0hFks5Ytb1 (accessed online October 10, 2024).

7. The Quarterly Journal of the Society of American Indians, V. 1 No. 1 (January-April 1913).

8. SAI Quarterly Journal, V. 1 No. 1 (January-April 1913), p. 69.

9. SAI Quarterly Journal, V. 1 No. 1 (January-April 1913), p. 3.

10. SAI Quarterly Journal, V. 1 No. 1 (January-April 1913), p. 4.

11. SAI Quarterly Journal, V. 1 No. 1 (January-April 1913), p. 5.

12. SAI Quarterly Journal, V. 1 No. 1 (January-April 1913), p. 5.

13. Annual Report of the Board of Indian Commissioners, 1907 (Washington: Government Printing Office), p. 3. https://babel.hathitrust.org/cgi/pt?id=hvd.32044097929608&seq=5 (accessed online October 5, 2024).

14. SAI Quarterly Journal, V. 1 No. 1 (January-April 1913), p. 5.

15. SAI Quarterly Journal, V. 1 No. 1 (January-April 1913), pp. 7-10. American Indian Digital History Project. https://aidhp.com/items/show/174 (accessed online October 8, 2024).

16. Society of American Indians, "The Quarterly Journal of the Society of American Indians, v. 1 no. 1 (January-April 1913)," pp. 71-73. American Indian Digital History Project. https://aidhp.com/items/show/174 (accessed online October 8, 2024).

17. Report of the Commissioner of Indian Affairs to the Secretary of the Interior, Office of Indian Affairs, United States. U.S. Government Printing Office, 1861, p. 93.

18. Annual Report of the Board of Indian Commissioners to the Secretary of the Interior, 1922-23, p. 8.

19. Annual Report of the Board of Indian Commissioners to the Secretary of the Interior, 1901, p. 5.

20. Society of American Indians, "The Quarterly Journal of the Society of American Indians, v. 1 no. 1 (January-April 1913)". American Indian Digital History Project. https://aidhp.com/items/show/174 (accessed online October 8, 2024).

21. Report of Special Agent Edwin Brooks to Commissioner of Indian Affairs E.A. Hayt, dated January 18, 1878. https://search.library.wisc.edu/catalog/9910707404302121 (accessed online June 21, 2022).

22. Society of American Indians, "The Quarterly Journal of the Society of American Indians, v. 1 no. 1 (January-April 1913)," pp. 71-73. American Indian Digital History Project. https://aidhp.com/items/show/174 (accessed online October 8, 2024).

23. *Indians of Fort Berthold Indian Reservation in the State of North Dakota v. United*

States, 71 Ct. Cl. 308 (1930), pp. 308-341.

24. Report of the Commissioner of Indian Affairs to the Secretary of the Interior, Reports of Agents in Arizona, United States, Office of Indian Affairs, U.S. Government Printing Office, 1893, p. 109.

25. Report of the Commissioner of Indian Affairs to the Secretary of the Interior, Office of Indian Affairs, United States. U.S. Government Printing Office, 1882, p. 128.

26. Society of American Indians, "The Quarterly Journal of the Society of American Indians, v. 1 no. 1 (January-April 1913)," pp. 71-73. American Indian Digital History Project. https://aidhp.com/items/show/174 (accessed online October 8, 2024).

27. 7 Report of the Annual Lake Mohonk Conference on the Indian and Other Dependent Peoples (1889), p. 7.

28. Society of American Indians, "The Quarterly Journal of the Society of American Indians, v. 1 no. 1 (January-April 1913)," p. 72. American Indian Digital History Project. https://aidhp.com/items/show/174 (accessed online October 8, 2024).

29. Hoxie, Frederick E. A final promise: The campaign to assimilate the Indians, 1880-1920. U of Nebraska Press, 2001, p. 201.

30. https://en.wikipedia.org/wiki/Society_of_American_Indians#:~:text=The%20university%20lectures%20were%20well,than%20a%20'Mohonk%20for%20Indians (accessed online November 5, 2024).

31. Society of American Indians, The Quarterly Journal of the Society of American Indians v. 1 no. 4 (October-December 1913), *American Indian Digital History Project.* https://aidhp.com/items/show/153 (accessed online April 29, 2024).

32. SAI Quarterly Journal, V. 1 No. 4 (October-Dec. 1913), p. 411.

33. SAI Quarterly Journal, V. 1 No. 4 (October-Dec. 1913), p. 411.

34. The Quarterly Journal of the Society of American Indians, V. 1 No. 4 (October-Dec. 1913), p. 352.

35. Letter from Charles H. Burke (Rep. SD) to Chairman Committee on Indian Affairs, House of Representatives. March 1, 1912. https://www.google.it.ao/books?pg=RA28-PA1&dq=editions:UOM39015035795981&lr=&id=YeR-TAAAAIAAJ&output=text
(accessed online November 26, 2024).

36. Report of the Commissioner of Indian Affairs to the Secretary of the Interior, Office of Indian Affairs, 1913, p. 7.

37. SAI Quarterly Journal, V. 1 No. 4 (October-Dec. 1913), p. 411.

38. 15 CONG. REC. 4074 (1884).

39. Ross-Mulkey, Mikhelle Lynn. *Locating the resiliency & survivance in the "Cherokee Phoenix".* The University of Arizona, 2010.

40. Teller quoted in Hoxie, Frederick E. A final promise: The campaign to assimilate the Indians, 1880-1920. U of Nebraska Press, 2001, p. 58.

41. SAI Quarterly Journal, V. 1 No. 4 (October-Dec. 1913), p. 412.

42. Annual Report of the Board of Indian Commissioners to the Secretary of the Interior (1904), p. 7.

43. SAI Quarterly Journal, V. 1 No. 4 (October-Dec. 1913), p. 412.

44. Annual Report of the Board of Indian Commissioners to the Secretary of the Interior, 1901, p. 8.

45. SAI Quarterly Journal, V. 1 No. 4 (October-Dec. 1913), p. 412.

46. Society of American Indians, "The Quarterly Journal of the Society of American Indians, v. 1 no. 1 (January-April 1913)," p. 32. American Indian Digital History Project. https://www.aidhp.com/items/show/174 (accessed online October 8, 2024).
47. https://en.wikipedia.org/wiki/Society_of_American_Indians#:~:text=The%20university%20lectures%20were%20well,than%20a%20'Mohonk%20for%20Indians (accessed online October 8, 2024).
48. Society of American Indians, "The Quarterly Journal of the Society of American Indians (April-June 1914).
49. Society of American Indians, "The Quarterly Journal of the Society of American Indians (July – September 1914).
50. Society of American Indians, "The Quarterly Journal of the Society of American Indians v. 3 no. 4 (October-December 1915)," American Indian Digital History Project. https://aidhp.com/items/show/161 (accessed online April 29, 2024).
51. Society of American Indians, "The American Indian Magazine, v. 4 no. 3 (July-September 1916)," American Indian Digital History Project. https://www.aidhp.com/items/show/164 (accessed online October 9, 2024).
52. Society of American Indians, "The American Indian Magazine, v. 4 no. 3 (July-September 1916)," American Indian Digital History Project. https://www.aidhp.com/items/show/164 (accessed online October 9, 2024).
53. Society of American Indians, "The American Indian Magazine, v. 4 no. 3 (July-September 1916)," pp. 223-224. American Indian Digital History Project. https://aidhp.com/items/show/164 (accessed online October 8, 2024).
54. Society of American Indians, The American Indian Magazine, v. 5 no. 4, (October-December 1917), pp. 213-215. American Indian Digital History Project. https://www.aidhp.com/items/show/169 (accessed online September 10, 2024).
55. Society of American Indians, The American Indian Magazine, v. 5 no. 4, (October-December 1917), pp. 218-219. American Indian Digital History Project. https://www.aidhp.com/items/show/169 (accessed online September 10, 2024).
56. The American Indian Magazine v. 7 no. 3 1919, p. 139. https://babel.hathitrust.org/cgi/pt?id=coo.31924102392515&seq=26 (accessed online November 6, 2024).
57. The American Indian magazine v. 7 no. 3 1919, p. 150. https://babel.hathitrust.org/cgi/pt?id=coo.31924102392515&seq=26 (accessed online November 6, 2024).
58. https://en.wikipedia.org/wiki/Society_of_American_Indians#cite_note-96 (accessed online August 21, 2024).
59. https://en.wikipedia.org/wiki/Society_of_American_Indians#cite_note-97 (accessed online August 21, 2024).
60. Society of American Indians, "The Quarterly Journal of the Society of American Indians v. 3 no. 3 (July-September 1915)," p. 232. American Indian Digital History Project. https://aidhp.com/items/show/160 (accessed online April 29, 2024).
61. The Purpose and Achievements of the Rodman Wanamaker Expedition of Citizenship to the North American Indian, Joseph Kossuth Dixon, 1913.
62. Barsh, Russel Lawrence, "An American Heart of Darkness: The 1913 Expedition for American Indian Citizenship," *Great Plains Quarterly*, 1993), 91–115. Society of

American Indians, "The Quarterly Journal of the Society of American Indians, v. 1 no. 1 (January-April 1913)," American Indian Digital History Project. https://aidhp.com/items/show/174 (accessed online October 8, 2024).

CHAPTER 54: Dr. Carlos Montezuma

Dr. Carlos Montezuma of Chicago, a full-blooded Apache, was captured by the Pimas, who were enemies of his people, as a child. He was ransomed by a reporter and photographer. He was taken to Chicago and when his benefactor died, Carlos became the protégé of the Chicago Press Club. He was the first American Indian student at the University of Illinois and Northwestern University, and only the second American Indian to earn a medical degree in an American University. After graduation Dr. Montezuma was sent by the Government as a physician to an Indian agency in Montana, and later transferred to the Carlisle School. In a few years he returned to Chicago and opened an office.

Dr. Montezuma dogmatically argued for abolishing the Indian Office, along with reservations. He insistently demanded a public school education for Indians, along with citizenship for all Indians. With only 225,000 Indians among 10,000,000, he wanted to obliterate anything Indian which, according to him, created prejudice and did the Indian more harm than good. "Indian Schools, Indian Hospitals, Indian Churches, Indian Missions, Indian Music, Indian Shows, Indian Reservations. Indian Day, Indian this and Indian that, or anything Indian" was to be expunged. For him, total assimilation was the solution for Indian progress. His scornful, scathing rhetoric against the Indian Bureau's system is set forth as a part of the history of the pan-Indian reformers. It is important to let him speak for himself.[1]

It is important to note that the BIC and LMC had been collaborating for twenty-nine years with the legislation for achieving their objectives already enacted. Also, Commissioner Sells and Dr. Montezuma detested each other so the probability of Dr. Montezuma's influence was low.

September 1915: What Indians Must Do, Free Ourselves, Speech by Carlos Montezuma, M.D. (Apache)

WE MUST free ourselves.[2]

Abolish Indian Bureau

Dr. Montezuma, in his speech, "Let My People Go!", delivered in 1915 at the SAI conference, argued for the abolition of the Indian Bureau:

> The Indian Bureau system is wrong. The only way to adjust wrong is to abolish it, and the only reform is to let my people go. After freeing the Indian from the shackles of government supervision, what is the Indian going to do? Leave that with the Indian, and it is none of your business. ...

> The iron hand of the Indian Bureau has us in charge. The slimy clutches of horrid greed and selfish interests are gripping the Indian's property. Little by little the Indian's land and everything else is fading into a dim and unknown realm.
>
> The Indian's prognosis is bad—unfavorable, no hope. ... when all the Indian's money in the United States Treasury is disposed of; when the Indian's property is all taken from him; when the Indians have nothing in this wide, wide world; when the Indians will have no rights, no place to lay their heads; and when the Indians will be permitted to exist only on the outskirts of the towns; when they must go to the garbage boxes in alleys to keep them from starving; when the Indians will be driven into the streets, and finally the streets will be no place for them, then, what will the Indian Bureau do for them? Nothing, but drop them. The Indian Department will go out of business.
>
> [B]y doing away with the Indian Bureau you stop making paupers and useless beings and start the making of producers and workers.[3]

Dr. Montezuma's WASSAJA Newsletter, 1916-1922

From 1916 to 1922, Dr. Montezuma published his own monthly newsletter, WASSAJA. WASSAJA is an Apache word for beckoning or signaling, and was the name given to Dr. Montezuma by his mother and father. The masthead showed an Indian lying crushed under a huge log labeled "Indian Bureau," and proclaimed that WASSAJA was "Freedom's Signal for the Indians." It went on to say that it existed only to hasten abolishment of the Indian Bureau and that it would be published monthly so long as the Bureau existed.

WASSAJA, July 1916: Churches "Tolerate Monstrous, Conscienceless Devil-Fish Indian Bureau Which Squeezes and Sucks Life-Blood Out of Indians"

Dr. Montezuma made blistering attacks on the Christian religious societies in Indian country, as well.

> The churches preach and preach, they tell of Christ and the Fatherhood of God. Their preaching is "as sounding brass or a tingling cymbal," and cold as ice to the Indians of America. ... The churches must stand in the right; they must not waver. *It is not right-it is wrong, in the sight of God, to confine the Indians as prisoners without cause, and preach to them Christianity.* It is a mockery, a blasphemy to their Great Spirit that gave them the continent of America. ... Churches, you are weighed and found wanting in the scale of justice with the Indian ... you have not turned one finger

> to show your interest in the direction of uplifting the MAN part of the Indian. ... Churches, you fought against slavery and yet you tolerate this monstrous, conscienceless devil-fish-the Indian Bureau-which squeezes and sucks the life-blood out of the Indians. ... They [Churches] deserve the punishment of the damned-damned. (Emphasis added).[4]

WASSAJA, October 1916: WASSAJA Attacks SAI Indians Employed by Indian Bureau; SAI "Arm in Arm" with Indian Bureau

WASSAJA claimed that the SAI was "arm in arm" with the Bureau on certain issues and accused that their election of officers was suspect. Of Coolidge's assertion that he could serve both Indians and the Bureau, Dr. Montezuma proclaimed - "if he serves God and the Devil the same way." (Emphasis added).[5]

Indian Bureau's Object – Save - Not Sever Ties of Bureauism; Helped by Indian Organizations Internal Squabbling

> *The spectacle of the Indians disagreeing, throttling each other, stirring up confusion and killing their organization is exactly what the Indian Bureau likes to see in all Indian organizations whose object is to sever the ties of Bureauism.* (Emphasis added).[6]

Indians Must Become Own Emancipators

> *The Indians must become their own emancipators. There is none to carry the burden for them.* (Emphasis added).[7]

WASSAJA, November 1916: Indian Reform Organizations in League with Indian Bureau

Properly, Dr. Montezuma vociferously challenged the interlocking government organizations aligned against the Indians. As stated previously, Indian Bureau officials routinely attended, spoke at and were welcomed by the Indian Rights Association's Lake Mohonk Conferences that went on for thirty years. After Congress declined to fund the Board of Indian Commissioners, they joined hands with the Lake Mohonk Conferences, as well. Year after year, they attended, congratulated themselves and even printed the Proceedings of the Lake Mohonk Conferences in their Annual Reports to the Secretary, including their Platforms.

Dr. Montezuma was not overstating the **profligate relationship between the government and private groups in determining Indian policy.** He *began to refer to cooperation with the Bureau as "Parkerism" and to lump the SAI with other groups he felt were proBureau--the Indian Rights Association, the Friends of the Indian, and various missionary groups.* (Emphasis added). He coined the terms Mohonkism, Indian Friendism, Missionaryism, and Indian Bureauism.

He printed his slogan on the WASSAJA Newsletter: THE ONLY WAY TO GET THE INDIANS OUT OF THE CONTROL OF THE INDIAN BUREAU, IS TO GET THEM OUT OF THE CONTROL OF THE INDIAN BUREAU

WASSAJA, December 1916: Dr. Montezuma Questioned Every Aspect of Indian Bureau

In his article on the **INDIAN OFFICE** he derisively questioned every aspect of its handling of Indian issues. "WASSAJA is emphatic in claiming the Indian Office has done all the harm that has come to the Indians; it is now doing great harm to the Indians, and *it will suck the life-blood out of the Indians and that is not FOR THE BEST INTEREST OF THE INDIANS*."

>If the Indian Office is in existence for the best interest of the Indians, why does it not work FOR THE BEST INTEREST OF THE INDIANS?
>
>Is working on the Indians as Indians, FOR THE BEST INTEREST OF THE INDIANS?
>
>Keeping the Indians as Wards, is that FOR THE BEST INTEREST OF THE INDIANS?
>
>Is caging the Indians on reservations FOR THE BEST INTEREST OF THE INDIANS?
>
>Does opening the Indian lands for settlers work FOR THE BEST INTEREST OF THE INDIANS?
>
>Are the Reimbursement Funds (Government Mortgage) FOR THE BEST INTEREST OF THE INDIANS?
>
>Are dams built on reservations FOR THE BEST INTEREST OF THE INDIANS?
>
>Giving five or ten acres of irrigation land to the Indian and taking the rest of his land away for land-grabbers, is that FOR THE BEST INTEREST OF THE INDIANS?
>
>Is selling the Indians' surplus land FOR THE BEST INTEREST OF THE INDIANS?
>
>To dispose of the Indians' mineral lands, is that FOR THE BEST INTEREST OF THE INDIANS?

> Selling the timber land of the Indians, is that FOR THE BEST INTEREST OF THE INDIANS?
>
> To discriminate and keep back the Indian race from other races, is that FOR THE BEST INTEREST OF THE INDIANS?
>
> Are Indian schools for the papooses FOR THE BEST INTEREST OF THE INDIANS?
>
> Is keeping the Indians from opportunities FOR THE BEST INTEREST OF THE INDIANS?
>
> Is doing everything for the Indians, without their consent, FOR THE BEST INTEREST OF THE INDIANS?
>
> Keeping the Indians from freedom and citizenship, is that FOR THE BEST INTEREST OF THE INDIANS?
>
> Is keeping six thousand employees in the Indian Service FOR THE BEST INTEREST OF THE INDIANS?
>
> For you to have sole power over the Indians, is that FOR THE BEST INTEREST OF THE INDIANS?
>
> Speak as we may, there is not one redeeming feature in the Indian Bureau FOR THE BEST INTEREST OF THE INDIANS. (Emphasis added).[8]

It became a divisive issue and led to the decline of the SAI and Dr. Montezuma's temporary departure from the SAI *because it would not take the strong anti-Bureau position he espoused.*

WASSAJA, January 1917: 6000 Indian Bureau Employees Used to Destroy other Indians

Dr. Montezuma detested the Indian Office and was convinced the Society was a puppet of the Bureau. He continually challenged the loyalty of Indian employees of the Indian Bureau.

> The Indian Bureau is hanging by a thread of 6000 employees, interwoven with whom are Indian employees. Indians have always been used by the Government to destroy other Indians, and it is the same old story here... If Indians in the Indian Service were loyal to their race, they would all scramble out and stampede for all they are worth, and apply themselves in other lines outside of the Indian Service, and cry out Freedom for their race.[9]

Dr. Montezuma openly quarreled on the floor of the SAI conference with ex-president Sherman Coolidge, directing his remarks critical of the Indian Bureau at Coolidge personally. *When Coolidge replied to his charges, Dr. Montezuma leapt to his feet and shouted, "I am an Apache and you are an Arapahoe. I can lick you. My tribe has licked your tribe before."* Coolidge, who stood at least a head taller than his rival, replied calmly, "I am from Missouri." The remark made no sense, but it did break the tension. (Emphasis added).[10]

WASSAJA, February 1917: SAI Divided

Unfortunately, the deep schism over the fate of the Indian Bureau led to the disintegration of the SAI.

WASSAJA Pigeon-Holed as "DESTRUCTIVE AND NOT CONSTRUCTIVE"

Dr. Montezuma responded to his criticism of the Indian Bureau and Indian employees of the Bureau as constructive:

> "DESTRUCTIVE AND NOT CONSTRUCTIVE." Some good people say WASSAJA is working on a destructive basis. ... To place the Indians on a solid foundation, instead of a wrong and rickety foundation, is not a destructive process but is a constructive act that will last forever.[11]

WASSAJA, May 1917: Half-White Indians Given Control of Their Property; Indians Judged "Competent" by Indian Office Will Also Be Given Such Control

> Washington, D.C., April 17. "In announcing its policy of discontinuing guardianship of all competent Indians and giving closer attention to the incompetent, the government has taken the most important step it has ever taken in connection with dealing with the Indian," said Indian Commissioner Sells today in promulgating regulations for the new policy.
>
> How many thousands of Indians will be affected by the new order is not yet known, but all half white Indians will soon come into complete possession of their property, as well as many others equally competent.

The new policy, he added, means the beginning of the end of the Indian problem.[12]

WASSAJA, June 1917: Reservations Are Prisons

The WASSAJA newsletter had numerous references to reservations as "prisons."

> June 1917 Caging the Indian is not freedom for the Indian. The reser-

vation is a prison for the Indian, and the Indian Bureau is supported to keep up the reservation system. To hire six thousand employees to dominate over three hundred thousand Indians, is not democracy. The Indian Bureau works against democracy for the Indians. It is: "You stay down there, Mr. Indian, and shut your mouth and don't you dare to dictate to me (Superintendent) or you will be jailed."[13]

WASSAJA, June 1917: Indian Bureauism is Kaiserism of America

Indian Bureauism is the Kaiserism of America toward the Indians. It enslaves and dominates the Indians without giving them their rights. ... But the question may well be asked, "Why does this liberty-loving country discern injustices across the sea, and close its eyes to the same thing at home?" Does this not show that America has failed at home? On the same principle, we Indians ask the Congress of the United States to give us our freedom from the Indian Bureau by abolishing the same-give us our citizenship that we may share in the glorious dream of the future of America. (Emphasis added).[14]

WASSAJA, June 1917: How Reservation Indian Complaints Are Treated

If you have any complaints to make against your slave owner the Indian Bureau, handle them with care. You can hardly afford to do it all for several reasons. *In the first place, most Indians are afraid to make a complaint because you know that if you do you will antagonize the Indian Office which is the one power that arbitrarily controls your life, liberty and property.* However, if you are brave enough to make a complaint as to your treatment, the process which is followed is about this: After your complaint reaches Washington it is referred to some subordinate who cubbyholes it where it lays a long time. The Indian Office has two methods of investigation which it follows, when your complaint is finally dug up. One is to send the complaint and your name to the superintendent where you live. This immediately puts you in bad with the superintendent, who at once commences his systematic course of persecution. *The other method is to send out an inspector who goes to the superintendent and sends the Indian police out to bring you to the office. And then-woe to you-for by the time the superintendent, inspector and third degree get through with you, you poor helpless brother, there isn't anything left of either your complaint or you.*

The gang-system is just this: The superintendent and inspector are each appointed by Cato Sells. One official in the Indian service is sent out to check up on a brother official, so Cato Sells, really makes his own investigation and obtains his own information from himself. (Emphasis added).[15]

WASSAJA, July 1917: When Are Indians Competent?

> **WHEN ARE INDIANS COMPETENT?** Indians are competent to be soldiers, but are denied the ballot. *The true Americans are not citizens. They are enslaved, dominated and handicapped by the United States Government in death chambers (reservations) and their blood squeezed out by the Indian Office, (political and ambitious greed.)* (Emphasis added).[16]

WASSAJA, September 1917 - What Indian Office or Reservation Life Does for Indian; What Freedom, Rights and Citizenship Will Mean for Indian; Constructive & Destructive Basis of Each

WASSAJA, January 1918: Plea to Indians for Unity

> We must be united; there must be harmony; we must stand together. We must be of one accord. We must get together and walk in the same trail. We must bring all of our forces and all pull together in one direction-namely free ourselves from the Indian Office and become American citizens, entitled to the rights and privileges thereof.[17]

WASSAJA, March 1918: Indians Wake Up, Protect Your Rights

His call for unity never materialized.

> Indians, wake up! If you have money in the treasury, you have a voice in the matter; if you have land, you have a voice in the matter; if you are not free, you have a voice in the matter; if you have a string tied to your citizenship, you have a voice in the matter. You are a man and as such you are entitled to the rights of a man. NOW IS THE TIME TO EXERT YOUR RIGHTS. No one can do it for you. You must do it yourself. You have been asleep long enough. Stir yourself to your manhood and look after your own interest. The future is just as bright for you as for any man in the world.[18]

WASSAJA, March 1918: Indian Bureau Doesn't Want to Go Out of Existence; Dr. Montezuma Opposed to Competency Determinations for Indians

> No one likes to die. Just so, the Indian Bureau does not want to go out of existence. It has been as poisonous as a rattle snake to the Indians, and it will die hard like a rattle snake. Its life is fed by sucking the blood from incompetent Indians, which it has manufactured from the most competent human beings on the face of the earth, and now, the *Indian Office is assorting the Indians— separating the chaff from the seed. Just hear their pious voices: "This is a perfect*

one, this is a rotten one; this one is an exception, this one we must leave for evolution; this one is competent, this one is incompetent; put that one over there and this Indian over here." (Emphasis added).[19]

1910: Competency Commission for Omaha Indians Divides Them into Three Groups

A competency commission was created to do this work, and it reported March 11, 1910. The commission divided the Omahas into three classes: (1) Composed of those fully competent to receive patents in fee for their land; (2) those partially competent and capable of making business transactions in connection with their allotted holdings, but not sufficiently competent to receive patents in fee; (3) those who were wholly incompetent and should remain under the supervision and jurisdiction of the Government for a further period of tutelage.[20]

WASSAJA, April 1918: Reservation Indians Ruled by Czar of America

Dr. Montezuma further denounced the despotic control Indian Bureau exercised over reservation Indians by continual analogous references to the tyrants Kaiser Wilhelm II of Germany and Tsar Nicholas II of Russia from World War I.

Forced by the point of bayonets or with impossible promises the Indians were inhumanly and illegally placed on reservations. The Indian Agent or Superintendent is the one who rules the Indians as slaves. The Indians believe that he has all power. *He is the Kaiser and the Czar of America. All power is given to him on earth and heaven for the Indians. He rules by might with imaginary bug-a-boo with the "Washington Father" behind him in the East.* This has been drilled into the Indians over a half century and you can just imagine, the Indians cringe under his words; they obey him with trembling fear; they take him as a great sovereign empowered with death if they least anger his displeasure. The Superintendent has become all powerful and the Indians dare not open their mouths or think for themselves. If that is not fake justice, what is it? It is an awful ghost to have in mind. *It is horror's dream of a dungeon prison, where you are hounded by brute force and tortured by threats.* (Emphasis added).[21]

WASSAJA, July 1918: Dr. Montezuma Denounced Despotic Control Indian Bureau Exercised over Reservation Indians

I am the Indians Kaiser of America. The redskins must do what I dictate and fear me, so says the Indian Bureau. With the Indians, all power is given unto me. There is nothing that rules me but the almighty dollar, so says the Indian Bureau. I am law and everything else unto the Indians and there is no way out of it. In my presence, no Indian dares to open his mouth. If they do, I will show them WHO IS THEIR MASTER savage brutes! so says the Indian Bureau. *Let them tremble at my feet and beg for the crumbs that fall from my table, so says the Indian Bureau.* (Emphasis added)."

WASSAJA, October 1918: SAI Condemns Indian Bureau

The Society of American Indians' platform and resolutions condemned the Indian Bureau.[23]

WASSAJA, November 1918: Demoralization of Reservation; Reservation Indians Lives Permeated with Fear

His life is permeated with fear. He lives by being ruled as cattle. The jail is always ready for him; with suspicion he roams the reservation cage. He lives on the past and groans under the present. He knows not what hope is; he only expects to breathe and die where he buried his father. (Emphasis added).[24]

Dr. Montezuma admired General R.H. Pratt who he considered "the life giving power" of Carlisle, and "the most esteemed white man by the Indian race." On the closing of Carlisle, he wrote: "No other institution in the United States has done more for the Indians than the Carlisle Indian Industrial School. It stood as a light-house on a hill to enlighten the world and to place the Indian where he rightly belongs."[25]

WASSAJA, December 1918: Reservation Indians Forced to Cower as Dogs at Dog Pound

Every branch of the Indian Bureau is working might and main to keep intact the system that defies the rights of man. If there is a system that keeps the Indians from what is right and just, IT IS THE INDIAN BUREAU. On reservations you see the power of one man over the Indians. The power is so great that the Indians dare not resent or they will suffer the consequences. *The Indians must cower as dogs at a dog pound.* On reservations the Indians live, breathe and jump at the voice of the SLAVE MASTERS. On reservations the Indians are considered not anything but Indians and as such, they must not raise a voice against Washington (Indian Bureau.) (Emphasis added).[26]

WASSAJA, February 1919: Indian Bureau Cracks Whip

The Indians are handicapped by the Indian Bureau and the Indian is NOT A FREE MAN AS A WARD. The Indians move and have their beings as the INDIAN BUREAU CRACKS THE WHIP AT THEM. (Emphasis added).[27]

WASSAJA, March 1919: Indian Bureau Sells Indian Lands and Spends Indian Money without Approval of Indians

The Indian Office seems to think unto themselves that it is their duty to dispose of all Indian lands without the consent of the Indians, after the Indians have been allotted. The money derived from selling the surplus land after the allotment is deposited in the Treasury and expended without the consent of the Indians. It appears to us that if the surplus land belongs to the Indians, after the Indians have been allotted, the Indians ought to have something to say as to whether they want the land sold or not. But to sell their surplus land without the voice of the Indians who own the land, is not treating the Indians right.[28]

WASSAJA, June 1919: Is It Legal? Dr. Montezuma Questioned Indian Bureau's Tyrannical Authority over Indians

Dr. Montezuma rightly questioned the authority of the Indian Bureau to (1) "dispose of the Indians lands without consent;" (2) "spend Indians' money without consent;" (3) sell deceased Indians' lands, again without consent; (4) sell surplus land without consent; (5) sell Indians' timber; (6) lease minerals on Indian land; (7) lease agricultural lands; (8) lease grazing lands; (9) use Indian money for irrigation projects that did not benefit them; (10) construct dams that flood Indian lands; (11) build railroads across Indian country; and (12) otherwise use Indian lands."[29]

WASSAJA, July 1919: Bleeding Indians More; Indian Bureau Leasing Indian Mining Lands

If the appropriation of $15,000,000 is true for Indian Affairs and a rider authorizing the Secretary of the Interior to lease 30,000,000 acres of Indian mining lands, it is getting worse and worse. It is bleeding the Indians without mercy! The people of the country thinks this $15,000,000 comes from taxation of the general public and that the government is getting generous to the Indians from year to year. *The Indians own the mineral lands. If they want to lease or sell the land, let the Indians say so or not. The land, mineral and riches of the soil are as good to the Indians as to capitalists. The Indians are foolish to sell any land. Let them hold their property for commercial purpose. It will come good in the future for their* children. *Just as long as the Indian Bureau exists the Indian property will fade away. That is the business of the Indian Bureau, to dispose of the Indians property and spend their money.* (Emphasis added).³⁰

WASSAJA, August 1919: Indian Bureau's Duty to Teach Indians to Manage Their Natural Resources

The Indian Bureau's duty is to teach the Indians to mine their mineral lands; to teach the Indians to construct oil wells and run them; to teach the Indians to cultivate and apply every space of their property to commercialism, and thus start its wards-its Indians-on the road to prosperity. (Emphasis added).³¹

WASSAJA, January 1920: Indian Bureau's Leasing 30,000,000 Acres of Indian Mining Land

There is a great stir among Indians about leasing their mining land. Naturally there would be, because the Indians knew nothing about it, when it passed as a rider with the Indian appropriation bill. It appeared to be backed by a great financial force. *These men do not believe that great wealth underneath Indian land should remain idle. The country demands that the mineral land should be worked for the best interest of industry. The Indians have no use for such rich layers underneath their grounds. So, it is a blessing that Congress gave the authority to the Secretary of the Interior to lease 30,000,000 acres of Indian mining land.* (Emphasis added).

The Indians are dumbfounded. They do not know what to say. *If there is wealth underneath their grounds, they want it themselves. Leasing their land for mining purposes is like taking their land away from them. If there is any money there he wants that money himself. He believes that he can work the mines as well as the white people. Leasing the top of his land to cattle men and now leasing the bottom part to others, he wants to know where he gets off at?* (Emphasis added).³²

WASSAJA, December 1920: Who Would Like It? Reservation Indian Has No Rights

Indian lands are sold and leased without the consent of the Indians. Timber on reservations is sold without consent of the Indians. If there is mineral on a reservation, it is leased without saying a word to the Indians. If there is a dam site on a reservation, the Indians are disregarded, and the process of constructing a dam goes on. A pipe line or anything else may go through a reservation.

The Indians have nothing to do but acquiesce. To-day that old saying has more truth than ever before: "When a white man wants the Indian's land, the Indian must move on." In other words, the guardian thinks more of his friends than of the Indians. (Emphasis added).[33]

The Indians on reservations are not treated as human beings. In the first place, the Indians were not considered as human beings when, by force of arms, they were placed on reservations. *It is a dreadful thing to live in fear. No one knows any better than the Indians on reservations*. One man's power is a dangerous thing. Indian agents, and their Indian policemen, have not benefited the Indian on reservations. They have been hard masters by disregarding the rights of the Indian. For fifty years the Indian Bureau has created fear in the reservation Indians. Indians are always afraid to do anything in their own interest on reservations. The policeman lurks around to take anyone who has a thought of his own. The jail is ready to quench his spirit to bring light of liberty to his people. If the agent says so, there is no redress whatever on a reservation. *Every Indian who has tried to help his people by telling the reservation Indians their rights has been silenced or put off the reservation.* An Indian agent claims that he is an undesirable person to have on a reservation. This may appear that the agent is guarding well his wards, but were the truth known, he is safeguarding the crookedness of the reservation system. If everything was earned on right and for the interests of the Indians, there would be no need of suspicion of anyone who speaks to the reservation Indians. But words cannot express the darkness of the reservation system to the rights of the Indian people. ... *At the altar of man, the red men are being sacrificed, scathed and punished without a cause by hearts of stone and passion of greed that know no mercy. The Indian race is being hurled into the oblivion of the archives of the dark intrigue mysteries of mysteries of man's inhumanity to man*; there to smoulder until the morn of the Judgment Day--when by the sweep of the sword of Justice, the Indian will come forth supreme, in that he served his fellow-man as he served himself, and heeded the light of heaven to lighten his pathway in the trail of life. (Emphasis added).[34]

An Indian has his being on a reservation and moved by the will of the agent. *An Indian agent, or as he is called now, 'superintendent,' is invested with greater power over the Indians than the Czar or the late Kaiser over their subjects*. (Emphasis added).[35]

WASSAJA, February 1921: Indian Appropriations Are Mockery

> Congressman M. Clyde Kelly, of Pennsylvania stated: Mr. Chairman, it would be difficult to put more of irony and mockery into words than are contained in this provision: "For the support and civilization of the Indians of the Umatilla Agency, Oregon, $3,000."
> ... This $3,000 goes, every cent of it, for the pay of the employees of the Indian Bureau. ... The money belonging to these Indians is spent in ways they know not of, and desire not. They get only an infinitesimal benefit from such expenditures...[36]

WASSAJA, April 1921: Dr. Montezuma Despised Reservations

Dr. Montezuma wanted to abolish reservations entirely. In a 1914 speech entitled "The Reservation is Fatal to the Development of Good Citizenship," which he delivered at a regional SAI meeting in Philadelphia, Dr. Montezuma pointed out that reservations kept Indians from learning English, the first step in their acculturation, and from interacting with whites or bettering themselves with education or industrial employment.

WASSAJA, April 1921: Indian Bureau Is Army of Blood-Sucking Grafters

> The nearer we advance to the goal of freedom and citizenship, the more opposition we will meet. The dog, while it is filling its stomach and is let alone, does not growl or show its teeth; but look out when you disturb him. The Indian Bureau, with its army of blood-sucking grafters, has the Indians to fill their stomachs and they are in power; they are worse than the dog; they are on guard and using every means to have the Indians in their charge, taking everything away from them.[37]

WASSAJA, April 1921: Reservations Are Czars Siberia, Dungeon of Human Crimes

> Liberty is one of the vital principles for which the American flag stands for. Have the Indians their liberty? No. They are under the human bondage system of the Indian Bureau. The Indian people do not know what liberty or freedom mean. *They are colonized on reservations away from all opportunities that liberty gives to all mankind. It is the Czars Siberia, a dungeon of human crimes.* There you find corruption, stagnation and misery and where there is no life, but sure death. Equal rights is the cry of man and the law that governs nature. Do the Indians on reservations enjoy equal rights? *The Indian Agents and Indian Bureau are their lords and little Czars in this land of democracy.* The Indian Bureau system for the Indians is a sham and a mockery to democracy. (Emphasis added).[38]

WASSAJA, September 1921: Indian Bureau Will Relinquish Its Throttle Hold on Indians Only when Every Indian Dollar Is Spent

> Congressman Kelly:
> It is clear to every observer of the actual situation that the Indian Bureau will voluntarily relinquish its throttle hold on the Indians only when every dollar of their money is spent and their property has been dissipated. When the Indians have nothing left and when Congress refuses to appropriate further funds, the Indian Bureau will decide it is time for their gigantic organization to go out of business.[39]

WASSAJA, December 1921: Indian Bureau - Cold Blooded Greed

> *There are many hundreds of Indians in the Indian Service. Of course, they are dependent on the Indian Bureau. It would not do for them to say anything against their master, even though, they know they are working against the best interest of their people.* (Emphasis added).
>
> The Indian Office system has converted the Indians into automatous tin-soldiers. They have nothing to say or do. They have no rights or privileges whatsoever. *The Indian Commissioner says, their rights are invested in his office-he is the King, the Kaiser and the Czar of America over the first Americans.* It is a mockery to our democracy. It is a mockery to our late war, where we fought for freedom. It is a mockery to justice, where it holds down the rights of man endowed by God. (Emphasis added).[40]

WASSAJA, March 1922: Indian Bureau - "Perpetual Machine"

Dr. Montezuma gave an excellent example of the well-oiled machinery of the Indian Bureau:

> In 1887 there were in the bureau an account division, finance division, files and record division, land and law division, and education division. Since that time there has been added a purchase division, a probate division, an inspection division, and forestry and irrigation divisions. The number of employees has been multiplied many times.
>
> Over and above all these divisions and sections is the inspection division, with its supervision of activities in the field and in the office. In the inspection division there is a special supervisor over the reimbursable industrial appropriations. There are two special supervisors over the probate division. There are two supervisors, one hospital

supervisor and one chief supervisor, over the health division. There is a chief supervisor and an assistant supervisor over the irrigation division. There are ten district supervisors over the schools. There is a chief supervisor and an assistant supervisor over the different courses of study in the schools. There is a chief supervisor over the agricultural division. There is a chief supervisor over the live stock division. There are three supervisors over the receipts and disbursements of funds. There is a supervisor over Indian employment. There is a supervisor over Indian trades. Then over all this vast inspection service there is a chief inspector and four separate assistants whose duties are to make special investigations presumably of the work of other inspectors.

The forestry division was organized in 1902. The diagram furnished by the bureau shows that it contains six sections. Protection of forestry, forest surveys, sales of lumber, manufacture of lumber, forest extension and grazing. These are in turn divided into a host of subsections, each with its employees. These subsections are as follows: (1.) Construction of roads, trails, bridges and telephone lines. (2.) Establishment of range stations. (3.) Maintenance of forest control. (4.) Suppression of forest fires. (5.) Prevention of timber trespass. (6.) Prevention of destruction by insects. (7.) Education as to proper use of forests. (8.) Establishment of boundaries. (9.) Examination of timber. (10.) Detailed estimate of amount of timber. (11.) Systematic appraisals of timber values. (12.) Preparation of contour maps. (13.) Regulation for particular salaries. (14.) Preparation of contracts and bonds. (15.) Presentation of sales to timber operators. (16.) Supervision of logging operations. (17.) Disposition of slash from lumbering. (18.) Records of transactions. (19.) The conducting of logging operations. (20.) Establishment and manufacture of sawmills. (21.) Operation of saw-mills. (22.) Sale of saw-mill products. (23.) Supervision of cutting operations by Indians. (24.) Encouragement of natural reproduction. (25.) Planting of trees. (26.) Assistance in management of stock. (27.) Supervising grazing in Indian lands. (28.) Preventing damage to forests.

That whereas in 1887 the expenses of the Indian Bureau were $5,000,000.00, in 1920 they were more than $15,000,000.00, an increase of $10,000,000.00 a year, long after Congress had decided to make the Indians self-supporting men and women. How has this gigantic organization, with its tremendous expenses, been built up? How has it been possible to not only perpetuate, but to increase greatly, the task definitely undertaken thirty years ago, that of making competent, self-supporting Americans out of some 300,000 assimilable American Indians. It could be done in but one way-making the Indians incompetent and keeping them incompetent. The system depends upon branding the Indian race as inferior and incapable of looking out for their own welfare and taking care of themselves.

Further, in great detail, Congressman Kelly pointed out the system now existing in the Indian Bureau whereby the bureau can indefinitely perpetuate itself and said: "If it is to be continued, generation after generation we'll see a segregated group in our midst, never assimilated or Americanized."

"It is infamous to wait until that far-off day. This is an American problem and should be met by Congress."[41]

1909: Board of Indian Commissioners - Is Indian Bureau No More than Well-Oiled Machine?

WORK OF THE OFFICE OF INDIAN AFFAIRS.

Does the entire system of caring for the Indians by an Indian Bureau tend to become a machine which calls for so much care to keep its multitudinous parts in position and well-oiled for running, that too little attention goes to the actual results for the Indians? ...[42]

WASSAJA, October 1922: Dr. Montezuma Ill, End of WASSAJA Newsletter

Dr. Montezuma became ill in 1922 and ceased publication of WASSAJA.[43]

NOTES

1. WASSAJA, Vol. 1, No. 11, February 1917. https://d1rbsgppyrdqq4.cloudfront.net/prism/s3fs-public/c195/WHS_Wassaja_V1_No11OCR.pdf?VersionId=dIQBoD-8MC9syA_VXC6DDtyEF35BTJ2y5 (accessed online October 10, 2024).
2. Society of American Indians, "The Quarterly Journal of the Society of American Indians v. 2 no. 4 (October-December 1914)," American Indian Digital History Project. https://aidhp.com/items/show/157 (accessed online October 8, 2024).
3. "Let My People Go": An Address delivered at the conference of the Society of American Indians in Lawrence, Kansas, by Carlos Montezuma (Apache, September 30, 1915). Society of American Indians, "The American Indian Magazine, v. 4 no. 1 (January-March 1916)," American Indian Digital History Project. https://www.aidhp.com/items/show/162 (accessed online October 9, 2024).
4. WASSAJA, Vol. 1, No. 4, July 1916. https://d1rbsgppyrdqq4.cloudfront.net/prism/s3fs-public/c195/WHS_Wassaja_V1_No4OCR.pdf?VersionId=fY979GM3UfAh_19ZjVaSLEpxdOJDYA.m (accessed online October 10, 2024).
5. WASSAJA, Vol. 1, No. 7, October 1916. https://d1rbsgppyrdqq4.cloudfront.net/prism/s3fs-public/c195/WHS_Wassaja_V1_No7OCR.pdf?VersionId=CijE0M-b9j7jQ079mnXIcMRXf_lUmY6Qm (accessed online October 10, 2024).
6. WASSAJA, Vol. 1, No. 7, October 1916. https://d1rbsgppyrdqq4.cloudfront.net/

prism/s3fs-public/c195/WHS_Wassaja_V1_No7OCR.pdf?VersionId=CijE0M-b9j7jQ079mnXIcMRXf_lUmY6Qm (accessed online October 10, 2024).

7. WASSAJA, Vol. 1, No. 7, October 1916. https://d1rbsgppyrdqq4.cloudfront.net/prism/s3fs-public/c195/WHS_Wassaja_V1_No7OCR.pdf?VersionId=CijE0M-b9j7jQ079mnXIcMRXf_lUmY6Qm (accessed online October 10, 2024).

8. WASSAJA, Vol. 1, No. 9, December 1916. https://d1rbsgppyrdqq4.cloudfront.net/prism/s3fs-public/c195/CHM_Wassaja_V1_No9OCR.pdf?VersionId=GKcIQidk6Yl-NTpaQyXY0hFks5Ytb1 (accessed online October 10, 2024).

9. WASSAJA, Vol. 1, No. 10, January 1917. https://d1rbsgppyrdqq4.cloudfront.net/prism/s3fs-public/c195/WHS_Wassaja_V1_No10OCR.pdf?VersionId=Of4rX-wKQlICN27QpQdTflF9h3NLemdR1 (accessed online October 10, 2024).

10. Indianapolis News, Indianapolis, Marion County, September 29, 1916, Cedar Rapids, IO, SAI Conference.

11. WASSAJA, Vol. 1, No. 11, February 1917. https://d1rbsgppyrdqq4.cloudfront.net/prism/s3fs-public/c195/WHS_Wassaja_V1_No11OCR.pdf?VersionId=dIQBoD-8MC9syA_VXC6DDtyEF35BTJ2y5 (accessed online October 10, 2024).

12. WASSAJA, Vol. 2, No. 2, May 1917. https://d1rbsgppyrdqq4.cloudfront.net/prism/s3fs-public/c195/UofA_Wassaja_V2_No2OCR.txt?VersionId=rDBp0O36bUIBsr-1phjg2LX8fi.SIWG3L (accessed online October 10, 2024). Indian Commissioner Sells, A Declaration of Policy. Report of the Commissioner of Indian Affairs, 1917, pp. 3-4.

13. WASSAJA, Vol. 2, No. 3, June 1917. https://d1rbsgppyrdqq4.cloudfront.net/prism/s3fs-public/c195/UofA_Wassaja_V2_No3OCR.pdf?VersionId=AdhtKn0Mw (accessed online October 10, 2024).

14. WASSAJA, Vol. 2, No. 3, June 1917. https://d1rbsgppyrdqq4.cloudfront.net/prism/s3fs-public/c195/UofA_Wassaja_V2_No3OCR.pdf?VersionId=AdhtKn0Mw..fhmjBxhE.kB0XmRF1qfVe (accessed online October 10, 2024).

15. WASSAJA, Vol. 2, No. 3, June 1917. https://d1rbsgppyrdqq4.cloudfront.net/prism/s3fs-public/c195/UofA_Wassaja_V2_No3OCR.pdf?VersionId=AdhtKn0Mw..fhmjBxhE.kB0XmRF1qfVe (accessed online October 10, 2024).

16. WASSAJA, Vol. 2, No. 4, July 1917. https://d1rbsgppyrdqq4.cloudfront.net/prism/s3fs-public/c195/WHS_Wassaja_V2_No4OCR.txt?VersionId=FPYg14WZrB9RX-fBNfEsVJpM3wQiFAdA9 (accessed online October 9, 2024).

17. WASSAJA, Vol. 2, No. 10, January 1918. https://d1rbsgppyrdqq4.cloudfront.net/prism/s3fs-public/c195/LAB_MSS_60_Box_1_Folder_6_Vol_2_No_9OCR.txt?VersionId=.sxG32mDLzWv8sMzbAgR3im7uAmsauLt (accessed online October 9, 2024).

18. WASSAJA, Vol. 2, No. 12, March 1918. https://prism.lib.asu.edu/items/51767 (accessed online October 10, 2024).

19. WASSAJA, Vol. 2, No. 12, March 1918. https://prism.lib.asu.edu/items/51767 (accessed online October 10, 2024).

20. Report of the Commissioner of Indian Affairs (1910), Office of Indian Affairs, United States. U.S. Government Printing Office, 1911, p. 48.

21. WASSAJA, Vol. 3, No. 1, April 1918. https://d1rbsgppyrdqq4.cloudfront.net/prism/s3fs-public/c195/WHS_Wassaja_V3_No1OCR.txt?VersionId=iJMLCu10r-8W8DbxtKk4DbGqzzFP.KbVL (accessed online October 9, 2024).

22. WASSAJA, Vol. 3, No. 4, July 1918. https://d1rbsgppyrdqq4.cloudfront.net/prism/s3fs-public/c195/WHS_Wassaja_V3_No4OCR.txt?VersionId=rI8XKqbU9U_l43wBsRGxvzgMV7alHxmE (accessed online October 9, 2024).

23. WASSAJA, Vol. 3, No. 7, October 1918. https://d1rbsgppyrdqq4.cloudfront.net/prism/s3fs-public/c195/CHM_Wassaja_V3_No7OCR.txt?VersionId=EcbBmQnzZ49LoS1QIOXkGZYxEeueVbNj (accessed online October 9, 2024).

24. WASSAJA, Vol. 3, No. 8, November 1918. https://prism.l ib.asu.edu/node/51390 (accessed online October 9, 2024).

25. WASSAJA, Vol. 3, No. 8, November 1918. https://prism.l ib.asu.edu/node/51390 (accessed online October 9, 2024).

26. WASSAJA, Vol. 3, No. 9, December 1918. https://d1rbsgppyrdqq4.cloudfront.net/prism/s3fs-public/c195/WHS_Wassaja_V3_No9OCR.txt?VersionId=cFp5_pS_rpqYHFhg2ogjPQYgvDOCopxF (accessed online October 9, 2024).

27. WASSAJA, Vol. 3, No. 11, February 1919. https://d1rbsgppyrdqq4.cloudfront.net/prism/s3fs-public/c195/WHS_Wassaja_V3_No11OCR.pdf?VersionId=FKHb8Imjv0e8js_cudRDd5v_lHtRA4nQ (accessed online October 9, 2024).

28. WASSAJA, Vol. 3, No. 12, March 1919. https://d1rbsgppyrdqq4.cloudfront.net/prism/s3fs-public/c195/WHS_Wassaja_V3_No12OCR.pdf?VersionId=W4oCCvNdeVozAZauM.tBlNWqUUqllqpE (accessed online October 9, 2024).

29. WASSAJA, Vol. 4, No. 3, June 1919. https://d1rbsgppyrdqq4.cloudfront.net/prism/s3fs-public/c195/CHM_Wassaja_V4_No3OCR.txt?VersionId=vgUeFBPrLwdyEBM2JRE66.6gKFh_V7Te (accessed online October 9, 2024).

30. WASSAJA, Vol. 4, No. 4, July 1919. https://d1rbsgppyrdqq4.cloudfront.net/prism/s3fs-public/c195/WSU_Wassaja_V4_No4OCR.pdf?VersionId=Bl1Thpjt4S6JeYRlFHkI.fVjVCBNcqc7 (accessed online October 9, 2024).

31. WASSAJA, Vol. 4, No. 5, August 1919. https://d1rbsgppyrdqq4.cloudfront.net/prism/s3fs-public/c195/CHM_Wassaja_V4_No5OCR.pdf?VersionId=eM796.CL7sqLrKIIacE4IOMU7b29JRuQ (accessed online October 9, 2024).

32. WASSAJA, Vol. 4, No. 10, January 1920. https://d1rbsgppyrdqq4.cloudfront.net/prism/s3fs-public/c195/MHM_Wassaja_V4No10OCR.pdf?VersionId=nkJXL_ijtSmLMMgfHTYv5jpqq7gI5kqy (accessed online October 9, 2024).

33. WASSAJA, Vol. 5, No. 9, December 1920. https://d1rbsgppyrdqq4.cloudfront.net/prism/s3fs-public/c195/MHM_Wassaja_V5No9OCR.txt?VersionId=23_lXg9ITUOhujos4TTsFW0GLxDy.fF2 (accessed online October 9, 2024).

34. WASSAJA, Vol. 5, No. 9, December 1920. https://d1rbsgppyrdqq4.cloudfront.net/prism/s3fs-public/c195/MHM_Wassaja_V5No9OCR.txt?VersionId=23_lXg9ITUOhujos4TTsFW0GLxDy.fF2 (accessed online October 9, 2024).

35. WASSAJA, Vol. 5, No. 9, December 1920. https://d1rbsgppyrdqq4.cloudfront.net/prism/s3fs-public/c195/MHM_Wassaja_V5No9OCR.txt?VersionId=23_lXg9ITUOhujos4TTsFW0GLxDy.fF2 (accessed online October 9, 2024).

36. WASSAJA, Vol. 5, No. 11, February, 1921. https://d1rbsgppyrdqq4.cloudfront.net/prism/s3fs-public/c195/UofA_Wassaja_V5_No11OCR.txt?VersionId=gwU40voDg.psHkDuNnzE3zjm7UnBjYZ3 (accessed online December 11, 2024).

37. WASSAJA, Vol. 6, No. 1, April 1921. https://d1rbsgppyrdqq4.cloudfront.net/prism/s3fs-public/c195/MHM_Wassaja_V6No1OCR.txt?VersionId=6M7Rh9.rSck75O7bscVgD6ZJ1c3JPOvu (accessed on-

line October 9, 2024).

38. WASSAJA, Vol. 6, No. 1, April 1921. https://d1rbsgppyrdqq4.cloudfront.net/prism/s3fs-public/c195/MHM_Wassaja_V6No1OCR.txt?VersionId=6M7Rh9.rSck75O7bscVgD6ZJ1c3JPOvu (accessed online October 9, 2024).

39. WASSAJA, Vol. 7, No. 9, September 1921. https://d1rbsgppyrdqq4.cloudfront.net/prism/s3fs-public/c195/WHS_Wassaja_V7_No9OCR.txt?VersionId=F.r3nDlBuzN0ud2_FayRTLZPDxTqlTcb (accessed online October 9, 2024).

40. WASSAJA, Vol. 7, No. 12, December 1921. https://d1rbsgppyrdqq4.cloudfront.net/prism/s3fs-public/c195/MHM_Wassaja_V7No12OCR.txt?VersionId=x5y_IEgzhWaJbWGX4nIRIsSjEnJkqRX (accessed online October 9, 2024).

41. WASSAJA, Vol. 8, No. 3, March 1922. https://d1rbsgppyrdqq4.cloudfront.net/prism/s3fs-public/c195/LAB_MSS_60_Box_1_Folder_6_Vol_8_No_3OCR.txt?VersionId=hYVbYIroWRLe0IXulX7PHscK6cltywUK (accessed online October 9, 2024).

42. Annual Report of the Board of Indian Commissioners, 1909 (Washington: Government Printing Office), p. 3. https://babel.hathitrust.org/cgi/pt?id=hvd.32044097929384&seq=5 (accessed online October 5, 2024).

43. WASSAJA, Vol. 8, No. 20, October 1922. https://d1rbsgppyrdqq4.cloudfront.net/prism/s3fs-public/c195/UofA_Wassaja_V8_No20OCR.txt?VersionId=Ez9HRACZHI02Tui6MwwE61N92RhHyYpc (accessed online October 9, 2024).

CHAPTER 55: 2024: Centennial Anniversary of Indian Citizenship Act

~

2024: Southern Ute Indian Tribe: "Indian Citizenship Act Offered Citizenship on Paper, But Also Sought to Dismantle Our Identity"

Southern Ute Indian Reservation – Today marks the 100th anniversary of the Indian Citizenship Act, also known as the Snyder Act, a landmark piece of legislation that granted U.S. citizenship to Native Americans born within reservation boundaries. Prior to the Snyder Act, the path to citizenship for Native Americans was a patchwork of treaties, federal policies, and court rulings that varied by Tribe and region.

The Snyder Act, passed on June 2, 1924, was a complex and controversial measure. While it extended citizenship rights, it also aimed to assimilate Native Americans into mainstream American society. This followed a dark period of forced relocation and the establishment of Federal Indian Boarding Schools. Before 1924, paths to citizenship were limited and conditional. Common routes included land cessions, honorable military service, or marriage to a non-Tribal male.

"The Snyder Act was a double-edged sword," said Chairman Melvin J. Baker. "It offered citizenship on paper, but also sought to dismantle our identity. We were expected to abandon our traditions and languages to fit a mold. True citizenship, however, is about respect, not assimilation. It's about honoring our shared history and upholding our right to self-determination. *This fight for genuine citizenship and recognition continues to this day.*" (Emphasis added).

"Though the path has been long, 100 years of Native American citizenship stands as a testament to our resilience. We acknowledge the challenges that remain, yet we celebrate the vibrant cultures that continue to enrich this land. May the next century be one of true partnership, where the Indigenous spirit and identity thrives in the American story," said Vice Chairman Lorelei Cloud.[1]

2024: Ute Mountain Ute Tribe: History Was Too Fraught to Warrant "Celebration"

The Ute Mountain Ute tribe did not have a special event to commemorate the anniversary. The history was too fraught to warrant a "celebration," [Chairman] Heart said.

Native Americans had endured the westward expansion of settlers into their lands and the violent assaults on their communities and cultures. Native children were forced into boarding schools where they were punished for speaking their language and endured conditions that resulted in deaths that are just now being uncovered.

Some states continued to bar Native Americans from voting until the 1965 Voting Rights Act, despite their status as citizens and even while tribal members were defending the country in the U.S. military.

Tribes are still advocating for inclusion and equality, Heart said. In May, school officials confiscated a Native American student's beaded graduation cap in Farmington, New Mexico, he said. The move sparked an outcry among the Indigenous community in the city. (Emphasis added).

"Even today, the United States and states still have this mentality of not recognizing who we are," Heart said.[2]

NOTES

1. Southern Ute Indian Tribe Press Release: June 2, 2024: Strands of Strength: The Indian Citizenship Act 100th Anniversary.
2. The Indian Citizenship Act marks its 100th anniversary. What does that mean to tribes in Colorado? https://coloradosun.com/2024/06/05/tribal-leaders-colorado-indian-citizenship-act/#:~:text=Some%20states%20continued%20to%20bar,inclusion%20and%20equality%2C%20Heart%20said (accessed online September 4, 2024).

APPENDICES

APPENDIX A: 1885: WASH, Yakama Reservation, A Story of One 'Suspended' Despotic Indian Agent

APPENDIX B: DECLARATION OF POLICY IN THE ADMINISTRATION OF INDIAN AFFAIRS By HON. CATO SELLS, Commissioner of Indian Affairs, Report of the Commissioner of Indian Affairs to the Secretary of the Interior, Office of Indian Affairs, 1915

APPENDIX C: Lake Mohonk Friends of the Indian Annual Conferences: Platforms 1883-1916 (34 Years)

APPENDIX D: Lands in Severalty to Indians, Minority Report of Committee on Indian Affairs, Rep. Russell Errett, *et al.*, H.R. Rep. No. 1576, 46th Cong., 2nd Sess. (1880)

APPENDIX E-1: Society of American Indians Petitions to President of the United States
APPENDIX E-2: Society of American Indians Memorial to Congress
APPENDIX _E-3: Highlights from Quarterly Journals of the Society of American Indians, 1912-1916

APPENDIX F: Excerpts from Charles Eastman's Books

APPENDIX A: 1885: WASH, Yakama Reservation, A Story of One 'Suspended' Despotic Indian Agent

When any Indian parents failed to send their children after I had sent word to them to do so, I sent the Indian police after the children, with orders that if parents hid or attempted to forcibly prevent the bringing of the children to bring such parents to me; when if they could furnish no reasonable excuse for their conduct they were punished by fine, or imprisonment and labor. The class of Indians opposed to sending their children to school are those who are untouched by civilization and opposed to everything that looks that way. The great body of such Indians belonging to this agency remain off this reservation, but a portion of them have homes, or rather hovels, on the reservation. The chief of the most refractory band of these is Cotiahan (Co-ti-a-han). He has a boy of about ten years, and there were nine children of school age belonging to other members of his band. In the early part of 1884 I sent word to these people to send their children to school. Cotiahan returned answer that they could teach their own children all they wanted them to know, and that they did not want them to leave off their old ways and take the white man's ways. His people said Cotiahan's talk was good, and they would send none of their children, unless he sent his boy. I then sent my police with orders to gather up all children of school age, and bring them to school, and if they could not get the children to bring Cotiahan. The police could find none of their children of school age, and the parents refused to tell where they had them hid. So Cotiahan was arrested and brought here a prisoner. I told him he could take his choice either to remain here in the fool's school or have his boy come and attend the wisdom school.

He answered, he would not permit his boy to come to school. So I had him taken to the blacksmith shop, and a heavy chain securely attached to his leg, and put him to sawing wood, and told him if he refused to work, he would be tied to a tree and whipped. He went to work sullenly, and was locked up in prison of nights. I told him that was the discipline of the fool's school of experience in which he would take lessons till his boy came. Every few days some of his people, 20 miles distant, would come to see how he was getting along. He stood this for about two weeks then sent word to his wife to bring in their boy, which she speedily did. I at once set Cotiahan at liberty and told him I hoped he would never need any more lessons in the fool's school; he grinned a ghastly smile and went home with his wife. His boy, after being sheared, scrubbed, and dressed up, proved to be a bright fellow; learned rapidly and became much attached to the school. All the children of school age belonging to the band of Cotiahan came in soon after his boy did, and all got along well until the vacation of 1884, when they, with all other Indian pupils, returned to their parents. (Emphasis added).

In the meantime this agency was visited by Major McMurray, of the Army, as more fully set forth in my last annual report. (See report of Commissioner on Indian Affairs for 1884, p. 184, "Conflict of Departments.") In his clandestine council with Cotiahan's band, as therein stated, he told them among other things that I had no authority or right to compel them to send their children to school, and that it was wholly optional with them to send their children or not. His speech, or, rather, speeches, pleased them so well that they at once renounced my authority over them, and transferred their allegiance from me to McMurray as their tyhee and agent.

Not having had a leave of absence from duty during twelve years in the Indian service, I obtained one of sixty days last year to attend some reunions and visit old friends, &c., in the East, and left during the vacation of the school here, my son, with the approval of the Department, being authorized to act as agent in my absence. When the school vacation ended and the school children returned to school, those of Cotiahan's band failed to come. After waiting a reasonable time my son sent the police to notify them to send their children. Cotiahan said that their children would not come, and that he would not recognize my authority to bring them. My son then sent two of the oldest reservation judges, being the most influential Indians on the reservation, to council with Cotiahan and his band and to try to persuade them to peaceably submit and send their children to school. But in vain. The judges were told that I was no longer their tyhee; that he told them not to send their children to school if they did not want to do so. *My son afterwards took the police force to enforce the attendance of the children or make arrests. But Cotiahan had assembled his whole force, both male and female, and after much vain talk the police were ordered to make arrests of Cotiahan and some of his leading men. The police, being ordered not to use their pistols and being greatly outnumbered and forcibly resisted by men and women, were soon overpowered and forced to leave.* (Emphasis added).

My son then applied to General Miles, the military commander at Fort Vancouver, for a small body of troops to put down this Indian rebellion, but none were sent, though a military inspector was sent up to look into the matter. He held a council with Cotiahan and his band without any apparent result. *After my return here I made another urgent appeal to General Miles for not to exceed half a dozen soldiers, under an officer, commissioned or non-commissioned, he might think proper, to come here to act with my police a few days to show Cotiahan and his band that the military would help to uphold my authority and not abet them in their opposition to it. But they refused, though there were thousands of idle soldiers under his (Miles') command who would have enjoyed the jaunt. I then applied to the Commissioner of Indian Affairs, stating the facts, and requesting him to procure through the Secretary of the Interior an order from the War Department for a few soldiers to be sent here, not to fight, but simply to demonstrate to Cotiahan and his band that the two Departments were in unison and not in opposition, as they believed.* (Emphasis added).

The Commissioner replied by sending out Mr. Dixon, a special agent, to look into and report on the matter. Mr. Dixon went down and held a council of an entire day and part of the night with the rebellious chief and his band, and made his report, the result of which was that I got a communication directing me to inform the Indians that they must send their children to school. *I sent this talk to Cotiahan, and after waiting a number of days I directed the captain of police to assemble his force secretly and go down after night, quietly surround the dwelling of Cotiahan, capture and bring him here a prisoner; that if there was any opposition, to use their pistols till it was ended. They found Cotiahan asleep, captured him without opposition, and brought him here, and he again went into the fool's school.* Before leaving his home he directed one of his band to go and inform his military tyhee of his capture, which probably was done, and Cotiahan evidently expected that his military tyhee would come with soldiers and liberate him. I again assured him that he would be liberated when his boy came; but he waited doggedly from February 1 till March 27, when, despairing of a release by his military tyhee, he told me that his boy had been taken many hundreds of miles away to keep me from getting him; that if I would trust him to go for him he would agree to bring him back to school, or return and surrender himself within four weeks; that he would pledge himself to keep his word if I would trust him. I agreed to do so, but the lying scoundrel, as soon as he got away, instead of going for his boy, went with all speed to Fort Vancouver to report matters to his military tyhee. *He shortly afterwards returned to his band and informed them that he had been advised by the military to at once remove with his band and all their property outside the reservation beyond my jurisdiction and remain outside till I would be dismissed and driven off the reservation, which would be before July, when a new tyhee would come; then they could come back and not be any more molested about school matters. This is the talk that a number of my reliable Indians heard from Cotiahan, and he and his band have acted on it, and have been and still are off the reservation with all their property awaiting the advent of a new tyhee, who will, as they believe, permit their children to grow up in all the barbarism of their parents unmolested.* (Emphasis added).

Previous to the present year I had always assumed the authority of sending my police outside the boundary of this reservation when necessary after lawless Indians of this agency and runaway school children. I sometimes sent them as far as across the Columbia *River into Oregon. But several months ago I received stringent instructions from the Department at Washington that I had no legal authority to send my Indian police beyond the boundary of the reservation. This fact becoming known to the Indians, together with the triumph of Cotiahan and his band in preventing the return of their children to school, induced other anti-civilized Indians to take their children beyond the boundary of the reservation. These malign causes have combined to reduce the number of Indian pupils in the school here over fifty during the past fiscal year.* (Emphasis added).

Why Education of Indians Should Be Compulsory

(1) *Because it is high time for our Government to go out of the business of raising ignorant, lazy, worthless but costly savages to furnish material for occasional Indian wars, or rather hunts for the amusement of our Army, which wars it is estimated have on an average cost our Government $1,000,000 and the lives of 20 whites for every Indian killed.* (Emphasis added).

(2) Because our half million of Indians, though natives of the country, with their ancestors, from time immemorial, yet *none of them can be enfranchised with the rights and privileges of citizenship, for the reason that the mass of them are ignorant and barbaric below the degree of civilization required by the duties of citizenship*; and as they cannot cure themselves of ignorance and barbarism, which can only be reached and effaced in the rising generation through teachers in industrial boarding schools, and as *it is both the duty and interest of the Government to civilize and citizenize all Indians as speedily as possible, and melt them into the body politic of our nation, and thus terminate the expensive and troublesome Indian Bureau*; and as the Government has the right, power, and ability to put all Indian children as fast as they become of school age into such schools, and thus rescue them from the low barbarism of their parents, and bring them up to citizenship, self-government, self-support, and independence, the Government should not permit the ignorance and superstition of parents to interfere with this high duty, and Indian children thereby held down in the barbarism of

their parents. Education being compulsory upon white children, who could without education absorb sufficient civilization from their surroundings to qualify them for citizenship in a low degree, should surely be compulsory upon Indian children, who can only absorb barbarism from their parents and surroundings. (Emphasis added).

Where Should Indian Schools Be Located, and What Kind

I am convinced from thirteen years' continuous observation and experience among Indians that *all Indian schools, to be successful, should be located off and away from reservations and the homes of the pupils, and the further away the better*, and that all schools should be industrial boarding schools, where, besides the common English branches, the necessary industrial branches of civilized life are taught, for the following reasons: *The greatest obstacle to education and civilization of Indians is their barbaric languages*. No Indian children educated on a reservation, surrounded by and in daily contact with their people will ever get away from their mother tongues sufficiently to enable them to speak, write, and understand the English language correctly. They learn our language by the eye and not by the ear, as our children learn French or German by the eye from books, but never in that way learn to speak it correctly or to understand it clearly when they hear it spoken.

Their intellectual ability as a race is less than that of the white race. Indian children will acquire the elementary branches of education as readily as white children; will learn to handle pen and pencil fully if not more easily and skillfully than white children; in short, they will readily acquire those branches of education that require the use of the eye, the hand, and close observation only. But when they come to those branches that require a strong exercise of the reasoning powers, such as the higher branches of mathematics, natural and moral philosophy, logic, &c., they fall far behind the whites. They readily acquire a practical knowledge of the common mechanical arts, such as carpentering, blacksmithing, harness and shoe making, wagon and plow mending—not making-but they are deficient in the higher branches of carpentering requiring intricate planning, calculations, &c. *In short, they are not elaborate or laborious brain-workers by inheritance or otherwise, and must be muscle-workers and "hewers of wood and drawers of water," and earn their bread by the sweat of their faces for generations to come, and for this they need preparation and training*. Report of the Commissioner of Indian Affairs to the Secretary of the Interior, Reports of Agents in Washington Territory, Office of Indian Affairs. U.S. Government Printing Office, 1885, pp. 200-202.

MY LAST ANNUAL REPORT-LEAVING THE SERVICE. As I was, by order of the President, of the 28th ultimo, suspended from office, and am now only waiting the arrival of my successor to relieve me therefrom, and as I am now in my seventieth year, of course I am now leaving the Indian service forever. I have been in this service almost continuously for thirteen years. It is admitted to be the least honorable branch of the Government service, and is very laborious. No honest man, who feels and responds to his duties to God, country, and fellow beings, can pecuniarily acquire anything beyond an adequate subsistence in this service on the pay of an Indian Agent. I believe I have laid up some treasure in Heaven, but know I have laid up none on earth, while in this service, as I leave it as poor as when I came into it. Having honestly and faithfully performed my duty to the best of my ability, I quit this service without regret, but with some annoyance on one point-that is, the manner of leaving it, being thrust out through the suspended door constructed by Congress for Presidents to thrust out discovered rascals and incompetents from Government offices. R. H. MILROY, United States Indian Agent (suspended). **Report of the Commissioner of Indian Affairs to the Secretary of the Interior, Reports of Agents in Washington Territory, Office of Indian Affairs. U.S. Government Printing Office, 1885, pp. 204-205.**

APPENDIX B: DECLARATION OF POLICY IN THE ADMINISTRATION OF INDIAN AFFAIRS By HON. CATO SELLS, Commissioner of Indian Affairs, Report of the Commissioner of Indian Affairs to the Secretary of the Interior, Office of Indian Affairs, 1917

REPORT OF THE COMMISSIONER OF INDIAN AFFAIRS. DEPARTMENT OF THE INTERIOR, OFFICE OF INDIAN AFFAIRS, Washington, D.C., October 15, 1917.

Sir: I have the honor to submit this the eighty-second annual report of the Bureau of Indian Affairs for the fiscal year ended June 30, 1917.

A DECLARATION OF POLICY.
A careful study of the practical effects of governmental policies for determining the wardship of the Indians of this country is convincing that the solution is individual and not collective. Each individual must be considered in the light of his own environment and capacity for larger responsibilities and privileges. While ethnologically a preponderance of white blood has not heretofore been a criterion of competency, nor even now is it always a safe standard, it is almost an axiom that an Indian who has a larger proportion of white blood than Indian partakes more of the characteristics of the former than of the latter. In thought and action, so far as the business world is concerned, he approximates more closely to the white blood ancestry.

On April 17, 1917, there was announced a declaration of policy for Indian affairs, as follows:
DECLARATION OF POLICY IN THE ADMINISTRATION OF INDIAN AFFAIRS.

During the past four years the efforts of the administration of Indian affairs have been largely concentrated on the following fundamental activities--the betterment of health conditions of Indians, the suppression of the liquor traffic among them, the improvement of their industrial conditions, the further development of vocational training in their schools, and the protection of the Indians' property. Rapid progress has been made along all these lines, and the work thus reorganized and revitalized will go on with increased energy. With these activities and accomplishments well under way, we are now ready to take the next step in our administrative program. The time has come for discontinuing guardianship of all competent Indians and giving even closer attention to the incompetent that they may more speedily achieve competency. Broadly speaking, a policy of greater liberalism will henceforth prevail in Indian administration to the end that every Indian, as soon as he has been determined to be as competent to transact his own business as the average white man, shall be given full control of his property and have all his lands and moneys turned over to him, after which he will no longer be a ward of the Government. Pursuant to this policy, the following rules shall be observed:

1. Patents in fee.-To all able-bodied adult Indians of less than one-half Indian blood, there will be given as far as may be under the law full and complete control of all their

property. Patents in fee shall be issued to all adult Indians of one-half or more Indian blood who may, after careful investigation, be found competent, provided, that where deemed advisable patents in fee shall be withheld for not to exceed 40 acres as a home. Indian students, when they are 21 years of age, or over, who complete the full course of instruction in the Government schools, receive diplomas and have demonstrated competency will be so declared.

2. Sale of lands.-A liberal ruling will be adopted in the matter of passing upon applications for the sale of inherited Indian lands where the applicants retain other lands and the proceeds are to be used to improve the homesteads or for other equally good purposes. A more liberal ruling than has hitherto prevailed will hereafter be followed with regard to the applications of noncompetent Indians for the sale of their lands where they are old and feeble and need the proceeds for their support.

3. Certificates of competency.-The rules which are made to apply in the granting of patents in fee and the sale of lands will be made equally applicable in the matter of issuing certificates of competency.

4. Individual Indian moneys.-Indians will be given unrestricted control of all their individual Indian moneys upon issuance of patents in fee or certificates of competency. Strict limitations will not be placed upon the use of funds of the old, the indigent, and the invalid.

5. Pro-rata shares-trust funds.-As speedily as possible their pro rata shares in tribal trust or other funds shall be paid to all Indians who have been declared competent; unless the legal status of such funds prevents. Where practicable the pro rata shares of incompetent Indians will be withdrawn from the Treasury and placed in banks to their individual credit.

6. Elimination of ineligible pupils from the Government Indian schools.-In many of our boarding schools Indian children are being educated at Government expense whose parents are amply able to pay for their education and have public school facilities at or near their homes. Such children shall not hereafter be enrolled in Government Indian schools supported by gratuity appropriations, except on payment of actual per capita cost and transportation.

These rules are hereby made effective, and all Indian Bureau administrative officers at Washington and in the field will be governed accordingly. This is a new and far-reaching declaration of policy. It means the dawn of a new era in Indian administration. It means that the competent Indian will no longer be treated as half ward and half citizen. It means reduced appropriations by the Government and more self-respect and independence for the Indian. It means the ultimate absorption of the Indian race into the body politic of the Nation. It means, in short, the beginning of the end of the Indian problem. In carrying out this policy, I cherish the hope that all real friends of the Indian race will lend their aid and hearty cooperation.

CATO SELLS, Commissioner.
Approved: FRANKLIN K. LANE, Secretary.

The cardinal principle of this declaration revolves around this central thought-that an Indian who is as competent as an ordinary white man to transact the ordinary affairs of life should be given untrammeled control of his property and assured his personal rights in every particular so that he may have the opportunity of working out his own destiny. The practical application of this principle will relieve from the guardianship of the Government a very large number of Indians who are qualified to mingle on a plane of business equality with the white people. It will also begin the reduction of expenditures, and afford a better opportunity for closer attention to those who will need our protecting care for some years longer. A vitally important result also will be obtained in placing a true ideal before those Indians remaining under guardianship. It will be a strong motive for endeavoring to reach the goal of competency, and prove a material incentive to a sincere effort for that end. This new declaration of policy is calculated to release practically all Indians who have one-half or more white blood, although there will be exceptions in the case of those who are manifestly incompetent. It will also give like freedom from guardianship to those having more than one-half Indian blood when, after careful investigation, it is determined that they are capable of handling their own affairs. This latter class, however, will be much more limited since only about 40 per cent of the Indians of the country speak the English language and the large majority of this latter class still greatly need the protecting arm of the Government. As an additional safeguard for those Indians of half or less white blood, a homestead commensurate with the value of the property to be patented may be retained by the allottee and made inalienable except by approval of the Secretary of the Interior. In other cases of manifest incompetency, the trust period on their land will be extended whenever it is deemed beneficial and in the interest of the Indians themselves. As a corollary of this central idea of the declaration, a more liberal policy has been adopted in the sale of inherited lands and Indian allotments, and the Indians are urged to sell that portion of their land which is not available or adaptable for their own uses and utilize the proceeds for the improvement of their remaining land or increasing their facilities for its fuller development by purchasing stock, machinery, etc. A liberal policy is now being pursued in allowing the use of the proceeds of the sale of the lands of old and indigent Indians, and following the general line of procedure of State laws, in all sales of allotted lands where circumstances warrant it, a part of the allotment may be retained as a homestead so that the Indian may not be deprived of a home. Especially is this desirable where an Indian and his wife need such place during their declining years.

Report of the Commissioner of Indian Affairs to the Secretary of the Interior, United States, Office of Indian Affairs, U.S. Government Printing Office, 1917, pp. 3-5.

1 Report of the Annual Lake Mohonk Conference on the Indian and Other Dependent Peoples (1883).

II.-LAW FOR INDIANS.

The Conference recommends: 1st, that the laws of any State or Territory relating to crime, marriage, and inheritance, be extended over the Indians on reservations within the limits of such State or Territory, except in the case of the Indians in the State of New York and in the Indian Territory; the said laws of the State of Kansas to be extended over the Indians in Indian Territory, exclusive of the five civilized tribes.

2d. That the Indians be admitted to United States citizenship so soon, and only so soon, as they are fitted for its responsibilities.

3d. That all Indians who are ready and anxious to receive titles to separate homesteads, and are capable of taking care of property, should be empowered to do so by proper legislation, which shall, at the same time, secure the lands so allotted from alienation and incumbrance for a period of twenty-five years, or such time after this period as shall be determined by the President and Secretary of the Interior. 1 Report of the Annual Lake Mohonk Conference on the Indian and Other Dependent Peoples (1883), pp. 8-9.

VIII.-RATIONS ISSUED TO INDIANS.

The gradual withdrawal of the issue of rations to Indians as rapidly as other means of support may be supplied is earnestly recommended by the Conference. A steady continuance of the ration system and a neglect of earnest effort to train Indians in self-support tend only toward demoralization and ultimate pauperism. 1 Report of the Annual Lake Mohonk Conference on the Indian and Other Dependent Peoples (1883), p. 13.

IX.-RELIGIOUS INSTRUCTION TO INDIANS. The Conference cordially adopts the statements of Commissioner Price in his annual report for 1882, where he speaks as follows: Extended observation proves that the influence of Christian teaching and training has been one of the most influential factors in whatever has thus far been gained in Indian civilization. 1 Report of the Annual Lake Mohonk Conference on the Indian and Other Dependent Peoples (1883), p. 14.

2 Report of the Annual Lake Mohonk Conference on the Indian and Other Dependent Peoples (1884).

SECOND ANNUAL ADDRESS TO THE PUBLIC OF THE LAKE MOHONK CONFERENCE HELD AT LAKE MOHONK, N. Y., SEPTEMBER, 1884, IN BEHALF OF THE CIVILIZATION AND LEGAL PROTECTION OF THE INDIANS OF THE UNITED STATES

SEPTEMBER, 1884.

The motive, therefore, which has urged the members of the Mohonk Conference to issue their address to the public is twofold:

1st. To inform the people of the United States as to the most direct practicable way in which the Indian question may be solved.
2d. To stimulate the thoughtful and right-minded citizens of the country to take immediate steps toward the solution of the problem.
It was felt by all those who took part in the work of the Conference that a calm, definite, and earnest appeal made to the conscience and intelligence of the country in behalf of a poor and helpless people, and for the righting of a national wrong, would not be uttered in vain.

INDIAN CITIZENSHIP THE SOLUTION OF THE INDIAN PROBLEM.
PROOFS OF INDIAN CAPACITY FOR CITIZENSHIP.
II.-WHAT IS NECESSARY TO SECURE INDIAN CITIZENSHIP.

1st. Resolved, That the organization of the Indians in tribes is, and has been, one of the most serious hindrances to the advancement of the Indian toward civilization, and that every effort should be made to secure the disintegration of all tribal organizations; that to accomplish this result the Government should, except where it is clearly necessary either for the fulfillment of treaty stipulations or for some other binding reason, cease to recognize the Indians as political bodies or organized tribes.
2d. Resolved, That to all Indians who desire to hold their land in severalty allotment should be made without delay; and that to all other Indians like allotments should be made so soon as practicable.
3d. *Resolved,* That lands allotted and granted in severalty to Indians should be made inalienable for a period of not less than ten or more than twenty-five years.
4th. *Resolved,* That all adult male Indians should be admitted to the full privileges of citizenship by a process analogous to naturalization, upon evidence presented before the proper court of record of adequate intellectual and moral qualifications.
5th. Resolved, That we earnestly and heartily approve of the Senate Bill No. 48, generally known as the Coke Bill, as the best practicable measure yet brought before Congress for the preservation of the Indian from aggression, for the disintegration of the tribal organizations, and for the ultimate breaking up of the reservation system; that we tender our hearty thanks and the thanks of the constituency which we represent to those members of the Senate who have framed this bill and secured its passage. We respectfully urge upon the House of Representatives the early adoption of this bill, that its beneficent provisions for rendering the Indian self-supporting and his land productive may be carried out with the least possible delay.

Abstract of the Coke Bill.

LAND IN SEVERALTY FOR INDIANS, AS PROVIDED FOR BY THE COKE BILL.

Forty-Eighth Congress, First Session, S. 48.

An "Act to provide for the allotment of lands in severalty to Indians on the various reservations, and to extend the protection of the laws of the States and Territories over the Indians, and for other purposes."

For many years past those who have given earnest thought to the best method of placing the Indian on a right footing among us, and patient effort to accomplish this result, have united in the belief that the allotment of land to individual Indians by a secure title would prove one of the most powerful agencies in the advancement of the race.

It has been often pointed out that we have by our policy taken from the Indian the ordinary and essential stimulus to labor while under our system of pauperizing Indians by the issuing of rations we deprive them of the ordinary necessity for self-support, by our refusal to protect them in the possession of their land and by our incessant removals we take away the common motives for cultivating it. The great mass of men work from the imperative necessity for self-support, and from the knowledge that the law will protect them in the possession of their rightful earnings. We have so alienated the Indian from all natural and general conditions, we have placed him in such an artificial and unjust position, that he has neither the necessity for self-support nor any proper protection in the result of his labor. It is a matter of surprise to all who fairly consider all the elements in the case, not that the result is no better, but that it is not far worse.

To give the Indian, then, a secure title to land, so that he may have the assurance of reaping what he has sown, is the plainest justice and good policy.

The thought and labor of those who have long worked for this end has taken shape in a most carefully and skillfully prepared bill for the allotment to Indians in severalty of land on the reservations. This bill is the outcome of long and intimate experience in the condition of the various Indian tribes, the result of a rare combination of practical knowledge and legal training. Its passage will greatly affect for the better the lives of nearly three hundred thousand human beings, besides the incalculable and yet wider influence in the life of a race and in the settlement of a question of national importance. The bill passed the Senate at the last session of the present Congress, and only its passage by the House of Representatives this coming winter is required to make it a law.

§ I. *By the first section* the President is authorized to issue patents for Indian reservations, set apart by treaty or act of Congress, in favor of the several tribes occupying them. Under these patents the United States is to hold the patented land in trust for the several tribes for twenty-five years, and at the end of that time to convey it by patent to the different tribes clear of incumbrance. The President is also given authority to delay in any case the issuing of the final patent if he considers it best for the Indians to do so. These patents are to be recorded and open to inspection.
This first section simply secures the tribe as such in the possession of its reservation. It places the strong restraint of the law upon the unjust occupation of Indian lands in the incessant push of Western settlement.

§ II. *The second section* authorizes the President, whenever he thinks it for the best interests of the Indians on a reservation, to have it surveyed or resurveyed, and to allot it to the Indians in severalty-to the heads of families onequarter, to single persons over eighteen one-eighth, and to orphan children under eighteen one-eighth of a section; to other persons under eighteen one-sixteenth of a section. If there is not sufficient land on a reservation to make such allotment, the land is to be allotted pro rata.

Treaty stipulations setting apart a reservation and providing for the allotment of land in larger quantities are to be fulfilled. The taking of land for grazing purposes by two or more Indians in common is provided for.

§ III. *In section third* provision is made for the manner in which the allotments are to be selected by the Indians, with the proviso that if such selection is not made within five years from the direction to take allotments the agent shall be directed to select for Indians failing to do so.

§ IV. The allotments are to be made under such rules as the Secretary of the Interior may prescribe by agents specifically appointed by the President.

§ V. Any Indian not residing upon a reservation or belonging to a tribe for which no reservation has been provided is entitled to settle upon unappropriated land of the United States, and on applying to the local land office can have the land allotted to him and to his children in the same manner as Indians residing on a reservation take allotments under the act. The fees of the local land office are to be paid out of the United States Treasury.

§ VI. *The sixth section* provides that patents shall be issued to individual allottees, declaring that the United States will hold the land in trust for the allottee or his heirs for twentyfive years, and then convey it to him or them absolutely and clear of all incumbrance. The land cannot be conveyed or charged during the time it is so held in trust, all the patents to individual allottees shall override the patent issued to the tribe. After the issue of patents the land shall descend according to the law of the State or Territory in which a reservation is situated. After all the lands on a reservation have been allotted, or sooner, if the President deems it for the best interest of the Indians, the Secretary of the Interior may negotiate with a tribe for the purchase of any unallotted portion of its reservation. This purchase is not complete until ratified by Congress. The principal of the purchase money shall be held by the United States for twenty-five years to the credit of the tribe, and the interest at five per cent., paid annually to the Secretary of the Interior, to be applied to the education and support of the tribe. After twenty-five years, by express authority of Congress, the principal shall be payable to the tribe. Proper provision is made for religious bodies now occupying land on the reservation.

§ VII. *Section Seventh* extends over a tribe, upon the completion of the allotment, the laws, both civil and criminal, of the State or Territory in which they reside, and prohibits the passage by the local government of any law denying Indians the equal protection of the law.

§ VIII. *Section Eighth*, in view of the important fact that the value of land in the West often depends largely upon its proper irrigation, authorizes the Secretary of the Interior to prescribe such rules as he may deem necessary to secure a just distribution of water among the Indians.

§ IX. *Section Ninth* excepts the five civilized tribes of Indian Territory and the Seneca Indians of New York from the provisions of the act.

§ X. *Section Tenth* appropriates one hundred thousand dollars for the survey or resurvey of reservations necessary under the act, and provides that the sum expended be repaid out of the proceeds from the sale of reservation lands.

§ XI. *Section Eleventh* provides that, except as to the issuing of the tribal patents, the provisions of the act shall not extend to any tribe as such until the consent of two-thirds adult male members shall have been obtained, but that, notwithstanding this, the President may make allotments to individual Indians in the manner provided irrespective of the consent of the two-thirds.

§ XII. *Section Twelfth* provides that the act shall not affect the right of Congress to grant a right of way for railroads, highways, or telegraph lines for the public use through any lands granted to an Indian or to a tribe upon just compensation being made.

THE MAIN POINTS OF THE BILL.

The broad and general advantages of the bill may be summed up in a few words. *It secures the tribes in possession of their reservations, and ends the notorious wrong of taking the Indian's land by fraud or force without his consent*. The United States is to hold the reservations in trust for the tribes, but not as a permanent arrangement. *The bill contemplates the breaking up of the entire reservation system*; it contemplates the protection of the Indian land from the grasp of unscrupulous whites only until the Indian has been given the proper training and preparation to enable him to take care of his own. In the meanwhile, the bill provides an important part of this training. On the consent of two-thirds of the adult males, allotments are to be made to a whole tribe in severalty. The reservations are divided into separate farms, the members of the tribe are given time to firmly plant and settle themselves before, by the extinguishment of the trust in which the reservation is held for the tribe, they are left to take care of themselves. Should the consent of the two-thirds not be obtained, the individual Indians can at once take allotments under the act. There is neither a compulsion of the majority nor the slightest disregard of the wants of the minority. The law of the white man is to be extended when, by the completion of the allotments, the Indians have shown themselves reasonably fit for it. Nor does the act overlook the undoubted fact that it is neither wise nor right to let these great, solid blocks of reservations stand in the way of traffic and settlement. Right of way through Indian land can be granted at any time to railroads, highways, and telegraph companies, and *at any time* unallotted lands can be purchased, proper compensation being given. *Such is the wise admixture in this bill of what is best in the views of those who regard this question from a radical or a conservative standpoint; land in severalty is to be given at once to all who desire it; the Indian is protected against the greed of the whites; a process of tribal disintegration is at once started, and the blotting out of the reservations as fast as it can be safely done is the ultimate object of the bill.*

In the light of the lasting importance of this measure to so many who are unrepresented among the legislators we have selected to do our will, you are asked to fairly and honestly consider it, and if it seems to you desirable and right, you are most earnestly and respectfully reminded that there rests on you a personal responsibility to give your influence, your time, and thought to secure its passage.

Henry S. Pancoast, Chairman of the Committee on Laws

EDUCATION.

a. Industrial.

b. Intellectual.

c. Moral and religious.

6th. *Resolved,* That from testimony laid before the Conference, our confidence in the good results flowing from the education of Indians has been confirmed, and that we regard with great satisfaction the increasing appropriations made by Congress for Indian schools, for instruction in farming and trades, for supplies of cattle, for irrigation, and for other means to promote self-supporting industries. That our conviction has been strengthened as to the importance of taking Indian youth from the reservations to be trained in industrial schools placed among communities of white citizens, and we favor the use of a larger proportion of the funds appropriated for Indian education for the maintenance of such schools. The placing of the pupils of these schools in the families of farmers or artisans where they may learn the trades and home habits of their employers has proved very useful and should be encouraged by the Government.

Resolved, That from evidence brought before the Conference it is apparent that the plan carried out to a small extent at Hampton and elsewhere, of bringing young men and their wives to industrial schools and there furnishing them with small houses so that they may be instructed in work and a proper home life, has been successful and should be carried out more largely.

Resolved, That while we approve the methods of Indian education pursued at Hampton and Carlisle, we do not fail to recognize that the schools and other methods of instruction, industrial, intellectual, moral, and religious, as carried on within or near the reservations by Christian missionaries for the first fifty years, have lifted up tribe after tribe to civilization and fitted them to take lands in severalty, and the good already achieved should stimulate and encourage Christian people to continue efforts in the same direction.

7th. *Resolved,* That education is essential to civilization. The Indian must have a knowledge of the English language, that he may associate with his white neighbors and transact business as they do. He must have practical industrial training to fit him to compete with others in the struggle for life. He must have a Christian education to enable him to perform duties of the family, the State, and the Church. Such an education can best be acquired apart from his reservation and amid the influences of Christian and civilized society. Such Government industrial training schools as those at Carlisle, Hampton, Forest Grove, Lawrence, Chilocco, and Genoa should be sustained and their number increased. The Government should continue to avail itself of institutions such as the training schools at Albuquerque, New Mexico; Lincoln Institute, Pennsylvania, and others conducted by religious or philanthropic associations, and promote the placing of pupils educated in all these schools in the families of farmers and artisans. But since the great majority of the Indians cannot be educated away from their homes, it is a matter of the highest importance that the Government should provide and liberally sustain good manual labor and day schools on the reservations. These should be established in sufficient number to accommodate all Indian children of school age. The Christian people of the country should exert through the Indian schools a strong moral and religious influence. This the Government cannot do, but without this the true civilization of the Indian is impossible.

HOW TO SECURE THESE THINGS.

a. Public sentiment.
b. Legislation.

8th. *Resolved,* That since legislation in Congress and the benevolent work of the Christian people on behalf of the Indian is dependent upon public sentiment, every effort should be made to further the development of such sentiment. To this end we commend to the sympathy and support of the public the Indian Rights Association and the Woman's National Indian Association. We urge the organization of branches of these Societies in the principal cities and towns of the country. We think it extremely desirable that the press be enlisted in bringing the Indian cause to public attention, and we also rejoice in the efforts of the many benevolent societies belonging to the various religious bodies to diffuse information concerning the Indians and to arouse public interest in their behalf.

SECOND TOPIC.

1st. Treaties.

9th. *Resolved, That we are bound by many treaties with various Indian tribes. These treaties are the bases of our relations with them, and yet are in some instances prejudicial to the best interests of both the Government and the Indians. Nevertheless, the treaties are binding upon the Government and the tribes until they can be modified by mutual agreement. The only way, therefore, to escape their evils is to persuade the Indians to agree to some modification of their provisions.*

We rejoice that since March 3d, 1871, it has been the policy of the Government to make no fresh treaties with the Indians. We trust that this policy may be strictly adhered to, and that the Government will have no dealings with chiefs alone as the representatives of tribal organizations.

2d. Reservations.

10th. *Resolved, That careful observation has conclusively proved that the re-*

moval of Indians from reservations which they have long occupied, to other reservations far distant from the former and possessing different soil and climate, is attended by great suffering and loss of life. Such removals destroy the fruits of past industry and discourage the Indians from further effort in the habits of civilized life. These removals are usually made, not for wise reasons, but are instigated by the covetousness of the whites, who desire possession of the Indian lands or wish to rid themselves of the Indians' presence. We, therefore, earnestly protest against such Indian removals in the future, excepting in those cases where they shall be justified by full and sufficient reasons, and shall not be detrimental to the welfare of the Indians. When the removal of an Indian tribe becomes a necessity, individual Indians belonging to the tribe who have formed settled homes should have the privilege of taking homesteads upon the lands they occupy prior to the opening of the reservation and before white men are permitted to make landentries thereon.

11th. *Resolved*, That the Conference gives its hearty approval to Senate bill No. 1755, providing for the division of the Sioux Reservation, which passed the Senate at the last session; that we record our gratitude to Senator Dawes and his colleagues upon the Select Committee for the skill and care with which they have embodied in this bill the important points agreed upon by the first Mohonk Conference; that we heartily commend the bill to the support of all friends of the Indians, and hope that it may be considered and passed by Congress at its next session.

Resolved, That the bill be referred to the Committee appointed to advocate the bill on lands in severalty, and that this Committee bring it to the attention of the Committees of Congress on Indian Affairs soon after that body shall have met.

For the convenience of those who are not familiar with the provisions of this bill, and who may find it difficult to obtain, we insert a brief analysis of it prepared for the Indian Rights Association.

3d. Government aid.

12th. Resolved, That the Conference hereby calls attention to the fact that Government aid extended to Indians in the form of rations, implements, clothing, etc., is in many instances not a gratuity, but is given simply in fulfillment of treaty stipulations and in payment for land ceded by the Indians to the United States.

In cases where Indians have been rendered destitute by the sudden destruction of the game on which they subsisted, as in the case of many Indians in Montana, they should be supplied with rations until time has been given them and opportunity afforded them to become self-supporting.

4th. Agencies.

13th. Resolved, That since Indian agents are obliged to live, in many instances, at a distance from the conveniences of civilized life, and where, owing to difficulties of transportation, the cost of living is extreme, and that as they are, furthermore, cut off from all means of self-support beyond the salary paid to them by the Government, this salary should in some cases be much larger than it is at present. Such an increase of salary would not be more than just compensation for the difficult and laborious duties of Indian agent, nor more than sufficient to secure the services of a high grade of men.

From personal observation and the testimony of competent judges, we are convinced that in many instances the agency buildings on reservations are unsuited to serve as homes for agents and their employees. In such cases suitable buildings should be provided.

We desire emphatically to reaffirm our conviction, expressed in the address of the first annual Conference, that the success of the Government in its effort to elevate the Indians depends on the ability, integrity, and energy of Indian agents and their employees, and we protest against any return to a system by which agents and their employees are appointed on the ground of political or personal favoritism.

5th. Law.

14th. *Resolved,* That immediate efforts should be made to place the Indian in the same position before the law as that held by the rest of the population, but that if it is not advisable, under existing circumstances, to subject the Indian at once to our entire body of law, the friends of the Indian should promptly endeavor: **First, to provide for him some method of admission to citizenship so soon as he has prepared himself for its privileges and responsibilities; second, to give him at once the right to sue in our courts, and, third, to provide some system for the administration of certain laws on the reservations. We believe that the laws relating to marriage and inheritance and the criminal law affecting person and property should be extended over the reservations immediately.**

As may be seen from the above resolutions, the Conference unites in urging that plain and sensible policy the main points of which have been so long and patiently recommended to Congress by men of practical experience in Indian affairs.

As these resolutions show, the Conference recognized that to permanently keep Indians as tribes, under the control of agents on reservations set apart for them, is both impossible and undesirable.

They recognized that the Indian must be forced out into the current of ordinary life; that to make him a citizen is the solution of the Indian problem.

Yet the resolutions express with equal strength the conviction that Indians should not be at once made citizens in a mass. The *preparation* for citizenship should be general, vigorous, and immediate. The Indian is to be prepared for citizenship by giving him his land in severalty in the manner provided for by the Coke Bill, by larger appropriations for Indian education and the careful use of such appropriations in the establishment and support of schools, industrial and otherwise, and by the *education* of the race in the broadest and largest sense of the word.

By adequate provision for the administration of law among the Indians, and by giving the Indian the right to sue.

By Christian teaching and the establishing and support of churches.

By the gradual reduction of rations given to Indians, the systematic instruction in farming, and the encouragement in selfsupport.

By the appointment and support of agents of ability and integrity, uninfluenced by political preference, the only standard being that of individual fitness.

By proper provision for the immediate admission to citizenship of such Indians as are fitted for its duties and responsibilities.

These are substantially the recommendations which the Conference respectfully urges upon Congress and the people of the United States, as the just, obvious, and practical answer to the Indian question. **2 Report of the Annual Lake Mohonk Conference on the Indian and Other Dependent Peoples (1884).**

3 Report of the Annual Lake Mohonk Conference on the Indian and Other Dependent Peoples (1885).

THE PLATFORM.

Dr. Rhoads reported from the Business Committee the following statement, which he said received the cordial approval of every member of the Committee:

The Indian question can never be settled except on principles of justice and equal rights. In its settlement all property rights of the Indians should be sacredly guarded, and all obligations should be faithfully fulfilled. Keeping this steadily in view, the object of all legislative and executive action hereafter should be not the isolation of the Indians, but the abrogation of the Indian reservations as rapidly as possible, the permitted diffusion of the Indians among the people in order that they may become acquainted with civilized habits and modes of life; the ultimate discontinuance of annuities, so promotive of idleness and pauperism; the subjection of the Indians to the laws of the United States, and of the States and Territories where they may reside, and their protection by the same laws as those by which citizens are protected; the opening of all the territory of the United States to their possible acquisition and to civilization, and the early admission of Indians to American citizenship. These objects should be steadily kept in view, and pursued immediately, vigorously and continuously.

The measures we recommend for their accomplishment are the following:
1. The present system of Indian education should be enlarged, and a comprehensive plan should be adopted, which shall place all Indian children in schools under compulsion if necessary, and shall provide industrial education for a large proportion of them. Adult Indians should be brought under preparation for self-support. To this end the free ration system should be discontinued as rapidly as possible, and a sufficient number of farmers and other industrial teachers should be provided meantime to teach them to earn their own living.
2. Immediate measures should be taken to break up the system of holding all lands in common, and each Indian family should receive a patent for a portion of land to be held in severalty, its amount dependent upon the number of members of the family and the character of the land, whether adapted for cultivation or for grazing. This land should be inalienable for a period of twenty-five years. The Coke Bill, as embodying this principle, has our earnest support, and is urged upon all friends of the Indians as the one practicable measure for securing these ends.
3. All portions of the Indian reservations which are not so allotted should, after the Indians have selected and secured their lands, be purchased by the Government at a fair rate, and be thrown open to settlement.
4. The cash value of the lands thus purchased should be set aside by the Government

as a fund to be expended as rapidly as can be wisely done for their benefit, especially their industrial and educational advancement.

5. In order to carry out the preceding recommendations legal provision should be made for the necessary surveys of reservations; and wherever necessary, negotiations should be entered into for the modification of the present treaties, and these negotiations should be pressed in every honorable way until the consent of the Indians be obtained.

6. Indians belonging to tribes which give up their reservations and accept allotments of land in severalty, and all Indians that abandon their tribal organization and adopt the habits and modes of civilized life, should be at once admitted to citizenship of the United States, become subject to and entitled to the protection of the laws of the United States and of the States or Territories where they may reside.

7. During this process of civilization some representative of the United States Government should be charged with the protection and instruction of the Indians. But all such officers should be withdrawn as soon as the Indians are capable of self-support and self-protection.

8. We are unalterably opposed to the removal of tribes of Indians from their established homes, and massing them together in one or more Territories, as injurious to the Indian and an impediment to civilization. **3 Report of the Annual Lake Mohonk Conference on the Indian and Other Dependent Peoples (1885), pp. 48-50.**

4 Report of the Annual Lake Mohonk Conference on the Indian and Other Dependent Peoples (1886). [Resolutions and Statement]

Business Committee Resolutions.

Prof. Merrill E. Gates, President of Rutgers College, offered the following resolutions for the business committee:-

Resolved, That the public and private utterances of President Cleveland, expressing his interest in securing justice, education, and ultimately citizenship for the Indian, and that such wise and courageous acts of the present administration as the revocation of the order opening to white settlers the Crow Creek Reservation, and the ejectment from Indian lands of illegal occupants and armed intruders, have the unqualified approval of this conference.

Resolved, That the efficiency of our Indian service depends almost entirely upon the personal fitness and the experience of the inspectors, agents, teachers, and subordinates, who are brought into immediate and personal relations with the Indians, and that under previous administrations the uncertain tenure of place on the part of Indian agents has interfered materially with the work of civilizing the Indians.

Resolved, That while this conference is credibly informed that within the last two years new appointments of agents have been made on about four-fifths of the agencies, while very generally changes have been made in subordinates and teachers, and that since many of the most experienced men have thus been lost to the service, friends of the Indian must regard with solicitude the continuance of the system of appointment and removal which has not shown itself under either party or under any administration adapted to secure the best results.

Resolved, That this conference earnestly recommends the immediate application of the principles of civil service reform to the entire Indian service, with such expansion or modification of the present law and rules as may be necessary to secure the end in view.

Resolved, That in the opinion of this conference it is to the last degree important that the bills known as the Dawes land and severalty bill, the Sioux bill, and the Mission Indian bill, which have passed the Senate and have been favorably reported by the Committee on Indian Affairs, should in the interest of the Indian race be speedily passed by the House.

The business committee, reported the following additional resolutions:

Resolved, That we recognize gratefully the utterances of the President in regard to the extension of education among the Indians and the increasing appropriations of Congress from year to year for this purpose, and we earnestly urge the continuance of this work of the Government until every Indian child shall be furnished with a common school education.

Resolved, That although it is not the function of the Government to teach religion, yet its help hitherto extended to missionary and other religious bodies without discrimination, in the maintenance of primary, normal, and industrial schools, could be greatly enlarged to the advancement of the civilization of the Indians, especially in view of the increasing interest felt in the preparation of the Indians for citizenship and the readiness of the various church organizations to co-operate therein. We earnestly hope that greatly enlarged appropriations may be made by the Congress soon to be convened.

Resolved, That the best interest of the Indians requires that ample provision should be made for the instruction of the adult Indians in farming and other industries.

Resolved, That in the existing system of Indian schools the day school occupies a primary and important place in its relations to the parents and home no less than to the children.

Resolved, That the number of day schools on Indian reservations should be multiplied in accordance with treaty stipulations, which promise a school-house and teacher to every thirty children among the Sioux and other tribes, and that in these schools systematic industrial training should be furnished in addition to the elements of an English education.

This resolution, which was read yesterday, I will read by request again.

We are convinced that the advancement of the Indian race in civilization is impeded rather than helped by a continuance of the reservation and agency system; and that their progress will be aided by its abandonment, as soon as practicable, with due consideration of all rights in the land acquired by the Indians. For this outgrown system would be substituted the rights and responsibilities of citizenship with individual ownership of homestead farms, or grazing ranges, and the protection of the equal laws made for all citizens as administered by the courts of the country. This change of the relations between the Government and the Indians is especially urgent in the case of tribes already surrounded or closely approached by a population of white citizens. Under these conditions the segregation of the Indians on reservations and their confinement thereon, under the arbitrary control of an agent and his subordinates, and subject to the existing laws regarding intercourse and trade with the whites, operate to keep them ignorant, barbarous, poor, dependent, and deprived of those inducements to industry and prudence which are potent forces in developing the saving aspirations and energies of every race of mankind.

The duties of citizenship are of such a nature that they can only be learned by example and practice, and we believe that quicker and surer progress will be secured in industry, education, and morality by giving citizenship first than by making citizenship conditional upon the attainment of any standard of education and conduct:

Therefore, Resolved, That we urge upon Congress the necessity of ceasing to treat the Indians as incapable of bearing responsibilities, and the advantage of compelling them to undertake the same responsibilities that we impose upon all other human beings competent to distinguish right and wrong, whether they were born here or brought here, whether rich or poor, whether they know our language or do not know it, whether they are Christians or pagans or infidels.

The substance of that is that we shall cease to treat Indians as a foreign people incapable of becoming a part of this nation, but shall recognize them as entitled-as General Armstrong so forcibly puts it-to the rights of humanity, and bring them under the power and within the scope of the Declaration of Independence and the Constitution of the United States, giving them the same encouragements, the same hopes, and the same prospects which we have ourselves.

THE STATEMENT (pp. 45-46)

Mr. Gates.
The discussions of the conference have led us to a clearer recognition of a few principles which we believe furnish the key to the solution of the Indian problem. ***The application and enforcement of these principles by the immediate passage of the Dawes land in severalty bill, the Sioux reservation bill, and the bill for extending law over all Indians***, would at once do more for the cause of the Indians than can be done in years without such legislation. (Emphasis added).

It is our conviction that the duties of citizenship are of such a nature that they can only be learned by example and practice, and we believe that quicker and surer progress in industry, education, and morality will be secured by giving citizenship first than by making citizenship depend upon the attainment of any standard of education and conduct; and we therefore urge upon Congress the necessity of ceasing to treat the Indians as incapable of bearing responsibilities, and the advantage of compelling them to undertake the same responsibilities that we impose upon all other human beings competent to distinguish right and wrong.

The uncivilized tribe enforces no law. The tribal relation dwarfs family life and weakens family ties. The reservation shuts off the Indians from civilization, and rations distributed unearned tend to pauperize them. Therefore we are convinced that the sooner family ties and family homesteads replace tribal relations and unsettled herding upon the reservation, the better. Give to every Indian family a home, where needful, with a protected title.

The opening of large parts of our great reservations to actual white settlers by the sale, in the interest of the Indians and with their consent, of lands remaining after all Indians have received ample allotments of land in severalty, we believe can be accomplished by the proposed legislation now before Congress, with justice to the Indian and with advantage alike to him and to the whites.

While these results will follow the proposed legislation, we believe that the great work of education, general, industrial, and moral and religious, should be pressed forward, both by the Government and the religious societies with unflagging zeal, with larger expenditure of money and of teaching force, at schools in the East, and in the day schools and the boarding schools on the reservations, and with greater hope and confidence as we see such encouraging results as have been reported to us here.

We believe that the agency system in some form must be temporarily continued; and since the efficiency of our Indian service depends almost entirely upon the personal fitness and the experience of the inspectors, agents, teachers. and subordinates who come into immediate and personal relations with the Indians, we have declared our conviction, for these and for other reasons elsewhere stated, that the principle of civil service reform should be at once applied to our Indian service.

We thankfully express our conviction that each year sees a quickening of the public conscience in matters touching justice for the Indian, and a deepening public sentiment in favor of the full protection of his rights by law, and we invite all good citizens to join us in our efforts to protect, to civilize, and to Christianize the Indians. **4 Report of the Annual Lake Mohonk Conference on the Indian and Other Dependent Peoples (1886).**

5 Report of the Annual Lake Mohonk Conference on the Indian and Other Dependent Peoples (1887). No mention of platform.

1887: Final Report of Business Committee

I. We congratulate the country on the notable progress towards a final solution of the Indian problem which has been made during the past year. The passage of the Dawes Bill closes the "century of dishonor"; it makes it possible for the people of America to initiate a chapter of national honor in the century to come. It offers the Indians homes, the first condition of civilization; proffers them the protection of the laws; opens to them the door of citizenship. We congratulate the country on the public sentiment which has made this Bill possible, on the Act of Congress responding promptly to the sentiment all too tardily roused, and the action of the Executive welcoming the Bill and the policy which it inaugurates, initiating the execution of its provisions in a just and humane spirit, and pledging its cooperation with philanthropic and Christian societies in the endeavor to prepare the Indian for the change which this Bill both contemplates and necessitates.

II. The Dawes Bill has not solved the Indian problem. It has only created an opportunity for its solution. The acceptance of allotment and citizenship by all Indians on United States reservations must be a matter of several years' time, gradually extinguishing the Agency system, but requiring in consequence increased facilities for the administration of local justice, both civil and criminal, and methods of governmental supervision and protection during the transition period, wholly free from partisan control. Surrounded as the Indian is by those who have little sympathy with him in his ignorance, we are persuaded that further legislation will be required to guard him in his rights and to prevent his new liberty and opportunity from becoming a curse instead of a blessing. The *method* is yet to be determined. The *necessity* is a constant fact. (Emphasis in original).

III. While the Dawes Bill will change the Indian's legal and political status; it will not change his character. The child must become a man, the Indian must become an American; the pagan must be new created a Christian. His irrational and superstitious dread of imaginary gods must be transformed into a love for the All-Father; his natural and traditional hatred of the pale-face into a faith in Christian brotherhood; his unreasoning adherence to the dead past into an inspiring hope in a great and glad future. In his case religious education must precede and prepare for secular education, the Gospel for civilization, the story of God's love for the era in which the spear shall be beaten into a pruning hook and the sword into a plowshare. This is the work of the Christian churches, on them the new era lays new and grave duties, because before them it opens new and larger opportunities.

IV. This work necessitates cooperation, if not combination. The work of education, which has been heretofore desultory, individual, fragmentary, denominational, must be made systematic, harmonious, organic, Christian. For this purpose the various missionary and educational bodies working among the Indians are earnestly urged to secure at once a joint representative meeting to frame some plan of cooperative action that they may not conflict with one another in the field; that they may reduce expenses and increase efficiency; and that, especially, in dealing both with the Indian and the United States Government, they may act as one body representing the great constituency, and combining their various energies to one great end, the Americanizing, civilizing and Christianizing of the aborigines of the soil.

V. The abolition of the reservation system effected by the Dawes Bill necessarily involves the largest civil and religious liberty in the work of education in the reservations, and such liberty is required in order to carry on missionary and educational work. While government must still determine on what conditions it will make appropriations for education, and while it must control all educational operations which are supported by its appropriations, the way should be open for any and every voluntary organization to carry on instruction among the Indian tribes without hindrance or interference. Experience can alone determine what method promises the cheapest, quickest, and best results. Failures may be as suggestive of truth as successes, and no experiment should be forbidden by government authority if it is not made a charge upon the government purse. There is no danger of too many schools; a great danger of too few. No policy can be endured which forbids Christian men and women to teach Christian truth, or to prepare instruction in it in any way they deem right, in any part of this Commonwealth that is consistent with that civil and religious liberty which is unhampered in every other part of our land, and must hereafter be unhampered within all Indian reservations. We lay on every Christian organization in the land the duty, and, therefore, we claim for every Christian organization in the land the right, to push forward this work with all enthusiasm, directing their efforts according to their own judgment, not directed in them by any civil or political authority whatever.

VI. The United States Government, however, leaves this work wholly to voluntary effort. It possesses large funds equitably belonging to the Indian. These are trust funds. The Indian's greatest need is education in primary, industrial, normal, and other schools. To hold these monies in the treasury while the Indians are allowed to grow up in ignorance is a misuse of trust-funds. We call for an immediate enlargement of government educational work, largely increased appropriations for it, and a full recognition by Congress and by the Department, as well as by the churches, that the educational need of the Indian is instant, the exigency pressing, the perils in delay great, and the duty of action unmistakable. We urge the immediate establishment of Indian schools at every practicable point, an increase in the number of teachers, and whatever enlargement of salaries may be required to secure efficient teachers. The most vigorous and united efforts are required to prepare the Indian for citizenship as rapidly as the Dawes Bill will confer it upon him.

VII. In the work of secular education the true end must be kept constantly in view-to prepare the Indian for American citizenship. He must therefore be taught whatever appertains to successful citizenship-the economic virtues, temperance, thrift, self-reliance, the duties and responsibilities as well as the rights and privileges of citizenship; some practical knowledge of industrial arts, and above all the language of the country of which he is hereafter to be a citizen. The English language should therefore be made at the earliest practicable day the sole medium of instruction in all government Indian schools; and even in purely voluntary and mission schools the English language should be brought to the foremost place as fast as the requirements of proper religious instruction will permit.

VIII. The introduction of civil service reform into the Indian Department is essential to its honest and effective administration. For the work of protection and education, permanence and purity are an absolute necessity, and neither is possible under the partisan method. We therefore demand the absolute divorce of the Indian Bureau from party politics in all its appointments and removals. **5 Report of the Annual Lake Mohonk Conference on the Indian and Other Dependent Peoples (1887, pp. 104-106).** https://babel.hathitrust.org/cgi/pt?id=uc1.a0012443123&seq=7 (accessed online September 26, 2024).

6 Report of the Annual Lake Mohonk Conference on the Indian and Other Dependent Peoples (1888).

ADOPTION OF PLATFORM.

The Lake Mohonk Conference, at this its Sixth Annual Conference, reaffirms the principles of justice and equal rights affirmed at previous sessions, and, in the name of the people of the United States, demands their application in better and more thoroughly organized systems of jurisprudence and education.

1. The Indian is not a foreigner; the tribe is not a foreign nation. Whatever his past history may have been, the Indian now is, in point of fact, a member of this nation, and as such must be amenable to its laws, subject to its jurisdiction and authority, and entitled to the privileges and prerogatives which belong to and are inherent in citizenship. Among these are the right to protection in the ownership of property, liberty in his industry, and the freedom of an open market for his productions. The land laws already passed recognize these his inherent and inalienable rights. It remains for the Nation to protect him in them by some adequate system of courts organized by and vested with the authority of the Federal Government, and easily accessible to the poorest, the least influential and the most remote. During the present transition period, the Indian cannot with either safety or justice be given over to the protection of State and local courts, which are often inaccessible and not always impartial, nor left to petty police tribunals organized by and dependent on the will of the Indian agent; tribunals essentially inconsistent with the fundamental provisions of the Constitution. The Conference gives its hearty approval to these essential principles of organized justice, and urges upon the favorable consideration of Congress the bill proposed by the Law Committee of this Conference, now pending in the United States Senate, or some other bill embodying these principles.

2. Neither the law in severalty nor law administered by competent courts will suffice for the protection of the Indian. More fundamental than either is his education. The present ill-organized and unsystematic educational methods of the Government, the imperfections of which have necessitated the labors of voluntary and philanthropic societies, should give place to a well-organized system of popular education, framed in accordance with the principles of our American institutions, and competent to provide the entire Indian race with adequate education. It is the duty of the Federal Government to undertake at once the entire task of furnishing primary and secular education

for all Indian children of school age on the reservations under Federal control. It has no right to thrust this burden on the pioneer populations in the midst of which the Indians happen to be located. It has no right to leave this burden to be carried by the churches and private philanthropic societies which have taken it up only because the necessity was great and the neglect absolute. The cost of education is immeasurably less than the cost of war; the expense of educating the Indian for self-support less than one tenth the cost of keeping him in pauperism. We call upon the Department of the Interior to inaugurate at once a thorough and comprehensive system, providing at national expense, on principles analogous to those which experience has incorporated in our public school system, for the education of all Indian children in its ward and care, in all the elements of education essential to civilized life and good citizenship-the use of the English language, the common industrial arts and sciences, the habits and proprieties of domestic life, and the ethical laws which underlie American civilization. We call upon Congress to provide at once, and by wholly adequate appropriation, the necessary funds for such a system, for buildings, teachers, inspectors, superintendents. And, in the name of the Christian and philanthropic people of the United States, and of the people of those Western States and Territories who rightly demand that the charge and burden of a pagan and pauper population shall no longer be thrown upon them, we pledge their cordial co-operation in such an effort to remove at once the National dishonor of supporting ignorant and barbaric peoples in the heart of a Christian civilization, with only feeble and wholly inadequate endeavors to bring them into harmony with a free and Christian civilization.

3. This education should be compulsory; but on those principles of compulsion which are recognized as legitimate in the free commonwealths of the world. The Indian child should be required to receive such education as will fit him for civilized life and for self-support therein, but his parents should be left at liberty to choose between the Government and the private school, so long as the private school furnishes the elements required by civilized life, and conforms to a uniform standard prescribed by the Government and maintained in its own schools. A uniform standard of qualification should be required of all teachers receiving appointment, and should be enforced by rigid and impartial examinations. The tenure of the teacher's office should be permanent. Removals should be made only for inefficiency, incompetency, or other unfitness. And the entire educational service from the superintendents of schools to the primary teachers, should, in the interest of just administration and efficient work, be exempt from those changes and that instability of tenure which appertain to political and party appointments.

4. In view of the great work which the Christian churches have done in the past in inaugurating and maintaining schools among the Indians, and of the essential importance of religious as distinguished from secular education, for their civil, political, and moral well-being, an element of education which, in the nature of the case, the National Government cannot afford, the churches should be allowed the largest liberty; not, indeed, to take away the responsibility from the Government in its legitimate sphere of educational work, but to supplement it. to the fullest extent in

their power, by such schools, whether primary, normal, or theological, as are at the sole cost of the benevolent or missionary societies. And it is the deliberate judgment of this Conference that in the crisis of the Indian transitional movement, the churches should arouse themselves to the magnitude and emergency of the duty thus laid upon them in the providence of God.

5. Nothing should be done to impair or weaken the agencies at present engaged in the work of Indian education. Every such agency should be encouraged and promoted, except as other and better agencies are provided for the work. In particular, owing to the anomalous condition of the Indians and the fact that the Government is administering trust funds that belong to them, what is known as the "contract system" - by which the Nation aids by appropriations private and missionary societies in the work of Indian education - ought to be maintained by a continuance of such aid, until the Government is prepared, with adequate buildings and competent teachers, to assume the entire work of secular education. In no case should the Government establish schools to compete with private or church schools which are already doing a good work, so long as there are thousands of Indian children for whose education no provision is made. 6 **Report of the Annual Lake Mohonk Conference on the Indian and Other Dependent Peoples (1888), pp. 104-106.**

7 **Report of the Annual Lake Mohonk Conference on the Indian and Other Dependent Peoples (1889).**

The Platform.

I. We, the members of the Lake Mohonk Conference, in this our seventh annual meeting, reiterate the principles laid down in our former platforms concerning justice, equal rights, and education, both by government and by religious societies, for the Indian races on this continent; we maintain that the nation ought to treat the Indian as a man, amenable to all the obligations and entitled to all the rights of manhood under a free republican government; we congratulate the country on the progress made in the opening of reservations to civilization, on the allotment of land in severalty, and on the assent of Indians in increasing numbers freely given to this policy; we emphasize the importance of the Christian and missionary work of the churches as fundamental to the education and civilization of the Indians, and the necessity for the vigorous and unimpaired prosecution of such work; we welcome heartily the presence of the Commissioner of Indian Affairs at this session, and indorse heartily the general principles embodied in the paper presented by him outlining a proposed policy for the organization of a comprehensive system of Indian education by the Federal Government; we urge upon the administration the organization of such a plan, and upon Congress the necessary appropriations for its execution; and the chairman of this Conference is hereby authorized and instructed to appoint a committee of seven, of whom he shall be one, to render to the Commissioner of Indian Affairs such cooperation as he may desire in preparing such a system as shall best promote the universal and compulsory education of all Indian children, in harmony with the principles of our government, and with the concurrent work of the churches, missionary boards and societies, and philanthropic organizations, and to urge upon Congress such increased appropriations as may be necessary to carry this into effect.

APPOINTMENTS TO OFFICE.
II. As the efficiency of every plan for the care and education of the Indians depends upon the intellectual and moral character of the agents, superintendents, teachers, matrons, and, in a greater or less degree, of all the employees of the Indian Bureau, and upon the cumulative influence dependent on continuance of service and resultant experience, the Conference emphasizes its conviction of the fitness and necessity of separating absolutely the appointments to office from the mutations of parties. To remove agents and teachers who are faithful and efficient merely because of a change of the party in power is not only a direct assault upon the work and the morale of the workers, but intrinsically capricious and absurd. And to make such positions a reward for party services, the incumbents to be named by those whom they have served, is to make it improbable, if not impossible, that either the interests of the Indians or of the national government will be adequately cared for. When it is considered that there are between eight and nine hundred Indian agents and teachers and other employees in the field, and that their functions are chiefly either military, judicial, or educational, it is apparent that removals on other ground than that of demerit, or the filling of vacancies independent of merit, cannot but constitute an almost insuperable obstacle to effective work.

ADDITIONAL LEGISLATION.
III. While we hail with satisfaction the progress that has already been made in the execution of the act for the allotment of Indian lands in severalty, we recognize that the operations of this act are met by difficulties which make further legislation necessary, and we call upon Congress to take such steps, before the Indians to whom allotments are made shall become citizens of any State, as will secure to their children the sure inheritance of those lands upon the death of their parents, without the risk of disinheritance because of their not being legal heirs under the laws of such States; to provide for the expenditure of the income of the funds for education derived from the sale of surplus lands, under such restrictions as will compel its use for the purpose intended, and in such a manner in reference to State taxation as will be alike just to the Indians and to their fellow-citizens in their respective States and Territories; and to enact such other measures, while the Indians are still the wards of the nation, as will secure to them the fullest benefits of their allotted lands, and will encourage to the utmost habits of thrift, enterprise, and progressive industry. And, in order to correct these and other difficulties which may be discovered, the chairman of this Conference is hereby authorized and instructed to appoint a committee of three to examine the scope of existing legislation on this subject, and to suggest to Congress such amendments as shall be found necessary to accomplish the beneficent purposes of the act.

THE INDIAN TERRITORY.
IV. The condition of affairs in the Indian Territory demonstrates the futility of all efforts to secure adequately the civilization and development of the Indians under those tribal relations against which we have so earnestly protested. The complex questions arising

from the relations of Indian, negro, and white man, the fact that non-citizen whites already outnumber the Indian population in the proportion of two to one, and that this large white population is without schools, and, to a large extent, uncontrolled by law, render the question of the Indian Territory one of the gravest importance. The wonderful progress of the five civilized tribes, in the face of many difficulties and under the most unfavorable conditions, demonstrates the capacity of the Indians for a larger life and a better civilization; and the time has come when they are ready for the duties, responsibilities, and privileges of American citizenship. The Conference rejoices that there is a growing sentiment among these people in this direction. As the beginning of better things, the establishment of a United States Court, with partial jurisdiction, has had a beneficent influence; and it is urgently recommended that the same jurisdiction be given to this court as is possessed by any United States District Court.

THE MISSION INDIANS OF CALIFORNIA.
V. This Conference is deeply impressed with a sense of the injuries done to the Mission Indians of California by the repeated delays in settling their lawful claims, and urges upon Congress the passage of a bill at the next session which shall settle their claims justly and give the Indians a legal right to their lands.

THE INDIANS OF NEW YORK STATE.
VI. The condition of the Indian reservations in the State of New York, with some notable exceptions, continues to be not only unsatisfactory, but positively bad, degrading to the Indians themselves, demoralizing to their neighbors, and humiliating to those who have brought so imperfectly to them the appliances of Christianity and civilization. While there are many among them who have accepted, so far as their circumstances allow, our Christian and English civilization, yet the controlling influence on many of the reservations is still that of a pagan superstition which fosters ignorance and vice, and degrades or denies the family life. We owe gratitude to those who have called attention to their condition and have tried to correct it; and especially do we rejoice that the legislature of the State has been considering the subject. And we trust that such legislation will be perfected as shall supply these Indians with facilities for higher education similar to those provided for other tribes by the general government, and shall, in a way just and right, substitute the full operation of the laws of the State for the present laws of their tribal organizations, and thus secure all the rights and all the duties of citizenship.

LAW ON THE RESERVATIONS.
VII. The Conference renews its earnest request that Congress will consider the bill proposed by the Law Committee, still pending in the United States Senate, intended to provide needed facilities for the administration of law on the reservations. **7 Report of the Annual Lake Mohonk Conference on the Indian and Other Dependent Peoples (1889), pp. 107-110.**

8 Report of the Annual Lake Mohonk Conference on the Indian and Other Dependent Peoples (1890).

PLATFORM OF THE EIGHTH ANNUAL CONFERENCE OF THE FRIENDS OF THE INDIANS.

The members of this eighth annual Lake Mohonk Conference, looking back upon the past and forward to the future, thank God, and take courage. The workers in the missionary schools, who have been the pioneers of this movement, have, by the inspiring results of labors pursued with inadequate means and against great discouragements, demonstrated the capacity of the Indian for civilization, and created a public sentiment which demands his civilization. This growing sentiment has been demonstrated in the inauguration of the peace policy, the creation of the Board of Indian Commissioners, the gradual improvement in the personnel of the Indian Bureau, the organization and work of the Lake Mohonk Conference, the abandonment of the pernicious reservation system, the allotment of lands in severalty, the improved though still inadequate provisions for the administration of justice, the gradual discontinuance of the policy of feeding the Indian and making him a mendicant, the steady development of the policy of teaching him and making him a citizen, witnessed in the increased government appropriations for Indian education, from $20,000 in 1870 to $1,800,000 in 1890; and it reaches a fitting culmination in the admirable plan of the present Indian Commissioner for providing all children of school age with a commonschool education, at government expense, and in schools under governmental control.

Turning toward the future, this Conference Urges Congress to make such liberal and increasing appropriations as may be necessary to perfect and carry this plan into full operation;

Calls for a further extension of education in all the industrial arts, as essential to preparation for self-support;

Protests against the removal of capable officials for party reasons, and emphasizes the necessity of permanent tenure and non-partisan administration in the Indian Bureau;

Urges improvement in the provisions for the regular and legal administration of justice both toward and among the Indians, and indorses the specific recommendations for this purpose laid before the Conference at this session by its Committee on Laws;

Urges the churches to larger gifts and greater zeal in their distinctive Christian work among the Indians, without which all the efforts of the government for their civilization will be in vain;

And reaffirms, as the fundamental principle which should control all friends of the Indians, that all work for them, whether by private benevolence or by government, should be done in anticipation of and in preparation for the time when the Indian races of this country will be absorbed into the body of our citizens, and the specific Indian problem will be merged in that great problem of building up a human brotherhood which the providence of God has laid upon the American people. **8 Report of the Annual Lake Mohonk Conference on the Indian and Other Dependent Peoples (1890), pp. 111-112.**

9 Report of the Annual Lake Mohonk Conference on the Indian and Other Dependent Peoples (1891).

PLATFORM OF THE NINTH ANNUAL CONFERENCE OF THE FRIENDS OF THE INDIANS.

In no year since the General Severalty Bill was enacted have we had occasion to record so important an advance in the administration of Indian affairs. The year is signalized by the fact that the President of the United States has extended the provisions of the Civil Service Act to over six hundred employees of the Indian service, superintendents of schools, teachers, matrons, and physicians,- whose appointment and permanency of service will no longer be affected by political influences.

We also heartily thank Congress for the enactment of important laws. By one of these laws provision is made for the compulsory education of Indian children. By two laws the wrongs to the Mission and Round Valley Indians, against which this Conference has long protested, have been corrected, and their provisions are now being carried out, so that we may soon expect to see these Indians holding firm titles to their own individual lands. Congress has also made increased appropriations for the education of Indians.

Under the direction and with the sympathy of the President and Secretary of the Interior, the Indian service has had the rare fortune of being conducted by a Commissioner of Indian Affairs whose energetic, courageous, and skilful (sic) administration has our heartiest approval.

What has been gained the past year encourages us to renewed effort for further advance. We heartily thank the President and Secretary of the Interior for the partial extension of the civil service to the Indian service; and we ask them to complete their work by putting under the provisions of the same act, so far as possible, all other appointees, including farmers and carpenters, etc., if found practicable, amounting to as many more. And, if it is not thought possible to apply the letter of the Civil Service Act to the appointment of agents, we would most earnestly ask that the spirit, at least, of that law be applied in this case also, as it is especially important that their selection be for merit and competency only, and that their tenure of office be not limited by political considerations.

With the same purpose we would call attention to the importance of maintaining from one quadrennium to another a consistently wise line of Indian administration. The duties of a Commissioner of Indian Affairs are no more political than those of any agent or teacher. We therefore urge that the responsibility for results in the conduct of Indian affairs be left with him, including a return to the former custom of devolving upon him the selection of agents as well as other employees.

The amount of $2,216,000 appropriated by Congress last year for the education of the Indian was twenty per cent. larger than the amount appropriated in any previous year, but it yet leaves a third of the Indian youth unprovided with schools. We still ask for rapidly increasing appropriations until the Indian school system shall be perfected, and provision made for the education of all Indian youth. We warmly approve the extension of the national public school system, so administered as not to restrain the freedom of religious schools supported for the benefit of the Indians.

We look with satisfaction upon the allotments of lands in severalty, but with concern upon the rapidity with which they are being made. In order that public sentiment may not be impeded, that schools may be provided, and that justice may be done adjacent white settlers, we ask Congress to pass a law providing that the government shall pay all equitable local taxation, or its equivalent, assessed on allotted lands, so long as these allotments remain inalienable, either from proceeds of surplus lands or from the public treasury.

The legal status of the Indian who holds an allotment in a reservation not yet fully allotted should be speedily decided. Legislation by Congress should provide for easy access to duly established courts of law, and for competent legal advice and service for Indians, during the transition period which must precede their intelligent entrance upon the full duties of independent citizenship. We do not favor the establishment of an elaborate system of special courts for Indians; but we affirm unhesitatingly that legislation to secure immediate and easy access to regularly established courts for legal protection and remedies is greatly needed, and should be by law provided.

The policy of getting the Indians into civilization by keeping them out of civilization has never succeeded, and never will. We therefore commend the policy of mingling the Indians with the whites, by seeking employment for them in Christian families and on farms, by placing them in the public schools in the States, and by encouraging their settlement together.

We regret that we have occasion again to note that the lands of the New York Indian tribes have not yet been allotted, and the tribal system thus abolished. We hope that the State of New York will follow the United States in securing to the Indians within its limits the individual ownership of their lands under some just legislation; and, if for any reason it may be impracticable to at once do this, we urge that the legislature shall without delay extend the operation of the civil and criminal laws of the State to residents of such reservations, except so far as such laws relate to the ownership of lands.

The public exhibition of Indians in their savage costumes and customs is demoralizing and humiliating, and we ask that no permission be hereafter given to take Indians from the reservations for this purpose.

We protest most earnestly against the removal of the Southern Utes from Colorado, as against their best interests, as involving their pauperization and needless expense to the government, and as, in our opinion, dictated solely by a desire on the part of the white man to obtain the valuable lands now occupied by these Indians.

Believing that in education lies the chief hope for the future of the Indian people, the Conference rejoices in the increased facilities afforded by government schools, trusts that regulations enforcing the compulsory education law will be so wisely carried out as to allow to Indian parents all reasonable freedom in choice of a school for their children, while still preventing undue solicitation of pupils by rival schools, and expresses its conviction that, as the work of Indian education began with Christian missionary efforts, and has had its strength in mission effort, the Christians of America are called upon to-day more strongly than ever before, by the hearty and generous support of missions to the Indians, to make manifest the supreme constraining force in civilization, that love of Christ, in accomplishing the work that remains to be done for these our fellow-countrymen of Indian descent. **9 Report of the Annual Lake Mohonk Conference on the Indian and Other Dependent Peoples (1891).**

10 Report of the Annual Lake Mohonk Conference on the Indian and Other Dependent Peoples (1892).

PLATFORM OF THE TENTH ANNUAL CONFERENCE OF THE FRIENDS OF THE INDIANS.

As an expression of the views of this Conference the following platform is adopted:

I. They advise that the allotment of lands be persistently and judiciously continued until there shall be no further need of Indian agents or reservation agencies.

II. They desire to emphasize the fact that the national government must assume the common school education of Indian children, making it compulsory where necessary.

III. That it is the duty of the general government to enact and enforce such laws as will fully protect the Indian in his relation to other Indians, as well as in his relations to all other persons; that as soon as possible he shall become self-respecting and self-supporting; and that also, until he becomes so, he shall be protected from robbery through deceit or extortion by scheming lawyers or greedy land claimants.

IV. They are convinced that not only the principles of the Civil Service Law should be applied, so far as practicable, to the Indian service, but that the appointment of Indian agents, inspectors, and allotting agents should be on account of fitness only, and that those holding these offices should continue to hold them during good behavior; and they emphatically condemn the appointment and removal of these officers for partisan reasons.

V. They earnestly appeal to all Christian people everywhere to relax no effort, but rather to vie with one another in every effort to bring the benign influence of Christian truth to these people. **10 Report of the Annual Lake Mohonk Conference on the Indian and Other Dependent Peoples (1892), pp. 121-122.**

11 Report of the Annual Lake Mohonk Conference on the Indian and Other Dependent Peoples (1893).

PLATFORM OF THE ELEVENTH ANNUAL CONFERENCE OF THE FRIENDS OF THE INDIANS PLATFORM.

The celebration this year of the discovery of America recalls the injuries done by the white man during four centuries to the race which was found in possession of the continent. It is hardly two decades since our government began to try to make civilized citizens out of those it had allowed to remain barbarians. The progress made during this short time is gratifying, though much less than we might have made, considering how few in number the Indians are and how plain are our duties to them.

We believe that the United States government should apply to the Indian problem a well-defined purpose to hasten, as rapidly as possible, the complete absorption of the Indians into the body politic. ... (Emphasis added).

1. The extension of the rules or the principles of civil service reform, so as to remove utterly from party politics the appointment of Indian agents, allotment agents, and inspectors.
2. Appropriations sufficient to equip and maintain a system of schools adequate to provide for all Indian children of school age not otherwise provided for, and compulsory attendance of children at these or other schools.
3. The protection of Indian trust funds against unjust claims, and their expenditure as far as possible for the education and civilization of the Indians.
4. The breaking up of the reservations as rapidly as the interests of the Indians will allow, and the incorporation of the Indians in the mass of American citizens.
5. Due provision made by Congressional appropriations or from trust funds for the maintenance of legal protection, for schools, roads, and other public burdens, in counties where Indians have received allotments of lands which, by protected Indian title, are exempt from all taxation, in order that no unjust burden may be put upon other resident citizens of these counties. **11 Report of the Annual Lake Mohonk Conference on the Indian and Other Dependent Peoples (1893), pp. 141-143.**

12 Report of the Annual Lake Mohonk Conference on the Indian and Other Dependent Peoples (1894).

PLATFORM OF THE TWELFTH ANNUAL CONFERENCE OF THE FRIENDS OF THE INDIANS.

The Mohonk Conference has now completed twelve years of work in the Indian reform. In this period a large advance has been made. The interest of the nation in the condition of the Indian has been greatly increased. *Legislation has been secured of great value, culminating in the Severalty Law, the happy result of which will be to break up the reservation system and make the Indian a citizen.* Great principles have been established. This Conference regards it as settled that the Indian is to be treated as a man, and ought to be put on the footing of other men. The unfortunate relation which he has held as a ward of the nation is a relation which is incompatible with his manhood, and should be brought to an end as soon as possible. (Emphasis added).

We believe the Indian has all the natural qualifications necessary for his education, civilization, and Christianization; and we are satisfied that, while we must be careful not to deprive him of his rights, we must be equally careful not to pauperize nor enervate him by undue paternalism.

The wide-spread corruption existing in the Indian Territory, as the result of its present autonomous reservation system, should excite alarm and indignation in the minds of all good citizens. We earnestly hope that the measures now being taken by the government to induce the five civilized tribes to take land in severalty, and exchange their tribal governments for a territorial government, may prove successful.

Recent laws permitting Indians to lease their lands are widely resulting in dispossessing ignorant Indians of their property rights, without an adequate return, to their great disadvantage and the enriching of designing white men. We recommend, therefore, that the law be so modified as to render it possible for Indians to sell or lease their lands only by permission of a judge of the United States District Court, upon the same principles which protect the lands of minor heirs among the whites from alienation.

We regard it as of the utmost importance that the Indian be encouraged to support himself and his family by work. On this account we deprecate present conditions tending to make the Indian a pauper, such as issuing rations and annuities, and the lack of work and of markets for Indian productions.

We reiterate the affirmation of our platform of 1893: that, from funds now held by the United States or hereafter created for the benefit of the Indians, provision should be made by law for their fair share of the expense of local improvements and taxes, that these burdens may not rest unjustly on the communities and States which include in their territory the lands of Indians who hold under a protected title and are exempt from taxation.

The Severalty Law, and other reforms inaugurated for the benefit of the Indians, are effective chiefly as they are executed by fit men. It is of the utmost importance at this juncture that Indian and allotting agents be men of stanch (sic) integrity and high character. Their tenure of office should not be subject to political changes.

Indian matters are now in a period of transition. *The operation of the Severalty Law is steadily breaking up the reservation system and scattering Indians on individual holdings. The Indians are rapidly becoming citizens, with local rights and duties. In view of these facts, some of the Indian agencies should now be discontinued, the district-school system should be introduced as rapidly as possible; and the time is coming when the Indian Bureau, as a distinct department of government, may well be abolished, and the education of the Indian be placed - where it naturally belongs in the Bureau of Education, until it shall ultimately be relegated to the individual States.*

To recapitulate, we ask:
1. That the five civilized tribes of the Indian Territory be persuaded to accept a territorial government.
2. That the laws be modified so as to render it possible for Indians to sell or lease their lands only by permission of a judge of the United States District Court.
3. That, as far as possible, work and markets be provided for Indians by organizations and individuals, and that rations and annuities be stopped as rapidly as a proper equivalent is provided.
4. *That provision be made by law for meeting, from Indian funds, the expenses of local improvements and taxes which would naturally fall on Indians now made untaxable by law.* (Emphasis added).
5. That the duties, powers, and duration of office of the Superintendent of Indian Schools be defined by law, and his salary be made adequate.
6. That the spirit of the civil service reform should be applied to the appointment of Indian agents as well as other officials.
7. That larger appropriations be made to enforce law in Alaska, and also to provide reindeer for the natives.
8. That the work of transition be expedited by discontinuing some of the Indian agencies and introducing the district-school system among the Indians; while we look forward to the eventual abolition of the Indian Bureau and the relegation of Indian schools to the care of the individual States.
9. That all religious bodies now receiving government aid for contract schools follow the example of other denominations in withdrawing their request for such aid.
10. That the religious bodies redouble their efforts in distinctively religious and moral work on behalf of the Indians. (Emphasis added). **12 Report of the Annual Lake Mohonk Conference on the Indian and Other Dependent Peoples (1894), pp. 149-151.**

13 Report of the Annual Lake Mohonk Conference on the Indian and Other Dependent Peoples (1895).

PLATFORM OF THE THIRTEENTH ANNUAL CONFERENCE OF THE FRIENDS OF THE INDIANS.

We, the members of the Lake Mohonk Conference, in this its *Thirteenth* annual meeting, reaffirm its utterances of past years, and especially of last year. *The reservation system is an insuperable obstacle to civilization, and should be abolished, the tribal organization destroyed, the lands allotted in severalty, the Indians intermingled with the whites, and the Indians treated as other men.* (Emphasis added).

II. Until the Indian comes into complete ownership of his allotment, he should have the special protection of the federal government, special federal officers should be endowed with magisterial authority for the administration of local justice, the bureau should have power and means to employ and assign counsel for the legal protection of his rights, he should be guarded by adequate legislation from the land robber, the gambler, and the liquor-dealer, he should not be allowed to sell or lease his lands except upon permission first obtained from a federal judge, and provision should be made for the secular and industrial education of all Indian children of school age in schools supported by and under the exclusive control of the government, State or federal.

III. *It is unrepublican and un-American to permit the existence of any landed class in the community exempt from taxation. Such exemption is equally unjust to the taxed and to the untaxed. The taxes otherwise due on the allotment of the Indian citizen, so long as by a protected title his land is exempt, should be provided for out of Indian funds in the hands of the national government, or, if there are no such funds, out of the general treasury.* (Emphasis added).

IV. No Indian tribe should be transferred from one reservation to another without its consent, and rarely, if ever, even with its consent. Rations should be given only where required by existing treaty stipulations or to avert imminent starvation, and should be done away with entirely as soon as practicable. Distribution of money per capita is often disastrous, and should be made with increased caution.

V. The nation possesses a supreme sovereignty over every foot of soil within its boundaries. Its legislative authority over its people it has neither right nor power to alienate. Its attempt to do so by Indian treaties in the past does not relieve it from the responsibility for the condition of government in the reservations and in the Indian Territory; and, despite those treaties, it is under a sacred obligation to exercise its sovereignty by extending over the three hundred thousand whites and fifty thousand so-called Indians in the Indian Territory the same restraints and protection of government which other parts of the country enjoy.

VI. The best of laws are useless unless they are faithfully and equitably enforced. Such enforcement through the Indian Department is impossible unless appointments are made only for merit, removals only for cause; and the tenure of administrative officials is to this extent made permanent. We congratulate the country upon the evidence which the history of the past year has afforded that it is the purpose of the department to administer the Indian Bureau upon this principle, and we call upon Congress to cooperate with the Executive in such measures as may be necessary to secure permanently the Indian Bureau from the fatal incursion of the spoils system.

VII. The government alone cannot solve the Indian problem. Our American civilization is founded upon Christianity. A pagan people cannot be fitted for citizenship without learning the principles and acquiring something of the spirit of a Christian people. The duty of the Church is increased, and the hopefulness of accomplishing it is made more reasonable, by every advance the government makes in providing protection and secular education for the Indian race. The progress already made toward the dissolution of organic barbarism, the opening already afforded for free Christian work, eloquently summon Christian philanthropists to furnish that contribution which nothing but unofficial, voluntary, and Christian service can furnish toward the emancipation and elevation of the Indian. **13 Report of the Annual Lake Mohonk Conference on the Indian and Other Dependent Peoples (1895), p. 105.**

14 Report of the Annual Lake Mohonk Conference on the Indian and Other Dependent Peoples (1896).

THE MOHONK PLATFORM.

p. 149 The Mohonk Conference has now completed twelve years of work in the Indian reform. In this period a large advance has been made. The interest of the nation in the condition of the Indian has been greatly increased. Legislation has been secured of great value, culminating in the Severalty Law, the happy result of which will be to break up the reservation system and make the Indian a citizen. Great principles have been established. This Conference regards it as settled that the Indian is to be treated as a man, and ought to be put on the footing of other men. The unfortunate relation which he has held as a ward of the nation is a relation which is incompatible with his manhood, and should be brought to an end as soon as possible.

We believe the Indian has all the natural qualifications necessary for his education, civilization, and Christianization; and we are satisfied that, while we must be careful not to deprive him of his rights, we must be equally careful not to pauperize nor enervate him by undue paternalism.

New needs are constantly arising; and there is, undoubtedly, work still for all friends of the Indian in carrying out the principles already established to their logical results.

We find that, in the actual condition of the Indian, much yet remains to be done to secure him his rights, and to give him a proper place in the land as a man, a citizen, and a brother.

The wide-spread corruption existing in the Indian Territory, as the result of its present autonomous reservation system, should excite alarm and indignation in the minds of all good citizens. We earnestly hope that the measures now being taken by the government to induce the five civilized tribes to take land in severalty, and exchange their tribal governments for a territorial government, may prove successful.

Recent laws permitting Indians to lease their lands are widely resulting in dispossessing ignorant Indians of their property rights, without an adequate return, to their great disadvantage and the enriching of designing white men. We recommend, therefore, that the law be so modified as to render it possible for Indians to sell or lease their lands only by permission of a judge of the United States District Court, upon the same principles which protect the lands of minor heirs among the whites from alienation.

We regard it as of the utmost importance that the Indian be encouraged to support himself and his family by work. On this account we deprecate present conditions tending to make the Indian a pauper, such as issuing rations and annuities, and the lack of work and of markets for Indian productions. We commend the efforts of organizations and of individuals to provide work and markets, and we believe that rations and annuities should be discontinued as rapidly as proper equivalents can be provided.

We reiterate the affirmation of our platform of 1893: that, from funds now held by the United States or hereafter created for the benefit of the Indians, provision should be made by law for their fair share of the expense of local improvements and taxes, that these burdens may not rest unjustly on the communities and States which include in their territory the lands of Indians who hold under a protected title and are exempt from taxation.

We are glad to learn that the Secretary of the Interior has expressed his purpose to suggest to Congress at the coming session the passage of an act to define the duties, powers, and duration of office of the Superintendent of Indian Schools, thereby removing the office from the crippling influence of the spoils system, and securing men of the highest educational ability. Such a law would tend to place the Indian schools in a condition of efficiency equal to that of the best public schools in the land. The salary of this office should be commensurate with its importance. We regret that it has been recently reduced to a point wholly inadequate.

The Severalty Law, and other reforms inaugurated for the benefit of the Indians, are effective chiefly as they are executed by fit men. It is of the utmost importance at this juncture that Indian and allotting agents be men of stanch (sic) integrity and high character. Their tenure of office should not be subject to political changes. We therefore urge, in order that the best men possible be secured, that larger salaries be paid, and that the administration select these agents, in accordance with the spirit of the Civil Service Law for their fitness only.

We further respectfully urge the President of the United States to extend by executive order the operation of the Civil Service Law to the positions of disciplinarian, assistant matron, farmer, and industrial teacher in the Indian service; also, that agents' clerks and those of bonded superintendents of schools should be selected by the agents and superintendents themselves.

Our attention has been called to the needs of Alaska. This part of our country is peculiarly endangered from the introduction of intoxicating liquors among the Indians. We earnestly hope that the government will appropriate a larger sum for the enforcement of law. A further appropriation is also essential to provide the natives with reindeer. We also urge larger appropriations for schools, and we recommend that the advantage of appropriations for agricultural stations be extended to Alaska as to the other Territories.

Indian matters are now in a period of transition. The operation of the Severalty Law is steadily breaking up the reservation system and scattering Indians on individual holdings. The Indians are rapidly becoming citizens, with local rights and duties. In view of these facts, some of the Indian agencies should now be discontinued, the district-school system should be introduced as rapidly as possible; and the time is coming when the Indian Bureau, as a distinct department of government, may well be abolished, and the education of the Indian be placed where it naturally belongs in connection with the Bureau of Education, until it shall ultimately be relegated to the individual States. This Conference unhesitatingly disapproves the continuance of any appropriation of public moneys for sectarian schools for the Indians, and it rejoices that several denominations have withdrawn their requests for such appropriations: and it earnestly expresses the hope that all other religious bodies now receiving aid will follow this example, and so affirm the distinctively American principle of separation between Church and State. We strongly urge the religious denominations of this country thus released from the demands of the secular education of Indian youth to redouble their efforts in distinctly religious and moral work on behalf of the Indians. **14 Report of the Annual Lake Mohonk Conference on the Indian and Other Dependent Peoples (1896), p. 149.**

15 Report of the Annual Lake Mohonk Conference on the Indian and Other Dependent Peoples (1897).

Platform.

The Lake Mohonk Indian Conference, during the fifteen years of its existence, has seen vast changes for the better in the condition of the Indian. In this period the education of Indian youth has been systematically undertaken by government (the appropriations for this purpose having increased one hundred and thirty fold); this education has been for the most part freed from anomalous alliance with religious bodies ... has become more and more industrial in character; the Civil Service Reform has been extended to nearly all subordinate officials who have to do with the Indian; corruption and fraud in the purchase of Indian supplies are largely a thing of the past; Congress has given unwonted (sic) attention to Indian reform, and has framed wise laws for securing to the Indian his lands in severalty, thus breaking up the tribal relation, protecting him from injustice and securing order; Indian wars seem to have ceased; while the religious bodies of this land have increased their missionary effort, and brought the larger part of the Indian tribes under the influence of the gospel.

The most recent advance made has been in the line of an effective extension of law for protecting the Indian from the liquor traffic, and in the great reform inaugurated in the government of the Indian Territory. We congratulate the United States government on the success of the commission appointed to treat with Indians in that Territory, and we are glad that Congress has decided by legal enactment to put an end to the unhappy condition of affairs there, and to establish a government, essentially territorial in character, in the Territory.

In view of all these facts it is plain that the civilization of the Indian is steadily advancing, and that our great task must be to see that the machinery already provided to secure this end be kept at work, and be rightly worked. We have the following suggestions to make;

1. This Conference urges that the Civil Service Reform should on no account be impaired in its efficiency in Indian matters. There is reason to fear, however, that there is a failure in some quarters to enforce the law, both in its spirit and the letter, and there are abuses remaining on certain of the reservations which a strict application of the law would remedy.

2. *The severalty law has already proved itself a great blessing to the Indian, and we are convinced that the time has come when certain of the existing agencies should be discontinued, both for the better progress of the Indian, and in order to save the people of the country a needless expense.*

3. It is recognized that the issuing of rations to the Indians is a great injury, pauperizing them, and destroying their energy and character. We again affirm that in all cases where such rations are not issued under treaty obligations, wherever such action can be taken, they should speedily cease, and that it is most desirable that, as rapidly as possible, treaty rights or contracts which require the issuing of such rations be modified, so that national obligations to the Indians may be met in less objectionable ways.

4. We recognize the great value of industrial education for the Indian, but it is plain that, while we teach him habits of labor and ways of work, it is necessary also to help him to find a market for the results of his industry.

5. We commend the admirable system of the present superintendent of Indian education, and we think that it should be continued.

6. *We reaffirm our conviction that government appropriations to contract schools under the control of any religious body whatever should cease without further delay.*

7. During past years the friends of the Indian have been repeatedly obliged to raise considerable sums of money (this year amounting to over $6,000) to defend in the courts of law the rights of the Mission Indians of California, although such defense was conducted in the name of the government. Since this is a matter which properly belongs to the government, we urge upon it to make adequate provision for such legal defense in any emergency which may arise.

8. Recognizing the success of the effort of Dr. Sheldon Jackson to introduce domesticated reindeer among the Eskimos of Alaska, we urge Congress to increase the appropriation for this purpose. We request it also to furnish better postal facilities to missionaries and others in Alaska, using the reindeer, if necessary, for winter service.

9. We earnestly renew our request that the number of field matrons be increased, and that an additional appropriation be made to cover their needful expenses and supplies. We do this believing that their work is vital in its influence on Indian homes.

10. We recognize the wise liberality of the present Secretary of the Interior in restoring to the Indian youth of the State of New York the privilege of education at Hampton and Carlisle.

11. *In the progress of events a new emphasis must now be laid on the importance of religious training for the Indian. All doors are open as never before for him to receive the uplifting influence of the gospel.* We call upon the Christian people of this land, and especially upon the missionary societies, by no means to diminish, but rather to increase their missionary efforts, and to seek to win speedily as possible the Christianity which is the strength and blessing of this nation. (Emphasis added). **15 Report of the Annual Lake Mohonk Conference on the Indian and Other Dependent Peoples (1897), pp. 114-115.**
16 Report of the Annual Lake Mohonk Conference on the Indian and Other Dependent Peoples (1898).

PLATFORM OF THE SIXTEENTH ANNUAL CONFERENCE OF THE FRIENDS OF THE INDIANS.

Great progress has been made in dealing with the Indian races in our country. The nation no longer regards them as a hostile people, nor even as a foreign people. The reforms inaugurated under President Grant have been carried forward toward their logical results. The policy of discontinuing the reservation system has been accepted; in many of the reservations the land has been allotted in severalty, and the surplus land sold for the benefit of the Indians; less money is spent in rations, which pauperize, and much more in schools, which prepare for self-support; the Government has recognized the value of the education of the Indian women in their homes, in the domestic arts, and has increased the appropriations to carry on that work. The anomalous partnership between the National Government and the churches has been discontinued, and now only one denominational body looks to the Government for aid in support of its schools; the schools of the other denominations are supported by themselves, and the Government itself has assumed the responsibility for organizing and carrying on the work of the secular education of all Indian children of school age on the reservation.

Nevertheless, the Indian problem is still far from solution. A needlessly expensive system is maintained, nominally to care for the Indian, but in too large measure to care for party and political favorites. The schools, the clerks in the Bureau at Washington, and the Agency physicians have been brought under the Civil Service, but, with these exceptions, the Indian Bureau remains a political machine, subject to change in all its personnel after every Presidential election.

By both Democratic and Republican administrations men have been put at the head of the Indian Bureau who are neither familiar with Indian affairs nor acquainted with methods of education. Indian agents and Indian inspectors have been appointed without training or evidence of their fitness for the office. In more than one instance a drunken official has been appointed on a reservation, and well-authenticated complaints have failed to secure his removal, or have resulted only in his transfer to another field with an increased salary. In cases in which the reservation has been discontinued and the land has been allotted in severalty, the machinery of the agency has been retained, though no considerable service is required, and the retention is clearly against the spirit of the law. These evils have shown themselves alike when the appointments have been left with the Indian Commissioner, when they have been reserved by the Secretary of the Interior to himself, and when they have been practically left to local politicians.

Some excellent officials have been appointed, and some excellent work has been accomplished; but this is not because, but in spite of, the system. Two illustrations of the evils of the system have been afforded during the past year. The first is the removal of Dr. Hailmann, notwithstanding his splendid record as Superintendent of Indian Schools, attested by protest against his removal from men of all parties and all sections who are familiar with his work, including many educational experts. The second is the outbreak of some of the Chippewa Indians, whose valuable pine timber the Government, by the agreement of 1889, covenanted to sell for their benefit, and is still appraising and reappraising as a preliminary to such sale-two successive appraisements, extravagantly conducted at the expense of the Indians, having already been set aside as worthless, with a third appraisement now in progress.

We have appealed to successive administrations to remedy these abuses, and the abuses still continue. We now appeal to the people of the United States to demand of their Government that the Indian Bureau be taken out of politics, that the Indian Commissioner be no longer treated as a political officer, to be changed with every change of administration; that the work of the Bureau be entrusted to experts, and left in their hands until it is accomplished. And we also appeal to them to demand of Congress that it recognize that the Indian Bureau is of necessity a temporary institution, and should be discontinued at the earliest practicable moment; that it expedite the dissolution of the reservation, and the allotment of the land in severalty; that it give all Indians everywhere a right to appeal to the courts, and render all Indians everywhere accountable to the courts; and that it thus prepare the way for the abolition of a costly policy, unjust to the Indians, injurious to the whites, and an impediment to civilization.

Resolved, That a committee of seven, of which the Chairman of the Conference shall be the Chairman, and which shall have power to increase the number, be appointed by the chair to prepare during the next year a scheme adapted to carry out the policy outlined in the above platform and appeal, and to propose it to the next Conference for its action; that the Committee be also authorized to gather, in the interim before the next Conference, specific facts concerning defects and abuses on Indian administration, and in behalf of this Conference, in their discretion, to present them to Congress, the Executive, and to the Press.

Congress should pass the liquor bill approved by Commissioner Browning, or some other bill equally stringent.

We further recommend that special attention be paid to the subject of marriage and divorce among the Indians, so as to bring their family relations under the laws of the States or Territories within whose bounds they reside.

That the Indian agents should not be removed because of a change of administration.

Further, we commend the admirable methods of the present Superintendent of Indian Education, and we desire that he may be retained to carry out the plans that he has inaugurated.

That the Indian schools be incorporated in the school systems of the several States and Territories, the United States paying the expense of the education of the Indian youth so long as they are the wards of the nation.

That the work of surveying the reservations should as speedily as possible be completed, so that Indians may be enabled to locate their claims.

That Indians on reservations should not be allowed to connect themselves with shows travelling about the world to exhibit the savagery from which we are trying to reclaim them.

That the anomalous and deplorable conditions in the Indian Territory should be remedied. Convinced that this can be done with justice to all parties, we desire the *speedy passage of the Curtis Bill* which passed the House at the last session, with such modifications only as will promote its efficiency and enable the Dawes Commission to introduce the Indians of the Five Civilized Tribes to the full rights of American citizenship. The utter failure of these tribes to protect the rights of citizen Indians in the tribal property lays upon our government the obligation to enforce the fulfilment of the trust which the tribal governments assumed in behalf of the individual members of each tribe; and the duty of protecting life and property in the Territory devolves upon the United States.

That it is of immediate importance that the natives of Alaska be put under the protection of organized Territorial law, and be prepared for citizenship.

That coordinate with the work of the government in providing the best facilities for the intellectual and moral training of the Indian must be that of the preacher and teacher of religion. We therefore urge all Christian people to vigorously re-enforce the work carried on by their missionary societies during this brief transition period until the Indian shall be redeemed from paganism and incorporated into our Christian life as well as into our national citizenship. **16 Report of the Annual Lake Mohonk Conference on the Indian and Other Dependent Peoples (1898), pp. 112-113.**

17 Report of the Annual Lake Mohonk Conference on the Indian and Other Dependent Peoples (1899).

Preface.

Instead of formulating a platform, as has been the rule heretofore, the report of a special committee appointed last year, Mr. Philip C. Garrett chairman, was unanimously adopted, and at the conclusion of the meeting several paragraphs were added. These declarations will be found on page 88.

We are for a *vanishing policy* in Indian affairs-a policy that shall press Indian peculiarities to the vanishing point, and shall speedily give to all Indians the laws, the privileges, the schools and the opportunities which are good enough for all other American citizens, and are good enough, and none too good, for Indians! (Emphasis added). **17 Report of the Annual Lake Mohonk Conference on the Indian and Other Dependent Peoples (1899), p. 11.**

1. Abolishing the Indian agencies as rapidly as possible, and putting the Indians thereof who are not ready to be thrown wholly upon their own resources in the care of the superintendent of the agency school. Seventeen agencies are suggested which might soon be abolished.
2. The complete abandonment of the distribution of rations and annuities to the Indians by some process consistent with justice and wisely adapted to the conditions of the various tribes.
3. The placing of Indian agents in the classified list, thereby relieving the appointing officer from the pressure of politicians in this respect.
4. Enlarging the powers of the Commissioner of Indian affairs, so that he may no longer be held responsible for that which he cannot control. **17 Report of the Annual Lake Mohonk Conference on the Indian and Other Dependent Peoples (1899), p. 33.**

With reference to the last part of the resolution, suggesting a recital of facts including specific cases of defect and abuse in Indian administration, the committee have this to say: Most of the evils that now afflict the Indian service are due to what is known as the spoils system and the conclusion of the Executive Department of our Government to surrender the prerogative of appointing officials in the service to political leaders, who too frequently select them without regard to merit or special fitness from among those to whom they owe rewards for party and personal fealty; often in utter disregard of the adaptation of their nominees to the place to be filled, sometimes by persons notoriously intemperate, immoral and dishonest. Indian progress was formerly obstructed mainly by the hostility of the whites along the border, by false allegations of warlike uprisings and by robbery on a large scale.

To these evils has succeeded the spoils system, which deprives them of proper instructors and caretakers, and which wins the assent of many good men out of a blind sympathy for the administration or party of which they are honest adherents. **17 Report of the Annual Lake Mohonk Conference on the Indian and Other Dependent Peoples (1899), p. 34.**

1. The defense of the rights of allotted Indians, especially by the registration of family and individual names, and the protection of rights of inheritance.
2. The continued breaking up of reservations by allotment of land in severalty, yet not in anticipation of the ability of the Indians to support themselves. We especially direct attention to the New York Indians as ripe for allotment.
3. The prohibition of the taking of Indians from their reservation for the purpose of

perpetuating by public exhibition of the conditions of barbarism. **17 Report of the Annual Lake Mohonk Conference on the Indian and Other Dependent Peoples (1899), p. 88.**

There are four great institutions which are the true foundation of the higher civilization, and with them there are four corresponding passions dormant in each human soul which relate each human being to these four institutions. I use these words in the highest and largest sense in which it is possible to use them: home, society, country, and the church.

To know the power and influence of these four institutions is to comprehend the real power of modern civilization, and if the Indian is to come into contact with civilization it must be through the four great forces which are represented by them. No man knows what it is to live, in the largest and deepest sense, until he discovers his true and real self by feeling the four great passions of the human soul which express its real life: love of home, love of humanity, love of country and love of God. ... When love of home, love of humanity in its largest sense, love of country with its commanding loyalty to the Government as a government of the whole country, and above all, around and through all, there comes the supreme passion born of a love of God, then will the Indian become a citizen possessed of that life which makes him, as all other men, a being in whom civilization is finding its true self-realization and its deepest meaning. It is the giving of himself along the line of these four passions, to these four fundamental institutions, that will bear him into the very heart and make him a citizen of God's republic. (Emphasis added). **17 Report of the Annual Lake Mohonk Conference on the Indian and Other Dependent Peoples (1899), p. 39.**

18 Report of the Annual Lake Mohonk Conference on the Indian and Other Dependent Peoples (1900).

PLATFORM OF THE EIGHTEENTH ANNUAL LAKE MOHONK CONFERENCE OF FRIENDS OF THE INDIAN AND OTHER DEPENDENT PEOPLES.

This eighteenth annual session of the Lake Mohonk Indian Conference affirms its hearty and unanimous approval of the statement of the Indian Commissioner that it would be better for the Indians if they had been treated from the beginning as individuals subject to the laws of the land. To overcome the difficulties which the natural error of the past has created, and to bring the Indian into individual relations with the Government as a citizen of the United States with the least intermediate injustice and hardship, is the Indian problem. The discontinuance of treaties with the Indian tribes as separate nationalities, the allotment of land in severalty, the gradual decrease of rations, the increase of appropriations for providing all Indian children of school age with the essentials of an English education, the consequent discontinuance of the contract school system with the un-American union of the Church and State which that system involved, are all parts of this one coherent and consistent general policy.

Rations should be issued only when succor is indispensable to prevent what would otherwise be unpreventable distress.

Where allotments are made in arid districts an ample supply of water for purposes of irrigation and domestic requirements should be provided under such arrangements as, within their natural possibilities, will secure its permanence and will make its subsequent diversion impossible.

The family is the basis of civilization, and marriage is the basis of the family; therefore, marriage should be regulated and protected by law, and a system of registration of births, marriages and deaths should be provided such as will secure the legal recognition of the family, and thus protect the right of the Indian to transmit by inheritance his lands to his legal heirs.

The habit of leasing allotments converts the lessee from an industrious worker into an idle and improvident landlord. It should, therefore, be permitted only to allotees who suffer from some infirmity or disability which incapacitates them from obtaining in any other way the benefit of their allotment; and the power of the agent to authorize such leases should be strictly limited by law to such carefully defined exceptions.

This Conference believes that Indian legislation should continue to be so shaped and the Indian Bureau should continue to be so conducted as to render the need of Government supervision constantly less and to secure its total abolition at the earliest practicable moment... **18 Report of the Annual Lake Mohonk Conference on the Indian and Other Dependent Peoples (1900), pp. 7-8.**

19 Report of the Annual Lake Mohonk Conference on the Indian and Other Dependent Peoples (1901).

PLATFORM OF THE NINETEENTH ANNUAL LAKE MOHONK CONFERENCE OF FRIENDS OF THE INDIAN AND OTHER DEPENDENT PEOPLES.

REPORT OF THE BUSINESS COMMITTEE.

The nineteenth annual session of the Lake Mohonk Indian Conference congratulates the country on the gratifying evidence of healthy progress and important results attendant upon efforts that have been put forth in recent years for the education and elevation of the Indian race, seen in a federal school system providing for the education of upward of 25,000 Indian children, and the allotment of over 6,500,000 acres of land to over 55,000 Indians, with a secure individual title, and in the possession by these Indians of all the rights, privileges and immunities of citizenship. We note with special satisfaction the action of the Department of the Interior, since our last meeting, in issuing regulations for licensing and solemnizing marriages of Indians, for keeping family records of all agencies, and for preventing polygamous marriages. There still remain evils to be corrected and work to be done. The frequent changes in the Indian service, involving both removals and appointments for purely political reasons, lead us to suggest to the President the propriety of framing and promulgating some rules prescribing such methods in nominating agents as will put an end to this abuse. The same pressure for patronage operates to delay or prevent the abolition of needless agencies. Congress, at its last session, acting on the recommendation of the Indian Commissioner, abolished three such agencies. There are at least half a score more which, in the judgment of experts, should be abolished as sinecures, which not only involve needless expense to the country, but also operate deleteriously upon emancipated Indians.

We recognize the administrative perplexities attending the allotting and leasing of lands: there are the aged and infirm, the feeble and incompetent, women and children; many who prefer other occupations than that of farming or grazing; others who, by renting their lands, may be able to pursue their education; all of whom, under a just system of leasing, would derive great advantage from holdings which would otherwise be valueless. But indiscriminate leasing, which strengthens the white man's hold on the Indian's land, and encourages lazy landlordism in the Indian, should be prevented, either by more stringent legislation, or by a careful scrutiny of all leasing recommended by agents in the field.

The tribal funds held in trust for Indians by the Government of the United States should be placed to the credit of individual Indians, who are entitled to share in them as rapidly as lists of such individuals in each tribe can be prepared and recorded. Children born after the preparation of such lists should share in such funds only by inheritance, and not as members of a tribe; and, so far as possible, consistent with the spirit and the equitable intent of the special terms which created each such fund, these funds should thus be broken up into individual holdings, when provision shall have been made for certain educational uses for all the members of the tribe, and perhaps for payment of territorial, state and county taxes on allotted lands during all or part of the period of protected titles. The money which belongs to the Indian should be paid to the Indians as rapidly as they are pronounced fit to receive it, that by receiving and using, each his own money, Indian citizens may be educated to the use of money.

Improvements are doubtless required in our Indian schools. This Conference puts itself on record as believing in schools, both in the Indian neighborhoods and at a distance from them; and the proportion to be maintained between the two must be left to be determined from time to time by experience. The eventual result to be reached is the abolition of all distinctively Indian schools, and the incorporation of Indian pupils in the schools of the country.

The importance of the native Indian industries is such that the Government, and all teachers and guides of the Indian, should cooperate in the endeavor to revive them. To the Indian, they are valuable as a means of profitable occupation and natural expression; to the country, as specimens of a rare and indigenous art, many of them artistically excellent; some of them absolutely unique; all of them adapted to furnish congenial and remunerative employment at home, and to foster, in the Indian, self-respect, and in the white race, respect for the Indians.

The evil condition of Indian reservations in the State of New York has been a matter of frequent consideration. This Conference emphasizes the recommendation made in December, 1900, by a committee of five appointed by the then governor, Theo. Roosevelt, that these reservations be allotted in severalty; and it urges Congress to consider at an early day the practicability of enacting such legislation as will accomplish this result without further delay.

The experience of the past indicates the errors which we should avoid; the principles by which we should be guided; and the ends which we should seek in our relations with all dependent races under American sovereignty. Capacity for self-government in dependent and inexperienced races, is a result to be achieved by patient and persistent endeavor; it is not to be assumed that they already possess it. Meanwhile, the duty of administering government for the benefit of the governed involves the obligation of selecting all officials, not with regard to services which have been rendered to their party, but solely with regard to the services which they will render to the governed community. Loyalty to the American spirit requires us so to organize and administer government over dependent peoples, as will most speedily prepare them for self-government. All men under American sovereignty, whatever their race or religion, should be treated as equals before the law; amenable to the same legal penalties for their offenses, and secured in the same legal protection for their rights. The principle recognized by all experts in social science, and abundantly confirmed by American experience, should prevent the Federal Government from granting any permanent franchises in any of our territories. Lands which have come, or shall come, into the possession of the United States, should be held in trust for the people of the territory, and, as far as practicable, should be disposed of to actual settlers in the spirit of the homestead laws. In all territories of the United States the Federal Government should see that public schools are provided under federal control, and, when necessary, at federal expense, for the education of all children of school age, until permanent governments are organized able to provide and maintain such schools. The Christian religion is the basis of Christian civilization; and the new opportunities opened before the American people, and the new responsibilities laid upon them, demand the co-operation of all the Christian churches in an endeavor to inculcate the principles, and impart the spirit, of the gospel of Christ. In brief, the object of action, whether governmental, philanthropic or religious, should be to secure to these dependent peoples just government, righteous laws, industrial opportunities, adequate education and a pure and free religion. **19 Report of the Annual Lake Mohonk Conference on the Indian and Other Dependent Peoples (1901).**

20 Report of the Annual Lake Mohonk Conference on the Indian and Other Dependent Peoples (1902).

PLATFORM OF THE TWENTIETH ANNUAL LAKE MOHONK CONFERENCE OF FRIENDS OF THE INDIAN, 1902.

Much has already been accomplished. About thirty years ago our Government decided to make no more treaties with Indian tribes. Then in 1887 was passed the Dawes Severalty Act, securing the Indians possession of land in severalty, and with such possession making them American citizens. Since the passage of this law the work has gone steadily forward. Already over seventy thousand allotments have been made, and as many Indians have become citizens.

In this work of elevating the Indian and giving him his place in our land on an equality with the white man and enjoying the same privileges, what yet remains to be done? The work of dividing the Indian reservations and allotting to each Indian his own piece of land to be held in severalty, must be pushed to completion. Indian reservations must cease to be, together with all the machinery that has been connected with them. The Indian agent is less and less needed, and the office should be discontinued at an early date. In the meantime, we rejoice in what has been done by the Commissioner of Indian Affairs in breaking up polygamy, securing the purity of homes, and the proper registration of families. We desire to see this work go forward until every family is properly constituted and fully registered. We cordially approve the order emanating from the Commissioner's office to diminish, and as soon as possible, to prevent various savage and pagan practices. We believe that the Government is fully justified in efforts to break up habits and customs among the Indians that interfere with their advance in civilization. The action of the Secretary of the Interior in forbidding Indians to take part in Indian war-paint shows, especially at public expositions, is highly to be commended, and we trust that no influence will succeed in securing a reversal of this policy. We are glad to note that lately not less than twelve thousand Indians have been dropped from the ration rolls of the Government, and that the Government has encouraged them to earn their bread by furnishing them work and paying them with money which would otherwise have gone for rations.

We would reiterate the previous utterances of this Conference as to the importance of choosing trustworthy and fit men to carry on the duties of the Government in dealing with the Indian. Whatever dishonor has come to our nation from its dealing with the Indian has not come from its purpose, which has been just and humane, but from the fact that the execution of the purpose has frequently been committed to unworthy instruments. The choice of Indian agents and every other public servant connected with Indian affairs should be most carefully made.

Added evidence confirms this Conference in the belief heretofore expressed, that the Indian should be subject to all the rights and privileges of a citizen -- well secured in the General Severalty Act of Feb. 8, 1887. That act provides that trust patents issued in the allotment of lands shall be of legal effect, and declares that the United States does and will hold the land thus allotted for the period of twenty-five years in trust, for the sole use and benefit of the Indian to whom such allotment has been made. The decision of the Secretary of the Interior that he has authority to annul a trust patent at his discretion at any time during the life of the patent is opposed to the spirit of the act, and seems to us detrimental to the interests of the Indian, as it renders his holdings insecure, and thus lessens the incentive to industry and thrift. We are, therefore, of the opinion that any defects which may exist in the present statute to render such a decision possible should be remedied by new legislation.

Experience under the Severalty Act has shown the need of freeing the Indians from the restraints heretofore surrounding trade. The fullest opportunity should now be afforded him to sell in the highest and buy in the lowest market obtainable. We urge that former conflicting legislation be repealed, and that any person of good moral character shall, upon application, be granted a license by the Commissioner of Indian Affairs to trade within any Indian reservation; also, that when Indians have been allotted lands in severalty no such license shall be required within such allotted lands.

The necessity for allotting all Indian lands so that each Indian will hold his land in severalty applies with equal force to the Seneca Indians of New York, who were not included in the Dawes Severalty Act. This Conference is convinced that the social and political conditions existing on the reservations involved are most serious in their nature, and make it important that these Indians be at once brought fully under the laws of the State of New York and of the United States, and thus become citizens. We therefore respectfully urge upon Congress the prompt passage of H. R. Bill No. 12270, known as the Vreeland Bill, introduced at the last session of Congress, and already favorably reported by the House Committee. But we believe the bill should be passed without the amendment requiring the consent of the Indians affected, thus bringing it into harmony, in this respect, with the terms of the Dawes Severalty Act.

The next great step necessary for the good of the Indian, and for his protection from the machinations of designing white men, is to break up the great tribal funds held by the Government into individual holdings. A share should be apportioned to each individual member of the tribe, and placed to his credit on the books of the Treasury of the United States, interest being paid thereon, while as soon as practicable the principal itself of each individual share should be paid to the Indian to whom it belongs.

This Conference desires to call attention to the peculiar needs of the Navajo Indians. These people are especially worthy, being industrious and self-reliant; but they are the only tribe which has no adequate school privileges, while they are also in danger at this time of starvation. They are not to blame, but suffer from adverse conditions, and their necessities should be met by the Government.

The educational work that has been maintained by our Government among the Indians is admirable, and should be steadily extended till a good public school education is made possible to every Indian child. We are looking, however, to the time when schools maintained by the National Government shall be discontinued, and all Indian youth shall be trained in the public schools and higher institutions of the states or territories.

The most important work for man is his religious training. This necessarily falls to the missionary societies of our different churches. Their labors, ever important, have now become indispensable for the uplifting of the Indians. We are heartily in favor of such missionary effort, and warmly commend it to public sympathy and support. This is work the Government cannot undertake, and it must be done by private beneficence.

...

To recapitulate we favor:-

The allotment in severalty of the lands of the New York Indians, and to this end the prompt passage of H.R. Bill No. 12270.

The discontinuance of Indian agencies where no longer needed.

The breaking up into individual holdings of the great tribal trust funds.

The omission of the public exhibition of pagan customs.

The establishment of unrestricted trade at Indian agencies.

The still further development of the present policy of the Indian Bureau of furnishing work and paying for it instead of giving out rations.

We emphasize the importance of selecting only trustworthy men as the agents of the Government.

We urge that trust patents should be made, if not so already, independent of any power of annulment by any officer of the Government.

We approve the Government schools, but look to see them eventually superseded by the schools of the states and territories where the Indians live.

We especially commend all missionary work, in whatever form undertaken, by missionary societies for the moral and religious elevation of the Indians. **20 Report of the Annual Lake Mohonk Conference on the Indian and Other Dependent Peoples (1902), pp. 9-10.**

21 Report of the Annual Lake Mohonk Conference on the Indian and Other Dependent Peoples (1903).

1903 PLATFORM OF THE TWENTY-FIRST ANNUAL LAKE MOHONK CONFERENCE OF FRIENDS OF THE INDIAN.

The Indian problem is approaching its solution, leaving us confronting the larger problem of our duties toward the people who have recently become subject to our Government and dependent on our care. In dealing with the Indians the objects to be accomplished are no longer questioned: they are the abandonment of the reservation system; the discontinuance of Indian agencies; such education of all Indian children as will fit them for self-support and self-government; access to the courts for the protection of their rights; amenability to the law in punishment for their crimes; the same liberty that white men enjoy to own, buy, sell, travel, pay taxes, and enjoy in good government the benefits enjoyed by other taxed citizens; and by these means a speedy incorporation of all Indians, with all the rights of citizenship, into the American commonwealth.

The best methods to secure these results are not wholly clear, but the experience of the past points to the following conclusions: The agency should be discontinued in all cases where the land is ready for settlement, and the Indians, when necessary, should be temporarily placed under the care of a bonded superintendent with limited powers, and the policy of the Indian Bureau in this direction is strongly commended. Whenever practicable the education of Indian children should be provided for in the schools of the States or Territories, if necessary for untaxed Indians at Federal expense or out of Indian funds; wherever this is not practicable, provision should be made by the Federal Government in Indian schools. The Indians should be encouraged in arts, both in the preservation of their own and in the acquisition of ours; the end should always be their industrial and moral development. The work of the Government, whether National, State, or Territorial, in providing secular education does not lessen the responsibility of the churches for the religious education of the Indians; we regard with interest and hope the recent action of the Secretary of the Interior opening the way for the religious work of the churches in connection with Government schools, and we urge the churches to co-operate with each other and with the Government in this work. The same principle should govern us in all our dealings with other dependent people; their civil rights should be scrupulously safeguarded; liberal provision should be made by Congress for their development and civilization; their industries should be encouraged; and their education should be so provided for that, whatever may be their final political relations to the United States, they may be equipped, at the earliest possible day, for self-support and self-government. **21 Report of the Annual Lake Mohonk Conference on the Indian and Other Dependent Peoples (1903), pp. 112-113.**

22 Report of the Annual Lake Mohonk Conference on the Indian and Other Dependent Peoples (1904).

Resolutions.

The Twenty-second Annual Lake Mohonk Conference of Friends of the Indian and Other Dependent Peoples rejoices that so much has been accomplished, under the wise action of the National Government, in bringing the descendants of the aborigines of our land to the enjoyment of education, justice and equity and, to some of the benefits of our civilization... We are encouraged to hope that nearly all the difficult problems with which these various wards of the Nation have been surrounded will ultimately, and perhaps speedily, meet with satisfactory solutions. For the Indians, we feel that our paternal care must be continued for some time to come, while to prolong it unduly will result, as such care always does, in weakness and permanent injury. ... The experience of our people in Alaska shows how easy it is for our Congress to fail to act upon important interests that happen to be remote.

We desire to reaffirm the statement made last year that "in dealing with the Indians the objects to be accomplished are no longer questioned; they are the abandonment of the reservation system; the discontinuance of Indian agencies; such education of all Indian children as will fit them for self-support and self-government; access to the Courts for the protection of their rights; amenability to the law in punishment for their crimes; the same liberty that white men enjoy to own, buy, sell, travel, pay taxes, and enjoy in good government the benefits enjoyed by other taxed citizens; and by these means the speedy incorporation of all Indians, with all the rights of citizenship into the American Commonwealth."

In continuation of the foregoing, it is the sense of this Conference that the initial steps should early be taken by Congress looking to the closing up of the business of the Indian Bureau, so soon as it may safely be done, leaving to the operation of the laws of the Nation and of the several States and Territories.

RESOLUTIONS.

The following resolutions were adopted unanimously by the Twenty-second Annual Lake Mohonk Conference of Friends of the Indian and Other Dependent Peoples, October 21, 1904:-

LIQUOR IN THE INDIAN TERRITORY.

Whereas, The Indians of the Five Civilized Tribes of the Indian Territory made solemn agreements with the United States, in the years 1887, 1888, and 1902, for the surrender of their lands to the Commission to the Five Civilized Tribes, providing that the sale, barter, or giving of intoxicating liquors to any person within the district now constituting the Indian Territory shall be forever prohibited, which agreements were fully accepted and approved by the United States; and,

Whereas, The said agreements constitute a permanent, unalterable condition applicable to the disposition and use of the beforementioned lands; therefore,

Resolved, That we call upon the Congress of the United States to duly execute the said agreement by inserting in the Enabling Act that may be passed, to constitute a State of the Indian Territory, either separately or in conjunction with Oklahoma, such provision as will secure, by constitutional enactment, the permanent enforcement of the said agreements.

SCHOOLS FOR THE INDIAN TERRITORY.

Resolved, As the existing treaties and agreements with the Five Civilized Tribes of the Indian Territory provide for the abandonment of all tribal institutions before March 4, 1906; and as this will involve the termination of the school system upon which these tribes are spending nearly half a million dollars annually, this Conference urges that immediate provision be made to carry on these schools under the control and management of the Department of the Interior until such time as they may properly be made a part of the school system of the State or Territory which may eventually have jurisdiction over the Indian Territory.

APPROPRIATION FOR SCHOOLS IN INDIAN TERRITORY.

Resolved, That this Conference heartily approves the grant of $100,000 made at the last session of Congress for enlarging and multiplying the schools of the Five Civilized Tribes in Indian Territory, so that they might be made available for non-Indian children otherwise without any possible means of securing educational advantages, and urges that for the next fiscal year an appropriation of at least $250,000 be made for this purpose.

WATER RIGHTS OF THE PIMAS.
Resolved, That the condition of the Pima Indians in Southern Arizona calls for immediate relief, and we ask the Government authorities to secure a supply of water for their use, without unnecessary delay, by sinking such number of artesian wells as may be necessary for this purpose, and that the funds now available be promptly used.

We further recommend that in the construction of dams on the Gila and Salt Rivers, the interest of these people be carefully considered.

NORTHERN CALIFORNIA INDIANS.
Resolved, That we believe the Government to be in duty bound to provide homes for the landless Indians in Northern California, and thus redeem the provisional pledges made in the treaties with the Indians, whereby they were induced to vacate their lands, the Government, as the other contracting party, having failed to ratify the said treaties, and to execute its obligation;
Resolved, That we recommend that the Congress appoint a commission of three men of high character, at least one of whom should be a resident of California, and familiar with local conditions, to investigate the condition of these Indians with a view to the purchasing of lands and allotting homes of from five to ten acres each to these Indians among white settlers, where employment may be found for them and that this commission be directed to report at the earliest practicable moment. **22 Report of the Annual Lake Mohonk Conference on the Indian and Other Dependent Peoples (1904), p. 162.**

23 Report of the Annual Lake Mohonk Conference on the Indian and Other Dependent Peoples (1905).

PLATFORM OF THE TWENTY-THIRD ANNUAL LAKE MOHONK CONFERENCE OF FRIENDS OF THE INDIAN AND OTHER DEPENDENT PEOPLES.

3. We are gratified with the progress made by the Government for doing away with Indian agencies and reservations.

4. We heartily commend the effort made in the last Congress to provide for the distribution of tribal funds, in accordance with recommendations made by President Roosevelt in his first annual message to Congress, and we recommend the passage by the present Congress of an act whose object shall be that sought by the Lacey Bill for the division of such funds; and we further believe that an early date should be fixed by law, on or before which the registration of Indians and of their family relationships at each agency and sub-agency (already required by regula-

tion of the Indian Office), shall be thoroughly completed, and that each Indian so registered shall then be enrolled as a share-holder of tribal property; and that no Indian child born after that date shall have a right to any share in Indian lands or Indian funds in his own name, but shall have such rights as shall be his by descent or relationship under the laws of inheritance for citizens of the State or Territory where such child may reside or such land be situated.

5. We strongly recommend an enactment in the early days of the coming session of Congress to provide for the continuance of existing schools in the Indian Territory.

6. This Conference respectfully petitions Congress by legislation to pass upon the question whether any funds held in trust by the United States should be used for the support of any schools under denominational or ecclesiastical control. And the Conference records its conviction that the decision repeatedly embodied in the legislation of Congress against the appropriation of any public funds for the support of such schools, should also be by law enforced against the use of Indian tribal funds of which the United States Government is the trustee.

We recommend to the Secretary of the Interior and to Congress that such measures as are necessary be taken, to make possible the admission of full-blood children of the so-called Five Civilized Tribes residing in the Indian Territory into the government Indian schools of the country.

We believe that Congress at an early date should enact legislation requiring all Indian children of school age and in good health to attend some school.

This Conference expresses its hearty appreciation and approval of the very decided stand taken by the Senate of the United States at its last session in favor of the continued maintenance of prohibition in the state of which it was proposed to make Indian Territory a part, and urges that there shall be no receding from the position upon prohibition then taken by the Senate.

The Conference hereby resolves that a committee of five be appointed by the Chair with power to increase their own number, with authority to issue an address to the Churches on the necessity of more of Christian work among the Indians and in the Indian neighborhoods. **23 Report of the Annual Lake Mohonk Conference on the Indian and Other Dependent Peoples (1905).**

24 Report of the Annual Lake Mohonk Conference on the Indian and Other Dependent Peoples (1906).

PLATFORM OF THE TWENTY-FOURTH ANNUAL LAKE MOHONK CONFERENCE OF FRIENDS OF THE INDIAN AND OTHER DEPENDENT PEOPLES.

Unanimously Adopted October 19, 1906.

The work of this Conference is to consider and advise as to the present duties of our Government and our people in behalf of those peoples which are under our control, but are not yet fitted for self-government. It is the belief of this Conference that such a condition should not continue indefinitely. It should be the aim of our Government to develop these peoples by the processes of intellectual, moral and spiritual education into the exercise of full, self-governing citizenship, whether they be Indians, Eskimos, Porto Ricans or Filipinos. Much has been achieved already to this end. This has been made for the first time in the history of subject peoples the accepted policy of the governing nation. We acknowledge gratefully the good work already accomplished by the President and his Cabinet, by Congress, by the officers of the Army and Navy, and by a multitude of devoted men and women who have given their lives best service to uplifting those of other races. We believe that these Possessions have come into our hands, not that we may make them serve us, but that we may serve them. This is the prime principle of our duty, and we are to do this in no spirit of racial superiority, but in the faith that what we have acquired and done they also may acquire and do, and that freedom and self-government are to be the ultimate right and possession of all.

Each step gained requires other steps to follow. This Conference has made many recommendations, and has had the great pleasure of seeing many of them adopted. Without argument we now offer the following further recommendations as to future policy, some of which we would have embodied in legislation, while others are submitted to the executive departments or to individuals or organizations.

In particular, we recommend for our Indian tribes:
That the purpose of the Lacey Bill for the division of tribal funds into individual holdings be approved, and that such division be made effective as speedily as possible, and that Indians be paid their individual holdings as fast as they are able to learn the use of money.
That in one or more of the larger Indian industrial training schools the course of study be so extended that graduates can pass from them into the Agricultural and Mechanical Colleges maintained in the States and Territories.
That Congress by definite legislation prohibit the use of Indian trust funds by the Government for the instruction or support of Indian students in schools under ecclesiastical control.
We call the attention of the Christian Churches and all other religious bodies to the urgent need of co-operation in promoting the spiritual uplifting of the Indians.

In particular, for Alaska we recommend:

That Congress amend the law providing for the election of a Delegate from Alaska, by giving citizenship and the right of suffrage to such native men of twenty-one years and upwards as can read and write.
That the General Government provide an adequate system of industrial and day schools for the natives of Alaska, with compulsory attendance; and that it provide for hospitals

and sanitary care, and that such schools and also the care of the reindeer herds be kept under the charge of the Bureau of Education.

That a sufficient number of courts be established in Alaska for the effective administration of justice.

24 Report of the Annual Lake Mohonk Conference on the Indian and Other Dependent Peoples (1906), pp. 7-8

25 Report of the Annual Lake Mohonk Conference on the Indian and Other Dependent Peoples (1907).

PLATFORM OF THE TWENTY-FIFTH ANNUAL LAKE MOHONK CONFERENCE OF FRIENDS OF THE INDIAN AND OTHER DEPENDENT PEOPLES, 1907. (Unanimously adopted October 25th, 1907).

The Lake Mohonk Conference, at the close of its twenty-fifth annual session, congratulates the people of the United States upon the progress made in the education and development of the Indians in the last quarter of a century. The general policy toward Indians adopted by the Government in these later years we heartily approve. It establishes the Indian in citizenship, in a home of his own, charges him with responsibility for the ordering of his own life and the management of his own property, while for a term of years it protects his title to his land and helps him to begin life as a citizen of the State in which he lives.

Recent legislation which reverses the order contemplated in the Dawes Severalty Act, and grants citizenship to an allotted Indian only at the discretion of the Department or at the expiration of the period of protected title, is contrary to the convictions of the Mohonk Indian Conference as expressed in other years, and will tend to prolong indefinitely an Indian Bureau which we hope to see discontinued as early as possible.

We have confidence in the officers of the Government entrusted with the duty of carrying out our general Indian policy. We heartily commend the greater emphasis now laid upon labor by Indians as a means of self-support and preparation for citizenship, and the effective measures adopted to protect Indians against the evils of illicit liquor traffic. To keep clean, honest and efficient that work of administration which is now the chief task of the Government, we look with confidence to a continuance of hearty co-operation between the administrative officers and the intelligent friends of the Indian.

This conference urges upon the Christian people of the country greatly enlarged efforts toward Christian education and the evangelization of the Indian. **25 Report of the Annual Lake Mohonk Conference on the Indian and Other Dependent Peoples (1907), pp. 7-8.**

26 Report of the Annual Lake Mohonk Conference on the Indian and Other Dependent Peoples (1908).

PLATFORM OF THE TWENTY-SIXTH ANNUAL LAKE MOHONK CONFERENCE OF FRIENDS OF THE INDIAN AND OTHER DEPENDENT PEOPLES, 1908.

At the session of the Mohonk Conference a year ago the Platform adopted presented a preliminary review of the progress accomplished in behalf of the Indians during the twenty-five years of the history of these Conferences. That worthy story we do not need so soon to repeat. Suffice it to say that our Government has with general wisdom, and with a prevailing purpose to do justice to all our dependent peoples, carried on its good work under the charge of its various Departments. So far as the Indians are concerned, most of the principles we have contended for are accepted, and they are carried out by a body of officials who have never been surpassed in character and capacity. What remains is to complete what is begun, giving education and citizenship to the Indian, putting him, as soon as possible, under the same administration of law as governs other citizens about him, so that Indian administration as such may as soon as possible come to an end. To certain remaining incidental wrongs and needs we call attention.

I. Observing the confusion which comes from the complexity of the administration, particularly in Alaska, and the difficulty in securing prompt administration of justice, we ask Congress to consider whether some more united and responsible form of administration may not be devised; and particularly we ask that laws be enacted and executed which by imprisoning offenders shall prevent the sale of intoxicating liquors to the natives. We also ask that increased appropriations for the education of Alaskan youth be made.

II. The additional appropriation needed to purchase small homesteads for the rest of the wronged, dispossessed and homeless Indians of California, Congress should make at this coming session, to complete the work of justice and mercy so well begun by the Government last year.

III. [Allotting lands to] Navajo Indians who have for years lived on the public domain, should be completed under Section 4 of the General Severalty Act; and where the title to land and water, which due care of its wards by the Government as guardian would have secured to such Indians has been lost to them and taken up by white men, we believe that the Government should by law provide other land and water rights for such dispossessed Navajos.

IV. We warmly commend the policy of the Indian Bureau which puts emphasis on the education of Indian youth near their own homes, and the closing of the non-reservation schools or the modifying of the courses of study and methods of administration so as to admit white pupils and ultimately bring these institutions under the control of the states in which they are located. We also urge the enlargement of the system of day schools for the people. **26 Report of the Annual Lake Mohonk Conference on the Indian and Other Dependent Peoples (1908), pp. 8-9.**

27 Report of the Annual Lake Mohonk Conference on the Indian and Other Dependent Peoples (1909).

PLATFORM OF THE TWENTY-SEVENTH ANNUAL LAKE MOHONK CONFERENCE OF FRIENDS OF THE INDIAN AND OTHER DEPENDENT PEOPLES.

Twenty-six years have passed since the first Lake Mohonk Conference was assembled. Then it was the policy of the nation to push the Indians aside when they were an impediment to national progress; now it is the national policy to incorporate the Indians in the nation and enable them to contribute to the national progress. The most important of the reforms advocated by the Conference have been accepted by the nation, specifically the abolition of the reservation system, the establishment of a federal public school system for the education of the Indians, and the application to the Indian service of the Civil Service rules. This change in the nation's conception of the Indian problem and its true solution has been accompanied by a great improvement in the personnel of the Indian service, in public sentiment upon the Indian question and in the protection of the Indian properties. Meanwhile new obligations have been laid upon the nation toward other peoples who are not citizens of the United States but are subject to its jurisdiction and authority. We take this occasion to reaffirm certain fundamental principles which the nation's failures and successes in the Indian service have illustrated and enforced, and which are equally applicable to these new wards of the nation.

This means for the North American Indian the abolition of the tribal relation in which the fundamental rights of the individual are denied, the substitution of personal for tribal property, the recognition of the Indian's right to travel freely and peaceably and to buy and sell in the open market, and his ultimate admission to American citizenship.
27 Report of the Annual Lake Mohonk Conference on the Indian and Other Dependent Peoples (1909), p. 7-9.

28 Report of the Annual Lake Mohonk Conference on the Indian and Other Dependent Peoples (1910).

PLATFORM OF THE TWENTY-EIGHTH ANNUAL LAKE MOHONK CONFERENCE OF FRIENDS OF THE INDIAN AND OTHER DEPENDENT PEOPLES, 1910.

As the result of nearly thirty years of public debate the people of this country have wisely adopted as the policy of the nation the abandonment of the reservation system, the dissolution of the tribal organizations and the incorporation of the Indians as individual members of the American communities. The Indian problem has now become almost wholly one of administration in carrying this policy into effect. This involves: The protection by the Federal Government of the personal and property rights of the Indian.

The vigorous prosecution and condign (sic) punishment of all who by violence, fraud or corruption violate those rights.

The protection of the Indians during this transition period from the vices of drinking and gambling.

The sanitation of their homes and settlements.

The encouragement of friendly relations between the Indians and the local communities in or near which they are situated.

The taxation of the inherited and surplus lands of all Indians according to the precedent set by the action of the last Congress relating to the taxation of the Omaha Indians.

The extension of Indian education until provision is made for the education of all Indian children of school age.

Special emphasis upon industrial, moral and political education that the Indians may be enabled to become self-supporting and self-governing members of the community.

As rapidly as is consistent with securing for the Indians adequate educational advantages adapted to their special need, the transfer of schools and their plants to the state and local authorities.

And your committee recognize with grateful appreciation the steady improvement during the last quarter of a century in the personnel of the Indian service, the self-denying and sometimes heroic work of many of its representatives in the field, the efficiency and vigor with which those principles of administration are being carried into effect by the Indian Bureau, and it expresses the hope that within the lifetime of the present generation, the work of the Bureau may have been successfully accomplished, the Bureau itself may be discontinued and the Indian problem may have become an affair of the past.

SUPPLEMENTARY EXPRESSIONS UNANIMOUSLY ADOPTED BY THE CONFERENCE - MINUTE RESPECTING THE NEW YORK INDIANS.

This Conference expresses its very sincere appreciation of the valuable Report of the special Committee appointed a year ago to consider the interests of the Indians upon the several New York reservations, and adopts thereupon the following minute:

First In the judgment of this Conference the abandonment of the reservation system in the State of New York at the earliest practicable moment is desirable, in the interest alike of the Indians and of the white citizens.

Second-A committee of three members to be appointed by the Chairman of this Conference is associated with the special Committee; and the report and the accompanying recommendations are hereby referred back to such new Committee of three for appropriate action, in accordance with the intent of the same. In particular, such Committee is directed-

(a) To lay before the President of the United States the request that he recommend to the Congress the enactment of such legislation as will accomplish, at the earliest practicable moment, the abandonment of the reservation system in the State of New York, with suitable provision for the judicial determination and extinguishment of any claims that may stand in the way of the allotment of the reservation lands in severalty to the reservation Indians;

(b) To request of the President furthermore that he determine, or cause to be determined, the question whether the Federal or the State Government is now properly chargeable with the exercise of police powers over the New York reservations; and that, in so far as these powers belong to the Federal Government, he will take such steps, in the way of recommending legislation or otherwise, as will lead to the better regulation of the conduct of the residents of these reservations, with particular reference to sanitation, public health, public morals, and the manufacture and sale of intoxicants;

(c) To urge upon the Congress the adoption of the proposed remedial legislation;

(d) To request of the Governor of the State of New York that he cooperate in this matter with the Federal authorities, by urging upon the Congress the adoption of the proposed legislation, and by taking such steps, in the way of recommending State legislation or otherwise, as will facilitate the ultimate abandonment of the reservation system, and such as will lead immediately to the effective exercise of any police powers over the reservations which he shall find to be properly chargeable to the State Government.

Third-Meanwhile, the New York State Health Department is invoked to do all it may to improve the sanitary and health conditions upon the New York reservations and the State Excise Department is urged to enforce rigidly the liquor laws so far as it has power to do so.

RESOLUTION REGARDING ALASKAN NATIVES.

Resolved: That in any reorganization of the territorial government of Alaska provision should be made for educational service among the Alaskan natives on a plan at least as generous and effective as that now in operation.

REPORT OF THE COMMITTEE ON NEW YORK INDIANS.

In conclusion, your committee recommend:

That this Conference memorialize Congress to enact the necessary legislation for the extinguishment of the claim of the Ogden Land Company, and for the allotment of the lands of the Cattaraugus and Allegheny Reservations among the Indians entitled thereto, having regard to all interests involved.

2.-That the Legislature of this State be requested to cooperate with the general government in the matter.

3.-That the Legislature be also requested to place the reservations of the State under the control of the State Board of Health for sanitary purposes; to make the necessary appropriation for the erection and equipment of a building for a trade school in connection with the Thomas Orphan Asylum for the education of Indian children.

4.-That the officials be urged to exercise a prompt and effective administration of the excise laws on the Indian reservations.

SPEECH OF COMMISSIONER VALENTINE PP. 37-49

https://books.google.com/books?id=mgwQAQAAMAAJ&printsec=frontcover&-source=gbs_ge_summary_r&cad=0#v=onepage&q&f=false

28 Report of the Annual Lake Mohonk Conference on the Indian and Other Dependent Peoples (1910).

29 Report of the Annual Lake Mohonk Conference on the Indian and Other Dependent Peoples (1911).

Platform of the Twenty-Ninth Annual Lake Mohonk Conference of Friends of the Indian and Other Dependent Peoples, 1911.

INDIANS

The general principles which ought to govern our treatment of the American Indians have been fully laid down at previous Conferences. They are now accepted and largely control the policy of our Government. We gratefully recognize the sympathetic labors of the Indian Bureau to promote the interests of the Indians through legal protection and in matters of health, education and industry. Equally our Mission boards and other benevolent societies recognize their obligations to the Indian, and with no little success are giving to him the blessings of Christianity and civilization. *We note the organization during the past year of a society composed of Indians themselves whose object it is to direct public attention to present needs and to the righting of existing wrongs.* (Emphasis added).

By the faithful efforts of our Government and of associated benevolence the constructive policy of education, industrial training, individual ownership of land, and the abolition of the ration system, has been carried on with such success that the end seems in sight, the absorption of the Indian with the general body politic, when he shall receive only the same care and protection as are given to all other citizens, and when he shall accept equally with them the duties and responsibilities of all of us who make and who submit to the laws and perform the duties involved in a Christian state.

We accordingly present the following recommendations:

1. Since morality and religion are the basis on which social order must rest, and since it is held that no one religious system is to be supported or taught by public funds, we urge that religious boards and societies assume this duty of religious training, until through mutual comity, there remains not one tribe of Indians that is not brought out fully from paganism into the life of Christianity. We rejoice in all such service done by our Churches, Protestant and Catholic, and by their allied societies such as the Young Men's Christian Association and the Young Women's Christian Association.

2. All the agencies of law should be used by the Department of the Interior to enforce the acts prohibiting the sale of intoxicating liquors to the Indians; and punishment for violation should be as energetically sought as in the case of counterfeiting or tampering with the mails; and we are warranted in pledging the support of all law-abiding citizens to such enforcement.

3. We approve the policy of the Indian Bureau to reduce as rapidly as may be the number of its Indian Schools, and to transfer their pupils to the public schools of the State or Territory. Wherever Indian holdings are not taxed the Indian Office will gladly pay for such education. In no other way can the Indians be more speedily incorporated into the life of the people as a whole.

4. The accepted policy by which individual allotments break up tribal lands, and which in the case of large tracts mixes Indians with white people, should be extended as rapidly as the Indians are prepared to make proper use of their several holdings.

5. We further approve the policy now initiated which breaks up tribal funds by their assignment to the members of the tribe individually. As fast as they are fitted for it, the assigned portions should be given over to such Indians for their control, the remainder being held by the Bureau in severalty for their present advantage and future possession.

6. Certain tribes of Indians being devoted to agriculture need special and vigorous protection against violent dispossession of their lands which they have cultivated for centuries. To the need of their full protection we call the attention of our Government. The small scattered communities of Pueblo Indians hold and own their lands in common under a Mexican treaty which recognizes their rights. But they are in danger of being crowded out of their choice sections of irrigated land and being driven from their homes. We recommend that by mutual agreement their lands be allotted under Government control with special safeguards as to alienation.

7. We note with satisfaction the fact that the Indian Bureau has undertaken a thorough investigation of the case of the Pima Indians. Without undertaking to anticipate the results of that investigation, we express our profound conviction that these Indians should not be removed without their consent from lands which they have peacefully occupied and industriously cultivated for generations, and that their water rights should be as carefully protected as would be those of white settlers under similar circumstances.

8. We urge that in coming legislation to give Territorial Government to Alaska special care be taken that the interests and rights of the aboriginal population be fully guarded. **29 Report of the Annual Lake Mohonk Conference on the Indian and Other Dependent Peoples (1911), pp. 7-9.**

30 Report of the Annual Lake Mohonk Conference on the Indian and Other Dependent Peoples (1912).

PLATFORM INDIANS.

In reviewing the conditions of the Indians we find much to commend and some things to criticize. The principles which must govern the final solution of this problem are well established, but the application of those principles [are] beset by serious difficulties. To an increasing extent the Indians must be treated as individuals, not as groups or tribes, if their permanent establishment as useful citizens of our nation is to be realized. During this time of crisis in their history, we should provide protection for the weak with freedom for the strong. *As an important aid to this work, we urge the codification of the confusing multiplicity of laws now in force affecting the Indians and the speedy publication of the Indian data collected by the Census Bureau, showing the educational and industrial situation and development of each tribe.* (Emphasis added).

The enormous total of Indian tribal funds now held in the United States Treasury, amounting to about $50,000,000, should be made the subject of an accounting, looking towards its division in severalty among the members of the tribes concerned, subject to such restrictions as experience in the division of Indian lands has shown to be desirable. (Emphasis added).

The Indian should be given every consideration in handling his affairs, that his manhood and sense of personal responsibility may be duly stimulated. In this connection, we urge that the Apaches held as prisoners of war at Fort Sill, Oklahoma, for twenty-five years be treated with the utmost consideration in determining their permanent settlement under the recent action of Congress providing for their liberty.

As the work of the Bureau of Indian Affairs is a great social undertaking, we urge the elimination of such selfish interests as interfere with proper administration and thus increase the difficulties of effective governmental activity and seriously handicap the most capable official personnel. As an aid in securing the necessary protection, we urge the reorganization of the inspection service of the Indian Bureau and the adoption of measures for placing all branches of inspection work affecting Indians upon the highest plane of efficiency. The Indian Bureau should also be relieved from unfortunate legislation, such as the Amendment to the Indian Appropriation Act for 1907, which, however unintentionally, has in effect legalized many of the frauds perpetrated on Indians in the State of Minnesota.

With the admission as States of Arizona and New Mexico, the condition of the Navajo Indians should receive attention. We deplore any action which will not scrupulously safeguard their self-reliance as a people, based on the grazing industry, which in that desert region requires very extensive areas of land. Their history since 1868 has proven their capacity as stock raisers, and no attempt should be made to compel them to become farmers to the neglect of their herds. Congress should make provision whereby education may be secured for the 6,000 Navajo boys and girls who have never seen the inside of a school house, thus fulfilling our treaty pledge made over forty years ago.

In providing water for irrigation for the lands of the Yakima and other Indian tribes, the Government is duty bound to protect their vested and treaty rights to as full an extent as would be done in cases between citizens. We recommend, that, wherever practicable, proceedings be instituted by the Government to procure a judicial determination of the Indian rights.

We reiterate our former statements respecting the necessity for the continued improvement of the educational facilities afforded Indians, and the extension of vocational training. Our concern is that health conditions among them may be improved and the medical service increased and strengthened, while again insisting upon the adoption of the most drastic measures for the elimination of the liquor traffic. (Emphasis added). **30 Report of the Annual Lake Mohonk Conference on the Indian and Other Dependent Peoples (1912), pp. 9-10.**

[WHITE EARTH, NOT PART OF PLATFORM]

What should we do? First, have an inspection service worthy of the name. How could White Earth have reached its amazing condition had inspectors done their duty? We should have an inspection corps composed of men who know Indians and will go among Indians and study their wants. Previous inspectors at White Earth stayed about the agency, checked accounts, listened to employees disputes and condemned worthless articles. The Superintendent at White Earth, Major Howard, complained to me that I spent two weeks among the Indians before I called on him or looked through his schools.

Second, there should be prompt legal action in Indian matters, and all laws rigidly enforced. Three years have passed and the Department of Justice has not ended its White Earth cases. No one has gone to jail; no Indians are living on returned allotments. The Ojibwa naturally conclude that the white rascals at Detroit and Ogema are more powerful than the Great Father at Washington, for the simple reason that they obtain the Indian lands in a few days or weeks - or at the most months - whereas the Great Father spends three years and has not administered justice.

Fourth, competent ethnologists or a Committee of the Board of Indian Commissioners should make a list of the full blood Indians of the United States. All depends upon the blood status. Ordinary clerks cannot make an accurate roll.

Fifth, at Washington we should have a Commissioner big enough to realize the essentials in this great Service, and he should make protection the key-note of his administration rather than indiscriminate allotting.

Sixth, the Board of Indian Commissioners should be given broader powers by the Congress, and funds in order that its members might visit reservations.

Seventh, restrictions should be imposed on Indian lands in such a way as prevent fraud. Otherwise, the lands in thousands of cases, will be absolutely lost to the Red Man.

Eighth, the police force on every reservation should be greatly increased and given full authority.

Ninth, scant attention should be paid to the pleas or suggestions of people living about reservations with reference to a change of Indian conditions. Before changes are made the matter should be fully investigated by the Board of Indian Commissioners.

Finally, the Indian has lost much, but much remains. ***Our policy, weak but well-meaning, has plunged thousands of our wards into poverty.*** Let us give the Indian what we ourselves enjoy - full rights and privileges of citizenship, and the pursuit of happiness — not merely empty words. (Emphasis added).

Otherwise, history will record our short-sighted and disastrous policy in its true light, and we shall be condemned by future generations. (Applause.) **30 Report of the Annual Lake Mohonk Conference on the Indian and Other Dependent Peoples (1912), pp. 60-61.**

31 Report of the Annual Lake Mohonk Conference on the Indian and Other Dependent Peoples (1913).

PLATFORM OF THE THIRTY-FIRST ANNUAL LAKE MOHONK CONFERENCE OF FRIENDS OF THE INDIAN AND OTHER DEPENDENT PEOPLES, 1913.

On this thirty-first Lake Mohonk Conference of Friends of the Indian and Other Dependent Peoples, we meet under the shadow of the great loss suffered by us in the death of our inspirer and guide, Friend Albert K. Smiley, and his beloved wife. ...

The great principle that for thirty years has controlled the action of these conferences is, that humanity is one; that no one race or rank of culture has the right to look with contempt on another as inferior and therefore unworthy to be given equal opportunities to reach its highest limit of training in the arts of civilization, and to share with the best of us the rights of self-government. Furthermore, it has been our duty, in the love of God and man, to seek to protect those undeveloped peoples for whom our government is responsible, to seek for them proper legislation, to save them from those who would prey on their weakness, and to afford them that training and culture by which they will be able to care for themselves.

Our work for the American Indian is not yet completed. To be sure, the great principles have been established. ***It is the policy of the government to break up the tribal system, to give the Indian land in severalty, and to protect him in the possession of his holdings until he can be so far incorporated into the community about him that he can be trusted with their entire control. There are those who would take advantage of his ignorance to rob him.*** We particularly oppose and condemn national or state legislation which would hastily remove protection given by the laws, and make it easier to separate the Indian from his land and livelihood. (Emphasis added).

INDIANS.

1. That a vigorous campaign be waged against tuberculosis, trachoma and other diseases among the Indians, by the provision of medical supervision and care;

2. That the campaign against the liquor traffic be effectively carried on; and we note with pleasure the increase of appropriations in Congress for this purpose;

3. That the suggestion made at this conference, which is reported as advanced by the Secretary of the Interior, that all Indian affairs, including care of property valued at nearly a billion dollars, should be placed under the entire control of a national non-partisan commission to serve during long terms or during good behavior is worthy of serious consideration.

4. For the Five Civilized Tribes of Oklahoma we favor ample Congressional appropriations to secure:

a. A vigorous educational policy, including care of individual health and preparation for self-support;

b. The payment to all competent Indians of their equitable share in all tribal property, and the final closing of the door against the horde of applicants who are seeking a share in this distribution;

c. Continued protection to uneducated full-blood and others in the restricted class by state and national legislation;

d. Aid given by the Federal Government to supplement the effort of the state of Oklahoma in probate matters to protect the estates of helpless Indian children;

e. Prevention of further removal of restriction from the sale of Indian holdings except in individual cases approved by the Department of the Interior;

f. The modification of the present law which allows restricted Indians to lease not only their additional lands but their homesteads, which in a multitude of cases has led to the loss of their home and a life of vagrancy and beggary;

5. Vigilance should be exercised to prevent ill-advised action concerning the lands of the Navajos, who have signally prospered, that their right to allotment on the public domain may be carefully safeguarded. Their own lands should be classified and units established suited to conditions of agriculture, grazing and irrigation. In view of the demand of white settlers in Arizona and New Mexico, it is imperative that definite steps be taken immediately to settle the status of the Navajo Indians in their lands.

6. The Pueblo Indians of New Mexico need special protection from the government in the settlement of questions affecting title to their lands. We favor the acceptance by the United States from these Indians of their proffered trusteeship, in the event that it is finally decided that they are citizens, with a view to their better education for the duties of citizenship and allotment of their lands.

7. We recommend continued attention to the Indians of New York and their reservations, to the end that as soon as possible with entire justice to the Indians, the reservations may be abolished and the Indians admitted to full citizenship. **31 Report of the Annual Lake Mohonk Conference on the Indian and Other Dependent Peoples (1913), p. 9.**

32 Report of the Annual Lake Mohonk Conference on the Indian and Other Dependent Peoples (1914).

Platform.

It is evident that at certain points the dangers which threaten our Indian population are still so great as to call, not only for the maintenance of the governmental protection now afforded, but for a considerable increase of such protection. This is particularly the case where the property interests of the Indians, in money and in lands, are so great as to arouse the intense cupidity of powerful and unscrupulous foes, some of whom are white men while others are themselves of Indian blood. Conditions in the State of Oklahoma, affecting particularly the Five Civilized Tribes, call for the closest scrutiny. In the event that the Oklahoma legislature shall fail to give early and adequate protection to these Indians, we see no alternative but that the Federal Government should resume full jurisdiction over all of the "restricted" Indians of that State. The land suits begun by the Federal Government in the interest of the Indians of Oklahoma should be prosecuted, if necessary, to the courts of last resort, to the end that the lands of the restricted allottees shall be preserved from spoliation and that as much as possible of that which has been wrongfully taken from the unrestricted allottees may be recovered.

It is now well known that the increasing use among the Indians of the mescal bean, or peyote, is demoralizing in the extreme. We recommend accordingly that the Federal prohibition of intoxicating liquors be extended to include this dangerous drug. The codification of our laws relating to the Indians is a matter of vital importance. The Conference accordingly recommends the immediate adoption of the necessary measures to accomplish this. **32 Report of the Annual Lake Mohonk Conference on the Indian and Other Dependent Peoples (1914), pp. 7-8.**

33 Report of the Annual Lake Mohonk Conference on the Indian and Other Dependent Peoples (1915).

Platform.

The Thirty-third Annual Lake Mohonk Conference on the Indian and Other Dependent Peoples gratefully recognizes the progress secured toward comparative justice and right and fair administration for the Indian. It approves the stress laid by the present administration on the conservation of the health of the Indians and its insistence on more hospitals and greater medical care, and it applauds the efficient efforts to stop the sale of intoxicants and the use of peyote.

But though much has been done our national responsibility is scarcely less than at an earlier date.

The present condition of the Utes may point our contention and our general recommendations. The Government holds property for this tribe amounting to an average of about $5000 for each member of the tribe, and yet these people live in squalor, and in moral and spiritual barbarism. The undertaking of the Government to give them an irrigation system at a cost of $864,000, was so hampered by selfish legislation as to threaten the loss of their water rights, unless the prompt and hopeful action of the Commissioner shall be pursued persistently to the end.

For the Indians in general the Government holds a billion of dollars in property and funds, all open to constant attack from the cupidity and greed of the whites and recreant red men. There is no hope of ultimate justice save through an improvement in our laws and in more rigid enforcement of them.

We urge, therefore, that the government shall first define the Indian, that he may be protected from those who profess Indian relationship in order that they may share in funds, lands and timber and newly discovered oil and mineral rights.

We urge the defining of his legal status and the codification of the laws regarding him, that the confusion and uncertainty now existing may be done away.

We urge the extension of the merit system in all appointments in the Indian Service.

We urge increased attention to the educational need of the Indian and lay emphasis on agricultural and other vocational training.

We urge on Congress the need of larger appropriations for educational and medical work in Alaska, under charge of the Bureau of Education.

We urge that legislation shall be enacted that will insure the preparation of the Indians of the Five Civilized Tribes to assume intelligently the responsibilities of their citizenship, and the protection of those of them who still own their allotted lands when the restrictions on the sale of their lands shall cease.

And we urge, with profound conviction, that to these important efforts to improve his physical condition and conserve his material resources, there be added by our churches and philanthropic agencies a harmonious and larger activity in behalf of the moral and religious instruction of the Indian, without which these efforts for his material good will surely prove ineffectual.

Our present system is full of bad inheritances. We urge instant and more thorough attention to these things to the end that justice be done. **33 Report of the Annual Lake Mohonk Conference on the Indian and Other Dependent Peoples (1915), pp. 7-8.**

34 Report of the Annual Lake Mohonk Conference on the Indian and Other Dependent Peoples (1916).

Platform.

The Thirty-fourth Annual Lake Mohonk Conference on the Indian and Other Dependent Peoples recommends that the number of hospitals for the Indian service be increased and urges improvement of sanitary conditions where they are at present seriously deficient, and further recommends an increase of the annual appropriation by Congress for the educational facilities among the Navajos. The Conference wishes also to set its approval upon the progress made in industrial and vocational education and in health conditions.

We heartily commend the work of the various Christian missionary bodies, which are now more than ever before exhibiting a higher degree of cooperation in meeting the spiritual needs and longings of the Indian.

The Conference deplores the fact that the continued uncertainty as to the legal status of the Indians of the State of New York causes serious injury to their industrial, intellectual and moral advancement and prevents the enforcement of the laws of the State relating to vice and crime, the public health and education. It is a matter of congratulation that an able investigation into this legal status has been recently made by a Deputy Attorney General of the State. We recommend that the results of this investigation be submitted to the Department of Justice of the National Government for its consideration and also that Congress be requested to pass a broad enabling act, under which the State of New York may enact all needful legislation for the improvement of these Indians and the benefit of the State. The Conference makes this specific recommendation because of the exceptional historic and legal situation of these Indians.

The ultimate solution of the perplexing Indian problem will be reached only when the Indians by an academic, industrial and moral education have been prepared to receive all the privileges and assume all the duties of American Citizenship. Until that time such Indians as are not so prepared are the wards of the Nation. The Nation is in duty bound to protect their rights, promote their interests, and provide for their education. Experience has proved that it is fulfilled very imperfectly and under great disadvantages by special legislation enacted to meet special exigencies and administered by a Bureau whose head changes with every change in the national administration. A permanent, stable, and developing policy is essential. We therefore urge the creation of a non-partisan, independent commission, permanent in its character, which should make a careful examination of the mass of Indian legislation on our statute books, much of it local and fragmentary, and from it develop an Indian law, general in its provisions, comprehensive in its policy, forward looking in its purpose. Such law, when enacted by the Congress, should take the place of all existing legislation except permanent treaties, and thereafter the administration of this law and the application of its principles to the varying conditions of the various tribes should be left by the Congress to the commission, to which should be committed the entire charge of the Indian service. We urge this plan, not only to secure greater economy and efficiency but also to promote a consistent, continuing and developing policy - a need recognized as of the utmost importance by all workers in the Indian service. The ultimate object of this policy should be to bring the present abnormal condition of the Indian to an end as speedily as possible by the incorporation of the Indian in the general citizenship of the Nation.

Until the reorganization of the work for the Indian upon the principles above outlined, we deprecate as unwise and dangerous legislation which will remove all authority respecting our Western Indians from the control and supervision of the Secretary of the Interior and the Commissioner of Indian Affairs.

The policy of all Indian administration should include at the earliest possible date the segregation and individualization of Indian tribal property, in order that competent Indians may have available immediately all resources to which they are entitled and that they may be completely severed from the guardianship of the Government.

We urge that immediate steps be taken by the enactment of new legislation or otherwise, further to protect all incompetent Indians, especially the full bloods, in order that their property rights may be conserved and their resources expended for their benefit under proper supervision, looking to the correction of the flagrant abuses now rampant as particularly brought to our attention as existing among the Five Civilized Tribes and the Osages. **34 Report of the Annual Lake Mohonk Conference on the Indian and Other Dependent Peoples (1916), pp. 7-8.**

APPENDIX D: Lands in Severalty to Indians, Minority Report of Committee on Indian Affairs, Rep. Russell Errett, *et al.*, H.R. Rep. No. 1576, 46th Cong., 2nd Sess. (1880)

LANDS IN SEVERALTY TO INDIANS.

VIEWS OF THE MINORITY. Mr. Errett submitted the following as the views of the minority of the Committee on Indian Affairs:

The undersigned, members of the Committee on Indian Affairs of the House of Representatives, are unable to agree with the majority of the committee in reporting favorably upon this bill, for these, among other reasons, viz:

I. The bill is confessedly in the nature of an experiment. It is formed solely upon a theory, and it has no practical basis to stand upon. For many years it has been the hobby of speculative philanthropists that the true plan to civilize the Indian was to assign him lands in severalty, and thereby make a farmer and self-sustaining citizen of him; and so far back as 1862 Congress established the policy that

> Whenever any Indian, being a member of any band or tribe with whom the government has or shall have entered into treaty stipulations, being desirous to adopt the habits of civilized life, has had a portion of the lands belonging to his tribe allotted to him in severalty, in pursuance of such treaty stipulations, the agent and superintendent of such tribe shall take such measures, not inconsistent with law, as may be necessary to protect such Indian in the quiet enjoyment of the lands so allotted to him.

This law stands to-day on the statute book as the recognized policy of this government of the United States in its dealings with the Indians. It does not make allotments of land in severalty obligatory, but recognizing the plea of those who contend for the beneficent effects sure to flow from the allotment policy, it has opened the door to its establishment, allowing any Indian, in any tribe, desiring to try that policy, a full opportunity to do so under the protection of the government. That law has been upon the statute book for nearly eighteen years, and how many Indians have availed themselves of its provisions? Manifestly, very few; and yet we are told, with great pertinacity, that the Indians are strongly in favor of that policy, and will adopt it if they get a chance. It is surpassing strange, if this be true, that so few have availed themselves of the privileges opened to them by the act of 1862.

Being an experiment merely, it would seem to be the dictate of wisdom to make the trial of putting it into practice on a small basis, say with any one tribe that offers a good opportunity for trying it fairly. The Chippewa bands on Lake Superior, for instance, are alleged to be willing to enter upon the experiment. They have good agricultural lands, are partially civilized and educated, and are sufficiently removed from barbarism to give ground for hope that the experiment may succeed. There could be no very strong reason against trying the experiment merely as an experiment with them. *But this bill, without any previous satisfactory test of the policy, proposes to enact a merely speculative theory into a law, and to apply the law to all the Indians, except a few civilized tribes, and to bring them all under its operation without reference to their present condition. It includes the blanket Indians with those who wear the clothing of civilized life; the wild Apaches and Navajos with the nearly civilized Chippewas; and it applies the same rule to all without regard to the wide differences in their condition.* It seeks to make a farmer out of the roving and predatory Ute by the same process as would be applied to the nearly civilized Omahas and Poncas. It needs no argument to prove that these Indian tribes vary widely from each other in their civilized attainments, but this bill ignores all these variances as if they did not exist, and erects a Procrustean bed, upon which it would place every Indian, stretching out those who are too short, and cutting off the heads or feet of those who are too long. (Emphasis added).

It is true that the bill leaves a great deal as to the time of putting the bill in operation to the discretion of the Secretary of the Interior; but we submit that the interests of these tribes are of too great a magnitude to be left to the discretion of any one man, even though he be a Secretary of the Interior. We know of nothing in the constitution of that department that qualifies it peculiarly for such a great trust. Secretaries of the Interior change as frequently as the occurrence of a Mexican or South American revolution; and Congress, we think, is a safer depository for such trusts than any one man, no matter what place he may hold. Let us deal with these people intelligently and wisely, and not at haphazard.

We have said that this bill has no practical basis and is a mere legislative speculation; but it may be added that the experiment it proposes *has* been partially tried, and has always resulted in failure. In the hurry of drawing up reports we cannot be expected to be very specific in our citations, but we may cite the case of the Catawbas, who had lands assigned them in severalty, and who were protected by the inalienability of their homesteads for twenty-five years, just as this bill proposes; and the result was a failure-a flat, miserable failure. The Catawbas gradually withered away under the policy, until there is not one of them left to attest the fact that they ever existed, and their lands fell a prey to the whites who surrounded them and steadily encroached upon them. They were swallowed up as thoroughly as Korah, Dathan, and Abiram, when the ground opened beneath their feet and ingulfed them. (See Hist. Mag., 1st series, vol. 5, p. 46.)

II. The plan of this bill is not, in our judgment, the way to civilize the Indian. However much we may differ with the humanitarians who are riding this hobby, we are certain that they will agree with us in the proposition that it does not make a farmer out of an Indian to give him a quarter-section of land. There are hundreds of thousands of white men, rich with the experiences of centuries of Anglo-Saxon civilization, who cannot be transformed into cultivators of the land by any such gift. Their habits unfit them for it; and how much more do the habits of the Indian, begotten of hundreds of years of wild life, unfit *him* for entering at once and peremptorily upon a life for which he has no fitness? It requires inclination, knowledge of agriculture, and training in farming life to make a successful farmer out of even white men, many of whom have failed at the trial of it, even with an inclination for it. How, then, is it expected to transform all sorts of Indians, with no fitness or inclination for farming, into successful agriculturists? Surely an act of Congress, however potent in itself, with the addition of the discretion of a Secretary of the Interior, no matter how much of a *doctrinaire* he may be, are not sufficient to work such a miracle.

The whole training of an Indian from his birth, the whole history of the Indian race, and the entire array of Indian tradition, running back for at least four hundred years, all combine to predispose the Indian against this scheme for his improvement, devised by those who judge him exclusively from *their* standpoint instead of from *his*. From the time of the discovery of America, and for centuries probably before that, the North American Indian has been a communist. Not in the offensive sense of modern communism, but in the sense of holding property in common. **The tribal system has kept bands and tribes together as families, each member of which was dependent on the other.** The very idea of property in the soil was unknown to the Indian mind. In all the Indian languages there is no word answering to the Latin habeo-I have or possess. They had words to denote holding, as "I have a hatchet;" but the idea of the separate possession of property by individuals is as foreign to the Indian mind as communism is to us. (Emphasis added).

This communistic idea has grown into their very being, and is an integral part of the Indian character. From our point of view this is all wrong; but it is folly to think of uprooting it, strengthened by the traditions of centuries, through the agency of a mere act of Congress, or by the establishment of a theoretical policy. The history of the world shows that it is no easy matter to change old methods of thought or force the adoption of new methods of action. The inborn conservatism of human nature tends always more strongly to the preservation of old ideas than to the establishment of new ones. The world progresses steadily, but always slowly. There are singularities in the Anglo-Saxon character and peculiarities in Anglo-Saxon belief which run back over a thousand years, and which all the enlightenment of progressive centuries has been unable to overcome. There are, even in our own land system, peculiarities which are the remnants of feudal forms and practices, and which still inhere in our methods simply from the force of habit and the conservatism of forms. And if this is true of ourselves, with a written history running back well-nigh two thousand years, why should we be so vain as to expect that the Indian can throw off in a moment, at the bidding of Congress or the Secretary of the Interior, the shackles which have bound his thoughts and action from time immemorial? *In this, as in all other cases, it is the dictate of statesmanship to make haste slowly.* (Emphasis added).

We are free to admit that the two civilizations, so different throughout, cannot well co-exist, or flourish together. One must, in time, give way to the other, and the weak must in the end be supplanted by the strong. But it cannot be violently wrenched out of place and cast aside. Nations cannot be made to change their habits and methods and modes of thought in a day. To bring the Indian to look at things from our standpoint is a work requiring time, patience, and the skill as well as the benign spirit of Christian statesmanship. Let us first demonstrate, on a small scale, the practibility of the plans we propose; and when we have done that, if we can do it, a persevering patience will be needed to make the policy general.

III. The theory that the Indian is a man and a citizen, able to take care of himself, possessed of the attributes of manhood in their broadest sense, and fully responsible to all the laws of our civilized life-a man like other men, and therefore to be treated exactly as other men-is embodied in the first part of this bill, which provides for giving every Indian a farm, and leaving him then to take care of himself, because, as is assumed by the framers of the bill, he *is* able to take care of himself; but having thus launched the Indian upon his future course of life, the bill turns round upon itself and, assuming that the Indian *is not* and *will not be* able to take care of himself, at once proceeds to hedge him around with provisions intended to prevent him from exercising any of the rights of a land-owner except that of working and living on his allotment. He cannot sell, mortgage, lease, or in any way alienate his land; and although he is to be under and amenable to the laws, he is to be free from taxation for all purposes. He is to be treated as a man in giving him land and exacting from him the duty of maintaining himself upon and off of it, and all this upon the plea that he is simply a man, who is to be treated as other men are; and then, as soon as we do this, we proceed to treat him as a child, an infant, a ward in chancery, who is unable to take care of himself and therefore needs the protecting care of government. If he *is* able to take care of himself, all this precaution is unnecessary; if he is *not* able to take care of himself, all this effort to make him try to do it is illogical. If the Indian is a ward under the paternal care of government, he might as well hold his lands in common as in severalty. He cannot be made to feel the pride which a man feels in the ownership of property while he is made to feel that he does not possess one single attribute of separate ownership in the soil. In this respect the bill is like the old constitution of Virginia, which, when the convention which framed it put into it a clause providing a method for amending it, was said by John Randolph to bear upon its face the sardonic grin of death.

The main purpose of this bill is not to help the Indian, or solve the Indian problem, or provide a method for getting out of our Indian troubles, so much as it is to provide a method for getting at the valuable Indian lands and opening them up to white settlement. The main object of the bill is in the last sections of it, not in the first. The sting of this animal is in its tail. When the Indian has got his allotments, the rest of his land is to be put up to the highest bidder, and he is to be surrounded in his allotments with a wall of fire, a cordon of white settlements, which will gradually but surely hem him in, circumscribe him, and eventually crowd him out. True, the proceeds of the sale are to be invested for the Indians; but when the Indian is smothered out, as he will be under the operations of this bill, the investment will revert to the national Treasury, and the Indian, in the long run, will be none the better for it; for **nothing can be surer than the eventual extermination of the Indian under the operation of this bill.** (Emphasis added).

The real aim of this bill is to get at the Indian lands and open them up to settlement.

The provisions for the apparent benefit of the Indian are but the pretext to get at his lands and occupy them. With that accomplished, we have securely paved the way for the extermination of the Indian races upon this part of the continent. If this were done in the name of Greed, it would be bad enough; but to do it in the name of Humanity, and under the cloak of an ardent desire to promote the Indian's welfare by making him like ourselves, whether he will or not, is infinitely worse. Of all the attempts to encroach upon the Indian, this attempt to manufacture him into a white man by act of Congress and the grace of the Secretary of the Interior is the baldest, the boldest, and the most unjustifiable. (Emphasis added).

Whatever civilization has been reached by the Indian tribes has been attained under the tribal system, and not under the system proposed by this bill. The Cherokees, Choctaws, Chickasaws, Creeks, and Seminoles, all five of them barbarous tribes within the short limit of our own history as a people, have all been brought to a creditable state of advancement under the tribal system. The same may be said of the Sioux and Chippewas, and many smaller tribes. Gradually, under that system, they are working out their own deliverance, which will come in their own good time if we but leave them alone and perform our part of the many contracts we have made with them. But that we have never yet done, and it seems from this bill we will never yet do. We want their lands, and we are bound to have them. Let those take a part in despoiling them who will; for ourselves, we believe the entire policy of this bill to be wrong, ill-timed, and unstatesmanlike; and we put ourselves on record against it as about all that is now left us to do, except to vote against the bill on its final passage.
Russell Errett of Pennsylvania, Charles Hooker of Mississippi, and T M. Gunter of Arkansas

APPENDIX E-1: Society of American Indians Petitions to President of the United States

Society of American Indians Petition to the President of the United States, October 5, 1912

To His Excellency the President of the United States: The Society of American Indians, in conference assembled at Ohio State University, Columbus, Ohio, respectfully petition you as follows:

1. That the appointment of the Commissioner of Indian Affairs be made without regard to the political affiliations of the appointee. The Commissioner of Indian Affairs has to deal essentially with human problems, the problems of a primitive and hampered race. His work is in no sense political. There has never been a time in the history of Indian affairs when the filling of this was of such vital interest to the Indian as a race as at present, during this period of enforced transition.

2. The man to be appointed to this important position should be one whose honesty, integrity and sympathetic and practicable interest in the Indian race is beyond question. He should be a man whose standing is such that he would command the hearty support of the best people of the country, regardless of politics or religious affiliations. It is not the policy of the Society to become involved in politics, either directly or indirectly, and it will not endorse any particular candidate nor oppose him, unless there is some one up for consideration who is manifestly unsuited, and whose appointment would be detrimental to the race as a whole. We believe, however, that it is not only the right but the duty of every advanced-thinking Indian to assert himself in a matter of this kind, and we respectfully request that the opinions and wishes of these Indians, speaking individually, concerning the appointment of Commissioner of Indian Affairs be given not only consideration but weight.
THE SOCIETY OF AMERICAN INDIANS. SHERMAN COOLIDGE, President.

Society of American Indians, "The Quarterly Journal of the Society of American Indians V. 1 No. 2 (April-June 1913)," pp. 216-217. *American Indian Digital History Project*, https://aidhp.com/items/show/151 (accessed August 11, 2024).

The Quarterly Journal of the Society of American Indians, V. 2 No. 3 (October-Dec. 1914)
Dec. 10. 1914

The Awakened American Indian An Account of the Washington Meeting by Arthur Parker

The American Indian has written a new chapter in his life story. The tenth day of December, nineteen hundred and fourteen, marked a new beginning in Indian progress and proclaimed a new day for the red race. Upon that day *President Woodrow Wilson listened to the memorial of the Society of American Indians in behalf of the*

American Indian. Never before perhaps had there assembled so large a body of men and women of Indian blood, having so wide an influence in the world's affairs. Never before had the men and women of the race presented so definite an appeal covering the conditions of all Indians. (Emphasis added).

The memorial presented to the President was the outcome of an action by the University of Wisconsin Conference of the Society of American Indians, and was drawn up by order of the conference.

Dec. 10. The Society, represented by its active officers, associate officers, board, and by members of both divisions reached the White House... More than forty delegates were in the body.

The President stood in the center of his office and shook hands cordially as each member was presented. Then, after a short explanation Mr. Dennison Wheelock read the memorial, which follows:

SAI Memorial to President Wilson, 1914

DISTRICT OF COLUMBIA, CITY OF WASHINGTON.
His Excellency, the President of the United States:
Acting under instructions of the Fourth Annual Conference of the Society of American Indians, held on the 6th to the 11th of October, 1914, at the University of Wisconsin, in the city of Madison, Wisconsin, your petitioners respectfully present this memorial.

Congress has conferred special authority upon the President of the United States respecting the welfare of the Indians, regarded as wards of the Federal Government. We believe that this obligation lies close to your heart and we, therefore, feel free to suggest to you a few things which seem to us necessary to our welfare and progress, to our development as co-laborers and producers. We believe that you feel, with the progressive members of our race, that it is anomalous permanently to conserve within the nation groups of people whose civic condition by legislation is different from the normal standard of American life.

Definition of Legal Status.

As a race, the Indian, under the jurisdiction of the United States, has no standing in court or nation. No man can tell what its status is, either civic or legal. Confusion and chaos are the only words descriptive of the situation. This condition is a barrier to the progress of our people, who aspire to higher things and greater success.

We hold it incontrovertible that *our status in this nation should be defined by federal authority.* We request, therefore, that, as the first essential to a proper solution of the Indian Problem, and even for the benefit of the nation itself, this matter be placed in the hands of a commission of three men-the best, the most competent and the kindliest men to be found-and that they be authorized to study this question, and recommend to you and to the congress the *passage of a code of Indian law* which shall open the door of hope and progress to our people. Our Society since its beginning has pled for this fundamental necessity of race advancement. (Emphasis added).

Admission to the Court of Claims.

We ask, also that the Court of Claims be given jurisdiction over all Indian claims against the United States. (Emphasis added).

This done, a great barrier to race development would be removed for we should no longer be tied to the past with the feeling that the country had not fulfilled its obligations to our race.

We believe that more has been done, can be done to make Indian property an efficient instrument for Indian welfare; to make Indian intellect, statesmanship, and craftsmanship useful to the nation. We point with pride to the men and women, who by their achievements have demonstrated the inherent capacity of Indian blood. Our plea is that just opportunity be provided to insure the efficiency and enlarge the capacity of the thousands who have not had freedom to struggle upward and whose condition very shortly become not only a menace to themselves but a burden to the nation.

We plead, sir, that you give us the cheer of your word, that you consider our request and call upon Congress to grant the American Indians those fundamental rights and privileges, which are essential to release them from enforced wardship, dependence and consequent degeneracy; and that you advocate measures that will, according to the recognized principles of legal and economic development, speedily secure their admission to the field of even chance for individual efficiency and competency.

For the weak and helpless, for the discouraged and hopeless of our race scattered over this broad land we make this plea and petition. Through our annual conference we have carried our plea to the great universities of the land; we have striven to awaken the public conscience to the justice of our demands and now we ask you to consider the merits of our appeal. And for the boon we crave we shall ever pray. THE SOCIETY OF AMERICAN INDIANS

The President [Wilson] remained standing at one corner of his desk during the reading and was evidently impressed. After Mr. Wheelock had handed the memorial to the President, Mr. [Sherman] Coolidge, president of the Society, delivered a few word (sic) in explanation of the object of the Society. This was followed by an address by Mr. Wm. J. Kershaw. Mr. Kershaw's speech was an eloquent classic and profoundly impressive. As the years go by it will be regarded as one of the masterpieces of Indian oratory. Congressman Charles D. Carter, former chief of the Chickasaw Council and now vice-president on legislation of the Society, made the closing address, indorsing the memorial in its plea for a new and just code of law and greater opportunity for the red man.

President Wilson replied expressing his pleasure in receiving the delegation and stating that he had not given special thought to the Indian, though he had appointed the best man he could find as Secretary of the Interior and as Commissioner of Indian Affairs. He promised to give the memorial his most earnest consideration and to study the measures advocated by the Society. The Quarterly Journal of the Society of American Indians, V. 2 No. 3 (October-Dec. 1914), p. 272.

SAI Speech to President Wilson. 1914, by Wm. J. Kershaw

Mr. Wm. J. Kershaw, An Address to the President of the United States

MR. PRESIDENT: It is true, as our memorial states, that the Federal statute governing the Indian in nearly all of its provisions places the Indian directly and immediately under the hand of the President, so that the Government stands as their guardian and the President as a sort of guardian ad litem. This appeal is made in behalf of all the Indians of the United States; but it more particularly concerns the young Indians. The Indian is changed; he is not the same as he was fifteen years ago, because his vision has greatly broadened, but his opportunities have not been correspondingly enlarged. Our purpose is to secure for him opportunities.

It would seem of no avail for the Government to educate and graduate hundreds of young Indians and return them to reservations without preparing conditions there in accord with their education. These young Indians on returning to their reservations must live under the laws which were designed for the government of their ancestors when they were barbarians and virtual prisoners of war; laws under which they can do nothing for themselves or their relatives by their own initiative; laws that are very arbitrary; they must live under the government of superintendents or agents who have arbitrary power over all their affairs. They have no access to the courts of the land for the settlement of property rights or inheritances. (Emphasis added).

These rights are not determined by any tribunals known to our system of jurisprudence or to the common law; but by agencies upon which the Constitution of the United States has never conferred any judicial powers. In this behalf we must not forget the young Indian women. Estimates of Indian character or the Indian situation seldom take into account the influence of Indian women, who are good mothers, good housewives, frugal and saving, and exceptionally industrious. Indian women could develop a domestic or household manufactory exceeding in magnitude and diversity anything of the kind ever known to our history. While we are insistent and urgent in this appeal, yet we are desirous that no inference be drawn from such urgency adverse to the present administration of Indian affairs. We are especially proud of that administration. We appreciate that Commissioner Sells has done splendid work. We cannot but commend his administration. He has taken the Government machinery with all the ingrown abuses of forty years of ill advised legislation, and with it he has accomplished splendid results.

The Carter code bill, now pending before Congress, introduced by Congressman Carter, meets the situation as to the commission. The Court of Claims ought to be thrown open for settlement of tribal claims, which cannot be taken into Court except by consent of Congress, and branches of the court opened in every judicial district where reservations are located.

Mr. President, we are deeply in earnest in what we are seeking to do for the American Indians. Each of us could recite many instances within our personal knowledge of abuses of the reservation system but it would take too long to do so now. There is nothing that the young Indian cannot do, even those who are apparently stupid, showing exceptional mental capacity when once they strike their vocation.

We want to bring the young Indian to his place in society and we know that he will not come to that society empty handed; that he will bring to it the primary virtues of a strong self-reliant race.

We ask you to heed this appeal.

The Quarterly Journal of the Society of American Indians, V. 2 No. 3 (October-Dec. 1914), p. 275.

APPENDIX E-2: Society of American Indians Memorial to Congress

A Message to Congress
THE SOCIETY OF AMERICAN INDIANS
Office of the President
University of the State of New York, Albany, N. Y.
December 1, 1916.

TO THE CONGRESS OF THE UNITED STATES:
The administration of the affairs of 300,000 Indians in United States is costing the Government about ten millions of dollars each year. Added to this from Indian sources and others is another ten million.

The aim of the Government is to do full justice to the American Indian and to bring him into efficient citizenship.

Before there can be such an achievement for the Indian, tribes must be dissolved as social, commercial and political entities. The Indians must come into the nation as individual units. (Emphasis added).

Vast sums are now expended to conserve Indian property, to defray the expense of governmental guardianship and trusteeship and to educate the Indian for efficient citizenship. But while the nation is ostensibly protecting and educating the Indians we ought to ask whether the machinery it employs is fully efficient, and all obstacles to final success have been removed? If not, the money is proportionally wasted and both the nation and the Indian vitally wronged. We believe that there is both waste and wrong.

Able men and women in business and professional life among both Indians and whites have pointed out several obstacles that prevent the complete assimilation of the Indians; and result in direct injury to the Indians and expense to the nation. Some of these obstacles are here named:

1. Lack of a defined status with a series of grades leading to citizenship and uniform in all states in which Indians are under federal supervision.
2. Lack of a uniform code of law, fully meeting the situation.
3. Failure to individualize trust funds, so that each Indian may know his pro rata share on the books of the nation.
4. Failure to admit Indian claims directly to the United States Court of Claims without the specific consent of Congress in each instance.
5. Failure to give Indians an adequate understanding of the government's purposes and contemplated actions respecting them. The Indians have been placed in the attitude of passive spectators.
6. Lack of an adequate form of education, fitting the adult for the struggle of life in his changing environment and preparing the youth for the more intense struggle in

citizen communities. Nearly one-half the Indians today are still illiterate. (Emphasis added).

We appeal to the Congress to bring about a change in the conditions we have enumerated, for they all reflect vitally in determining the progress and assimilation of the Indian. With the continuation of the obstacles the Indians will remain confused in mind, remain broken in spirit, become pauperized by annuities and doles, waste their time in fighting for claims, (many just and many visionary), remain passive and lacking in initiative and ignorant and ill-prepared for a struggle in civilization.

Cannot the Congress awaken to the fact that it is expending millions to remedy conditions and ills that it has itself imposed or aggravated?

As long as Indians are segregated, because of the law, the evils of segregation will result.

As long as the present system of conducting the Indian Bureau continues there will be a vast wastage. Congress must make the administration of Indian affairs more efficient by constituting it upon a different basis or it must abolish the Bureau altogether and place the administration of Indian affairs in the hands of a non-political commission empowered to bring about a speedy assimilation of the Indians.

The remedies we seek are legislative and lie in the hands of Congress.

We direct the attention of every member of Congress to the Memorial of this Society presented to the President of the United States on December 10, 1914, which reads in part: (Emphasis added).

As a race, the Indian under the jurisdiction of the United States has no standing in court or nation. No man can tell what its status is, either civic or legal. Confusion and chaos are the only words descriptive of the situation. This condition is a barrier to the progress of our people, who aspire to higher things and greater success.

We hold it incontrovertible that our status in this nation should be defined by federal authority. We request, therefore, that, as the first essential to a proper solution of the Indian problem, and even for the benefit of the nation itself, this matter be placed in the hands of a commission of three men-the best, the most competent and the kindliest men to be found-and that they be authorized to study this question, and recommend to you (the President) and to the Congress the passage of a code of Indian law which shall open the door of hope and progress to our people. Our Society since its beginning has pled for this fundamental necessity of race advancement.

We ask, also that the Court of Claims be given jurisdiction over all Indian claims against the United States.

This done, a great barrier to race development would be removed, for we should no longer be tied to the past with the feeling that the country had not fulfilled its obligations to our race.

We believe that even more than has been done can be done to make Indian property an efficient instrument for Indian welfare; to make Indian intellect, statesmanship, and craftsmanship useful to the nation. We point with pride to the men and women who by their achievements have demonstrated the inherent capacity of Indian blood.

"Our plea is that just opportunity be provided to insure the efficiency and enlarge the capacity of the thousands who have not had freedom to struggle upward and whose condition very shortly become not only a menace to themselves, but a burden to the nation." (Emphasis in original).

May we not hope that Congress will awaken to the need of the hour and respond to these critical situations that affect the life, property, efficiency and happiness of 300,000 potential and actual citizens of Indian ancestry?

The need of haste is great for each year, nay each day, of delay, but aggravates the case and renders the injury more grievous. We look to you for action.
Respectfully, ARTHUR C. PARKER, President of the Society of American Indians
THE AMERICAN INDIAN MAGAZINE, October-December, 1916, Vol. IV, No. 4, 1916, pp. 282-284.

APPENDIX _E-3: Highlights from Quarterly Journals of the Society of American Indians, 1912-1916

Second Annual Conference of The Society of American Indians, Oct. 1912, Ohio State University

The Society American Indians held its Second Annual Conference at Ohio State University during the first week of October, 1912 *"An Indian must say with a man of any race who has risen, I am proud of my race. It is not an inferior race. It can advance; it can achieve; and by God's help I shall do my utmost to prove it."* (Emphasis added). Proceedings Of The Second Annual Conference Of The Society Of American Indians Held At Ohio State University Columbus, Oh., Oct. 1912. Published in the Quarterly Journal of the Society of American Indians By Order of the Executive Council, 1913, p. 64. https://aidhp.com/files/original/e293ef5647b96574987d8408e62d2435.pdf (accessed online September 9, 2024).

Objects of the Society:

First.-To promote and co-operate with all efforts looking to the advancement of the Indian in enlightenment which leaves him free as a man to develop according to the natural laws of social evolution.
Second.-To provide, through our open conferences, the means for a free discussion on all subjects bearing on the welfare of the race.
Third.-To present in a just light the true history of the race, to preserve its records and emulate its distinguishing virtues.
Fourth.-*To promote citizenship and to obtain the rights thereof.*
Fifth.-*To establish a legal department to investigate Indian problems and to suggest and obtain remedies.*
Sixth.-To exercise the right to oppose any movement that may be detrimental to the race.
Seventh.- *To provide a bureau of information including publicity and statistics.* (Emphasis added).
Proceedings Of The Second Annual Conference Of The Society Of American Indians Held At Ohio State University Columbus, Oh., Oct. 1912. Published in the Quarterly Journal of the Society of American Indians By Order of the Executive Council, 1913, p. 144. https://aidhp.com/files/original/e293ef5647b96574987d8408e62d2435.pdf (accessed online September 9, 2024).

1913

The Quarterly Journal of the Society of American Indians, V. 1 No. 1 (January-April 1913).

SAI Plan to Develop Indian Leaders

P. 3 *The open plan is to develop race leaders, to give hope, to inspire, to lead outward*

~ 593

and upward, the Indian American as a genuine factor in his own country and lead him to see that upon his individual effort depends his share in the salvation of his race and his value to his country.

The plan is so transparent, so simple, that those inclined to be sordid cannot believe that there is not some deep and hidden evil. Here lies a grave danger. Good men and good women fear. (Emphasis added).

U.S. Strategy: Setting Indians against One Another

Long ago, this principle of setting Indians against one another was understood and in the heat of the early contest for the Indians' country, it was no less than George Washington who said: "Unless we have Indians to oppose Indians we may expect but small success." For four hundred years this opposing of one's own people has been cleverly fostered. (Emphasis added). [P. 4].

Indians Have 72,535,862 Acres

Indians under government supervision, have in individual right, 31,383,354 acres of land and in tribal right 40,263,445 acres, making a total of 71,646,799. With the public domain added, the total swells to 72,535,862 acres. [P. 5].

Wealth of "Government" Indians Is $1,066,106,427

According to government appraisers the value of this property, together with the houses, barns, tools, lumber, furniture, stock and other properties, in the possession of government-controlled Indians is $387,542,166. Undivided tribal property amounts to $687,564,253. The grand total of the wealth of "government" Indians is $1,066,106,427. (Emphasis added). [P. 5].

Indians under Constant Exploitation by Whites; U.S. Government Acknowledges It Can't Protect Indians

Leave Indian to (1) Sink or Swim or (2) Educate Indian to Economic System of Modern Civilization

Unskilled, as yet in sharp business methods, and unfamiliar with values and indeed with the whole economic system of civilization, the Indian holds his property by only a slender grasp. This immense property protected only by the filmy tissue of law affords a tempting bait to the shrewd speculator, for, as Washington said of the white race, "our people are not to be restrained by any law now in being, or likely to be enacted." Until the Indian can be educated and adjusted to the economic system of modern civilization, he will suffer from constant exploitation. How shall he learn? "Throw every Indian upon his own responsibility now say some. Educate him more, allow him to develop, grow and gradually accustom him to independence by withdrawing supports one by one," say others. [P. 5].

SAI Free to Speak Truth, Non-Partisan, Non-Secular

Our great advantage is that we are free from any connection with political bodies, from churches and from the government or its dictation. Nobody may say what we shall do or say, save the Indian people themselves. We exist to afford them a right and an opportunity to speak out. We ask every Indian to speak, to voice his wrongs, to tell of injustice where he knows it to be, to mention his fears of any factor affecting the Indian. ... Your officials are but your servants, your society your means for work. ... We stand as the founders of the Society have said "for broad interests, not selfish interests." (Emphasis added). [P. 7].

What is best for the American Indian as a race? How shall his condition be bettered? How may he have justice and secure his natural rights? Who are his enemies? What forces are holding him down? Who are his friends? Who will help in his uplift? Should not the Indian people themselves be the chief factors in placing their own race on a solid foundation and in demanding for it a definite status in the country? [P. 8].

The Society of American Indians is not a political or a partisan organization. [P. 10].

Indian American-His Duty to His Race and to His Country

The Indian American-His Duty to His Race and to His Country, the United States of America Address of SAI President Rev. Sherman Coolidge, "Use Your Citizenship Worthily of the Gospel of Christ."

Citizenship for the native ward is the aim of the United States and he must ultimately assume the duties and responsibilities involved in a Christian nation. To that end the existence of the Indian bureau must be terminated and the elimination of the Indian as a national ward must be effected as soon as may be possible.

The dictates of patriotism and justice demand that the Indian shall not be left to work out unaided the peculiar problem thus thrust upon him; and the nation that created the problem must assist in the solution. [P. 20].

The Teaching of Ethnology in Indian Schools by J.N.B. Hewitt (Tuscarora), of the Smithsonian Institution

The well-attested fact that not one American Indian in 5,000 knows what his own tribe, not to say the American Indian race, has done in the past as expressed in terms of human culture, makes this question one that should receive the attention of this Society of American Indians, at this Conference. [P. 30].

Among the objects mentioned in the Statement of Purpose of this Society of American Indians are, to promote the advancement of the American Indian in enlightenment, to conserve the history of the American Indian race, without distortion from ignorance, misconception, or misinterpretation, and to promote all honorable means the social, ethical, political, and economic welfare and betterment of not only its members but also that of their other brothers of the American Indian race, by conserving and developing what is congruous to their attainment, and eliminating what is not. *It is true that before this great work can be done intelligently and effectively the past history and the culture of the people must be known.* (Emphasis added). [P. 32].

Dr. Carlos Montezuma: Wipe Out Reservation System; Permit Free Association with Whites

P. 50 Light on the Indian Situation by Carlos Montezuma, A.B., M.D. (Apache)

Senator Smith of Arizona, when a member of the House of Representatives, said, There is more hope of educating the rattlesnake, than of educating the Apaches. I am Apache.

P. 53 *I firmly believe that the only true solution of the so-called "Indian problem" is the entire wiping out of the reservation system; of the absolute free association of the Indian race with the paleface.*

PP. 71- 73 Platform of the Second Annual Conference of the Society of American Indians.

PP. 73-74 RESOLUTIONS INVOLVING SPECIFIC CASES DEMANDING ACTION

The Quarterly Journal of the Society of American Indians, V. 1 No. 1 (January-April 1913). https://www.aidhp.com/items/show/174 (accessed online September 9, 2024).

The Quarterly Journal of the Society of American Indians, V. 1 No. 2 (April-June 1913)

Proceedings of the Second Annual Conference (pp. 117- 222)
Constitution and By-Laws (pp. 223-230)

Recommended Reading: "The American Indian of Today and Tomorrow" by Prof. F. A. McKenzie. It advocates among other things the codification of Indian law and a competent inquiry into how Indian money is being spent. McKenzie, Fayette Avery. "The American Indian of Today and Tomorrow." J. Race Dev. 3 (1912): 135.

One Hundred Million People v. Two Hundred Thousand Indians

P. 114 *"But why should a nation of nearly 100,000,000 people trouble itself about 265,000 people scattered all over its wide domain and hidden in its deserts and mountains?"* (Emphasis added). The answer is plain. We owe something to the people whom we have supplanted. We owe the best of guardianship to our national wards. In themselves these people are worthy of adequate care. Rightly treated they will shortly become a national asset instead of a burden; it is economy to invest in them.

Belief that if Indian Will Work, No Need for U.S. Reservation System and BIA

P. 138 If the Indian will go to work, will form habits of industry, we will have no need of the reservation system that we complain of so bitterly, we will have no need for a Commissioner of Indian Affairs, no need for the establishment of Indian agencies, no need for Indian agents. We will be our own agents and commissioners. So, I say, tell the Indian to go to work.

Commercial Schemes to Exploit an Undeveloped Race - Indians

P. 143 *Its agents [Office of Indian Affairs] have trafficked in the well being of the generations of Americans of the future; trafficked in the welfare of the souls of men and women and children.* That is why I say it is a most serious matter - a religious matter. If ever a man needed to get down on his knees and ask his God for pardon, it is the craven who has entered into a commercial scheme to exploit an undeveloped race, and turn drops of human blood into gold. The money changers of the temple should find a paradise in comparison. If you deprave a man and give him an unequal chance to develop his highest character, you are robbing the American race of the future.

Economic Conditions on Jicarilla Reservation, Northern New Mexico

P. 154 Economic conditions on a reservation is presented to us in no more bold relief than that of the Jicarilla Reservation in northern New Mexico. These Indians live up in the mountains. The rock-ribbed, craggy mountains show their teeth at the inhabitants of the land and seem to flaunt defiance at any man who would try to eke out a living there. The stream that flows through the Jicarilla country is so alkali horses will not drink it. The water in some of the lakes is bitter. Here the Jicarilla Apaches, seven hundred strong, are trying to keep body and soul together year after year. *No one undertakes to farm, for their is no rain and no means of irrigation. No white people live in a land among whom they hire out as farmhands. They own no cattle, but one or two few sheep and goats.* They eat bread baked by the coals and drink black coffee for breakfast, bread and coffee at noon and the same at night. When the rigors of winter come on and the bread is gone they boil and eat the inner bark of the yellow pine on their reservation. *In the days gone by the mothers, not having any milk for lack of proper nourishment, took their babies into the mountain caves, waiting in solitude and going home alone*. The consumptives on this reservation, lacking that nutriment which plenty of healthy food gives to the blood to build up the waste tissues, die by the scores. *Last winter, through hunger, cold and disease, seventy of these Indians died*. These Indians are flesh of our flesh, bone of our bone. I need not prophesy their future. (Emphasis added).

Future of Indian Rests on Shoulders of Educated Indians

P. 160 We have a great many educated and intelligent Indians. The future of the Indian rests upon the shoulders of these Indians. In order that better management, legislation, and men and women to work among the Indians, be accomplished, we must be Christian men and women worthy of such.

U.S. Plenary Power over Indians Gives Power to Abrogate Indian Treaties, Allot Lands, Sell Surplus to White Settlers

P. 168 The fundamental part of the government which interests the Indian Conference particularly is controlled by Congress as the executive part of the government, which includes the President of the United States, and *the government under a recent decision, holds that, although that land has been set apart as a reservation for Indians, it is so far under the control of the government that the government may by act so dispose of that land as to change the title, to sell it, and they have provided an act, too, that when an Indian dies, a division of his lands should be made by the Secretary of the Interior, and his findings should be binding and conclusive*. (Emphasis added).

The Quarterly Journal of the Society of American Indians, V. 1 No. 3 (July-Sep. 1913)
Education

The Quarterly Journal of the Society of American Indians, V. 1 No. 4 (October-Dec. 1913)

Indian Must Fight Back Sickness, Misery, Poverty, and Grafters Successfully; No One Else Will Ever Do It as Well

To fight back sickness, misery, poverty, and grafters successfully the Indian himself must know how to do his own fighting. No one else will ever do it so well as the individual Indian for himself. Indian agents and government officials will never do it perfectly.

Legislation to Permit Indians to Submit Claims to U.S. Court of Claims

P. 352 *On February 3, 1912, Mr. Stephens of Texas introduced H.R.19414, authorizing any nation, tribe or band of Indians to submit claims against the United States to the Court of Claims*. (According to existing law, Indians cannot enter the United States courts without special enabling acts. This bill, on becoming law, would be the enabling act for all tribes suing the government for any moneys due or misappropriated under any treaties or laws.) It is provided that either party may appeal to the United States Supreme Court and a statute of limitation clause demands that all claims, based on facts, happening prior to the passage of this act, shall be barred unless suit is brought within five years after the passage of this act. ... The rights in the claims are to be settled by the Court of Claims regardless of the lapse of time or statutes of limitation prior to the passage of the act. (Emphasis added).

PP. 353-355 **Stephens Bill, H.R.19414**

1914

The Quarterly Journal of the Society of American Indians, V. 2 No. 1 (Jan.-March 1914)

P. 2 Warning: Need for Vigilance; Impending Crisis

Keen political minds are at work to control Indian interests, to remove supervision, to entrench themselves and promote their own ends. This is no open fight; it is an entangled, hidden one. Many good men will be deceived, many will awaken when it is too late, many will be led far away from real issues through created dissensions. There is an impending crisis that will result in good or evil for the red man, take time to investigate, act wisely and be vigilant. We cannot tell the story now. We only warn; take nothing for granted.

Dixon/Wanamaker Expedition of Citizenship

P. 85 **Wanamaker Expedition** Fort Wadsworth in New York Harbor. There were several Indians present from the far west and a large company of citizens. The irony of building a gigantic statue to a race of men who have been so grossly injured by the evils of civilization cannot but be apparent to those who think even superficially. The idea of the statue, however, is a noble one, and it is to be hoped that it will correctly portray the tribes that welcomed and nursed the feeble colonists.

The Quarterly Journal of the Society of American Indians, V. II No. 2 (April-June 1914).

Editorial Comment: Equal Status of Indians Imperative; Legislative Needs of Indians Need to Be Understood

P. 95 The Indian cannot compete in civilization unless placed on the same footing as other men. An equal status is imperative. If the Indian does not become an equal before the law he will be robbed, plundered, trampled upon, and finally die out. ... To obtain legal equality the law must pave the way. There is a primary need, therefore, for legislative action.

The Editor's Viewpoint: Indians Need Equal Rights; Equal Responsibility; Equal Education

P. 118 Out of this belief sprang the Society of American Indians as a race organization. Its purpose is to attain three great ideals for the American Indian, not only in order to benefit the Indian but to benefit the great American people.

These ideals are: First, *the obtaining of rights equal to those of the governing powers.* This ideal seeks out an equal opportunity to compete with other men and to enjoy the same privileges that they do. The Indian deserved all his rights and every power for achievement, liberty of action and chance for success that any man in civilization has. Second, the *American Indian*, as interpreted by this Society, *asks for equal responsibility.* With equal rights must come an equal opportunity to serve the greater nation and all the human race. With the power that comes, comes the duty to use that power for the betterment of others. The Indian must be a producer, a worker, a builder, a maker of things, a grower, give largely of his fortunes, and do it consciously and intelligently because he wills to do it. Third, *the Indian must in order to have equal rights and to perform equal service be equally equipped. Education is that equipment.* (Emphasis in original).

Equal opportunity, equal responsibility and equal education.

Indians' Lack of Trust with U.S.

P. 153 **The Murderer of Desota Tiger Caught**. Mr. Tiger was a Seminole Indian. Without the help of SAI, the murderer would have gone unprosecuted.

The Quarterly Journal of the Society of American Indians, V. II No. 3 (July-September 1914).

SAI Opposed to Wild West Shows

PP. 174-175, 224-225, 226-227 The Wild West show has done a lot of harm in the way of deceiving the public. It has made most persons think that the Indians are still wild savages. ... And here is something the Indians themselves should consider. There would be no such degenerate antics if the public opinion of the Indians themselves was against it.

The Loyal Indians in Government Employ; Rumors Started to Cause Dissension: SAI Has Hostile Attitude toward Indians in Federal Employ (Divide and Conquer Strategy)

PP. 176-177 But we find ourselves rudely shocked. A rumor has gone forth that "the Society" has a hostile attitude toward Indians in Federal employ. Some one seems to have spread the idea that, through our members so employed, "the Bureau" was endeavoring to control the Society. Of course this is untrue and unjust. ... our Indian membership employed by the Bureau is absolutely loyal to the race.

Let Us Discover the Human Elements of this Indian Problem

SAI Needs Data on Indians

PP. 183-184 This lack of data leads to an inability on the part of social and religious workers, educators, and physicians to handle systematically their special fields. For the sake of efficiency and economy we plead for vital facts. The Indian problem is a human problem and we must know its human elements if we are to handle it concretely.

The Society of American Indians as an organization should like to know the following things

Vital Statistics-Tribe, age, married or single, size of family, full blood, degrees of white, Negro, Mongolian blood, lives on or off reservation.

Educational Facts-Grade of education, where obtained, Government day or boarding school, public or private school, speaks good English, imperfect English, only Indian, ever employed in educational work.

Industrial Facts-Occupation, degree of success yearly income, regular or irregular employment, own stock, owns acres, acres cultivated, grazed, rented out, has no land, rents land, sole income from rentals; leases.

Housing and Health Statistics-Lives in house, number of rooms, lives in tent, lives in shanty or earth lodge, earth or board floor, sanitary condition, water from well, spring, stream, water hole, food principally meat, vegetable, mixed, tubercular, trachoma, health in general, insured, number of sick persons in family, takes patient medicines, consults physician when ill, consults medicine man, uses alcoholic liquor.

Religious and Social Facts-Attends church regularly, irregularly, no church, member peyote society, other native society, member American fraternity or lodge, member local social, educational club or society, reads daily paper, weekly and monthlies, what grade.

Legal Statistics-Ward, allotted ward, limited citizen, full citizen and voter, can sue and be sued.

Environmental Facts-Lives near white settlement, near agency, remote from white communities, near mission.

P. 186 The Function of the Society of American Indians by SHERMAN COOLIDGE, President of the Society.

Successes to Date

PP. 188-189 We aided in liberating two hundred and sixty Apaches who had been held in bondage as prisoners of war for twenty-six years, and persuaded Congress to appropriate $300,000 for land and homes for them.

We helped the Cayugas in getting $247,000 due them from the State of New York.

The murderer of Desota Tiger is in irons, thanks to some of our active and associate members and to Hon. Cato Sells, Commissioner of Indian Affairs.

An Indian woman out west tried to get her money through the Indian agent and was put off – we helped her get her money.

The fate of a $50,000 item in the last money appropriation bill was uncertain; it was for the education of about two thousand Papago children; but the bill passed with our assistance.

Continue advocating for the passage of the Carter and the Stephens bills.

Government Oversight of Expenditure of Indian Funds Important to Indians

P. 189 The Government has charge of $900,000,000 worth of property for the three hundred thousand Indians under its care; $100,000,000 worth of timber land, but will this timber be turned into lumber for the use of Indians, or will it be turned over to some corporation? Again, the Government holds $60,000,000 in cash for our national wards. What shall be done with it? These subjects are of vital interest to the Indian. Besides all this there are millions annually appropriated by Congress for our civilization and education. The Society of American Indians asks: "Are we getting a proportionate good out of this vast expenditure?"

P. 196 The Indian Must Assume Responsibility if He Demands Rights

Hon. William Howard Taft, Letter of President Taft to Secretary of Interior, 1912.

> Citizenship involves more than benefits to the individual. There are obligations and burdens toward the community which he must recognize and assume. Any plan for the development of the Indian as an individual must, to be successful, include efforts to impress upon him the fact that he must accept the responsibilities if he demands the benefits of citizenship.

P. 209 **Commissioner Sells Visits Hampton**

While at Hampton, Commissioner Sells remarked upon the vast property holdings of the Indians, stating their value as about a billion dollars. White men are waiting to determine whether or not the young Indians can demonstrate their capacity for self-support. *If the young Indians fail, then the next generation will not be given an opportunity, for by that time the white race will have sufficient excuse for appropriating what the Indians have.* "Young Indians," he continued, "must meet new conditions and do the things that their mothers and fathers could not do, thereby justifying themselves and those who come after them." He repudiated the doctrine that the Indian is a vanishing race, and added that *the Indians should be treated in the personal and property rights just as so many white persons under like conditions.* (Emphasis added).

Open the Court of Claims

P. 228 Not all the legal tangles in Indian property affairs can be straightened out in a single year, but the discussion of the years past has made fairly clear what the initial step should be. All the property claims against the United States government, whether they should prove to amount to fifty or even one hundred in number, should be given a prompt hearing and a final disposition. With them out of the way another remedy or method will be at hand for the solution of the next large group of legal problems. The remedy is a simple one: Open the United States Court of Claims to Indian tribes and groups.

Open Forum

PP. 246-248 The Apache Situation

> FORT APACHE INDIAN AGENCY, Whiteriver, Ariz., Sept. 22, 1914.
> To THE SECRETARY-TREASURER, The Society of American Indians, Washington, D. C.
>
> You ask for the "situation in Arizona." I am very glad to have this opportunity to submit the following to the Society for careful consideration:
>
> Condition of the Apache Indians off the Reservation. At Globe, Ariz., the Apache Indians live in teepees on the desert lands outside of the city limits. They have no farms there, and simply live there waiting for some work to turn up in the vicinity. The same condition exists at Miami.
>
> At Wheatfields the Indians live in the teepees on the hill tops. They have no farms there and a number of them work for Chinese farmers. *The white community there is prejudiced against the Indians and do not want them to live there.*

At Green Back Valley the Indians live in teepees and have no lands of their own. Mr. Packard, who owns most of the valley at this place, told the Indians that if they would clear the land and irrigate they could raise as many crops as they wished. They cleared the land, and after three crops he told them he wanted the land for himself.

At Sallymay there are 30 families living in teepees in a canyon. They have some small patches of corn. They are 25 miles from the nearest store.

At Gisela there are about 25 families living in teepees. Some of them have small farms. *The white people in this vicinity don't want them*. When the cow-boys have their cattle roundup they tear down the Indians' fences and turn their cattle into the Indians' corn fields. When the Indians are out hunting their ponies, the cow-boys would draw guns on them even when they are out on the road with their families. They have appealed to the civil authorities, but have received no protection from the cow-boys.

At Angora the Indians had small farms in good condition, but *they were driven away by the white men* and appealed to the civil authorities, but nothing was done to help them to hold their homes.

At San Pedro Valley, 18 families live in teepees on small farms which the white men have not been able to take away from them. Formerly the Apaches owned the whole valley and used it. *The white men have gained possession of about nine-tenths of the land, and continually annoy the Indians by tearing down fences and turning their cattle and horses into the Indians' cornfields.*

The old Indians tolds me that General Crook, in rounding up all the Apaches, told them that if they would help him to get rid of the troublesome Apaches and after settling the troubles they would be allowed to return to their various homes, and live in peace, and that they would not be in need. They said that they did their part and nothing has been done by the Government to carry out the promises made to them by General Crook. They have gone back to their various homes and found the white people occupying their old farms, and the only thing left for the Indians to do was to pitch their teepees on hilltops and look at the white men in the valleys deriving the benefits from the farms that were at one time their own.

I was informed by the Indians off the reservation that four Indians were killed by white men, but nothing was done by the civil authorities to punish the murderers. A white man was killed and an Indian was sent to the penitentiary. The Indians claimed that the white men were killed by a Mexican.

At one instance a white man killed an Indian at Globe. The white man fled. An Indian was blamed for the murder and went to the penitentiary for life. The white man, who committed the murder, was in California and while he was under the influence of liquor confessed that he killed the Indian at Globe and that an innocent Indian was serving a life term for it. The white man was brought back to Globe, tried, and was released. The innocent Indian was also released.

There ought to be something done to help these Apache Indians off the reservation. They ought to have some protection.

I am informed by the Indian Office that the Government has no jurisdiction over these Indians off the reservation and that they are amenable to the laws of the State. I think this would be true if those Apaches owned farms and lived in houses and citizens, but when they have nothing and simply exist in teepes, I think the Government still has jurisdiction over them.

VINCENT NATALISH.

The Quarterly Journal of the Society of American Indians, V. III No. 1 (January – March 1915).

P. 150 When something is going to happen that affects his human interests or his property rights, the policy of fairness, if not simple decency, would dictate letting these potential citizens know why the contemplated act is inaugurated. *We call for the publication of a set of simply-worded books setting forth, for each tribe its legal rights and the agency rules regulating their control*. (Emphasis added).

1910 Census
P. 185 Population, age, blood, sex, stock, fecundity and vitality was issued as a special bulletin two years ago. It was prepared by Prof. Dixon. The part on education, illiteracy, school attendance, occupations and taxation was prepared by Dr. McKenzie.

The Quarterly Journal of the Society of American Indians, V. III No. 4 (October-December 1915).

P. 252 **Congress Strikes at the Root**

A new bill has been introduced by Congressman Stephens of Texas, providing for the segregation and allotment of Indian tribal and trust funds and other property. The bill bears the numbers H.R. 6888, of the 64 Congress. The time has come to place to the credit of each Indian the share of the tribal fund due him as an individual. No longer should Indians be taught to expect monthly payments in small amounts, or annual payments of tribal funds, and to spend days and weeks of valuable time in waiting to collect it. "Annuities and doles foster pauperism and are a curse to any people that expects to develop independence," says the S.A.I. platform.

Where to Get Good Land Cheap [Land for Sale and Lease on Shoshone Indian Reservation]

P. 253 Report of A.L. Campbell, County Agricultural Agent of Fremont County, Wyoming. In an officially signed article in the Wyoming Farm Bulletin, Mr. Campbell says: "Seeing great possibilities in these heavy crop yields many old residents as well as new settlers, are acquiring farms upon the *land for sale and lease on the Shoshone Indian Reservation*. This reservation lies in the central and best part of Fremont County. Those who are buying these irrigated lands at the present low prices are indeed fortunate. About one hundred new farms have been made on these lands this year. In some cases the original cost of the land and water-right has been regained from the first year's crop of grain. Judging from the number of sales and leases lately contracted at the office of Supt. J.W. Norris at Fort Washakie there will be many more new settlers next year. On these lands the irrigation ditches are already constructed. A perpetual water right goes with each tract of land sold or leased under these ditches. The price of fifteen to thirty-five dollars an acre, including both land and water right, is only about one-half what water alone costs under other large projects. The quality of the land is unexcelled, the water supply is more than sufficient, and the climate is delightful both summer and winter. In forty years of farm practice under irrigation in Fremont County there have been no crop failures. Truly this is land where the settlers are satisfied and making good from the start."

PP. 285-287 Platform of the Fifth Conference

Sep. 1916 Demise of SAI due to internal conflict led by Dr. Montezuma over the loyalty of Indian Bureau employees in SAI.

American Indian Magazine Jan.-March 1916

Study of Indian Claims

We are glad to see an item in the Indian Appropriation Bill empowering the Commissioner of Indian Affairs to make a study of these claims and to report such as seem equitable and to report these claims to Congress for its action. Such a measure strikes at the very roots of a fundamental matter. It will mean the saving of large sums of money to the Indians and the removal of chains that now make the settlement of the Indian problem difficult indeed.

P. 4 Mr. Merrit, the Assistant Commissioner, in testifying before the Indian Committee during the hearing on the Indian Bill ...: These Indian tribes should not be required to expend their moneys in the payment of attorneys to formulate and prosecute claims against the Government. The most equitable arrangement would seem for the Government to establish a commission to investigate these various matters, prepare reports setting forth the claims in an intelligent manner and present for the consideration of Congress facts on which an adjudication could be made and the matters disposed of for all time.

April-June 1916

P. 107 *"Can they stick together, can they take a stand on moral issues and maintain it?" were questions asked as soon as this Society was organized. Men shook their heads and said the Society was foredoomed.*

P. 108 Our first duty, then, is to stand the test of cohesiveness, the test of responsiveness and the test of concerted action. All this requires the losing sight of self and the exercise of great patience. After a complete demonstration of these things we can expect to reach out in matters of legal dispute, in bills in Congress, in a campaign for governmental reform, and only then we can expect success in every thing we desire.

As a journal of constructive thought our publication has been a success.

P. 118 Until a codified law with the proper changes has been provided and tribal claims settled we shall expect the Indians and the Indian Office to suffer.

In his column of Arrow Points, "Wassaja" takes some long shots at the Society of American Indians and this Magazine. We have ever been glad for honest criticism and even invited it. Here are some of the arrows that transfix us against "Wassaja's" war post.

> PP. 170-171 *Indian Day proclamation is a farce and worst kind of a fad. It will not help the Indians, but the Indians will be used as tools for interested parties. To the Indian it is a laughing mockery because he does not enjoy freedom, but is a ward and is handicapped by the Indian Bureau.*
> *"'The Journal of the Society of American Indians' has turned into a magazine. Now it can straddle any old thing that comes along. Like all magazines, it cannot have any definite object but to tickle its readers at the expense of the Indians. Buffalo Bill and P. T. Barnum used the Indians. Now it is the American Indian Magazine's turn."*

July-Sept. 1916

The Cedar Rapids Platform
PP. 223-224

The Society of American Indians assembled in the Sixth Annual Conference in the

City of Cedar Rapids, Iowa, September 26-September 30, 1916, more conscious than ever of the complex situation in which a kindly and benevolent Government has placed the Indian of the United States, and appealing to the people, the Congress and the Executive officers of the Nation for such sympathetic counsel and assistance as may be necessary in working out a plan for a legal, educational and administrative policy, which, when adopted, shall contemplate the speedy and just settlement of all causes of Indian discontent, by placing them on an equal footing with other Americans, do adopt the following platform:

1. Closing the Indian Bureau. We believe the time has come when we ought to call upon the country and upon Congress to look to the *closing of the Indian Bureau, so soon as trust funds, treaty rights and other just obligations can be individualized, fulfilled or paid*. It should be clearly seen that the Indian Bureau was never intended as a permanent part of the Interior Department, but merely to perform a temporary function. With the progress and education of Indians, they should be invested with the full privileges of citizens without burdensome restrictions. As its jurisdiction is removed, the books of the Bureau should be closed until there is a final elimination. As citizens and taxpayers struggling side by side with other Americans, we are willing to entrust our liberties and fortunes to the several communities of which we form a part.

2. Schools for Citizenship. It is believed that the preparation and introduction in Indian schools, of the new vocational courses of study marks an epoch in Indian education. Furthermore, we cannot urge too strongly upon the Congress that provision should be made, and Indian pupils encouraged, to *make use of the Federal schools merely as stepping stones to the attendance of white schools, where contact with other American youth makes for patriotic, competent citizenship*. Furthermore, we believe that all Indian pupils over twenty-one years of age, having completed a prescribed course of study, should be deemed fully competent, given control of their property and thrown upon their own resources.

3. *Liquor Traffic an Evil*. We commend the efforts of the officials of the Bureau for the suppression of the liquor traffic among Indians and we urge upon our own people the adoption of habits of total abstinence which we are convinced are conducive to happiness and prosperity. We urge unequivocally upon Congress the passage of the Gandy bill to prohibit the commerce in and use of peyote among our people, because of its known baneful effects upon the users in mind and morals.

4. *Health Conditions on Reservations*. We commend the efforts to improve sanitary and health conditions on the reservations and to save the lives of the Indian babies, which efforts have already resulted in greatly reducing the death rate. We trust that the health campaign will continue unabated until the baneful effects of reservation life and ignorance shall have been wiped out for both infants and adults.

5. *Former Principles Reaffirmed*. We reaffirm the principles so ardently and justly urged by former Conferences of this Society. We reiterate our pleas made in our Denver, Madison and Lawrence platforms calling for *(a) a definition of the legal status of*

the Indians; (b) for the individualization of trust funds; (c) and the early adjudication of all tribal claims. We renew our appeal as made in our memorial to the President of the United States, December 11, 1914.

P. 227 Certain Addresses and Discussions at the Cedar Rapids Conference

P. 230 *The financial position of the Society, therefore, has in all its activities, almost from the very beginning of the year, been crippled.*

P. 252 Open Debate on the Loyalty of Indian Employees in the Indian Service The question was raised by Dr. Montezuma that Indian employees in the service of the Indian Bureau could not be loyal to the Indian race and to their real interests. His argument was that the Indian Bureau did not conserve the best interests of the Indians.

P. 266 Dr. Carlos L. Montezuma, an Apache Indian, had just concluded an impassioned speech in which he spoke his mind freely about the Indian Bureau and criticized the society for its failure to do many things for the betterment of the Indian. His remarks seemed to be directed toward the Rev. Sherman Coolidge, an Arapahoe. When Montezuma concluded he sat down and President Coolidge took the floor to answer some of the charges. His replies seemed to fire the blood of the Apache. Montezuma jumped to his feet, waving his arms wildly. "I am an Apache," he shouted to Mr. Coolidge, "and you are an Arapahoe. I can lick you. My tribe has licked your tribe before." "*I am from Missouri,*" replied Mr. Coolidge. His remark broke the tension by creating a laugh and what promised to be an exciting incident soon simmered down and the discussion continued.

April-June 1917
DECLARATION OF POLICY IN THE ADMINISTRATION OF INDIAN AFFAIRS
By HON. CATO SELLS, Commissioner of Indian Affairs

**1918 SAI QUAR JOUR EXCERPTS NONE
NO MORE SIGNIFICANT ACTION**

APPENDIX F: Excerpts from Dr. Charles Eastman's Books

Dr. Charles Eastman's Indian Boyhood

p. 191 As our cone-shaped teepees rose in clusters along the outskirts of the heavy forest that clothes the sloping side of the mountain, the scene below was gratifying to a savage eye. The rolling yellow plains were checkered with herds of buffaloes. Along the banks of the streams that ran down from the mountains were also many elk, which usually appear at morning and evening, and disappear into the forest during the warmer part of the day. Deer, too, were plenty, and the brooks were alive with trout. Here and there the streams were dammed by the industrious beaver.

In the interior of the forest there were lakes with many islands, where moose, elk, deer and bears were abundant. The water-fowl were wont to gather here in great numbers, among them the crane, the swan, the loon, and many of the smaller kinds. The forest also was filled with a great variety of birds. Here the partridge drummed his loudest, while the whippoorwill sang with spirit, and the hooting owl reigned in the night.

To me, as a boy, this wilderness was a paradise. It was a land of plenty. To be sure, we did not have any of the luxuries of civilization, but we had every convenience and opportunity and luxury of Nature. We had also the gift of enjoying our good fortune, whatever dangers might lurk about us; and the truth is that we lived in blessed ignorance of any life that was better than our own.

p. 252 I was scarcely old enough to know anything definite about the "Big Knives," as we called the white men, when the terrible Minnesota massacre broke up our home and I was carried into exile. I have already told how I was adopted into the family of my father's younger brother, when my father was betrayed and imprisoned. We all supposed that he had shared the fate of those who were executed at Mankato, Minnesota.

p. 259 My father, accompanied by an Indian guide, after many days' searching had found us at last. He had been imprisoned at Davenport, Iowa, with those who took part in the massacre or in the battles following, and he was taught in prison and converted by the pioneer missionaries, Drs. Williamson and Riggs. He was under sentence of death, but was among the number against whom no direct evidence was found, and who were finally pardoned by President Lincoln. (Emphasis added).

When he was released, and returned to the new reservation upon the Missouri river, he soon became convinced that life on a government reservation meant physical and moral degradation.

p. 263 Late in the fall we reached the citizen settlement at Flandreau, South Dakota, where my father and some others dwelt among the whites. *Here my wild life came to an end, and my school days began.* (Emphasis added).

Dr. Charles Eastman's Book - From Deep Woods

One can never be sure of what a day may bring to pass. At the age of fifteen years, the deepening current of my life swung upon such a pivotal day, and in the twinkling of an eye its whole course was utterly changed; as if a little mountain brook should pause and turn upon itself to gather strength for the long journey toward an unknown ocean.

From childhood I was consciously trained to be a man; that was, after all, the basic thing; but after this I was trained to be a warrior and a hunter, and not to care for money or possessions, but to be in the broadest sense a public servant. After arriving at a reverent sense of the pervading presence of the Spirit and Giver of Life, and a deep consciousness of the brotherhood of man, the first thing for me to accomplish was to adapt myself perfectly to natural things in other words, to harmonize myself with nature. To this end I was made to build a body both symmetrical and enduring a house for the soul to live in a sturdy house, defying the elements. I must have faith and patience; I must learn self-control and be able to maintain silence. I must do with as little as possible and start with nothing most, of the time, because a true Indian always shares whatever he may possess. I felt no hatred for our tribal foes. I looked upon them more as the college athlete regards his rivals from another college. There was no thought of destroying a nation, taking away their country or reducing the people to servitude, for my race rather honored and bestowed gifts upon their enemies at the next peaceful meeting, until they had adopted the usages of the white man s warfare for spoliation and conquest.

There was one unfortunate thing about my early training, however; that is, I was taught never to spare a citizen of the United States, although we were on friendly terms with the Canadian white men. The explanation is simple. My people had been turned out of some of the finest country in the world, now forming the great states of Minnesota and Iowa. The Americans pretended to buy the land at ten cents an acre, but never paid the price; the debt stands unpaid to this day. Because they did not pay, the Sioux protested; finally came the outbreak of 1862 in Minnesota, when many settlers were killed, and forthwith our people, such as were left alive, were driven by the troops into exile. My father, who was among the fugitives in Canada, had been betrayed by a half-breed across the United States line, near what is now the city of Winnipeg. Some of the party were hanged at Fort Snelling, near St. Paul. We supposed, and, in fact, we were informed that all were hanged. This was why my uncle, in whose family I lived, had taught me never to spare a white man from the United States.

The thought of my father's wish kept me on my true course. Leaving my gun with Peter, I took my blanket on my back and started for the Missouri on foot. "Tell my father," I said, "that I shall not return until I finish my war-path."

My older brother John, who was then assistant teacher and studying under Dr. Riggs, met me at the school and introduced me to my new life.

My brother got me a suit of clothes, and had someone cut my hair, which was already over my ears, as it had not been touched since the year before. I felt like a wild goose with its wings clipped.

It seemed now that everything must be measured in time or money or distance. And when the teacher placed before us a painted globe, and said that our world was like that - that upon such a thing our forefathers had roamed and hunted for untold ages, as it whirled and danced around the sun in space - I felt that my foothold was deserting me. All my savage training and philosophy was in the air, if these things were true.

In September, 1876, I started from Santee to Beloit to begin my serious studies.

It was here and now that my eyes were opened intelligent to the - greatness of Christian civilization, the ideal civilization, as it unfolded itself before my eyes. I saw it as the development of every natural resource; the broad brotherhood of mankind; the blending of all languages and the gathering of all races under one religious faith. There must be no more warfare within our borders; we must quit the forest trail for the breaking-plow, since pastoral life was the next thing for the Indian. I renounced finally my bow and arrows for the spade and the pen; I took off my soft moccasins and put on the heavy and clumsy but durable shoes. Every day of my life I put into use every English word that I knew, and for the first time permitted myself to think and act as a white man.

At the end of three years, other Sioux Indians had been sent to Beloit, and I felt that I might progress faster where I was not surrounded by my tribesmen. Dr. Riggs arranged to transfer me to the preparatory department of Knox College, at Galesburg, Ill., of which he was himself a graduate. Here, again, I was thrown into close contact with the rugged, ambitious sons of western farmers.

I went on to Dartmouth College, away up among the granite hills. At Kimball Union Academy, the little ancient institution at which I completed my preparation for college by direction of President Bartlett of Dartmouth, I absorbed much knowledge of the New Englander and his peculiarities.

I was treated with the greatest kindness by the president and faculty, and often encouraged to ask questions and express my own ideas. My uncle's observations in natural history, for which he had a positive genius, the Indian standpoint in sociology and political economy, these were the subject of some protracted discussions in the class room.

After my graduation with the class of 1887, it was made possible for me to study medicine at Boston University.

The Pine Ridge Indian agency was a bleak and desolate looking place in those days, more especially in a November dust storm such as that in which I arrived from Boston to take charge of the medical work of the reservation.

An Indian agent has almost autocratic power, and the conditions of life on an agency are such as to make every resident largely dependent upon his good will. We soon found ourselves hampered in our work and harassed by every imaginable annoyance. My requisitions were overlooked or "forgotten," and it became difficult to secure the necessaries of life. (Emphasis added). I would receive a curt written order to proceed without delay to some remote point to visit a certain alleged patient; then, before I had covered the distance, would be overtaken by a mounted policeman with arbitrary orders to return at once to the agency. On driving in rapidly and reporting to the agent's office for details of the supposed emergency, I might be rebuked for overdriving the horses, and charged with neglect of some chronic case of which I had either never been informed, or to which it had been physically impossible for me to give regular attention.

This sort of thing went on for several months, and I was finally summoned to Washington for a personal conference. I think I may safely say that my story was believed by Senators Dawes and Hoar, and by Commissioner Morgan also. I saw the Secretary of the Interior and the President, but they were non-committal. On my return, the same inspector who had whitewashed the payment was directed to investigate the "strained relations" between the agent and myself, and my wife, who had meantime published several very frank letters in influential eastern papers, was made a party in the case.

I will not dwell upon the farcical nature of this "investigation." The inspector was almost openly against us from the start, and the upshot of the affair was that I was shortly offered a transfer. The agent could not be dislodged, and my position had become impossible. The superintendent of the boarding school, a clergyman, and one or two others who had fought on our side were also forced to leave. We had many other warm sympathizers who could not speak out without risking their livelihood.

We declined to accept the compromise, being utterly disillusioned and disgusted with these revelations of Government mismanagement in the field, and realizing the helplessness of the best-equipped Indians to secure a fair deal for their people. Later experience, both my own and that of others, has confirmed me in this view. (Emphasis added). Had it not been for strong friends in the East and on the press, and the unusual boldness and disregard of personal considerations with which we had conducted the fight, I could not have lasted a month.

It was a great disappointment to us both to give up our plans of work and our first home, to which we had devoted much loving thought and most of our little means; but it seemed to us then the only thing to do. We had not the heart to begin the same thing over again elsewhere. I resigned my position in the Indian service, and removed with my family to the city of St. Paul, where I proposed to enter upon the independent practice of medicine.

I wished very much to resume my profession of medicine, but I was as far as ever from having the capital for a start, and we had now three children. At this juncture, I was confronted by what seemed a hopeful opportunity. Some of the leading men of the Sioux, among them my own brother, Rev. John Eastman, came to me for a consultation. They argued that I was the man of their tribe best fitted to look after their interests at Washington. They had begun to realize that certain of these interests were of great importance, involving millions of dollars. Although not a lawyer, they gave me power of attorney to act for them in behalf of these claims, and to appear as their representative before the Indian Bureau, the President, and Congress.

After signing the necessary papers, I went to Washington, where I urged our rights throughout two sessions and most of a third, while during the summers I still traveled among the Sioux. I learned that scarcely one of our treaties with the United States had been carried out in good faith in all of its provisions.

My work for the International Committee of Young Men's Christian Associations brought me into close association with some of the best products of American civilization. I believe that such men as Richard Morse, John R. Mott, Wilbur Messer, Charles Ober and his brother, and others, have through their organization and personal influence contributed vitally to the stability and well-being of the nation. Among the men on the International Committee whom I met at this time and who gave me a strong impression of what they stood for, were Colonel John J. McCook, David Murray, Thomas Cochrane, and Cornelius Vanderbilt. I have said some hard things of American Christianity, but in these I referred to the nation as a whole and to the majority of its people, not to individual Christians. Had I not known some such, I should long ago have gone back to the woods.

From the time I first accepted the Christ ideal it has grown upon me steadily, but I also see more and more plainly our modern divergence from that ideal. *I confess I have wondered much that Christianity is not practised by the very people who vouch for that wonderful conception of exemplary living. It appears that they are anxious to pass on their religion to all races of men, but keep very little of it themselves. I have not yet seen the meek inherit the earth, or the peacemakers receive high honor.* (Emphasis added).

Why do we find so much evil and wickedness practised by the nations composed of professedly "Christian" individuals? The pages of history are full of licensed murder and the plundering of weaker and less developed peoples, and obviously the world today has not outgrown this system. Behind the material and intellectual splendor of our civilization, primitive savagery and cruelty and lust hold sway, undiminished, and as it seems, unheeded. When I let go of my simple, instinctive nature religion, I hoped to gain something far loftier as well as more satisfying to the reason. Alas! it is also more confusing and contradictory. The higher and spiritual life, though first in theory, is clearly secondary, if not entirely neglected, in actual practice. *When I reduce civilization to its lowest terms, it becomes a system of life based upon trade. The dollar is the measure of value, and might still spells right; otherwise, why war?* (Emphasis added).

Yet even in deep jungles God's own sunlight penetrates, and I stand before my own people still as an advocate of civilization. Why? First, because there is no chance for our former simple life any more; and second, because I realize that the white man's religion is not responsible for his mistakes. There is every evidence that God has given him all the light necessary by which to live in peace and good-will with his brother; and we also know that many brilliant civilizations have collapsed in physical and moral decadence. It is for us to avoid their fate if we can. (Emphasis added).

I am an Indian; and while I have learned much from civilization, for which I am grateful, I have never lost my Indian sense of right and justice. I am for development and progress along social and spiritual lines, rather than those of commerce, nationalism, or material efficiency. Nevertheless, so long as I live, I am an American. (Emphasis added).

Dr. Charles Eastman's Book - Soul of Indian

The red man divided mind into two parts—the spiritual mind and the physical mind. The first is pure spirit, concerned only with the essence of things, and it was this he sought to strengthen by spiritual prayer, during which the body is subdued by fasting and hardship. In this type of prayer there was no beseeching of favor or help. All matters of personal or selfish concern, as success in hunting or warfare, relief from sickness, or the sparing of a beloved life, were definitely relegated to the plane of the lower or material mind, and all ceremonies, charms, or incantations designed to secure a benefit or to avert a danger, were recognized as emanating from the physical self.

The rites of this physical worship, again, were wholly symbolic, and the Indian no more worshiped the Sun than the Christian adores the Cross. The Sun and the Earth, by an obvious parable, holding scarcely more of poetic metaphor than of scientific truth, were in his view the parents of all organic life. From the Sun, as the universal father, proceeds the quickening principle in nature, and in the patient and fruitful womb of our mother, the Earth, are hidden embryos of plants and men. Therefore our reverence and love for them was really an imaginative extension of our love for our immediate parents, and with this sentiment of filial piety was joined a willingness to appeal to them, as to a father, for such good gifts as we may desire. This is the material or physical prayer.

The elements and majestic forces in nature, Lightning, Wind, Water, Fire, and Frost, were regarded with awe as spiritual powers, but always secondary and intermediate in character. We believed that the spirit pervades all creation and that every creature possesses a soul in some degree, though not necessarily a soul conscious of itself. The tree, the waterfall, the grizzly bear, each is an embodied Force, and as such an object of reverence.

The Indian loved to come into sympathy and spiritual communion with his brothers of the animal kingdom, whose inarticulate souls had for him something of the sinless purity that we attribute to the innocent and irresponsible child. He had faith in their instincts, as in a mysterious wisdom given from above; and while he humbly accepted the supposedly voluntary sacrifice of their bodies to preserve his own, he paid homage to their spirits in prescribed prayers and offerings. (Emphasis added).

Yet the religion that is preached in our churches and practiced by our congregations, with its element of display and self-aggrandizement, its active proselytism, and its open contempt of all religions but its own, was for a long time extremely repellent. To his simple mind, the professionalism of the pulpit, the paid exhorter, the moneyed church, was an unspiritual and unedifying thing, and it was not until his spirit was broken and his moral and physical constitution undermined by trade, conquest, and strong drink, that Christian missionaries obtained any real hold upon him. Strange as it may seem, it is true that the proud pagan in his secret soul despised the good men who came to convert and to enlighten him!

Nor were its publicity and its Phariseeism the only elements in the alien religion that offended the red man. To him, it appeared shocking and almost incredible that there were among this people who claimed superiority many irreligious, who did not even pretend to profess the national faith. Not only did they not profess it, but they stooped so low as to insult their God with profane and sacrilegious speech! In our own tongue His name was not spoken aloud, even with utmost reverence, much less lightly or irreverently.

More than this, even in those white men who professed religion we found much inconsistency of conduct. They spoke much of spiritual things, while seeking only the material. They bought and sold everything: time, labor, personal independence, the love of woman, and even the ministrations of their holy faith! The lust for money, power, and conquest so characteristic of the Anglo-Saxon race did not escape moral condemnation at the hands of his untutored judge, nor did he fail to contrast this conspicuous trait of the dominant race with the spirit of the meek and lowly Jesus.

It is my personal belief, after thirty-five years' experience of it, that there is no such thing as "Christian civilization." I believe that Christianity and modern civilization are opposed and irreconcilable, and that the spirit of Christianity and of our ancient religion is essentially the same. (Emphasis added).

Dr. Charles Eastman's Book - The Indian Today

pp. 18-19 This transition period has been a time of stress and suffering for my people. Once they had departed from the broad democracy and pure idealism of their prime, and undertaken to enter upon the world-game of competition, their rudder was unshipped, their compass lost, and the whirlwind and tempest of materialism and love of conquest tossed them to and fro like leaves in the wind.

p. 19 *"You are a child," said the white man in effect to the simple and credulous native. "You cannot make or invent anything. We have the only God, and he has given us authority to teach and to govern all the peoples of the earth. In proof of this we have His Book, a supernatural guide, every word of which is true and binding. We are a superior race—a chosen people. We have a heaven fenced in with golden gates from all pagans and unbelievers, and a hell where the souls of such are tortured eternally. We are honorable, truthful, refined, religious, peaceful; we hate cruelty and injustice; our business is to educate, Christianize, and protect the rights and property of the weak and the uncivilized."* (Emphasis added).

p. 19 I have tried to set forth the character and motives of the primitive Indian as they were affected by contact with civilization. In a word, demoralization was gradual but certain, culminating in the final loss of his freedom and confinement to the reservation under most depressing conditions.

p. 37 Who is this Indian agent, or superintendent, as he is now called? He is the supreme ruler on the reservation, responsible directly to the Commissioner of Indian Affairs; and all requests or complaints must pass through his office. The agency doctor, clerks, farmers, superintendents of agency schools, and all other local employees report to him and are subject to his orders. Too often he has been nothing more than a ward politician of the commonest stamp, whose main purpose is to get all that is coming to him. His salary is small, but there are endless opportunities for graft.

p. 37 *If any appeal from the agent's decisions, they are "kickers" and "insubordinate." If they are Indians, he can easily deprive them of privileges, or even imprison them on trumped-up charges; if employees, he will force them to resign or apply for transfers; and even the missionaries may be compelled, directly or indirectly, to leave the reservation for protesting too openly against official wrongdoing. The inspector sent from Washington to investigate finds it easy to "get in with" the agent and very difficult to see or hear anything that the agent does not wish him to hear or see. Many Indians now believe sincerely in Christ's teachings as explained to them by their missionaries, but they find it impossible to believe that this Government is Christian, or the average official an honest man.* (Emphasis added).

p. 48 The Indian Rights Association maintains a representative in Washington to cooperate with the Indian Bureau and to keep an eye upon legislation affecting the tribes, as well as a permanent office in Philadelphia. Its officers and agents have kept in close touch with developments in the field, and have conducted many investigations on Indian agencies, resulting often in the exposure of grave abuses. They have been courageous and aggressive in their work, and have not hesitated to appeal to the courts when necessary to protect the rights of Indians. They have also done much to mold public sentiment through meetings, letters to the press, and the circulation of their own literature to the number of more than half a million copies.